DICTIONARY
FOR
BUSINESS & FINANCE

DICTIONARY
FOR
BUSINESS
&
FINANCE

SECOND EDITION

John V. Terry

The University of Arkansas Press
Fayetteville 1990 London

94 93 92 91 90   5 4 3 2 1

Designer: B. J. Zodrow
Typeface: New Baskerville

The paper used in this publication meets the minimum requirements of the
American National Standard for Permanence of Paper for Printed Library
Materials Z39.48-1984. ∞

Library of Congress Cataloging-in-Publication Data

Terry, John V., 1920 –
    Dictionary for business & finance/John V. Terry. — 2nd ed.
       p.   cm.
    ISBN 1-55728-169-6 (alk. paper). — ISBN 1-55728-170-X (pbk. alk. paper)
    1. Business – Dictionaries.   2. Finance – Dictionaries.   I. Title.
    II. Title: Dictionary for business and finance.

HF1001.T43   1990
650'.03 – dc20   90-33432
                                          CIP

To my wife Fern, who gave me John Mark, Joan, Luanne, and Clay, who in turn took as life-mates Barbara, Bob, Dennis, and Trish, who in turn gave us our grandchildren, Joanna, Tyler, Tara, Micah, Nicolas, and Nathan. To these, who make up my greatest wealth, I lovingly dedicate this publication.

Contents

Preface

As the world develops a more global economy, the terminology of that economy will become increasingly common. Students in colleges and universities and professional people everywhere will find that they must adapt to an entire world of business, not just to the practices of a particular region or country; the first prerequisite for this adaptation will be a knowledge of the special language of world business.

The second edition of the *Dictionary for Business & Finance* has broadened the scope of the first edition by adding many terms in the field of economics, statistics, and management.

John V. Terry

Preface to the First Edition

Dictionary for Business & Finance is the product of many years of thought, college teaching, public lecturing, conducting business and financial seminars, consulting with the world of business, and the training of financial planners.

When I started my first financial planning class, I had about a dozen such dictionaries in my library, but, while they were helpful to a degree, they were not what I needed. Not enough of the terms were relevant to the wide-ranging business areas of banking and financial institutions, investing, insurance, real estate, estate planning, economics, management, communications, and employee benefits (both social and private).

My first thought was to put together a comprehensive glossary for my own classes; then I decided to prepare a complete dictionary that would serve the needs of all the professions mentioned, as well as those of my business students.

The business and industrial world is changing rapidly, and the walls separating industries, as well as those between financial and quasi-financial institutions, are disappearing. We can no longer be content with understanding the jargon of one profession; it is becoming increasingly necessary to be acquainted with terminology from many. This dictionary is dedicated to that purpose.

It is helpful to segregate certain types of information for quick reference; this has been done by appendices offering ready access to formulas, addresses, acronyms, etc.

If errors are found, they are mine.

If this dictionary accomplishes a small part of the purpose for which it was put together, the time and effort will have been well spent.

J. V. T.

Acknowledgments

One does not "author" a dictionary. I owe thanks to every textbook I have read and taught from, a host of periodicals from the various fields of business and finance, every seminar I have attended, and every person I have talked business with.

I acknowledge especially my debt to Nancy Bayley, who, while a senior at John Brown University, did the first word processing which helped me get started. Kelly Fields, now a student at the University of Arkansas, spent an entire summer on the word processor, putting together the collection of words and phrases I had decided to use. Loretta Ingram, a trusted assistant, spent countless hours sorting the words and phrases, and assisting in the many revisions which had to be made to arrive at the finished copy. I could not have completed the manuscript in an acceptable period of time without her. Jerry Hunter, a computer "whiz kid," wrote the necessary programs for the word sorting—no mean task when a dictionary is involved.

I owe a debt to my first class of Certified Financial Planners, whose needs, along with mine, inspired this work. To my friends of the Federal Reserve Banking System, I am grateful for the privilege of using their material. The same thanks go to the College for Financial Planning, Denver, Colorado, for allowing the use of some of their material, and for their encouragement. Houghton-Mifflin Company, Boston, is to be commended for their aid in securing a source to certain Latin terms.

I wish to acknowledge the grace of Almighty God, who has given me health and the desire to continue to be productive.

To any person, or group, who may have been left out of these acknowledgments, it is my hope that the success of the publication will serve as thanks.

J. V. T.

Introduction

Any professional person will spend countless hours consulting dictionaries and other professionals. Almost every distinct discipline has dictionaries which deal in an encyclopedic manner with major terms. However, the walls between professions are rapidly breaking down. The dictionaries and references, which once served well, now come up short as the need for a wider vocabulary is increasingly required.

It was the breakdown between the various professions in the field of finance which occasioned the compiling of the *Dictionary for Business & Finance*.

Though a practicing economist for many years, I found, several years ago, that I needed to know more legal, insurance, real estate, investment, marketing, accounting, and banking terms. Some of the dictionaries in my library gave only brief definitions of highly complex terms. Therefore, I often found myself consulting half a dozen different volumes to get an encyclopedic answer relating to one word or phrase. I combed the nation looking for a combined dictionary, but discovered that one did not exist or was well hidden in some ancient library.

Over the years banks have accepted deposits, made commercial and consumer loans, and served various smaller needs of clients. Now they make real estate loans—something generally left to savings and loan companies in the past. They also offer discount brokerage services through various agencies. In the near future, they will have full-blown mortgage banking services, sell both equity and fixed income investments, and deal in all types of insurance, annuities, and employee benefit plans. Brokerage houses will offer financial planning, sell retirement plans and insurance, and do investment banking. Insurance people will be involved in loans, insurance and annuities, and financial and estate planning. Real estate firms will make loans, do financial planning, conduct appraisals, and sell certain types of insurance. Economists and marketing and finance specialists will overlap fields until none will be distinct from the other. Accountants will offer financial planning, estate planning, and setting up of trusts, and they will try to keep abreast of what other professions are doing, so that this knowledge will be available for interpretation and application in tax accounting. Attorneys will have to know about every field in order to be equipped to work as legal advisors. As long-recognized barriers break down between professions, the terminology and jargon of each will have to be understood by all the others.

An encyclopedic dictionary for all professionals, businesses, industries, students of business, and scholars who want to understand the professions better is much needed. It will aid professional and research libraries at the senior high, junior college, college, and university levels.

Dictionary for Business & Finance goes beyond the boundaries ordinarily set by business dictionaries and gives encyclopedic explanations of thousands of terms all professions must work with every day. It is hoped that it will save many hours of valuable time, while adding to the store of general knowledge about business and finance.

J. V. T.

DICTIONARY
FOR
BUSINESS
&
FINANCE

abandonment 1. *insurance* The relinquishment of ownership of lost or damaged property to the insurer when permitted under the contract. 2. *law* Voluntary relinquishment of property or a right by the owner or holder, with the intention of terminating ownership and without vesting ownership in another person. Abandonment is composed of two concurring elements: intention to relinquish the right or property without intending to transfer title to any particular person and an external act by which such intentions are carried into effect.

abandum; abandun Anything abandoned, sequestered, or proscribed.

abatement Proportional diminution or reduction of the monetary legacies, when funds or assets out of which such legacies are payable are not sufficient.

abdication The act of voluntarily giving up or renouncing a throne, an office, a function, or a trust.

ability-to-pay principle 1. *economics* A theory of wages and salaries which states that employee's compensation should rise and fall with company profits. 2. The philosophy that it is "just" for people who earn more (or own more) to pay more taxes.

ab initio *law From the beginning.* A term used specifically in law with reference to the question of illegality as to whether a sale, contract, etc., is to be set aside from the genesis, or from the time of the action by the party.

ab intestato *From the intestate.*

abrogate *law* To alter or modify a previous agreement by a later one; to repeal a statute, ordinance, or by-law by express words or by implication; to repeal, annul, or abolish. (E.g., a law is abrogated by legislative action, constitutional authority, or usage.)

absentee *real estate* A person who is not present; one who is away from, as in "absentee landlord."

absentee owner Owner who does not personally manage or reside at property owned.

absentee rate *economics* The ratio of lost work days in relation to possible work days.

absoluta sententia expositore non indiget *Language is plain* (as in statute or deed); *no explanation is required.*

absolute advantage 1. Condition that exists when one producer can produce a product more efficiently than another. Both benefit when each produces the product in which it has an absolute advantage and trades part of the output for the other. 2. The ability to produce a good for less cost (less factor inputs) than anyone else.

absolute estate *law* Estate in which the owner is entitled to the entire property with unconditional power of disposition during the owner's life, and which descends to the heirs and legal representatives should the owner die intestate. Often used synonymously with fee simple.

absolute gift *law* A gift of property, given through a will, which carries with it complete and unconditional access to and control over the property.

absolute income hypothesis *economics* The concept that many will increase their consumption as their income increases, but not by as great a percentage as the increase in income. This would tend to make the consumption rate less, and the savings rate more, as income increases.

absolute interest Full and complete ownership.

absolute liability Indebtedness that arises and is imposed on a person regardless of the circumstances leading to it.

absolute title *real estate* An exclusive title, or one that excludes all others not compatible with it.

absorption rate *real estate* Estimate of the expected annual sales or new occupancy of a particular type of land use.

absque impetitione vasti *Without impeachment of waste.* Clause contained in an instrument granting a life estate that indicates the life tenant takes the estate without liability of impeachment for waste. (*See* waste)

abstinence theory of interest *economics* A concept of interest that says interest is the price paid by a borrower to a lender for the latter's abstinence from consumption.

abstract of title 1. Historical summary of all recorded instruments and proceedings that affect the title to property. 2. Abridged history of the title recording all the conveyances, transfers, liabilities, covenants against or burdens upon the land, and other facts pertinent to such title that would be of interest to a prospective purchaser. 3. Condensed history of the title to land appearing on the public records consisting of a summary of the relevant portion of all conveyances which affect said land or any estate or interest, together with a statement of all liens or liabilities to which the land may be subject.

abuse 1. Damage by careless use or deliberate misuse. 2. Any act of a corporation in violation of its charter and which detracts from the public right.

abusive dismissal *management* The discharge of an employee in which harsh methods are used, even though proper company termination procedures have been followed.

abusive tax shelter *investing* A tax deduction the Internal Revenue Service deems illegal, usually a limited partnership.

abut To touch, border upon, be contiguous to.

abutting owner *real estate* Owner of property that touches, is contiguous to, or in close proximity to other property.

Academic Consultants An advisory group initiated by the Federal Reserve Board in the 1960s to provide a forum for the exchange of views between the Board and members of the academic community in economics and banking.

accelerated cost recovery system (ACRS) 1. A provision in the Economic Recovery and Tax Act of 1981 that allows investors in a limited partnership to depreciate an asset faster in the first three years, then slower in the final years of the typical ten to fifteen year life of the partnership. 2. *corporate finance* System under which fixed assets put into service since 1980 may be written off much more rapidly than before. (E.g., equipment and machinery can be amortized in five instead of fifteen years. Most buildings can be depreciated in eighteen years instead of twenty to forty years.) Sometimes called the 3-5-10 rule, referring to periods in which vehicles, equipment and machinery, and leased buildings, respectively, are depreciated under the system. 3. Method of depreciation under which most buildings acquired in 1981 and thereafter may be depreciated using a fifteen year life. Owners may also select thirty-five and forty-five year lives. Accelerated depreciation approximating 175 percent declining balance may be used resulting in depreciation recapture. (*See* Appendix G)

accelerated cost recovery system (ACRS) deduction The percentage deduction for depreciation one may take in any given year, using a percentage of the basis price. (These deductions will vary according to the type of property, and the number of years chosen as the write-off period.) (*See* Appendix G)

accelerated depreciation *accounting* The action of allocating a greater portion of the depreciation of an asset to its earlier years of life by using (a) declining balance of (b) sum of the years digits method. (*See* Appendix G)

acceleration The hastening of the enjoyment of an estate which is otherwise postponed to a later period; a remedy used when there has been an anticipatory repudiation of a contract or a possibility of a future breach.

acceleration clause 1. Loan provision giving the lender the right to declare the entire amount immediately due and payable upon the violation of a specific loan provision, such as failure to make payments on time. 2. Clause often used in reference to contracts for payment by which the time for payment of the debt is advanced because of breach of some condition such as failure to pay interest when due. Such clauses are often bargained for elements of mortgages and notes to protect the mortgagee from risks connected with the transfer of the mortgaged property.

acceleration coefficient *economics* The additional amount of capacity needed to produce another unit of output.

acceleration premium *economics* The increase in pay allowed a worker with increased production. Sometimes relates to piecework where the per-unit pay is increased as the number of units produced increases. May also relate to an incentive pay plan, where the more one produces, the greater the pay per marginal unit produced.

acceleration principle *economics* A theory that asserts that the changes in demand for consumer goods and services tends to give rise to much greater changes in demand for producer goods.

acceptable paper *finance* Notes, drafts, bills of exchange, etc., which the Federal Reserve will accept for discount, or as collateral.

acceptance 1. The agreement to accept an offer. 2. The reception of something offered with the intention of keeping it, such receipt generally being considered an unspoken agreement to some earlier act or understanding. 3. A deliberate intentional agreement or consent (may possess a special meaning or significance in connection with a particular subject matter).

acceptance criterion Any minimum standard of performance in investment analysis. (*See* hurdle rate)

access 1. Approach, admittance, admission, entrance, or passage to anything. 2. A right vested in owner of land which adjoins a road or highway to go and return from one's land to the road or highway without obstruction. 3. Means of entry and exit from land.

accessio cedit principali Accession or annexation of a thing to another by which the thing annexed becomes part of that to which it is annexed and the property of the owner of the latter.

accession rate *economics* The ratio of the number of workers added to the payroll in a month to the average work force during the same month.

accessory 1. An adjunct, accompaniment, or anything which is joined to another thing as an ornament. 2. One who contributes to or aids in the commission of a crime.

accidental bodily injury *insurance* Unexpected and unintended physical harm. (Only the result, not the cause, must be unanticipated.)

accidental death and dismemberment benefits Low cost, psychologically appealing insurance which usually offers the same death benefits as group life. Dismemberment benefits are fixed by a schedule based on accidental death benefits. The principal sum of such benefits is payable for loss of one hand and one foot or one foot and one eye, while one-half is payable for loss of one hand, one foot, or one eye.

accidental means *insurance* A clause requiring the injury to result from causes that were accidental.

accommodation An arrangement, such as a loan, made by one person as a favor to another.

accommodation indorsement *economics* The signing of one's name to a negotiable instrument for the benefit of another person, with the intent of lending the creditability of one's name to the document, so that it will be more acceptable and circulate more freely. The accommodation indorser thus becomes for all intents and purposes a surety for the party at whose request he or she indorsed the instrument.

accommodation indorser *law* Person otherwise unconnected with a negotiable instrument who may indorse the instrument for the purpose of lending his credit to the instrument. Should the primary indorsers default for any reason, the accommodation indorser is held liable, but also has the right of recourse against the original indorser.

accommodation line *insurance* A policy written by an agent, and accepted by the insurer, because of the satisfactory nature of the account in general, even though the individual policy might not be accepted under strict underwriting standards.

accomplice A person who knowingly, voluntarily, and with common intent unites with another in the commission of a crime. (*See* accessory)

accord and satisfaction *law* An agreement between two people, one of whom has a claim against the other, to accept something in settlement of that claim.

account 1. Detailed statement of the mutual demands in the nature of debt and credit between parties, arising out of contracts or some fiduciary relation. 2. A statement of debits and credits, or receipts and payments.

accountancy conventions   *accounting*
Basic practices, consistent in nature, used
in the accounting profession.

accountant   Individual or group authorized under applicable law to practice public accounting, including authorized
professional accounting associations, corporations, or partnerships.

account executive   The individual representing the brokerage house with whom
one deals.

accounting   The act of recording, classifying, and summarizing in a significant
manner, and in terms of money, transactions and events which are, at least in part,
of a financial character and interpreting
the results thereof. (This is the official
definition of the American Institute of
Certified Public Accountants.)

accounting cycle   A recording process
for each accounting period which begins
with transactions recorded in a journal
and ends with a post-closing trial balance.

accounting, double entry   *See* double
entry accounting.

accounting income   An economic
agent's realized income as shown on financial statements. (*See* economic income,
realized income)

accounting period   Any time period for
which an income statement is prepared.

accounting principles   Broadly
defined rules which have been adopted
over time by accounting professionals for
use as guides in recording and reporting
the financial affairs of business.

accounting projection   *limited partnerships* A section in an offering memorandum which projects earnings based on
preconceptions of the performance of the
project.

accounting rate of return   A figure of
investment merit, defined as average
annual cash inflow divided by total cash
outflow. (*See* internal rate of return)

account in trust   *finance* An account
which is opened by one person but held in
trust for another. Unless this is a trust
fund, the person who opened the account
must approve withdrawals.

account payable   Amount owed to an
ordinary business creditor as distinct from
long-term liability.

account receivable   Amount due in the
short-term from a business debtor as
distinct from long-term debt.

accounts payable   Money owed to suppliers. Also called payables.

accounts receivable   1. Money owed by
customers. 2. The short-term claims of
business entities against their debtors.
Also called receivables.

accredited   Recognized as meeting a
given set of standards (e.g., accredited law
school, accredited hospital).

accretion   *investing* The growth of a
fund, such as a pension fund, by virtue of
new contributions and/or interest
received on the principal.

accrual accounting   1. Method of
accounting in which revenue is recognized
when earned and expenses are recognized
when incurred without regard to the timing of cash receipts and expenditures. 2.
Method of accounting that requires
income or expense to be entered when
the amount is earned or the obligation is
payable.

accrued depreciation   A loss which is
not restored by current maintenance and
which is due to all factors involved causing
ultimate nonuse of the property (includes
normal wear and deterioration).

accrued expense   *accounting* Expense
that has been incurred but has not been
paid.

accrued expenses payable   Obligations such as wages and salaries, interest of
borrowed funds, and pensions.

accrued interest   Interest that has been
earned but not paid.

accrued revenue   *accounting* Revenue
which has been earned but has not been
received.

accrued taxes and interest   *accounting* Money set aside to pay taxes and interest which are accrued (accumulated) but
not yet paid.

accumulated income   *investing* That
income earned by a trust which is retained
in the trust, rather than being paid out.

accumulated profits tax   *finance* A
surtax which is levied on earnings retained
in a business to avoid the higher personal
income taxes they might be subject to if
paid out in dividends to the stockholders.
Retained earnings must be justified as necessary for the growth and development of

the business to avoid the surtax. (*See* Appendix G)

accumulation plan *investing* A method for the systematic accumulation of mutual fund shares through periodic share buying and the reinvesting of individual dividends and capital gains distributions.

ac etiam *And also.* Used to introduce the real cause of action in writs that allege a fictitious cause of action.

acid test A method of determining the short-term liquidity of a company by dividing current assets, less inventory value, by current liabilities. (*See* quick ratio)

acknowledgment *law* 1. The formal declaration by a person, before a competent authority such as a notary, that the signature on a legal document is the signer's free act and deed, and therefore subject to any legal scrutiny. 2. A formal declaration before a proper officer that an instrument, act, or deed is that of the person executing it.

acquiescence *law* 1. Passive compliance or satisfaction; as distinguished from avowed consent on the one hand and from opposition or open discontent on the other hand. 2. A consent inferred from silence, a tacit encouragement.

acquisition cost The price and all fees required to obtain a property.

acquittance *law* 1. The relief of an obligor from a specific obligation. 2. A written, legal document which relieves the obligor from some type of obligation, financial or otherwise.

acre A two-dimensional measure of land equaling 160 square rods, 10 square chains, 4,840 square yards, or 43,560 square feet.

acre foot *economics* Approximately 325,850 gallons of water, or the volume required to cover one acre of land to a depth of one foot.

action to quiet title *law* A remedy by which the party who believes himself to be the owner can clear up defects in his title to the land.

actio personalis moritur cum persona *Personal action dies with a person.* Maxim which does not apply to actions founded on contract. Various statutes such as the Provincial Fatal Accidents Act

have curtailed the application of this maxim.

active equity management strategies The conscious selection of investment securities, intentional diversification to balance risk, following trends and indices. An individual who invests in an active management fund will pay fees for buying and selling specific securities.

active life reserve *insurance* In health and accident insurance, the type of reserve held when level premiums are charged, but when claim rates increase as the ages of the policy holders increase.

active trustee Trustee who has active duties to perform in connection with the trust property, such as managing it. (*See* trustee)

activities analysis *management* One of three techniques espoused by Peter Drucker to be used in deciding the appropriate organizational structure of a given company. The other two techniques are decision analysis and relations analysis.

act of God 1. An event that happens purely through the operation of nature unmixed with any human agency or human negligence. 2. An act accomplished exclusively by violence of nature without the intervention of any human agency; any accident produced by any physical cause which is beyond resistance, such as lightning, earthquake, or floods and not preventable by human care, skill, or foresight. (Primarily used in insurance contracts and, as such, is an exemption whereby the insurer does not have to pay for damages or loss caused by such an occurrence. There are, however, exceptions to this rule.)

actual cash value 1. Original cost of property minus that sum equal to accrued financial depreciation, technological obsolescence, and location deterioration. Homeowner's insurance would pay the actual value of the building minus depreciation in the event of the total destruction of the building. 2. The fair or reasonable cash price for which the property could be sold in the market in the ordinary course of business. 3. *insurance* The sum of money the insured goods would have brought at market price at the time of the loss.

actual notice   Knowledge that may be positively proven to have been communicated to a person directly and personally or that is presumed to have been received personally. (*See* notice)

actuals   *investing* Any physical commodity which is ultimately delivered to the buyer upon expiration of the contract (i.e., gold, soybeans, pork bellies, etc.).

actuarial assumption   *pension plans* The reasonable expectation of time period, amount of contribution, and amount of earnings in a defined benefit plan. Since the future is unknown, an actuarial assumption must be made with respect to these three variables. A plan may be reviewed periodically, and adjustments made as necessary. Other variables may include mortality, turnover, settlement factors, etc.

actuarial cost methods   Recognized actuarial techniques utilized for establishing the amount and incidence of the annual actuarial costs of pension plan benefits and expenses. Six of the more popular methods are: (a) individual level premium cost; (b) entry age normal with frozen initial liability cost; (c) aggregate cost; (d) modified aggregate cost; (e) modified entry age normal with frozen initial liability cost; and (f) modified individual level premium cost. These cost methods are normally used only by experts in the field.

actuary   1. Person skilled in calculating life expectancy to determine the value of life interests, reversions, and annuities; frequently used in fatal accident cases to compute the monetary benefits which the deceased would have given to the immediate family had the person lived. 2. *insurance* One who is schooled in mathematics and uses those statistical skills to figure premium rates for insurance companies, plus feasible numbers for pension plans. The actuary will use every kind of demographic information, mortality tables, and the experience of the company to arrive at actuarial conclusions.

act within scope of employment   *law; insurance* An act performed while on duty and in the course of performing those duties. The test of whether an employee is acting within the scope of his or her employment at the time of the accident or wrongful act is whether the act was done while the employee was doing the employer's work.

additional extended coverage   *insurance* An additional policy on an extended coverage homeowner's policy, which insures against such perils as damage from vandalism, glass breakage, falling trees, and water damage from heating or cooling systems.

additional living expense form   A form attached to DB&C (dwelling, building, and contents) basic form and used to recover additional living expenses within reason, when a family must find lodging after the residence is lost.

add-on charge   A method of advertising the interest rate on installment loans that understates the true interest rate (no longer permissible).

add-on clause   A proviso allowing additional purchases on an existing installment credit agreement which often states that default on the addition constitutes default on all purchases.

add-on interest   Interest added to the principal of a loan. The amount of interest for length of term is computed on the original principal.

ademption   *law* The extinction or withdrawal of legacy by testator's act equivalent to revocation or indication of intent to revoke. If a bequest is of specific property and the property has been sold or otherwise disposed of before death, that's generally the end of the matter. The legatee gets nothing, unless some other provision is made in the will. The legatee's loss is technically known as ademption. Similarly, if the estate owner, after having made a specific bequest of property, puts a mortgage on the property, the legatee generally takes the property, subject to the mortgage, which will have to be paid by the legatee to get the property free of encumbrance. There you have a partial ademption.

Aden Analysis, The   Newsletter once published by the Aden sisters of Costa Rica extolling the virtues and predicting the price of gold.

adhesion   *insurance* Contract prepared and made available by an insurer to an applicant who must accept or reject it in the form offered.

adjustable benefits *insurance* Insurance which allows a policyholder to increase or decrease the face amount of the policy according to changing needs. Proof of insurability is necessary before the face value can be increased.

adjustable life A type of insurance policy introduced in 1971, which provides policy owners the option of adjusting various components of the policy to meet their needs and ability to pay.

adjustable peg System which permits changes in the par rate of foreign exchange after a nation has had long-run disequilibrium in its balance of payments and which allows for short-run variations within a few percent of the par value.

adjustable rate mortgage (ARM) Mortgage loan that allows the interest rate to be changed at specific intervals over the life of the loan.

adjusted basis Base price from which to judge capital gains or losses which entails tax deductions, cash distribution, and depreciation.

adjusted gross estate Gross estate less administrative costs, funeral expenses, debts, and claims against the estate.

adjusted gross income 1. Income on which an individual computes federal income tax. It is determined by subtracting from gross income unreimbursed business expenses and deductions (e.g. IRA and Keogh payments, moving expenses, alimony payments, special deductions for working married couples, and disability income). 2. Income before itemized deductions for medical expenses, interest payments, and real estate taxes.

adjusted tax basis Original basis of property reduced by depreciation deductions and increased by capital expenditures.

adjusted taxable gift A decedent's taxable gifts made after December 31, 1976, which are not otherwise included in the gross estate. In 1976, the gift tax and the estate were "unified" in order to determine the combined tax owed by the estate upon the death of a person. If the decedent had unpaid gift taxes at the time of death, and also estate taxes, the two will be considered together to determine the ultimate tax owed. (*See* unified credit)

adjusted trial balance *accounting* The trial balance which results from combining adjusting entries with the unadjusted trial balance.

adjuster *insurance* Person employed by an insurance company to investigate and settle claims for personal injury or property damage, as between the insurer and insured in property losses. May be independent or a paid employee of the insurer. (*See* independent adjuster)

adjustments to income Expenses related to the taxpayer's employment and miscellaneous expenses which reduce the total income figure to the adjusted gross income for income tax purposes.

administered price *economics* A price attached to a product by the producer who appears willing to produce only as much as consumers will buy at that price. Such an action makes a product to appear in short supply, and thus "worth" the asked price, whereas the producer could produce much more, and at less cost.

administration of estates The collection of the assets of the deceased, the payment of debts, and the distribution of the surplus to the persons beneficially entitled to the estate remainder.

administrative assistant *banking* One who serves the bank president in many and different ways, usually handling activities which the president does not have time for, but which need the stamp of the president's office.

administrative secretary *banking* Secretary who usually works closely with a number of bank officials, attends executive meetings to take minutes of the meetings, and attends meetings of the board of directors to take the official minutes there. Will normally have a wide knowledge of the bank personnel and all the bank's operations. Position is sometimes combined with that of executive secretary.

administrative services only (ASO) health insurance An arrangement by which an employer is allowed to self-insure. The employers who utilize this plan usually have highly predictable claims rates. Approximately 18% of group health plans are now written under ASO.

administrator 1. Person appointed by the court to settle the affairs of one who dies intestate. 2. A person authorized to manage and distribute the estate of one who dies intestate or of a testator who has no executor.

ad pios usus   For pious, religious, or charitable purposes.

ad valorem   *According to value.* Describes tolls, duties, or levies payable according to the value of the subject.

advance funding   Money put aside in excess of that required to pay current pension benefits for retired employees held by a trustee, a bank, or an insurance company.

advancement   Gift of money or property in anticipation of the share that an heir will inherit from an estate with the intention that the amount of the gift will be deducted from that share.

advance-premium mutual   *insurance* Mutual that charges annual premiums large enough to provide funds to pay claims and expenses and strengthen surplus. Large advance-premium mutuals have accumulated sufficient surpluses to write nonassessable policies.

advance refunding   *investing* A situation in which the U.S. Treasury may offer the owners of a given issue the opportunity to exchange them for debt instruments of longer maturity, but with a greater yield to maturity.

adverse action   1. Unfavorable change in terms that affects some debtors. 2. Refusal to grant credit in the amount or under terms requested. 3. Termination of an account. 4. Refusal to increase the amount of an existing credit line when requested in accordance with the creditor's procedures.

adverse possession   1. Occupancy of real property to which the occupier has no title, in continuous, open defiance of another person's legal title to it. 2. *law* A method of acquiring title by being in actual, peaceful, continuous, and open possession of realty not consistent with the title of the owner and not recognized or acknowledged by the possessor of that title. 3. The period or length of time (governed by statute) during which such possession continues before the possessor acquires title to the realty.

advertisement   Nonpersonal sales presentation directed to potential customers. A commercial message which is delivered or made available to a customer or prospective customer in any manner, such as through print or broadcast media, in direct mail literature, on signs or displays, in point-of-transaction literature, or on price tags.

advertising agency   *marketing* Professional organization, sometimes very large, that does research, market surveys, and public relations for clients, followed by promotional campaigns for the company's products or services. Most agencies place the advertising with the media at 15% less than they charge the client, which amount is their fee. Often, special research and market surveys done for a company will entail special payments to the agencies according to a pre-arranged price schedule.

advisory   Pertaining to counseling, suggesting, or advising which is not imperative or conclusive.

advisory opinion   An opinion sought or offered which is binding on no person and which has no legal status.

aequitas   *Equity.*

aequitas sequitur legem   *Equity follows the common law.*

affected with a public interest   Clearly devoted to the public use or interest, as concerns a business or property.

affiant   *law* A person who makes and swears to an affidavit.

affidave   *To pledge one's faith.*

affidavit   *law* A statement or declaration in writing sworn to or affirmed in front of a person having the authority to administer the oath.

affiliate   1. To join or associate with. 2. An associate.

affiliated service organization   Corporation established to service a parent organization. Most are single purpose, as for instance to handle insurance of parent.

affiliated service organization regulations   *retirement plans* Rules for Affiliated Service Organizations as contained in Internal Revenue Code 414(m), essentially establishing that all employees of such groups must be included in retirement plan eligibility, coverage, and vesting tests. (Refers to actual "service groups"; i.e., groups providing services for other groups.)

affinitas affinitatis Remote relationship arising by marriage, as distinct from blood relationship.

affinity A relationship by marriage to blood relatives of a spouse. Direct affinity is one that a spouse has with the relatives of the other spouse. Secondary affinity is that which subsists between the husband's and the wife's relatives by marriage. Collateral affinity is that which subsists between one spouse and the relations of the other spouse's relations.

affirmative action program A program devised and frequently mandated by government to increase the hiring of women and minorities.

a fortiori Much more so; by so much stronger reason.

after-born child *law* A child born after the execution of a will by the parents.

after-tax cash flow 1. Cash flow, less income taxes, attributable to the income-producing property. The resultant tax saving is added to the cash flow that is earned by the property. 2. *financial management* Total cash generated by an investment annually, defined as profit after taxes and depreciation, or, equivalently, operating income after tax plus the tax rate times depreciation. 3. The cash flow resulting from different methods of cost recovery and different marginal tax rates.

after-tax return The return on an investment after all taxes on the earnings have been paid; also referred to as after-tax yield.

after-tax yield The true earnings of an investment after taxes on the earnings have been paid.

agency 1. An entity acting for or representing another by the latter's authority. 2. The legal relationship between a principal and an agent arising from a contract in which the principal engages the agent to perform certain acts on the principal's behalf.

Agency for International Development (AID) Semiautonomous unit of the State Department which administers funds voted by Congress for economic, technical, and defense assistance to nations identified with the free world.

agency relationship *insurance* Relationship established between principals and agents by mutual assent usually given in an express agreement or by one party sanctioning the actions of another, thereby creating an agency by ratification.

agent 1. A person authorized by another to act for that person in the transaction of business, the management of property, or the performance of miscellaneous tasks. 2. *insurance* In property and casualty insurance, one allowed by the company to initiate, modify, and cancel insurance contracts. In life insurance, the agent will commonly be in sales and service. 3. *real estate* Anyone who undertakes to transact business on behalf of another person, provided the other person has given full and explicit authority for that specific transaction.

agent, general *See* general agent.

agent, special *See* special agent.

aging schedule *accounting* A summary of accounts receivable in which accounts are categorized by number of days outstanding.

agio theory of interest *economics* The concept that interest is a payment to the saver by the borrower for the postponement of the saver's current consumption. In short, the saver gives up the pleasure of consuming in this period in order to have more money to spend (saving plus interest) at some future time.

aggregate concentration Total sales of all industries measured against the sales of the largest firm or firms in the country.

aggregate demand Total spending in the economy, including consumer spending, planned investment, government spending for goods and services, and net exports.

aggregate indemnity *insurance* The upper limit the insurer will pay the insured for liabilities assumed under a specific type policy.

agreement An understanding or contract between two or more parties in respect to some common purpose, such as the transfer of property, rights, or benefits.

agreement among underwriters *investing* A contract between participating members of an investment banking syndicate. (*See* syndicate)

agreement corporation A federally or state-chartered corporation that has entered into an agreement or understanding with a corporate board of directors that it will not exercise any power not permissible under the Edge Act. (*See* Edge Act)

agreement of sale   *real estate* A written agreement by which the purchaser agrees to buy certain real estate and the seller agrees to sell same on terms of the agreement.

Agricultural Adjustment Act (1938) Basic farm law (with subsequent amendments) of the United States which provides for: (a) price supports of selected farm products at specified levels, to be implemented by purchases and nonrecourse loans by the Commodity Credit Corporation; (b) production control through acreage allotments of certain crops; (c) marketing agreements and quotas between the Department of Agriculture and producers in order to control the distribution of selected commodities; (e) payments to farmers and others who follow approved soil conservation practices; and (f) parity payments to farmers for selected agricultural staples.

agricultural labor Services performed on a farm for the owner or tenant (exempted from the Unemployment Compensation Law).

agriculture futures (*See* commodity futures)

aid and abet To assist by words, acts, encouragement, or presence, actual, immediate, or not, or constructive, in the commission of a crime.

Aid to Families with Dependent Children (AFDC) A federally subsidized public assistance program to provide income maintenance and social services to needy families with dependent children.

Airline Deregulation Act (1978) A law adopted by Congress that reduced the regulatory powers of the Civil Aeronautics Board (CAB) and mandated its abolition in 1985.

air-pocket stock   *investing* A name given to a specific stock that plunges rapidly on the market, usually due to a bad earnings report, or some other negative variable. As shareholders sell rapidly, and buyers are few, the plunge becomes precipitous.

air rights The right to use, control, or occupy the space above a designated property which can be leased, sold, or donated to another party.

aleatory contract   *insurance* A contract in which the dollar amount to be exchanged will be unequal; e.g., if a loss is suffered, the payment will be far greater than the premium, and if there is no loss, there is no payment.

alien Any person not a citizen of a given nation; a person who owes allegiance to a foreign government; a foreigner. In the U.S., an alien is entitled to the same protection of life, liberty, and property under the due process clause of the U.S. Constitution as is afforded a citizen, according to the Immigration and Nationality Act.

alimonia Sustenance, nourishment.

alimony Allowance made by court order to a person from his or her spouse's estate or income to support that person after divorce or legal separation from the spouse or while a divorce action is pending. Originally based on husband's common law duty to support his wife. (*See* alimony in gross, alimony pendete lite, permanent alimony)

alimony in gross Alimony paid in a lump sum in final settlement.

alimony pendete lite   Alimony allowance made during the pendency of a matrimonial action.

alley   *real estate* A type of street running between the back property lines. A narrow public way unless otherwise designated.

Alliance for Labor Action (ALA) Federation of unions started in 1968 by the United Automobile Workers and the International Brotherhood of Teamsters.

allocate To apportion, allot, assign, or set aside according to a predetermined schedule or with some particular purpose in mind.

allocated annuity distribution Deposits made by an employer to a retirement plan which are identifiable for each participant. Distribution of the funds is made periodically, and the entire amount (if the employee has made no contributions) must be reported as ordinary income.

allocated costs Costs systematically

assigned or distributed among products, departments, or other elements.

allocated funding A pension-funding instrument in which funds are specifically allocated to a particular participant. Trust fund plans usually are unallocated while insured plans may be allocated or unallocated, depending on the plan used.

allocation formula Method of distribution. Allocation or distribution of Individual Retirement Account funds must begin by April 1, in the year after the participant has reached the age of seventy years and six months. If the funds are not taken in a lump sum, they can be removed from the fund on a proportionate basis, with mortality tables being used to determine the expected life span of the individual. (E.g., John Doe has one hundred thousand dollars in an IRA. At the appropriate time, if his expected life is figured to be ten more years, then approximately ten thousand dollars per year will be removed from the fund for ten years. This is highly simplistic, inasmuch as each allocation formula must be calculated on an individual basis, and often must be changed each year.) All funds being distributed by the fund will be taxed as ordinary income.

allocation method The process of comparing each participant's compensation or service to that of all other participant's to determine the allocation of defined-contribution deposits.

allocation of expenses *limited partnerships* The distribution of deductible expenses between the general partner of a limited partnership and the limited partners. Sometimes tax laws may have a bearing on such allocations.

allocation of income and profits *limited partnerships* Part of the agreement between the general partner and the investors, or limited partners. Usually, the investors put up a larger percentage of the money than they receive back, proportionately, in profits. The structure of fees paid to the general partner will control the return to the investor, to a marked degree.

allocation of resources and goods A plan for the distribution of resources to be used for particular purposes and the distribution of income derived from them.

allodial system The legal system and basis for property rights in the United States that allocated full property ownership rights to individuals. (*Cf.* free hold)

allot 1. To apportion, to set aside for a specific person; to indicate that a portion of property held by one or more persons is to belong in the future exclusively to another specific person or persons. 2. To distribute or appropriate a share of a corporation to a specific recipient who then becomes a shareholder.

allotment A distribution, as of shares in a corporation to purchasers of such shares; apportionment; division.

alloy *economics* A mixture of baser metals used in gold and silver coinage to give greater strength to the coins and allow them to better resist wear during circulation.

all risks coverage *insurance* Protection against all risks or perils that may cause loss to the covered property, except those specifically excluded in the policy.

alter ego *The other self.* Under doctrine of alter ego, the court may disregard the corporate entity and hold individuals responsible for acts knowingly and intentionally done in the name of corporations.

alternate valuation date *estate planning* The date six months after the date of death which the executor may elect to use as the date of valuation. If no date in the sixth month corresponds numerically to the date of death, the alternate valuation date is the last day of the sixth month. The valuation date for property disposed of within the six month period is the day of disposition. The executor's election to use the alternate valuation date applies to all assets included in the decedent's gross estate.

alternate valuation election *estate planning* The right of the executor of an estate to choose an alternate valuation date (usually six months after the date of death). Usually appreciation or depreciation of assets would set the tone for such a decision.

alternative *law* Option or choice; as when two remedies are possible to redress the same wrong and the litigant must choose one of the two; if both can be resorted to they are considered cumulative.

alternative cost *See* opportunity cost.

alternative minimum tax Federal tax designed to close certain loopholes in the income tax law to ensure that all wealthy taxpayers pay some income tax. Computed by adding tax preference items (such as tax shelter deductions) to adjusted gross income, subtracting forty thousand dollars for a married couple filing jointly or thirty thousand dollars if filing singly, to determine the taxable income, approximately 20% of which is payable tax. Different from the minimum tax which usually sets a base level for taxation of corporations. With tax law changes, specific figures may change.

alternative mortgage instrument (AMI) Any property lien agreement other than a fixed interest rate, level payment amortizing loan.

altum mare *The high seas.*

ambulance chaser A lawyer or lawyer's agent who tries to persuade victims of accidents to institute lawsuits for damages.

American Depository Receipts Claims to share certificates that are held in a foreign bank.

American Federation of Labor-Congress of Industrial Organizations (AFL-CIO) Organization of labor unions formed in 1955 by a merger of the AFL and CIO to improve wages, hours, and working conditions through free collective bargaining. It exercises no authority or control over member unions other than its constitution and code of ethical practices.

American Institute of Real Estate Appraisers (AIREA) A professional organization of real estate appraisers affiliated with the National Association of Realtors.

American Real Estate and Urban Economics Association (AREUEA) An organization of scholars, researchers, and practitioners concerned with economic analysis of real estate related problems.

American Society of Appraisers (ASA) A professional organization of appraisers (not restricted to real estate). (ASA publishes the biannual journal, Valuation.)

American Stock Exchange (Amex) The second most important exchange in the United States. Amex lists the stocks of small companies not listed on the New York Stock Exchange, though some are national in scope. Qualified regional companies may be listed on the Amex if they wish to be.

amortization 1. Payment of indebtedness, such as bonds or mortgage, by installments or a sinking fund. 2. Reduction of debt by regular payments of interest and principal sufficient to pay off a loan by maturity. 3. Process of paying off indebtedness by installments of principal and earned interest over a definite time. 4. Accounting procedure that gradually reduces the cost value of a limited life or intangible asset through periodic charges to income. For fixed assets the term used is depreciation. For "wasting assets" it is depletion. The purpose of amortization is to reflect resale or redemption value.

amortization term For a loan, the period of time during which principal and interest payments must be made; generally the time needed to amortize the loan fully.

amortize To repay a loan in periodic payments over a stated period of time.

analysis, logical *See* logical analysis.

analyst One who dissects and evaluates available information in the securities markets relating to certain securities or industries.

anchor tenant *See* prime tenant.

ancillary letters testamentary *law* Those letters issued in a jurisdiction for probate of property owned by a nonresident decedent.

ancillary probate procedure A procedure by which, when a decedent owns property in more than one state, the probate courts of the state involved will cooperate in the probating of the entire estate, usually by each affected state dealing with the property under its jurisdiction and sharing the information with the other state.

ancillary time *See* machine ancillary time.

and interest *investing* A phrase used in the quotation of bond prices, denoting that, in addition to the price quoted, the buyer will also receive accrued interest.

animo felonico *With felonious intent.*

animus cancellandi *With intention of cancelling* (as applied to the revocation of wills).

animus dedicandi   *With intention of donating.*

animus donandi   *With intention of giving.*

animus manendi   *With intention of establishing a permanent residence.*

animus revocandi   *With intention to revoke.*

animus testandi   *With intention to make a will.*

annexation   The process by which an incorporated city expands its boundaries to include a specified area. The rules of annexation are established by state law and generally require a public ballot within the city and the area to be annexed. Incorporated areas are generally protected from annexation by an adjacent city.

annual   Of or pertaining to a year; continuing for the period of a year; occurring or recurring once in each year.

annual additions   *pension plans* The additions which can be made each year to an employee's pension plan. The Employee Retirement Income Security Act set the limitation on annual additions at the lesser of either thirty thousand dollars or 25% of compensation. (This limit became exorbitant under ERISA, so the original maximum of thirty thousand dollars was imposed. Beginning in 1986, this will be adjusted annually for inflation.) (*See* Appendix G)

annual budget   A systematic listing of anticipated yearly expenditures.

annual contributions   *pension plans; profit sharing* Those contributions made by the employer on an annual basis to an employee's retirement plan. Because they are tax deductible for the employer, their amounts are prescribed by law. Of critical importance to defined-contribution plans is the concept of "maximum annual contributions." Were it not for this restraint, an employer could make tax-free contributions (so far as the company is concerned) far in excess of what Congress intended. The maximum annual addition for any participant is computed by adding the following: employer contributions allocated to the participant during the plan year; plus the lesser of: (a) one-half of a participant's contributions or (b) all of the participant's contributions in excess of 6% of the compensation; plus reallocated forfeitures.

annual debt service   Amount required to cover annual principal and interest payments for a loan.

annual gift tax exclusion   That dollar amount which can be given annually by a donor to a donee without triggering a gift tax to the donor. The Economic Recovery Act of 1981 allowed a ten thousand dollar federal gift tax exemption per recipient. Where husband and wife agree to the gift, twenty thousand dollars can be exempt per recipient. Gift taxes are not levied against the donor, nor income tax against the donee. (*See* Appendix G)

annually balanced budget   A budgetary principle calling for revenue and expenditures to be equal during the course of a year.

annual percentage rate (APR)   1. Finance charge over a full year, expressed as a percentage, reflecting all costs of the loan (required by the Truth in Lending Act). 2. The effective yearly rate of interest for a loan, disclosure of which is required by the Truth in Lending Act. 3. The cost of credit on a yearly basis expressed as a security.

annual report   A corporation's financial statement prepared yearly for stockholders. Annual reports of most large corporations are available to persons other than stockholders upon request and are often used as public relations vehicles. Besides giving comparative financial statements for the current and past years, some give divisional reports of past activities and future plans.

annuitant   Person receiving the proceeds from an annuity, may be the person originally named in the annuity, or that person's beneficiary, such as a spouse or heir.

annuitize   *investing* The commencement of a series of payments from the principal which has been built up in an annuity.

annuity   1. A yearly payment of a stipulated sum paid for a definite number of years or for life. Also used to refer to recurrent payments at shorter intervals as in annuity policies where an insurance company, in consideration of a lump sum, agrees to pay to an investing party equal monthly or yearly payments, for a definite number of years or until that person's death. 2. A series of annual payments purchased or arranged for with a sum of money or other capital assets which may be for life, terminable on the death of the investor or at the expiration of other terms. 3. A sum paid periodically in equal installments to annuitants or their beneficiaries under the terms of an insurance policy or a bequest. 4. A level stream of cash flows for a limited number of years. (*See* perpetuity)

annuity certain Benefits payable for a given time period regardless of the life or death of the annuitant.

annuity contract An agreement by which a person makes an investment which will assure payment of an annual sum to one's self during the person's life and of any yet-unpaid balance to his or her estate or beneficiary after death.

annuity due Periodic payment made by an annuity to the recipient, such payment being made at the beginning rather than the end of the year (i.e., January 1, 1988, rather than December 31, 1988).

annuity factor Figure that shows present value of an income stream that generates one dollar each period for a specified number of periods.

annuity table List of annuity factors for different time periods at different rates of interest.

ante mortem interest An interest that exists prior to but not after the transferor's death.

antenuptial settlement An agreement or contract made by a couple before marriage to determine the interests and property rights of both and to set aside property for the benefit of the prospective husband, wife (or both) and/or others, such as their children.

anticipation note 1. A short-term liability to be retired by specific expected revenues (e.g., expected tax receipts). 2. A short-term municipal debt instrument issued to obtain funds in anticipation of revenues or permanent financing. (*See* revenue anticipation note, tax anticipation note)

anticipation of elasticity The recognition that changes in price bring about changes in production, and vice versa. Galiani recognized that the distribution of wealth had an effect on the quantities of goods consumed. For example, a needed good, if it fell enough in price, would then be available to low-income classes, and more would be demanded.

antidumping duty *economics* A tariff designed to prevent countries with a surplus of a goods from selling them to importing countries, so that they will be retailed at a lower price in the importing country than in the producing country. (*See* dumping)

anti-trust legislation Laws which protect trade and commerce by prohibiting or limiting monopolies and monopolistic practices.

apparent authority *law* That power which a principal does not actually grant an agent but knowingly permits the agent to exercise or holds agent out as possessing. The doctrine of apparent or ostensible authority is applicable when a principal places an agent in such a situation that one would reasonably be led to believe that person has authority to perform the acts that are being performed.

appellant *law* Party who takes the appeal of a case decision from one court to another, usually called an appeals court.

appellate court *law* A reviewing court; not a trial court or court of first instance, excepting special cases where original jurisdiction is conferred.

application of funds *finance* A statement usually accompanying the annual financial statement of a company indicating the funds available during the year, how they were obtained, and how they were used.

apportionment 1. The proportional assignment of rights or liabilities to several persons according to their respective interests in the subject matter involved (e.g., division of rent among a number of owners of a building). 2. Division and distribution of property in proportionate parts. 3. The process by which legislative seats are distributed among units entitled to representation. (*See* districting)

appraisal 1. An expert or official evaluation. 2. Valuation or estimation of value of property by any qualified impartial, disinterested person. 3. An estimated value set on property by two qualified persons (does not have the legal authority of an appraisement).

appraisal approach A method of estimating the value of property. (*See* cost approach, income approach)

appraisal fee Charge for estimating the value of property, especially when offered as security.

appraisement A true valuation of property given by qualified person(s) under the authority of a court or legislature.

appraiser 1. One qualified to determine the price or value of goods, land, building, shares, and stocks. 2. *real estate* One who is schooled and skilled in the evaluation of real estate. Appraisers are often called upon by a court of law to give expert testimony in a trial.

appreciable Measurable; capable of being estimated, weighed, judged, or recognized by the mind; perceptible.

appreciate To increase, as in "appreciate in value."

appreciation *economics* The increase of the market value of a specific asset over its value at some other point in time. Appreciation of an asset is usually not recognized as a gain until it is realized (actually sold and obtained). (Cf. depreciation)

apprentice One employed to learn an art or trade.

appropriate 1. To set apart for or assign to a particular purpose, person, or use to the exclusion of others (e.g., to appropriate land for road widening purposes). 2. To apply funds for a particular purpose, as when a creditor appropriates payments made to an earlier debt.

appropriated surplus *economics* A part of the surplus funds of a corporation which have been earmarked by the board of directors for a specific purpose. Such an appropriation can be set aside by the board at a subsequent date, and the surplus funds recognized as an existing liability.

appurtenance 1. Something annexed to a more important thing; that which belongs to something else. 2. *real estate* All rights and interests which attach to or pass with that necessary for the full enjoyment or use of the property (e.g., easements and servitudes).

appurtenant Belonging, attached, annexed, incident, accessory, subsidiary, or appended to something else more important (e.g., right of way to a piece of land).

a priori From the cause to the effect; from the antecedent to the consequent.

arbitrage *investments* Buying something in one market and selling it in a different market at the same time to make a profit (e.g., buying francs in New York and selling them in London when the price is lower in New York). Arbitrage tends to equalize prices of a commodity in different markets, except for differences in the costs of transportation, risk, etc.

arbitration 1. A judicial or quasi-judicial proceeding; a trial out of court; a substitute for the ordinary method of trial. 2. An arrangement for taking and abiding by the judgment of selected persons instead of carrying the dispute to established tribunals of justice which is intended to avoid the formality, delay, expense, and vexation of ordinary litigation. 3. A contractual remedy for settlement of disputes by extra-judicial means. National policy encourages arbitration of labor disputes to avoid industrial strife. 4. *insurance* Process in which insured and insurer are represented by disinterested parties who choose a third party to be an objective participant with the understanding that the agreement of any two becomes binding on both the insured and the insurer. In liability lines, the court becomes the arbitrator, and the policy has no arbitration clause.

arbitrator *law* Person, not always a lawyer, who is chosen to be the referee in a dispute. Often used in disputes over insurance settlements.

archives Backup storage for computer files on magnetic tape.

area sampling A method of obtaining a random poll when population lists are unavailable whereby everyone on a designated block is interviewed. In some cases, respondents are randomly selected from each designated block.

arising out of and in the course of employment A natural and reasonable connection between the risk employment requires of the workman and the resulting injury. Frequently used in workmen's compensation cases in reference to an injury sustained by a worker while doing something reasonably incidental to the requirements of one's employment.

arithmetic average; arithmetic mean *statistics* A measure of central tendency arrived at by dividing the sum of various items in a list by the number of items in the list.

arithmetic straight line trend A simple method of showing the relationship between variables by drawing a straight line through the scatter diagram, which seems to best fit the majority of the dots in the diagram.

arm's length transaction Business dealing between or among parties, each acting in his or her own best interest with no special duty, obligation, or relation to one another.

arrangement *law* Any plan of a debtor for the settlement, satisfaction, or extension of the time of payment of the debtor's unsecured debts, upon any terms proposed by the debtor before or after the adjudication in bankruptcy.

arrearages Unpaid dividends.

arrears An overdue and unpaid debt or liability; what remains after part of a debt has already been paid.

arithmetic straight line trend A simple method of showing the relationship between variables by drawing a straight line through the scatter diagram which seems to best fit the majority of the dots in the diagram.

arson *law* At common law, the malicious and voluntary or willful burning of another's house, dwelling, or outhouse appurtenant to or a parcel of the dwelling house. (A crime against another's habitation, not against that person's property.) Statute law extended the definition to include the burning of other structures or personal property including one's own property when done for the purpose of making a claim on the insurer of the property.

articles of agreement A written memorandum of the terms of an understanding between two or more people.

articles of commerce Commodities shipped or forwarded from one state to another and put up for sale.

articles of incorporation The instrument by which a corporation is formed which states the purpose, place of business, amount of capital stock, amount of paid-in capital, and the number and names of officers.

artificial person Entity created by laws (e.g, a corporation).

art object Painting, sculpture, graphics, etc.

Art of Contrary Thinking *investing* A book by Humphrey Neill which discusses how "contrarian thinking" in investing works.

as agent Phrase describing the role of a broker in a transaction in which the broker acts as a commission agent only.

ascendants Persons related or connected in the ancestral line, by consanguinity or affinity.

ascertainable standard A standard wherein a holder's duty to exercise power is reasonably measurable in terms of one's needs for health, education, support, or maintenance.

as is Without guarantees as to condition.

asked price *investing* 1. The wholesale price asked for a security for interdealer trading purposes. This does not represent prices to the public. 2. The price the security owner wishes to get when selling. (Cf. bid price)

asportation The carrying away of goods one of the circumstances requisite to constitute the offense of larceny).

assay *investing* The test of a metal's purity to verify that it meets the standard for trading on a commodities exchange. E.g., a 100 troy-ounce of refined gold must be assayed at a fineness of not less than 995 before the Comex will allow it to be used to settle a gold contract.

assemblage 1. A collection of persons. 2. The combining of two or more parcels of land.

assess To ascertain; to fix the value of; to levy a tax in the manner authorized by law.

assessed value or valuation An estimated worth and appraisement of taxable property by authorized officials. Generally, it is the value as assessed by municipal or local government on which a percentage is to be paid as taxes by the owner of the property. Each jurisdiction constitutionally limits the indebtedness of such municipal or local government on which, and, to meet this indebtedness, properties may be subject to taxation.

assessment *limited partnerships* In reference to oil, additional cash contributions an investor must make to a program after the initial drilling period, to develop the discoveries made with the initial investment. The money paid will generate tax deductions just as the initial investment did. Investors not paying assessments suffer various penalties provided for in the initial agreement.

assessment ratio *economics* The ratio of the assessed value of property to the market value of the property.

assessor 1. An official who determines property tax assessments. 2. One skilled in ascertaining value of some specific thing or class of things; one who assists the court in trying a scientific or technical matter because of his or her specialized knowledge.

asset 1. Resource having commercial or exchange value that is owned by or due an individual, business, institution, or corporation. 2. A person's property, as contrasted with liabilities or debts. 3. A thing owned, including money, land, buildings, and receivables. 4. Property of any kind, real or personal, tangible or intangible, legal or equitable, which can be made available for the payment of debts. The assets of an individual are often categorized as liquid (cash or near cash) assets, invested assets, and assets in use.

asset-based loan Loan for which fixed assets (e.g., real estate, machinery, etc.) serve as collateral.

asset category Class assigned to investment vehicles according to the goal or objective of the investor (e.g., funds invested in highly liquid vehicles to give the situation adequate liquidity for emergencies).

asset depreciation range Limitations on the period over which assets may be depreciated. Generally applies to property purchased before 1981 and allows depreciable lives 20% longer or shorter than the guidelines provided by Internal Revenue Service. Also provides maximum amounts that can be spent annually on assets and still be a deductible repair. (*See* Appendix G)

asset shiftability doctrine *finance* A concept which maintains that a bank does not need to seek supplementary liquidity in its loan portfolio, since liquidity can be maintained through the shifting of the short-term assets.

asset turnover ratio A measure of asset efficiency; net sales divided by total assets.

assign To transfer, set over, appoint, allot, or designate for a particular purpose.

assigned risk *insurance* In a case in which certain persons applying for insurance are considered sub-standard risks, some states make it possible for such insurance to be purchased at a premium by assigning the policy to a certain company. Normally such adverse selections are given out over time to a number of insurers so that no one company is overburdened.

assignment The transfer of property or some interest in property (e.g., the transference of interest of the mortgagee or lessee in a property or the unexpired residue of a lease). An equitable interest can be assigned under an agreement for sale.

assignment for the benefit of creditors The transfer, without compulsion of law, by a debtor of property to an assignee for application of property or proceeds thereof in payment of debts and return of any surplus.

assignment of dower The act by which a widow's share in her late husband's realty is apportioned and set aside for her.

assistance and cooperation *insurance* Provisions included in crime and liability policies requiring the vital mutual agreement between the insurer and the policy owner in dealing with third parties after a loss.

assistant vice president *banking* Title, given to a person in any department of a bank, which indicates authority and prestige above the level of nontitled employees, but below the level of vice president. Usually indicates the growth and promotability of the person.

associated service organization (ASO) A company set up to provide services to the "mother" company. This ploy was often used, particularly by professional companies, to exclude ASO personnel from fringe benefits offered to employees of the mother company. While ASOs may still be lawfully set up, the personnel must be given the same benefits as personnel in the mother company.

association   1. A union of persons for a common purpose; a confederacy.   2. The parties to such a union.   3. A body of persons not invested with corporate status.   4. A corporation formed not for profit but for the advancement of some objective.

assumpsit   Undertaken or promised (originally used to refer to all contracts, verbal or written, but not under seal). Action brought for the recovery of debt or damages for breach of contract not under seal.

assumption of mortgage   The purchase of mortgaged property whereby the buyer accepts liability for the debt, but the seller remains liable to the lender unless the lender agrees to a release.

assumption of risk   *law*   A voluntary and willing encounter of risk of a danger which is known, understood, and appreciated by the party.   In such a defense, the defendant must prove that plaintiff subjectively and consciously appreciated the danger and willingly chose the risk.   (*See* contributory negligence)

assurance   *insurance*   A policy designed to cover an event which is sure to happen, but the time is not known.   Normally, an insurance policy is taken out to protect against an event which might happen.

assured   That person in whose favor an insurance policy is issued.

at-risk   Describes the total amount of cash invested plus the total debt for which the investor is liable.

at-risk exemption   *limited partnerships*   Tax deduction for exposure to danger of loss.   Investors in a limited partnership can claim these deductions if it can be proved that there is a possibility of realizing no profit and of losing the investment as well. Deductions will be disallowed if the limited partners are not exposed to economic risk.   (E.g., the general partner guarantees to return all capital to limited partners even if the business venture should lose money.)

at-risk rules   Tax laws which limit the amount an investor can lose to the amount that the investor actually has invested in the deal.   Generally does not apply to real estate owners or partnerships whose principal asset is real estate.

attachment   1. The seizure or taking of property for placement under the control

of the court to be held pending judgment. 2. An involuntary disposition of the defendant prior to any adjudication of the rights of the plaintiff; a seizure in advance of trial and judgment.

attained age level funding   A method by which client deposits are made in the exact amount required to fund a participant's retirement benefit over the years of service remaining in that participant's employment (assuming level compensation from the date of computation to the date of retirement).   This actuarial method is favored by many insurance companies and a large segment of the small business pension market because: (a) it generates a specific cost for each employee and lends itself to individual funding products like annuities, and (b) it can absorb the problems caused by the historical instability of small business payrolls.

attempt   An endeavor or effort to do, get, or have.   In civil matters, the term indicates the endeavor to do something that falls short of full execution.   In criminal matters, it indicates that the culprit had commenced the action which, if uninterrupted, would have resulted in a criminal offense.   Mere preparation for or intent to commit a crime does not constitute an attempt.

attestation   The act of witnessing the execution of a document and signing of one's name as a testament to that fact.

at-the-opening order   *banking*   An order for a securities transaction to be executed at the opening of the market or not at all.

attitude of consumers   *marketing*   That frame of mind that is essential for the consumer to actively demand the good or service.   Normally such a frame of mind is based on reasons which are both logical and emotional.

attorney   1. Agent; a person appointed to do certain acts in the place and name of another.   (*See* power of attorney)   2. An officer of the court with an obligation to the court, as well as to the client, to aid in the administration of justice.

attorney-at-law   *law*   A person who has been formally trained and licensed by special examination by the state to practice civil and criminal law and to author legal documents, such as contracts.

attorney-in-fact   1. A person chosen by another and given authority to act in that person's place in a situation that is nonlegal in character.   2. *insurance* One who is empowered, by power of attorney, to act for another.   In a reciprocal group insurance situation, one who is empowered to commit the members as insurers of each other.   One who is empowered to execute a surety bond for the company he represents.

attornment   Agreement that a tenant will continue to hold the leasehold and pay the rents to the new owner when ownership of property changes.   Originating in feudal English law, the term has in recent times been loosely used to refer to a new owner's demand, generally accompanied by a direction from the previous owner, for rents from the tenant.

attractive nuisance   *insurance* Anything particularly attractive to children and potentially dangerous to them (creating also a significant liability hazard to the owner).

attractive nuisance doctrine   The principle that one who maintains on his or her premises a condition, instrumentality, machine, or other agency which is dangerous to children by reason of their inability to appreciate the peril and which may reasonably be expected to attract children to the premises, is under a duty to exercise reasonable care to protect against danger of attraction.

auction   1. A method of marketing property to the highest bidder.   2. A public sale of land or goods transacted by open competitive bidding with goods going to the highest bidder.

audit   1. An examination and full scrutiny of accounts.   2. The act of examining and scrutinizing accounts to weigh and judge their truth and correctness; verification.   3. *accounting* A procedure, usually performed by an outside agency, that passes judgment on the fairness of a financial statement, and on the accounting procedures used in arriving at the conclusions contained in the statement.

auditor   1. One who is qualified to examine and scrutinize accounts.   2. One who officially examines and allows as proper and lawful, or rejects as unlawful, the items of an account or accounts.   3. *bank-*

ing One who provides to top management in the bank periodic financial reports, mode of operations reports, and reports suggesting areas of change which will make the bank more efficient.   In an audit program, the emphasis is normally on preventive measures rather than on curative measures.   At any point in time, the auditor will submit reports to top management which will reveal to them exactly how the bank is functioning.   While the reports are often financial, they may also be operational.   The task of the auditor is a control function.

audit trail   *accounting* A recordkeeping method which leaves a clear path for auditors to follow.

Austrian school   *economics* A school of thought founded by Carl Menger, Eugene Böhm-Bawerk, and Friedrich Wieser in Austria in the nineteenth century, also know as the marginal utility school.   It deals with the problem of "value" and generally affirms that value is dependent upon utility, and more particularly on the utility of the marginal unit consumed.

Austrian theory of capital   *economics* The theory that capital is created when the factors of production finally become a finished product or service, and is ultimately destroyed when such goods or services are utilized.

authentic   Genuine, true; having the character and authority of an original.

authentic copy   A copy which is of such authority, complies with all due formalities, and has been legally certified to prove the form and contents of the original from which it is taken.

authoritarian leader   *communication* Director who determines policy, procedure, tasks, and roles of members.   (An old-fashioned managerial style in which the employee is considered unable to make proper decisions.)

authoritarian socialism   A command economy in which all means of production are in the hands of the state and decision making is centralized.

authoritarian theory   *management* A theory of human nature which declares that human beings are essentially selfish and indolent, requiring strong, authoritarian leadership, and discipline, to achieve their goals.   This is generally known

19

in management as "Theory X."

authority Jurisdiction; judicial or legislative precedent; permission; power delegated to one person by another. Such a power may be express, implied, or imposed by law. (*See* express authority, apparent authority, authority by estoppel)

authority by estoppel Authority which is not actual, but imposed where conduct of principal has been such that it would be against good conscience and unjust to let the person deny it.

authorized dealer *finance* A bank which is permitted by regulators to deal in foreign exchange.

authorized investment *investment* An investment vehicle which is specifically approved by a trust instrument.

automated clearinghouse (ACH) A computer-based clearing and settlement operation, often operated by a Federal Reserve bank, established for the exchange of electronic transactions to make recurring payments such as payroll or preauthorized insurance premium payments. The U.S. Treasury uses the ACH extensively to pay certain obligations of the government.

automated teller machine (ATM) Computer-controlled terminal located on the premises of or belonging to financial institutions through which customers may, by the use of a magnetically encoded card, make deposits, withdrawals, or other transactions. Groups of banks sometimes share ATM networks throughout a region that may include portions of several states. Also known as customer-bank communications terminal (CBCT) and remote service unit (RSU).

automatic fiscal stabilizers 1. Nondiscretionary or built-in features that cushion recession by helping to create a budget deficit and curb inflation by helping to create a budget surplus (e.g., income tax receipts, unemployment taxes and benefits, agricultural price supports, and corporate dividend policies). 2. Built-in features of the economic system which tend to minimize fluctuations in spending (e.g., progressive income tax which automatically pulls more money out of the income stream as total spending increases, and unemployment payments which automatically push more money into the

income stream when the economy slows down).

automatic premium loan provision *insurance* A provision by which the premium will be paid from the policy loan value if the policyholder fails to pay when due.

automation Production techniques that adjust automatically to the needs of the processing operation by the use of self-functioning control devices.

autonomous variable *economics; statistics* An economic variable which is determined by a non-economic event, such as a political action impacting directly upon the economy.

availability *finance* The lag time between the deposit and the date it is credited to the collected balance.

availability schedule *finance* A timeframe showing the lag time between the date checks drawn on banks in different locations are deposited and when they are made available to the depositor.

available unified credit *tax law* Dollar for dollar reduction of taxes which is available to the decedent after provisions have been made for the paying of gift taxes which may be due on lifetime transfers. Inasmuch as the unified credit has increased every year from 1977 through 1987, the available credit (in total) would be $30,000 in 1977 and $192,800 in 1987. From this available credit would be subtracted all gift taxes on a cumulative basis, at the time of death to determine the credit available to offset estate taxes.

average 1. Medium, mean proportion. 2. *marine law* The equitable principle that where an expense is incurred, sacrifice is made, or damage suffered for the safety of a vessel, its cargo, or freight an equitable adjustment and distribution of the loss shall be made and proportionately borne by all interested parties. (E.g., in order to save the ship, some cargo is thrown overboard; in such a case, the several persons interested in the ship, cargo, and freight must contribute ratably to indemnify the person whose goods have been sacrificed.) A general average is to be distinguished from a particular average in that the latter is an expenditure made for the purpose of forestalling the occurrence of disaster to a particular interest or diminishing the loss therefrom. 3. Mathematical compilation by which market performances are measured (often in reference to Dow Jones). 4. *statistics* Any one of several measures of central tendency of a list of items. (*See* measures of central tendency.)

averageable income 1. The amount by which adjusted taxable income exceeds 133⅓% of average base period income. 2. Adjustment in certain cases for capital gains. (E.g., if the average base period capital gain net income exceeds the capital gain net income for the computation year, then the amount determined is reduced by an amount equal to such excess.)

average annual compound return The result of averaging the interest earned on interest over several years to test the yield on the security.

average base period income 1. One-fourth of the sum of the base period income for the base period. 2. Base period income.

average collection period The number of days spent collecting accounts receivable in a given period, such as a month, divided by the number of collections. (E.g., in 1987 the XYZ company spent 1,182 man-days collecting on 52 separate accounts. The average collection period would be 1,182 divided by 52, or 22.7 days.)

average cost 1. Total costs divided by the number of units produced. 2. *accounting* Figure determined by dividing the cost of goods in beginning inventory, and the costs of goods purchased, by the number of units, and then multiplying that average cost by the number of units in the ending inventory.

average daily balance Sum of the daily balances for the interest period divided by the number of days in the interest period.

average deviation *statistics* The total sum of the deviations of the items of a distribution from the median, or from the arithmetic mean, divided by the number of items. Also called mean deviation.

average income tax rate The percent arrived at by dividing tax liability by taxable income.

average index monthly earnings (AIME) An income index based on Social Security earnings for years after 1950.

average-marginal relationship *investments* The relationship between all corresponding average and marginal curves such that: when an average curve is rising, its corresponding marginal curve is above it; when an average curve is falling, its corresponding marginal curve is below it; and when an average curve is neither rising nor falling (i.e., it is either at a maximum or a minimum) its corresponding marginal curve intersects (is equal to) it.

average propensity to consume 1. The average percentage of after-tax income which consumers spend on goods and services. 2. The portion of disposable income spent for consumer goods. (*See* Appendix D; cf. marginal propensity to consume)

average propensity to invest The ratio between new capital formation and national income.

average propensity to save That portion of disposable income which is not spent for consumer goods, paid as taxes, or spent for imported goods. (*See* Appendix D)

average revenue Ratio of total revenue to output, or price per unit of quantity sold. (*See* Appendix D)

average tax rate Ratio of total tax to base on which it is imposed. (*See* Appendix D)

averaging down The process of reducing the average cost basis of a security by buying more of its shares at a lower price.

avoidable expense *See* escapable expense.

avoidance of risk The act of eliminating danger of loss or damage by avoiding their potential causes.

avulsion 1. A sudden and perceptible loss or addition to land by the action of water or a sudden change in the bed or course of a stream. 2. Transference, by the perceptible action of a watercourse, of a piece of a person's property to that of another. Differs from accretion or alluvion in that the ownership of the soil so removed does not change.

B

baby bond   *investing* A bond which may be either a convertible or straight debt bond, with a denomination of from twenty-five to a thousand dollars. Used to reach a market of investors with less money than regular buyers of corporate bonds.

back casting   *economics* The determination by statistical methods of the relationships between dependent variables and independent variables in past economic data. The reverse of forecasting.

backdating   *finance* Dating any statement, document, check, etc., earlier than the date drawn.

backhaul   *economics* A load arranged for at the destination of a planned trip by a commercial freight carrier to be delivered to or near the home terminal. (*See* deadheading)

back spread   *economics* In the study of arbitrage, a less-than-normal spread between the prices of a given product in two markets. (*See* arbitrage, spread)

back up   *investing* A sudden downward spiral of the market after a period of upward movement. The same expression is sometimes used when the trend of the market is downward.

backwardation   *investing* A situation in which the prices of commodities, or foreign exchange, tend to be higher for quick delivery than for later delivery. This occurs when current demand is greater than anticipated future demand.

backward integration   *economics* The takeover of a manufacturing firm by a wholesaler, or by a retailer or group of retailers, who wish to assure their future supply of products.

bailee   *law* The receiver of property to be held in trust for a specific purpose and a specific time.

bailment   *law* Delivery of property upon agreement, express or implied, that after a specific purpose is accomplished the property shall be returned to the bailor or disposed of according to the bailor's direction.

balance   Residue; remainder; what remains or is left over. In relation to accounts, denotes equality between the debit and credit totals.

balanced budget multiplier   1. *eco-nomics* The proposition that when the federal government balances its budget, taxes levied result in a reduction of expenditures, but less than the amount of the taxes. The reason for this is based on the assumption that not all of the untaxed money would be spent, but part would be saved. When tax monies are spent by the government, spending is increased over what it would have been had there been no tax. 2. Principle that if government spending and taxes are increased or decreased simultaneously by an equal amount, national income will be increased or decreased by the same amount. (E.g., a balanced increase in government spending and taxes of one dollar will raise national income by one dollar, and a balanced decrease of one dollar will lower national income by one dollar.) The effects of balanced increases in government spending and taxes are equal but opposite, and hence the two multiplier processes cancel each other out—except on the first round when the full amount of government spending is added to national income.

balanced fund   1. A mutual fund that invests in many types of securities rather than concentrating on a single kind. 2. A conservative type of mutual fund. Balanced funds invest in common stocks, preferred stocks, and bonds, but the investment objective is security of principal, reasonable current income, and reasonable capital appreciation in the long term.

balance of payments   *economics* An annual statement of international transactions prepared by the Department of Commerce, which includes every action that gives rise to money payments between nations. The more important among these actions are: (a) current accounts involving international trade and services as between nations; (b) capital accounts, whether long-term or short-term; (c) movements of gold and silver; (d) unilateral transfers of gifts of governments and individuals. The statement accounts for all of the wealth flowing out of a country, and the wealth flowing in.

balance of trade   *economics* An annual accounting for goods and services exported, and goods and services imported. In theory, it is better when outflows and inflows are essentially equal. Trade is the largest component in the balance of payments report.

balance of trade deficit Condition in which value of imports is greater than the value of exports. More is spent for goods and services than is received from the sale of goods and services.

balance sheet 1. A statement showing an entity's financial position at a specific date: what it owns (assets), what it owes (liabilities), and what is left over (net worth). 2. A statement which shows a summation of all accounts, but not the particular items which make up the several accounts. 3. *accounting* A report made for a business, or an individual, that shows total assets, total liabilities, and net worth. Net worth is total assets minus total liabilities.

balance sheet equation *economics; finance* An algebraic expression of the balance sheet in which assets equals liabilities plus owner's equity.

balloon maturity *finance* 1. A loan which requires a larger payment at the end than the previous payments have been. 2. A bond issue with larger payments due at later maturity dates. 3. A mortgage which is amortized by periodic payments, with a large payment on the date of the last payment period.

balloon mortgage A contract requiring a certain number of payments at stated regular intervals with a final payment substantially greater than the periodic payments.

balloon payment Any payment which is more than twice the amount of any other regularly scheduled payment.

banding *economics* The practice of grouping pay scales into a few major categories instead of having many multiple rates.

band of investment technique An income property appraisal technique by which the capitalization rate is derived as a function of mortgage and equity rates.

bank 1. An association or corporation whose business it is to receive money on deposit, cash checks or drafts, discount commercial papers, make loans, and issue promissory notes. 2. *real estate* Any moundlike formation or ridge; raised ground; the slope of land at the edge of a watercourse.

bankable paper *See* bank paper.

bank bill *See* bank note.

bank check A check drawn by a bank on its account in another bank. (The drawer bank on such a check has the right to issue a stop payment to the drawee bank.)

bank credit An arrangement by which a bank engages to honor drafts drawn pursuant to its terms and with authority to pay or to purchase such a draft. (A bank making such an engagement is an issuer.)

bank credit card A card issued by a bank which enables the customer to buy goods and services on credit or obtain cash loans from banks or businesses which honor that card.

bank draft Instrument of one bank drawing upon its deposits with another bank.

bank eligible securities *finance* Securities which are seen as safe by bank regulatory agencies and thus are approved as investment vehicles for banks.

banker's acceptance A time draft drawn on and accepted by a bank as a customary means of effecting payment for merchandise sold in import-export transactions and a source of financing used exclusively in international trade. With the credit strength of a bank behind it, the banker's acceptance usually qualifies as a money market instrument. The liability assumed by the bank is its acceptance liability. (*See* letter of credit)

Bank for International Settlements (BIS) Central bank for large international banks serving somewhat the same purpose internationally as the Federal Reserve does domestically. Located in Basle, Switzerland, the BIS was established in 1930 to administer the post-World War I reparations agreements. Since the 1960s, it has evolved into an important international monetary institution and has provided a forum in which central bankers meet and consult on a monthly basis. As an independent financial organization, the BIS performs a variety of banking, trustee, and agent functions, primarily with central banks. The Federal Reserve is represented at BIS meetings, but is not a member. The BIS is the only international financial institution in which most Eastern European countries, excluding the Soviet

Union, East Germany, and Albania, are members.

bank holding company A corporation created for the purpose of holding the stock in one or more commercial banks. Bank holding companies often own other financial corporations such as consumer finance companies.

Bank Investment Contract (BIC) A 1989 ruling of the Federal Deposit Insurance Corporation that the FDIC insure individual components of pension funds held by banks up to $100,000 per component.

bank note A promissory note issued by an authorized bank made payable to bearer on demand and intended to circulate as money. Unlike a check, which is not currency although it may pass readily from hand to hand, a bank note is issued as currency under legal restrictions and authority. Also called bank bill.

bank overdrafts A check written by a depositor which cannot be honored because of insufficient funds in the account. Some banks may honor the check but make a special charge for this service.

bank paper Negotiable, discountable, commercial paper, such as securities, bank drafts, bills of exchange; high credit paper which, if the time of payment was reasonable and the bank had loanable funds, would be discountable. Also called bankable paper.

bank rate *economics* In the main, an expression which refers to the Federal Reserve discount rate, or the rate of interest the Fed charges member banks for borrowings. Sometimes the expression is used simply to denote the rate at which banks loan money to customers.

bank rate, international *See* international bank rate.

bank regulation The formulation and issuance by authorized agencies of specific rules or regulations, under governing law, for the conduct and structure of banking.

bankrupt A person who is unable to pay a just debt when payment is due and demanded of that person; an insolvent.

bankruptcy 1. The state or condition of one who is a bankrupt; the status of one who has committed an act of bankruptcy; insolvency. 2. A court action declaring a

person free of most debt, due to the person's inability to pay. All the estate of the bankrupt vests in a trustee in bankruptcy for the benefit of the creditors. Bankruptcy proceedings contemplate the taking of possession by the trustee of the property of the bankrupt actually or constructively in that person's possessions at the time of filing of petition in bankruptcy, the distribution of the proceeds received from such property, ratably among bankrupt's creditors whose claims have been filed and allowed, and the discharge of the bankrupt from liability for the unpaid balance of such claims.

bank service charge Charge made by a bank to a customer, according to a specific schedule, and debited to a customer's account. (Charges differ among banks, and some banks have no service charge if the balance in the account does not fall below a prescribed level.)

bank statement reconciliation The process by which the depositor checks the statement against his or her cancelled checks and check stubs to reveal checks outstanding and provide a double check on the accuracy of the records.

bank supervision The general and continuous oversight of the activities of the banking industry to ensure that banks are operated prudently and in accordance with applicable statutes and regulations.

Bankwire An electronic communications network owned by an association of banks and used to transfer funds and convey messages between subscribing banks. (*See* Cashwire)

bargain in good faith *labor law* Exploration of a transaction with an eye to agreement of compromise rather than mere adherence to pre-formed opinions.

bargaining theory of wages *economics* A general theory that wages tend to fall between two limits. The upper limit is break-even production as viewed by the entrepreneur, and the lower limit is the subsistence level for workers. It is assumed that the equilibrium point between the two levels will depend upon the bargaining power of the two groups.

bargaining unit *labor law* A group of employees who have banded together for purpose of bargaining wages and/or benefits with their employer.

bar graph 1. Chart on which factors such as the high, low, and closing price of a security are indicated by solid columns or bars. 2. A price-time axis chart which depicts changes of a stock or a market index and its volume over a period of time and usually presents high-low closing data.

barometer *economics* A selective compilation of economic data, usually including sectors such as housing starts, consumer spending, interest rates, inflation, etc., which tend to reveal larger trends in the total economy.

barratry *law* 1. In foreign trade, any unlawful dealing with a ship, or its cargo, by the captain or crew of the ship. 2. In pure law, the inciting of a quarrel or litigation.

barrier to entry An obstacle to the entry of new firms into an industry.

Barron's confidence index Index that compares yields on high grade bonds against yields on low grade bonds. As yields move down on lower grade bonds, the index reflects an increased confidence in the economy by investors.

barter To exchange goods for goods without the use of money or other medium of exchange.

base market value *finance* The average market price of a select group of securities at a specific point in time.

base period *economics* A point in time which is used to make comparisons to other points in time. The value for base period is always 100%, and that of the comparative points, more or less than 100%. In gauging inflation, if 1976 is the base year (or, 100%), then years prior to, or subsequent to, 1976 can be compared to that base year to determine the increase or decrease in price levels.

base period income For any taxable year, the taxable income for such year first increased and then decreased (but not below zero) in the following order: (a) Taxable income shall be increased by an amount equal to the excess of the amount excluded from gross income under section 911 (relating to earned income from sources without the United States) and subpart D of part III of subchapter N (sec. 931 and following, relating to income from sources within possessions of the United States) over the deductions which would have been properly allocable to or chargeable against such amount but for the exclusion of such amount from gross income. (b) Taxable income shall be decreased by the capital gain net income. (c) If the decrease provided by paragraph (2) of subsection (b) applies to the computation year, the taxable income shall be decreased under the rules of such paragraph (2) (other than the limitation contained in subparagraph (c) thereof).

base rate *economics* When referring to wages, the rate of pay for a specific output, or for a specified period of time.

base year The beginning year or reference year for constructing a price index. (*See* Consumer Price Index)

base-year analysis *finance* An analysis of a financial statement in which the figures of all years are compared to one year, known as the base year.

basic coverage *insurance* Insurance against damage or loss by fire, lightning, vandalism, malicious mischief, and theft of dwelling buildings, their contents, and personal property, and including comprehensive personal liability insurance.

basic deficit The excess of import-type transactions over export-type transactions in a country's current, long-term capital and noninduced short-term capital movements in the balance of payments.

basic insurance amount *employee benefits* The amount of each type of group term insurance offered to an employee based on annual salary. An allowable amount of insurance determined by rounding the employee's annual salary to the next highest multiple of one thousand dollars and adding two thousand dollars.

basic medical insurance The traditional coverage of hospital, surgical, and regular medical expenses that provides benefits for specified kinds of care, usually starting with the first dollar of expense incurred, but with relatively low maximum benefits.

basing point *transportation* A rate established between two fixed points which serves as a base for rates in between the points, or beyond the points.

basing point system A pricing procedure in which the selling price includes the price at the factory plus freight charges from the basing point nearest the buyer.

basis 1. Fundamental principle; the foundation of any reasoning. 2. *tax* The point from which gains, losses, and depreciation deductions are computed; usually the cost or purchase price of an asset; original cost of property plus any additional money put into the property less the deductions. 3. A term for the cost of property which generally includes mortgages assumed. 4. *investing* Original cost plus out-of-pocket expenses that must be reported to the Internal Revenue Service when an investment is sold. This constitutes the total cost used in calculating gains or losses in the investment.

basis book *finance* A book of mathematical tables used to convert yields to maturity into equivalent prices at various rates of interest.

basis point *finance* One hundredth of one percent (0.01%). Generally refers to the interest rate on a bond.

basis reduction The amount by which the original basis is reduced by different methods of decreasing the value of the asset over time.

bathtub theorem *economics* An analogy in which the water in a bathtub is compared to the stock of goods, the faucet flow to production, and the drain flow to consumption. Thus, the rate of accumulation would be the excess of inflow over outflow.

Bayesian analysis *statistics* A method in statistics for assigning subjective probabilities to uncertain possible events. (I.e., a way of assigning best judgments to each alternative development, which are compared to the real world once all the figures are in. From that time on, real world figures are used for further projections. This usually must be done when projecting the sales of a new product.)

Bayes criterion *statistics* The theory that if we know of no reason why probabilities should be different from each other, we should assume they are equal.

BD form *finance* A document which must be filed with the Securities and Exchange Commission by every brokerage house. The form reveals the firm's financial position, its officers, and other pertinent information, which must be constantly updated in the SEC files as changes occur in the company.

bear One who thinks that the trend of the market or the price of a security is downward.

bearer 1. A person in possession of a bill, note, check, draft, or any negotiable instrument presented for payment. 2. Person in possession of a bill of exchange which is "payable to the bearer." In law of negotiable instruments, anyone in actual possession of such a note is entitled to payment and is not affected by any disability of the nominal payee.

bearer bond Bond that passes title simply by delivery. Such bonds have coupons attached and by delivery of the coupons on the due dates, interest on the bond can be collected. Also called bonds to bearer.

bearish The stock market philosophy that prices of stock, in general, will go down.

bear raid *investing* A term denoting an attempt by market speculators to manipulate the price of a stock by selling a large number of shares short. This would tend to push the price of the stock down, which would then yield a good profit to the seller, as he or she fulfilled the short obligations by buying stock in the market at the new and lower price. This maneuver is illegal, since short sales are supposed to be made on the uptake.

bedroom community A residential area, often near an employment center, which provides few employment opportunities within its borders, but whose residents commute to another city for work.

before-tax dollars Income prior to deductions for taxes.

behavioral equation *economics* In econometrics, an equation denoting the economic behavior of an individual or the whole economy. This behavior is stated as a functional relationship to many aspects of economic life rather than an identity or a definition (e.g., expenditures on VCRs depend upon population and the income of that population).

bellwether *investing* A stock which is so well known, and which is held in such high regard, that its movement is looked upon as a signal of the direction the market may take in the near term.

benchmark A permanently affixed mark used to establish the elevation and position of a place; used by surveyors as a referent point for determining other positions and elevations.

bench warrant A writ issued by the presiding judge directing that a person be brought before the court. Commonly used to compel attendance before the court to answer a charge or to appear as a witness after failure to respond to a subpoena.

beneficial association Organizations formed for the mutual protection, relief, or benefit of their members or their families, relations, dependents, or designated beneficiaries. Also known as benefit societies, benevolent societies, and fraternal or friendly societies.

beneficial owner *investing* A person who receives the benefits of an investment, though it may be held in the name of another (e.g., a minor child receiving all the benefits from an investment held for the child by an adult).

beneficial use Right to occupancy and use of a property, including any benefits or profits that may be derived from such property. (A person does not have to own property to have the beneficial use of it.)

beneficiary 1. One entitled to the benefit of property; one for whose benefit a trust is created; one for whose benefit a trustee or an executor holds the property; one who receives a benefit or advantage. 2. One who may receive and use the profits and proceeds of an estate or property even though the title is vested in another.

benefit-cost ratio Index of profitability.

bequeath *estates* Real property derived under a testamentary instrument. In modern usage, the word has been used to describe any kind of testamentary disposition of property real or personal.

bequest A gift of personal property by will; legacy. (*See* devise)

best efforts agreement An arrangement with an investment banker to make every attempt to sell a security with no guarantee of sale.

best evidence *law* Most reliable proof obtainable under existing circumstances. The best proof of the terms or contents of a document is the original document itself. However, other evidence of the terms of a document is allowed when the absence or unavailability of the original is satisfactorily accounted for.

Best's rating *insurance* A well known rating service known for its analysis of insurance companies, and its annual publication of ratings of these companies. Best's top rating for a company is A+. These ratings are valuable for purchasers of insurance, and for anyone to whom the knowledge of an insurance company's soundness is important.

beta coefficient *finance* A measure of the volatility of a stock. A stock is said to have a high beta when the beta is more than 1, indicating that stock is more volatile than the market average. To measure the beta of a stock, divide the percentage change of the market index by the percentage change in the price of the stock. This is a measurement of risk. (*See* Appendix C)

betterment 1. An improvement to real estate. 2. *accounting* The replacing of one asset by another which is deemed to be better, at a price usually higher than the original asset.

betting The backing of a guess by offering to forfeit, in the case of error, a sum of money or article of value to one who holds the opposite position and who backs that opinion by corresponding stipulation; the staking of money or other value on the event of a doubtful issue.

biannual Occurring twice a year. Same as semiannual. Sometimes used loosely to mean every two years. (*See* biennual)

bid 1. An offer to buy goods or services at a stated price or an offer to perform a contract for work, labor, or materials at a specified price. 2. The amount one offers to pay. 3. Indication of the highest price for which a security may be sold.

bid price *finance* The price at which a market-maker (dealer) will buy stock on the over-the-counter market. (Cf. asked price)

biennual 1. Biannual. 2. Occurring every two years.

big bang *finance* A slang term used to describe the deregulation of the London-based securities markets on October 27, 1986. Some experts consider the step in

London as a start toward a single world financial market.

Big Board *See* New York Stock Exchange.

Big Eight *accounting* Formerly, the eight largest accounting firms in the United States as measured by annual revenues. Recently two mergers occurred so that the eight firms are now six.

bilateral contract 1. A contract under which each party promises performance. 2. Mutual promises between two parties of a contract, each party being both a promissor and promissee. Such a contract is created when the offeror extends a promise and asks for a promise in return and the offeree accepts the offer by making the requested promise.

bilateralism *economics* Economic policy on an international scale designed to achieve a balance of trade between two countries. (This is often done when one country has a very favorable balance of trade, and the second country has an deficit balance, in which event the country with the deficit balance may resort to high tariffs, quotas, etc., to gain trading clout. This action will normally put the first country into the position of needing to bargain with the second to achieve a better relationship.)

bilateral monopoly Market structure in which a monopsonist buyer faces a monopolist seller.

billing cycle Time interval between periodic statement dates. Such intervals may be considered equal unless the date varies more than four days.

billing error Mistake in a periodic statement. (*See* Regulation Z)

bill of exchange A written agreement under which title to personal chattels is transferred in consideration of some value other than money.

bill of lading Written acknowledgment, signed by the carrier, of the receipt of goods to be transported on the terms therein expressed and delivered to the consignee or parties therein designated.

bill of rights That portion of the U.S. Constitution which states the guaranteed rights and privileges of the individual and the general principles and fundamental ideas of free government.

bill of sale 1. A written agreement under which title to personal chattels is transferred in consideration of money received. 2. A written instrument given to pass title of personal property from a seller to a buyer.

bimetalism *economics* A monetary system in which both gold and silver are minted and the coins are used as legal tender. There is usually a stated ratio of exchange between the two established by government.

bimetallic standard Monetary standard per unit of currency in terms of a fixed weight of two metals, usually gold and silver. The United States was on this standard during the nineteenth century.

binder 1. *real estate* An agreement, accompanied by a deposit, for the purchase of real estate, to evidence good faith on the part of the purchaser. 2. *insurance* A memorandum of a verbal contract, given by the company to the insured, which provides for temporary protection until a formal policy is issued.

bivariate analysis *statistics* An analysis of the values of two variables, which results in the determination of the coefficient of correlation.

black capitalism An effort begun in the late 1960s to increase Negro ownership and control of business. Its objectives are to improve the job market, the ghetto economy, and the condition of the black community.

black economy; black market *economics* 1. Transactions which evade government controls and taxation, and are thus illegal. 2. An illegal free market which tends to develop when government restrictions prevent prices from reflecting the true demand and supply conditions. 3. Economic activity which is not reported in official statistics and which usually pays no taxes because it is not reported. Also called underground economy.

blank endorsement An instrument which specifies no particular party to whom it is payable but authorizes negotiation by the bearer upon delivery.

blanket encumbrance Lien, including an option or contract to sell or a trust agreement, affecting a subdivision or more than one lot offered within a subdivision, except such lien arising as the result of tax assessment by public authority.

blanket insurance Policy which covers changing membership groups such as students or spectators at sports events. No insured is named and no certificates are issued.

blanket mortgage Single lien that covers more than one parcel of real estate.

blended rate An interest rate on a refinanced loan that is higher than that of the old loan but lower than the current rate. (Offered by lenders to induce home buyers to refinance existing, low-interest rate loans as an alternative to assuming such loans.)

blighted area Section of a city in which a majority of the structures are dilapidated.

blind figure *accounting* A term which denotes a figure which is indistinctly written, so that it may be read as an altogether different figure (e.g., an 8 which is written to look like a 3).

blind pool 1. Investments in the petroleum industry by an investor who does not know what specific properties were invested in. (Units of investment are usually small in such pools.) 2. An investment program in which monies are invested into an association without investors knowing which properties will be purchased.

blockage discount Discount seldom allowed by the Internal Revenue Service which applies only to stock listed with a public exchange. This discount is determined as a percentage of the decrease in realizable price below current market price, so only stock that is listed and quoted may take advantage of the valuation technique. The theory behind the blockage discount is that a sizable amount of stock contained in the decedent's gross estate cannot be readily sold at one time without decreasing the stock's market price. Based on this market factor, the stock is allowed a blockage discount computed on the basis of the decrease in the realizable price below the current market price.

blockbusting A discriminatory and illegal practice of coercing a party to sell a home to a member of a minority, then using scare tactics to influence others to sell at depressed prices.

blocks *investing* A large quantity of stock, or a large dollar amount of bonds, either held or traded. Usually, ten thousand shares of stock, and $200,000 worth of bonds, would be considered blocks.

blood relationship *law* The relationship between persons who stand in lawful descent from a common ancestor.

blowout *See* out the window.

blue chip stock 1. Stock in an old company with a long history of profitability and stable dividend payments. Usually, a blue chip company is engaged in an industry which is more likely to grow than to decline. (e.g., IBM, AT&T) 2. High-grade securities issued by mature companies that are well established, have great financial strength, and are leaders in their industry. (Often used to describe the thirty companies listed in the Dow Jones Industrial Average.)

Blue Cross/Blue Shield An independent, non-profit plan available to groups in place of commercial insurance. Such groups have a tax advantage in most states because they are non-profit. Blue Cross/Blue Shield works from the experience of the one insured group and is essentially a producer's cooperative. Benefits are provided on a service basis rather than a reimbursement basis, including complete coverage for either a semiprivate hospital room or ward accommodations (length of stay is commonly limited to 90, 120, or 365 days), and full coverage for hospital extras for the benefit period. Some Blue Shield plans will allow full service benefits to lower income groups. A form of medical coverage is often included in the Blue Shield contract. Blue Cross and Blue Shield extended benefits programs are similar to comprehensive medical plans offered by insurance companies. The plans of these non-profit organizations may exclude blood and plasma, expensive drugs, and nursing services. Separate deductibles are used for Blue Cross and Blue Shield.

blue law 1. Laws or ordinances for the regulation of personal conduct on Sundays. Blue laws are often concerned with gambling and the sale of liquor. 2. Laws, usually localized, which inhibit the ability to do business on Sunday.

blue list *investing* A daily financial publication listing bonds offered for sale by

29

about seven hundred dealers, and banks, representing more than $3 billion in par value. Bonds listed are mainly municipals.

blue-sky law 1. Act providing for the regulation and supervision of investment companies, which are aimed at preventing fraud in the sale of securities. 2. Law enacted to regulate the sale of stocks and bonds, intended to protect inexperienced investors from fraudulent exploitation. 3. State regulation on securities that were begun before federal regulations (Kansas, 1911). The laws passed controlling the sale of securities were frequently called "blue sky laws" because they protected the securities markets from fraudulent securities referred to as "pieces of the blue sky." Although there are differences in state laws, generally the four "blue sky laws" components are: (a) security firms and brokers must be licensed; (b) financial information concerning issues of new securities must be filed with state regulatory bodies; (c) new securities must meet specific standards before they may be sold, and, (d) regulatory bodies must be established to enforce the laws. (See securities law)

board of equalization A government entity whose purpose is to assure uniform property tax assessments.

Board of Governors Group of seven people that supervises the Federal Reserve System. Members are appointed by the President and confirmed by the Senate for terms of fourteen years each, one term expiring every two years.

board of realtors A local group of real estate licensees who are members of the State and National Association of Realtors.

board room *investments* A portion of a brokerage office in which the client and/or account executive may sit and follow the stock exchange tapes and the market news events as disseminated.

bodily heirs Lineal descendants. The class of persons who, by law, take property by inheritance or succession from another, exclusive of adopted children.

body language *See* nonverbal communication.

bogus check Check drawn on a nonexistent bank or by or payable to a fictitious person.

boiler plate Stereotypical wording

found in contracts, such as in preprinted material.

boilerplate legends Standardized provisions printed in very small print on a formal paper such as a contract, a deposit slip, the content of which is so routine and common that it does not generally require reading.

boiler room *investing* A name given to a place where high-pressure salespeople use telephones to attempt to sell securities to lists of customers. Usually the securities being hawked are highly speculative, and sometimes fraudulent. Such activities may be illegal, or, at the least, contrary to the Rules of Fair Practices of the National Association of Securities Dealers.

bona Movable goods.

bona fide *In good faith*, honestly, without fraud, collusion or participation in wrongdoing. Real, actual, genuine, and not feigned. (Often used to describe a person who acquires property honestly, giving good consideration for the same and without any notice of the claim of a third party to the property.) A bona fide holder for value takes a negotiable instrument in good faith for valuable consideration without any notice of the defect in the title of the person from whom it was acquired.

bond 1. Contract under seal to pay a sum of money; contract under seal acknowledging a debt (usually future). (See double bond, performance bond) 2. Instrument of indebtedness issued by companies or governments to secure repayment of borrowed money (sometimes accompanied by a mortgage of hypothecation of the property of the borrower). Sometimes the mortgage is in favor of a trustee for the benefit of bond holders. (See bearer bond) 3. A contract between surety and government that surety will undertake that a defendant who has been released will appear at a specified time and place. 4. To establish a contract binding a party financially for the performance by another in completing an obligation.

bond-a-month plan A plan through which a bank debits the customer's account monthly for a Series EE bond.

bond, coupon *See* coupon bond.

bond, discount *See* discounted bond.

bond rating 1. The varying degrees of status given to bonds, usually in direct relationship to the credit worthiness of the issuing institution. Ratings are given by independent rating agencies, and may run from AAA to D, according to the posture of the company at the time. 2. An appraisal by a recognized financial organization of the soundness of a bond as an investment.

book inventory *accounting* A system of accounting for inventory that perennially records incoming and outgoing items. It is not based on periodic physical counts, and therefore does not account for deterioration, destruction, or theft of inventory.

book entry Entry on the records of the United States Treasury Department, a Federal Reserve bank, or a financial institution, in which Treasury and certain government agency securities are held.

book-entry securities *investing* Securities which are not represented by certificates, but which are recorded in a book of customer accounts. Municipal bonds are often handled in this manner.

book value 1. The value of a business or an item of property as shown on the balance sheet. 2. In a corporation with only one kind of stock outstanding, the net worth of the corporation divided by the number of shares of stock outstanding. 3. A firm's total assets minus its total liabilities (i.e., equity or net worth). 4. The value at which an item is reported in financial statements; value after crediting surpluses or losses, or in the case of depreciable capital assets, after deducting the permitted amount of depreciation each year. (*See* market value)

book value per share Measurement of the assets a corporation has working for each share of common stock. It is arrived at by taking the net balance sheet value of the corporate assets, subtracting the face value of creditors' and preferred stockholders' claims, and dividing the remainder by the number of outstanding shares. Also known as net asset value per share.

boom and bust cycles *economics* Cyclical movements in the stock market which carry the market index from a very high point down to a very low point.

boot Unlike property included in an exchange to balance the value of the like properties exchanged. Money or property given to equalize values between other property exchanged.

borrowing power An unfunded indebtedness, such as a line of credit with a bank; the authority or the legal right of a corporate body to borrow. Where there is no fixed line of credit, often used to denote an individual's ability to borrow.

bottleneck inflation *economics* Condition of generally rising prices or drop in real income caused by uneven upward demand or cost pressures in some key industries (e.g., automobiles, construction, or steel) even if aggregate demand is in balance with aggregate supply for the economy as a whole. This is commonly caused by changes in the structure of the nation's economy, and inability to quickly shift productive resources. Also called structural inflation.

bottom fisher *investing* An investor who looks for a security which, in the investor's opinion, has hit bottom, and can be purchased at a low price. The investor then buys the stock with the hope that it will move to a much higher level. Some such investors even buy stock in companies near bankruptcy with the hope that the stock will make a come-back.

bottomry bond Mortgage of a ship, by which her keel or bottom is pledged. Security given by the master of the vessel pledging the vessel, its cargo, and freight as security for money borrowed to meet an emergency at a time when no other source of funds is available to the ship's master. The debt is not recoverable in the event of the nonarrival of the ship at its destination. Such a bond has priority over all other claims. (Cf. respondentia)

bottoms-up approach to investing A method of investing in stocks that seeks out high-performance securities, and especially those which seem relatively immune to the impact of economic trends.

boundary 1. A limiting line, marked or unmarked, by which lands are known and ascertained. 2. A dividing line between two pieces of land.

bourgeois *economics; political science* Citizens of a country who are in the upper middle class with respect to annual income. Karl Marx made much use of the term, denoting those he deemed to be exploiters of the laboring masses. (*See* proletariat)

31

bourse *investing* A word of French derivation which refers to a stock or commodities exchange.

boutique *investing* A small brokerage firm which is highly specialized, and may deal in only a few select stocks and have only a few select clients.

box *investing* The physical location of securities, or other important documents, which are kept by the broker for the client.

boycott 1. A form of coercion directed against an individual, corporation, or group, especially used in labor disputes. A primary boycott occurs when employees of an organized union, acting in concert, refuse to have anything to do with the products or services of an employer in order to force that employer to accept certain conditions desired by the union. A secondary boycott occurs when pressure is applied on customers, actual or prospective, to coerce them to withhold or withdraw patronage from a particular business. 2. To refrain from commercial dealing by a concerted effort. Refusal to work for, purchase from, or handle the products of an employer. Within the meaning of the Sherman Act, this includes even peaceful persuasion of a person to refrain from doing business with another.

bracket creep Movement of taxpayers into higher marginal tax brackets in the progressive income tax schedule, as a result of inflation.

brain drain *economics* The loss by one nation of professional people, or skilled craftsmen, who choose to migrate to another country, usually to work for more pay and better living conditions.

brainstorming *communication* Procedure in which a group discusses problems and alternative solutions to problems.

branch manager *banking* Person responsible for a branch bank whose duties may vary relating to the site of the operation. Many of the primary functions of a commercial bank will be carried on in the branch, such as accepting deposits, cashing checks, making loans (under specifically prescribed rules), marketing, public relations, etc. The branch manager may report directly to the president, but in most situations would answer either to the senior vice president for administration, the executive vice president, or the vice president for branches.

brand A name, term, sign, symbol, design, or some combination used to identify the products of one firm and to differentiate them from competitive offerings.

brand awareness *marketing* The degree to which a brand name or logo is recognized by people who are shopping for a specific product or service.

Brandeis brief Method of appellate briefing developed by Louis Brandeis, former Justice of the United States Supreme Court, which in addition to legal citations includes economic and sociological data.

branding 1. Marking of cattle for the purpose of identification. 2. Formerly, in England, mode of punishment by inflicting a mark with a hot iron on the offender.

Brannan plan Proposal made by Secretary of Agriculture Charles F. Brannan in 1949 designed to eliminate parity payments to farmers and give them direct payments. Under the plan, agricultural prices would be determined in a free market by supply and demand; farmers would then be compensated by a subsidy from the government for the difference between the market price they receive and some higher target price established according to a selected base period in the past.

brazen law of wages *See* subsistence theory of wages.

breach of contract A violation of the terms of a legal agreement; default. Breach of contract allows the nonbreaching party to rescind the contract, sue for damages, or sue for performance of the contract.

breach of duty *law* A situation in which the tort-feasor (wrongdoer) had a duty to the injured person and failed to honor that duty.

breach of warranty *law* 1. The violation of a contract of warranty. 2. Non-performance of a specific or essential condition.

break-even analysis 1. A tool that allows decision makers to compare the profit consequences of alternative prices. The break-even point (in units) equals total fixed cost divided by the per unit contribution to fixed cost. 2. Analysis of the level of sales at which a firm or product will just break even.

break-even chart *economics* A graphic presentation showing how total revenue and total costs vary with the quantity of goods or services produced. The break-even point occurs at that level of production where total costs and total revenues are equal.

break-even point 1. *real estate* The amount of rent or the occupancy level needed to pay operating expenses and debt service. 2. *accounting* That point at which total revenue is equal to the sum of the fixed and variable costs at that specific level of activity, i.e., total costs and total revenues are equal. 3. *economics* That intersection in the marginal cost curve and the marginal revenue curve which indicates that one is equal to the other.

breakout *investing* An increase in the price of a stock above its resistance level, or the drop in the price of a stock below its support level, which usually indicates the continuing movement of the stock.

breakpoint 1. *health insurance* That point at which the insured has paid the necessary deductible and the coinsurance, and at which, from that point on, the insurer pays all costs up to the limits of the policy, if any (also called stop loss). 2. *pension plans* The point at which Social Security taxes are no longer paid on a salary because they exceed covered compensation as defined by the government.

break-up value *economics* The immediate cash value of the assets of a company should it cease to function and go out of business.

Bretton Woods agreement An agreement reached at the the Bretton Woods conference in 1944, which established the International Bank for Reconstruction and Development and the International Monetary Fund in order to avoid many of the problems which had been experienced after other major conflicts.

Bretton Woods conference *economics* A conference of forty-four countries held in Bretton Woods, New Hampshire, in 1944, for the purpose of discussing post–World War II international finance. (*See* Bretton Woods agreement)

breve de recto A writ of right available

to one who is dispossessed of an estate to recover the possession thereof.

bribery The corruption of any person in public or official capacity by gifts or promises of money, favors, property, advantage, privilege, or anything of value. The giving, offering, receiving, or soliciting of anything of value to influence the actions of an official in the discharge of a legal or public duty.

bridge loan *finance* Mortgage financing between the termination of one loan and the beginning of another loan.

B-risk Systematic risk; nondiversifiable risk; risk that cannot be neutralized by diversification. This is the beta coefficient or market risk which measures the risk on a certain stock, as related to the risk of the whole market. A specific stock may rise or fall more sharply than the market as a whole. Such stock is risky; while the stock may rise more than the market when the action is bullish, it will also fall more rapidly than the market when the action is bearish.

broad form CGL endorsement *insurance* Endorsement adding coverage for a broad range of liability exposures faced by firms but often overlooked. Twelve coverages are included.

broad form coverage *insurance* Coverage differing from the basic form in that one additional loss and several additional perils are included. The additional loss covered is additional living expense coverage. The additional perils are glass breakage, burglary, falling objects, weight of ice, snow, or sleet, structural collapse, rupture or bursting of steam or hot water systems, freezing or water damage from plumbing and heating systems, and damage to electrical appliances or wiring (except television picture tubes) caused by manufactured electricity.

broad form theft policy *insurance* More limited form of theft policy which is written to cover the value of personal property not covered in the homeowner's policy. The schedules for personal property rarely insure for more than a fraction of the worth of valued personal property, such as coin collections, etc. This type policy covers only loss from theft, robbery, and larceny.

broad market *economics* 1. A specific market situation in which a broad spectrum of goods are being traded. 2. A market situation in which geographical boundaries are broad, or where prices of goods may vary widely from the very high to the very low.

broad tape Printed tape recording releases concerning the affairs of companies.

broker 1. One who handles negotiations between parties in the business of buying or selling or any other lawful transactions. A person whose business it is to bring a buyer and seller together. 2. *real estate* One who has taken courses prescribed by the state board and has been duly examined and licensed to transact business on behalf of others in the purchase and sale of real estate. (In most states, the broker is more completely qualified in the real estate business than a salesperson.) 3. *insurance* An agent of the insured, paid a commission by the insurance company and authorized to deliver contracts and collect premiums on behalf of the insurer.

brokerage firm research report Results of research on various securities which can be purchased from brokerage houses. These should not be considered completely objective reports, since the firms involved may want to push a certain security or discourage purchases of another. While normally this bias is not flagrant, objective reports are looked upon as being more valuable.

broker-dealer Any person, other than a bank, engaged in the business of buying or selling securities on its own behalf or for others.

brokers' loans Money borrowed by brokers from banks for uses such as financing specialists' inventories of stock, financing the underwriting of new issues of corporate and municipal securities, and financing customer margin accounts.

brother-sister controlled group Relationship between mother companies and affiliated service organizations requiring that five or fewer shareholders own more than 80% of the voting power or 80% of all value (excluding classes of stock which are nonvoting and limited with preference for dividends) and the same five or fewer shareholders own more than 50% of the voting stock, taking into account ownership only to the extent of identical own-

ership of each corporation. For example, the XYZ company's stock is owned by five persons who have 87% of the voting power. They decide to set up an affiliated service organization to provide services for the XYZ company, and they own 62% of that ASO stock. This would constitute what the Internal Revenue Service calls a brother/sister relationship, and requires that fringe benefits for all employees of both groups be the same.

Bubble Act *investing* An act passed in England in the early eighteenth century prohibiting the issuing of stock certificates by firms, following prohibitive losses incurred by people who were "speculation mad" and who invested in almost any new venture promising great returns on investment.

bubble companies *investing* New companies which appeared in England in the early eighteenth century who managed, through false promises, to induce many speculators to buy new-issue stock which often turned out to be as unsubstantial as a bubble.

bucket shop *investing* A type of illegal brokerage firm almost non-existent today which accepted orders from clients but did not execute them immediately as required. Sometimes the stocks were kept by the broker until they could be bought or sold at a price advantageous to the broker, without regard to the interests of the client.

budget control form A standardized form on which a comparison for each item can be made of budgeted figures and actual expenditures.

budget deficit Expenditures in excess of receipts. (Normally refers to governments.)

budget mortgage A mortgage that requires monthly payments for taxes and insurance in addition to interest and principal.

budget surplus Receipts in excess of expenditures.

building and loan association Original generic designation for any institution of the type now referred to as a savings and loan association. The original name reflected the fact that all loans were made for building structures with almost all of these for residences. (*See* savings and loan association)

building line   A line fixed at a certain distance from the front and/or sides of a lot, beyond which the building may not project.

building permit   Permission granted by a local government to build a specific structure at a particular site.

building residual technique   An appraisal technique whereby income to land is subtracted from net operating income to obtain building income. Building income is then capitalized into building value.

built-in obsolescence   *economics* A part of the make-up of a product which causes it to cease operating after a given length of time so that it must either be repaired or replaced, or a style change in a product such as an automobile which makes it appear out-of-date. Many American-made products have had this accusation made toward them over the past forty years.

built-in stabilizers   *economics* The factors built into our economic functions which tend to lend stability to the economy through the various stages of the business cycle. (E.g., when we are in a rising cycle, government revenues tend to go up, even when tax levels remain the same. And, when unemployment is high, workmen's compensation kicks in for many of the unemployed, thus mitigating the loss of normal wage.)

bulge   *investing* A sudden, but often brief, rise in the price of a stock or a commodity, or in the market indices for either.

bull   One who feels that the trend of the market or of the price of a security is upward.

bullishness   The stock market philosophy based on the belief that the direction of the market will be up.

bundle of rights   *real estate* The recognized rights and interests one has in real property. Also, the exclusive right of the owner to occupy, possess, enjoy, use, and dispose of real property.

burnout   *investing* The point at which a tax shelter ceases to provide tax deductible benefits and begins to provide income for the investor.

business   Anything which occupies the time and attention and labor of people for the purpose of profit. The manner in which individuals make or earn a living.

business cycle   1. The phases of change an economy usually experiences from slump to recovery. The four typical phases used to describe economic activity in industrial nations are: depression, recovery, recession, and prosperity. 2. The recurrent speeding up and slowing down of the economy; macroeconomic fluctuations.

business day   A day on which business is usually conducted; excludes weekends and holidays.

business entity concept   *general business; law* The assumption that a business is separate and distinct from its owners. Proprietorships and partnerships cannot be viewed in this manner, since, legally, they do not exist apart from the owners. Corporations are legal entities, that is, separate and apart from the owners.

business indicators   *economics* The statistical data on factors in an economy which most nearly presage changes in the total economic climate, or in some specific industry. Some indicators have forecasting value, and are known as leading indicators.

business interruption form   Insurance against fire and other perils which covers loss of profits and those fixed charges that continue regardless of whether a business is operating. The insuring agreement states that the insurer shall be liable for the actual loss sustained for the time it would reasonably take to repair or rebuild the damaged property.

business interruption insurance   A coverage against the loss of business income caused by a covered peril, such as fire, explosion, etc.

business risk   1. Risk associated with a business itself; concerns the degree of uncertainty associated with earnings, ability to pay investors' dividends or interest, and ability to pay other debts due, with bankruptcy the most severe outcome. (E.g., risk associated with the stock of a public utility is obviously different than that associated with a high-fashion clothing manufacturer.) 2. *investing* Risk associated with uncertainty about investment outlays, operating cash flows, and salvage values without regard to how the investments are financed. (Cf. financial risk)

business transfer payment Outlay by business for which no good or service is exchanged, such as excise taxes, payouts under deferred compensation arrangements, gifts, and donations.

buy-and-hold strategy *investing* The simple technique of buying good stocks and holding them, rather than jumping in and out of the market on the basis of some technical system.

buy-and-write strategy *investing* A conservative strategy in options trading in which the investor buys stocks and then immediately writes covered call options on them.

buy a spread *commodities market* To simultaneously purchase a near futures contract and sell a far futures contract.

buydown A lump sum payment made to the creditor by the borrower or by a third party to reduce the amount of the consumer's periodic payments to repay the indebtedness.

buyer's market 1. A situation in which buyers have a wide choice and may negotiate lower prices; in real estate, often caused by overbuilding, local population decreases, or economic slump. 2. *economics* Any kind of market in which supply exceeds demand at the current price level, and which gives an advantage to the buyer.

buying climax *investing* 1. A sudden rise in the price of a stock or a commodity which may presage a rapid decline in the price of the same security. 2. A burst of buying which often signals the end of a strong market.

buying on the bad news Purchasing the stock of a firm that has issued bad news, under the assumption that as the stock has gone down on the bad news, good news will bring it back up again; i.e., a strategy of buying when the stock has gone down because of bad news, and holding until it has gone up in the wake of good news.

buying power The total value of securities that may be purchased in an account.

buying, reciprocal *See* reciprocal buying.

buy-sell agreement 1. Arrangement for the disposition of a business interest in the event of the owner's death, disability, retirement, or withdrawal from the business at some earlier time. This is normally drawn up in a written agreement stating the purchase price, terms, and funding arrangements. 2. A pact among partners or stockholders under which some agree to buy the interests of others upon some event. 3. A cross-purchase agreement or a stock retirement or stock redemption agreement providing for the sale and purchase of the stock of a deceased stockholder, often the best solution for disposing of a business interest. 4. An agreement which may exist in a partnership or a close corporation where the surviving partners or stockholders can either buy the interests in the partnership or close corporation or sell them as is deemed best for all persons concerned.

bylaws Set of rules adopted by an association, corporation, or the like and subordinate to its constitution or charter. Bylaws govern the internal mechanical procedures of a corporation and regulate its dealing with others. The word is also used to designate a law enacted by a subordinate legislative body such as a municipality.

bypass trust Situation in which part of the estate owner's property is given to the surviving spouse either outright or in a trust that qualifies for the marital deduction. The rest (often an amount equal to the exemption equivalent of unified credit available to the estate owner) is put into a non-marital trust which pays the surviving spouse income for life and possibly permits the use of the principal for the survivor's defined and ascertainable needs but carefully avoids giving too much control or rights in the trust property. In this way, the property will not be includable in the survivor's estate and can pass estate-tax free to the beneficiary or beneficiaries in line. Also known as a non-marital trust or a family trust.

by-product *economics* Products which are produced from the raw material remaining after the primary product has been produced. E.g., after chickens have been processed for the main carcass, the offal often goes into dog food, or some other feed additive, the feathers into feather meal, and the blood into blood meal.

by-product method of cost accounting
A system of cost-allocation between the primary product being produced and the by-product. Usually all costs are assigned to the primary product up until the by-product becomes distinguishable. Proceeds (net) from the by-products are looked upon as reductions in the cost of the primary product.

C

cabinet security *investing* A stock or bond which is listed on a major exchange, but which is not actively traded.

cadestre *economics* The tax inventory and assessment of real property in a particular governmental subdivision.

caducarry Relating to or of the nature of escheat, forfeiture, or confiscation. (*See* escheat)

cafeteria plan A written plan in which participants may choose among two or more benefits which may be cash or non-taxable. A participant in a plan will not be treated as having received taxable income solely because they had the opportunity to elect a cash benefit. Proposed regulations provide that the plan must offer at least one nontaxable benefit and a taxable benefit. (The only taxable benefit which may be offered effective January 1, 1985, is cash.) The plan must be maintained by an employer for the benefit of employees only. The term employees includes former employees (although the plan may not be established primarily for their benefit) but does not include self-employed individuals. Also called flexible benefit plan, flexible compensation plan, market basket plan.

calendar spread *investing* A method of buying options that entails buying two options on the same security with different maturity dates.

call 1. Demand for payment. 2. Demand by a corporation made on subscribers for shares to pay unpaid portion of a subscription. 3. Option to buy securities. A negotiable open contract which gives the bearer the right to buy from the promissor a specific number of shares of a specific class of stock on and for a certain agreed upon date and price. 4. *real estate* In instruments of conveyance of real property, landmark used to signify a boundary of described land. 5. *bankruptcy law* Assessment levied at the time petition of bankruptcy is filed, which can give rise to a fixed indebtedness provided that the trustee in bankruptcy disclaims all interest in the stock.

callable bond *investing* Bond which carries the stipulation that the issuer may call it in prior to the maturity date; usually a premium will be paid by the company for the privilege to call. Such bonds are often redeemed, and a new issue sold, to take advantage of a lower interest rate.

call date *investing* The date on which a callable bond may be redeemed by the issuer, at the issuer's option.

called bond *investing* A bond which the issuer has declared to be due and payable prior to the maturity date, and in accordance with the stipulations in the bond indenture.

call feature The right of an issuer to retire a debt issue before maturity.

call option *investing* Generally, a short-term instrument giving the owner the right to buy a specific security at a specific price until a specific future date.

call penalty A premium paid for exercising a call feature.

call premium *investing* The amount above the par value of a bond which the issuer must pay the holder if the bond is redeemed prior to the maturity date. The bond indenture specifies the amount this will be.

call price Price at which a security may be redeemed at the issuer's option.

call protection on bonds *investing* A stipulation in some tax-exempt bonds that, though they are callable, they cannot be called until a specified number of years have passed. At the time of the call, a stipulated premium must be paid by the issuer.

call provision   1. Clause in a loan that gives the lender the right to accelerate the debt upon the occurrence of a specific event or date.   2. Provision in a corporate bond which allows the corporation to call in the bond upon notice. A callable bond is usually not considered a good investment as the bonds are apt to be called when it is advantageous to the corporation and not to the bond holder.

Cambridge school   *economics*   A neo-classical school of economic thought which follows the theories of Alfred Marshall (1842–1924).

cameralism   Form of mercantilism extensively implemented by German governments during the eighteenth century. Its chief objective was to increase the revenue of the state, paying more attention to protecting domestic industries than to international trade.

canal   An artificial trench or ditch for the purpose of allowing water to flow for transportation purposes.

cancel   *law*   To erase, obliterate, strike, or cross out by drawing lines across the face of the document; annul, make void. So long as the instrument unequivocally shows that it has been cancelled, the cancellation can be done either by destruction of the instrument or by writing or stamping words on the face of the instrument.

cancellation clause   A contract provision that gives the right to terminate obligations upon the occurrence of specified conditions or events.

canned approach   *communication*   A memorized sales talk used to ensure uniform coverage of the points deemed important by management.

canons of professional responsibility   *law*   The standards of professional conduct expected of lawyers in their relationships with the public, the legal system, and with the legal profession; ethical considerations are aspirational in character and represent the objectives towards which every lawyer should strive; disciplinary rules are mandatory and state the minimal level of conduct below which no lawyer can fall without being subject to disciplinary action.

canons of taxation   *economics*   The principles of taxation espoused by Adam Smith: (a) taxes should be in proportion to revenue received, (b) should not be arbitrary, but certain, (c) should be collected at a time convenient to taxpayers, (d) should be collected as economically as possible.

capacity   1. The status or attributes necessary for a person in order that his or her acts may be legally allowed and recognized; legal qualification.   2. Testator's ability to rationally consider the claims of all those who are related to the person and who are supposed to have claim to the testator's consideration when dealing with personal property as it is to be disposed of after the testator's death. One must consider whether the testator was in such a state of mind that the testator could rationally take into consideration the amount and nature of his or her property and the interest of those who have claims upon the estate. The testator should understand the nature of the act and its effects and the extent of the property being disposed, be able to comprehend and appreciate claims to which he or she ought to give effect. The standard of capacity in the case of impaired mental power is the capacity on the part of the testator to comprehend the extent of the property to be disposed of and the nature of the claims of those who are being excluded.   3. *contract law*   Age of majority and soundness of mind; ability to appreciate the nature and extent of the testator's act. An agreement executed by an insane person or a person who is so intoxicated as to be deprived of understanding is voidable if the insanity or drunkenness was known to the other party to the contract, for the insane and the intoxicated are incapable of giving intelligent assent to a contract.

capacity utilization   Rate at which the capital assets of the corporation are being utilized in production, usually expressed as a percentage of maximum utilization. This is considered to be a short term concept, limited by the capital equipment existing at any point in time.

capital   1. Fund or the sum of money that one is willing to or actually has invested in a personal undertaking, trade, calling, or profession.   2. Total amount of money that can be subscribed for all the shares of the corporation, pursuant to the limitations laid down under its charter or articles of incorporation. 3. Aggregate of the face value of all shares that have been allotted in a corporation. 4. As a factor of production, produced means of further production such as capital goods or investment goods in the form of raw materials, machines, or equipment for the ultimate purpose of manufacturing consumer goods. Hence, human resources are also part of an economy's capital. 5. Funds which businessmen use to purchase capital goods. 6. *accounting* Net worth or the stockholders' equity in a business. 7. The amount of property owned by an individual or corporation at a specified time as distinct from the income received during a specified time. 8. Wealth in any form employed in or available for the production of more wealth or income.

capital accumulation The additions one may add to personal worth each year by saving or investing a part of total earnings, rather than by spending all of it.

capital adequacy *finance* Measures of the sufficiency of the capital of a bank, set out in regulations either by the Federal Reserve, the FDIC, or the comptroller of the currency. (*See* primary capital)

capital asset Long-term asset or an asset with a life exceeding one year that is not bought or sold in the normal course of business, and under Section 1221 of the Internal Revenue Code, can receive favorable tax treatment upon sale. This includes inventory, property held for resale, property used in a trade or business, copyrights in certain instances, and certain United States government obligations.

capital consumption allowance 1. *accounting* A charge against gross product which accounts for the depreciation of capital assets. 2. *economics* Sum attributed to the depreciation of capital goods in a year. In National Income accounts, capital goods depreciation is subtracted from Gross National Product to arrive at Net National Product.

capital deepening Increase in capital relative to other resources, especially labor. Usually applied to a nation, but can equally apply to a region or a firm.

capital equipment Machinery, tools, and other equipment used in production.

capital expenditure Expense incurred in acquiring or disposing of property. Also refers to improvements as distinguished from repairs, an expenditure in the nature of an investment for the future.

capital flight *finance* The movement of large amounts of capital from one country to another, sometimes for political reasons, but usually because return on the capital is greater.

capital gain 1. Profit received from the sale of an asset, such as securities or real estate equal to the difference between the asset's purchase price and selling price, when the difference is positive. Under United States law in the mid 1980s, the profit on an asset held for six months was considered a long-term capital gain and qualified for a lower tax rate. A capital gain can result from buying or selling assets of any kind covered by the Internal Revenue Service definition of capital assets. 2. The increase in the value of an asset over time. (*See* Appendix G)

capital gain net income 1. Amount equal to 50% of the excess of net long-term gain over net short-term capital loss. 2. Average base period capital gain net income, meaning one-fourth of the sum of capital gain net income for any base period year, shall not exceed the base period income for such year.

capital goods *economics* Assets used in the production of other goods.

capital investment Money paid out to acquire something of permanent use or value in one's business. Similarly, money spent to improve an asset.

capitalis debitor The chief or principal debtor as distinguished from a surety.

capitalism *economics* Economic system in which private individuals and businesses own the factors of production and make resource-use decisions based on markets and prices. Usually characterized by (a) private ownership of property; (b) assets, property or capital, that provides a source of income for the owners; (c) a marked degree of individual freedom, in all areas of life, including the ability of individuals to compete with each other for economic advantage; and (d) the profit motive. Reasonably synonymous with laissez-faire economy, private enterprise, free-price system, and modified market system.

capitalization A method of computation which gives value to land in relation to income it produces.

capitalized and amortized expenses Assets to be amortized or paid off over an extended period of time which may range from just over one year to as many years as the asset is supposed to last.

capitalized value The value of an asset as determined by the amount of discounted income which is expected to flow to its owner over the life of the asset.

capital loss 1. Loss incurred on the sale of an asset such as securities or real estate. Long-term capital losses are those that have been held long enough to receive special tax treatment. Short-term capital losses are those that may be deductible against ordinary income. 2. *tax law* Loss resulting from the sale or exchange of a capital asset.

capital loss carryover A tax benefit that allows a company or an individual to apply losses to reduce a tax liability. A company may offset the current year's capital or net operating losses against profits in the three immediately preceding years, with the earliest year first. After this (a carryback), it may carry forward (carryover) capital losses five years and net operating losses up to fifteen years. Individuals may carry over capital losses until they are used up for an unlimited number of years to offset capital gain. Individuals generally cannot carry back losses, however. (*See* Appendix G)

capital market *finance* An informal financial market in the economy in which stocks and bonds are bought and sold and where businesses obtain funds for long-term investments.

capital-output ratio *investment* The ratio of the cost of new investment goods to the value of the annual output produced by those investment goods. (*See* capital productivity ratio)

capital productivity ratio *economics* The quantity of capital of a firm, industry, or whole economy divided by the quantity of output.

capital rationing *finance* The action by a firm to allocate capital expenditures to most-necessary items, in the face of a shortage of capital.

capital stock 1. Unit of ownership in a corporation representing the stockholder's proprietary interest. Two major classes are common stock and preferred stock. 2. Property received in exchange for all issued stock and not the other capital or assets of the corporation.

capital-stock insurer Business corporation engaged in issuing various types of insurance coverages. This company is owned by the stockholders and has the duty of earning a profit for them. This is in contradistinction to a mutual company where the firm is ostensibly owned by the policyholders.

capital-stock mutual Insurance company in which the company theoretically belongs to policyholders. The company is usually run by a manager and staff, and, in most mutual companies, the policyholders, in practice, have little to do with the company.

capital structure Mixture of long-term debt and equity (i.e., common and preferred stock) used to finance a corporation's operations.

captive agent *insurance* Agent who writes insurance for only one company, and who is tied to that company by contract for a specified period of time.

captive finance company *finance* A financial subsidiary of a large corporation which has been established specifically to finance the products of the parent company.

captive shop *economics* A company that produces all of its product for another company, usually the parent company. This sometimes comes about due to mergers, where the mother company buys all the product of the subsidiaries. While this is acceptable when kept within a family of companies it is a dangerous practice as between independent companies. Some companies have a maximum percentage of their total production they will agree to sell to one buyer.

cardinal utility theory *economics* The proposition that economic analysis should proceed from the absolute measurements of pleasure derived from consumption.

career average pay *pension plans; profit sharing* Plan that would require complete payroll records on every participant from the beginning of employment and which allows for a slightly higher excess benefit rate.

careless   Negligent, failing to take due care. The law concerns itself with carelessness only when there is a duty to take care and where failure in that duty has caused damage. In such circumstances, carelessness assumes the legal quality of negligence and entails consequences in the law of negligence.

carrier   A person or company that transports persons or goods for hire.

carrying charges   Expenses necessary for holding property, such as taxes and interest on idle property or property under construction.

carryover   *investing* The net capital loss of a taxpayer which is used to reduce capital gains, or other income, in the future. (*See* Appendix G)

carryover basis   In a tax-deferred exchange, the adjusted tax basis of the property surrendered that is used to determine the tax basis of the property acquired.

cartel   *economics* A group of nations or business firms within a nation, or a firm specifically selected by a government, which conspire to influence prices by regulating the production and marketing of a product. In recent years, the best known cartel has been the Organization of Petroleum Exporting Countries (OPEC). Cartels, particularly those granted by government, go back many thousands of years. They are generally considered illegal in our time.

case study   A method of teaching in multiple disciplines where the student is asked to analyze a true-life (or pseudo) situation.

cash account   1. Condition in which the investor must pay in cash for the securities as purchased. 2. *investing* An account in which the securities are paid for in full.

cash basis accounting   A method of accounting based on cash receipts and disbursements. Cash is recorded in the period received, and expenses are recorded in the period paid. This system is most often used in small businesses, and only rarely in larger ones.

cash conversion cycle   *finance* The time that elapses between a firm's outlay for raw materials and the time cash is received by the firm for finished product.

cash cow   *finance* A company, or a specific product, which generates more cash than needs to be reinvested in that operation, and can thus be used in other company activities.

cash discount   1. Price reduction offered by merchants to customers paying in cash or by check instead of by credit card. 2. *marketing; accounting* Discount allowed on invoices when payment is made early. (E.g., the notation 2/10, n 30 would indicate a 2% discount if the invoice is paid within ten days, and net at thirty days.)

cash equivalent   Any asset which can be turned into cash quickly.

cash flow principal   *finance* A concept of investment evaluation which states that only actual cash movements are relevant and that they should be recorded on the day they move.

cash flow statement   A statement for a specified period of time showing income (inflow) and expenditures (outflow) and the difference between the two.

cashier   *banking* One who provides general supervision for the operations department; is often influential in changing modes of operations to achieve maximum efficiency. This person usually gives particular attention to customer service, but also gives direction to the behind-the-scenes operations supportive to all customer service. This position normally answers to the senior vice president of operations or administration or executive vice president.

cash market   *investing* Transactions in the commodities markets where the commodity is transferred to the buyer, perhaps immediately, and payment is made upon delivery.

cash or deferred arrangement (CODA) 401(k) plan   Option provided by employer that some or all of the annual profit sharing contribution can be designated as a 401(k) contribution. In a typical cash or deferred plan, the employer makes a conventional profit sharing contribution for eligible employees with the additional caveat that all (or part) of that contribution is subject to a 401(k) election option. Under the option, each employee can elect to take his or her profit sharing contribution either in cash or

41

on a deferred basis. If the employee elects cash, the employee is immediately taxed on the distribution and the elected portion obviously does not find its way into the shelter of the employee's 401(k) account. If the employee elects deferral, the deferred amount is credited to the employee's 401(k) account and is 100% vested.

cash over and short account *accounting* A recording made in a special account for those times when the actual cash in the register is less than the sales rung up during the day.

cash surrender value *insurance* The cash value of an insurance policy if the policy is surrendered.

cash surrender value option *insurance* The option, elected by the policyholder, to surrender the policy for its cash value at the time. This option should not be elected if it can be avoided if there is still the need for insurance protection.

cash value fund *insurance* One component of universal life, by which a company deducts the cost of life coverage and costs from the premium, and the remainder goes into a fund, usually made up of high-yielding government securities. After the first year, approximately 90–93% of each premium dollar goes into the cash value.

cash value insurance Insurance on which premiums are paid in excess of the cost of pure insurance. These excess premiums accumulate in the accounts of the policyholders and are then available for borrowing, usually at interest rates lower than market rates. While the policy is usually sold as a savings policy, many investors doubt the validity of an insurance policy as a savings vehicle. Sometimes referred to as whole life insurance.

Cashwire A clearing service offered by Bankwire that includes a settlement facility. (*See* Bankwire)

castle-in-the-air theory *investing* A theory, especially in stocks, which has nothing to do with intrinsic values, but rather centers on psychic values. The theory is based on the assumption that a few investors want to avoid the analysis of intrinsic value in favor of trying to guess how people will react to certain stimuli, and thus push the prices of stocks either up or down. John Maynard Keynes was a proponent of this method.

casualty An accident, an event that cannot be guarded against.

casus fortuitus A fortuitous event; an accident.

catalog retailer A mass merchandise retail store that operates from a showroom displaying single units of each item listed in a catalog with orders filled from a backroom warehouse.

Catt concept *management* A theory devised by management specialist Ivor Catt which reveals the methods used by employees to assure the continuation of their jobs, including: (a) Make the job last as long as possible. (b) Be as secretive as possible about the job and its progress. (c) Keep information which may be used against the boss.

causa causans The immediate cause; the nearest cause of an event.

causa mortis In contemplation of impending death.

cause of action *See* claim.

caveat *Let him beware.* 1. An instrument which, when registered, secures priority for the estate or interest claimed. 2. A formal notice or caution given to a person interested by a court, judge, or public office against the performance of certain judicial or ministerial acts.

caveat emptor *Let the buyer beware.* A legal doctrine warning that without a warranty a purchaser buys at his or her own risk and must make sure that the goods bought are what they purport to be. Recent consumer laws have considerably weakened the doctrine.

caveat subscriptor *Let the signer beware.*

caveat venditor *Let the seller beware.*

C corporation The most general form of a corporation. The corporation, which is a taxable entity, may range from a one-person service organization to a business with millions of shareholders. Three main characteristics of a corporation are: (a) the limited liability of shareholders, (b) the advantage of perpetual life, and (c) generally unrestricted transfer of ownership interests.

cease-and-desist order 1. An order issued by a court or an administrative agency of the nature of an injunction prohibiting an individual or business from continuing an activity. Such orders are proper only after a hearing or waiver of right to a hearing. 2. An order issued after notice and opportunity for hearing, requiring a depository institution, a holding company, or depository institution official to terminate unlawful, unsafe, or unsound banking practices. Cease-and-desist orders are issued by the appropriate federal regulatory agencies under the Financial Institutions Supervisory Act and can be enforced directly by the courts.

ceded amount The amount of insurance placed with a reinsurer.

Celler Antimerger Act (1950) Major antitrust law which was an extension of Section 7 of the Clayton Antitrust Act. It prohibits a corporation from acquiring the stock or assets of another corporation if the effect would be a substantial lessening of competition or the tendency toward monopoly. Prior to this law, only the acquisition of stock by competing corporations was illegal under the Clayton Act.

census The official counting or enumeration of people of a state, nation, or district.

Central American Common Market (CACM) An organization established in 1960 to promote a free-trade area between Costa Rica, Guatemala, Honduras, Nicaragua and Salvador.

central bank 1. A government institution that controls the issuance of currency, provides banking services to the government and to other banks, and implements the nation's monetary policy; in the United States, the Federal Reserve is the central bank. 2. The official bank of a nation that regulates other banks, controls the money supply, performs fiscal functions for the government, and helps to balance international payments.

central limit theorem *statistics* The hypothesis that the distribution of the sample mean approaches a "normal distribution" as the number of samples increases.

centrally directed economy Economic system in which the basic questions of what, how, and for whom to produce are resolved primarily by governmental authority. Also called command economy.

central planning A method of resource allocation in which the governmental authority makes the major decisions on production, distribution, and coordination.

certainty equivalent *finance* An amount of money which is guaranteed and which could induce a decision maker to accept it in lieu of the actual cash flow.

certificate 1. A statement in writing by a person having public or official status, or a representation or assurance from such person, concerning some matter within that person's knowledge or authority. 2. A printed or engraved piece of paper evidencing ownership of stock.

certificateless municipal *investing* Municipal bond which has a master certificate and does not supply certificates to the individual bondholders.

Certificate of Accrual on Treasury Securities (CATS) *investing* United States Treasury issues which are sold at a deep discount, and which have no coupons. The principal, plus interest, is recovered at maturity. These are often used for educational, or retirement, funds.

certificate of authenticity Common merchandising technique used in the sale of reproductions of coins, antiques, and objects of art.

certificate of deposit (CD) 1. Savings account that carries a specified minimum deposit and term and provides a higher yield than passbook-type savings accounts. 2. Paper evidencing the existence of a time deposit with a bank or trust company. 3. Negotiable money market instrument issued by banks for $100,000 or more for at least thirty days with negotiated rates. These trade on the open market and offer the investor an excellent return and high degree of safety. 4. Non-negotiable instruments issued by banks to individuals offering an excellent return and a high degree of safety but with penalties for early withdrawal.

certificate of eligibility *real estate* Paper issued by the Veteran's Administration to those who qualify for a VA loan.

certificate of incorporation Formal document issued by the secretary of state recognizing the formation and existence of a corporation.

certificate of stock Written acknowledgment by a corporation of the stockholder's interest in its property and franchises. It has no value except that derived from the issuing company and its legal status in the nature of a chose in action. The value of all property owned by a corporation, including its franchise, is the value of all its stock.

certified check   Check that has been accepted for payment by the drawee. A check drawn by a depositor upon funds to the depositor's credit in the bank, which the proper officer of the bank certifies will be paid when duly presented for payment.

certified copy   Document signed and verified as a true copy by the officer to whose custody the original is entrusted.

Certified Financial Planner (C.F.P.) *finance* A designation granted by the College for Financial Planning, Denver, Colorado, upon the completion of six sections of study, and associated testing. The sections of study, each comprising about four months, are financial planning, risk management, investments, tax planning, employee benefits, including Social Security, and estate planning.

certified historical structure   A structure older than forty years of age which has been certified by the Office of the Secretary of the Interior as being historic. If a building invested in lies in a district, all of which has been properly certified, then special certification is not necessary. A tax credit of 25% will be granted to the restorer of such a building. (*See* Appendix G)

certified residential broker (CRB) *real estate* Person in real estate who is specifically qualified by study and experience to deal in residential housing. The CRB designation is awarded by the Realtors National Marketing Institute.

certified residential specialist (CRS)   *real estate* Realtor who holds the GRI (Graduate of the Realtors Institute) designation, which denotes that he or she is a practiced professional in the sale and purchase of residential housing.

cessio   A relinquishment, a surrender.

cessionary bankrupt   One who gives up one's estate to be divided among one's creditors.

cestui que trust   *law* The person for whose benefit a trust is created, i.e., the beneficiary.

ceteris paribus   Assuming that everything else remains unchanged. (E.g., if the price of imported champagne goes down to fifty cents a bottle, ceteris paribus, people will buy more champagne.)

chain   A linear unit of land measurement used in surveying equaling sixty-six feet in length. Each chain consists of one hundred links.

chain of title   1. A history of conveyances and encumbrances affecting a title from the time that the original patent was granted, or as far back as records are available. 2. *law; economics* A series, sometimes quite long, of conveyances, probate proceedings, court decrees, etc., by which the current owner of real estate has title to the property. Often, the beginning point in the series is a patent (deed) from the government to the first legal owner.

chain stores   Number of retail stores under the same ownership with a central management selling uniform merchandise and following a uniform policy.

chance of loss   The long-run relative frequency of loss, expressed as a fraction or percentage.

change   Alteration an investor may make, or has made, in an investment portfolio as goals or objectives change.

change in amount consumed Increase or decrease in the amount of consumption expenditure due to a change in income. It may be represented by a movement along a consumption-function curve.

channel   The bed of a stream or river over which waters run, a passageway between banks through which flow waters of the stream or river. Applicable to any watercourse whether a river, creek, slough, or canal. By analogy of the common-law rule pertaining to nontidal stream boundaries, boundary between countries separated by navigable waters is the geographical center between the banks of those waters.

charge   1. Security which does not transfer the property to the chargee but gives him or her the right to payment out of the property and entitles the chargee to have the property sold to raise the money charged. Unlike a mortgage, a charge is not a conveyance of the fee with a condition for repayment. 2. Expense, cost, or disbursement incurred.

charge account *See* open-end credit.

charitable 1. Having the character or purpose of a charity. A charitable institution is one organized for the promotion of some public object, such as relief of aged and infirm persons or an institution for the care of children on philanthropic principles and not for the purpose of gain or profit. Directed to or proceeding from charity. 2. Promoting welfare of mankind at large, or of community, or of some part of it indefinite as to numbers and individuals. In order for a gift or a trust to be characterized as charitable, it must be for the benefit of an indefinite number of unascertained persons. Charitable designation in the legal sense falls into four principal divisions: trust for the relief of poverty; trusts for the advancement of education; trusts for the advancement of religion; and trusts for other purposes beneficial to the community not falling under any of the preceding heads.

charitable deduction A reduction of income, gift, or estate tax for transfer of property to charitable, religious, scientific, educational, and other specified organizations, allowed if the donee falls within categories designated by law.

charitable devise *real estate* A gift of real property made to a legal charity through the the vehicle of a will.

charitable lead trust Trust designed to provide the charity with a determinable amount of income for a determinable period of time at the end of which individual beneficiaries are to receive a remainder interest; the income is given to the charity but the property is retained by the donor. Basically this is the reverse of the charitable remainder trust in which individuals start out as the income beneficiaries and the charity holds a remainder interest. Also called charitable income trust or front trust.

charitable organizations—20% Tax exempt institutions or organizations which are deemed by the IRS to be nonprofit, and the activities of which are are deemed to be in the public good. Churches, private schools, veteran's groups, and many others are in this category. Deduction is limited to 20% of the taxpayer's adjusted gross income for gifts of long-term capital gain appreciated property to private nonoperating foundations.

charitable organizations—50% Public charities, such as churches, schools, hospitals, and governmental units, to which donations may not be deducted over the amount of 50% of the taxpayer's adjusted gross income. Other organizations which allow charitable deductions up to 50% of adjusted gross income include operating, conduit, passthrough, distributing, community, and pooled-fund foundations.

charitable remainder A gift to the charity of what remains from specific property. Donor can give a present gift of future interest. If the gift is cash, a trust must be established. If the gift is property, the donor can create a remainder interest without a trust. A remainder trust can be set up so that any number of beneficiaries can benefit from the income, after which time the remainder goes to the charity. Thus, it can be set up to encompass a number of years at the death of a beneficiary.

charitable remainder annuity trust Trust, either testamentary or inter vivos, that requires the creator of the trust to set aside certain assets, with specified amounts payable either for a period of years (no more than twenty) or for the life of the settlor, his or her spouse, or other persons named by the creator, with the remainder going to a qualified charity. The trust must be set up for beneficiaries living at the time the trust is set up and periodic payments, at least annually, be made to these beneficiaries. The trust requires a rate of return of at least 5%, and the principal may not be used for the beneficiaries except to satisfy the specific payout requirements of the trust.

charitable remainder unitrust A trust from which a fixed percentage of the net fair market value of the trust's assets, valued annually, is paid each year to the beneficiary. This trust, either testamentary or inter vivos, is similar to the charitable remainder trust with specific property set aside in the trust. However, the return to beneficiaries must be no less than 5%, calculated on the basis of the value of trust assets as determined annually (as opposed to a 5% calculated on the initial net worth of the assets transferred to the trust). It may provide that the corpus may not be invaded in order to meet the 5% annual payout to beneficiaries. When this is true, the trust must provide that deficiencies in one year when income is below the required level will be made up in subsequent years when the income is greater. Also, a unitrust may have additional contributions on specified terms and conditions.

charitable stock bailout Situation in which an owner of stock in a closely held corporation wants to donate to a charity but is short on cash. The donor will give stock to the charity, with a prearranged agreement that the charity will sell the stock back to the corporation. The donor makes the gift he or she wants to make and gets the tax deduction while the charity gets cash on the sell-back; both donor and charity are helped. While the closely held stock is given by an individual owner, the stock is sold back to the corporation, eventually getting back into the proper hands.

charitable trust A trust set up for the benefit of the public or of some part of the public.

chart *economics* A graphic method of presenting statistical data. Some popular forms are pie charts, bar charts (vertical), and band charts (horizontal). Line graphs are still widely used.

charter 1. Originally, the document evidencing the transaction between two persons and, by extension, of any deed relating to hereditaments. 2. Grant, particularly one incorporating corporations and other bodies such as universities.

chartist *investing* A technical market analyst who charts the patterns of commodities, stocks, and bonds in order to make buy or sell recommendations to clients. These market analysts believe that the recurrent trends of the markets can help forecast future market movements.

chattel Personal property. Anything owned and tangible, other than real estate. Chattels can be divided into two classes. Personal chattels are those which are movable and would include animals as well as goods. Chattels real concern or arise out of lands. Where the duration of an estate is uncertain it is characterized as a freehold. If the duration is fixed then it is a chattel real. Thus, a lease for a term

of years is a chattel real, while a gift to the same person for life will be, under common law, a freehold estate.

chattel mortgage 1. A contract between parties, whereby the mortgagor transfers the property in chattels to the mortgagee, subject to the mortagor's right to retain possession and to redeem the chattels. Conveyance of some present legal or equitable right in personal property as security for the payment of money or for the performance of some other act. A contract between the parties importing transfer of property in the chattels from the mortgagor to the mortgagee as security for a debt, defeasible on the payment of the debt. 2. A document offering property as security for payment of a debt. 3. A pledge of personal property as security for a debt.

cheap money *economics* A situation in which money loses its purchasing power, sometimes because the money supply is too large for the needs of the economy. As a rule, this situation also produces low interest rates.

check Written order on a bank for payment of money on demand. This represents a conditional payment only and therefore the holder may sue on the original claim which revives when payment on the check is refused. The drawer of a check can stop payment until the time of payment by the bank. The giving of a check does not operate as an assignment of the drawer's funds on credit at the drawee's bank. Differs from a bill of exchange in that commonly a check is honored by presentment for payment while a bill exchange is honored by presentment for acceptance.

checkable deposits Deposits which can be transferred by check, including demand deposits in commercial banks; NOW accounts at savings and loans, mutual savings banks, and some commercial banks; and share drafts at credit unions.

check clearing Movement of checks from the banks or other institutions where they are deposited back to those on which they are written, and funds movement in the opposite direction. This process results in credits to accounts at the institutions of deposit and corresponding debits to the accounts at the paying institutions. The Federal Reserve participates in check clearing though many checks are cleared by private sector arrangements.

check-off agreement *economics* A method of collecting union dues where the firm deducts the dues from the member's paycheck and sends them directly to the union. This plan is usually arrived at through collective bargaining, and is much loved by union leaders since it relieves them of the task of collecting the dues.

Chicago Board of Trade (CBT) An organized commodities market located in Chicago, Illinois, which is the oldest and largest in the nation.

Chicago Board Options Exchange (CBOE) The first organized exchange in the United States to trade in stock option contracts.

Chicago school of economics A school of thought known as monetarism that was born at the University of Chicago and is identified with Nobel laureate economist Milton Friedman.

chief executive officer (CEO) *See* president.

chief place of business The place where any person or a corporation conducts the greatest volume of business.

child An infant; an offspring of human parents; progeny. Except as where modified by statute, at common law, child or children as used in a legal document always means a legitimate child or children.

child and dependent care credit *tax law* Tax credit for a portion of the expenses incurred, ranging from 20–30% on qualifying income, to pay someone to care for dependents under the age of fifteen, a disabled dependent, or a disabled spouse if necessary in order to work full-time. A tax credit up to twenty-four hundred dollars for one qualifying dependent or forty-eight hundred dollars for two or more qualifying dependents is allowed. (*See* Appendix G)

chose A chattel personal. Choses are of two kinds: in possession and in action. (*See* chattel, chose in action, chose in possession)

chose in action An incorporeal right to something not in one's possession covering numerous rights, diverse in their nature, such as debts, company shares,

negotiable instruments, and rights of action founded on tort or breach of contract. A thing recoverable by action which may be either legal or equitable, the words "in action" being used merely by way of distinction from a chose in possession. The common law did not recognize assignments of a chose in action except those by or to the Crown and later, under the influence of the law merchant, of bills of exchange and promissory notes. It was thought that to recognize such assignment would be to encourage litigation. In contrast to this, Chancery assisted the assignee in two ways: firstly, where the chose in action was purely equitable and was absolutely assigned leaving no interest in the assignor, so that the assignee could proceed in his or her own name; and secondly, by compelling the assignor of a legal chose in action to collaborate with the assignee in asserting a claim in the common law court. (*See* chose; cf. chose in possession)

chose in possession A movable chattel, such as furniture, animals, goods, and merchandise. (*See* chose; cf. chose in action)

churning *investing* The creation by a broker of numerous transactions in a client's account in order to collect the transactions fees.

circular flow diagram A schematic drawing showing the economic relationships between the major sectors of an economic system.

circular flow of the economy A simplified view of a market-directed economic system illustrating payments from businesses to households in exchange for input factors and payments from households to businesses in exchange for output products.

citizen bond *investing* A specific type of municipal bond, which does not give individual certificates, but which can be registered and traded on a stock exchange.

citizenship The state of being vested with the rights and privileges of a citizen.

city A municipal corporation of statutory creation having only such limited powers of legislative enactments as are conferred by law of its creation.

Civil Aeronautics Board (CAB) A federal government agency composed of five members appointed by the president, whose duty it is to police the air carrier industry with respect to safety rules, rates and other regulations.

civil embargo Embargo applied to ships belonging to citizens of the state imposing it.

civilian labor force *economics* The labor force minus those persons who are on active duty in the military. (Sometimes this also excepts those institutionalized.)

civil law That rule of action which every nation, commonwealth, or city has established, more familiarly referred to as municipal law. Used to distinguish the system of jurisprudence from the common law. Historically, however, the term has come to mean that law which the Romans compiled from the laws of nature and nations.

civil rights Those rights which are the outgrowth of civilization arising from the needs of civil, as distinguished from barbaric, communities and are given, defined, and circumscribed by such positive laws enacted by communities as are necessary to the maintenance of organized government. The distinction between private and public wrongs or civil injuries and crimes is that when the wrong is a civil injury, the sanction is enforced at the discretion of the party whose rights have been violated; when the wrong is a crime, the sanction is enforced at the discretion of the government.

Civil Service Includes all appointive positions in the executive, judicial, and legislative branches of the government of the United States, except positions in the armed forces, the commissioned corps of the Public Health Service, and the commissioned corps of the Environmental Science Services Administration.

claim *law* The assertion of right to a remedy, relief, or property. The right to demand something of another. Frequently used to refer to a pleading delivered on behalf of a plaintiff; also used as denoting the assertion of a right to a payment in money, as in a claim against a fund. A challenge of interest of anything which is in another's possession, or at least out of a one's own possession, as a "claim by character, descent, etc." Often used as synonymous with cause of action.

claimant One who makes a claim.

claims investigation *insurance* Process that involves ascertaining whether a loss occurred, determining whether the actions of the insured have invalidated the claim, and establishing the amount of loss. The investigation involves validation of facts submitted in the proof-of-loss statement.

clandestine mortgage A second mortgage on lands where the existence of the first mortgage was not disclosed in writing.

class action An action brought by one or more plaintiffs on behalf of other persons who are similarly situated or have suffered a similar wrong. The essential condition of a representative action is that the persons who are to be represented have the same interest as the plaintiff in one and the same cause or matter. There must, therefore, be a common interest in the sense that the plaintiff and all those who are being represented will gain some relief by the plaintiff's success, though possibly in different proportions and degrees.

classical economics Body of economic thought dominant in the Western world from the late eighteenth century until the 1930s. Among its chief proponents were Adam Smith (1723–1790), Jean-Baptiste Say (1767–1832), Jeremy Bentham (1748–1832), Thomas Robert Malthus (1766–1834), David Ricardo (1772–1823), and John Stuart Mill (1806–1873). They emphasized a person's self-interest and the operation of universal economic laws which tend to automatically guide the economy toward full employment equilibrium if the government adheres to a policy of laissez-faire or noninterventionism. (*See* neoclassical economics)

classification issue An issue in which the Internal Revenue Service can, under certain circumstances, reclassify a partnership into a corporation for the purposes of taxation. Out of six attributes of a business, with the IRS eliminating the first two, at least two of the remaining four attributes must be present for the firm to be classified as a partnership. The four attributes are: continuity of life, centralized management, limited liability, and free transferability of interest.

classified balance sheet *accounting* A

balance sheet on which assets and liabilities are categorized for better understanding. (E.g., assets may be divided into such categories as cash and cash equivalent, invested assets, and assets in use. Liabilities are often categorized as long-term or short-term.)

classified income statement *accounting* A profit and loss statement that classifies revenues and expenses according to business function.

classified stock *investing* Different classes of common stock which may exist in the same firm. Usually called "A" or "B." Stock is differentiated by voting privileges.

class struggle *economics; politics* The basis of a theory propounded by Karl Marx which outlined the inherent antagonism between certain economic, political, and social groups and which, in Marx's view, could not be resolved without the use of revolutionary methods.

Clayton Antitrust Act (1914) Amendment to the Sherman Antitrust Act enacted into law in 1914 which was aimed at preventing unfair, deceptive, dishonest, or injurious methods of competition. It declares the following as illegal where the effect is a substantial lessening of competition or tendency toward monopoly: (a) price discrimination, except where there are differences in grade, quality, or quantity sold, or where the lower prices made due allowances for cost differences in selling or transportation, or where the lower prices are offered in good faith to meet competition; (b) tying contracts between sellers and purchasers; (c) intercorporate stockholdings among competing corporations. It also makes illegal, regardless of the effect on competition, interlocking directorates if the corporations involved are competitive and if any one of them has capital, surplus, and undivided profits in excess of a million dollars.

clearing entries *accounting* Entries that clear and close out the revenue and expense accounts. Also called closing entries.

clearinghouse 1. Voluntary association or institution created for the benefit of bankers for adjustments and for clearing checks. 2. An institution where mutual claims are settled between accounts of member depository institutions. Clearinghouses among banks have traditionally been organized for check-clearing purposes, but more recently have cleared other types of settlements, including electronic fund transfers.

Clearinghouse Interbank Payments Systems (CHIPS) An automated clearing system, owned and operated by the New York clearinghouse banks, used primarily for international payments.

clear title 1. Title free from encumbrances. 2. A marketable title; one free of clouds and disputed interests.

client 1. One who engages a broker, lawyer, accountant, appraiser, or another professional. 2. *real estate* Person who seeks the advice and help of a realtor in the matter of the sale or purchase of real estate.

Clifford trust 1. Short-term reversionary trust whose purpose is to provide the income from the trust to the beneficiary for a limited period of time, normally ten years. During this time, the income from the trust is taxed to the beneficiary. The recipient may be in a lower tax bracket or may need the income from the property for a relatively short period of time. After the trust period is over, the property in the trust reverts to the creator of the trust. Also called short-term trust. 2. A trust whereby the grantor reserves the right to repossess property transferred in trust upon the occurrence of a specific event or the expiration of a period of time. 3. A temporary shifting of ownership of assets, along with income from the assets, which must last for ten years and one day but which then can be recaptured by the original donor. This is a method used to reduce the taxes of the donor, while perhaps providing for some specific financial need of the donee. (*See* Appendix G)

clog on equity of redemption Any stipulation in a mortgage that prevents redemption on payment of principal, interest, and costs owing on the mortgage or on performance of the obligations for which the security was given.

clone fund *investing* In a family of mutual funds, a new fund that emulates a successful, existing one.

close corporation A corporation in which the stock is held by a few people and in which the stockholders are often employees of the firm in management positions. The stock is not publicly traded. Unlike a partnership, which is dissolved upon the death of a partner, the close corporation, which is a business entity within itself, continues to live after the death of one or more stockholders. (In many family-oriented close corporations, the death of a stockholder often provides a myriad of problems.) Sometimes called a closed corporation.

closed-end company Company which raises capital by a single offering of its stock to the public. (Cf. open-end company)

closed-end credit Loan or credit sale agreement in which the amounts advanced plus any finance charges are expected to be repaid in full over a definite time. Most real estate and automobile loans are closed-end agreements.

closed-end fund *See* closed-end investment fund.

closed-end investment company 1. Company that operates a mutual fund with a limited number of shares outstanding. These are often listed on an exchange, where they are traded like any other stock. The company can issue bonds and preferred stock so as to leverage the position of the common shareholders. 2. Investment fund that issues only one offering of shares to the public. The shares then trade on the open market and are not redeemable upon demand as in mutual funds.

closed-end investment fund Fund that sells its own securities and invests the proceeds in the securities of other companies. May also be called mutual fund. (*See* money-market mutual fund)

closed-end mortgage *finance* A bond issue secured by real estate which does not allow the mortgaged property to be used as collateral for other loans.

closed indent *economics* The purchase order sent by an importer to an exporter in which the manufacturer of the goods purchased is specifically named.

closed sales territories A practice in which some manufacturers restrict their distributors' geographic territories.

closed shop clause Clause in a labor contract which requires that an employee

be a member of the union as a requisite for employment.

closed system *economics* A method of analysis borrowed from the natural sciences in which some factors are excluded or severely controlled while other factors are variable. (E.g, in international matters, one nation will be isolated for analysis as though the rest of the world did not exist.)

closely held business Business, either a sole proprietorship, a partnership, or a close corporation, in the hands of one or a few persons, the death of any one of which may alter the course, or even the life, of the business. Thus, such a business has specific needs with respect to how it will be handled once a principal has died.

close off the top *finance* A term used in finance indicating the rejection of further debt financing.

close position *investing* The act of eliminating a security from one's portfolio, usually by selling it.

closing 1. The transfer of ownership of a property from seller to buyer in accordance with a sales contract. 2. The time when a closing takes place.

closing costs *real estate* Various fees and expenses payable by the seller and buyer at the time of a real estate closing. Also called transaction costs.

closing entries *See* clearing entries.

closing statement An accounting of funds from a real estate sale made to both the seller and the buyer separately.

cloud on title *real estate* An outstanding claim or encumbrance upon property that, if not proved to be invalid or inapplicable, renders the owner's title to the property defective.

cluster housing A subdivision technique in which detached dwelling units are grouped relatively close together, leaving open spaces as common areas.

cobweb effect; cobweb theorem Generic name for a theory of cyclical fluctuations in the prices and quantities of various agricultural commodities—fluctuations which arise because, for certain agricultural products (e.g., hogs and beef cattle), the quantity demanded of the commodity at any given time depends on its price at that time, whereas the quantity supplied at any given time depends on its price at a previous time when production plans were initially formulated. This causes low production and high prices in one year, followed by high production and low prices in the following year.

code channel *communication* Medium which carries the symbols of the message to the other person.

code of ethics Guidelines of conduct for dealing with clients, peers, and others.

codex A code or collection of laws.

codicil A supplement or an addition to a will which explains, modifies, adds to, subtracts from, qualifies, alters, restrains, or revokes provisions in the existing will. A codicil normally does not revoke the will, but simply modifies it in some manner, usually by a written page to be inserted in the original will.

coefficient of alienation *statistics* The square root of the unassociated variance divided by the total variance.

coefficient of correlation *statistics* A measure of the degree of the comovement of two variables. (I.e., the movement of a stock index as related to the movement of a specific stock for the same time period.)

coefficient of determination *statistics* The ratio of the associated variance due to the independent variable to the total variance of the dependent variable. Symbol of the ratio is r^2.

coefficient of expectation *statistics* The percentage of change in the output of the prior period which is expected to be the change in the output of the present period.

coefficient of multiple correlation *statistics* The degree of association between a dependent variable and two or more independent variables. The symbol for this coefficient is r.

coefficient of nondetermination *statistics* The ratio of the non-associated variance to total variance.

coefficient of partial correlation *statistics* The square root of the coefficient of partial determination.

coefficient of partial determination *statistics* In multiple correlation, the ratio of the associated variance of one independent variable to the total variance with the effect of the other independent variables held statistically constant.

coefficient of regression *statistics* The slope of a regression line; the average unit increase or decrease in the dependent variable associated with a unit increase of the independent variable. (Cf. beta coefficient)

coefficient of relative effectiveness (CRE) Phrase used in the Soviet Union to mean the expected payoff or percent rate of return on a capital investment; akin to the concept of marginal efficiency of investment in Western economics.

coefficient of variation *statistics* The measure of relative dispersion of data. The standard deviation divided by the arithmetic mean gives the coefficient of variation.

coercion Threats of force or intimidation.

co-executor A person named with one or more persons in a will to perform the duties of executor.

cognitive note *law* A legal form of evidence of indebtedness in which the debtor acknowledges personal liability and allows the creditor to take judgment, without a legal suit.

Cohan principle *tax law* Rule in effect where a taxpayer has proven a credit for a particular deduction but is unable for lack of adequate records to prove with certainty the amount. The Internal Revenue commissioner or the courts are required to make an approximation of what would be a reasonable allowance under the circumstances.

coin Metallic money of all types, specifically a piece of gold, silver, or other metal stamped by authority of the government in order to fix its value.

coincident indicator *economics; statistics* A series of economic data that tends to follow the general economic activity with a marked degree of consistency.

coinsurance 1. Certain portion, commonly 20–25%, of covered expenses that most major medical policies require the covered person to bear with the insurer paying the remainder. 2. Stipulation in an insurance policy that the underwriter shall be liable for such proportion only of the property at risk, lost, or damaged, as the amount of the insurance may bear to the value of the entire property at risk. A coinsurance clause is designed to compel the insured, either as self-insurer or otherwise, to carry insurance. 3. Clause restricting the amount paid for partial losses if the damaged property is not covered for at least a stated percentage of its actual cash value at the time of the loss. The purpose of coinsurance clauses is to help achieve rate equity and adequacy. 4. A system of insurance in which there is a relative division of risk between the insurer and the insured.

coinsurance provision Clause allowing the insured and the insurer to share in the expenses up to a certain point, called the stop-loss or breakpoint, after which the full expenses are paid by the insurer up to the policy limits.

cold canvass The process of contacting homeowners without appointment in an area to solicit listings.

collapsible corporation A corporation formed principally for the purpose of purchasing property with a view to transformation or dissolution prior to the realization of a substantial part of the income to be derived from such property and prior to the realization of such gain by the corporation's shareholders. Such corporations are normally dissolved within three years. The Internal Revenue Service treats gain on the sale or liquidation of the corporation as ordinary income to the stockholder.

collateral Property that is offered to secure a loan or other credit and that becomes subject to seizure on default; security.

collateral agreement A second of two agreements, which is independent, separate, and distinct from the original agreement but is consistent with the provisions of the original.

collateral assignment Assignment of only certain rights, perhaps serving as collateral for a debt.

collateral heir Heir not of direct line of descent, but from a collateral line (e.g., a brother, sister, uncle, aunt, nephew, niece, or cousin).

collateral mortgage Mortgage in which money is not directly advanced but is given to secure an indebtedness that is pre-existing, contemporaneous, or may spring in the future. It is given to secure a

mortgage not pledged as collateral security for debt or succession debts.

collateral promise Promise to pay the debt of another, made either before, after, or contemporaneously with the promise of the primary debtor; it is a promise to answer for the debt, default, or miscarriage of another person.

collectible Tangible property purchased in the hope of selling in the future for a substantial profit (e.g., a painting, piece of antique furniture, rare edition stamp, book, paperweight, etc.). An investment-grade collectible is an item that is relatively scarce, as well as historically significant, within the context of the collectible genre itself and, preferably, within the larger context of the culture that produced it. Should be in excellent condition and attractive to display.

collection ratio *accounting* A ratio of a firm's accounts receivable to its average daily sales.

collective bargaining Union-management negotiations.

collective bargaining agreement An agreement between an employer and a group of employees, generally organized as a union, as to wages and conditions of employment.

collectivism *economics* A theory advocating the public ownership of property. In extreme cases, only personal property is excepted. In less extreme views, only some property, such as basic industries, is publicly owned, and individuals are allowed to own homes, etc.

collusion Conspiracy by sellers to set prices and outputs.

color of title That which appears to be but which, by reason of some defect, does not in fact amount to good title.

co-maker *See* co-signer.

combination, horizontal *See* horizontal combination.

combination in restraint of trade Any combination of two or more individuals or corporations having as its purpose the illegal restraint of trade or commerce in some particular commodity, as by the regulation of production, restriction of sales, establishment and maintenance of prices, or the stifling or exclusion of free competition. Prohibited by the Sherman

Antitrust Act, such a combination is characterized by an express or implied agreement or understanding that participants will jointly give up their trade freedom or help one another to take away the trade freedom of others through the use of such devices as price-fixing agreements or boycotts.

comfort letter *accounting; law* 1. The letter of an independent auditor which is required in securities underwriting agreements to assure that the data in the agreement is properly prepared, procedurally. The "lack of comfort" rests in the fact that while procedures used are verified, factual information is not. 2. A letter from one party of a legal agreement to another indicating that some provisions in the agreement are not clear. Usually these are small matters which can quickly be resolved.

command economy *See* centrally directed economy.

commerce Interaction for the purpose of trade in any and all its forms. Denotes the exchange of merchandise on a large scale between different places or communities. Describes any commercial interaction between nations and parts of nations and is regulated by the prescribing rules for carrying on that interaction.

commercial annuity Systematized capital-consuming device meant to give the annuitant more than would be received if the annuitant had taken the capital paid into the annuity, invested it personally, and tried to live off the income. A person can buy a commercial annuity in one or more of a variety of forms. All of these guarantee the annuitant annual or more frequent payments consisting of interest income and a return of capital for a lifetime or for some specified period.

commercial bank A privately owned financial institution authorized to provide a variety of financial services, including consumer and business loans (generally short-term), checking services, credit cards, and savings accounts. Certain deposits at most commercial banks are insured by the Federal Deposit Insurance Corporation. Commercial banks, which may be members of the Federal Reserve System, are owned by stockholders and are operated for profit.

commercial broker *real estate* Realtor who specializes in the purchase and sale of commercial properties which may include shopping, office, industrial, and apartment projects.

commercial hedgers *investing* Firms that actually use the commodities in which they trade, and thus take positions in the market to assure a price at a specific time. Often these traders will hedge by buying and selling futures at the same time.

commercial industrial *real estate* Commercial property, as opposed to residential property, which is specifically zoned for industrial concerns, usually manufacturing or warehousing.

commercial paper *investing* Short-term obligations with maturities ranging from 2 to 270 days issued by banks, corporations, and other borrowers to investors with temporarily idle cash. Such instruments are unsecured and usually discounted, although some are interest bearing. They can be issued directly or through brokers and trade on the open market. Ratings are assigned to commercial paper by both Moody's and Standard and Poor's.

commission Amount earned by a real estate broker for services.

Committee on Uniform Securities Identification Procedures (CUSIP) A committee that assigns all identification numbers and codes to securities. These numbers and codes are used in electronic reporting of markets and in the recording of all buy and sell orders.

Commodity Credit Corporation *economics* A federal corporation, the task of which is to finance public price supports for farm commodities. This organization also sells, stores, transports, and sometimes subsidizes such commodities.

commodity futures Purchases or sales in the commodity market for redemption or delivery at some future time. (In actuality, few commodities futures are expected to reach maturity date, since it is a part of the speculation which lends stability to the commodities market.)

commodity markets Exchanges which make the trading of various commodities possible in contrast to security markets.

common area *real estate* Area of a property used by all owners or tenants.

common budget *economics* A budget

made up of contributions of European Common Market countries out of which they finance certain programs for the benefit of the organization.

Common Business Oriented Language (COBOL) A computer language developed specifically for the business data processing industry.

common carrier *economics* A transportation organization operating under a license from government which requires that the carrier serve all customers, as contrasted with a contract carrier, a private carrier, or an industrial carrier.

common law *law* Accepted customs which have come down to us over time, and which are considered sanctioned precedents, though they may never have been codified. In specific instances, a court will decide what common law is. Common law is distinguished from statutory law which has been reduced to codes. Equity consists of changes in common law after it has been frozen with time.

common market Association of trading nations which agrees to impose no trade restrictions such as tariffs or quotas among participants, establish common external barriers (such as a common external tariff) to nonparticipants, and impose no notion restrictions on the movement of labor and capital among participants (*See* European Economic Community).

common-size financial statements *finance* A concept used in comparing financial statements of companies of varying size, whereby all balance sheet entries are divided by total assets and all income statement entries are divided by net sales.

common stock Ownership shares in a corporation. Shares of common stock are sold by a corporation to get money to buy capital equipment. The price of a share of stock is determined by the demand for and supply of that stock on the exchanges and is influenced by the assets and earnings (and expected future earnings) of the corporation.

common stock warrant Certificates that give the holder the option to buy the common stock of a corporation at a stated price which normally is higher than the market price at the time the warrant is issued. Some warrants are perpetual, but most expire five to ten years after issue.

Warrants represent a call on the future earnings of a corporation. Their value is speculative, and they are generally used by investors following an aggressive plan.

commonwealth 1. A nation with a republican form of government in which the administration of public affairs is open to all, with few, if any, exceptions, and in which the welfare and rights of the entire mass of people are the main consideration, rather than the privileges of a class or the will of a monarch. 1. Any of the individual states of the United States and the body of people constituting a state or politically organized community. 3. A body politic, hence a state, especially one constituted by a number of persons united by compact or tacit agreement under one form of government and system of laws.

communibus annis *On the annual average.*

communication 1. The process of sharing thoughts, ideas, and feelings with others in commonly understandable ways including all oral and written exchanges of ideas and information between persons directly or indirectly involved in the organizational setting. 2. Deliberate interchange of thoughts and opinions between two or more persons. Such communication may also be implied by conduct intended to convey a message.

communism 1. Social, economic, and political theory or system based on common ownership of property; in those countries which describe themselves as communist, control of the means of production and distribution is held by the government. 2. According to Karl Marx (1818–1883), the last stage of economic development after the state has withered away and work and consumption are engaged in communally.

communis stipes A common line of descent or ancestor.

Communist Manifesto *economics; political science* A document published by Karl Marx and Friedrich Engels in 1848, setting forth the basic tenents of Communism. Specifically emphasized were the materialistic interpretation of history and the proposition of the class struggle. The basic recommendation was for the workers of the world to organize, rise up, and overthrow the capitalistic system.

community Quality of holding goods in common, as in community property.

community integration *management* A theory that states that employees are less strike prone if they live in an integrated community (where several trades are represented).

community property 1. Property owned in common by husband and wife, each having an undivided one-half interest by reason of their marital status. The eight states with community property systems are Louisiana, Texas, New Mexico, Arizona, California, Washington, Idaho, and Nevada. The rest of the states are classified as common law jurisdiction. The difference between common law and community property systems centers around the property rights possessed by married persons. In a common law system, each spouse owns whatever he or she earns. Under a community property system, one-half of the earnings of each spouse is considered owned by the other spouse. 2. Property and income accumulated by a married couple and belonging to them jointly. The two have equal rights in the income from stocks, bonds, and real estate, as well as to the appreciated value of those assets.

Community Reinvestment Act (CRA) statement A description available for public inspection at each bank office indicating, on a map, the communities served by that office and the types of credit the bank is prepared to extend within the communities served.

co-mortgagor One who signs a mortgage contract with another party or parties and is thereby jointly obligated to repay the loan. Generally a co-mortgagor provides some assistance in meeting the requirements of the loan and receives a share of ownership in the encumbered property.

company An organization engaged in doing business as a sole proprietorship, partnership, corporation, or other form of enterprise.

company union A union composed of workers within one company and having no outside affiliation, considered to be dominated by the employer. Illegal under the National Labor Relations Act.

comparative advantage 1. The ability to produce a product for an opportunity cost which is lower than anyone else's opportunity cost in producing that product. 2. *economics* A complex theory used in the analyzing of international trade. The primary principle is that mutually profitable trade can arise between two regions when the ratios between production costs on specific commodities are different from those of another region. The tendency is for a nation or region to sell those products in which its ratio of costs is low in comparison to other countries, and buy those commodities where the other country's ratios are lower. This makes trade a mutually beneficial activity. (Cf. absolute advantage)

comparative advertising A type of persuasive product advertising that makes direct promotional comparisons with leading competitive brands.

comparative negligence *law* A situation in which the plaintiff may recover in an action on account of the negligence of a defendant even though the plaintiff was also guilty of negligence. In such cases damages are apportioned according to the degree of negligence of each party.

comparative statement *accounting* Financial statement which contains figures from previous years for the purposes of making comparisons. Companies with good growth records like to use these to graphically accent the progress they are making.

comparison shopping *finance* Evaluation of a lender's annual percentage rate (APR), which tells the borrowers the relative cost of credit, against the APRs quoted by other lenders.

compensatory transaction Transaction among nations that is a direct response to balance-of-payments considerations. They may be thought of as balancing items which arise to accommodate differences in money inflows and outflows resulting from so-called autonomous transactions. The two main classes are short-term capital movements and shifts in gold holdings.

competent party *law; insurance* Person legally capable of entering a contract. Must be of legal age and mentally competent.

competition Interaction among sellers

of a product. Tends to hold down prices and maintain product quality based on the belief that buyers tend to move toward the lower-priced, higher quality products. Opposite of monopoly. In any market, the greater the degree of competition, the smaller the degree of monopoly power. (*See* pure competition, perfect competition)

competitive bidding Bidding that is free of the presence of monopoly or collusion; requires that everyone be given the opportunity to bid on the same conditions and terms.

competitive trader *See* registered competitive trader.

complementary goods 1. Two or more commodities that are related in that a change in the quantity demanded of one results in a direct change in the quantity demanded of the other, within a consumer's given budget. 2. Goods which are used together, like lumber and nails.

complete audit *accounting* An audit in which the outside auditor examines the methods, accounts, and all supporting documents used by the internal auditor. This audit is supposed to be legal, mathematically correct, and accomplished with the use of all accepted accounting principles.

completed contract method of accounting Method of accounting under which authorization of gross income or a tax deduction is delayed until the entire contract has been completed. Prior to completion, the taxpayer records all advance receipts and disbursements in a suspense account which is cleared when each project is finished.

completed gift Gift where the donor has completely and irrevocably parted with dominion and control. A transfer is normally completed by the physical delivery of the property to the donee, though it may be completed by delivery to the donee's agent (but not to the donor's agent) or to someone acting in a fiduciary capacity on the donee's behalf. The general rules for determination include the following: (a) a competent donor, (b) a clear intent to make a gift, (c) an irrevocable legal title barring further control by the donor, (d) a delivery to the donee of the gift or of evidence of title such as a deed or stock certificate, and (e) acceptance of the gift by the donee.

completion program *investing* A limited partnership, usually in the field of gas and oil production, that takes over the operation once the levels of commercial resources are known to exist. This partnership does not offer the large tax write-offs available in an exploration partnership but usually returns more to the investor with less risk.

composite account method *income tax* Depreciation method under which all of the property items utilized by a taxpayer in operations are grouped into one account, and one composite rate of depreciation is applied to the group, with the rate based on the average useful life of all property included in the group. This rate is applied to the average of beginning and ending balances of asset accounts for the taxable year.

composition 1. Agreement between a borrower in financial difficulty and a lender, allowing the borrower to eliminate debt by paying only a portion of the total amount owed the lender. 2. A settlement between an insolvent debtor and creditors; in order to obtain immediate payment or payment earlier than when due, they agree to accept less than the total amount of their claims as satisfaction for the whole.

compos mentis *Of sound mind.*

compounding Process by which interest earned in the previous period along with the principal draws interest in subsequent periods.

compounding period The period, from a year to any period less than one year, on which interest is figured before proceeding to the subsequent period.

compound interest Interest computed on the original principal together with its accrued interest.

compound rate Rate used to compute interest on the principal along with interest personally accrued.

comprehensive insurance Broad automobile coverage including all risks except collision, which is written as a separate coverage. Technically called physical damage coverage on one's own car.

comprehensive medical expense coverage Policy, widely used in group insurance, that combines basic hospital, medical, surgical, and major-medical (catastrophic) benefits. This comprehensive policy may or may not have a coinsurance clause and usually has a deductible. When one goes beyond the deductible, there is usually a coinsurance clause up to a certain limit, after which the policy pays all costs up to some maximum limit, frequently as much as one million dollars.

comprehensive medical expense protection Policy under which hospital, surgical, medical, and diagnostic expenses are combined, with the insured required to pay a single deductible amount prior to receiving any reimbursement (except for in-hospital expenses). After satisfaction of the deductible amount, the plan will commonly pay 80% of expenses. Most plans limit the amount the insured employee must pay under this 20% coinsurance requirement, so that after a specified dollar maximum has been incurred by the employee, the insurer pays 100% of the expenses.

comprehensive personal liability coverage Insurance that covers all sums, up to the policy limit, that the insured becomes legally obligated to pay as damages because of bodily injury and property damage. The insurer also agrees to defend the insured in any suit that would be covered by the policy. (The insuring agreement is quite broad but still is limited by certain exclusions which will be specifically outlined in the policy.)

comprehensive zoning plan A general plan to control and direct use and development of municipal property by dividing the municipality into districts according to the present and potential use of the properties. Such a plan must be based on considerations concerning the common needs of the area and must be designed to accomplish the most appropriate uses of land consistent with public interest and the safeguarding of the interest of the individual property owners.

compromise 1. To adjust or settle differences or conflicting claims between parties; implies a mutual agreement. 2. A coming to terms or arrangement of a dispute by concessions on both sides.

comptroller One charged with the duties of examining and auditing the collectors of public money, keeping records, and reporting the financial situation from time to time. (*See* controller)

comptroller of the currency Officer of the Treasury Department responsible for chartering national banks and with primary supervisory authority over them.

comptroller's call *banking* A term applied to a Federal Reserve regulation requiring banks with a national charter (or national banks) to submit specified financial reports at least three times each year. These same reports must be published in local newspapers.

concealment *law* The failure to disclose known facts when obliged to do so.

concentrated marketing Practice of selecting a small segment of the total market and devoting all marketing resources to satisfying this single segment.

concentration ratio *economics* 1. Percentage of the total output of an industry that is produced by the few (usually four) largest firms in the industry. Rough way of measuring market structure and competitiveness. 2. The percentage of sales accounted for by the largest eight firms.

concentric chart *management* A circular chart depicting the president of the company in the center of the circle, and the concentric circles indicating different levels of authority and responsibility in the company. The chart indicates that as the lines move farther from the center, the numbers of people occupying the circles increase. This indicates that while there is need for, and room for, a few leaders, there is a far greater need for supporting personnel, or followers.

concept stocks *investing* Common stocks which seem to move on the basis of how people feel a given stock should do, in some general or specific field, rather than on the performance of stocks which have already been tried. (E.g., the youth movement in the United States, which lasted nearly two decades, produced a lot of ideas of how companies producing for the younger set should do. While the concepts often appeared good, many companies started on the concept did not do well.)

concordia *An agreement.*

concurrent jurisdiction *law* Several different levels of the judiciary, each of which is authorized to deal with the same legal subject matter.

concurrent policies *insurance* Policies in force at the same time covering identical risks.

condemn To expropriate a property for public use under the right of eminent domain. (*See* eminent domain)

condemnation *law* 1. The process in law by which private property is claimed for public use, and the owner compensated accordingly. (*See* eminent domain) 2. Elimination of property because it is hazardous to health, etc., because of the operation of the law.

conditio *A condition.*

condition 1. State or mode in which a person or thing exists. 2. *real estate* Any qualification, restriction, or limitation annexed to a gift, modifying or destroying its full enjoyment and disposal. 3. *insurance* Ground rules of the transaction that control the insurer's liability for covered losses by imposing obligations on the policyholder and insurer. Typical conditions are those related to a policyholder after a loss.

conditional contract *insurance* Contract requiring the insured to meet specific conditions in order to collect for losses.

conditionally renewable A condition under which the insured is guaranteed that renewal will not be denied solely on the basis of deterioration in health.

conditional sale A sale in which transfer of title to the purchaser is contingent upon fulfilling a certain condition or conditions, usually the full payment of the purchase price. The purchaser is entitled to the possession of the goods until default.

conditional sales contract A document used in installment sales credit arrangements, withholding ownership title from the buyer until the loan has been paid in full.

condition precedent 1. *law* Condition which delays the vesting of a right until a specific event occurs. 2. *real estate law* A fact or event which must exist or happen before a right becomes vested.

condition subsequent *real estate* Condition that operates upon an estate conveyed or gifted and renders it liable to be defeated for breach, in which event the estate conveyed or gifted reverts to the grantor.

condominium 1. A system of ownership of individual units in a multi-unit structure, combined with joint ownership of commonly used property such as sidewalks, hallways, or stairs. 2. An apartment house in which the units are owned separately by individuals.

conduit principle *trusts* Trust through which income is passed to the beneficiaries. Income generally will be taxable to the beneficiaries to the extent that it is actually distributed or made available to them by the trust. Income is taxable to the trust if it is accumulated by the trust; however, the trust can be set up so that part of the income is taxable to the trust and part to the beneficiaries. In this way, the income can be split in at least one more portion than there are beneficiaries.

conduit taxation Partnership taxation process in which certain items of income, deduction, and credit are passed through to partners as through a conduit. These items are treated as personal income on the partners' individual tax returns.

confession of judgment *law* A written acknowledgment by a defendant in a case which permits judgment to be entered against the defendant without the benefit of a trial in court. This is normally done by the defendant to save court expenses.

confidence coefficient *statistics* The probability that the value of a statistical measure, such as the arithmetic mean, determined from a given sample of a population will fall within a given range either side of the true value of that measure in the population. (E.g., in ninety-three cases out of a hundred, the statistical measure will be within a certain range of the true value of the two measures.)

confidential As occurring in the Freedom of Information Act, information as is likely, if disclosed, to impair the government's ability to obtain necessary information in the future or cause substantial harm to the competitive position of the person from whom the information was obtained.

confirmation 1. The act of conveying the interest of a person in lands and tenements to one who has possession, thereby enlarging a particular estate or affirming what would otherwise be a voidable estate. 2. *investing* A written description of a stock transaction given by a broker to a client, or to another broker.

confirmed letter of credit *banking* A letter issued by a bank guaranteeing the payment of all credit issued under it. Used prolifically in international trade.

confiscation *law* 1. The expropriation by the state of private property without indemnity. The essence of confiscation is the appropriation without any indemnity or compensation; a punitive action. 2. The appropriation for public use of private property that the owner has forfeited.

conflict of laws The disagreement between the laws of different states or nations as it affects the rights of persons acting under the laws of more than one jurisdiction.

conglomerate *economics* A combine of separate and different companies under one corporate head. Such business structures were popular in the 1960s, but have since declined in popularity due to the difficulty of operating widely diverse companies at a profit.

conglomerate merger The combining into one firm of two or more previously separate business firms which produce unrelated products. The new combined firm would be called a conglomerate corporation.

consanguinity The relationship that proceeds from a common ancestry. It is distinguished from affinity or relationship by marriage.

conscious parallel action Identical price behavior among competing firms that may or may not be the result of collusion or prior agreement, but has been held illegal by the courts in various antitrust cases.

consensus ad idem *A meeting of minds;* one of the essential requisites of the formation of a valid contract.

Consensus of Insiders *investing* One of a number of investment newsletters specifically devoted to monitoring and interpret-

ing insider activities in the stock market.

consent decree A means of settling cases in equity among the parties involved (such as a defendant firm and the Department of Justice). The defendant does not declare guilt, but agrees to cease and desist from certain practices and abide by the rules of behavior set down in the decree. This is the chief instrument employed by the Justice Department and by the Federal Trade Commission in the enforcement of the Sherman and Clayton acts. The majority of antitrust violations are settled in this manner.

conservatism *accounting* A principal of accounting specifying that when choosing among alternative accounting methods, the one least likely to overstate assets or net income should be selected.

consideration 1. *law* A requirement in contract law for making the contract valid; i.e., something of value which is given by one person to another in exchange for a promise, or for a specific act. 2. *insurance* Anything of value (e.g., money, personal services, love and affection, etc.) given to induce entering into a contract without which no contract is valid. In certain policies, the promise to pay is the consideration, such as in most property and liability policies. In life insurance, the first premium is the consideration, and for the insurer, the promise to pay as stipulated in the written contract is consideration.

consignment 1. The act of forwarding or delivering something to be sold, disposed of, or cared for, as merchandise or movable property. 2. The thing that is forwarded or delivered.

consistency *accounting* A basic principal which requires that methods be consistent over time, for the purpose of making reasonable comparisons.

consociatio An association or partnership.

consol *investing* A bond which pays interest perpetually, but never repays the principal. Such bonds were first issued by the British government in 1814.

consolidated statements *accounting* Financial statements which combine the financial statement of the mother company with all the subsidiaries.

consolidation loan One loan used to pay several smaller debts, usually to reduce the annual percentage rate or the dollar amount of payments made each month by extending them over a longer period of time.

conspicuous consumption The purchase of consumer goods for the purpose of impressing others. This expression was originated by Thorstein Veblen (1857–1929), to mean that those above the subsistence level (i.e., the so-called leisure class) are mainly concerned with impressing others through their standard of living, taste, and dress through what he called pecuniary emulation.

constant dollar accounting *See* current dollar accounting.

constant dollar GNP The gross national product expressed in the monetary value of a specific period in time, such as a particular year. (*See* gross national product)

constant dollars Dollar figures which have been deflated by using a price index to eliminate the effect of inflation.

constant purchasing power *economics* The amount of a currency needed over time to purchase the identical "market-basket" of goods or physical assets. (This relates to a period of inflation in which the purchase price of a select grouping of goods or material assets may change over time.)

constitution 1. The established form of government in a state, kingdom, or country. 2. System of fundamental rule, principles, and ordinances for the government of a state or nation, either contained in a written document or established by prescriptive usage. 3. Body of fundamental laws which recognize the basic rights of the citizens and define and govern the distribution or exercise of the sovereign power.

constraint 1. *real estate* General limitations that affect the selection of an estate planning technique to achieve a client's objectives. The nine general constraints are value of gross estate, amount of estate and gift tax liability, types of property, health and life expectancy, financial needs, title to properties, competency of beneficiaries, marginal income tax brackets, and state law. 2. *insurance* Forces which bear upon the categories of investment vehicles one is able to buy for a port-

folio. For example, if safety was a primary objective, constraint would be put upon the portfolio manager to avoid speculative investments.

construction period interest and taxes Interest and taxes paid or accrued during the period of construction which must be capitalized and deducted over a number of years. Rather than benefiting from the deduction all at once, the deduction is spread out over a number of years, like a depreciation deduction. (*See* Appendix G)

constructive Assumed or inferred by legal interpretation, used to describe an act or condition that is not the thing named but that acquires the character of the thing named because of the way it is regarded by the law. (E.g., a landlord's failure to maintain a tenant's apartment in livable condition would constitute constructive eviction of the tenant.)

constructive conflict *management* A theory, usually attributed to Mary Parker Follett, which states that conflict in industrial relations can serve the purpose of bringing into the open hidden grievances which are causing unrest.

constructive contract Obligation created by law for reasons of justice without regard to expressions of assent by either words or acts of the parties; sometimes known as a quasi contract, implied when one person has received money which is the property of another and which the former is obliged to refund.

constructive dismissal *management* A situation in which an employee leaves the job, apparently of his or her own accord, but who, in reality, was hounded from the job by an intolerable work atmosphere created by the employer.

constructive notice 1. Knowledge which a reasonable person would acquire through the exercise of ordinary care. A party will be deemed to have notice of a fact if that person had knowledge of facts which would naturally suggest that particular fact's existence and where, if the person had made reasonable inquiries, the existence of that fact would have been disclosed. Information of a fact imputed by law to a person because it could have been discovered by proper diligence and the situation was such as to make the act of inquiring a duty. (*See* notice) 2. *law* Information which is made public through notices in newspapers, or in other prescribed public documents. The law presumes that everyone has knowledge of a fact when it is a matter of public record.

constructive receipt The date when a taxpayer received dividends or other income. Internal Revenue Service rules say that constructive receipt of income is established if the taxpayer has the right to claim it, whether or not the choice is exercised. For instance, if a bond pays interest on December 29, the taxpayer must report the income in that tax year and not in the following year. However, income is not constructively received if the taxpayer's control of its receipt is subject to substantial limitations or restrictions.

constructive trust Trust raised by implication by a court of equity where a person achieves some personal advantage by becoming a trustee. The doctrine of constructive trust is a remedial device created by the court to compel a person who holds legal title to property subject to an equitable duty to convey to another to do so because that person would be unjustly enriched if permitted to retain the property. A resulting trust is based upon the presumed or inferred intent of the settlor of the trust whereas the constructive trust is imposed upon parties without regard to their intent.

consuetudo ex certa causa rationabili usitata privat communem legem *A custom that is certain and reasonable prevails over the common law.*

consuetudo vincit communem legem *Custom supersedes the common law.*

consumer One who actually uses the goods.

Consumer Advisory Council (CAC) A statutory body established by Congress in 1976 consisting of thirty members who represent a broad range of consumer and creditor interests. The council advises the Federal Reserve Board on the exercise of its responsibilities under the Consumer Credit Protection Act and other matters on which the Board seeks its advice.

consumer behavior The actions of individuals in obtaining and using goods and services, including the decision pro

cesses that precede and determine these acts.

consumer credit Credit offered or extended to a natural person in which the money, property, or service involved is primarily for personal, family, household, or agricultural purposes. A finance charge may be imposed, and/or, by agreement, credit extended may be payable in more than four installments.

consumer credit controls *economics* 1. A situation in a nation during a national emergency, such as a war, when credit is not extended, or is seriously curtailed by making the downpayment and/or the length and size of the loan a legal matter. 2. Normal use of credit rules by a company dictating the percentage of the downpayment and the length of time credit will be extended.

Consumer Credit Protection Act (1968) Legislation designed to give consumers full information on transactions between lenders and borrowers. The information required by the Act includes annual percentage interest rates paid by the borrower, potential total cost of the loan, special provisions bearing on the loan, and language which can be clearly understood by the average consumer.

consumer equilibrium Condition in which consumers allocated their income in such a way that the last dollar spent on each good or service and the last dollar saved provide equal amounts of utility.

consumer goods Products purchased by the ultimate consumer for personal use and not intended for resale or further use in the production of other goods.

consumerism 1. Demand that marketers give greater attention to consumer wants and desires in making their decisions. 2. More recently, the various movements working to protect consumer interests.

Consumer Price Index (CPI) Most commonly used measure of changing consumer prices in the United States; this index is calculated and published monthly by the Bureau of Labor Statistics, U.S. Department of Labor. The index expresses the price of consumer goods in a given month as a percentage of the price prevailing in some earlier period, known as a base period. (*See* cost-of-living index)

consumer sovereignty 1. *marketing* Concept of the consumer as "king" in that the consumer is free to buy what one wishes where one wishes, and by these actions determines what will be produced. In a highly competitive economy, competition will cause producers to adjust their production to the changing patterns of consumer demands. In less competitive economies resources will not be allocated in accordance with consumer wishes. 2. The condition of a market economy by which consumer decisions about which goods and services to purchase ultimately determine resource allocation.

consumer's surplus Satisfaction (utility) which a consumer receives and does not have to pay for.

consumption 1. Expenditures for consumer goods. 2. The using up of goods and services or wearing out of goods.

consumption tax *economics* A tax, such as a sales tax or an excise tax, which is levied on expenditures for consumption goods and services.

containerization *international trade* The combination of several unitized loads of products into a single load in order to facilitate intertransport changes in transportation modes.

contemplation of death Phrase used where the expectation of impending death influences someone to make a gift.

contestable period Certain length of time (normally two years) after an insurance policy has been in force in which the insurer agrees not to deny a claim because of an error, concealment, or misstatement (generally including even fraud) on the part of the insured.

contiguous Actually touching; contiguous properties have a common boundary.

contingent Likely, but not certain to occur; possible; accidental or incidental; dependent upon an uncertain future event.

contingent beneficiary *insurance* The person who will receive the death proceeds from an insurance policy in the event the primary beneficiary dies prior to the death of the insured.

contingent claim A claim which may or may not ever ripen into a debt, depend

ing on whether some future event does or does not happen.

contingent debt A debt that, either as to its existence or as to its amount, depends on some event uncertain either as to its occurrence altogether or to the time of its occurrence.

contingent fee 1. A fee payable to an attorney measured exclusively or predominantly by financial results accomplished and only in the event that the attorney wins the case; paid out of recovery in the action and is a proportionate part of the amount recovered. 2. A fee payable to an attorney representing a client only in the event that a certain result is achieved.

contingent interest Interest which is uncertain either as to whom it will go to or when it will occur.

contingent remainder Remainder which is limited to a person either not in existence or not certain or ascertained, or an estate which is limited to take effect either to a dubious and uncertain person, or upon a dubious and uncertain event which may never happen or be performed. Thus, a gift in remainder to a life tenant's issue surviving on the date of the life tenant's death is a contingent remainder and not a vesting one.

continuous stocktaking A British term synonymous with perpetual inventory.

contour map A map that displays the topography of the site with contour lines that indicate various elevations of the land.

contra bonos mores *Against good morals.*

contract A deliberate engagement between competent parties upon a legal consideration to do or abstain from doing some act. It is essential to its creation that the parties shall have intended that their agreement shall have legal consequences and be legally enforceable. The essential elements of a contract are an offer and acceptance thereof, the capacity of the persons to contract, consideration to support the contract, and a mutual identity of consent or consensus ad idem.

contract carrier A carrier that establishes specific contracts with a few customers and does not offer its services to the general public.

contractor One who contracts to supply labor and materials; one who undertakes to perform work for another.

contractor's bond A bond which guarantees that a contractor will perform or which guarantees that all material and labor used by the contractor has been paid for. In the event of default by the contractor, the surety is liable.

contractor's lien A statutory lien for the benefit of a contractor to the extent of the contractor's labor and materials on the structure which the contractor has worked.

contractual liability Obligation to repay all debts made in accordance with a contract.

contractus ex turpi causa, vel contra bonos mores, nullus est *A contract arising out of base consideration or against good morals is null.*

contraetatio rei alienae animo furandi, est furtum *Theft is the touching or removing of another's property with the intention of stealing.*

contra jus commune *Against common law.*

Contrarian Investment Strategy A book by David Dreman published in 1984 which attempted, with much success, to show that stocks with low P/E ratios outperformed stocks with high P/Es.

contrary thinking *investing* The concept that entails taking an opposite view from that which is currently popular with regard to a specific stock, or to market movement in general. The rule of thumb is that only if the bullish consensus goes above 80% should one take a position opposed to the trend.

contribution The satisfying by each of two or more persons, jointly liable by contract or otherwise, of his or her share of the liability.

contribution clause *insurance* The clause in a policy that states that if more than one policy covers a loss, the insurers share the loss in proportion to the face amounts of the policies.

contributions for social insurance *economics* All payments made by employers and employees for FICA taxes.

contributory A person liable to contribute to the assets of a company upon its being dissolved. Generally, this is a shareholder who has not paid for the stock in full.

contributory infringement *patent law* The intentional aiding of one person by another in the unlawful making, selling, or using of a patented invention.

contributory infringer *patent law* A person who induces, aids, or contributes to wrongful acts of another which constitute infringement of a patent.

contributory negligence *law* Conduct or performance that fails to meet the standard required for protection, which failure contributes in causing injury or damage.

contributory pension plan A pension plan in which both employer and employee make contributions to the plan.

contributory plan An employer-sponsored insurance plan to which the employee also makes contributions. This can be a group-life or pension or profit sharing plan. Group plans normally are contributory.

control 1. To exercise or to have the right to exercise a directing or governing influence over a thing. 2. The power of authority to manage, direct, superintend, restrict, regulate, govern, administer, or oversee.

controlled group regulation *close corporations* Regulation requiring that all members of the controlled group be considered for purposes of meeting eligibility and nondiscrimination requirements. Controlled group regulations are brought into play with a parent-sub relationship or with a brother-sister relationship.

controller A person who checks expenditures and finances; especially, an officer appointed by a state, by a municipal or other public corporation, or by a private corporation to examine and audit the accounts of collectors of the public or private money. (*See* comptroller)

control ratio *finance* A measure indicating management's control over a specific current asset or liability.

convenience goods *marketing* Common consumer goods, such as bread and milk, for which consumers do not shop around, or compare quality, price, etc.

convenience store *marketing* A store located to meet the needs of a neighbor-

63

hood for convenience goods, including gasoline.

conventional annuity Annuity where the annuitant is guaranteed a specified minimum dollar amount for each payment period, subject to increase if the annuity was issued on a participating basis.

conventional loan A mortgage loan other than one guaranteed by the Veterans Administration or insured by the Federal Housing Administration or any other agency of government.

conversion 1. A wrongful interference with goods, as by taking, using, or destroying them, inconsistent with the owner's right of possession. 2. The changing of property to a different use or form of ownership, such as when apartments are transformed to condominiums. 3. Wrongful disposition or detention of the personal property of others by one who has the lawful possession of the property. 4. The exchange of real to personal property, or the reverse, that is considered to have taken place where no actual exchange has been affected, as in settling the affairs of an estate.

conversion ratio *investing* The relationship between a preferred stock, or a bond, and the number of common shares which will be exchanged for it at the time of conversion. The holder is usually assured of full value, without dilution, at the time of conversion. (Cf. convertible bond)

convertible bond Bond that can be exchanged for stock of the issuing corporation under stated conditions, which may carry as much as a 1% difference in interest earned, but gives the investor the possibility of earning more, if the stocks to which the bonds are converted are at a favorable price at the time. However, since convertible bonds are normally callable, the issuer is more apt to call the action favorable to them. The importance of the callability feature combined with the conversion feature is that it may be used to shorten the bonds' maturity.

convertible debenture *finance* An unsecured bond or note which must be converted into the common stock of the issuing company at a specified future date.

convertible security A debt instrument (or sometimes an equity instrument) issued with the privilege of conversion for

another security of the same issuer at a specific price at a specific point in time as dictated by the issuer.

convertibility *economics* The degree to which a currency, such as the U.S. dollar, can be exchanged for gold, silver, or another currency, if it can be exchanged at all.

convey 1. To deed or transfer title to another. 2. To take from one place to another; to lead or conduct the channel or medium, transmit.

conveyance 1. The transfer of the title of real estate from one to another; the means or medium by which title of real estate is transferred. 2. A mode by which property is voluntarily transferred from one person to another by means of a written instrument and other formalities; it also signifies the instrument itself. This includes every instrument which transfers an interest in or creates a charge of lands. A conveyance can also take place independent of the will and intention of the grantor, and, in such case, is known as a conveyance by matter of record as in a court order vesting title to property in the plaintiff.

cooperative 1. A corporation organized for the purpose of rendering economic services, without gain to itself, to the owning and controlling shareholders or members. 2. An apartment building in which the owner holds title to all premises and grants rights of occupancy to particular apartments by means of proprietary leases or similar arrangements. 3. Type of corporate ownership of real property whereby stockholders of the corporation are entitled to use a certain dwelling unit or other units of space. Special income tax laws allow the tenant stockholders to deduct interest and property taxes paid by the corporation.

cooperative advertising The sharing of advertising costs between the retailer and the manufacturer or vendor.

cooperative association 1. An association of individuals formed with the object of providing for certain pre-existing common needs of the members. 2. A jointly owned union, as of laborers, farmers, or consumers, operated for the mutual benefit of all the persons making up the union, its profits being shared by all according to the capital or labor they contribute.

cooperative bank *See* savings and loan association.

coordination of benefits Provision included in most group medical expense contracts which has the effect of limiting the total amount recoverable from group contracts in effect for a person to have 100% of the expenses covered under any of the contracts. This serves to avoid duplication when a person may be covered under more than one group contract. (Hospital income benefits are usually an exception to this. Also, individual policies usually differ.)

co-owners Persons owning property jointly or as tenants in common.

coparcenary *law* Common ownership arising by descent as when lands descend on an intestacy to several persons as co-heirs; the persons so inheriting are called coparceners.

copy A reproduction or duplication of a document taken or written from another, as opposed to an original.

copyright 1. An incorporeal right existing in a work of art, literature, music, film, or pictures, usually in favor of the author of such work and governed by the provisions of the copyright act. 2. An author's right of literary property, recognized by common law, in unpublished literary and artistic productions. 3. *economics* A registration made of a writing, a work of art, a design, etc., with the Library of Congress, upon publication of the work, and which is done to help assure the registrant of the exclusive right to reproduce the material.

corner In speculation, the manipulation of the market in such a manner as to make the thing involved (stocks, grains, etc.) scarce or plentiful in the market at the will of the manipulator, that the latter may fix the price.

corollary A proposition appended to another which has been demonstrated and following obviously from it; an immediate inference, deductions, consequence. Something additional or resulting from.

corporate bond 1. Debt security issued by a public corporation and backed by either specific assets of the corporation or the credit worthiness of the corporation. Corporate bonds normally have a stated life and pay a fixed rate of interest semi-annually but do not represent ownership in the corporation. The principal classes of corporate bonds are mortgage bonds, collateral trust bonds, equipment trust certificates, guaranteed bonds, and debentures. 2. A written promise under seal, according to which a corporation pledges to pay a sum of money at a specified future time with interest set to be paid on a fixed date or at fixed intervals.

corporate dividend exclusion Subtraction from dividends qualifying as taxable income under Internal Revenue rules, limited to one hundred dollars for individuals and two hundred dollars for married couples filing jointly. Dividends from money market funds, foreign corporations, and exempt organizations do not qualify for the exclusion. Dividends from mutual funds generally do qualify. Although the 1986 Tax Reform Act repealed the exclusions, they should be understood since there is the possibility of their being restored.

corporate franchise The right to exist and do business granted by a government to a private corporation.

corporate image *marketing* The impression made by a corporation on employees, vendors, customers, and the public in general (i.e., how people view the corporation).

corporate insider *See* insider.

corporate liquidation The dismantling of a corporation, paying off debts in order of priority and distributing the remaining assets in cash to the owners. This creates a disadvantage of the corporate form, the potential for taxation upon liquidation. The shareholders will generally be required to recognize gain to the extent that the value for the property and cash distributed by the corporation exceeds the shareholder's adjusted base in the stock cancelled by the corporation.

corporate reorganization *economics; finance* A series of major changes made in a corporation, usually with the intent of streamlining it for subsequent years. The changes may include changes in top management, restructuring of debt, a new brand name or logo, etc.

corporate vertical marketing system Condition created through single ownership of each stage of the marketing channel.

corporation Form of business organization in which the business is an artificial person, an entity in its own right, owned by stockholders. The stockholders elect the directors, who hire the management. The management runs the corporation, and the corporation usually pays out a part of its profits as dividends to stockholders. Being a creature of the law, it possesses only those properties which the charter of its creation confers upon it, either expressly or incidental to its very existence. A corporation is endowed by the law with the capacity of perpetual succession—it remains the same though its members may die or change—and is empowered to act as a unit or as a single individual. Professional associations, as among doctors or lawyers, are looked upon by law and are taxed as corporations. (Cf. unincorporated association)

corporeal Having an objective material existence.

corporeal hereditament Any inheritable property that is tangible, such as land.

corporeal property Property which has a physical existence, such as lands or goods.

corpus 1. *The body;* an aggregate or mass; the principal or capital of a fund. 2. *trusts* All assets surrendered by the donor to the trust. 3. *investing* The principle sum, as contrasted to interest or other income received on that sum.

corpus juris *A body of laws.*

corpus juris civilis The Justinian Code.

correlation *statistics* The degree of relationship between variables or sets of data. Simple correlation may be figured as the square root of the associated variance divided by total variance, or as the geometric mean of the slopes of the two regression lines.

correspondent bank Bank that accepts deposits of and performs banking services for other depository institutions.

corroborate *law* To strengthen; to give increased support or credibility to something as evidence by furnishing additional or different evidence, confirming facts.

corrupt *law* Spoiled; tainted; depraved; debased. With an improper motive, an evil or wicked purpose.

co-signer 1. A person, other than the borrower, who signs a note in order to give additional protection to the creditor granting the loan because of the uncertain credit quality of the borrower. Also called a co-maker. 2. *finance; law* One who signs a legal instrument with another person and who is equally responsible for whatever the obligation is. (This is often done on a friendship basis, since it is widely agreed that it is not good business practice.)

cost The price paid for anything; outlay; expense.

cost approach A method of appraising property based on the depreciated reproduction or replacement cost (new) of improvements plus the market value of the site.

cost basis The original cost of the asset.

cost-benefit analysis A comparison of all the project costs to the value of the project benefits.

cost center *accounting* A unit or activity in a company for which costs are accounted as a separate entity.

cost depletion The writing off of a capital investment (e.g., a mine) over its projected life. To compute cost depletion, the cost or basis in the property must first be determined. Then the basis is divided by the number of estimated units (e.g., barrels of oil), and that fraction multiplied by the number of units (barrels) sold in a given year. This effectively guarantees the right of a taxpayer to recover an original capital investment in a mineral property, assuming production. (*See* Appendix D)

cost effectiveness study *economics* The analysis of a project for the purpose of determining if the benefits received are as great as they would be on an alternative, similar project costing the same amount of money. Such studies also normally concentrate on the methodology used in the projects to see if they are as effective as they should be per dollar spent.

cost method of inventory valuation *accounting* A method of valuing inventory after a physical count, or by using the balance from the control account, where the count is multiplied by the average cost determined by taking the weighted average of the unit cost of the beginning inventory and the unit cost of those units produced or bought during the fiscal period.

cost of capital   *See* risk-adjusted discount rate.

cost of capital theory of rate making   *economics* A concept which allows a public utility to earn a return sufficient to meet bond interest payments and any preferred stock dividends, and to give the common stock the rate of return currently prevailing in the market.

cost-of-living adjustment (COLA)   *economics* A provision in Social Security, and in many labor contracts, which allows adjustments in wages or payments to make up for the loss of purchasing power due to inflation. Adjustments are normally made annually.

cost-of-living index   An indicator of the current price level for goods and services related to some base year.

cost-plus contract   *economics* Contract which bases the delivered cost of the product on the cost of production, plus an additional fee, usually a percentage of the cost. Such contracts cannot always be deemed wise and are most often used when no guide to the cost of production of the specific product exists.

cost-plus pricing   Approach to price determination that takes some base cost figure per unit and adds a markup to cover unassigned costs and provide a profit. The two most common cost-plus procedures are full cost pricing and incremental cost pricing.

cost principal   *accounting* The principal that all properties and services acquired by a business are entered in the accounting records and are carried at their cost.

cost-push inflation   Price increases in the economy caused by increasing costs of factors of production (not by increased demand for the output).

cost recovery   Methodology used to recover the cost of a fixed asset over time.

co-tenancy   Any of a number of forms of multiple ownership, such as tenancy in common and joint tenancy.

counsel   *law* A person authorized by law to practice law.

counselor of real estate (CRE)   *real estate* Member of the American Society of Real Estate Counselors. The designation is given for experience and professional conduct in real estate counseling.

counterclaim   *law* A claim alleged by a defendant seeking to reduce the plaintiff's claim or provide grounds for a judgment in favor of the defendant to whatever extent the counterclaim exceeds the plaintiff's claim.

countercyclical policy   Government policy designed to work against the business cycle, the purpose of which is to stabilize the rate of output and income and prices in the economy.

counterfeit   To forge, copy, or imitate without lawful authority and with a view to deceive or defraud by passing the copy for that which is original or genuine.

countermand   To recall or revoke an order, authority, or instruction previously issued.

counter offer   A reply to an offer, though purporting to accept it, which adds qualifications or requires performance of conditions.

counterpart   The corresponding part of an instrument or a duplicate originally executed.

countervailing power   *economics* A principle, generally attributed to economist John Kenneth Galbraith, which asserts that the power of one sector of the economy must be balanced with the power of other sectors to have harmony in the economy. (I.e., the power of employers must be countervailed by the power of labor, or else labor will be exploited.)

country bank   *banking* Any bank which is not located in a city with a Federal Reserve Bank or a Federal Reserve Branch Bank.

county   A geographical area composed of local or minor municipalities, established by authority for municipal purposes.

coupon   1. A sales promotion technique that offers a discount on the purchase of a product. 2. Interest and dividend certificate. 3. Part of a commercial instrument which is to be cut off and submitted as evidence of something connected with the contract mentioned in the instrument. (*See* coupon bond)

coupon bond   *finance* A bond which has a series of small slips of perforated paper attached, usually at the bottom, indicating

67

when interest is due. The holder of the bond tears off the appropriate slips and presents them to the paying agent for payment of interest.

coupon rate   Rate of interest paid on a bond, represented by an attached coupon which must be presented to collect the interest.

course   In land surveying, the direction of a line with reference to a meridian.

covariance   *statistics*   The correlation between two variables multiplied by the standard deviation for each of the variables.

covariation   The inner relationships between assets in a portfolio.

covenant   1. *common law* An agreement or promise under seal.   2. A promise or obligation as contained in an instrument.

covenant not to compete   A clause in an agreement where one party promises not to offer to sell or produce the same goods and services in proximity to the other party.   (Occurs occasionally where one businessperson has sold the business to another and promises not to compete with that business for a stipulated period of time.)

covenant of seisin   *law*   An assurance that the grantor of land has the estate in quantity and quality which the grantor purports to convey.

covenant personal   Classification including all covenants except those so closely connected with realty that their benefit or burden passes with the realty.

covenant running with the land   *real estate law*   A covenant of such character that its performance or nonperformance will so affect the use, value, or enjoyment of the land itself that it must be regarded as an integral part of the property.

coverage   *insurance*   The risks insured against and the monetary amount of insurance.   Refers not only to risk of loss or type of risks assumed but also to dollar limits of liability or amounts of indemnity.

coverage analysis   *marketing*   A mathematical technique used to determine what level of inventory should be maintained, relative to the capital tied up in it, to provide the level of service the firm wishes to give its customers.

coverage requirements   *pension plans*

Determinations for coverage of a specific employee or class of employee dependent upon the laws governing the plan.   The originator of the plan can, within limits of the law, tailor the plan according to the originator's desires to reward or deny certain employees.   As laws are changed, however, these plans become more stringent with respect to discrimination.   (*See* Appendix G)

covered compensation   1. Level of pay up to which an individual participant's Social Security benefits are presumed to be provided.   The government publishes covered compensation tables periodically in two forms: Table 1, which provides covered compensation amounts for bracketed (average) ages; and Table 2, which provides covered compensation amounts for individual ages.   2. The projected average of the taxable wage bases to which an employee will have been subject during his or her working life.

covered earnings   Maximum amount on which FICA insurance is paid each year by the participant in the plan.

covered option   An option for which the seller owns the securities.

crawling peg   System of foreign exchange rates which permits the par value of a nation's currency to change automatically by small increments, downward or upward, if in daily trading on the foreign exchange markets the price in terms of other currencies persists on the floor or ceiling of the established range for a specified period.

creative financing   1. Any financing arrangement other than a traditional mortgage from a third-party lending institution.   2. Any new method to raise capital without use of bank loans, stock offerings, or other conventional steps.

credit   1. Trustworthiness. Credibility.   2. The time allowed to the purchaser of goods or services for payment.   3. A sum placed at a person's disposal in the books of a bank, etc., upon which he or she may draw to the extent of the amount; any note, bill, or other document on security of which a person may obtain funds.   4. The promise to pay in the future in order to buy or borrow in the present. The right to defer payment of debt.   5. The right hand side or page of a ledger in which are shown all items that reduce the charges of the account; opposite of debit.

creditable service *civil services* Total service of an employee or member of Congress measured in full years and months (anything less than a month is not counted) from the date of original employment to the date of separation. No credit is allowed for a period of separation from the service in excess of three calendar days.

credit agency An agency engaged in the business of collecting information as to the financial status and credit worthiness of individuals, partnerships, and corporations for distribution to subscribers.

credit analysis A financial and management review conducted by a lender or a credit-rating agency to determine the financial soundness and debt-repayment ability of a corporation, municipality, foreign government, or an individual.

credit application A form or an interview which seeks information about an applicant wanting credit regarding residence, employment, income, and existing debt.

credit bureau A reporting agency which assembles credit and other information on consumers to supply such information to others concerning a consumer's credit worthiness, credit standing, and/or capacity.

credit card A plastic card issued by a creditor, representing a charge account which allows individuals to obtain cash, goods, or services according to (and within the dollar limits of) an established credit arrangement.

Credit Control Act (1969) *economics* An Act of Congress, very broad in scope, which gives the President of the United States complete control over any type credit when it is deemed necessary for the health of the economy. (In the past, similar powers have been used in time of war, or in the years just following a war.)

credit history A continuing record of a borrower's debt commitments and how well these have been honored. A record of how a person has borrowed and repaid debts.

credit investigation An inquiry undertaken by a lender to verify information supplied by a borrower on a credit application.

credit life Insurance covering the unpaid balance of a loan in the event of a borrower's death.

creditor 1. A person to whom money is owed as the result of a financial or business transaction, not ordinarily including a person who has a contingent or future claim against the debtor. 2. Person or business who, in the ordinary course of business, regularly extends or arranges for the extension of consumer credit or lends money.

credit rating An evaluation of a person's capacity (or history) of debt repayment. Generally available for individuals from a local retail credit association; for businesses, by companies such as Dunn & Bradstreet; and for publicly held bonds, by Moody's, Standard & Poor's, and Fitch's. Individuals have access to their own files.

credit reduction election Method of tax credit reduction a taxpayer may use to reduce the basis of an asset.

credit risk Possibility of loss to a lender resulting from nonpayment by a borrower.

credit sale Any sale in which credit is extended or arranged by the seller.

credit scoring system Statistical measure used to rate credit applicants on the basis of various factors relevant to credit worthiness.

credit union Cooperative organization of individuals with a common affiliation (such as employment, labor union membership, or place of residence) which makes loans to members at low rates of interest, accepts deposits of members, and pays interest (dividends) on these deposits out of earnings.

credit worthiness 1. The ability to repay debts. 2. A creditor's measure of a consumer's past and future ability and willingness to repay debts.

creeping inflation Modest increases in the general price level.

crime of 1873 *economics* Popular name for the revision in that year of the coinage laws, with the omission of the silver dollar. This took place because very little silver had come to the mint after 1834, and because the price paid by the mint was below the market price.

critical path The sequence of tasks in a Project Evaluation and Review Technique (PERT) network that require the longest total completion time.

cross-action An action brought by a defendant against a plaintiff in the same suit.

cross elasticity of demand and supply *economics* The relationship between the relative change in the quantity of one product in response to the relative change in the price of another commodity.

crossover point The particular time when a tax shelter moves from producing losses to producing taxable income. It is also known as the turnaround point.

cross-purchase agreement *management; insurance* An arrangement made between partners through some specific plan allowing the partner(s) to buy out the interest of another partner in the event the partner leaves or wishes to leave the partnership for any reason, including death. Normally, insurance policies are purchased to cover these cross-purchase agreements.

cross-purchase plan Agreement, entered into during the partners' lifetimes, between the individual partners as to how the interest of a deceased partner may be purchased by the surviving partner(s). (Cf. entity plan)

crowding-out *finance; economics* The situation in which too much government borrowing reduces the funds available to private borrowers, pushing up interest rates and causing a decrease in private investment spending.

Crown loan A demand loan to the children or parents of lenders. Named for Chicago industrialist Harry Crown (b. 1896), who first used it. It puts the money in the lower tax category that applies to the loan recipients. For years, the Crown loan provided a substantial tax benefit for all parties involved since such loans could be made interest-free. In 1984, the United States Supreme Court ruled that such loans had to be made at the market rate of interest or be subject to gift taxes.

Crumney trust Trust which permits the accumulation of income in order to allow contributions to the trust to satisfy the present interest requirement for the annual exclusion. The beneficiary is given limited power to withdraw income, principal, or both. Generally the power is exercisable only during a limited period of time (fifteen to thirty days) each year and is noncumulative; i.e., if not exercised in one year, the power of withdrawal for that year is lost. The power of withdrawal is usually limited to the amount excludable from gift tax under the annual exclusion.

cujus est solum, ejus est usque ad coelum et ad inferos *The owner of land owns everything above it (to the sky) and everything beneath it (to the depths).*

cujus juris (i.e., jurisdictionis) est principale, ejusdem juris erit accessorium *An incidental or accessory matter is subject to the same jurisdiction as its principal.*

cul-de-sac *real estate* Street with an intersection on one end and a closed turning area on the other. Often valued in the design of residential subdivisions for the privacy provided to homes on the street.

cum aliquis renunciaverit societati, solvitur societas *A partnership is dissolved by any partner renouncing the same.*

cum dividend *investing* With dividend. The buyer of stock sold cum dividend will receive the dividend which has already been declared but not paid.

cum onere Subject to a burden encumbrance.

cum rights *investing* With rights. Stock sold cum rights gives the buyer the right to subscribe to a new issue of stock currently being issued.

cum testamento annexo *With the will annexed.* Condition in which a testator fails to name an executor or the executor named is unable or refuses to act, then letters of administration may be granted to a fit person found by the court, with the will annexed, so that the person so appointed has to dispose of the estate in accordance with the terms of the will.

cumulative Increasing by successive additions.

cumulative gift tax Tax on gifts which accumulates over the lifetime of the donor with respect to its effect on the Unified Credit. Since the gift tax laws were changed and merged with estate tax requirements in 1976, the planner must look at gift taxes due prior to 1977 before merging them with gift taxes made in 1977 or after. For example, a donor makes taxable gifts to various donees over a period of years, but does not pay the gift taxes. When the donor dies, the gift taxes will be combined with the estate taxes owed to determine the ultimate unified tax.

cumulative voting *investing* A method of stockholder voting in which the number of shares held is multiplied by the number of directors to be elected to determine the number of votes a shareholder may cast.

cura *Care, guardianship.*

curable depreciation Depreciation or deterioration that can be corrected at a cost less than the value that will be added.

currency 1. Coins and paper money. The medium of exchange circulating in a country. 2. The period during which anything is in force. (E.g., the currency of a mortgage is the continuance of the security.)

currency depreciation or devaluation *economics; finance* 1. Reducing or eliminating the gold, silver, or other commodity for which the currency can be exchanged. 2. Altering all or some of the ratios of foreign exchange. 3. Changing the supply of currency without requiring a corresponding change in the goods produced.

currency futures Contract for the future delivery of foreign exchange.

current account In banking practice, an open, running account of a customer from which the customer draws money from time to time.

current account balance The difference between the nation's total exports of goods, services, and transfers and its total imports of them, excluding transactions in financial assets and liabilities.

current assets 1. Cash and other liquid assets that can easily be converted into cash. Those assets that will be turned into income within a year or less. 2. Cash and equivalents owned by a company.

current disbursement plan *pensions* Plan in which employers pay retirement benefits out of current earnings directly to their employees as their pension benefits come due. (*See* funded pension plan)

current dollar accounting A system of accounting used during an inflationary period in which historical-cost items are restated to adjust for price changes caused by changes in the purchasing power of the monetary unit.

current income interest trust Trust that provides a stream of income to the spouse or other person with income distributions made at least annually. The "Q-tip" or "C" trust, as it is also called, qualifies for the marital deduction and is included in the surviving spouse's gross estate if elected by decedent's executor. A noncumulative right of invasion is limited to 5% of corpus or five thousand dollars, whichever is greater. The surviving spouse cannot have a general power of appointment and cannot be the ultimate beneficiary of the property when the trust terminates. If the income stream goes to the surviving spouse, it cannot be split. The funding amount is usually an amount remaining after a nonmarital trust has first been funded. It can be used in combination with other trusts to achieve maximum estate tax saving.

current liability 1. A liability that is presently enforceable; i.e., trade debts as distinct from long-term indebtedness such as mortgages. 2. Short-term debt that is due and payable in one year or less.

currently deductible expenses Expenses which pertain to the specific tax year in question. They include such expenses as goods or services used up within a year, intangible drilling and development costs, and state and local taxes.

currently insured Condition met under Social Security laws if one has at least six quarters of coverage in the thirteen-quarter period ending with the quarter in which one becomes entitled to old-age benefits or disability benefits or dies.

current maturity *investing* The length of time between the present time and the maturity date of a bond issue. (*See* original maturity)

current portion of long-term debt *finance* That part of long-term debt payable in the current year.

current production rate *investing* The top interest rate on current Government National Mortgage Association government-backed mortgages.

current ratio Measure of liquidity calculated by dividing current assets by current liabilities and used to measure the short-term financial strength of a company. (*See* Appendix C)

current yield 1. Measurement of investment returns based on the percentage relationship of annual cash income to the investment cost (not acquisition cost). (Annual interest on a bond divided by market price.) 2. Annual amount of income received from an investment compared with that used for common and preferred stocks and frequently that used for bonds as well. (*See* Appendix C)

curtesy *common law* The right by which a man is entitled to enjoy all or part of his dead wife's estate, regardless of the provisions of her will, during his lifetime. Exists in only a few states.

custodial account Type of account necessary to purchase stock for minors since minors are not permitted to buy or own stock.

custodian 1. Receiver or trustee of any of the property of the debtor, appointed in a case or proceeding. A general term to describe one who has been given legal charge or custody of property, papers, and/or people. 2. Assignee under a general assignment for the benefit of the debtor's creditor. 3. Trustee, receiver, or agent under applicable law or under a contract that is appointed or authorized to take charge of property of the debtor for the purpose of enforcing a lien against such property or for the purpose of its general administration for the benefit of the debtor's creditors.

custody *law* The care and keeping of anything; safekeeping; protection; charge; guardianship.

custom Usage, having the force of law, being established by long use and consent of ancestors.

custom builder *real estate* Builder of residential housing who specializes in building individual residences to the specifications of the client, as opposed to a developer who may build several residences with similar specifications in the same area.

customer In the special sense, natural person to whom consumer credit is offered or to whom it is or will be extended including a co-maker, endorser, guarantor, or surety for such natural person who is or may be obligated to repay the extension of consumer credit.

customs duties *economics* Taxes on imports. They are collected from the importer, who normally would build them into the cost of the goods bought and thus into the price at which the goods would be sold. The ultimate burden of the tax would fall on the consumer.

custos statum haeredis in custodia existentis meliorem, non deteriorem, facere potest *A guardian can improve the estate of an existing heir but cannot make it worse.*

cutoff rate *economics; finance* In capital budgeting, the rate of return at which no capital investments will currently be made.

cyclical balanced budget *economics* The concept of a federal budget which is balanced over the business cycle, with deficits occurring in low periods, and surpluses occurring in peak periods.

cyclical stock Stock from a company whose earnings tend to fluctuate sharply with the business cycle and the level of economic activity. When earnings are good, the price of the stock usually rises sharply, and when the down-cycle is on, the inverse is true. Automobile companies and machine tool companies are good examples of this situation.

cyclical unemployment *economics* Unemployment in the economy which is related to phases of the business cycle.

cy pres *law* As nearly as possible. Doctrine whereby a gift or trust impossible to administer as the testator directed may be used or administered as nearly as possible in accordance with the testator's intentions. This enables the court to carry out the general intention of the donor or settlor of a fund when the particular method of carrying it out indicated by the instrument fails or when the instrument fails to indicate fully the method of fulfilling the general intention.

D

daily balance Balance for a day in the period for which interest is to be paid. (*See* average daily balance)

daily trading limit *investing* The maximum amount that many commodities and options markets are allowed to rise or fall in one day. The limits are imposed to prevent panic buying or selling in the markets.

damage Loss, injury, or deterioration caused to a person or a person's property by the negligence, design, or accident of another.

damaged *law* Describes property when the action of a public authority results in diminution of property value, under the constitutional provision that private property shall not be taken or damaged except for public purposes and after just and adequate compensation is paid.

damages *law* Pecuniary compensation or indemnity which may be recovered in the courts by any person who has suffered loss, detriment, or injury whether to his or her person, property, or right, through the unlawful act, omission, or negligence of another.

damnosa haereditas 1. *civil law A losing inheritance.* 2. Property which a trustee in bankruptcy declaims as being a burden to the creditors.

damnum absque injuria *law An injury without a wrong.* A loss without a remedy provided by law.

damnum emergens *law Loss arising.* In a breach of contract, one aspect of damages is the actual loss, as distinguished from the loss of profit.

Danish income tax *economics; political science* The state income tax of Denmark, which is highly progressive. It is levied on total income, with an additional flat tax levied on dividends, and capital gains. There are also local and county income taxes.

data Facts from which to draw a conclusion. Known facts; collected information.

data integrity *computers* The degree to which computer-stored data corresponds to original source data.

data manipulation *marketing* Methods of introducing bias into data for the purpose of making the results appear what the company wants them to be.

data survey form A special form on which a financial planner can gather both qualitative and quantitative data on a prospective client.

Data Universal Numbering System A numerical method of identifying businesses designed and maintained by Dun and Bradstreet and published as part of a list of firms, giving information on the firms, such as management personnel, finances, size, etc. Also called Dun's number or Dun's Market Identifier.

date of record *finance* The date by which a stockholder must appear on the list of stockholders to qualify for participation in the dividend payment.

day *common law* The full twenty-four hours from midnight to midnight.

day book *accounting* A record book in which financial transactions of the day are noted without regard to debits and credits. (Antiquated.)

daylight trade *See* day trade.

day loan *finance* A loan which is made and repaid the same day, the proceeds from which are used to buy securities. Usually, the loan will then be secured by the securities purchased.

day order A buy or sell order that expires at the end of the day entered.

day rate *accounting* Pay for work by the hour or by the day, as distinguished from piece work. (Antiquated.)

day trade Purchases and sale or short sale and cover of the same security in a margin account on the same day. Also known as a daylight trade.

days of grace The days (usually three) allowed for payment of a note or bill after its stated due date.

day's sales in cash Cash divided by sales per day. Measure of management's control of cash balances.

deadheading *transportation* The return of an empty truck or railroad, along with the crew, after completing a shipment. While this is still common with rail traffic, trucking has put much emphasis upon the backhaul to at least make expenses on the return trip. (Cf. backhaul)

deadweight In shipbuilding contracts, the quantity of cargo, expressed in tons, a ship will take on board.

deadweight tonnage, vessel *See* vessel deadweight tonnage.

deal An arrangement to attain a desired result by a combination of interested parties.

dealer 1. *investments* Market maker for over-the-counter securities. Dealers buy for their own accounts, but also facilitate the exchange of stock by buying from those who wish to sell and selling to those who wish to buy. Markets for stocks would probably not be operable were it not for these people. 2. One who buys to sell again.

dealer financing *marketing; finance* A common situation in which a dealer sells durable goods to consumers on credit, then sells the loans to a bank. The consumers then become effective borrowers of the bank.

de arbitratione facta *As a result of arbitration.* A writ for enforcing a judgment of arbitrators.

death benefit Insurance benefit under group plans covering the deaths of employees, the amount of which is a flat rate or determined by a schedule related to earnings or position. Generally, death benefit payments, up to a total of five thousand dollars with respect to one employee, are exempt from income tax under Section 101(b) of the Internal Revenue Code. It makes no difference whether the death benefit is payable to the employee's estate or personal beneficiary. However, the five thousand dollar exclusion is available only to the extent that the employee did not have a nonforfeitable right to receive the payment had the employee lived. (*See* Appendix G)

death certificate Official proof of death as noted in an official registry of death.

debased currency *economics* A monetary system which no longer has a commodity base. The original base might have been gold, or gold and silver, or, in the case of small countries, the base might have been the monetary unit of a large country which had a commodity base for its currency.

debenture *law* 1. Any writing that acknowledges a debt. 2. Something other than money such as goods or services that is owed by one person to another. 3. An obligation of corporations or large-moneyed co-partnerships, issued in a form convenient to be bought and sold as investments. 4. *See* debenture bond.

debenture bond *investing; finance* 1. An unsecured bond. 2. An unsecured long-term instrument backed by the general credit of the issuer but has no special lien on the issuer's property. The bond indenture may stipulate certain safety measures to protect the bondholders. Debentures normally have first claim on assets not specifically pledged under mortgage bond indentures.

debet sua cuique domus esse perfugium tutissimum *Every man's home must be a perfectly safe refuge.*

debit 1. A sum shown in the books of account as due and owing. 2. The left hand side or page of a ledger in which are shown all items that are charged to the account.

debita sequuntur personam debitoris *Debts follow the person of the debtor.* Thus an action founded on a debt may be commenced and the debt itself enforced from the debtor in the locality where the debtor resides.

debit card A card that resembles a credit card but which debits a transaction account (checking account) with transfers occurring with customer's purchases. A debit card may be machine readable, allowing for the activation of an automated teller machine or other automated payments equipment.

de bonis asportatis Action of trespass for damages for taking away goods.

de bonis intestati Judgment against the property of a deceased who died intestate. (Cf. de bonis testatoris)

de bonis non administratis *Relating to goods or assets which have not been administered.* Where an executor dies intestate or an administrator dies without fully having administered the assets of the deceased, a grant of probate or letters of administration de bonis non may be granted.

de bonis propriis *Of his own goods.* Where an administrator or an executor has been guilty of waste, the judgment obtained against the administrator to make good the loss is known as a judgment de bonis propriis.

de bonis testatoris Judgment against the property of a deceased who died testate. (Cf. de bonis intestati)

de bonis testatoris ac si *From the goods of the testator, if any,* and if not, from those of the executor.

debt 1. A specified sum of money owed by one person to another because of an express or implied contract. 2. Something other than money that is owed by one person to another, as goods or services.

debt capacity The total amount of debt a company can prudently support, given its earnings expectations and equity base.

debt collector Anyone, other than a creditor or a creditor's attorney, who regularly collects debts for others.

debt crisis A situation which exists when debt is growing, annual deficits continue, and there seems to be little hope that the situation will change.

debt crisis, national *See* national debt crisis.

debt limit *economics* 1. In federal government, the limit placed upon debt by Congress, which can be changed by a joint resolution of Congress. Since the change is a mere formality, in essence there is no ceiling on the federal debt. 2. Debt limitations built into state constitutions, which usually allow for no debt at all. 3. Limitations on debt which are built into the articles of incorporation of a corporation.

debt monetization *economics; finance* The method by which the national debt is used to create money or get more money in circulation. This is accomplished by having the Federal Reserve System purchase the debt instruments and release Federal Reserve notes in payment.

debtor 1. A person from which something is due to another, as money, goods, or services. 2. One who owes a debt or anyone who is liable on a debt, whether due or to become due.

debt-to-assets ratio A measure of financial leverage, calculated by dividing debt by total assets. (*See* debt-to-equity ratio)

debt-to-equity ratio A measure of financial leverage calculated by dividing debt by shareholders' equity. This is used to measure the risk associated with the capital structure of the corporation.

de caetero *Henceforth.*

de catallis reddendis Writ for the restoring of specific chattels detained from the owner.

decedent A deceased person.

deceit Fraud, cheat, craft, or collusion used to deceive and defraud another.

decentralize *economics; marketing* 1. To delegate authority and responsibility to lower echelons in the organization. 2. A term often used to describe the spin-off of subsidiaries of a company, usually to different geographic locations, where they become separate profit centers.

decimal Pertaining to or founded on the number ten. (E.g., the decimal system is a system of reckoning by tens and tenths.)

decision theory *management; statistics* A body of knowledge resting on measurements of probabilities which involve determination of the possible strategies available and the probabilities attached to each situation that may develop for the purpose of selecting the course of action most likely to achieve the defined goal(s). Prolific use is made of probability theory.

declaration 1. The act of declaring or announcing. Affirmation; explicit assertion; open expression; avowal. 2. A formal statement intended to create, preserve, assert, or testify to a right. 3. *insurance* Descriptive material relating to subjects covered, persons insured, premiums charged, period of coverage, policy limits, and warranties or promises made by the insured regarding the nature and control of the hazard. 4. *finance* An authorization passed by the board of directors of a corporation to pay a dividend on a specified date. Once a dividend is declared it becomes an obligation of the issuing company.

declaratory judgment *law* A court's decision that either interprets an instrument or declares the meaning of the law under a statutory proceeding which authorizes the court to enter such a decision, even when the case is not being litigated.

declining balance Decreasing amount owed on a debt as monthly payments are made.

declining yield curve *investing* A graphic presentation which shows that rates of return on long-term maturities are lower than on short-term maturities. (Normally this illustrates a strong belief that interest rates are currently too high and will will decline in the long-term.)

decreasing cost industry *economics* 1. Any industry for which the average total unit cost decreases as the volume of production increases, over the normal range of production. 2. Industry which experiences decreases in resource prices or costs of production during expansion because of entering firms. This situation might arise as a result of substantial external economies of scale.

decree An edict; a law.

decree nisi *law Decree unless.* A temporary decree which will become final with the passing of time alone if no further action is taken.

dedication 1. The act of setting aside private property for public use. Such an act is done by the property's owner with the consent and agreement of the public authority involved. 2. Gift from the owner to the public of land, streets, roads, or highways. In order to constitute dedication, there must be an offer, either express or implied, by an owner to appropriate land or some interest or easement therein to public use and an acceptance of such offer, either express or implied, when acceptance is required by the public.

de die in diem *From day to day.*

de dolo malo *Arising out of fraud.*

deductible 1. That which may be subtracted, particularly from income for tax purposes. 2. *insurance* Amount the insured is required to pay before the insurance comes into play. The use of deductibles results in lower premiums for the insured, since it requires the insured to pay the first portion (e.g., one hundred dollars) of the covered loss before the insurer begins to pay anything on the loss.

deductible employee contribution Limited amount of voluntary contribution to certain plans sponsored by an employer allowed if an employee has not reached the age of seventy and one-half and is still getting compensation. Certain types of plans for employee thrift allow for contributions with before-tax dollars. Such contributions must not exceed limitations on deductions in order to be qualified voluntary employee contributions.

deduction for adjusted gross income Items that can be subtracted from adjusted gross income to calculate taxable income. These are: employee business and trade expenses; moving expenses of employees and self-employed persons; deductions attributable to a business or trade; limited deduction for charitable contributions for individuals who do not itemize personal deductions; disability income exclusion; and alimony payments.

deduction from adjusted gross income Itemized deduction allowed for subtraction from adjusted gross income, including medical and dental expenses (including medical expense insurance premiums); taxes; charitable contributions; interest expense; casualty losses; and miscellaneous deductions.

deed A written instrument, signed, sealed, and delivered, whereby an interest, right, or property passes, an obligation binding on some person is created, or which is in affirmance of some act whereby an interest, right, or property has passed.

deed of arrangement *law* A document through which an individual or company assigns or conveys property to a trustee for the benefit of creditors.

deep discount bond Bond selling substantially below face value because it was issued when interest rates were lower (e.g., bond with a face value of one thousand dollars selling below eight hundred dollars).

de facto *In fact; actually.* (Cf. de jure)

defalcation *law* Outright embezzlement or some other form of misappropriation of money or property.

default 1. Failure to perform what is required by terms of a credit agreement. 2. Failure to fulfill a legal obligation or requirement, such as failure to pay money due or to appear in court to answer a summons.

default premium Increased return on a security required to compensate investors for the risk that the company will default on its obligation.

defeasance clause *law* 1. A provision found in some debt agreements whereby the contract is nullified as the result of the ommission of certain specified acts. 2. A clause in a mortgage which defeats the forfeiture of the property as long as the debtor performs one's obligations under the contract.

defeasible Subject to being defeated, annulled, or abrogated; subject to defeasance (e.g., a legal estate vested in a mortgagee which is defeated upon the repayment of the mortgage debt as provided in the mortgage).

defect 1. Lack, want, or absence of something legally requisite; a deficiency. 2. The lack or absence of something necessary for completeness or perfection.

defendant *law* Person or entity who must defend himself or herself against a complaint of wrong doing made by the plaintiff, in court of law. Defendants have only to defend themselves; plaintiffs bear the burden of proof that the defendant is guilty as accused.

defendemus *We will defend.* The term as used in a grant amounts to a warranty of title whereby grantors are obliged to defend the title of their grantee.

defensive issues Securities that remain relatively stable even in periods of economic slumps. Some defensive issues include high grade corporate bonds, government and municipal bonds, certificates of deposit, commercial paper, and utility stocks.

defensive stock Stocks which do not fluctuate wildly during the ups and downs of the economy, but remain rather stable over time. Companies issuing such stock tend to produce products or services which are needed in good times and in bad. Shares in utilities, banks, and food companies usually come under the category.

deferral 1. Charge made to defer payment. 2. Deferring of tax liability from one year to the next, or to some subsequent year.

deferred annuity Annuity where benefits begin after a given number of years or at optional ages as specified in a contract purchased with a single premium or annual premiums. Benefits under a deferred annuity are payable after the expiration of a given period. The deferred period is usually one that lasts until retirement.

deferred availability *banking* The time lag between the deposit of a check and the availability of the funds to the depositor. This is due to the length of time it takes the check to clear.

deferred compensation plan Plan by which a certain portion of a person's compensation will be deferred to a later time, usually after retirement when taxes are apt to be less. This plan is often used by executives of large companies. The compensation which is deferred must be guaranteed by the firm; no trust with an outside agency can be used.

deferred tax liability Estimated amount of future income taxes that may become payable from income already earned but not yet recognized for tax reporting purposes.

deficiency 1. Lack. 2. *law* That part of a secured obligation which remains after crediting the net proceeds accruing from the sale of the security by the creditor.

deficiency bill An act by a legislature which authorizes an additional appropriation of funds for a project when the original appropriation was not sufficient.

deficit 1. *government finance* Condition existing when expenditures by the government are greater than total revenues being collected so that the balance must be made up by borrowing and/or by creating money. 2. *international finance* Condition created when import items exceed export items.

defined-benefit plan *pensions* Plans in which the benefits are defined and categorized as follows: a flat amount, a flat percentage of earnings, a flat-amount unit, or a percentage-unit benefit.

defined-contribution plan Plan in which the amount of an employee's retirement benefit will be determined by how much the contributions in the pension fund made on the employee's behalf can buy. (In this plan, the employee does make contributions, usually a percentage of gross pay, and the employer also makes contributions in the employee's name.) The amount of retirement benefit that can be purchased with each dollar of contribution will decrease as the employee grows older. Also known as a money-purchase plan.

defined performance A sales device used by mutual funds to prove they have superior management. In short, if one fund had a 19% yield performance in one period, and others were below that, they would tout this performance as a reason to buy shares of the fund. (Percentage yields vary from time to time among similar funds, and vary widely as between funds, usually related to the degree of risk in the fund's portfolio.)

definite loss   *insurance* A loss which can be defined with approximate accuracy. Covered and noncovered losses are specified in the policy.

definitely determinable benefits   *pensions* Ultimate proceeds which an employee may receive from an employer through a pension or profit sharing plan. Benefits are considered to be determined if each participant in the plan receives a proportionate share of the contributions. In such a plan, it is the benefit which must be prescribed rather than the contribution. Any qualified plan must be non-discriminatory. The cardinal rule in retirement benefits is equity.

definitional equation   *economics* An equation stating alternatives, equilibrium conditions, or a mathematical necessity.

definition of disability Provision outlining what is required to be considered disabled for purposes of collecting benefits. Generally, there are three classifications of definitions. "Any occupation type" refers to the complete inability of the person to perform the work required in any occupation. "Own occupation" is when the covered person is prevented by disability from performing any and all of the duties required by the occupation. "Split definition" refers to the performance of any duties of occupations for which the person was formerly suited.

definitive Describes a permanent certificate or document replacing one temporarily issued.

deflation   *economics* That part of the downward phase of a trade cycle where there is a decided decline in economic activity, often followed by unemployment and generally depressed economic conditions.

deflationary gap 1. Amount by which aggregate demand falls short of full-employment aggregate supply, thereby pulling down the real value of a nation's output. 2. *economics* The difference between the amount of spending in the economy theoretically necessary to maintain full employment and that which is actually being spent.

deflection of tax liability The legal shifting of one's personal tax burden to another, usually a person in a lower tax bracket, through some vehicle such as a trust, where assets are transferred out of one's estate and into the estate of another. Some such vehicles, such as the well-known Clifford Trust, were curtailed by the 1986 Tax Reform Act, but not eliminated completely.

defraud 1. To deprive of some right, interest, or property by fraud, deceit, or artifice. 2. To cheat, trick, or swindle; to deprive a person of property, an estate, or the like by fraud.

de furto   *Concerning theft.*

degree of risk A function of the probability distribution of losses over time. The more predictable the loss, the less is the degree of risk.

degressive tax   *economics* A progressive tax where the tax rate increases at a decreasing rate.

dei gratia   *By the grace of God.*

dei judicium   *The judgment of God.*

de jure   *By law; by right.*

del credere   *Of belief or trust.*

delay clause   *insurance* Clause included in life insurance contracts to permit an insurance company to postpone payment of the cash surrender (or loan) value for a period of six months after requested by the policyholder. By law, insurers must include this in their contracts, but it is rarely invoked.

delayed call   *investing* A provision in a security which gives the issuer the right to call the security, but only after a specified length of time has elapsed. (Cf. call provision)

delinquency Neglect of duty; failure to do what is legally required to be done.

delinquent Describes a credit account which is past due and for which no satisfactory repayment arrangement has been made.

delisting   *investing* The removal of a company's security from an organized exchange because of the violations of exchange regulations, or the failure of the company to meet continuing financial requirements.

delivery The act by which an object or thing is placed within the actual or constructive possession or control of another.

Delphi forecast *See* jury of executive opinion.

Delphi technique *statistics; marketing* A method of forecasting, the technique of which is to get independent opinions on a problem from a number of experts. The opinions are then grouped, analyzed, and passed along to the individual participants who express second opinions in the light of previous opinions. This procedure is repeated until a reasonably common opinion is reached. (The technique is named for the ancient Greek temple of Delphi, whose oracle was given to making obscure, ambiguous pronouncements.)

demand The desire to possess plus the ability to purchase.

demand curve *economics* A graphic presentation, showing the specific quantities that will be demanded by any given price, with dollars on the vertical (y) axis and quantity of product sold on the horizontal (x) axis. Also called demand schedule.

demand deposits 1. Checking account deposits held by commercial banks. The deposits can be withdrawn on demand and can be transferred to others by writing checks. 2. A deposit payable on demand or a time deposit with a maturity period or required notice period of less than fourteen days. Commonly takes the form of a checking account.

demand, derived *See* derived demand.

demand elasticity *economics* Changes in demand for a good or a service in response to a relatively minor change in price. (I.e., if the price of a good increases 10%, and the demand by 15%, the demand is said to be elastic. If the percentage drop in demand is the same as the increase in price, unitary elasticity exists. If the percentage drop in demand is less than the percentage increase in price, demand is said to be inelastic.)

demand, law of *See* law of demand.

demand note 1. A note payable on demand. 2. Bill of exchange which is expressed to be payable on demand.

demand-pull inflation 1. Rises in prices caused by "too many dollars chasing too few goods," or by putting too much pressure of demand on existing supply. 2. Rising prices in the economy caused by increased aggregate demand (total spending) which is not matched by increased aggregate supply (total output).

demand schedule *See* demand curve.

demand-side economics Economic analysis and/or policy which focuses attention on aggregate demand for output (total spending) and on the factors which influence this. (*See* Keynesian economics)

demarketing The process of cutting consumer demand for a product back to a level that can reasonably be supplied by the firm.

de melioribus damnis *Of the better damages.* Describes a judgment a plaintiff might take against one defendant in a situation in which a jury returns by error the verdict assessing damages separately against each individual defendant.

demesne Domain; ownership.

demise 1. A conveyance of an estate for life, for a term of years, or at will. 2. Death; decease.

democratic leader *communication* Style of a leader who suggests alternatives, but allows the group to decide specific policy, procedure, tasks, and roles of members. Group discussions are encouraged and assisted by the leader with everyone free to participate.

democratic socialism Economic system that combines state ownership of some of the means of production and some democratic political institutions.

demographics Characteristics of potential buyers, such as locations, age, sex, and income level.

demolish To throw or pull down; to raze; to destroy the fabric of; to pull to pieces.

demonstrative gift A bequest, by will, of a specified sum of money which will be paid from a designated fund or asset (e.g., a gift of two thousand dollars from the sale of a deceased person's house).

demurrage *economics* The penalty charged when freight cars, or trucks, are held up for loading or unloading, or instructions, beyond the accepted time limit, which is usually forty-eight hours.

dental expenses *insurance* Benefits that

provide reimbursements for all types of dental fees, including limited orthodontia care, with a maximum benefit, a deductible amount, and coinsurance. A typical plan utilizes a calendar year deductible, 80%–20% coinsurance, and a lifetime maximum. Dental examinations are exempt from the applicability of the deductible amount. The policy covers these costs from the first dollar of expense in order not to discourage periodic routine examinations.

dependency Relationship between two persons, one of whom is sustained by, looks to, or relies on the aid of the other for support or reasonable necessities consistent with the dependent's position in life.

dependency and indemnity compensation Compensation for the surviving spouse, children, and dependent parents of military personnel who die in service. This is paid by the Veterans Administration upon proper application by survivors and is payable to survivors of servicemen or reservists who died from disease or injury incurred or aggravated in the line of duty while on active or inactive duty training or from disability compensable under laws administered by the VA.

dependent 1. One who is unable to subsist without the aid of another. A person who depends on another for support or favor, such as a child. 2. *tax law* One whose relationship to a taxpayer is such that the latter, in determining personal income tax, is granted an exemption for this person.

dependents' coverage *insurance* Plan which includes dependents of the employee for both health and life coverage. Health plans normally have the same coverage for both employee and dependents, but group life insurance normally has lesser amounts for dependents and is not allowed in all states.

dependents' group life Life insurance on eligible dependents including the employee's spouse and unmarried children, normally issued only in conjunction with the employee's coverage. The amount of insurance on dependents will be less than that on the employee with policies differing widely as to the coverage on children. For example, a wife may be covered for the maximum of five thousand

dollars and dependent children for lesser amounts.

dependent variables *statistics* A variable which is determined by another factor. (E.g., in a time series of corn output per year and annual rainfall, corn output is the dependent and rainfall the independent variable.)

depletion *economics* The act of using up a natural resource. Normally it is stated in terms of dollars or a percentage, as related to a specific period of time.

depletion allowance Tax deduction given to compensate the investor for the using up of minerals or other property in one's investment. Applicable to all types of mining activity and for timber operations.

deposit That part of the purchase price prepaid by way of security in contracts for sale, particularly the sale of land. If the contract is completed, then the deposit is applied against the purchase money. Its primary purpose is that it is a security for the completion of the contract, a guarantee that the purchaser means business.

deposit ceiling rates of interest Maximum interest rates that can be paid on savings and time deposits at federally insured commercial banks, mutual savings banks, savings and loan associations, and credit unions. Ceilings on credit union deposits are established by the National Credit Union Administration. Ceilings on deposits held by the other depository institutions are established by the Depository Institutions Deregulation Committee (DIDC). Under current law, deposit interest rate ceilings are being phased out over a six-year period, ending in 1986 under the supervision of the DIDC.

deposit expansion multiplier A magnified increase in the deposits of a banking system as a whole, caused by an increase in its excess reserves. The converse of this in the case of a deposit decrease is also true. The total cumulative expansion (or contraction) will be some multiplier, calculated by dividing one by the legal reserve ratio. There are leakages, however, which prevent this multiplier from exerting its full impact. They include: the leakage of cash into circulation, since some deposits will be withdrawn in cash and some checks will be cashed instead of deposited; a margin of excess reserves which banks for one reason or another may not lend out; and the failure of businessmen to borrow all that the banks want to lend. (*See* Appendix C)

deposition   Testimony of a witness taken outside a court and set down in writing for use as evidence in court.

deposit liabilities   The amount that a depository institution is obligated to pay out to its depositors.

depository   Party receiving the deposit; one with whom anything is lodged in trust. A place where something is deposited or stored as for safekeeping or convenience.

depository institution   Financial institution which maintains deposit account obligations to customers; includes commercial banks, savings banks, savings and loan associations, and credit unions.

Depository Institutions Deregulation and Monetary Control Act (1980)   *finance* Comprehensive federal legislation providing for deregulation of the nation's banking system which applied uniform service requirements to and required reports from all depository institutions with certain types of accounts. Among the Act's provisions are: (a) Establishment of the Depository Institutions Deregulation Committee, charged with the phasing out of regulation of interest rates of banks and savings institutions over a six year period ending in 1986. (b) Authorization of interest-bearing Negotiable Order of Withdrawal (NOW) accounts to be offered anywhere in the country. (c) Overruling of state usury laws on home mortgages over twenty-five thousand dollars and also the modernization of mortgages by eliminating dollar limits, permitting second mortgages, and ending territorial restrictions in mortgage lending. It also extended access to the Federal Reserve discount window and to other Federal Reserve services in step with the implementation of a fee schedule.

Depository Institutions Deregulation Committee (DIDC)   The committee responsible for the orderly phase-out, over a six-year period ending in 1986, of interest rate ceilings on time and savings accounts at depository institutions. Voting members of the DIDC are the Secretary of the Treasury and the chair-

men of the Federal Reserve Board, the Federal Deposit Insurance Corporation, the Federal Home Loan Bank Board, and the National Credit Union Administration Board. The Comptroller of the Currency serves as a nonvoting member. (*See* Depository Institutions Deregulation and Monetary Control Act)

deposit ratio   *banking* The ratio of total deposits to total capital accounts.

depreciation   1. Diminution in value, particularly the deterioration or the loss or lessening in value arising from age and use of a property. 2. The reduction in the value of a long-lived asset from use or obsolescence. The decline is recognized in accounting by a periodic allocation of the original cost of the asset to current operations. (*See* accelerated depreciation, Appendix G) 3. *accounting* A systematic process of allocating and charging the cost of a capital asset over the accounting periods expected to receive benefits from its use.

depreciation reserves   *accounting* The recording of periodic charges to income to reflect the portion of the cost of a long-term capital asset recovered. If a fund is kept, it will accumulate as the capital asset depreciates, and the money will be on hand, at least in part, to buy a new capital asset once the old one is completely depreciated. Often, the original asset can be used in the productive process long after it has been depreciated out.

depredation   The act of plundering, robbing, or pillaging.

depression   *economics* That period in an extreme business cycle when unemployment is highest, production lowest, prices lowest, and where pessimism prevails. A depression cannot be linked to any specific period of time, since it can last from months to years.

depression, Hayek's concept of   *See* Hayek's concept of depression.

deprivation   Taking of property, rights, or privileges from a person.

derivative action   A suit brought by one or more shareholders of a corporation on behalf of the corporation.

derivative deposit   *banking* A bank deposit that comes as a result of the bank making a customer a loan, and the loan proceeds being deposited in the same

81

bank. Under a fractional reserve system, loans can be made in excess of actual money deposited.

derived demand 1. *economics* The demand for a product which derived from the demand for another product. (E.g., the demand for brick creates a derived demand for cement.) Also called indirect demand. 2. In investment studies, the equivalent of the acceleration principle.

descend To pass or be transmitted by succession, as when an estate becomes the property of an heir as an immediate result of the death of the ancestor.

descendant Person who is descended from another; one who proceeds from the body of another, however remotely, such as a child, a grandchild, or great-grandchild. Generally used as equivalent to issue.

descending tops *investing* A graphic presentation of stock prices over time in which each new high is lower than the previous high, indicating that a bear market is in progress.

descent Taking of real estate by inheritance, as heir of the former owner. The passing of title in realty from a person dying intestate to a blood relation.

descriptive labeling *marketing* A method of labeling consumer products naming the ingredients, proclaiming the quality, and usually ignoring recognized standards or grades. (In fact, it is not now required that most food products be labeled as to grade or standard, although most of them are graded in the factories and warehoused by grade.)

descriptive statistics A branch of statistical studies that makes a comprehensive summary of the group characteristics of sets of observed data.

desirable coverage *insurance* That coverage which is needed, not because the lack of it would ruin the family or business finances, but because it is to be preferred over the possibility of the loss.

desire *law* Request or recommendation in a will.

desk, the Trading desk at the New York Federal Reserve Bank, through which open market purchases and sales of government and federal agency securities are made. The desk maintains direct telephone communication with major government securities dealers. (*See* foreign exchange desk)

de son tort *Of his own wrong.* (*See* executor de son tort)

destroy *insurance* To render the subject useless for its intended purpose, though not literally to demolish or annihilate same.

detailers Missionary salespeople of the health care industry.

determinable Liable to come to an end upon the happening of a certain contingency susceptible to being determined. An interest or estate in land is said to be determinable when it is liable to be determined or come to an end whether by limitation, passage of time, merger, surrender, or otherwise.

determination Extinguishment; putting an end to. In contract law, the determination of an agreement is its extinguishment by judicial pronouncement after the contract has been affirmed; distinct from rescission.

detinue *common law* Action in tort based upon the wrongful detention of goods by a defendant and where the plaintiff seeks to recover goods in specie (i.e., money in lieu of goods).

detriment *law* In the law of contracts, an element of consideration meaning that promisee has, in return for the promise, forborne some legal right which the promisee would otherwise have been entitled to exercise.

deus solus haeredem facere potest, non homo *Only God and not man can make an heir.* An heir is a descendant by blood.

devaluation *economics; finance* The action by a country to lower the official rate at which a currency is exchanged for another currency. (Often a floating exchange rate accomplishes the same purpose, in that a given currency will become weaker compared to other currencies, if domestic inflation reduces the purchasing power of the monetary unit.)

devastavit *He was wasted.* Has particular reference to any acts of waste or mismanagement committed by an executor or administrator in relation to the trust property. An administrator or executor guilty of devastavit is liable to the beneficiaries of the estate.

developer Any person who, directly or indirectly, sells, leases, offers to sell or lease, or advertises for sale or lease any lots in a subdivision.

development *mining* Preparation of the explored deposit for extraction and exploitation and the techniques employed, such as stripping, shafting, or tunneling, where techniques have as their immediate object the opening up of or the gaining of access to the deposit so that actual mining may take place.

development economics A general field of study, expanded by Simon Kuznet, which deals primarily with those forces which either promote or impede economic development in different areas of the world. Some factors considered are natural resources, labor force literacy, per capita income and its distribution, etc.

development mortgage *banking; finance* A loan made to develop the land on which specific types of buildings will be constructed.

development well Well drilled close to proven reserves to expand an existing site. This is contrasted with exploratory wells where nothing has as yet been proven related to the presence of oil or gas.

deviation 1. Departure from the norm. 2. *insurance* A material departure from or change in the risks insured against without just cause. The varying from the route insured against, without necessity or just cause, after the risk has begun.

devise Gift or disposition by will, particularly a testamentary disposition of land or realty. A devise may be either specific, such as a devise of a particular piece of land, or residuary as where a testator devises the residue of the testator's land and realty to a beneficiary. Also used in distinction from a general devise which is a devise of all the lands of the testator without specifying any particular land.

devisor Testator who gives lands or real estate by will.

devolution *law* Transmission of an interest in property from one person to another by operation of law, particularly on the death of the former person.

devolve To pass or be transferred from one person to another, particularly the passing of an estate from a deceased person.

diagnostic services *insurance* Services such as x-ray and laboratory expenses that can be covered under a comprehensive plan by adding riders to the policy.

dialectical materialism A logical method of historical analysis developed by Karl Marx, who employed the philosopher Hegel's concept that historical change is the result of inherently conflicting or opposing forces in society, and that the forces are basically economic or materialistic.

Diamond Investment Trust A unit trust started by Thomas McKinnon in the early 1980s, the major investment of which is high quality diamonds. This allows an individual to invest in diamonds without owning an actual stone. However, the shares do not trade actively, which could create a liquidity problem for some investors.

differential *investing* A small additional charge made by the dealer when selling odd lots (less than one hundred shares) of stock. Normally, this is one eighth of a point, or 12.5 cents.

differentiated competition An industry in which a large number of firms produce similar but not identical products. Sometimes called monopolistic competition.

diffusion index *economics* A measure of the time spread of the movement among economic indicators.

diffusion process Acceptance of new products and services by members of a community or social system.

diffusion theory of taxation *economics* A hypothesis that all taxes are spread eventually over all the population, through price changes, rather than stopping with the person who pays the tax.

diligence Prudence, attentiveness, care. Persevering application and untiring efforts in good earnest, a steady application to business of any kind, or constant effort to accomplish any undertaking. Law recognizes three degrees of diligence: common or ordinary, high or great, and low or slight.

dilution Reduction from use or obsolescence in the value of a long-lived asset. The decline is recognized in accounting by a periodic allocation of the original cost of the asset to current operations. (*See* accelerated depreciation)

dilution of common stock   *finance* The decrease in book value of common stock brought about by increasing the number of shares of common stock without increasing the net income or assets of the company.

diminishing balance accrual   *accounting* An accrual method for recognizing earned income by applying the Rule of 78 to the unearned interest balance on the account. (Cf. rule of 78s)

diminishing marginal productivity, law of   *See* law of diminishing marginal productivity.

diminishing marginal utility, law of *See* law of diminishing marginal utility.

diminishing return   *economics* A point beyond which the employment of additional resources will not result in a proportionate increase in output.

diminishing return, law of   *See* law of diminishing return.

dip   *investing* A slight drop in the securities markets after a prolonged uptrend. Usually, this is considered a short-term aberration which may well be followed by a continuing uptrend. Some financial advisors advise buying during the "dip" under the assumption that the market will resume its bullish trend after the dip.

directed verdict   *law* In a lawsuit where reasonable jurors could not disagree as to the facts or inferences to be drawn from them, the judge instructs the jury what the verdict must be, or gives the verdict personally.

director   1. One who directs. Person appointed or elected according to law, authorized to manage and direct the affairs of a corporation. Generally, a director is elected by the body of shareholders. 2. Member of the board of directors of a corporation. These persons, ostensibly, are elected by the stockholders and advise top management in determining the goals and policies of the corporation. In some corporations this is a time consuming job and pays a handsome fee. Directors are normally stockholders, but not always. At times, the expertise of people who are not holders of stock is needed on the board.

director of building and equipment *banking* Where bank buildings are large enough to lease out space to other tenants, person who handles that and is a part of the decision making team with respect to building renovations, furniture and equipment changes, etc. In very large banks, this is a more-than-full-time job, whereas, in smaller banks, this task may be handled in tandem with others.

director of economic development *banking* Job which may carry a number of different titles, according to the size of the bank or the banking system, the duties of which normally include serving on the area economic development commission, entertaining prospects for new industry, and being a liaison between the bank and the businesses and industries located within the geographical area. The person will often supervise or set up economic development meetings, including foreign trade seminars. Depending on the size of the bank, he or she may answer directly to the president or the the senior vice president for administration.

director of financial planning   *banking* Supervisor of certified financial planners who, operating at different levels, assist bank clients in a total program of financial planning, from the making of the first budget, until all estate planning matters are settled. This planning is carried out in the context of the client's resources and objectives. It requires a knowledge of risk management vehicles, taxes, employee benefits, government social programs, investing, and estate planning. Normally, financial planners, including the director, will work in close concert with all the other departments of the bank. If a bank is part of a group, there may be a director of financial planning for the bank group, and financial planners needed would depend upon the size of the bank. Since financial planning is still relatively new to banking, this position may still not exist in many banks. (*See* Certified Financial Planner)

director of public relations   *banking* The person who has a part, along with the director of marketing, in advertising services of the bank, keeping good relationships with the media, reporting on all bank activities, and participating, on behalf of the bank, in community activities.

director of training   *banking* Person

who normally carries on or supervises all in-bank training programs. This person is responsible for scheduling for outside training for personnel, though decisions for the training will probably be made at a higher level. This person must be adept at meticulous scheduling and human relations. The position may be called by a number of different names, such as supervisor of training, manager of the training department, etc.

direct paper *finance* Commercial paper which is placed directly on the market by the issuer, rather than through a dealer. Only large organizations with outstanding credit standings can sell paper in this manner. (Cf. commercial paper)

direct tax *economics* A tax, such as the personal income tax, which cannot be easily shifted to someone else.

direct transfer Conveyance of securities to investors (usually individual), and the direct movement of savings to a company in payment for securities (new issue). (This does not occur often in finance.)

disability 1. Legal incapacity or inability to act, as that of infants or lunatics. 2. The state of being physically disabled, as from an accident.

disability income rider *insurance* Attachment allowed by some insurance companies adding disability income benefits, based on the face amount of the insurance, to permanent life insurance policies for an extra premium. Such disability income riders often provide a disability benefit of 1% of the face amount of life insurance per month (or ten dollars per one thousand dollars of life insurance).

disability retirement Retirement allowing an immediate annuity payable to an employee when two conditions are met: the employee has completed five years of civilian service and the employee has become totally disabled for useful and efficient service in the position occupied or the duties of a similar position. (It need not be shown that the applicant is disabled for all kinds of work.)

disagio *economics* The charge for exchanging a depreciated foreign currency.

disbar *law* Expel. Deprive of the privilege of practicing law.

disbursement *law* Express necessarily paid or incurred by a party.

disbursing agent *See* paying agent.

discharge 1. To pay a debt or satisfy a claim or an obligation. 2. To release a bankrupt from the obligations of one's debts, following adjudication of bankruptcy and the administration of the bankrupt's estate. 3. An instrument by which the binding force of a contract is terminated. 4. To release; to cancel; to extinguish an obligation; to revoke; to rescind.

discharge of lien Recorded release of a lien when debt has been repaid.

disciplined creativeness *marketing* The application of the scientific method to an activity that requires both a marked degree of conceptual ability and innovativeness, sometimes to the point of daring. The scientific method does serve to impede the more reckless side of creativity.

disclaim To renounce all claims to or refuse to accept a right, an interest, or an office.

disclaimer Absolute, unqualified renunciation of any beneficial interest, enjoyment, or ownership of property. Commonly, it is an executed refusal (in writing) by a would-be beneficiary who will not accept a bequest or a lifetime gift. If executed properly, the disclaimer is regarded for tax purposes as if the transfer had never occurred.

disclaimer trust A trust established, which is irrevocable, where the property in the trust is the result of disclaimed bequests. The living spouse will then receive the income benefits from the trust. Thus an irrevocable trust, known as a disclaimer trust, can be established through a testamentary trust in the decedent's will.

disclose To reveal; to make known.

disclosure 1. Information lenders must give to borrowers before a credit contract is signed. 2. The act of making known, of revealing; revelation. 3. That which is disclosed or revealed.

discommodity *economics* A theory proposed by Jevons in which he reasoned that we make goods commodities by giving them utility, and thus make goods "discommodities" by failing the give them utility. (Although Jevons could not have been aware of the current problem of waste, it would fit well with his theory of discommodities.)

discontinuous variable *See* discrete variable.

discount 1. Allowance or deduction from a gross sum for a particular reason, such as to encourage immediate cash payment. 2. The interest deducted beforehand from an advance or loan of money. 3. An allowance or deduction made from a gross sum on any account whatever. Relating to bills of exchange, it denotes the sum of money deducted from its face value in consideration of its payment before the stipulated time.

discount broker *investments* Broker who buys and sells for customers at a discount, without giving advice on the purchase or sale of securities. Often the business is conducted by phone without a meeting between the broker and the client. In a sense, these discount brokers are order processors, since no advice is given to clients. Rates may be from 25% to 50% below normal fees.

discount charge Finance charge deducted in advance.

discounted bond 1. Bond sold for less than its face amount or principal. 2. Bond for which the current market value is below face value. (E.g., if a thousand dollar face value bond sells for nine hundred dollars, the investor should receive interest each year that the bond is held plus one thousand dollars at maturity.)

discounted cash flow 1. Value of future expected cash receipts and expenditures at a common date, which is calculated using net present value of internal rate of return and is a factor of both capital investments and securities investments. 2. The method of evaluating long-term projects which explicitly takes into account the time value of money.

discounted cash flow rate of return Internal rate of return.

discounted note receivable *accounting* A note sold to a bank by a merchant for less than its face value. The amount discounted is the interest paid by the merchant to the bank. Usually, if the signer of the note defaults, the merchant again becomes responsible for the note.

discounted rate Value of future expected cash receipts and expenditures at a common date, which is calculated using net present value or internal rate of return

and is a factor in analysis of both capital investments and security investments. Net present value (NPV) method applies a rate of discount (interest rate) based on the marginal cost of capital to future cash flows to show them at present value.

discount house Store that charges lower-than-usual prices and does not offer such traditional retail services as credit, sales assistance by clerks, and delivery.

discounting 1. Finding the present value of a sum of money which is not going to be received until some time in the future. 2. The process of compounding in reverse, where a future value has deducted from it a specified rate of interest for a specified number of periods to arrive at the present value. 3. Making a loan with the interest subtracted in advance from the principal.

discounting period That period of time used to deduct a specified rate of interest from a future value to find the present value.

discount on stock *finance* The issuance and sale of stock which sells for less than its par value. In some states, stock sold at a discount becomes a contingent liability to the stockholders, since the corporation cannot carry it as a loss.

discount point *See* point.

discount rate 1. Interest rate used to calculate the present value of future cash flows. 2. That rate of interest deducted at specified intervals from the future value to arrive at the present value. 3. *See* rediscount rate.

discount window Figurative expression for the Federal Reserve facility for extending credit directly to eligible depository institutions (those with transaction accounts or nonpersonal time deposits).

discrete variable *statistics* A variable whose values by necessity are spaced by a definite interval. (E.g., the number of people can vary only by individual units.) Also called discontinuous variable.

discretion Power to act on one's own judgment and conscience uncontrolled by the judgment or conscience or others.

discretionary fiscal policy Any direction the federal government may choose to take relative to taxing, spending, and budget management.

discretionary income Income that is

left after meeting all essential expenses to maintain one's current standard of living.

discretionary stabilization policy Government policies aimed at stabilizing the economy and maintaining full employment and which are adjusted by government policy makers at their discretion to reflect changing economic conditions.

discrimination 1. Failure to treat all persons equally, generally arising out of a prejudice against a class of persons regarding national origin, race, age, sex, religion, etc. 2. A general failure to treat all persons equally where no reasonable distinction can be found between those favored and those not favored. 3. *pension plans* The distribution of funds to participants in such a manner as to give one group a higher percentage than another group. (E.g., a nonintegrated plan would discriminate against higher paid employees, in that Social Security payments tend to be higher, on a percentage basis, to those with lower salaries than to those with higher salaries.)

diseconomy of scale *economics* The tendency for certain types of costs to grow as a company becomes larger or its volume of business becomes larger. Condition that exists when a large-scale plant is less efficient than a small-scale plant.

disenfranchise *See* disfranchise.

disequilibrium 1. State of imbalance. E.g., a situation in which the quantities supplied and demanded of a commodity at a given price are unequal. 2.*economics* The lack of equilibrium, or balance, in the economy. This is indicated when unemployment is high, when prices are high, or when any sector of the economy is out of line with the other sectors. (It should be remembered that, while the economy is always tending toward equilibrium, it never reaches equilibrium. In short, it never truly reaches the point where the sectors are perfectly balanced.)

disfranchise Act of depriving of a franchise, immunity, or privilege. In election law, a voter is said to be disfranchised when that voter is denied the right to vote or when the voter is permitted to vote but the vote, by reason of fraud, violence, or other wrong, is not counted as cast. Also called disenfranchise.

dishonor To refuse or decline to accept a bill of exchange or to refuse or neglect to pay a bill or note at maturity.

dishonored note receivable *finance* A note which is not paid by maturity date and which will likely not be paid.

disinflation *economics* That point in the downcycle of an economy when economic activity lessens enough to discourage inflation, but not enough to increase unemployment. At this stage in the economy, if actions to improve are not taken immediately, deflation will result.

disinherit To prevent an heir from coming into possession of any property or right that, by law or custom, would become the heir's in the course of descent; to deprive of an inheritance.

disinheritance Act by which the owner of an estate deprives an heir of the right to inherit it.

disinterested person One who has no interest in a transaction in any manner at all (e.g., not a creditor, an equity security holder, or an insider).

disintermediation *investing; finance* A situation in which withdrawals of money are made from conventional financial institutions and put into investment vehicles because the rate of interest is higher in those investments than financial institutions can pay on deposits. This often occurs during periods of inflation and can cause short-term cash problems for the financial institutions. (Cf. intermediation)

disinvestment Reduction in the total stock of capital goods caused by failure to replace it as it wears out (e.g., the consumption or using up of factories or machines at a faster rate than they are being replaced so that the productive base is diminishing).

dispersion Statistical term indicating how closely to a return, such as the expected return, the actual returns for specific periods are congregated. If the dispersion is large and without symmetry, this indicates that the risk is large on the security.

disposable income Take-home pay or net pay. The money households actually have to spend. Personal income which is left over after all taxes have been paid and all transfer payments have been received.

disposal Sale, pledge, giving away, use,

consumption, or any other disposition of a thing.

dispose To alienate or direct the ownership of property. To make over, as by gift, sale, or other means of alienation; to bestow.

disposition Getting rid or making over of anything; relinquishment; alienation; disposal; plan or arrangement of the disposal; distribution; final settlement with regard to some matter; ultimate destination; order.

dispossess To oust; to deprive a person wrongfully of the possession of a thing or land. Includes abatement, intrusion, disseisin, discontinuance, and deforcement.

dispossession The ejecting of a person from the occupancy of real property by legal process.

dissaving Expenditure on consumption in excess of income. This may be accomplished by drawing on past savings, borrowing, or receiving help from others.

disseisin *law* Wrongful putting out of one who is actually seised of a freehold. The act of wrongfully depriving a person of a seisin of land, rents, or other hereditaments. In the case of land, the disseised person has both a right of entry and a right of action.

dissolution Act of putting an end to a legal relationship. Thus the dissolution of a contract is the cancellation or abrogation of it by the parties. The dissolution of a corporation means the termination of its existence as a body politic, either by an act of the legislature, by the surrender or forfeiture of its charter or articles of incorporation, or by appropriate proceedings under the applicable laws.

distrain *law* 1. To seize goods by way of distress. To detain personal property from the rightful owner under color of some right or interest in the same. 2. Common law procedure whereby a creditor might obtain security without resorting to legal process.

distress *law* 1. To take, without legal process, a personal chattel from the possession of a wrongdoer into the hands of an aggrieved party, as a pledge for the redressing and injury, the performance of a duty, or the satisfaction of a demand. 2. Property distrained.

distress selling *investing; marketing* 1. A rush to sell stocks during a bear market in the fear that the value will drop further. 2. Selling of assets during bankruptcy proceedings, or because of foreclosure. 3. Selling is of excess inventory which could endanger the future of the business if held.

distributable net income Amount of trust income available for distribution after the payment of trust taxes. However, there is no accumulation distribution for a taxable year if the amounts paid, credited, or required to be distributed by the trust for the year don't exceed its accounting income for the year. Accounting income in this connection is trust income determined under the terms of the trust and local law.

distribute To deal or bestow in portion or share among many; to allot or apportion.

distributee Any person, other than a creditor or purchaser, who has received property of a decedent from a personal representative. A testamentary trustee is a distributee only to the extent of distributed assets or increment remaining in the trustee's hands. A beneficiary of a testamentary trust to whom the trustee has distributed property received from a personal representative is a distributee of the personal representative. For purposes of the provision, testamentary trustee includes a trustee to whom assets are transferred by will to the extent of the devised assets.

distribution 1. Act of parceling out, apportioning, especially in profits. 2. The fund out of which distributions to shareholders are made.

distribution date Date on which a dividend or other payment or distribution is made to holders of an instrument. Also known as payment date.

distribution question Question of how the output of the economic system will be divided among the people—which people will get how much and how that will be decided.

distribution strategy *marketing* A plan to make a product available to consumers at the times and in the places desired.

distributive share Share or portion which a given heir receives on the legal distribution of an intestate estate.

districting Process by which legislative seats are distributed by the establishment of precise geographical boundaries. (*See* apportionment)

disutility *economics* Any economic entity which tends to cause pain rather than pleasure and which is relatively useless rather than being useful.

disutility of labor *economics* A concept proposed by Jevons in his theory of exchange that, if the value of a unit of labor is not equal to whatever it is exchanged for, exchange will soon stop and labor will be said to have disutility. (E.g., if a unit of labor and a unit of capital investment have the same value, yet the unit of capital produces more than the unit of labor, labor will begin to have disutility, or lack of usefulness, and capital will be substituted for labor in the process of production.)

diversifiable Describes a portfolio of investments which can be diversified for the purpose of equalizing risk and return.

diversifiable risk Risk which is eliminated when an asset is added to a diversified portfolio. (*See* B-risk)

diversification Use of several different types of investment vehicles in an investment portfolio to help the investor achieve personal goals, such as a need for safety. These vehicles may include tax-free municipal bonds, blue-ribbon stocks, growth stocks, corporate bonds, government debt instruments, certificates of deposit, and real estate. The reasons for diversification vary according to the individual investor.

diversified common stock fund Funds which invest mainly in good quality common stocks and tend to be quite conservative. Their objective is long-term capital growth with reasonable, but varying, current income.

divest To take away from a person an estate of interest which has already vested in that person.

dividend 1. Number or quantity which is to be divided by another. 2. A sum of money to be divided among a number of persons, especially the total sum payable as interest on a loan or the profit of a joint stock company divided among the creditors of an insolvent estate.

dividend growth model Valuation model that deals with dividends and their growth which have been discounted back to present value.

dividend option *insurance* Avenue open to the policyholder for the utilization of dividends paid by the policy.

dividend paying agent *finance* An organization, usually a financial institution, that assumes the responsibility of paying the dividends to stockholders which have been declared by the board of directors of the corporation. Usually, this same organization will serve as a transfer agent for the corporation, and will file all the necessary tax reports to the proper governmental authorities.

dividend payment ratio Measure of the level of dividends distributed, calculated by dividing dividends by earnings.

dividend reinvestment plan Program offered by mutual funds that allows shareholders to have their dividends automatically reinvested in additional shares of the corporations.

dividend rollover plan *investing* A plan for buying and selling stocks around their ex-dividend dates, generally in order to make a small amount on the dividends collected, and perhaps a little more after the stock price has adjusted for the dividend payment and has edged up a bit.

dividends in arrears *finance* Unpaid dividends on cumulative preferred stock.

dividend yield Periodic return received by the investor on a security. Yield is usually quoted as a percentage of current market price.

divisible That which is susceptible of being divided. A contract is said to be divisible when it contains considerations for several acts and neither party to the contract is discharged from the performance of the whole or a particular part by reason of the fact that the other party has failed to do his or her part in relation to one of the matters into which the contract is divided.

division of labor Breaking down of the production process into several small tasks so that each worker can become specialized in doing one thing (e.g., an assembly line).

doctrine *law* Rule or principle of law developed by decisions of the courts.

document 1. Any solid substance having on it marks capable of being read expressing or describing any matter; all material substances on which thoughts are represented by writing or any other species of conventional mark or symbol. 2. An instrument on which is recorded, by means of letters, figures, or marks, matter which may be evidentially used.

documentary stamp A stamp, looking much like a postage stamp, which is attached to documents and which represents the tax levied by the state on the transfer of real property.

document of title Document which in the regular course of business or financing is treated as adequately evidencing that the person in possession is entitled to receive, hold, and dispose of the document and the goods it covers; includes bill of lading, dock warrant, dock receipt, and warehouse receipt.

Doe, John 1. Fictitious name frequently used to indicate a person for the purpose of argument or illustration or in the course of enforcing a fiction in the law. 2. Fictitious name used to designate a party until a real name can be ascertained.

dole *economics* Formerly, a method of social welfare used in England. Sometimes used to denote welfare expenditures of any kind.

do, lego *I give and bequeath.* The formal words of a bequest or legacy in a will.

dollar cost averaging 1. Purchase of securities at different intervals to reduce the impact of price fluctuations. When prices are high, fewer shares are purchased and, when prices are low, more shares would be purchased. 2. One technique for long-term investing in which the investor will decide on a specific amount of money which will be invested at intervals, regardless of the price of the stock at the time. Over time, the investor will buy more "lows" than "highs" and thus average a lower cost per share overall.

dollar diplomacy *economics* Dealings between nations motivated by financial interests, rather than political interests.

dolo malo pactumse non servaturum *A contract founded upon fraud will not be upheld.*

dolus *Fraud;* deceit.

dolus dans locum contractui *Fraud or deceit giving rise to the contract.* A false representation or misrepresentation that is not innocent and that is material in the formation of a contract.

Domar's fundamental equation A concept with two main corollaries of the fundamental equation: (a) saving and investment must grow in absolute amount from year to year, and (b) on the assumption of a constant income velocity, money must be injected into the system in increasing absolute amounts, thus allowing the economy to expand at a given percentage rate. (This to maintain a full-employment equilibrium in the economy.)

domestic Pertaining, belonging, or relating to a home. Thus a domestic servant is one who is employed in and about the house on household affairs, whose business it is to serve the employer and the employer's family.

domestic system *economics* One stage in the development of an economy. The stages usually appear in this order: (a) Handicraft done in the home, often for home consumption. (b) A merchant capitalist begins to buy the handicraft and contracts for more to be done, but still it is done in the home. (c) The factory system usually follows this on a small scale. (It is interesting to note that in our advanced economy, work is now being "put out" into homes to accommodate people who need to earn income but want to stay at home.)

domicile Permanent home of a person; that place where one has one's true, fixed, and permanent home and principal establishment and to which, whenever a person is absent, the person has the intention of returning. A person may own a number of residences, but, according to law, only one domicile, namely one's primary place of residence, probably where the person is recognized as a citizen for voting purposes.

dominant tenement Tenement or land in favor of which an easement is constituted.

dominium directum *Strict ownership.* The mere right of property as distinct from its possession and enjoyment.

dominium plenum *Full (or complete)*

ownership, including possession of the property.

donated stock   *investing* Stock, fully paid up, which is donated back to the issuing corporation without any payment. The stock becomes a part of the donated-stock account of the corporation, at the fair market value.

donatio inter vivos   *A gift between living persons.* Gratuitous transfer of property by the donor to the donee during the donor's life, with full intent to pass title to the donee and, unless made by deed, accompanied by delivery.

donatio mortis causa   A gift made while the donor is under the apprehension of death. It is made in contemplation, fear, or peril of death with the intent that it shall take effect only in the event of the death of the donor.

donation   *A gift.*

donee   One to whom a gift is made or a bequest given.

donor   One who makes a gift.

do not reduce (DNR)   Instruction given by an investor regarding a limit-order to buy, or a stop-order to sell, not to reduce the order when the stock goes ex-dividend and the price is temporarily lower. If the broker has an open order or price at which the stock is to be purchased for a client, that price remains the same until the order is either carried out or cancelled, and the price is not to be reduced in the amount of any dividend declared upon each ex dividend happening.

don't fight the tape   *investing* A general rule which indicates that it is usually not wise to trade against the market trend. (*See* contrary thinking)

double-barreled   *investing* A guarantee by a larger entity of government that a municipal revenue bond will pay the principal and interest as noted on the certificate. A town builds a bridge and pledges to pay the bonds from the revenue earned from use of the bridge. If such revenues prove to be inadequate, the bonds will be paid off by some higher entity to avoid default.

double bond   Bond which has a condition added that if the obligator does or forbears from doing some act the obligation shall be void. A common illustration is the so-called performance bond preva-

lent in the construction industry, where in construction projects involving large sums of money or government or municipal lands, the owner requires that the contractor obtain such a bond to indemnify the owner against nonperformance by the contractor; such a bond has the condition that performance of the work voids the bond.

double deduction rule   Rule under the Internal Revenue Code Section 691 allowing administrative expenses to be deducted on the estate tax return and against the estate's liability on income in respect to the decedent. (Actually, the rule extends further than other items that have accrued at the date of the decedent's death and are thus claims against the estate. These expenses may be claimed both as estate tax deductions and income tax deductions under Section 691.)

double-entry accounting   A system for recording transactions such that the effect of every transaction is recorded in two or more accounts and transactions have equal amounts of debits and credits.

double exemption   *finance* A situation which allows municipal bonds to be exempt of taxes, both federal and state, because the bonds were issued by a municipality within the state. (Municipals which are out-of-state bonds will be federal tax exempt, but not state.)

double indemnity rider   *insurance* Provision in a life insurance policy by which a payment of double the face value of the policy is to be made in the event of the accidental death of the insured in circumstances covered by the policy.

double jeopardy   *law* Situation in which a person is tried more than once for the same charge. Provisions in the United States Constitution and in state constitutions prevent this from happening. However, more than one charge can emerge from the same set of facts. While this rule applies to criminal law, in civil cases, a similar provision exists called the rule of res judicate.

double possibility   *law* Gift by way of contingent remainder preceded by an estate which is also a contingent remainder (e.g., a gift to an unborn child for life with remainder to another unborn child), considered void under common law.

double taxation Taxing of corporate profits twice—once when the corporation is taxed and again when the shareholder pays taxes on dividends.

doubtful title Title where the holding party is exposed to the hazard of litigation.

dow To give or endow.

Dow Jones Industrial Average Average computed from thirty leading blue-chip industrial stocks using an unweighted arithmetic mean and quoted in terms of points rather than dollars.

Dow theory Analytical theory based on present movements of the Dow Jones Industrial Average and the Dow Jones Transportation Average. The theory states that if either of these averages moves in the other index, the market in general is moving upward. When both averages fall below an important previous low, it is considered confirmation that the market in general is on a downturn.

dower That portion or interest in a deceased husband's real estate given by law to his widow during her life. A wife acquires the life interest on her husband's death in one-third of all the real estate of which he may have been seised or possessed at any time during their marriage. This right vests in the wife upon the death of the husband.

down payment Cash sum required at the outset of a credit transaction which together with the outstanding loan balance comprises the total cost.

downstairs merger *economics* The merger of a parent company with a subsidiary.

downtime *See* machine downtime.

downward communication *communication* Type of communication which flows from superiors to subordinates.

draft Order for the payment of money drawn by one person and directed to another.

draining reserves *money; banking* Periodic actions by the Federal Reserve to reduce the amount of loanable funds held by the banks. Three methods are used: (a) raising reserve requirements, i.e., the reserves held with the Fed by specific banks; (b) increasing the discount rate, i.e., the amount of interest the Fed charges member banks for funds bor-

rowed; (c) selling bonds on the open market, which banks will usually buy, thus reducing their funds available for lending.

drive Any strong stimulus which impels action.

dual banking system *banking* A situation in which a bank can be chartered by either the federal government or the state government.

dual economy The economy of a less developed country with unbalanced growth where some parts of the economy are modern and efficient and some of the people live by modern standards, while elsewhere in the economy primitive conditions and poverty are widespread.

dual fund Fund organized as a closed-end investment company with half the shares sold as capital shares and the other half as income shares. The capital shares benefit from any capital appreciation of the entire fund, while the income shares receive all the income. Dual funds are based on the fact that some investors are interested exclusively in capital gains while others are interested only in income.

duality theorem *statistics* In linear programming, the theory that the solution of the problem of the optimal production program (i.e., the most profitable combination of resources) solves the problem of the valuation of the limiting factors of production.

due date Day of the month by which payment must be made.

due diligence meeting *finance* A meeting often held by the underwriter of a new issue of stock, in which the prospective buyers ask questions about the issuing company. When securities are recommended by a broker who does not exercise due diligence, the broker may be subject to prosecution later, if the securities end up being a bad investment.

due process of law Phrase used in reference to certain fundamental rights or principles of justice that limit the government's power to deprive a person of life, liberty, or property.

dues Ascertained payments, rates, or taxes. Sums of money paid towards support of a society by its members and which payment entitles that member to retain membership.

dummy 1. One who holds legal title for another; a straw man. 2. Sham; make believe; pretend. (*See* dummy director)

dummy director *management* Impotent member of a Board of Directors who generally accepts without question the decisions of the management of the company, or of a combination of management and a few powerful board members.

dumping *economics* The practice of selling exported goods at less than they sell for domestically. A way of ridding the domestic market of goods it does not need, by enticing exports based on low prices, often, in fact, lower than production costs. This tends to upset all markets concerned since it may well undermine the markets of the importing countries as well.

Dun and Bradstreet, Inc. A credit reporting agency that supplies credit information, primarily on businesses, and used primarily by businesses. A directory is published, periodically, in which businesses are listed, along with all pertinent financial information.

dunnage *transportation* Materials packed around goods being shipped, particularly in rail cars, to protect the goods from damage. (In recent years, a small businessman invented an inflatable dunnage which could be re-used several times.)

Dun's Market Identifier; Dun's number *See* Data Universal Numbering System.

duopoly Oligopoly consisting of two sellers. Hence it may be either a perfect duopoly or an imperfect one, depending on whether the product is standardized or differentiated.

duplex house Dwelling which is constructed internally so as to provide two sets of distinct apartments.

duplicate 1. Document substantially the same as another and having the validity of the original. 2. That which exactly resem-

bles or corresponds to something else.

durable goods Commodities which serve consumers over an extended period of time, such as cars.

durable power of attorney *law* A power which remains effective even after the disability or incompetence of the person granting the power. Often, a power of attorney will be conferred with the stipulation that it will become effective only upon such disability or incompetence.

durante absentia *During absence.* Where a grant of letters of probate is made to a person not named as an executor of a will by reason of the absence of the named executor.

durante minore aetate *During minority.*

durante viduitate *During widowhood.*

Dutch auction *investing* A type auction dealing in securities where the price begins high and is reduced until prospective buyers are enticed to buy. U.S. treasury bills are sold by Dutch auction.

duty A tax, an impost, imposition, or obligation. Also the correlative of right.

duty, retaliatory *See* retaliatory duty.

dwelling House in which a person lives with his or her family; a residence.

dynamic equilibrium *statistics; economics* Offsetting changes in one variable by changes in some proportion of other variables in order to avoid disequilibrium. Based on the realization that changes come over time. While it might be assumed that the variables in the economy would have to change proportionately with each other to maintain equilibrium, this is not true.

dynamics *economics* The consideration of the effect of the time dimension on economic situations. (Cf. statics)

dynamic theory *economics* The concept that a rapidly moving economy produces disequilibrium in the economy, which is a general part of the well-known business cycle.

E

each way *investing* Describes profit of a broker who makes a commission on both the purchase and sale of a security.

eagle *economics* The name given a former coin of the United States, a ten dollar gold coin. There was a double eagle worth twenty dollars, the quarter-eagle worth two and a half dollars, and the half-eagle worth five dollars. The coins that remain of these issues are collectors items.

early withdrawal penalty   *investing* A penalty charged holders of fixed term investments if the investment is liquidated prior to the maturity date.

earned income   Wages, salaries, and other employee compensation plus self-employment earnings.

earned premium   *insurance* That part of an insurance premium which the insurer can credit to a past period of time.

earned surplus   1. *finance* Profits earned by a corporation which have not been paid out in dividends, but have been transferred to the surplus account. Some commercial banks do this to increase their lending capacity. 2. *See* retained earnings.

earnest money   1. Deposit made by a purchaser of real estate to evidence good faith. 2. Something given or done in advance as a pledge or an indication of good faith; a partial payment of the purchase price of goods sold or a delivery of part of the goods themselves, for the purpose of binding the agreement.

earnings   1. That which is earned. The price of services performed. The gains derived from a person's services or labor without the aid of capital. 2. The excess of revenues over all related expenses for a given period (i.e., income, net income, net profit, profit).

earnings drift   *economics* The tendency of earnings in some regions of the country to rise above the national average because of some economic development in that region. Usually this occurs under conditions of full employment.

earnings per common share   1. Total earnings available to common stock divided by the number of shares outstanding. 2. *See* earnings per share.

earnings per share   *investing* A number arrived at by dividing the net income of a corporation by the number of outstanding shares of stock. This number is considered important in that it reveals the capacity of the company to properly recompense its stockholders.

earnings yield   *investing* Earnings per share divided by the current stock price.

easement   1. Right of the owner of a parcel of land to use the land of another for a special purpose not inconsistent with the general property of the owner. 2. A liberty, privilege, or advantage obtained by will, deed, prescription, or necessary implication that the owner of one parcel of land holds or enjoys in the land of another. It entitles the holder to some limited use of the other's land, such as the right to cross it in order to reach a highway.

easement by prescription   Conditions under which continued use of another's property for a special purpose can ripen into a permanent use.

ecclesiastical   Pertaining to the church; as distinguished from anything civil or secular.

econometric model   1. Empirical statement of economic theory that utilizes mathematics and analytical technique to estimate or explain an economic relationship. Such a model relates economic theory to actual economic events. 2. Integration of economic theory, mathematics, and statistics consisting of expressing economic relationships in the form of mathematical equations and verifying the resulting models by statistical methods.

econometrics   *economics* A technique of computer analysis and modeling which describes in mathematical terms the relationships between economic variables (e.g., the relationship between government fiscal policy and interest rate levels).

economic base   Industry within a geographic market area that provides employment opportunities that are essential to support the community.

economic depreciation   Loss of property value from all outside causes.

economic dynamics   A concept propounded by Samuelson which, because of econometrics, could incorporate the theories of price, public finance, international trade, etc., and emerge with a single concept of economic movement.

economic goods   All physical goods and services produced which have utility for people, and thus have a market value.

economic imperialism   Practice of expansionism where control of a country is maintained by economic power rather than by political action or military force.

economic income *economics; finance*
The amount of money an economic agent could spend during a specific period without affecting the agent's wealth. (*See* accounting income)

economic indicator Situation in one sector of the economy or in one industry which gives some indication of the economy's future direction. There are more than a thousand indicators in all, the three types being leading, coincident, and lagging. Twelve leading indicators (including interest rates, unemployment, and inflation) are most often used officially to forecast the future of the economy.

economic life 1. *real estate* Remaining period for which real estate improvements are expected to generate more income as compared to operating expenses. 2. That period of time over which a capital investment continues to yield a profit.

economic man theory Theory that each individual in a capitalistic society, whether the individual is a worker, businessman, consumer, or investor, is motivated by economic forces and will always act to obtain the greatest satisfaction for the least cost. Satisfaction may take the form of profits to a businessman, leisure hours to a worker, or pleasure to a consumer from the goods that the consumer purchases.

economic profits Earnings on invested capital that are in excess of the normal rate of return.

economic reasoning Application of theoretical and factual tools of economic analysis to explain economic developments or to solve economic problems; basic concept in economics.

Economic Recovery Tax Act (ERTA) (1981) A general tax-cutting piece of legislation passed in 1981 and containing major changes in tax laws, some of which are: (a) An across-the-board tax cut which took effect in three stages, ending in 1983. (b) Tax brackets to be indexed to the inflation rate. (c) The lowering of top tax rates on long-term capital gains from 28% to 20%. Also, top rate on dividends, interest, rents, and royalties income lowered from 70% to 50%. (Cf. Appendix G) (d) The lowering of the marriage penalty tax, as families with two working spouses could deduct 10% from the salary of the lower-paid spouse, up to $3,000. (Cf. Appendix G) (e) Expanded Individual Retirement Accounts (IRAs) to all working people who can contribute up to $2,000 a year, and $250 for non-working spouses. Also, expansion of the amount that self-employed people can contribute to Keogh Plan account contributions. (Cf. Appendix G) (f) Creation of the all-savers certificate, which allowed investors to exempt up to $1,000 a year in earned interest. The authority to issue these certificates expired at the end of 1982. (g) Approval of deductions for reinvesting public utility dividends. (h) Reductions in gift and estate taxes, phased in so that the first $600,000 of property can be given estate tax free starting in 1987. Annual gifts that can be given free of gift tax were raised from $3,000 to $10,000. Also unlimited deduction for the transfer of property to a spouse at death. (i) Lowered rate on the exercise of stock options. (j) Changed rules governing "Depreciation and Investment Credit." (The Tax Reform Act of 1986 changed some of these provisions.)

economic rent 1. In an industry characterized by a reasonable state of economic equilibrium, the excess received by one factor in a productive process over what is required to retain it in the current process. 2. According to Samuelson and Stigler, the difference between the current earnings of a resource and what that resource could earn in an alternative use. 3. *economics* Cost commanded by a factor that is unique or inelastic in supply.

economics 1. Social science concerned chiefly with the way society chooses to employ its limited resources, which have alternative uses, to produce goods and services for present and future consumption. 2. The systematic study of how humans attempt to meet unlimited wants and needs with limited resources.

economics of public policy and administration Jean Bodin's theory of public finance based on the premises: (a) raising revenues by honest means; (b) employing revenues for the profit and honor of the state; (c) saving some portion of the revenues for emergencies. Bodin's primary publication, *The Six Books of the Republic* (1586), referred to the proper management of the public finances as "the nerves of the state." He approved of direct taxes on individuals if the individuals had a voice in the matter. He believed in taxing business (domains), and in some customs duties. He also assumed that as long as the state had excess revenues in savings, it would have no occasion to borrow.

Economic Table A book written by François Quesnay in 1758, in which he developed the first integrated theory of the production and distribution of wealth.

economic warfare Punitive actions by one country against another which hinder the free exchange of goods and services between the two. Actions may appear as high tariffs, quotas on specific goods, etc.

economy of scale A reduction in per unit cost of a specific good occasioned by the growth of the size of the plant. While increasing unit outputs usually decreases per unit cost for a time, as the size of the plant increases, diminishing marginal utility begins, and prices per unit tend to go up. The ideal size of a plant occurs when the marginal cost of a unit of good exactly equals the marginal revenue from the sale of that good.

e contra *On the contrary.*

e converso *On the other hand;* conversely.

Edge Act *banking* Banking legislation passed in 1919 which gives national banks the right to conduct foreign banking operations through federal or state chartered subsidiaries. This act was further strengthened by the International Banking Act (1978).

Edge Act Corporation Organization chartered by the Federal Reserve Board to engage in international banking operations. The Board acts upon applications by United States and foreign banking organizations to establish Edge corporations; it also examines Edge corporations and their subsidiaries. The corporation gets its name from Senator Walter Edge of New Jersey, the sponsor of the original legislation to permit formation of such organizations.

edict Command or proclamation; carrying the authority of law issued by the sovereign; positive law, as contrasted with a mere proclamation which may be a declaration of what the law is.

effective age Age of a property based on the amount of wear and tear it has sustained.

effective debt *finance* The total debt owed by a company including the capitalized value of lease payments.

effective demand *economics* 1. The actual purchase of a good, as opposed to the expression of a desire for the good. 2. The quantity of a good demanded at a specific price.

effective income tax rate *See* average income tax rate.

effective rate True rate of return considering all relevant financing expenses.

effects Personal estate or property; movable property or chattel of any kind.

efficient market *stock market* Market in which asset prices instantaneously reflect new information. (*See* efficient market theory)

efficient market theory A concept that states that the stock market is highly efficient, and able to assimilate all information relative to its activities, prior to the time an individual investor would be privy to the knowledge. This results in the idea that it is generally impossible to outguess the market, and that a technical approach to investing is better than a "seat-of-the-pants" approach. (Cf. new investment technology)

efficient portfolio *investing* A variety of securities held in a portfolio which yield the highest possible return at the lowest possible risk.

egoistic needs *management; psychology* A term used to describe the needs of individuals other than remuneration. These may include a feeling of self-worth, acceptance by peers, job status, etc.

egress 1. Means of exit, usually from land or a building. 2. Access from a land parcel to a public road or other means of exit.

80/20 law *See* Pareto's law.

ei incumbit probatio, qui dicit, non qui negat; cum per rerum naturam factum negantis probatio nulla sit *The proof lies upon he who affirms, not upon he who denies, since, by the nature of things, he who denies a fact cannot produce any proof.*

ejectment 1. Mixed action in which recovery of land, rents due, and damages could be recovered in the same action. 2.

An action at law for the termination of a claim of right of possession to and recovery of possession of corporeal hereditaments. 3. The common law action now brought in the United States to determine who has title to or ownership of land.

ejusdem generis *law Of the same kind.* When a series of terms with common characteristics is used, an ambiguous term in the same series will be presumed to mean about the same as the other terms.

elasticity, anticipation of *See* anticipation of elasticity.

elasticity, finite *See* perfect elasticity.

elasticity of demand, income *See* income elasticity of demand.

elasticity of demand and supply, cross *See* cross elasticity of demand and supply.

elasticity of demand and supply, price *See* price elasticity of demand and supply.

elasticity of expectations *economics* The ratio of the relative rise in expected future prices of a commodity to the relative rise in price in the preceding period.

elasticity of production *economics* The ratio of the relative change in output to a relative change in input.

elasticity of substitution 1. *economics* The rate at which one factor of production will be substituted for another in response to a change in their relative prices. 2. With consumers, the rate at which one commodity will be substituted for another in response to their relative prices.

elasticity, perfect *See* perfect elasticity.

elasticity, promotional *See* promotional elasticity.

elasticity ratio Measurement of the degree of the response of a change in quantity to a change in price (normally stated as a percentage).

elderly applicant Credit applicant aged sixty-two or over, as defined in the Equal Credit Opportunity Act.

election *estates* Choice by a surviving spouse either to accept the provision made for him or her in the deceased spouse's will or to disregard that provision and claim what he or she is entitled to by that state's laws of descent and distribution.

election against the will *law* Use of will stipulations, as opposed to the marital deduction, or some other techniques of reducing the size of the estate or evening the size of the estate the surviving spouse may leave for purposes of taxation. Most states provide a right of election to take against the will unless the survivor leaves a certain portion of the real estate and, in many states, personal property to the spouse.

election option *pensions; profit sharing* Employee's option to receive a profit-sharing contribution, either in cash or on a deferred basis.

elective share statute Statute providing the surviving spouse protection from being disinherited. Typically, these statutes enable the surviving spouse to make an election within a specified time following the death of the first spouse and to take a specified percentage of the value of the decedent's property, even if the decedent chose to leave no property to the surviving spouse under the terms of the will.

electric utility company Company which owns or operates facilities used for the generation, transmission, or distribution of electric energy for sale, excluding the operation of such facilities for employees' own use or for sale to tenants.

electronic fund transfer (EFT) Movement of funds initiated other than by check. Withdrawals or transfers at automated teller machines and debits to accounts at point of sale are EFTs. This includes Fedwire, Bankwire, automated clearinghouses (ACHs), and other automated systems.

eleemosynary Having to do with, derived from, or dependent on charity.

eleemosynary corporation A corporation created for and having to do with charitable purposes. This is a vital concept in tax planning and management, inasmuch as the Internal Revenue Service allows deductions to individuals and companies contributing to nonprofit organizations and allows tax exemptions on income received by the organizations.

eligibility requirements *retirement plans* Requirements designating which employees are eligible for the plan, usually related to age and length of service. Many variations qualify according to the laws, and the company may choose the plan which most nearly meets its goals and objectives.

eligibility year *social security* Year in which the worker reaches sixty-two years of age, becomes disabled, or dies.

eligible paper *banking* Commercial paper, drafts, bills of exchange, and other negotiable instruments that a bank can acquire at a discount and that the Federal Reserve will accept for rediscounting.

elimination period Period of time that must elapse after a covered disability starts before disability income begins. The time range may be from thirty days to six months, and usually the benefit payments are not retroactive. The premiums decrease substantially with an increase in this period. Also called waiting period.

eloigne *law* To take away goods from a person or from a premises; to take away or conceal anything beyond the jurisdiction of the court.

emancipation *law* The gaining of freedom, usually of a minor, to assume the posture of an adult, and which generally requires an action by a court.

embankment Artificial bank or mound of earth raised for any purpose, such as to carry a canal, road, or railway. Synonymous with levee; however, while every levee is an embankment, every embankment is not a levee.

embargo Prohibition to pass. In times of war or hostilities, order of the government prohibiting ships from leaving certain ports until further order. (*See* civil embargo, hostile embargo)

embezzlement Fraudulent taking of money or goods for personal use by one to whom they have been entrusted, such as an agent, a public officer, or any other person who acts in a fiduciary capacity.

emblement *law* Growing crop. Annual crops are generally considered personal property.

emergency fund Cash, or cash equivalent, fund held for the purpose of meeting emergency situations. Three to six month's earnings equivalent is usually considered sufficient.

Emergency Home Finance Act (1870) An act of Congress creating the quasi-governmental Federal Home Loan Mortgage Corporation, (Freddie Mac), the purpose of which was to encourage and enlarge the development of a secondary mortgage market. Freddie Mac packages FHA and VA mortgages for resale to investors. This is considered a good investment since the federal government guarantees some part, or all of the loans under FHA and VA.

emergency provision *law; finance* The stipulation in a will or a trust which allows the trustee to pay out principal or accumulated interest to the beneficiary to meet unforeseen circumstances such as an illness or an accident.

eminent domain 1. Inherent sovereign power of the state to take private property for public use. The power of eminent domain is paramount to all private rights vested under the government which rights are held in subordination to this power, yielding in every instance when the powers of eminent domain are properly exercised. 2. The right of the government or a public utility to acquire property for necessary public use by condemnation. (The owner must be fairly compensated.)

empirical credit system Credit scoring system, based on creditor's experience with borrowers, allotting certain points to attributes describing the applicant.

empirical information Facts derived through experience or observation.

employ To engage, have, or keep for or in service or duty; to procure or retain the services of; to furnish work or occupation for.

employee business expense Expense incurred in an employee's normal business activity and which is tax deductible (e.g., nonreimbursed car expenses made on behalf of the company by the employee or tools purchased by an employee to enable one to follow one's trade).

Employee Retirement Income Security Act (ERISA) (1974) Act passed to police employee retirement plans and attempt to guarantee their provisions. The act also tries to determine the equity of such plans.

employee stock ownership plan (ESOP) Program which allows employees to purchase stock in the company they work for. Under this plan, employees may participate in the company management, even taking control to rescue the company or a particular plant that would otherwise go out of business. Employees may offer wage and work-rule concessions in return for ownership privileges to keep a marginal facility running. In a typical profit-sharing plan, no more than 10% of the trust portfolio can be made up of employer securities; the ESOP allows employees to own stock in excess of this 10% limitation. This plan has positive motivational aspects which apply to the employee and allows a cashless contribution to be made by the employer.

Employment Act (1946) Act of Congress passed in 1946 which requires the government to attempt to maintain high levels of employment, production, and purchasing power. To assist the President in this task, the act authorizes the President to appoint a panel of experts known as the Council of Economic Advisors.

Employment, Interest and Money (The General Theory of) Book published by John Maynard Keynes, an English economist and civil servant deriding the writings of Jean-Baptiste Say and Say's Law. His primary premise is that the private enterprise system will not work under all circumstances and sometimes the need arises for government to intervene with injections of capital in order to restore equilibrium in the economy. The United States government adopted Keynesian philosophy during the Great Depression.

employment multiplier *economics* The reciprocal of the ratio between the people initially employed as a result of additional expenditures to the total increase in employment, which also includes the consequent increases in employment caused by the first increase.

emptor *Buyer* or purchaser. (*See* caveat emptor)

empty nesters Couple whose children have established separate households; important segment of the housing market, since empty nesters often seek to reduce the amount of housing space they occupy, becoming one source of demand for smaller housing units.

enact To establish by decree or by law.

enactments Acts of Congress or various state legislatures.

en bloc Describes goods sold as a whole, rather than by measurement.

enclosure *See* inclosure.

encroach To intrude upon the possession or right of another by stealth; to trespass.

encroachment 1. A building, part of a building, or obstruction that physically intrudes upon, overlaps, or trespasses upon the property of another. 2. The unauthorized extending of the boundaries of one's land into that of another. To unlawfully gain the lands, property, or authority of another by gradual or partial assumption of right.

encroachment *law; real estate* An improvement to property that illegally intrudes upon the property of another, or the easement rights of another.

encumber To impede; to hinder; to obstruct.

encumbrance *law* Claim, lien, charge, or liability attached to property. Any right to or interest in land which subsists in another to diminution of its value, but consistent with passing of the fee, including outstanding mortgage loans, unpaid taxes, easements, and/or deed restrictions. Also spelled incumbrance.

endogenous theory of the business cycle *economics* Any theory relating to the business cycle that relates it to movements or adjustments in the economy, which are indigenous to the economy.

endorse 1. To sign one's name, as payee, to a check or note, with or without further qualification (originally on the back of the document; sometimes now on the face). By extension, any signature or statement of approval, as of a political candidate. 2. *insurance* To add special provisions to an insurance policy, usually in property or liability policies, which complete the contract concerning special kinds of coverage desired by the insured. In life insurance, endorsements are usually called riders.

endorsement, restrictive *See* restrictive endorsement.

endowment 1. Assignment of a woman's dower. 2. The bestowal of money, income from a fund, and/or use of property for public use. 3. A permanent fund of property or money bestowed upon an institution or a person, the income from which is used to serve a specific purpose.

endowment fund *finance* The accumulated fund of an organization such as a college or a university which serves to guarantee the future life of the organization. Such funds usually result from gifts or bequests from alumni and friends.

endowment insurance Policy offering insurance protection for a specified period of time, such as ten, twenty, or thirty years, or to age sixty-five; if the insured lives to the end of the specified period, the contract pays the face amount either in a lump sum or in installments. Endowment life insurance contracts are basically savings plans with an insurance element added.

energy mutual fund *investing* A mutual fund that invests only in energy stocks and in stocks of companies that manufacture energy-saving equipment.

energy tax credits Reduction in income tax which is no longer allowed by law, generally based on the cost of installing insulation and other energy-saving devices. (*See* Appendix G)

enfeoff *law* To invest a person of an estate by means of a feoffment (gift of property).

enfranchise 1. To make free or to confer a liberty. 2. To confer on one the right of voting at elections.

engagement Undertaking or contract.

engagement letter *accounting* A proposal from an external auditor indicating the scope of a proposed audit, including the time it will require, the procedures to be followed, and the reports to be submitted.

Engel's laws Set of relationships between consumer expenditures and income derived by a nineteenth-century German statistician, Ernst Engel, based on research into workingmen's purchases in Western Europe during the 1850s. The relationships state that as a family's income increases: the percentage it spends on food decreases; the percentage it spends on housing and household operations remains constant (except for fuel, light, and refrigeration, which increase); and the percentage it spends on all other categories and the amount it saves increas-

es (except for medical care and personal care items, which remain constant). In general, the total amount spent increases as a family's income increases. (Note: only the first relationship above is attributed to Engel; the other two are modernized versions of his early findings, based on more recent research.)

engrossing Copying of a legal document in a legible form.

enhance To increase or improve the value of.

enjoin To command or instruct with authority; to abate; to suspend or restrain; to issue an injunction.

enjoy To have, possess, and use with satisfaction; to occupy or have benefit of.

enroll To register or make a record of; to enter a document or name on an official record.

entail 1. To settle or limit the succession to real property. 2. *law* The order of succession created by an owner of land so that those following the owner cannot sell or convey the land.

enter To go upon the land; to go into, as to enter a building.

enticement 1. Act of attracting by arousing hope of pleasure or profit. 2. Act of wrongfully inducing, persuading a person to do anything.

entire contract Contract where the entire fulfillment of the promise by either party is a condition precedent to the right to call for the fulfillment of any part of the promise by the other.

entitle To give title or right to; to qualify for; to provide proper grounds for relief.

entitled Having a right or grounds for laying claim to benefits based on the provisions of the Social Security Act applicable at the time.

entity Legal person; the legal form under which property is owned which includes a person, an estate, a trust, or a governmental unit. (*See* corporation, limited partnership, partnership)

entity plan Plan made by the partnership as an whole as to how matters will be handled in the event of the death of a partner. (Cf. cross-purchase plan)

entrap To ensnare; to trick into danger or difficulty.

entrepreneur 1. A production innovator who perceives the opportunity to provide a new product or implement a new production method, and then organizes the needed production inputs and assumes the financial risk. 2. The person or persons who assume the risk of doing business in a private business economy. 3. *real estate* "Spec" builder; one who builds or develops an area in the hope of making a profit. One who bears the risk of doing business.

entropy *statistics; communications* The frequency of random occurrence of an event within a closed system, allowing a sequence of outcomes; i.e., a measure of the probable uncertainty content of a message.

entry age normal with frozen initial past service liability (EIPSL) Plan which assumes that the person has always had a pension plan. The key flexibility is the unfunded past liability. This represents a hypothetical pool of money which would have been available if the pension plan had always been in effect. The individual funds future benefits currently, as with the attained age level. The person may selectively amortize the initial unfunded past service liability over an extended period. In general, the amount can be paid off over anywhere from ten to thirty years, at one's own discretion.

entry book Log book for recording changes in estates of land generally under the names of grantor and grantee.

en ventre sa mere *law In its mother's womb.* A phrase descriptive of an unborn child; it may take a legacy or have a guardian.

environmental impact statement (EIS) Analysis of the expected effects of a development or action on the surrounding natural and fabricated environment. Such statements are required for many federally supported developments under the National Environmental Policy Act (1969) and under some state laws.

Environmental Protection Agency (EPA) Independent agency of the United States government established in 1970 to enforce federal pollution abatement laws and to implement various pollution prevention programs. This agency is charged with the responsibility of reducing air and water pollution, noise pollution, and radiation, and of ensuring the safe handling and disposal of toxic waste. It works with state and local agencies to prevent all types of pollution.

eo nomine *By that very name; under that very name.*

epochal innovation *economics* A major addition to the stock of human knowledge which provides a potential for sustained economic growth during any given era.

equal Of the same degree (relative to size, weight, or any quality); equivalent.

equal and uniform rule of taxation Tax that reaches and bears with a like burden upon all property within a given district, county, or municipality.

Equal Credit Opportunity Act (ECOA) *finance* Federal law, enacted in 1974, aimed at discouraging discrimination by lenders on the basis of gender or marital status. Amended in 1976 to prohibit discrimination on the basis of age, race, color, religion, national origin, receipt of income from public assistance programs, or past exercising of rights under the Consumer Credit Protection Act. The law further prohibits certain questions or actions when one is obtaining credit information.

equalization *economics; government* A method which attempts to assure a uniformity of the tax burden borne by real property owners. Since most states, or lower governmental units, have equalization systems for property taxes, but assessment is carried out on a local basis and applied to several local governmental units, it is necessary to have coordination which recognizes the difference between local units in assessing. It is rarely agreed by property owners that the tax burden is uniform, however.

equalization board Government agency that determines the fairness of taxes levied against properties.

equal protection under the law The right of any individual, in any legal jurisdiction, to be treated by the law exactly as is every other citizen in the jurisdiction.

equation, Domar's fundamental *See* Domar's fundamental equation.

equation of exchange *monetary theory* A concept of Marshall's which states that

101

the money supply multiplied by the velocity is equal to the price level times the number of transactions; $MV = PT$. This amounts to the common-sense statement that the larger the proportion of their income that people hold in money, the more slowly money moves from one income recipient to another; or, any reduction in cash balances held speeds up monetary circulation. Also called quantity equation.

equilibrium   *economics* A state of balance in the economy which will normally be accompanied by the following phenomena: (a) full employment, (b) proper payment to each of the four factors of production, (c) equilibrium points in the various demand/supply curves are relatively easy to achieve, and, (d) moderate and acceptable interest rates, as pertains to both savers and investors. While it is generally thought that the economy tends toward equilibrium, it seems rarely, if ever, to be achieved.

equilibrium point   *See* Marshallian cross.

equilibrium price   1. *economics* Price at which both buyer and seller agree (demander and supplier) and at which, theoretically, the market will be cleared. 2. *manufacturing* Price at which the manufacturer's profits are maximized.

equimarginal principle   *economics* Principle that, in dividing a fixed quantity of anything among a variety of uses, it will be apportioned to each use so that the gain from putting one unit into one use is just equal to the loss in the uses from which the unit has been taken.

equipment trust certificate   1. Serial bond secured by specific equipment. 2. Debt instruments issued by companies for purchasing rolling stock equipment, such as rail cars. The equipment serves as collateral for the debt.

equitability   *tax law* Social or economic objective achieved by the use of tax credits for taxpayers in various marginal tax brackets where it is felt that equitability is not fully achieved through exclusions and deductions.

equitable adoption   Situation that exists under the law of certain jurisdictions where a child had certain inheritance rights of estate of an individual who con-

tracted to adopt the child but did not do so. Such a contract may be in writing or oral. (*See* equitable conversion)

equitable asset   *law* An asset held by the executor of an estate but subject to debts only by the decree of an equity court for the satisfaction of certain obligations.

equitable conversion   *law* Rule applied when a court of equity gives effect to those things intended to be accomplished even though all the legal formalities have not been finished, based on the principle that equity regards that as done which ought to have been done. (E.g., if a contract to sell land has been entered but death intervenes before the deed is executed, equitable conversion will be applied so that the estate of the deceased vendor will be considered to have money and not land.)

equitable estate   Interest in land by operation of equity, such as the estate or title of a person for whose benefit lands are held in trust by another, the latter having the legal estate.

equitable execution   Mode of obtaining payment of a judgment debt by the appointment of a receiver of a defendant's property.

equitable interest   1. Beneficial interest in an estate left to be administered by a trustee. (E.g., if Mr. Doe dies leaving his estate in trust with Bank X, with his wife, son, and daughter the recipients of the estate, the wife, son, and daughter have equitable interests in the estate.) 2. Interests in property which, though not recognized at law, will be recognized and enforced by a court of equity. While a trustee has the legal estate in the trust property, the trustee is compelled to hold the property for the benefit of the beneficiaries whose interests are called equitable. The right of a mortgagor in the mortgaged lands is an equitable interest while the legal estate vests in the mortgagee.

equitable lien   Right to have specific property applied toward payment of a debt, declared by a court of equity. A court of equity may impose a lien as a remedial device where possession of property has changed, thus terminating the legal lien.

equitable mortgage   Equitable interest

analogous to a legal mortgage, generally arising where the mortgage instrument is not effective as a mortgage at law. A transaction which vests a grantee-mortgagee with a right to bring action for foreclosure in the event that the obligation of the grantor-mortgagor has not performed. The doctrine has also been extended to other cases such as where a deed is granted in a form that is absolute but in fact was intended to secure an indebtedness.

equitable owner   Owner whose rights of ownership are recognized only in a court of equity and are enforceable only under the rules of equity. The beneficiary of a trust is thus an equitable owner.

equitable right   *law* A right recognized in a court of equity.

equitable title   Interest held by one who has agreed to purchase but has not yet closed the transaction.

equity   1. Ownership interest of common and preferred stockholders in a company; on a balance sheet, equity equals total assets less all liabilities. Also known as owner's equity, net worth, and shareholder's equity. 2. *law* Aequitas. Fairness or impartiality. Justice according to natural reason and good conscience as distinct from that which is strictly according to law. 3. The interest or value that the owner has in real estate over and above the liens against it.

equity financing   1. *finance* Raising funds for a firm by selling stock rather than issuing bonds.   2. Method of financing a business, often used when venture capital is necessary for startup situations, in which partial ownership is used as collateral.

equity-linked product   *insurance* Hybrid product which has elements of regular insurance policies, such as protection and savings functions, but also has an equity function whereby a part of each premium paid is used to purchase equities, usually common stock (e.g., a variable life policy).

equity of redemption   Right of an owner to recover property that has been foreclosed.

equity security   1. Share in a corporation, such as transferable or denominated stock or similar security.   2. Interest of a limited partner in a limited partnership.

3. Right, other than a right to convert, to purchase, sell, or subscribe to a share, security, or interest of a share of a corporation or of a limited partner.

equity security holder   Holder of an equity security of the debtor.

equivalence   Economic concept which states that two cash flows occurring at different times are of equal value if the earlier cash flow can be converted into the later cash flow by investing at the prevailing interest rate. Time value of money concept.

equivalent   Equal in work or value, force, power, effect, or import.

equivalent taxable yield   *investing* A comparison of the yield on a tax-free municipal bond and a taxable corporate bond. This is simply computed: the tax-exempt yield is equal to the taxable yield multiplied by the reciprocal of the tax bracket.

equivalent tax benefit   *See* Appendix C.

equivocal   Having several meanings.

equivocation   Use of equivocal expressions to mislead.

erasures   Obliteration of words in a document by rubbing or scraping them out.

ergonomics   *management; psychology* The study of the relationships between a person and the type of work that person does. It is a comprehensive study, both intensive and extensive, that includes anatomical, physiological, and psychological studies of the individual, in relation to the makeup of the individual's job.   (*See* occupational psychologist)

erosion   Gradual wearing away of land by the currents of water or tides.

erroneous   *law* Involving error; deviating from the law. There is a distinction in law between a process which is erroneous and one which is irregular. The former stands until it is set aside, while the latter is completely void.

escalator clause   1. Clause in a contract that stipulates the increase, under certain conditions, of amounts to become due under the contract.   2. A provision in a lease that requires the tenant to pay more rent based on an increase in costs. Same as a stop clause.   3. *economics* A special clause in an agreement providing for an adjustment of price based on some event or index. It can be the effect of rising costs, or, in a labor contract, it can be the effect of an increase in the Consumer Price Index (CPI).

escapable expense *finance* Expenses that can be avoided by a company by closing a department, or branch, which is unprofitable.

escheat *law* Reversion of property to the state in the event that the owner dies without leaving a will and has no legal heirs.

escrow 1. Deed, bond, or other legal instrument delivered by a grantor to a third person, who in turn delivers it to the grantee upon proof of the performance or fulfillment by the grantee of some condition stated by the grantor. 2. A fund of money (called escrow fund) similarly delivered by a grantor. 3. *law; finance* An account held by a third party on behalf of two other parties, who have agreed to the arrangement. (E.g., if a buyer pays a downpayment on a house, the seller will usually put the money in an escrow account in a bank where it is held until the deal is consummated.)

escrow account *See* trust account.

essence That which makes a thing what it is. A provision in a contract is said to be of the essence when, at the time of entering into the contract, both parties knew that performance of the contract without compliance with such provision may be of no avail. Whether a provision in a contract is or is not the essence thereof, in the absence of any express stipulation in the contract, will depend on the circumstances of each case, such as the purpose of the contract.

essential coverage Insurance covering any possible loss which could be disastrous. It is not the frequency but the size of a possible loss which is most important.

establish To fix immovable or firmly; make stable and permanent; to originate and secure the permanent existence of; to found; to institute; to create and regulate; to prove by evidence or argument.

estate The amount, degree, nature, and extent of interest to which a person is lawfully entitled with regard to the ownership or use of real or personal property.

estate by entirety A form of co-ownership held by husband and wife with right of survivorship by virtue of title acquired jointly after marriage, and upon the death of either of the spouses, the survivor inherits the estate.

estate for life *See* life estate.

estate for years An estate that is less than freehold, where a person has an interest in the lands with possession for some fixed and determinable period (e.g., a leasehold estate).

estate in expectancy Estate where right to possession of the property is postponed to a future time pending the determination of an intermediate estate, such as that of a life tenant. A reversionary or a remainder estate is one in expectancy. (Cf. estate in possession)

estate in inheritance A freehold estate that descends to the heirs of the holder of the estate upon the holder's death under the laws relating to succession. Estates of freehold are divided into those of inheritance and those not of inheritance. While all estates of inheritance are freehold, the converse is not true; a life estate and other estates of indefinite duration are also freehold but not of inheritance.

estate in possession An estate which entitles the owner to immediate possession of the property. (Cf. estate in expectancy)

estate liquidity Pertains to the cash which will be needed to properly take care of all the details of an estate upon the death of the principal, such as debts and administrative costs. Estate liquidity is particularly applicable in partnerships and corporations.

estate planning Planning involving three dimensions: (a) the acquisition and use of property during one's productive years, to provide a balance between current enjoyment of the assets, security, and provision for the future; (b) adequate assets to enable one to maximize enjoyment during retirement years; and (c) the disposal of assets at death to ensure where, to whom, and in what form they should go, at the least possible drain on the asset corpus.

estate pur autre vie *law* An estate in land that endures during the life of a person other than the one entitled to such estate. A form of life estate that lasts for the lifetime of another person.

estate tax   Tax imposed by a state or federal government on assets left to heirs in a will. Under the Economic Recovery Act (1981), there is no estate tax on transfers of property between spouses. There is also an exclusion for all estates amounting to $250,000 in 1982 and rising to $600,000 in 1987. Further changes may come in subsequent years.

estimated tax   *economics* The estimated tax for the coming tax year, minus tax credits, which is based on the higher of the regular tax, or the alternative minimum tax. (Cf. alternative minimum tax)

estoppel   *law* A legal doctrine by which a person is prevented from attempting to prove facts contrary to the person's own actions.

estovers   Necessities. The right of a tenant to take wood for fuel, fences, and similar purposes from the premises the tenant has leased.

ethical responsibility   Responsibility one has to act in a moral and correct manner, as required by circumstances, toward clients, peers, and all persons with whom one works.

ethics   The basic principles of right action. The ethics of a profession are the general body of rules, written or unwritten, intended to guide members in maintaining certain basic standards of behavior.

et seq   *And the following.*

et ux   *And wife.*

Eurodollar   United States dollar deposited at banks and other financial institutions outside the United States. Although the name originated because of the large amounts of such deposits held at banks in Western Europe, similar deposits in other parts of the world are also called Eurodollars.

Eurodollar CDs   *investing* Investments often made by brokerage houses which are based on Eurodollars. Since Eurodollars are dollars held by foreign banks, they are not under the control of the United States government, and are considered by some to be more speculative than other CDs. Normally, these CDs (usually six months maturity) pay ½ to 1% more than traditional CDs.

European Economic Community   *economics* A cooperative system established by the Treaty of Rome in 1957, the goal of which is to break down economic barriers between the participating countries. Founding members were France, West Germany, Italy, the Netherlands, Belgium and Luxembourg. The membership roll now includes Belgium, Denmark, France, West Germany, Greece, Ireland, Italy, Luxembourg, Netherlands, and United Kingdom. Also called the Common Market.

European Free Trade Association (EFTA)   *economics* Originally set up by seven countries—United Kingdom, Sweden, Norway, Denmark, Switzerland, Austria and Portugal—this organization was viewed as an answer to the Common Market. The idea was for these seven countries to form the same sort of union that the European Economic Community had, thus reducing barriers between themselves to free and mutual trade. The union did not last, and some members then sought membership in the Common Market. (Cf. European Economic Community)

European Recovery Program (ERP)   Comprehensive recovery plan for European countries, financed by the United States, for the purposes of: increasing their productive capacity; stabilizing their financial systems; promoting their mutual economic cooperation; and reducing their dependence on U.S. assistance. The ERP was terminated in 1951 after considerable success, and its functions were absorbed by other government agencies and programs. Commonly known as the Marshall Plan, after Secretary of State George C. Marshall, who proposed it in 1947.

event   Anything that happens or comes to pass. The consequence of anything; conclusion; that in which an operation or series of operations terminates; an occurrence.

eviction   Dispossession of a tenant by a landlord. Expulsion by the assertion of a paramount title or by process of law.

evidence   *law* Anything that furnishes or tends to furnish proof at the trial of an issue, such as the testimony of witnesses, documents, and objects.

ex aequo et bono   *According to equity and good conscience.*

ex-all *investing* The sale of a security without dividends, rights, warrants, or any other privilege related to the security.

ex ante saving *finance; economics* Planned saving.

ex assensu patris *With the consent of the father.*

ex cathedra *From the seat of authority;* authoritative.

ex causa *By title.*

exceptional equilibrium *economics* A situation in which the the expectations of people, though changing, come to pass as anticipated.

exceptio probat regulam *The exception proves the rule.*

excess accumulation Amount an individual contributes to an Individual Retirement Account over the two thousand dollar/100% of compensation limit; the excess will not be income tax deductible.

excess capacity *See* overcapacity.

excess contribution *pension plans* Amount in excess of 25% of salary or thirty thousand dollar maximum that is contributed to a pension plan. The excess amount can be suspended or put into a suspense account and carried over until a subsequent year, when contributions do not reach the maximum level. (*See* Appendix G)

excess itemized deduction On the personal income tax form, any deduction from adjusted gross income which exceeds in total the standard deduction (1987 and after). The standard deduction for single persons is $2,540 in 1987, and $3,000 in 1988; married persons filing jointly, $3,760 in 1987, and $4,400 in 1988. (Payments that are deductible as itemized deductions save no tax unless they exceed the standard deduction.)

excessive Greater than what is usual and proper; characterized by or exhibiting excess; greater than usual amount or degree; exceptional; very great.

excess liability insurance Sometimes called an umbrella policy, a policy created to cover excess liability not covered by other insurance.

excess-line broker/agent *See* surplus broker/agent.

exchange 1. Transfer of property for property or some value other than money. Barter; trade. Includes situations in which money changes hands in addition to property, it would still be an exchange. 2. *See* New York Stock Exchange.

exchange privilege *investing* A right of the shareholder to exchange shares in one mutual fund for shares in another, offered by the same company, and at little or no cost.

exchange rate The value of a nation's currency measured in the number of units of a foreign currency for which it can be exchanged (e.g., 1 U.S. dollar = 2.07 German marks).

exchange value *economics* The value of any good measured by the quantity of other goods for which it might be exchanged.

excise tax Tax imposed upon the manufacture, sale, or consumption within the country of certain commodities, upon licenses to pursue certain occupations, and upon corporate privileges. A form of indirect tax imposed upon the acts of persons.

excludable personal income Income that is not taxable, such as interest on municipal bonds and most employee benefits.

excluded class Specific categories of employees who do not have to be included in a tax-exempt pension plan for it to be qualified by the Internal Revenue Service.

exclusion 1. *insurance* Statements in a policy which reduce the broad coverage provided in the agreement. 2. *tax* Item that would be considered part of a more general class of items or events that has been the basis for a tax but has been specifically removed by law from the tax base.

exclusion allowance That part of an annuity payment which is excluded from income taxes of the recipient, in that the employee participated with the employer in purchasing the annuity, and the employee's part was paid with after-tax dollars. The concept is simple in that the government is not requiring the employee to pay taxes on the same money twice. The formula is complex in that it must consider the proportion of the employee's payments to the total annuity, the interest-free buildup in the account, and how the payments are being received.

exclusion of gain on sale of residence One-time exclusion from capital gains, or income tax, on proceeds received from sale of a home by a person age fifty-five or older. The excluded amount may not be more than $125,000.

exclusion ratio formula Method used to assure that contributions made to a retirement plan by an employee using after-tax dollars, is not again taxed as ordinary income as the proceeds of the plan are distributed.

exclusive Intended for or pertaining to the subject alone; not shared.

exclusive-right-to-sell listing *real estate* A contract between the real estate broker and the seller that the broker has exclusive rights to sell the property, and will receive a commission even if the property is sold by someone else. While brokers like such an agreement, sellers usually don't, and will usually refrain from making such a contract.

ex contractu *Arising out of a contract.* One of the divisions of all actions is those that arise out of contracts and those that arise ex delicto (from a tort).

exculpate *law* Absolve, clear, or tend to clear of fault or guilt.

exculpatory provision *law* A provision in a will or trust instrument which relieves or attempts to relieve an executor or trustee from liability for breach of trust.

excuse *law* A reason alleged for doing or not doing a thing. Not synonymous with an alibi as the former deals with justification and the latter negates the physical possibility that the suspected individual could have committed the crime.

ex debito justitiae *Arising as a matter of right;* a debt of justice.

ex demissione *Upon the demise.*

ex dividend *Without dividend.* Describes sale of stock in which the buyer does not receive the recently declared dividend. Every dividend is payable on a fixed date to all shareholders recorded on the books of a company at a previous date of record. (E.g., a dividend may be declared as payable to holders of record on the books of the company on a given Friday. Since five business days are allowed for delivery of a stock in a "regular way" transaction on the New York Stock Exchange, the Exchange would declare the stock ex dividend as of the opening of the market on the preceding Monday. That means anyone who bought it on and after Monday would not be entitled to the dividend.) When stocks go ex dividend, the stock tables include the symbol "x" following the name.

ex-dividend day Day on which the stock starts trading without the dividend. This is usually four days before the date of record. Owners of record prior to the ex-dividend date are entitled to the dividend.

execute To complete, as a legal instrument; to perform what is required to give validity to, as by signing and perhaps sealing and delivering. To perform; to finish; to accomplish an act.

executio est finis et fructus legis *Execution is the end and fruit of the law.*

executive department Branch of the United States government which is charged with powers and duties of carrying the law into effect. The government of the United States is divided into three branches: the executive, the judicial, and the legislative.

executive officer Official of high rank in many different kinds of business organizations who is likely to have authoritative input into company policy and procedure. Such a person may carry any one of a dozen different titles.

executive secretary *banking* Secretary who usually serves the president as a personal secretary. Position is sometimes combined with that of administrative secretary.

executive vice president *banking* Individual who has the responsibility for the administration and operations of the bank. The person reports directly to the president. Usually, this person will be on the executive committee, and perhaps on the board of directors. In a manner similar to the president, this person stays close to all the functions of the institution. Some banks may not use this title at all, but rather the title of senior vice president for administration.

executor Person designated to carry out the wishes expressed in a will pertaining to the administration of the estate and the distribution of the assets; this may be a bank officer, family member, or trusted friend. A woman thus appointed may be called an executrix, although executor applies to a woman if that is the term written in the will by the testator. An executor holds strictly a representative capacity, standing in and enforcing the right of the testator. The executor in equity is looked upon as a quasi-trustee for the beneficiaries.

executor commission Fees set by state law for the skills and time of the executor. The executor may accept a bequest in lieu of fees.

executor de bonis non *law* The person or firm named in a will to take over and complete the provisions of the will, in the event the original executor cannot or will not perform.

executor de son tort *law* Person who by intermeddling with the estate of a deceased person takes on the office of executor, although not constituted by the deceased and not appointed to act as administrator by a court of competent jurisdiction.

executory devise A gift of anything by will which is not to take place upon the testator's death but upon the happening of some specified event.

executory interest Interest that may be created not only by will but by grant inter vivos.

executory trust One in which a further conveyance is to be made by the trustee.

executrix A female executor.

exempli gratia *As for an example.*

exempted security A security that is exempted from most provisions of the securities laws, including the margin rules. Such securities include United States government and agency securities and municipal securities designated by the Securities and Exchange Commission.

exempt employees *law* Persons working under the Fair Labor Standards Act who do not have to be paid additional compensation for overtime hours worked. (Often this has to do with the title the person has, or the specific kinds of duties performed.)

exemption Freedom or immunity, as from a tax or obligation.

exemption equivalent *law* The amount of property which can be given away, or descend, at death without a transfer tax being imposed under the federal unified credit.

exempt securities *investing* Stocks or bonds which are exempt from certain rules of the Securities and Exchange Commission. Among these exempts are treasury securities and municipal bonds.

exercise price 1. The price per share at which the holder of a stock option contract may purchase the underlying security on a call option, or sell the underlying security on a put option. 2. The price per share at which stock may be purchased if the option is exercised; also called strike price.

ex facie *On the face; apparently.*

ex facto jus oritur *The law follows the facts.*

ex gratia payment *law* A payment paid even when it is not owed to avoid the cost of litigation.

existing use value *economics* The price that land will bring when its use is confined to the purpose for which it is currently being used, as contrasted with some alternative use.

ex-legal *investing* A municipal bond that has not been examined by a bond law firm, and thus has no legal opinion to support its value.

ex maleficio non oritur contractus *A contract cannot arise out of an act that is immoral* (or illegal).

ex mero motu *Of his own accord.* Voluntarily.

ex officio *By virtue of the office.* Powers that are necessarily implied in an office may be exercised by the holder of the office without any further instrument concerting such power specifically on that person.

exogenous theory of the business cycle *economics* Any theory which attributes the problems in the economy to an outside agent, such as inclement weather, new inventions, etc.

ex pacto illicito non oritur actio *No action can arise from an illegal contract.*

ex parte *law From one side.* A proceeding which is unopposed but required to establish the legality of the court or commission judgment, or order desired, as a result of the proceeding.

ex parte materna *On the mother's side.*

ex parte paterna *On the father's side.*

expectancy The interest of one who foresees that he or she may receive a future benefit but has no present enforceable right. The hope of succession to the property of another as may be entertained by an heir apparent. An interest in expectancy is therefore called an inchoate interest.

expectant heir Person who has a vested or contingent remainder in property or who hopes to succeed to property and is tempted to make improvident bargains in such hope and thereby needs the protection of the court.

expectation of life The number of years which a person of given age may be expected to live.

expected return Average of possible returns weighted by their probability.

expedient At and suitable to the end in view; furthering or adapted to further what is proposed; practical and efficient.

expedit reipublicae ne sua re quis male utatur *It is in the interest of the public that one should not use his own property improperly* (so as to cause injury to others).

expenditure Using up or consumption of property; laying out or disbursement of money; the act of expending; payment.

expense ratio *investing* An amount, expressed as a percentage of total investment, that shareholders pay for mutual fund operating expenses and management fees.

expert witness A witness having special knowledge of the subject about which the witness is to testify (e.g., a forensic scientist or polygraphist). A person possessing, with reference to particular subjects, knowledge not acquired by ordinary persons. Expert evidence is only admissable when the subject matter is such that inexperienced persons are unlikely to prove capable of forming a correct judgment without such assistance.

expire To cease; to end; to die.

explicit Plainly expressed.

exploitation Obtaining labor services, raw materials, or finished goods for a price below their true value.

exploitation of labor *economics* 1. In the theory of Karl Marx, giving labor less than the total value of its production, after capital maintenance. 2. In the theory of Alfred Marshall, paying labor less than its marginal product.

exploratory well Well drilled in uncharted territory where geologists have little or no geological information from other wells, only data from seismic and other tests conducted.

exponential smoothing *statistics* Mathematical techniques for improving the accuracy of forecasting, particularly in the short-term, by weighting variables to include the most recent statistical trends.

export To carry or send abroad to foreign countries in the way of commerce. To send from one country to another.

export finance house *finance* A financial organization which specializes in arranging non-recourse financing for exporters.

ex post facto *law After the fact.* An ex post facto law makes punishable as a crime or increases the punishment for an act that was not punishable at the time it was committed, or for which the penalty was then less severe.

express 1. Clear; definite; explicit; unmistakable; not dubious or ambiguous. 2. Explicitly set forth in words; stated, not implied.

express authority Power usually granted by a formal document, such as a power of attorney.

expressly In direct or unmistakable terms; in an express manner.

expresso unius est exclusio alterius *The expression of one specific thing is the exclusion of another.*

express trust A trust created or declared, usually in writing, as distinguished from one inferred by law from the conduct or dealings of the parties, and wherein the terms of the trust are specifically set out. An express trust can only arise by direct act of parties, and should directly and expressly point out the person, property, and purposes of the trust.

expropriation The compulsory purchase of land or other property of a person by a municipal or other governmental authority usually in return for fair compensation.

ex provisione mariti   *From the provision of the husband.*

ex tempore   *By reason of time;* by lapse of time; also, without preparation.

extend   To broaden the application or action of; to expand; to enlarge; to prolong; to lengthen; to widen; to carry out further than the original limit. To extend a lease or contract is not necessarily the same as to renew it, for the stipulation to renew requires the making of a new lease while one to extend does not.

extended-area service   That type of service in which a subscriber of one telephone exchange may call a subscriber of a second exchange without being required to pay a separate charge.

extended coverage endorsement   *insurance* Coverage against each of the following perils: windstorm, hail, explosion, riot, civil commotion, damage by aircraft or by vehicle, and smoke damage. Specifically excluded are war and related hazards, the nuclear hazard, and water losses. When written on dwellings, a one hundred dollar deductible is often used and is required in some states.

extended term insurance option   Nonforfeiture option allowing the policyholder to exchange the cash value for the full face amount of the original insurance contract. The duration of the coverage is that which can be purchased with the net cash value applied as a single premium at the insured's attained age.

extension   Agreement with the lender to allow the borrower to make smaller payments of an outstanding debt over a longer period of time.

extensive growth   Economic growth that results from an increase in population and in proportionate quantities of other factor inputs; does not generally raise a country's standard of living.

extensive margin of cultivation   *economics* A situation in which the last unit of labor and capital applied to specific land on which previous additions have been applied yields just enough product to pay for the additional application.

external audit   *accounting* A review of auditors from outside the firm who seek to verify the accuracy of the financial statements.

external bond   *investing* A bond which is issued in one country and sold in another country, and which is payable in the second country's currency.

external funds   *finance* Funds which are not generated from within the company, but which come in the form of a loan, the proceeds of a bond offering, or funds from venture capital.

extinguishment   *law* Event that takes place when the right or interest comes to an end. A debt is extinguished when it is paid or the creditor releases the debtor from the obligation to pay.

extortionate means   *law* Any means which involves the use or threat of use of violence or other criminal means to cause harm to the person's self, reputation, or property. An extortionate extension of credit is any extension of credit with the understanding of the creditor and the debtor at the time it is made that delay or failure in making repayment could result in the use of violence or other criminal means to cause harm to the person or to the reputation or property of any person.

extractive industry   *economics* An industry which uses up irreplaceable natural resources such as oil or coal.

extra-expense form   *insurance* Insurance covering the added cost of continuing operations following damage from a covered peril. It does not cover loss of income profits, fixed charges, or the usual expenses of a business-interruption form. Many times, these two coverages are written together.

extraordinary items   *finance* Items which will significantly affect the financial position of a company, but cannot be looked upon as normal expenses, or normal practice, in the operation of the business. The Financial Accounting Standards Board (FASB) does not recognize many items as extraordinary, but has allowed for gains and losses from the early extinguishment of debt to be so accounted.

Extraordinary Popular Delusions   *investing; psychology* A book written by Charles MacKay recounting the great "tulip bulb" investment explosion which took place approximately from 1634 to 1638. This was one of the first investment delusions of great magnitude of which we have seen many.

extra praesentiam mariti   *Out of her husband's presence.*

extra vires   *Beyond powers.*

extreme care   Degree of care a reasonable person would exercise in dangerous circumstances.

extrinsic evidence   External evidence, or that which is not contained in the body of an agreement, contract, or will. Since only the words of a document may be considered by the court in interpreting or giving effect to it, extrinsic evidence is normally inadmissible.

extrinsic fraud   Type of fraud which prevents an adversarial trial. (Cf. intrinsic fraud)

F

Fabian socialism   *economics* Form of socialism introduced by the Fabian Society in England in 1884, the primary hypothesis behind which is that struggle and violence are unnecessary to introduce socialism to a nation, since it will evolve in any event; emerged as an outgrowth of utopian socialism.

face   Front of the check or money order where the payer writes all the particulars of these instruments, in contrast to the back where it is endorsed by the payee.

face amount   Amount indicated by the language of an instrument, without taking into consideration any accrued interest, dividends, or discounts.

face amount certificate   *investing* A debt security on which the holder makes periodic payments to the issuer, and the issuer promises to pay to the holder the face value of the security at maturity, or the surrender value, if presented prior to maturity. This is one of three categories of mutual funds defined by the Investment Company Act of 1940.

face interest rate   Percentage of interest that is shown on the loan document. (*See* annual percentage rate, effective rate)

face value   1. Dollar amount shown by words and/or numbers on a document. 2. The value that can be ascertained from a document without aid from extrinsic facts or evidence. In respect to corporate stock, face value means par value. The face value of an interest bearing note is the principal plus accrued interest.

facilitating agencies   Organizations, such as marketing research firms, transportation and storage companies, advertising agencies, insurance companies, and financial institutions, that provide specialized assistance for channel members in moving products from producer to consumer.

facility   *investments* In an exchange, the premises, tangible or intangible property whether on the premises or not, and any right to the use of such premises or property or any service for the purpose of effecting or reporting a transaction on an exchange (including any system of communication to or from the exchange, by ticker or otherwise, maintained by or with the consent of the exchange).

facility of payment clause   *insurance* Clause in life policy or industrial life policy permitting an insurer an option to make payments to any person appearing equitably entitled. If such payment is made in good faith, the insurer is liable to no one else on the policy.

facio ut des; facio ut facias   *I do so that you may give; I do so that you may do.* Forms of consideration for a contract where the consideration is mutual.

facsimile   Exact copy, preserving all the marks of the original.

fact   A thing or an event.

factor   1. *economics* One of the four necessary ingredients in the productive process. The four are land, labor, capital, and entrepreneurship. 2. *finance* Organization whose primary business is that of buying accounts receivable from businesses at a discount and collecting such accounts from the debtors. This is common practice in international accounts. 3. *marketing* An agent who accepts the goods of another for the purpose of selling the goods. The sale is made on a commission basis, and often the buyer does not know the original source of the goods.

factor cost   *economics*   Payments to the four factors of production, namely, rent, wages, interest and profit.

factoring   1. System involving notice to trade debtors, confined principally to the textile industry. 2. *economics* A specific type of financial service that buys accounts receivable from companies and then acts as the principal in collecting them. Factors sometimes make cash advances to the companies in anticipation of sales and ultimate accounts receivable.

factor market   Market in which resources and semifinished products are exchanged.

factor of production   Anything used as an input in the production process. In economics, usually grouped as land, labor, capital, and (sometimes) the entrepreneur.

factor's lien   Possessory lien that a factor has on goods consigned and possessed for all advances to the consignor.

factory   Building or part of a building where the business of making, altering, repairing, ornamenting, or finishing any article is carried on. Implies the presence of machinery on the premises for use in the process.

factory mutual   *insurance* Insurance putting the emphasis upon fire prevention, not loss coverage, though loss coverage is provided; not available to the average fire insurance buyer. Although they are restricted, the four factory mutual fire insurance companies now operating do hold an important place in the business. They generally charge a very large advance premium which covers the amount needed for claims and expenses.

factory overhead   *accounting* All costs related to the productive (manufacturing) process other than for direct materials and direct labor.

factory price   Price for which a good is sold at the location where it is produced.

facts of independent significance   *estates* Doctrine which permits reference to an act, fact, or writing outside of a will when necessary to ascertain the testator's intent, but the facts or writing must have some independent, nontestamentary significance.

factum   *A fact.*

factum probandum   Facts that are in issue, that are to be proved.

faculative reinsurance   Arrangement to insure a specific risk on a reinsurance basis, allowing the accepting company to accept or reject it.

fail   *estates* To decline or leave unperformed. A legacy or bequest is said to fail when it lapses never having vested or taken effect.

failure of consideration   Loss of significance of a legal consideration. Differs from "want of consideration," which denotes that nothing of value was ever received.

failure of issue   Death without issue (i.e., children).

fair actual value   Price which a prudent person desiring to invest in property might reasonably be expected to pay. Also referred to as fair market value.

Fair Credit Reporting Act   *economics* An act of Congress passed in 1970 that guarantees individuals the right to inspect all information about them on file with a credit reporting agency and permits them to change information that is incorrect.

Fair Labor Standards Act   Federal statute, enacted in 1938 and amended several times, which regulates hours worked, minimum wages, and overtime compensation of employees engaged in interstate commerce or in the production of goods for interstate commerce; prohibits discrimination by sex in pay rates and limits the employment of children. Also called the Wage-Hour Law.

fair market   A market that is not temporarily prone to fluctuation.

fair market rent   Amount that a property would command if it were available for lease.

fair market value   1. Price at which a seller and buyer, dealing at arm's length and without compulsion, will trade. The price that the property will fetch in the market place. Fair implies the presence of a market which is not disturbed by factors similar to transient boom or depression and where vendors, ready but not overanxious to sell, meet purchasers ready and able to buy. 2. As used in property tax and condemnation legislation, the market value of a property. 3. The price a willing buyer would pay and a willing seller would accept for a piece of property in ordinary circumstances.

fairness doctrine   Doctrine which gives broadcasters the responsibility to provide adequate coverage on issues of public importance that fairly reflects differing viewpoints.

Fair Packaging and Labeling Act (1967)   Legislation requiring disclosure of product identity, name and address of manufacturer or distributor, and information about the contents' quality.

fair rate of return   *investing*   The level of profit a public utility is allowed to earn as determined by federal and state regulations.   Public utility commissioners (by whatever name) of the various states set the rate of return for each utility based on the need to provide adequate services to customers, pay reasonable and regular dividends to stock and bond holders, and to retain earnings for upgrading old facilities or building new ones.

fair trade acts   Statutes which provide that the sale of trademarked or trade-named commodities shall not violate general monopoly prohibition by the producer's regulation of a resale price.

fair use   *copyright law*   The privilege to use certain copyrighted material under certain circumstances without the copyright holder's consent.

fait accompli   *An accomplished fact.*

falsa demonstratione legatum non perimi   *A bequest is not vitiated by an erroneous description.*

falsa demonstratio non nocet   *False description does not vitiate,* provided the thing or person described is sufficiently identified.

falsa orthographia non vitiat chartam, concessionem   *Erroneous spelling does not vitiate a deed.*

false   Contrary to fact.

false advertising   Description of property in a misleading fashion.

false presentation   An untrue representation deliberately made by a person who does so in order to deceive, thereby injuring another.

false return   Income tax return in which the information presented by the person making the return is entirely or in part false.

falsify   To counterfeit or forge; to tamper with any document in order to change the context.

falsity   An untrue statement.

family allowance   *finance*   An allowance out of the estate of a deceased person to be used for family expenses while the settlement of an estate is going on.

family brand   One brand name used for products made by the same firm, (e.g., Johnson & Johnson or General Electric).

family car doctrine   Doctrine resting on the theory that since parents furnish a car for the family's use, any family member who drives the car does so as the parents' agent in pursuance of the parents' business, so that if a family member inflicts injury by negligent operation of the car, the parents are held responsible.

family life cycle   Process of family formation and dissolution.   The stages include unmarried, young married couple with no children, young married couple with children, older married couple with dependent children, older married couple with no children at home, and solitary survivor.

family of funds   *investing*   A grouping of mutual funds managed by the same company and set up to meet the varied needs of investors, such as income, capital growth, tax-free income, etc.   The funds may either be load or no-load funds.

family partnership   Partnership which exists between members of a family, referring to an individual's spouse, ancestors, lineal descendants, and any trusts established primarily for the benefit of such persons.   If a partnership among family members is genuine, it will be taxed the same way as any other partnership and serve as an acceptable way to split income among family members.   There are usually no legal problems with a family partnership in which each of the family members who are partners contributes his or her own services or capital to the business.   Partnerships and S corporations both utilize the conduit approach to transfer income, deductions, and credits directly from the business to the personal returns of the owners.   To minimize taxation of closely held business profits, the high bracket owner might transfer ownership of a percentage of the partnership or S corporation to a family member. Thus, the proportionate income attributable to the new partner or shareholder's ownership percentage is shifted to the lower taxpayer's income. Therefore, the net wealth of the family increases at the expense of the loss of tax revenues to the government.

family S corporation An S corporation, the stock of which is held by family members. (See subchapter S corporation)

family settlement agreement Settlements made to shift property interests from one beneficiary to another. While such family agreements must have court approval, they may take place among family members without court supervision. They are often called favorites of the law, since little court time and expense is involved. The reasons for the shift can be many, ranging from personal concerns to the avoidance of taxes.

family trust Vehicle funded by income-producing property through which income may be split among family members. The income from the trust can be distributed in accordance with the directions of the grantor by means of the trust document. Therefore, the income is disbursed among many taxpayers instead of just one. However, the grantor may not retain too much power over the trust or it will be deemed a grantor trust and all the income will be taxable to the grantor. A family trust is particularly useful when the grantor would rather not divide an asset. It is also useful if minor children are the income recipients because the administrative problems of the guardianship are avoided. (See Appendix G, bypass trust)

Fannie Mae Nickname for Federal National Mortgage Association.

farm Tract of land held for the purpose of cultivation; sometimes used to denote land used for dairy, poultry raising, and such similar purposes. Originally, denoted an agricultural holding on a lease.

farmer Agriculturalist; a husbandman; a cultivator; one who owns and operates a farm. A farm is defined by the United States Census Bureau as a business that earns a thousand dollars or more per year from the sale of agricultural products.

Farmer's Home Administration (FmHA) Agency within the United States Department of Agriculture that administers assistance programs for purchasers of homes and farms in small towns and rural areas.

farming operation Agricultural property which may include farming, dairy farming, tillage of the soil, ranching, production or raising of crops, poultry, or livestock, and production of poultry or livestock products in an unmanufactured state.

farming property Agricultural property bought as an investment, especially by high-income persons who have no desire to live on the land. Normally, the land is leased out to tenants. The rent is business income, and the expenses are business expenses. There are also tax benefits which are not available to owners of raw land. Recently, much land has been bought on speculation related to the rapid inflation of a few years ago.

farming/ranching land Land suitable primarily for row cropping or grazing. Marketability differs from decade to decade, and liquidity would usually be low to moderate. Historically, such land has increased in value over time. (Caution should be exercised in such an investment.)

farm syndicate Purchasers of a cattle feeding operation (in a limited partnership), which prior to tax reform (mid-1970s) could profit by borrowing much of the money required to participate and then taking large tax deductions relative to the actual cash invested. Often nonrecourse notes were also used. At that time, the lack of at-risk rules made this a sought-after shelter. In form, today's farm syndicates are merely a rehash of the old multi-investor limited partnership cattle shelters. In substance, however, because of the mid-seventies reforms, they are mere ghosts of those earlier, popular tax bonanzas. (See Appendix G)

fashion goods *economics* Goods, the primary appeal of which is the frequent change in design or appearance.

favor To give support or to sustain; to aid; to show partiality or unfair bias towards.

favorable balance of trade Surplus

in a country's merchandise trade when exports during the year are greater than imports.

feasibility study Determination of the likelihood that a proposed development will fulfill the objectives of a particular investor.

feasible Capable of being accomplished.

featherbedding Coercing employers to hire union workers to perform unneeded or nonexistent jobs. This was outlawed by the Labor-Management Relations (Taft-Hartley) Act of 1947.

Federal Advisory Council Committee within the Federal Reserve System that advises the Board of Governors on important current developments. This group consists of one member (usually a banker) from each Federal Reserve district to be elected annually by the Board of Directors of each of the twelve Federal Reserve banks. They meet with the board to discuss business and financial conditions and to make advisory recommendations.

federal agency bonds Debt investments issued by agencies of the federal government.

federal agency securities *investing* Debt instruments issued by agencies of the federal government, such as the Federal National Mortgage Association, the Federal Farm Credit Bank, etc., which securities are not general obligations of the treasury of the United States, but which are considered low-risk securities because of their sponsorship by the federal government.

Federal Communications Commission (FCC) Independent federal agency that regulates radio and television broadcasting and interstate and foreign telephone and telegraph services. The seven members on the commission are appointed by the President to seven-year terms.

federal debt Total amount of government bonds and other securities which have been sold by the United States government to private individuals, businesses, and the Federal Reserve banks.

Federal Deposit Insurance Corporation (FDIC) Government agency that insures deposits up to a maximum amount per account in participating savings and commercial banks.

Federal Fair Housing Law Federal law that forbids discrimination on the basis of race, color, sex, religion, or national origin in the selling or renting of homes and apartments.

Federal Farm Credit Bank *finance* A financial institution sponsored by the federal government which consolidates the financing activities of the Federal Land Banks, the Federal Intermediate Credit Banks, and the Banks for Cooperatives.

Federal Financing Bank (FFB) *finance; investing* A special kind of bank established by the Federal Financing Bank Act (1973), the purpose of which is to coordinate the financing activities of federal agencies, whose obligations are guaranteed by the federal government.

federal funds market *finance; investing* The market among depository institutions for very short-term borrowing and lending of excess reserves in order to keep reserves at the required level.

federal funds rate *finance; investing* The rate of interest banks charge for excess reserves which are loaned, above that rate required by the Federal Reserve to those banks with deficient reserves.

Federal Home Loan Bank Board (FHLBB) Agency of the federal government that supervises all federal savings and loan associations and federally insured state-chartered savings and loan associations. The FHLBB also operates the Federal Savings and Loan Insurance Corporation, which insures accounts at federal savings and loan associations and those state-chartered associations that apply and are accepted. In addition, the FHLBB directs the Federal Home Loan Bank System, which provides a flexible credit facility for member savings institutions to promote the availability of home financing. The FHL banks also own the Federal Home Loan Mortgage Corporation, established in 1970 to promote secondary markets for mortgages.

Federal Home Loan Bank System Federally created banking system intended to assure liquidity to member savings and loan associations.

Federal Home Loan Mortgage Corporation (FHLMC) Government-sponsored corporation that was established to develop a secondary market in conventional residential mortgages. Its function is to buy mortgages from financial institutions that have deposits or accounts insured by a federal agency and then resell them in pools and by issuing notes and bonds which are publicly traded. Usually called "Freddie Mac," it was established to help maintain the availability of mortgage credit for residential homes. It purchases a large volume of conventional residential mortgages and sells them by means of mortgage-related investment instruments.

Federal Home Loan Mortgage Corporation (FHLMC) participation certificate *See* guaranteed mortgage certificate.

Federal Home Loan Mortgage Corporation (FHLMC) mortgage certificate *See* guaranteed mortgage certificate.

Federal Housing Administration (FHA) Agency within the United States Department of Housing and Urban Development that administers loan programs, loan guarantee programs, and loan insurance programs designed to make more housing available.

Federal Intermediate Credit Bank *finance* One of twelve banks that loan funds to production credit associations, commercial banks, agricultural credit corporations, livestock loan companies, etc., who make loans to farmers and ranchers.

federalism Relationship among the different levels of government (national, state, and local) in a system of federal government such as that in the United States. In a centralized federalism more of the functions are performed and more of the powers exercised by the highest level of government (the federal government in Washington) and in a decentralized federalism more of the power and functions are exercised at the lower levels of government (state and local).

federalists Political party formed in 1787 by Alexander Hamilton, John Jay, James Madison, and others. The party favored a strong, central (federal) government, and members wrote eighty-five articles setting forth their views and urging the ratification of the constitution.

Federal Land Bank *finance* One of

twelve banks working under the U.S. Farm Credit Administration that extend long-term loans to farmers and ranchers. To obtain a loan, a farmer must purchase stock in one of the more than five hundred local land bank associations to the extent of 5% of the loan.

federal margin call Broker's demand upon a customer for cash or securities needed to satisfy the required Regulation T down payment for a purchase or short sale of securities.

Federal National Mortgage Association (FNMA) Corporation that specializes in buying mortgage loans, mostly from mortgage bankers. It adds liquidity to the mortgage market. Nicknamed Fannie Mae, FNMA is owned by its stockholders, who elect ten of the Board of Directors. The United States president appoints the other five directors.

Federal Open Market Committee Committee consisting of the Federal Reserve Board of Governors and the presidents of five regional Federal Reserve banks that decides on the purchase or sale of government securities by the Federal Reserve to implement monetary policy. This is the most important policy-making body of the Federal Reserve System.

federal question *law* Legal issue which involves interpretation of the Constitution of the United States, statutes enacted by the U.S. Congress, or treaties. Jurisdiction of such matters is vested in federal courts.

Federal Register Daily publication containing executive orders and presidential promulgations as well as rules and regulations of the federal agencies.

Federal Reserve Act (1913) *banking* The federal law which brought into being the Federal Reserve Bank system of the United States.

Federal Reserve Bank One of the twelve banks (and branches) which make up the Federal Reserve System. Each serves as a "banker's bank" for the member banks in its district by acting as a source of credit and a depository of resources, and by performing other useful functions.

Federal Reserve Board of Governors Governing body of the Federal Reserve System consisting of seven members appointed by the President of the United States for fourteen-year terms, with terms arranged so that one expires every two years. Its primary duty is to supervise all operations of the Federal Reserve System including the Federal Reserve banks, the Open Market Committee, and the Federal Advisory Council. In addition, it sets current margin requirements, bank reserve requirements, the discount rate, and the execution of the open market operations.

Federal Reserve city *banking* A city that has a Federal Reserve Bank, or a Federal Reserve Branch Bank, located in it.

Federal Reserve currency *money; banking* Paper money circulated by the Federal Reserve Banking System which is legal tender and is used as a medium of exchange.

Federal Reserve district One of the twelve geographic subdivisions into which the Federal Reserve System is divided, with one primary Federal Reserve bank in each of the twelve districts. There may be one or more branches, depending upon the needs of the region.

Federal Reserve float Checkbook money that for a period of time appears on the books of both the payer and payee due to the lag in the collection process. Federal Reserve float often arises during the Federal Reserve's check collection process. In order to promote an efficient payments mechanism with certainty as to the date funds become available, the Federal Reserve has employed the policy of crediting the reserve accounts of depository institutions depositing checks according to an availability schedule before the Federal Reserve is able to obtain payment from others.

Federal Reserve note Paper money which makes up most of the currency in the United States.

Federal Reserve System (FRS; Fed) Central banking system of the United States; a system established by the Federal Reserve Act (1913) to issue paper currency, supervise the nation's banking system, and implement monetary policy. It is not owned by government, but by the member banks. The Fed does have the primary power over monetary policy in the U.S.,

however, and serves as a lender of last resort to the government and to member banks.

Federal Savings & Loan Association Member of the Federal Home Loan Bank System and the Federal Savings and Loan Insurance Corporation (a federally chartered savings and loan).

Federal Savings & Loan Insurance Corporation (FSLIC) Agency of the federal government that insures depositors in savings and loan associations against loss of principal. Most deposits, including passbooks and savings certificates, are insured up to a maximum amount per account.

Federal Trade Commission (FTC) Federal agency responsible for enforcement of antitrust laws in conjunction with the antitrust division of the Department of Justice. The FTC, with a five member governing board and national network of offices, attempts to counter deceptive actions and practices and anticompetitive behavior among businesses through regulations.

FedWire *finance; investing* A high-speed, computerized network that connects all twelve Federal Reserve Banks, their twenty-four branches, the Federal Reserve Board office in Washington, D.C., the U.S. Treasury offices in Washington and Chicago, and the Washington, D.C., office of the Commodity Credit Corporation.

fee A reward, compensation, or wage given to a person for performance of professional services.

fee absolute; fee simple *law; real estate* Absolute ownership of real property; the greatest estate that any person can have in land under the common law. The holder of an estate in fee simple has unconditional power of disposition and, upon the owner's death, the estate descends to the owner's heirs. Also called fee absolute or fee simple absolute.

fee simple defeasible *law* Type of property ownership in which the grant of title or duration of ownership is dependent on a specified condition.

fee structure Fees charged for getting into the tax shelter, no matter if done through a brokerage house, a promoter, or a salesperson.

feedback *communication* Verbal and visual responses to messages. Feedback is a self-monitoring response that allows individuals to modify their behavior until their expectations are met. Feedback is also the only way a person can know whether messages sent are interpreted as intended.

feme *A woman.*

feme covert *law A married woman.*

feme sole *law A woman alone.* Divorcee, widow, or unmarried woman.

fence Colloquially, a receiver of stolen goods who disposes of the goods for profit.

feoffment *law* The conveying by gift of the fee simple title in land.

ferry Place of transit across a stretch of water, such as a river, lake, or arm of the sea.

feudalism *economics* An ancient form of government and the economic system thereof which came into being after the dissolution of the Roman Empire. There was a strong central government, usually with a system of feudal lordships reigning under the auspices of a king or central ruler. The land was held by the lords and worked by the subjects of the lord. There was little private ownership of real property as we now know it, but sometimes the subjects were permitted to use small plots of land for their own use, and a part of the produce from it went to the lord as rent.

fiat *Let it be done.* Decree; an authority issuing from some competent source of the doing of some legal act. In English law refers to a short order or warrant of some judge or public officer making out and allowing certain processes. (*See* fiat money)

fiat money Paper money issued by governments or central banks which is not backed by or convertible into anything, but is money because the government declares it to be legal tender.

fictio *A fiction;* a legal fiction.

fictitious payee Nonexistent or fictitious person who, although named on a bill of exchange as payee, has no right to it, and the maker does not intend that such payee shall take anything by it.

fidelity bond 1. Guarantee of a person's honesty furnishing indemnity against embezzlement or negligence. 2. An assurance, generally purchased by an employer, to cover employees who are entrusted with valuable property or funds. 3. Bonds that guarantee the principal's honesty.

fides *Faith;* trust; confidence, honesty.

fiducia *law* One form of mortgage or pledge whereby property was transferred from the debtor to the creditor with an implied understanding that upon the repayment of the debt it will be retransferred back to the debtor.

fiduciary 1. Of the nature of trust; having the characteristics of a trust; related to or grounded upon trust or confidence. 2. A person holding the character of a trustee or a character analogous to that of a trustee, derived from Roman law. 3. A person who acts for or handles the money or property of another in a capacity that involves a confidence or trust. 4. *insurance* Position of trust whereby an individual or a corporation handles business deals and money on behalf of another person(s).

fiduciary money *economics; finance* Paper money which is legal tender in a country and is convertible in gold and silver. However, the paper money is not fully backed by a commodity, thus the simultaneous conversion of all paper money into a commodity would be impossible. Faith in the system is thus required to make the monetary system function.

field supervisor *insurance* Salaried employee of an insurance company who covers a prescribed territory for the company to encourage sales through existing agents, appoint and train new agents, and otherwise promote the interests of the company in that area.

field warehousing *finance; marketing* A method by which a business firm finances inventory. The inventory is placed in the custody of a lender's agent in a warehouse near the business firm. The inventory becomes the collateral for the loan. As the inventory is sold the funds are transferred to the lender.

fieri facias; fi fa *law That you cause to be made.* A writ of execution levied on the lands, tenements, goods, and chattels of a judgment debtor.

figure of merit *investing* A number which summarizes the investment worth of a project.

filiatio non potest probari Doctrine that evidence to show that a person is the child of his or her mother's husband is inadmissable, for the law will presume the husband to be the father if the child is born during coverture.

filing and hoping Action by a banker who fails to adequately review reports on a loan's collateralized inventory and receivables. So called because the lender simply files the loan and hopes for the best.

filius *Son; a child.*

filius nullius *Illegitimate child.*

filtering down Process whereby over time a housing unit or neighborhood is occupied by progressively lower income residents.

filter system *investing* A theory of investing that recommends an investor buy stock when it moves up a few percentage points from its low, and sell when it moves down a few percentage points from a subsequent high.

filum aquae Middle line of a stream or body of water.

final equation *economics* Essentially a difference equation, in one endogenous variable expressing the current value of that variable as a function of a number of the lagged values and of parameters, exogenous variables and disturbances.

final prospectus Stock or bond prospectus issued after the new issue has been approved by the Securities and Exchange Commission which is almost a duplicate of the original prospectus. The red lettering on the original (making it known as a red herring) is listed along with financial information on the company made available since the original prospectus.

finance 1. To provide capital or loan money as needed. 2. To borrow money to buy property.

finance charge 1. Cost of a loan in dollars and cents as required by the Truth in Lending Act. 2. A service agreement or membership fee imposed as a condition before credit is extended; the charge must be payable directly or indirectly by the person to whom credit is extended. If the charge is paid solely by the creditor and absorbed as a cost of doing business it is not a finance charge.

finance company *finance* A company engaged in making loans to individuals or businesses. Although most loans are individual, and relatively small, some large finance companies make large loans to businesses. Finance companies do not accept deposits, but are capitalized by borrowings from banks, and other money market services. The rates of interest charged tend to be higher than market, because sometimes the risks are greater than with conventional loans.

Financial Accounting Standards Board (FASB) *accounting* A private, nongovernmental, organization that sets standards for financial accounting.

financial flexibility Ability to raise sufficient capital to meet company need under a wide variety of future contingencies.

financial institution Institution that uses its funds chiefly to purchase financial assets (deposits, loans, securities) as opposed to tangible property. Financial institutions can be classified according to the nature of the principal claims they issue: nondeposit intermediaries include life and property/casualty insurance companies and pension funds, whose claims are the policies they sell or the promise to provide income after retirement; depository intermediaries obtain funds mainly by accepting deposits from the public. The major depository institutions are commercial banks, savings and loan associations, mutual savings banks, credit unions, and thrift institutions. Although historically they have specialized in certain types of credit, the powers of nonbank depository institutions have been broadened in recent years. For example, NOW accounts, credit union share drafts, and other services similar to checking accounts may be offered by thrift institutions. (*See* commercial bank, savings and loan association, mutual savings bank, credit union, thrift institution)

financial intermediaries 1. Nonbank saving and lending institutions such as savings and loan associations, insurance companies, personal finance companies, and credit unions. These organizations do not create demand deposits, but have large volumes of savings that they invest or lend to the public. Hence they may sometimes help to offset restrictive monetary policies which the Federal Reserve authorities are pursuing. 2. Financial institutions which receive deposits from savers

119

(investors) and facilitate getting these funds into the hands of those individuals or companies that want to borrow.

financial leverage   1. Use of borrowed funds to acquire an asset; the use of debt financing.   2. A financial structure having a large amount of debt and a relatively small amount of common stock equity.   3. Use of debt to increase the expected return and the risk to equity. (*See* operating leverage)

financial mania   Obsession or unreasonable fear about risks which play a role in why and how one invests in securities.

financial planning   *finance*   The development and implementation of coordinate plans through which one seeks to achieve lifetime overall financial objectives.

financial pyramid   *finance*   A graphic presentation of an investment portfolio showing the value of the portfolio invested in high-risk, medium-risk, and low-risk securities. Normally, the low-risk securities provide the base for the pyramid, with the risk factor increasing toward the peak.

financial responsibility laws   *insurance*   Laws providing that all drivers and owners involved in an accident causing a given amount of property damage or any bodily injury must immediately post security to guarantee judgments that could arise.

financial risk   1. Risk associated with the mix of debt and equity used to finance a firm or property. The larger the proportion of debt used, the greater its financial risk. (A firm with no debt financing has no financial risk.)   2. The risk associated with a firm's sources of finance.   3. Risk taken when the individual buys many types of debt or equity instruments. Risk that the company issuing the instruments may suffer financial hardships and be unable to pay the sums the investor had expected; firm in which one holds stock might do the same, or merely suffer hard times when dividends are not paid.   4. *finance; investing*   Risk distinguishable from interest rate risk and purchasing power risk in that it denotes a risk of the default of the security in performing the normal obligations of a security which are a return of principal and interest earned on the prin-

cipal. (*See* interest rate risk, purchasing power risk)

financial statement   Written record of the financial condition of an individual, business, or association. Normally it will contain both a balance sheet and a profit and loss statement, and possibly include written notes on substantive changes in financial condition from the time of the last report.

financial suitability   *limited partnerships*   Requirement of sophisticated investors to have a certain minimum net worth and be in a high tax bracket, often 50%. The standards vary from state to state. The net worth requirement is to make sure one can afford to lose the money if the deal goes under. (*See* Appendix G)

financial supermarket   *finance*   Companies, often nonfinancial companies, which offer a wide array of financial services under one roof. (Sears is a prime example.) Some people believe that the financial supermarket is the wave of the future, and that conventional financial institutions will also become supermarkets.

financing fee   Fee including costs incurred in securing the construction loan, brokerage fees, and appraisal fees which are amortized over the life of the loan.

finder's fee   Money paid to someone other than a broker who locates suitable property or a purchaser. Prohibited or limited in most states.

finite elasticity   *See* perfect elasticity.

finite real estate investment trust (FRIET)   *investing; real estate*   A real estate investment trust that pledges to sell its holdings after a certain period of time to realize capital gains.

firm   1. Style or title under which one or more persons carry on business.   2. The partnership itself; i.e., the individual members forming the partnership. Although commercially a firm is treated as though it is a separate legal entity, strictly, it is not. For the sake of convenience, rules of practice may permit a firm to sue or to be sued in the firm name.

firm foundation theory   *investing*   A theory that insists that each investment instrument, whether a share of common stock or a piece of real estate, has a firm intrinsic value. When prices fall below this value, it is time to buy, and when they go above this value, it is time to sell.

first devisee *estate planning* First person who is to receive an estate devised by will. (*See* next devisee)

first index investment fund A mutual fund that is internally managed and that invests in stocks of the Standard and Poor's 500 stock index purchased in the same proportion as their weight in the index. Each investor in this fund shares proportionately in the net income and in the gains and losses in the portfolio.

first-in, first-out (FIFO) Method of inventory accounting in which the oldest item in inventory is assumed to be sold first. (*See* last-in, first-out)

first mortgage *finance* Mortgage that has priority as a lien over all other mortgages against a specific property, and, in cases of foreclosure, will be satisfied before other mortgages.

fiscal agency services Services performed by the Federal Reserve banks for the United States government, including maintaining deposit accounts for the Treasury and issuing and redeeming savings bonds and other government securities.

fiscal dividend Disbursement of accumulated budgetary surpluses by the federal government to society, thereby offsetting the effect of fiscal drag. The fiscal dividend may consist of increased federal spending on public goods, reduced taxes on the private sector, and larger grants-in-aid to state and local governments. Any of these would help stimulate further consumption and investment expenditures.

fiscal drag 1. Tendency of a high-employment economy to be held back from its full growth potential because of incurring budgetary surpluses. Such surpluses may arise because a progressive tax system tends to generate increases in revenues relative to expenditures during periods of high employment. 2. *economics* The time lag between the start of a specific fiscal policy of government before it begins to show results in current economic events.

fiscal federalism Tax collection and disbursement of funds by a higher level of government to lower jurisdictions.

fiscalist Economist or other person who believes that the use of fiscal policy is the way to achieve equilibrium in the economy.

fiscal monopoly *economics* A somewhat antiquated term denoting the monopolization by a government of the manufacture and/or sale of certain commodities in order to get the profits from sales for government. Some commodities so used in the past are tobacco, salt, camphor, spices, etc.

fiscal policy 1. Taxation, expenditures, and debt management of the federal government. 2. Adjusting government expenditures and taxes to try to stabilize the economy and overcome inflation and/or unemployment.

fiscal year 1. Twelve-month time interval used for financial reporting; the period starts on any date after January 1 and ends one year later. 2. Year by or for which accounts are reckoned, or year between one annual settlement or balancing of accounts and another.

Fisher effect *finance* A theory named for economist Irving Fisher which states that the nominal rate of interest should approximately equal the real rate of interest plus a premium for expected inflation. (*See* real amount, nominal amount, real rate of interest, nominal rate of interest)

Fitch Investors Service, Inc. *finance; investing* A rating service which has bases in New York and Denver and specializes in rating commercial and municipal bonds, preferred stock, commercial paper, and obligations of health-care and not-for-profit institutions.

fixed amount annuity Annuity which specifies the amount of each periodic payment.

fixed amount option *insurance* Option that provides a stated amount of income each month until the proceeds are exhausted. (E.g., the insured or beneficiary may desire that the proceeds be paid at a rate of five hundred dollars a month for as long as the proceeds last.) (*See* settlement option)

fixed asset 1. Real estate, machinery, and other asset on which immediate liquidity is unlikely. 2. Asset essential to the undertaking or proper operation of business.

fixed asset turnover   Ratio of sales to fixed assets; tells the amount of fixed assets necessary to generate sales.

fixed budget   *accounting* A budget predicted on a fixed level of business activity, whether by units produced, units sold, or whatever.

fixed capital   Cost of total plant and general equipment.

fixed cost   1. Any cost which does not vary with changes in volume over the observation period.   2. Cost of production that does not change as output is increased or decreased in the short run.

fixed dollar investments   Investment which has a constant rate of return.

fixed exchange rates   Currency exchange rates legally set by the respective countries.

fixed income security   Security which promises an unvarying payment stream to holders over its life (e.g., a savings account, certificate of deposit, or corporate bond).

fixed period annuity   Annuity which specifies the number of periods it will be paid.

fixed period option   Option, similar to the fixed amount option, in which the period the payments are made is fixed and amount of each monthly installment varies accordingly. (*See* settlement option)

fixed prices   Agreed or set price, sometimes unlawful.

fixed rate   Traditional approach to determine the finance charge payable on a credit extension where a predetermined, specific interest rate is applied to the principal.

fixture   *real estate; law* Personal property affixed to realty in such a way as to become a part of it and to pass to a grantee when the realty is transferred, e.g., bathroom fixtures. The test of determination is the intention of the person affixing it. That is determined, in the absence of direct evidence, by the physical difficulty of removal, custom, the nature of the fixture in connection with the tenure of the occupant, the intention of the annexing party, and the degree and the object of the annexation. Even articles no further attached to the land than by their own weight may become fixtures if the circumstances are such as to show that they were intended to be part of the land.

flag   *investing* A technical pattern chart that resembles a flag, with the two masts being the two sides of the chart, i.e., a parallelogram. The chart which represents a daily recording of a stock price, or a stock index, may contain an indication of a period of consolidation within a trend. If that consolidation was preceded by a rise, the rise is liable to continue after the consolidation. If the period was preceded by a fall, the fall is likely to continue after the period is over.

flash   *investing* A signal on a market tape indicating that the tape is five or more minutes behind regular trading, because of the volume of trades. The flash will interrupt the regular tape display to show the price of a specific stock which is being heavily traded.

flat   Describes a bond upon which no interest is presently being paid.

flat cancellation   *insurance* The cancellation of a policy as of its effective date without a premium charge.

flat market   *investing* A market which is represented by a trend line that is nearly horizontal. This is often the result of very slow activity; however, a stable period or a period of consolidation may result in a flat market regardless of the activity.

flat tax   A proposed income tax plan that would tax all levels of income at the same rate. Those who favor such a plan oppose the progressive rate, saying that it tends to inhibit the incentive to earn and may inhibit the ability to save. The simplicity of a flat tax also makes it acceptable to some. Opponents of the flat tax say that it is really a regressive tax in that it puts more of a real burden on lower income earners. In some such proposed plans, lower income earners are excused from paying any income tax at all. The 1986 Tax Reform Act, which limited income tax brackets to three, is considered one step toward a flat tax.

flat yield curve   *finance; investing* A graphic presentation revealing that interest rates on long-term maturities are essentially equal to rates on short-term maturities.

fleet policy   *insurance* An auto liability policy issued by one insurer and covering all vehicles owned by the insured.

flexible benefit plan   *See* cafeteria plan.

flexible budget   *accounting* A budget developed to show revenue and expense levels at various levels of business activity.

flexible compensation plan   *See* cafeteria plan.

flexible past service liability   *profit sharing* Plan that assumes that the money-purchase plan has always been in force for the purpose of rewarding long-term employees. Applying the plan's contribution formula to average compensation for the number of years of an employee's past service yields a special "pot" for each participant. Under the money-purchase plan approach this pot can be amortized over anywhere from ten years to the number of years remaining until the employee's retirement. The annual amortization is subject to the discretion of the employer. Therein lies the flexibility with this approach. In a good year the employer can make contributions for current compensation plus a large amount (based on the most rapid amortization—ten years) for past service. In years the company is experiencing poor profits, the payments made to the plan may be low or nonexistent.

flexible payment mortgage (FPM) Home-purchase loan plan that allows the borrower to pay interest only for the first several years of the term. FPMs were authorized by the Federal Home Loan Bank Board in 1974 with two restrictions: monthly payments must be sufficient to cover interest, and after five years payments must be sufficient to amortize the principal over the remaining term.

flexible premium payments   *insurance* Premiums allowing the policyholder to determine when and in what amounts payments are to be made (a component of universal life). The policyholder can choose to pay for the cost of a lifetime of insurance with a single payment, payments for five years, ten years, or whatever payment schedule the policyholder chooses. Premiums may be made at differing intervals of time or stopped temporarily and resumed later. This type of payment pattern does not initiate a policy loan. The only limitation placed on these flexible payments is that the premium be sufficient to cover the next month's insurance protection.

flexible working hours; flextime *economics; management* A system under which an employee works a given number of hours per day, but not necessarily consecutive hours, and often hours which best meet the needs of the employee. (While this plan is being experimented with all over the world, there is no evidence as yet that it is a viable concept for many industries.)

floater policy   *insurance* A policy designed to cover property for all risks regardless of the location of the property at the time of the loss.

floating charge   Form of charge, mortgage, or pledge on the assets of a business, present and future, but which allows the charger to deal with the assets in the usual course of business until the chargee intervenes when the charge is said to be crystallized. When that occurs, the charge attaches and is enforceable against all the assets of the business then available.

floating exchange rates   Exchange rate between the monies of different nations which are allowed to move up or down in response to supply and demand conditions in the foreign exchange markets.

floating notes   Notes on which the interest rate varies, often with stated limitations regarding the minimum rate of interest that will be paid for the duration of the notes.

floodplain   Level land area subject to periodic flooding from a contiguous body of water. Floodplains are delineated by the expected frequency of flooding (e.g., an annual floodplain is expected to flood once each year).

floor broker   *investing* A member of the stock exchange who executes orders on the floor of the exchange.

floor plan rule   Rule stating that when a dealer in new automobiles has stock encumbered with a mortgage (a floor plan mortgage), such a mortgage is void as against a bona fide purchaser without notice. This is based on the theory that, notwithstanding the conditions of the mortgage and its record, an inference of apparent authority in the dealer to sell arises from the fact of the dealer's permission to exhibit the property, precluding the mortgagee from asserting the mortgage against such a person.

floor trader   *See* registered competitive trader.

flotation cost   *finance* The cost to a corporation of issuing new stocks or bonds. These cost include legal fees and advice, printing, etc., in preparing for the issue, and the costs of underwriters who sell the issue. Underwriter's costs will vary according the the the worth of the issue.

flowage   Natural flow of water from an upper estate to a lower one.

flow of funds   *economics; finance* In economics the term is used to describe the transfer of funds from an agency with a surplus to an agency with a deficit. In finance, regarding municipal bonds, it is a statement in the bond resolution showing how priorities will be applied to the revenue of the municipality.

foemina viro co-operta   *A married woman.*

foenus   Interest on money lent.

Follett, Mary Parker (1868–1933)   *management* A social worker born in the United States, who became a specialist in management, focusing on vocational guidance and leadership qualities. She was among the first to focus attention on personal and group relationships.

Food and Drug Administration (FDA)   Agency within the United States Health and Human Services Department, created by the Food and Drug Act of 1906, which is responsible for the protection of the public from health hazards posed by harmful or mislabeled foods, cosmetics, medical devices, and drugs. The FDA tests products prior to approval and distribution and licenses biological product manufacturers.

food stamps   Certificates issued by the U.S. government to low-income households to be used in place of money to purchase food items.

footing   *accounting* The total of both sides of an account, giving a net increase or decrease, called the balance of the account.

Forbes 500   *finance* A special annual edition of *Forbes* magazine which lists the five hundred largest U.S. companies, with the companies ranked by sales, assets, profits, and market value.

force conversion   To force owners of a convertible security to convert by calling a security at a time when its call price is below its conversion value. (*See* call provision, convertible security)

forced heirs   Descendants or ascendants whose rights to a fixed portion of a person's estate cannot be denied without a plausible reason to disinherit.

forced sale   Sale by compulsion on the part of either the seller or buyer.

forced saving   Situation in which consumers are prevented from spending part of their income on consumption (e.g., prices rising faster than money wages, causing a decrease in real consumption and hence an increase in forced saving; a corporation which plows back some of its profit instead of distributing it as dividend income to stockholders; or a government which taxes its citizens and uses the funds, thereby preventing the public from utilizing a portion of its income for the purchase of consumer goods).

forcible detainer   *law* Refusal to restore another's goods after sufficient amends tendered, the original taking having been lawful.

forcible entry   *law* Offense of entering any land or tenements in a violent manner in order to take possession thereof, whether the violence consists in actual force applied to any person, in threats, or in breaking into any building.

forcing conversion   *investing* The strategy a firm uses to force owners of a convertible security to convert by calling the security at a time when its call price is below the conversion value. (Cf. call provision, convertible security)

forecasting   *economics; marketing; statistics* Anticipating future events on the basis of historical data, including past events, current events, and the probability of events in the future. Some methods used are moving averages, regression analysis, and operational research.

foreclosure   1. Any one of several methods used in various states to enforce payment of a debt secured by a mortgage by taking and selling the mortgaged property. This is a remedy available to a mortgagee when the mortgagor commits a default under the terms of the mortgage.   2. A termination of all rights of a mortgagor or the grantee in the property covered by the mortgage. Statutory foreclosure is effected without recourse to courts, but must conform to laws. Strict foreclosure forever bars equity of redemption.

foreign   Belonging to another nation, country, or jurisdiction.

foreign corporation   *economics* A corporation which is chartered in a state other than that in which it is doing business.

foreign exchange   1. Instruments used for international payments consisting not only of currency, but also of checks, drafts, and bills of exchange (which are orders to pay currency). 2. The money of any other country. (E.g., to exchange dollars for Mexican pesos is to buy foreign exchange.)

foreign exchange desk   Trading desk at the New York Federal Reserve Bank. The desk undertakes operations in the exchange markets for the account of the Federal Open Market Committee and as agent for the United States Treasury and foreign central banks.

foreign exchange market   Set of institutions, including large banks, private brokers, and government central banks, that deal in the exchange of one country's money for another.

foreign exchange transactions Purchase or sale of the currency of one nation with that of another. Foreign exchange rates refer to the number of units of one currency needed to purchase one unit of another, or the value of one currency in terms of another.

foreign market   *marketing* Places in foreign country which may be prospective market for goods or services produced in one's home country. Business firms often erroneously assume that other countries are so different from theirs that the people would not be interested in their products. While many market studies place emphasis upon the differences in people in different parts of the world, in marketing it is wise to explore the many ways in which people all over the world are alike.

foreign-trade multiplier   *economics* Principle which states that fluctuations in exports or imports may generate large variations in national income. It is based on the idea that a change in exports relative to imports has the same multiplier effect on national income as a change in autonomous expenditures; similarly, a change in imports relative to exports has the same multiplier effect on national income as a change in withdrawals from the income stream. (This is analogous to the concept of the investment multiplier.) In general, an increase in exports tends to raise domestic income, and the money received will be spent on domestic goods which will demand greater domestic investment in capital goods and greater production. The increased income also induces some imports which act as leakages tending to reduce the full multiplier effect that would exist if imports remained constant.

foreseeable   Reasonably anticipated.

forfeit   To surrender to an individual or the state money, property, a right, or a privilege because of a fault, omission, misconduct, or crime.

forfeiture   1. Loss of right, property, benefit, or privilege by a person as a result of having committed a crime or breached some legal obligation imposed on the person. 2. Loss of money or anything else of value because of failure to perform under contract. 3. *pension plans* Division on a pro rata basis of the remainder in an employee's account to other participants active in a plan, after the termination of an employee for whom contributions have been made, but who has qualified for only partial or no vesting. Such forfeitures can add up to a considerable amount over the years, especially when the company has a high turnover of employees.

forge   To counterfeit or falsify by imitation; to fabricate a written instrument with the intention of substituting the false for the genuine or of deceiving or defrauding the public.

forisfactum   Forfeiture of goods.

form   *law* Technical manner or order to be observed in legal documents or proceedings; the requirements that a document has to meet to satisfy law as distinct from its substance.

125

forma *Form.*

formal communications network
Network where messages flow along the official paths prescribed by the organization's chain of command.

forma legalis forma essentialis
Legal form is essential form. Law is not concerned merely with the letter of a statute but also with its essentials.

formal pension plan Plan which defines the rights and benefits of the employees in advance, setting forth eligibility standards for participation in the plan and for the receipt of benefits. It also establishes a formula for determining the amount of pension and other benefits under the plan. Pension plans today generally are formal plans.

forms of action *law* Division of personal actions under common law into several categories, such as trover, trespass, assumpsit, or debts. Each has its own strict requirements in the matter of pleading and evidence, and a case could be lost simply because the plaintiff chose a form of action inapplicable to the plaintiff's cause.

form 1040 Basic individual Internal Revenue Service tax return form.

form 1065 Internal Revenue Service form for return of partnership income.

form utility Utility created when raw materials are converted into finished products.

forthwith *law* In a statute, within a reasonable time in view of the circumstances of the case and subject matter.

Fortune 500 *finance* An annual special issue of *Fortune* magazine which lists the five hundred largest industrial (manufacturing) corporations, as ranked by sales. Other rankings are made by assets, net income, stockholder's equity, earnings per share, and total return to investors.

Fortune Service 500 Special edition of *Fortune* magazine which lists the top five hundred nonmanufacturing companies. This group of five hundred is broken down into categories such as commercial banking, diversified service, diversified financial, life insurance, retailing, transportation and utilities.

forum non conveniens Principle that venue or place where an action is to be tried may be changed to another by court order if it appears that the place chosen by the plaintiff is not convenient to the litigants and the witnesses and if in the interest of justice the venue should be changed. A decision relating to change of venue is dependent upon various factors such as the ease of access to sources of proof, the residence of witnesses, and/or the cost of compelling their attendance at another place.

forum originis The court of the place of a person's domicile by birth.

forward integration *economics* A situation in which a manufacturer will take over wholesale or retail outlets in an endeavor to assure future outlets for goods, as well as the opportunity to expand the manufacturer's markets.

for-whom question, the *economics* Deciding which members of society will receive how much of the goods and services produced; the process of allocating income.

foster child Child brought up by someone other than parents.

foster parent One who brings up the child of another as one's own.

four corners *law* The face of a written instrument.

Fourth World Poorest countries of the underdeveloped regions characterized by the lack of intensive growth and valuable export resources.

fractional interest rule Internal Revenue Service Code Section 2040(b) that establishes that only 50% of the value of jointly owned personal and real property held by spouses in joint tenancy with right of survivorship or as tenants by the entirety will be included in the estate of the first spouse to die regardless of the consideration furnished by each spouse.

fractional money *finance; economics* Coins of a value smaller than the nominal monetary unit. In the U.S., these include the half-dollar, quarter, dime, nickel, and penny; in England, the shilling, penny, and half-penny.

frame of reference *communication* Point of view determined by one's educational background, race, sex, home environment, attitudes, personality, past experiences, etc.

franchise License granted by the

owner(s) of a company name to others who have paid a fee for doing business under the copyrighted name. In commercial usage, denotes some right, privilege, license, or monopoly granted to a person called the franchise holder to enable that person to carry on some business. It is, in this context, created by contract between parties.

franchise health insurance Insurance designed primarily for small groups unacceptable to most group insurers. Premiums are less than individual policies, but more than group plans. Also called wholesale health insurance.

franchise life insurance Policies which adopt some group insurance principles to cover groups ineligible for true group insurance. No master policy is issued; participants receive individual policies after application has been approved. (Normally used by a small firm with ten or fewer employees.) Also called wholesale life insurance.

franchise tax *economics; finance* A state tax, usually regressive, imposed on a state-chartered corporation for the right to do business under its corporate name. Franchise taxes are usually based on a number of different characteristics of the corporation, such as capital stock, capital stock plus surplus, or profits.

franking *economics; government* The privilege of the free use of the mails as granted to Congressmen and to federal agencies.

frater *Brother.*

fraternal insurance Plan organized under a state's insurance code related to social organizations, usually a lodge system, that provide insurance benefits for members.

fraud Infraction of the rules of fair dealing. Intentional deception in order to cause another person to suffer loss.

fraud in execution Misrepresentation of the contents of a document which one is induced to sign thinking it to be other than what it is. In such a case there is no contract.

fraudulent conveyance Transfer made by a debtor with intent to hinder, delay, or defraud creditors by placing the debtor's own property beyond a creditor's reach; transfer is characterized by lack of fair and valuable consideration.

fraudulent preference *law* Law discouraging debtors, on the eve of bankruptcy, from making a voluntary distribution of their assets in contravention of the provisions of bankruptcy laws providing for orderly distribution without any preference shown to one creditor as against another.

fraus est celare fraudem *It is a fraud to conceal a fraud.*

fraus legis *A fraud upon law (i.e., bringing a fraudulent suit).*

Freddie Mac Nickname for Federal Home Loan Mortgage Corporation.

free alongside (F.A.S.) *economics* Agreement in which the seller must deliver goods alongside a ship with all charges included in the sales price. From that point the buyer is responsible for any loss and for loading on the ship.

free and clear Phrase used to describe title to property when it is not encumbered by any liens, mortgages, charges, etc.

free and open market *economics* A market in which the price is determined by the laws of supply and demand and the interaction between the two.

Freedom Share *investing* A nonmarketable U.S. Treasury note which has not been issued since 1970, but which has outstanding obligations until 1994.

free enterprise An economic system based on the competition of business firms privately owned and operated for profit. Under a free enterprise system most goods and services are provided by the private sector.

free goods 1. Product free of charge and available to anyone who desires it. 2. A product for which the market price is zero at a particular time and place. 3. Goods furnished by nature freely without human effort because of their abundance (e.g., air and, formerly, water). Somewhat antiquated usage.

freehold *law* Estate in land of indeterminate duration. It may be one of inheritance (i.e., in fee simple), or not of inheritance but of life. An estate held by free tenure as distinguished from copyhold or villenage. It was originally an estate held by a free man, as opposed to villenage.

freely fluctuating exchange rates Exchange rate system by which the relative values of different currencies are determined by supply and demand rather than by government fiat.

freeman Person possessed of all the civil and political rights accorded to people under a free government. In the feudal system, the term denoted a proprietor as distinguished from a vassal or feudal tenant.

free of all average (FAA) Describes insurance is against total loss only.

free on board (f.o.b.) *economics* A term used in quoting prices for both foreign and domestic shipments and meant to indicate that all charges are paid including the delivery of the goods on board the ship, or loaded on the truck or railcar. The term may denote delivered charges either at the point of origin or destination.

free on board (f.o.b.) plant— freight allowed *See* freight absorption.

free trade International trade that is unrestricted by government protectionist measures.

free-trade area Association of trading nations whose participants agree to impose no restrictive tariffs or quotas on one another, but are free to impose whatever restrictive devices they wish on non-participants (e.g., the European Free Trade Association).

freight *marine law* Charges paid for the carriage of goods by sea from port to port. Normally it becomes payable once the voyage is completed and the goods are carried to their destination. If the consignee accepts the goods at an intermediary port voluntarily, then freight is payable for that part of the voyage that has actually been performed.

freight absorption Pricing system by which the seller permits the buyer to subtract transportation charges from the bill. Also known as free on board (f.o.b.) plant—freight allowed.

freight forwarder Wholesaling middleman who consolidates shipments of several shippers to enable them to achieve the cost savings of truckload or carload shipments. (Usually pertains to foreign trade.)

frequency curve *statistics* A curve on a graph depicting the frequency count on the "Y" axis and the magnitude on the "X" axis, connecting the plotted points of a frequency distribution.

frequency distribution *statistics* A method of classifying data showing the number of items having the same value.

frequency polygon *statistics* A graphic line presentation based on a specific distribution and essentially showing the same thing one sees on a histogram. While the histogram is a bar-chart of the distributions, the polygon is a line graph drawn to the mid-points of the values in the distribution. (*See* histogram.)

frictional unemployment *economics* 1. Unemployment which is caused by the temporary lack of a balance between supply and demand of the product being produced by specific labor. (E.g., when the temporary demand for autos is less than the supply, plants may have to close for a short time until some balance is achieved.) 2. Lack of work that occurs from time lost changing jobs (not considered as real unemployment).

fringe benefits Nonwage returns to workers for labor services; includes retirement benefits, health care, time off with pay for holidays, vacations, sick leave, and similar benefits.

frontage Property line immediately abutting a street or highway.

front-end fees *limited partnerships* Payment charged when a business is set up and the investment is made. Made up of two parts: reimbursement of the promoter for out-of-pocket expense in setting up the deal and payment of profits to promoters.

front foot Standard measurement of land, applied at the frontage of the street line. Used for cost of generally uniform depth in downtown acres.

front money Cash necessary to start a development project.

frozen account 1. *banking* An account from which funds cannot be withdrawn by the owner due to a lien against it. Usually, a court order is required to free the funds. 2. *investing* A brokerage account which may be under disciplinary action for violation of Regulation T. Usually the account is frozen for ninety days, and is often the result of freeriding.

frozen convertible *investing* Convertible security which has been outstanding for several years and which cannot be forced to convert because its conversion value is below its call price. Also called hung convertible. (Cf. forcing conversion)

fructus *Fruits,* produce, profit.

fructus industriales *The profits or fruits of industry,* as distinct from fructus naturales (e.g., crops grown as a result of human labor).

fructus naturales *Produce that occurs naturally* (e.g., grass, milk, minerals, etc.).

frustration *law* Unforeseen termination of a contract or the prevention of its performance by reason of the destruction of the subject matter of the contract or by reason of the impossibility or impracticability of its performance.

frustrum terrae *A parcel of land.*

full age Age of majority or legal maturity.

full-bodied money *money; banking* Currency which is made from material which is as valuable as the face value of the money (e.g., a fifty-dollar gold piece which contains fifty dollars worth of gold).

full-cost broker *investing* A sales agent for a brokerage firm who advises clients on investments, and who arranges the purchase and sale of securities for the client. The agent usually works on a commission basis, and the commission may be from 50% to 70% more than a discount broker.

full disclosure Revelation of all information pertinent to a transaction.

full disclosure requirements Obligation to provide all terms and components of an agreement, policy, or other transaction in readable and understandable prose before policyholder, consumer, or other party agrees to and signs such transaction. This requirement holds, for example, for universal life policies.

full employment Situation in which everyone who desires a job can find one without unreasonable difficulty and at prevailing rates of pay. Does not denote a situation in which all employable people in the economy are employed at a specific time, since there is constant frictional unemployment such as during labor strikes, etc.; a figure of about 4–5% of the labor force unemployed is usually considered to be full employment.

Full Employment and Balanced Growth Act (1978) Federal law enacted by Congress setting forth national goals for employment, economic growth, and development.

full faith and credit *law* Requirement of the U.S. Constitution that a state accord the judgment of a court of another state the same credit that it is entitled to in the courts of that state.

full-function merchant wholesaler Wholesaling middleman who provides a complete assortment of services for retail customers, including storage, regular contacts through a sales force, delivery, credit, returns privileges, and market information.

full-line forcing *marketing* The practice of a manufacturer or wholesaler of requiring a buyer to purchase all items in a line as a prerequisite for getting a specific item in the line which the purchaser wants.

fully funded pension plan Plan in which the employer puts away enough each year to fund the accruing pension liability for the current service of covered employees, and in addition accumulates sufficient assets to offset the initial past-service liability (pension credits earned before the plan was installed). (*See* funded pension plan)

fully insured *social security* 1. Having worked and paid into the social security system for forty quarters (a total of ten years in covered work). Once a person has acquired forty quarters of coverage, the person is fully insured for life, even if that person spends no further time in covered employment or covered self-employment. (Quarters or years of covered work do not need to be successive.) 2. Having both (a) at least six quarters of coverage and (b) at least as many quarters of coverage as there are years elapsing after 1950 (or, if later, after the year in which one reaches age twenty-one) and before the year in which one dies, becomes disabled, or reaches age sixty-two, whichever occurs first. (However, if a year or any part of a year fell within an established period of disability, that year need not be counted.)

fully registered *investing* A non-negotiable bond which is registered in the name of the owner with respect to both principal and interest. The periodic interest is paid to the registered owner by the disbursing agent.

functional allocation *limited partnerships* 1. Most used way of allocating the expenses and profits between the general partner and investors. In functional allocation, the limited partners are allocated 100% of the currently deductible expenses while the general partner is allocated the costs that must be amortized over a period of years. 2. A cost allocation method whereby investors are allocated most of the early expenses of the project so that tax deductions come quickly and are maximized. This method is favorable to the promoter because it shifts most of the risk to investors.

functional approach *personnel; industrial psychology* The study of jobs and people according to how they function in the work situation, rather than who or what they are.

functional finance Principle which holds that the government should pursue whatever fiscal measures are needed to achieve noninflationary full employment and economic growth, without regard to budget balancing per se. The federal budget is thus viewed functionally as a flexible fiscal tool for achieving economic objectives, rather than as an accounting statement to be balanced periodically.

fund Sum of money set apart for a specific purpose. It can be used to denote capital assets, liquid assets, money in hand, or notes and/or bills, depending on the context.

fundamental analysis 1. *economics* The analysis of various factors in the economy such as interest rates, inflation, gross national product, unemployment, etc., for the purpose of forecasting the future of the economy. 2. *investing* The analysis of the balance sheets of companies in the attempt to forecast future stock prices of the company. 3. Examination and interpretation of all relevant factors that can influence the direction of a corporation's growth, earnings, and dividends. This includes the analysis of economic data, industry conditions, company fundamentals, and corporate financial statements.

fundamental equation, Domar's *See* Domar's fundamental equation.

fundamental methods of managing tax liability Means used by individual income tax payers to mitigate the ultimate tax liability. Tax liability is usually reduced by the use of one or all of the following: exclusions, deductions, income averaging, and tax credits. (*See* Appendix G)

fundation A foundation such as a corporation.

funded agreement *pension plans* Agreement where property is put into a trust for the employee or an annuity is purchased in the employee's name to fund a nonqualified deferred compensation agreement with different tax consequences set forth in the Internal Revenue Code. Funded deferred compensation may take the form of either a salary continuation or a pure deferred plan. (Certain exceptions exist in the code for some organizations.)

funded insurance trust A personal trust which is funded from the proceeds of an insurance policy. The trust only becomes funded when the insured dies, and the proceeds of the policy are put into the trust.

funded pension plan Plan in which the employer puts aside money, usually on an annual basis, to fund a pension plan. When the money is in excess of that required to pay current pension benefits to retired employees, and this money is transferred to a trustee (usually a bank) or an insurance company, the plan is considered to be advanced funded. Plans today are usually funded, but not always fully funded. (*See* fully funded pension plan, current disbursement plan)

fundi patrimoniales Inheritance.

funds Any means of payment. (Along with cash flow, funds is one of the most frequently misused words in finance.)

fundus *Land;* the foundation of a thing.

fungibiles res *Movable things* of the same class (e.g., corn, rice, etc.) which may be sold by a general description of weight, measure, and number.

fungible goods *economics; marketing* Movable goods that are standardized so that one unit is essentially the same as another, which may be estimated and replaced by weight, number, and measure (e.g., grain, wheat, coal, or gravel). Where the subject matter of a contract is the delivery of movable goods of a class, then any goods of the same quantity, number, or weight of that class would satisfy the contract; but where the contract calls for delivery of the property in specie, then the same is not fungible.

funnel sequence *communication* Questions moving from the general (open-ended questions) to the specific (closed questions). The funnel sequence is probably the most often used method of organizing the interview.

furisos nulla voluntas est *A lunatic has no free will.* Thus the person lacks the capacity to enter into contracts and is incapable of conceiving the *mens rea* essential for culpability under criminal law.

furlong Measure of distance equal to one-eighth of a mile.

furlough Leave of absence. An authorized leave of absence given to an enlisted person or any employee of a government.

furnish To fit and equip with what is appropriate or necessary by way of personal chattels for ornament, to promote personal comfort, or to facilitate the business being done on the premises being furnished.

furtum 1. *Theft.* 2. Thing stolen.

furtum est contrectatio rei alienae fraudulenta, cum animo furandi, invito, illo domino cujus res illa fuerat *Theft is the fraudulent appropriation of another man's property, without the consent of that other and with the intention of stealing it.*

furtum non est ubi initium habet detentionis per dominium rei *There is no theft where the possession of the thing was based upon the ownership of the same.*

future interest Property right or estate that may not be enjoyed until some time in the future.

futures Contracts that require delivery of a commodity of specified price on a specified future date. Commodity futures are traded on a commodity exchange and are used for both speculation and hedging.

Futures Commission Merchant (FCM) A person, or a business firm, that handles orders for the purchase or sale of futures contracts. They are subject to the regulations of a futures exchange and must be licensed by the Commodities Futures Trading Commission.

futures contract 1. Present right to receive at a future date a specific quantity of a given commodity for a fixed price. Futures markets do not involve face-to-face negotiations between the buyers and sellers; instead brokers act as their agents and negotiate the sales. 2. An agreement to buy or sell a commodity at a price stated in the agreement at a future date. While futures contracts call for the delivery of the commodity (unless the contract is liquidated before it matures), this is rarely done, and the speculator in commodity futures almost always closes out his or her position in a futures contract before the contract matures. This way, the commodity itself never changes hands among speculators.

futures market Market in which a contract can be made to buy something at a specified future date for a currently agreed-upon price. If the price of what was bought increases between the contract date and the delivery date, a profit will be made. If it decreases, a loss will be suffered.

future sum Sum one would expect to have at some future date, beginning with a specific principal and taking into consideration time periods, compounding, and rate of interest.

future value Value of a deposit at any given time in the future.

future value factor The $(1+r)n$ portion of the future value equation, used to make simpler, multiple-period problems.

future value of an annuity *insurance* Value to which the annuity will accumulate at the end of the annuity period.

future value table Table constructed to show the future value factor for different time periods and different interest rates.

G

gain Profits, winnings, or increments of value; not limited to pecuniary gain nor confined to commercial profits only. It includes a benefit or advantage as well.

gainful Lucrative; remunerative; profitable; advantageous.

gain realized On like-kind exchange, the fair market value of the property acquired less the adjusted basis of the transferred property plus the sum of the boot received and mortgage transferred less the sum of the boot paid and mortgage assumed.

gain recognized On like-kind exchange, the boot received plus the difference between the mortgage transferred and the mortgage assumed (if such difference is greater than zero) all reduced by the difference between the adjusted basis of the property transferred and the fair market value of the property acquired (if such difference is greater than zero). In no event may the gain recognized be less than zero.

gains to net debtors *economics* The increase in a debtor's wealth attributable to a decline in the purchasing power of the debtor's liabilities.

gallon United States measure containing 231 cubic inches. An imperial gallon is a measure containing 277 cubic inches. The metric equivalent of one gallon is 3.7853 liters.

galloping inflation *economics* A rapid acceleration in the rate at which general price levels are rising which, if not checked, can lead to an economic breakdown.

gamble To play for money or other stakes.

Gantt Chart *management* A graphic presentation of an employee's performance on the job, measured against some predetermined standard.

Gantt, Henry Lawrence (1861–1919) *management* A management specialist who worked closely for many years with Frederick W. Taylor. He emphasized the methodology of work and sharpening the skills of workers. Later he became interested in motivation and in the social responsibilities of business.

Gantt premium plan *economics* One of a number of incentive wage plans for employees wherein the employee receives a flat hourly rate for production up to a certain point and a piece rate for all production after that. The piece rate may exceed the normal wage by as much as 50%. Other similar plans were introduced by Emerson, Halsey, Taylor, Rowan, and others.

gap 1. *finance; securities* That part of a project which is left unfunded after an original borrowing has been exhausted and there is a remaining need for money to complete the project. Sometimes the original lender will make the loan; at other times the gap must be filled by finding another lender. 2. *finance; securities* A term used in the securities industry, usually in the commodities market, where the opening price on one day is higher (or lower) that the closing the day before. This is usually the result of some bit of news that has had an immediate impact on the market. 3. *banking* The difference between the maturities of a bank's assets and liabilities. (Cf. negative gap, positive gap)

gardia Custody; wardship.

garnish *law* To warn; to serve notice of proceeding; to attach a debt.

garnishee *law* One against whom a garnishment order has been made; a person who owes money to a judgment debtor and who has been ordered to pay all or part of it into court to satisfy the judgment debt. Such person, once the process is served, cannot lawfully pay the debt owed the defendant to the latter but must obey the order of the court.

garnishment *law* 1. Notice to a person holding money or property belonging to a defendant not to turn it over to the defendant but to appear and answer the plaintiff's suit. Many states still permit creditors of wage earners to obtain an order of garnishment requiring the debtor's employer to deduct a specified amount from each paycheck and to pay that amount to the creditor until the debt is paid off. 2. Court-ordered procedure by which a portion of a debtor's wages is set aside to repay creditors.

gathering in the stops *investing; finance* A tactic in stock trading that involves selling enough of the stock to drive down the price to a point where stop orders (orders to buy or sell at a certain price) exist and must be exercised. This further selling often pushes the price down to the next stop level. This action can turn into snowballing (a rush of selling downward) until it is stopped by the authority of exchange floor officials.

Gaussian curve   *statistics* A type of normal curve devised by Gauss which depicts the probable distribution of large numbers.

gemstone   Any relatively scarce natural stone, used primarily in decorative jewelry with a value that quite commonly increases over time, such as diamonds, rubies, sapphires, and emeralds. Among the oldest economic investment vehicles, they are often used as a hedge against inflation.

General Accounting Office (GAO)   A federal office founded by Congress in 1921 to coordinate and supervise the accounting for government expenditures.

general agent   1. *insurance* Agent who represents a company as an independent contractor in a given territory performing all operating functions of the company, including claims adjusting, collections, and underwriting. 2. *law* One who has almost unlimited authority to act for the appointer. Since the assumed powers are so broad, a general agent is rarely appointed.

General Agreement on Tariffs and Trade (GATT)   *economics* A rather informal agreement among many nations, which had its beginning in Geneva in 1947, to reduce tariffs between nations and promote free trade. The nations that are informal members of the group account for about 80% of world trade.

general assignment   *bankruptcy law* Any conveyance by which one intends to make an absolute and unconditional appropriation of all one's property to pay creditors, share and share alike.

general average   *insurance* A provision that the loss of any cargo from navigation risks will be borne proportionately to value by all the cargo.

general contractor   *real estate* One who bids in an entire building or improvement job, and who assumes the responsibility for its completion. The general contractor may sub-contract work, such as the plumbing, but he remains generally responsible for the satisfactory completion of the project.

general creditor   *finance* An unsecured creditor.

general damages   Damages that the law will presume to be the direct natural or probable consequence of an act complained of.

general endorsement   Endorsement of a negotiable instrument made without qualification or restriction.

general equilibrium   *economics* 1. Under monopoly or monopolistic competition, a relatively stable situation under which there is little incentive to enter or leave an industry, or expand or contract. While under monopoly the situation could remain stable over time, under monopolistic competition there may be attempts to differentiate products through subtle change or through advertising which could upset the equilibrium. 2. Under pure competition, essentially a static state where all prices are at their long-run equilibrium, individuals are spending their incomes to yield maximum utility, and the demand for and supply of factors of production are generally equated.

general equilibrium theory   *economics* 1. A hypothetical framework of the national economy (U.S.), recognizing the interrelation of price and output for both goods produced and the factors of production. 2. An economic theory developed in the nineteenth century by Léon Walras that attempts to trace the effect of a single economic change on the economy as a whole. It was Walras's belief that in order to understand what is happening in the economy as a whole, one must study the impact of changes in parts of that whole.

general ledger   *accounting* A consolidated summary book of accounts for any business enterprise, including a bank.

general legacy   Bequest to be provided out of the testator's general estate, which does not earmark any particular thing; designated primarily by quantity or amount which may be paid out of the general assets in the estate with no regard to any particular fund or thing.

general letter of credit   Open letter whereby the issuer proposes to undertake certain obligations to the person who will deal with the customer; these obligations primarily consist of the payment of a specific amount for a specific purpose.

general liability policy   *insurance* Program, similar to many fire and inland marine programs, which is written as a form attached to a standard policy (known as a jacket). The standard policy contains the common provisions, conditions, and definitions applying to all policies in the program. The form added to the standard policy divides the general liability exposures into three broad areas: personal liability, professional liability, and business liability.

general lien   Lien that includes all of the property owned by the debtor, rather than specific property.

general-obligation (G.O.) bond Largest category of municipal bonds, which are secured by the full faith, credit, and taxing power of the issuing municipality.

general partner   1. One of two or more partners who are jointly or severally responsible for the debts of the partnership. All partners in an ordinary partnership are general partners.   2. The managing partner of a limited partnership who is responsible for its operations and, ultimately, any debts taken on by the partnership. He or she is the partner with unlimited liability. (*See* limited partnership)

general power of appointment Power given to one person by another to take charge of the grantor's assets after death and appoint those assets as the grantee sees fit. Under a general appointment, the one with the general power may appoint the property to whomever he or she will, even to one's own estate. In short, it is the power to invade the corpus of the estate. Should the grantee die with the general appointment still intact the property will be considered as part of the estate.

general power of attorney   Power of attorney by which the attorney-in-fact has authority to act in all matters for the principal.

general price-level index   *economics* An index, the base year of which is 100%, which shows the changing purchasing power of the dollar in general.

general property form   *insurance* Form common for covering commercial buildings and contents. When attached to the standard property form, it is widely used because of its versatility.

general property tax   *economics* A tax on wealth and property, usually at a semi-local level, often regardless of the nature of that property. Often, certain types of property are exempt. This is unquestionably the most important tax at the local level and, in some states, at the state level also.

general revenue sharing   *finance; government* Unrestricted funds, usable for any purpose, that the federal government passes down to states, or to more than thirty-eight thousand municipalities, counties or townships. These funds were established under the Local Fiscal Assistance Act of 1972 (expired in 1987), and included Indian tribes and Alaskan native villages.

general sales tax   *economics* A tax levied on all goods as they are sold through retail outlets. Some states give exemptions for food and prescription drugs as protection for the poor and/or elderly citizens. Sales taxes continue to escalate due to the ease of raising the tax. Sales taxes are now levied at state levels, and sometimes county and municipal levels.

general union   *economics; management* A union that draws members from several different occupations, as opposed to craft guilds, which draw members from one trade only.

general warranty deed   Deed in which grantor agrees to protect grantee against any other claim to title of the property along with other promises.

generation-skipping tax   *law* A tax imposed on any generation-skipping transfer of property. Ostensibly, this tax is about equal to what it would have been if the same assets had been transferred to each succeeding generation.

generation-skipping trust   *tax law* Trust in which beneficiaries are two or more generations younger than the generation of the person creating the trust. The tax on generation-skipping transfers is imposed on such trusts by treating the property in trust as includable in the gross estate of the intervening life beneficiary of the trust, who belongs to a younger generation than the creator of the trust and is referred to as a deemed transferor. The generation-skipping trust involves skipping in two senses: there is the skipping of trust property for the use of the income by one generation to its use by another generation, and to yet another; and the skipping of estate taxes as the trust property passes to the service of succeeding generations. Thus, one could set up a trust to pay the income to a surviving spouse for life, then to the children of the couple for their lives, all tax free, except for the initial transfer to the trust. (*See* Appendix G)

generic name 1. Relating to a whole group or a class. 2. Brand name that has become a descriptive term for a product (e.g., nylon, zipper, aspirin). When this occurs, the original owner loses exclusive claim to the brand name.

generic product Food and household staple characterized by a plain descriptive label, little or no advertising, and no brand name. Such products compete on the basis of price.

gentrification Displacement of lower-income residents by higher-income residents in a neighborhood. Generally occurs when an older neighborhood is rehabilitated or revitalized.

genuine *law* Free of forgery or counterfeiting.

geometric mean *statistics* A complex method of determining the mean of a distribution when the relationship of the values is multiplicative rather than additive. Its most familiar role is that of finding the average rate of interest in a transaction when compound interest is used.

geometric progression *economics* A series of terms (values) which increases or decreases by multiplication of the preceding term by a constant factor (e.g., 2, 4, 8, 16, 32, or 32, 16, 8, 4, 2) but cannot be below zero. The Rev. Thomas Malthus (1766–1834), built an entire system on the premise that world population would grow in geometric progression, but foodstuffs by arithmetic progression, thus bringing a time when the earth could not sustain the population, and starvation on a worldwide scale would ensue.

Gibrat's distribution *economics* A statement by a French economist in 1931, explaining the size distribution of firms.

He stated specifically that the distribution of percentage changes in size of the firms in a given size class is the same for all firms above the minimum size class.

Giffin Effect *economics* A premise noted by Sir R. Giffin of England that a rise in the price level of all goods will, in the case of the poor whose incomes do not increase, cause an increase in the quantity of staple items consumed despite the increase in price in order to make the income cover the needs.

gift Voluntary transfer of property made without consideration or expectation of consideration. The essential components of a valid completed gift of personal property are: competency of the donor to give the gift; voluntary intent on the part of the donor to make a gift; delivery, whether actual or symbolic; acceptance, actual or imputed; complete divestment of all control by the donor; and a lack of consideration. (*See* Appendix G, donatio inter vivos, donatio mortis causa)

gift deed Deed for which consideration is affection, with no material consideration involved.

gift inter vivos *See* donatio inter vivos.

gift mortis causa *See* donatio mortis causa.

gift of a present interest A gift in which the beneficiaries have unrestricted right to the immediate use, possession, or enjoyment of the property or resulting income.

gift of future interest Any interest or estate, whether vested or contingent, and whether or not supported by a particular interest or estate, limited to commence in use, possession, or enjoyment at some future date in time. Gifts of future interests in property do not qualify for the annual gift tax exclusion.

gift tax 1. Federal tax upon a gift of money or property given to a relative or friend. Generally, each person may give up to ten thousand dollars per year to each donee without imposition of a federal gift tax. On higher gifts, there may be a gift tax if the gift may affect the donor's estate tax. 2. Tax on the transfer of ownership of an asset when the value of the asset exceeds a specified amount.

gift tax annual exclusion Provision allowing every donor to make tax-free gifts

135

each year of up to ten thousand dollars each to however many persons the donor wishes. Gifts within the annual exclusion do not reduce the donor's unified credit. (The annual exclusion pertains only to gifts of a present interest.) (*See* Appendix G)

gift tax charitable deduction Provision allowing a deduction for the value of a gift to charity. Unlike the income tax charitable deduction, there is no dollar limit on the amount of the gift tax charitable deduction. In order to qualify, the gift must meet certain requirements. The gift must be to a qualified donee and cannot be conditional unless the possibility that the charitable transfer will not occur is so remote as to be negligible. In the case of a partial gift, the gift must be in specified forms.

gift tax marital deduction Provision allowing a donor who is a citizen or resident of the United States to get an unlimited marital deduction for qualified interspousal gifts made after 1981. Before 1982, the marital deduction was a limited amount. The gift tax marital deduction is one of the most important gift tax elimination devices as well as an important estate planning tool for the married donor.

gifting Act of giving to a person or a charitable institution gifts of assets, in trust or outright. Such gifts are generally not taxable to either the donor or the donee, provided that no more than the maximum of ten thousand dollars is given by one person or entity to the same given person in a year's time.

gifting of life insurance Transferring of a life insurance policy during the lifetime of the donor. Like the gift of other property, such a gift may be subjected to federal gift taxation. Thus, if the policyholders absolutely assign a life insurance policy on their life to someone else (a child or trust, for example) they have made a current gift to the donee of the then value of the insurance policy. The insurance company will supply the gift value of the policy upon request. If the insured continues to pay the premiums on the gift policy(s), each such premium constitutes a gift to the new policyholder.

gift-leaseback Situation where a person owning property used in personal business or practice transfers it to a short-term trust, usually set up for the children's benefit although it may be used for other family members. The trust then leases the property back to the settlor at a rental price based on the property's fair rental value. The goal is for the settlor to get a deduction for the rent paid to the trust, which makes income available to members of the family in a lower tax bracket. The most frequently transferred property is an office building. Often the transfer takes place when the settlor has begun to run out of depreciation deductions, and the lease expense will be substantially higher than any depreciation deductions one might have. (*See* Appendix G)

GI loan Loan popular after World War II designed to assist veterans to acquire residential housing. The loans are made by conventional mortgage lenders or individuals and usually have a lower interest rate. The mortgage can be for 100% of the appraised value of the property.

gilt-edged bond *investing* A high-grade bond issued by a highly reputable company, which, over time, has paid interest regularly on this and other bond issues.

Gini coefficient *statistics* A measure of the degree of inequality in the distribution of two variables arranged cumulatively in a Lorenz curve (e.g., percentage of population and percentage of income).

Ginnie Mae Nickname for Government National Mortgage Association.

Ginnie Mae pass-through Investment vehicle guaranteed by the federal government which earns high mortgage yields and has an average life of ten to twelve years. Minimum investment is twenty-five thousand dollars. The investment is in residential mortgages which have been guaranteed by the Veterans Administration or FHA, and have been purchased by the Government National Mortgage Association. They are then packaged by Ginnie Mae and sold to investors. (*See* pass-through certificate)

giro *banking; finance* A method of bill-paying or transfer of funds which is widely used in Europe. It allows the account holder to make a single payment order which will implement transfers from one account to several other accounts on the books of the same institution. (E.g., if one has an account at the same bank as do five of one's creditors, one can give a payment order of a thousand dollars and transfer two hundred dollars each to the five accounts owed.)

giveback Withdrawal of a labor benefit prior to the end of a collective bargaining agreement by mutual agreement of the employer and the union, normally to avoid closure of plants due to business losses.

glamour stock *investing* A stock which may have a large public and institutional following. Usually it is a stock that sells well, and can even be a "blue-ribbon" stock. It is usually well-known, however, for its earnings growth.

Glass-Steagall Act *banking* A part of the Federal Banking Act of 1933, which deals specifically with the separation of commercial banking and investment banking.

global fund *investing* A mutual fund that invests in both domestic and foreign stocks.

Gnomes of Zurich *finance* A term coined by the Labor ministers of Great Britain to describe the financiers and bankers in Zurich, Switzerland, during the sterling crisis of 1964, when the Swiss engaged in speculation in foreign exchange.

goal *finance* Objective which a client wishes to achieve in a given period of time. Goals should always be specific (e.g., I will want to have a fund of twenty-five thousand dollars eleven years from today to start my youngest child in college) versus nebulous (e.g., I would like to do well enough to send my youngest child to college).

go around *finance; investing* Process whereby the trading desk at the New York Federal Reserve Bank ("the desk"), acting on behalf of the Fed Open Market Committee, contacts primary dealers for the bid and offer prices on securities. Primary dealers are those banks and investment houses approved for the direct purchase and sale transactions with the Federal Reserve Open Market Committee.

go-go funds *investing* Mutual funds which are often constructed of portfolios of current stocks with young, gung ho managers. These funds do occasionally prosper for short periods of time, but seldom in the long term.

going ahead *investing* An unethical practice in the securities market whereby a broker will trade first for the broker's own account, particularly under favorable circumstances, before executing trades for customers. Violates the Rules of Fair Practice.

going away *investing* Bonds which are purchased for immediate sale to buyers, as opposed to those purchased to go "on the shelf."

going concern *accounting* Assumption made in accounting, usually on the basis of existing financial conditions, that the business will continue operations unabated for an indefinite period of time.

going concern value *See* going value.

going public *finance; investing* The process through which a privately owned company becomes publically owned, with the ability of trade shares of stock on some stock exchange. The normal procedure is for an investment house to sell the first issue of stock, after which it is traded on the open market.

going short *investing* Selling a stock or commodity which the seller does not own. Short sales are usually covered by the seller by borrowing from the broker in hopes that the seller will be able to get into the market soon and buy the stocks at a lower price.

going value *economics* The value that a business has as an operating enterprise unit as opposed to the value of the individual parts taken separately. (E.g., the value of a retail store, still operating, usually will be much greater than if the store closes and sells inventory, fixtures, etc.) Also called going concern value.

gold Precious metal that has long served as a metaphor for excellence and desirability. Considered a good investment over the long term because of its universal acceptability. Gold responds less to the normal market factors of basic producer supply and consumer demand than it does to political and psychological forces in the marketplace. The price of gold is a sensitive barometer of world anxiety over economic conditions.

gold and foreign exchange reserve The supply of gold, along with the currencies of other countries, a nation will hold to settle debts that are called in and to remedy deficits in balance of payments accounts.

gold bond   *investing* A bond backed by gold and issued by gold-mining companies. Interest rates on the bond are pegged to the price of gold. Investors who buy these bonds, and similar bonds backed by silver, anticipate rising prices in these precious metals.

gold bullion   Most obvious form of gold, cast in bars or ingots. Generally for investment purposes. Bullion is bought outright and usually held as a long-term investment.

gold bullion standard   Monetary standard under which the national unit of currency is defined in terms of a fixed weight of gold; gold is held by the government in the form of bars rather than coin. There is no circulation of gold in any form within the economy, and gold is available solely to meet the needs of industry (e.g., jewelry, dentistry) and settle international transactions among central banks or treasuries. This is the standard that the United States and most advanced nations adopted when they went off the gold coin standard in the early 1930s.

gold certificate   Dollar bill backed by and convertible into gold. The only gold certificates now in use in the United States are those which are issued by the Treasury and held by the Federal Reserve banks.

gold clause   *economics; finance* A provision in a contract calling for payment in a specific amount of gold, or a specific number of dollars at the option of the one being paid. (Such a contract has not been binding in the United States since 1933.)

gold coin   Coin minted of gold, rarely used as a coin; usually considered a collector's item. Canada and South Africa still mint gold coins of differing values, and they are normally bought by small investors for value appreciation and for collection value.

gold coin standard   Monetary standard under which the national unit of currency is defined by law in terms of a fixed weight of gold; there is a free and unrestricted flow of the metal in any form into and out of the country; gold coins are full legal tender for all debts; there is free convertibility between the national currency and

gold coins at the defined rate; and there are no restrictions of the coinage of gold. Nearly fifty countries of the world were on this standard in the late nineteenth and early twentieth centuries.

gold currency system   *economics* A monetary system in which paper currency and gold can be freely exchanged for each other at established rates.

golden handcuffs   *investing* A contract which ties a broker to a brokerage house. Generally, if the broker remains with the house for a long time, the broker may expect to earn large fees, and perhaps part ownership in the business. If the broker leaves the firm, he or she is restricted in the matter of absconding with the firm's clients by having to repay some of the prior compensation. Brokers historically move frequently, and this is a method of restricting such movement.

golden handshake   *management* A term used to describe the negotiations between management and labor, when both sides approach the bargaining table with good intentions of reaching a quick agreement.

golden parachute   *management; finance* Lavish benefits provided to a top executive of a company in case a company is taken over by another firm, resulting in termination. This plan may include generous severance pay, stock options, or a bonus payable when the executive's employment with the company ends.

gold exchange standard   *economics* Monetary standard under which a nation not on a gold standard will redeem its money on demand in the form of drafts written against bank deposits in a gold-standard country. In this way, the non-gold-standard country can keep its money on a par with gold without having to maintain gold reserves. This standard was particularly popular among nations which lacked gold or were politically dependent on other nations after World War I (e.g., British Commonwealth countries). However, it ceased to exist with the worldwide abandonment of gold in the 1930s.

gold exporting point   *economics* A rate of exchange at which the importer of goods can at the same cost buy gold and export it in payment for imports. Before 1931, the gold exporting point between the United States and England was about $4.88, or two cents (the cost of shipping the gold) above the par of gold exchange ($4.86).

gold futures contract An aspect of gold trading which has expanded to such a degree that the spot price of gold on the major futures exchanges is read along with the Zurich price and the London gold-fixing as one of the authentic market indicators of gold's value. Gold futures are traded exactly as are other commodities.

gold importing point *economics* A rate of exchange at which the exporter can at the same cost arrange to have gold sent in payment for goods. Prior to 1931, the gold importing point between the United States and England was about $4.84, or two cents (the cost of shipping $4.86 worth of gold) below the par of gold exchange ($4.86).

gold mining stocks Shares in gold mines which trade on the exchanges as do stocks in other companies. While gold objects have the disadvantage of offering no current return, shares in gold mining companies frequently do pay dividends, some quite generous by market standards.

gold mutual fund *investing* A mutual fund that invests in stocks of gold mining companies. Many restrict their investments to North American mining concerns, while others are international in scope.

gold standard *economics* A monetary system under which currency is convertible into gold at a specified rate, and vice versa, and the free shipment of gold on an international basis is allowed.

good *economics* 1. Any material thing that is capable of satisfying a human need or want, as distinguished from a service rendered. 2. Generally in economics no substantive difference is made between a material good and a service sold for money; both are considered goods.

good delivery *investing; finance* A securities industry designation denoting that a certificate has necessary endorsements and meets all other qualifications for transfer to the broker.

good faith Honesty. (*See* bona fide)

good money *banking; finance* 1. Federal funds which clear the same day as opposed to clearing house funds which usually require three days to clear. 2. Money with intrinsic value. (*See* Gresham's law)

goods and chattels *law; finance* Personal property as distinguished from real property.

good-this-month order *investing* An order by a customer to a broker to buy or sell specific securities by the end of the month. (It should be understood that the order stands until the end of the current month, but the purchase or sale is to be made at the most advantageous time for the customer.)

good-till-cancelled order Order placed with a broker that remains in effect until it is executed by the broker or cancelled by the investor.

good will *accounting* An intangible value often attached to a business enterprise as a result of the satisfactory operation of that enterprise in a community over an extended period of time. While this is sometimes the capitalized estimated increase in the business done over time, more often it is a guess by the businessperson (usually a sole proprietor) of what the business is worth over and above its intrinsic value. Sometimes good will is a line item in the balance sheet. Any person buying such a business must be informed as to the nature of the good will and the fact that it may not accrue to the business after it is sold by the current owner.

go private *finance* The action of a corporation of buying up its own stock from the public that owns it.

gosbank Soviet bank that handles all financial transactions between firms, extends credit to firms for purchasing productions inputs, and audits firms' plan fulfillment.

government publications Material published by the United States government. (E.g., *The Survey of Current Business* presents business statistics and the *Business Conditions Digest* provides information on business indicators. The *Economic Report of the President* and the *Annual Report of the Council of Economic Advisors* are published annually and give statistics covering virtually every sector of the economy, besides providing economic forecasts.) The Federal Reserve System publishes both periodicals and ad hoc reports on economic conditions, many of which are available without cost.

government purchases of goods and services   *economics* Amount of the gross national product which is purchased by the federal government in a given period of time, usually one year.

governments   *investing* 1. Securities issued by the Treasury of the United States such as bills, notes, or bonds. 2. Securities issued by government agencies which are not directly backed by the United States government.

government sector spending Spending by various levels of government on goods and services, including public investment.

government security Government bond, Treasury bill, or any other debt instruments sold by the government to finance the government debt. (*See* security)

government subsidy Economic benefits provided by the government to investors, as for instance in certain low- and moderate-income housing tax shelters. To induce investment in these projects (which would otherwise attract little interest from investors), the government provides a variety of direct and indirect subsidies, often in low-interest rates and long pay-out periods. Subsidies may also be directed to producers of farm and dairy and certain manufactured products.

grace period   1. Period of time after a due date not subject to late charges. 2. *insurance* Period after the premium due date for a life insurance policy during which the policy remains in force even though the premium has not been paid, commonly thirty-one days. This provision is designed to protect the policyholder against inadvertent lapse of the policy.

grade labeling   *marketing* The practice of indicating the quality of a canned fruit or vegetable by letter, such as A, B, C, etc., or by some other symbol used by the Food and Drug Administration to denote specific standards of excellence. Currently such designations are not required by law and are therefore not found on many labels.

graduated payment Repayment terms calling for gradual increases in the payments on a closed-end obligation. A grad-

uated payment loan usually involves negative amortization.

graduated payment mortgage (GPM)   *finance* Mortgage requiring lower payments in early years than in later years. Payments increase in steps each year until the installments are sufficient to amortize the loan. This type of mortgage fits the needs of young professionals whose incomes begin low, increase in the middle years, and level off at a later time.

graduated security   *investing; finance* A security, the listing of which has increased in value by moving from one stock exchange to another; i.e., moving from a regional exchange to a national exchange

Graham and Dodd Method of Investing An approach to investing first outlined in the book *Security Analysis* by Benjamin Graham and David Dodd, a 1930 publication. It was an introduction to investing by the use of technical analysis.

grandfather clause   *law* Special provision in legislation which allows people already engaged in something which is prohibited by the new law to continue that practice, though new entries into the field are not allowed.

granger movement   *economics* A movement which became popular in the late nineteenth century, primarily in the farm states of the upper Mississippi valley, when farmers took issue with the monopolistic control of railroads and railroad warehouses, and attempted to control them through legislation. The movement ultimately spread from direct farm concerns to other types of businesses such as public utilities. The original movement resulted in some of the well-known farm organizations of today, along with the cooperative movement in farm buying and marketing.

grant   1. Formal transfer or conveyance of real property. 2. The instrument by means of which such transfer is made. 3. The property transferred.

grantee Person to whom a grant is made.

grantor Person by whom a grant is made.

grantor annuity trusts Irrevocable trust to which money or property is transferred in exchange for an annuity in a fixed dollar amount payable to the grantor for a specified period of time. At the end of such period, the trust principal may be paid to family members (or others) outright or may continue to be held by the trust for their benefit.

graveyard market   *investing* Situation in which an investor in a bear market cannot get out without sustaining substantial losses. At the same time, those with money to invest will not get in the market in its unsettled condition. Thus, like a graveyard, those who are in cannot get out, and those who are out do not wish to get in.

graveyard shift   *economics* A term used to denote the third shift in a twenty-four hour plant, i.e., the shift from twelve midnight to eight in the morning.

Great Depression   Period of worldwide economic crisis during the 1930s that closed banks, created 25% unemployment, and led to increased government intervention in the economy of the United States under New Deal legislation.

greater fool theory   *investing* A theory that states that if you have been a fool for buying over-priced stock, there may be a greater fool somewhere who will buy from you at a higher price, thus giving you a profit. This happens sometimes when a stock "goes wild" in the market and ascends to heights neither expected nor justified.

greenbacks   *economics; finance* A paper currency which was first printed during the Civil War on the faith and credit of the Federal government, without any commodity backing. They were identified by the green ink used for printing one side of the bills.

greenmail   *investing* The practice of buying up large portions of a company's stock in an apparent hostile takeover attempt, thus driving up the price of the stock, which forces the original major stockholders to buy back the stock at a much higher price.

Green Revolution   Revolutionary agricultural breakthroughs of the 1960s and 1970s: fast-growing, high-yielding plants and new agricultural chemicals. Initially thought to be a possible long-run answer to hunger in the world.

Green River ordinances   Local law limiting door-to-door selling. Named for Green River, Wyoming, where such an ordinance was first enacted.

green shoe   *finance* A clause put in an underwriting agreement which says that in the event of rapid sales of the security the issuer will authorize additional shares to the syndicate.

Greenwich Standard Time   The local time at Greenwich, in southeast England, on the zero meridian. It is used as a world datum time for such purposes as international air travel, meteorological reports, etc.

Gresham's law   *economics; finance* Bad money drives out good money. Generally, where some of the nation's money has intrinsic value (e.g., gold coins) and other money does not (e.g., paper money) or is less valuable (e.g., silver coins), people tend to hoard the good money and leave the less valuable money in circulation. This happened in the United States under the bimetallic standard during the nineteenth century. The law is named after Sir Thomas Gresham, master of the mint under Queen Elizabeth I during the sixteenth century. (*See* bimetallic standard)

grid theory   *management* A theory that the three universal factors interacting in any organization are (a) people, (b) production of goods or services, and (c) the management hierarchy.

gross estate   1. Starting point for calculating how much federal estate tax the estate must pay. It includes the property in the probate estate; life insurance owned jointly by a husband and wife; and all the value of property owned jointly by persons other than husband and wife, except to the extent that the survivor can show that he or she contributed to the purchase of the property. 2. *law; finance* The total value of a person's assets before liabilities such as debts and taxes are deducted. (Cf. net estate)

gross income   1. Entire receipts or revenue of a business before any expenditure, such as payment of wages or payment for materials. 2. The total income of a taxpayer from all sources before deductions or exemptions. The first basic rule of federal income taxation is that all income is taxable income unless the taxpayer can find good authority for excluding it. Thus gross income is all income from whatever source derived. 3. Total earnings of a wage-earner prior to deductions for taxes, health insurance, employee benefit plans, etc. 4. Total income from property before any expenses are deducted.

gross lease Lease of property whereby the lessor is responsible for paying all property expenses, such as taxes, insurance, utilities, and repairs.

gross margin percentage Revenue minus cost of goods sold divided by revenue.

gross national income Income equivalent of the gross national product; consists of national income at factor cost (i.e., the sum of wages, rent, interest, and profit) plus two nonincome or business expense items, indirect business taxes, and the capital consumption allowance.

gross national product (GNP) *economics* Total gross value of all final goods and services produced in the economy in one year. GNP figures reflect the annual rate of gross output of the economy. Sum total of final goods and services produced in an economy in a year, stated in terms of dollars.

gross private domestic investment *economics* Business investment in a year with no deduction for the depreciation of capital goods.

gross profit 1. Profit an investor receives before allowing for commissions, taxes, or other deductions. 2. *accounting* Profit after subtracting the cost of goods sold and overhead, but before taxes.

gross spread *finance* The difference between the price paid by an investment bank for a new securities issue and the price paid by those who purchase the securities.

gross-up rule Rule stating that gift taxes payable upon gifts made within three years of death are included in the gross estate. This has the effect of increasing the descendant's estate tax liability.

ground rent Rent earned by leased land.

group annuity *insurance* A pension plan which provides annuities to retiring employees, but which is bought under a master plan instead of individual plans. Normally, the group annuity would be issued to the employer and would cover all participating employees.

group banking Normally, a holding company which is formed by a group of banks that supervises and coordinates the activities of all the banks in the group.

group credit insurance Policy designed to pay a disabled debtor's payments until the debtor recovers or the debt is paid. In some plans, payments are retroactive; in others, payments are made only after the normal waiting period.

group dynamics *management* A study of the behavior of groups and of individuals as members of a group.

group insurance Any of various systems of life, accident, or health insurance covering members of a group, as the employees in a business organization, under a single contract.

group maintenance role *communication* Role which aims at keeping a group in a mood to function properly. These roles include an encourager, a harmonizer, a tension reliever, and a gatekeeper. This person(s) and the role played is vital in the proper functioning of the group.

Group of Ten *government; finance* Ten major industrialized countries that try to maintain monetary stability through the use of monetary and fiscal policies in the various countries. They are the United States, West Germany, Belgium, Canada, France, Italy, Japan, the Netherlands, the United Kingdom, and Sweden.

group/ordinary Program which combines group term life insurance with individual life insurance. The total life coverage is determined in a manner similar to the coverage of the group life program using earnings, position, length of service, or a flat amount basis.

group/ordinary (section 79) Plan which allows employees to choose a certain type of permanent insurance for an off-setting amount of term. This plan may be initially elected or chosen at optional times later. It does not increase the death plan.

group paid-up plan Plan based upon a combination of accumulation units of single premium whole life insurance and decreasing units of group term life insurance, designed to meet the most serious defect of group term—its temporary nature.

group property and liability insurance Relatively new plan in which property and casualty insurance is written on a group basis. This plan is generally opposed by agents and makes underwriting difficult because of the differences existing within the group. The plan has been approved by the National Association of Insurance Commissioners although there are still many objections.

group task role   *communication*   Role of participant in a group. These include the initiator, the information giver, the information seeker, and the opinion giver.

group term life   Insurance providing for payment of face amount to designated beneficiary upon the death of the insured at any time and from any cause while the coverage is in effect. Over 90% of group life insurance in force is yearly renewable term. The popularity of this plan is due chiefly to its low cost, the simplicity of administration, and the tax advantages.

growing equity mortgage (GEM) Mortgage loan in which the payment is increased by a specific amount each year, with the additional payment amount applied to principal retirement. As a result of the added principal retirement, the maturity of the loan is significantly shorter than a comparable level payment mortgage.

growth stock   Security issued by companies whose sales and earnings are expanding faster than the economy and/or faster than the average of their particular industry. The company is usually aggressive and research minded and plows back most of its earnings into the company for future expansion. For this reason, growth companies, intent on financing their expansion from retained earnings, pay relatively small dividends and their current yield is generally low. Over time, however, investors hope substantial capital gains will accrue from the appreciations of the value of their stock as a result of the plowback and expansion.

growth stock fund   Mutual fund which may specialize in investing in stocks with the potential to grow rapidly and ultimately produce an outstanding return on investment. The goal is capital appreciation.

guaranteed annual income   Plan that awards all families under a certain poverty line level a straight allowance for each par-

ent plus specified amounts for each child according to the size of the family. No family receives less than a designated amount, and as a family's income rises, the payment from the government is reduced until a break-even level, which is a little higher than the poverty line, is reached.

guaranteed annual wage   *economics* A system proposed by organized labor wherein employees will be assured of sufficient work during the year to result in an agreed-upon annual income.

guaranteed dividend   *investing; finance* A payment made to the holders of the capital stock of a firm which is guaranteed and paid periodically.

guaranteed insurability option   Option that permits the policyholder to purchase for an additional premium additional amounts of insurance at stated intervals, without additional proof of insurability.

guaranteed interest certificate   *investing* A registered investment vehicle which is negotiable and which covers the guaranteed portion of a Small Business Administration loan. Such instruments are traded in the secondary markets.

guaranteed minimum annuity   Life annuity which requires a smaller periodic payment in exchange for a guaranteed return, either a full refund of the invested principal or a guaranteed number of payments.

guaranteed mortgage certificate (GMC)   Instrument created in 1975 by the Federal Home Loan Mortgage Corporation to encourage institutional investors in the capital markets to purchase mortgage-secured instruments. The guaranteed mortgage certificate was specifically designed to appeal to pension funds, trusts, and insurance companies that find that cash flow certainty and greater freedom from reinvestment problems make corporate bonds more appealing than the mortgages. Because of the complexity of the GMC, the total amount issued through mid-1978 was only $1.8 billion. The GMC represents an undivided interest in specific mortgages tailored so as to meet the requirements of institutional investors that dislike the servicing and origination costs and the inconvenience of the monthly principal and interest payments associated with mortgage payments. Also called FHLMC mortgage certificate or FHLMC participation certificate.

guaranteed renewable   Renewal provision in a health insurance policy providing that the insured will have the right to renew the coverage for a specified period of time, such as to age sixty-five or, in some cases, for life. During this time the insurer can make no changes in premium rates except for whole classes of policies.

guarantee of sale   Situation in which an underwriter agrees to take all of a new issue and guarantees payment whether or not the company is able to sell all of the issue. Most agreements are made between firms and underwriters on this basis.

guarantor   Person who makes or gives a guarantee.

guaranty of title   *insurance* A protection provided by some insurance companies to insure a buyer of real estate against an invalid title. Such protection is of value both to the buyer of the real property and the mortgage lender.

guardian   *law* Person designated by a court to administer the affairs of one who is legally incompetent.

guardian ad litem   *law* Person designated by a court to handle the affairs of a legally incompetent person in legal proceedings.

guardian de son tort   *law* A person, not appointed by the court, who takes possession of and manages a minor's property, or that of an incompetent person, thus making himself or herself accountable to the court.

guardianship   Custody and management of the minor's property with fiduciary responsibilities akin to those of a trustee but without holding legal title to property.

guest worker   A foreign national who is permitted to enter a country for work, but who is not allowed to move there or move family there. This is a common occurrence in the European Economic Community.

guild socialism   *economics* A socialistic system propounded in England after World War I, involving the organization of the economy into modern guilds (or industries) with minimum government interference.

gun jumping   *investing* The practice of trading securities on information before it is disclosed to the public, and the illegal soliciting of buy orders in an underwriting before the Securities and Exchange Commission registration.

H

Haavelmo principle   *econometrics* Principle that the statistical method used must be derived from a model that specifies the relations among the jointly dependent variables.

habeas corpus   *law You shall have the body.* Writ to produce the body of a person under detention before a court of superior jurisdiction with a view to testing the legality of the detention.

habendum   In conveyancing, that part of a grant which limits the quantity of the estate conveyed.

habendum et tenendum   *To have and to hold;* phrase used in a conveyance to delineate the estate granted.

habitable   Fit to be occupied, not only with safety but with reasonable comfort.

hade of land   Unplowed strip of land situated between two plowed portions of a field.

haeredes proximi   *Next of kin,* nearest heirs.

haeredes remotiores   *Remote heirs.*

haeredipeta   *The next heir to lands.*

haereditas, alia corporalis, alia incorporalis; corporalis est, quae tange potest et videri; incorporalis quae tangi non potest nec videri   *An inheritance is either corporeal or incorporeal. A corporeal inheritance is one which is tangible and visible; incorporeal is one which can neither be touched nor seen.*

haereditas damnosa   An inheritance which is more a burden than a benefit.

haereditas est successio in universum jus quod defunctus habuerit *Inheritance is the succession to all the rights that a deceased had.*

haereditas legitima Inheritance by operation of law (by devolution) as contrasted with a testamentary one.

haereditas testamentaria *Testamentary inheritance.*

haeredum in infinitum *Heirs to infinity.* Perpetual inheritance through endless lineage.

haeres factus An heir appointed as such by will.

haeres institutus *A testamentary heir.*

haeres legitimus est quem nuptiae demonstrant *The lawful heir is one whom marriage points out as such*; only a person born in lawful wedlock is capable of inheriting.

haircut *investing* A term used in the securities industry which refers to the formulae used in determining a broker/dealer's net capital. Since, at any point in time, securities may not be worth their face value, if anything, methods have been devised to determine the current value of any security.

half-life *investing* The point in time at which half the principal has been repaid on a mortgage-backed security guaranteed or issued by the Government National Mortgage Association (Ginnie Mae), the Federal National Mortgage Association (Fannie Mae), or the Federal Home Loan Mortgage Corporation (Freddie Mac). Many such securities have a half-life of twelve years, but they vary as to pay-out time.

half-stock *investing* Common or preferred stock with a fifty dollar par value rather than the usual hundred dollars.

half-year convention *tax* Principle which assumes that any property put into service during the year was acquired in the middle of the year, without regard to the actual date of purchase. The 1986 deduction is the same whether the equipment was purchased on January 15, 1985, or December 15, 1985. This allows the buyer to buy needed equipment near the year's end, and thus save tax dollars.

hammer *law* A forced sale.

hammering the market *investing* The intense selling of stock over a short period, usually by speculators, who believe the market is about to drop. In view of this, they will sell short, expecting to buy back in later at a lower price.

hand *law* Signature or handwriting.

hand-to-mouth buying *economics* A business's buying only as it sells, either because of financial problems, or because it does not want the expense of carrying inventory.

harbor Port or haven so protected, naturally or artificially, as to provide shelter for ships. Port has a larger meaning, for it implies the availability of such facilities as wharves, dock, etc.

hard dollars *investing* Actual dollar payments made to a brokerage firm by a client for services rendered, including research. This is held to be distinct from the usual transactional fees the client might pay. Such payments are said to be "soft dollars."

hard money *economics* 1. Metallic money (usually with intrinsic value) as opposed to paper money. 2. A stable monetary unit with little fluctuation in purchasing power.

harmonic mean *statistics* A value obtained by adding the reciprocals of all the values of the items in a series, then dividing this total by the number of items and taking the reciprocal of the quotient.

harmonic series *statistics* A series so composed that the reciprocal of each term forms an arithmetic series.

Harvard case method An educational method, first utilized at Harvard School of Business, which puts the accent upon case studies, usually from real-life situations.

Hawley-Smoot Tariff Act *economics* A tariff law passed in 1930 raising tariff rates on more than a thousand commodities but permitting variation of rates within a 50% limit by the President on the advice of the U.S. Tariff Commission. The law was passed ostensibly to protect U.S. industries as the Great Depression was getting underway. It had the effect, conversely, of further deepening and prolonging the Depression.

Hawthorne effect *management* The instinctive tendency of employees to group together, either formally or informally, and to improve performance when they know they are being watched.

Hayek's concept of depression *economics* A theory that denies that depressions are caused by excess savings. Rather, Hayek declares that a shortage of capital which prevents producers from using the full capacity of their facilities contributes to the business cycle on the down-side.

hazard 1. Condition that may create or increase the chance of loss from a given peril. Exposure to the chance of loss or injury. 2. *insurance* The risk, danger, or probability that the event insured against may happen, varying with the particular circumstances of the case.

head-and-shoulder pattern Tool of technical analysis; a pattern of security prices that, when graphed, resembles a head and a shoulder. A series of peaks with the central peak being higher than the previous or following peaks. It may be interpreted as a sell signal and the end of an upward trend.

header Person who simultaneously buys and sells to reduce the risk of loss inherent in commodities trading.

head hunter *management* A person or firm who serves as an agent for other companies to find specific types of personnel needed by the companies. This is most often done on a fee basis, and the fee is paid by the company retaining the services of the agent.

head note *law* Summary of an issue covered in a reported case; summaries of all points discussed and issues decided in a case, which are placed at the beginning of a case report.

head of a family Individual who supports and maintains in one household one or more individuals who are closely connected to that person by blood relationship, relationship by marriage, or by adoption.

head-of-household status Tax category that extends head-of household benefits to a single person who has responsibility for support of one or more dependent relatives. (*See* Appendix G)

head tax *economics* A tax of a specified amount per head (or per person).

health maintenance organization (HMO) 1. Formal organization of physicians who provide medical service to subscribers and divide earnings. Each subscriber to a group practice plan pays a premium in return for the right to medical care when desired. HMOs emphasize prevention. Their benefits are broader than group insurance or Blue Cross/Blue Shield plans. They are not limited to treatment resulting from accident or illness but extend to preventive medicine also. 2. Special health organization which restricts treatment to one clinic. They offer some benefits if the employees involved are willing to place all their health care in the hands of the one organization. Referrals will be made if the particular HMO does not have the needed service available.

"Heard on the Street" *investing* A column in the Wall Street Journal which often discusses stocks which have performed well and therefore deserve attention.

hearing A proceeding, marked by certain formalities, held by a court of law, judicial or quasi-judicial, or administrative tribunal where definite issues of fact or law are determined.

hearsay evidence Such evidence as derives its value not solely from the credit to be given to the witness upon the stand but in part from the veracity and competency of some other person.

heavy market *investing* A situation which exists in a bond, stock, or commodity market when prices are falling because the offers to sell far outnumber the bids to buy.

hectare Metric land measurement equal to about 2.471 acres or about 107,637 square feet.

hedge 1. To make a commitment on both sides of a transaction so that the risks offset each other. 2. Means by which a party who deals in the purchase of commodities in large quantities for actual delivery at some future time insures itself against unfavorable changes in the price of such commodities by entering into compensatory arrangements or counterbalancing transactions on the other side.

hedge clause *investing* In essence, a disclaimer, seen in many market letters, research papers, or other printed matter regarding the evaluation of securities, which is designed to absolve the writer of any responsibility with respect to investment decisions made on the strength of the writing.

hedge fund Unregulated investment fund in which speculative investments, such as margin, short selling, trading futures contracts, and buying and selling puts and calls, are used to achieve its objective of using relatively small amounts of cash to make quick profits.

heir *common law* 1. Person who, on intestacy, succeeds to the estate of the deceased. There can be no heir until after the death of the ancestor. 2. Person who inherits property, either real or personal, whether by will or by operation of the law from someone who dies without a will.

heir apparent One who has the rights to heirship or inheritance providing that one lives longer than one's ancestor.

heiress Female heir.

heirloom Personal chattel that goes to the heir, together with the inheritance. A chattel intended to pass on with land.

heir presumptive Person who would be an heir if the ancestor died immediately, but who is liable to be displaced by the birth of a nearer heir.

hemline theory *investing* Idea that stock prices tend to rise and fall as the hemlines of women's dresses rise and fall. Historically, this has been true on a few occasions, but it is obviously considered a theory without foundation in fact.

herbage License to pasture cattle on another's land.

herd instinct *investing* Tendency in people to follow the crowd when it comes to investing. Usually, this bears no relationship to the direction of the market at the time. This has a special meaning to the contrarian investor who often tends to pursue a path diametrically opposed to the crowd.

hereditament Any inheritable estate or interest in property. (*See* corporeal hereditament, incorporeal hereditament)

heredity Transmission of genetic characters from parents.

heritor One who owns an inheritance.

hermeneutics *law* Art of construing and interpreting documents, such as scriptural or legal writings.

Herzberg's theory *management* Theory of employee motivation devised by Herzberg, one of the better-known management specialists of the 1950s and '60s. His theory propounds two basic concepts: (a) There are such things in the workplace as "dissatisfiers" or "hygiene" problems. While these do not have the power to satisfy or motivate employees, they do have, in large proportions, the power to frustrate them. So, the employer must see that the dissatisfiers never reach the proportions to frustrate the employees. (b) There are also primary motivators, or "satisfiers," such as higher pay, status, a feeling of personal worth, etc. The two facets of Herzberg's theory must be used in tandem to promote a healthy, efficient workplace.

heuristic *statistics* Describes the process of arriving at the solution of a problem, not by a systematic step-by-step approach, but by the use of a series of plausible, proposed solutions whose testing determines in which direction to proceed.

HH bond *investing* Ten-year savings bond issued by the federal government, which pay interest semi-annually. HH bonds can be obtained only in exchange for EE bonds which have matured. At the end of the ten-year period, the HH bonds can be renewed for another ten-years, and another if so desired. Rates of interest vary according to the time the bonds are issued.

hidden inflation *economics* A noticeable deterioration in the quality of a good, while the price remains the same.

hidden tax *economics* An indirect tax which is included in the price of the good sold, thus not revealing how much of the price is actually tax.

hidden unemployment That part of the unemployed population not reflected in official unemployment figures (i.e., not legally counted as being in the labor force).

"Higgledy Piggledy Growth" *investing* An article written by Ian Little for some British companies, saying essentially that past growth and performance are almost useless in predicting future growth.

high flyer *investing* A high-priced, and usually highly speculative stock which tends to move up or down sharply in a short period of time. Stocks of new high-tech companies often fall into this category.

highest and best use   *real estate* The legally and physically possible use that, at the time of appraisal, is most likely to produce the greatest net return to land and/or buildings over a given period.

highgrading   *mining* Practice of stealing ore.

high-premium convertible debenture   *investing* A long-term bond with a high-premium stock conversion feature which also pays a competitive interest rate. (Cf. premium)

high-ratio loan   *banking* A mortgage loan which approaches the size of the value of the collateral securing it.

high rise   Building that exceeds six stories in height and is equipped with elevators.

high seas   Part of the sea outside territorial waters.

high technology   Production processes that utilize modern, especially electronic, techniques and are capital-intensive with a large investment in equipment per worker.

high-water mark   Part of the seashore to which the waters ordinarily reach when the tide is highest.

highway   *law* Passage or roadway open to the public. Thus, public rivers are in law considered as highways.

Highway Beautification Act (1965) Legislation regulating the use of outdoor advertising near interstate highways.

hinder   To cause delay, interruption, difficulty; to obstruct.

hindrance   The act of impeding, stopping, or preventing.

hire purchase   An installment purchase, one which is paid out over a period of time with periodic payments being made. Title usually does not reside in the purchaser until the last payment is made. A term used mostly in the United Kingdom and western Europe.

histogram   *statistics* A graph composed of a series of rectangles proportional to class frequency, and grouping all items by ranges.

historical-cost depreciation   Depreciation based on the amount originally paid for an asset.

historical school of economics   A group of nineteenth-century economists, primarily from Germany, which opposed the classic school because of its theoretical composition, and opted for theories based on historical facts.

historic structure   Building officially recognized for its historic significance. Such buildings have special status under the 1976 Tax Reform Act, which encourages their rehabilitation and discourages demolition or substantial alteration. In 1981 a special tax law allowed a 25% tax credit for rehabilitation of certified historic structures.

hit the bid   *investing* The action of accepting the highest price offered for a stock. (E.g., if the ask price for stock is 26¼, and the current bid is 26, the seller will hit the bid if the seller accepts the bid of 26.)

holder   Person who has legal possession of a check, promissory note, or bill of exchange and who is entitled to receive payment.

holder in due course   1. Someone acquiring in good faith a purchaser's note. A legal doctrine previously separated the purchaser's obligation to pay the note from the seller's obligation to meet the terms of the sale. 2. One who has taken a note, check, or other negotiable instrument, complete and regular on the face of it, in good faith and for value, without notice of any defect in the title of the person who negotiated it.

holder of record   Stockholder whose holdings are recorded in the books of the corporation.

hold harmless clause   *contracts* Clause or agreement in which one party agrees to release another from all legal liability resulting from the occurrence of specific events.

holding company   Corporation organized and authorized to hold common stock in one or more other corporations.

holding out   *law* To represent as true by words or conduct that which may not be true. In the law of agency, a person holds out another as having authority to act as agent when the person so acts as to induce third parties to believe in the existence of such authority, which the person is precluded from denying if the third parties act in that belief.

holding period   1. Time span of ownership, often for investment in real estate. 2. *investing* The length of time an investor holds a security. Prior to the Tax Reform Act of 1986, this was of vital importance since taxes paid on capital gains were different if a stock was held for the short-term (six months or less), the long-term (six-months), or longer. (Cf. Appendix G)

holding period return Income plus price appreciation during a specified time period; total return divided by the cost of the investment.

holding the market *investing* The action of entering the market with enough buy orders to create a price support for a security or a commodity, the trend of which is down.

hold over To remain in possession of land or building after expiration of the term of lease.

holograph *law* Will or deed written entirely by the testator or grantor with his or her own hand without being witnessed.

holographic will *law* A will handwritten by the hand of the decedent. These are acceptable in some states, but not all.

Home Mortgage Disclosure Act (1975) An act governed by Regulation C of the Federal Reserve System which requires lending institutions to disclose the amount and location of their home mortgage activities to the public and to government officials. The act is administered by the regulatory agency for lending institutions.

homeowner's policy Insurance policy designed especially for homeowners. Usually protects owner from losses caused by most common disasters, theft, and liability. Coverage and costs vary widely.

Homeowners' Series Series of policies, often called the "76" series because they were rewritten in 1976, which are more complete in coverage and more readable for the policyholder than prior policies. The series is composed of seven different policies. While the policies have some provisions in common, each offers distinct advantages to homeowners of different types. All policies have two sections; one section covers property exposures and another covers liability exposures. Within the scope of the seven types of policies are tenant's insurance, condominium insurance, normal home insurance, and insurance for more expensive homes. Also, there is one policy specifically written for lower-cost, usually older, homes.

home run *investing* A large gain, quickly accomplished, by an investor on a specific security. (More often hoped for than realized.)

homestead 1. Real estate obtained under the homestead laws of the nineteenth century which made it possible for people to settle on land and obtain it free of cost from the government after a period of occupation and land development. 2. A minimum amount of land and a house exempted from seizure by provision in the law of bankruptcy. Differs from state to state. 3. The provision in the laws of inheritance securing to a widow the right to live in the family homestead after her husband's death. Differs from state to state. 4. Status provided to a homeowner's principal residence by some state statutes which protects the home against judgments up to specified amounts. This includes the home, the house, and the adjoining land where the head of the family dwells. The exemption from seizure or forced sale is purely statutory.

homestead association *See* savings and loan association.

homestead rights Rights given to individuals by state statutes protecting certain property belonging to a debtor from the claims of creditors. (*See* homestead)

homogeneous products Identical product produced by different firms.

honorarium Gift in place of a salary or wage; generally given to one who volunteers services to cover out-of-pocket expenses.

Hopkinson rate *economics* In public utilities, a rate which is made up of two parts a specific charge for fixed capacity costs and a charge based on the variable output cost.

horizon analysis *investing* A method of measuring the discounted cash flow from an investment, using time periods which are different from the maturity dates of the securities.

horizontal combination *economics* The merging of companies, each producing similar products, for the purpose of commanding a larger percent of the market, and to eliminate competition.

horizontal communication Communication where messages flow laterally between persons of the same rank or position.

horizontal integration The putting together of various firms, all doing essentially the same thing, under one management either through merger or acquisition. (Cf. vertical integration)

horizontal merger Joining of two firms that produce the same good or service or close substitutes.

hospital expense *insurance* Provisions for reimbursement of expenses incurred up to specified maximum amounts or confinement from nonoccupational accident or sickness. The coverage can usually be written to provide a daily board and room allowance after six hours of confinement, generally for 90, 120, or 365 days for one confinement. As a rule the costs are covered from the first dollar without coinsurance.

hospital insurance benefits plan *social security* Benefits provided to all persons age sixty-five and over who are entitled to monthly Social Security cash benefits or monthly cash benefits under railroad retirement programs (whether retired or not). Persons not covered by Social Security can apply for Medicare at age sixty-five and pay a monthly fee for it. This plan pays basic hospital costs only, and the four areas covered are: in-patient hospital care for up to ninety days for each benefit period; post-hospital extended care in a skilled nursing facility for up to one hundred days in each benefit period; an unlimited number of post-hospital home health services; and hospice care for terminally ill patients. Under certain conditions, one will be eligible for hospital benefits even if one does not draw Social Security benefits or is in a certain category of aliens.

hostile embargo Embargo imposed on ships belonging to a hostile country.

hostile takeover Acquisition of a corporation against the wishes of the management. (*See* takeover bid)

hot assets Unrealized receivables, appreciated inventory, and recapture on cost recovery property, all of which can be potentially recognized as ordinary income proving the exceptions to the general rule that no income will be recognized on the liquidation of a partnership.

hot issue *investing* A new issue of stock which is met with a surge of demand from issue date, trading on the first day at a price much higher than the public offering price. For new issues, those buying the original issue can often get quick and positive results, sometimes quadrupling the investment cost in the first year. However, new issues also have a good chance of failing, and often do.

hot money *finance* A monetary unit attracted to a country because of favorable interest rates. Also, a currency may sometimes become "hot" because it is overvalued, and traders in currency will want to dump their currency holdings as quickly as possible, before devaluation takes place, or the currency loses value in the international markets via other means.

house call *investing* A notice sent to a client from a brokerage house alerting the client that the margin account is below maintenance level.

household 1. Economic unit consisting of an individual or a family. 2. An organized family; a domestic establishment. A collective group living in a house, acknowledging the authority of a head, the members of which are bound by marriage, blood, affinity, or other bond, between whom there is an intimacy and by whom there is felt a concern with and an interest in the life of all.

house of issue *investing* An investment banking house that underwrites a new securities issue and offers it for sale to the public. (*See* underwriter, syndicate)

house rules *investing* A term used to describe the rules peculiar to a specific brokerage house. Rules tend to be almost the same, and all houses have to follow SEC rules, but houses often have rules peculiar to themselves.

Housing and Urban Development (HUD), Department of Cabinet-level United States government agency established to implement certain federal housing and community development programs.

housing code Local government ordinance that sets minimum standards of safety and sanitation (i.e., plumbing, heating, lighting, number of houses in an area, number of people that can live in certain type dwellings, etc.) for existing residential buildings, as opposed to building codes, which pertain to new construction.

housing starts   Estimate of the number of dwelling units on which construction has begun during a stated period.

how question   The question of how to produce a good or service; the process of determining what mix of land, labor, and capital to use in production and what production methods to employ.

HR 10   *See* Keogh Plan.

Hulbert Rating   *investing* A rating, prepared by an agency, of financial newsletters that are of an advisory nature as to their predictions compared with actual facts over a period of time.

Human Action   *economics; finance* A 1966 book by Ludwig von Mises of the Austrian school of economics in which he reveals that governments, and commercial banks, cause the unending boom-and-bust cycles in the economy by artificially expanding the supply of money and credit in the economy.

human asset accounting   *management* A practice which evolved in the United Kingdom whereby employees are valued as a factor of production rather than just a cost of doing business.

human capital   Labor which is literate, skilled, trained, healthy, and economically motivated.

human relations school   *management; industrial sociology* A school of thought developed mainly in the United Kingdom in the 1930s and '40s by Elton Mayo. He saw good relations between employees and employers as the key to providing high morale and productivity. This discipline has risen and fallen many times in the estimation of management specialists and is usually debunked by organized labor as a way for management to take a manipulative approach to labor.

human resources planning   *management* A term used primarily in the United States which denotes planning for future manpower needs.

hung convertible   *See* frozen convertible.

hung up   *investing* The position held by an investor whose securities have dropped in value below the purchase value, and who would suffer a considerable loss if the investor sells.

hurdle rate   1. Minimum acceptable rate of return on an investment. (*See* acceptance criterion)   2. *See* risk-adjusted discount rate.

husbandman   Farmer; a tiller of the soil.

husbandry   Agriculture; farming the soil for food.

hyperinflation   Condition in which prices rise rapidly and people rush to spend more money before it buys less; runaway inflation.

hypermarket; hypermart   1. A rapidly growing method of mass merchandising in which many types of stores are situated under one roof, selling everything from fast food to groceries, to hardware, clothing, household goods, etc. The hypermart is usually located near the edge of a city, the suburbs, or the countryside. Usually, the entire market is based on discount selling. It is noted, also, for having vast parking areas and the check-out capacity to service thousands of customers in a relatively short length of time.   2. Giant mass merchandising retail outlet that operates on a low-price, self-service basis and carries lines of soft goods and groceries.

hypothecate   To pledge property as security without actual transfer of possession.

hypothecation   *banking; investing* 1. The act of pledging property as collateral for a loan.   2. Pledging securities as collateral for loans made to purchase, or cover the purchase, of short sales.

hypotheque   *civil law* Right acquired by the creditor over immovable property which has been assigned to the creditor by the debtor as security for the debt, although the creditor is not placed in possession of it.

hypothesis   1. *law* Supposition; an assumption; a theory set up by the prosecution or defense as an explanation of the facts in evidence.   2. Working guess about the behavior of things; an expression about the relationship between variables in the real world.   3. *statistics* A statement or tentative theory which attempts to explain certain facts about the real world.

151

hysteresis   *economics* A term referring to the nonreversibility of an economic function, e.g., if in expansion the cost curve goes down, then after the expansion an effort to contract to the original position will not proceed along the same cost curve. This is due to the fact that not all economies (or diseconomies) inherent in the expansion are lost in the contraction.

I

ibidem (ibid.)   *In the same place;* in the same book; in the same page.

iconic model   *economics* A model that differs from reality only in terms of scale.

idem semper antecedenti proximo refertur   *"Idem" (the same) always refers to the nearest antecedent.*

identification   *economics; statistics* The problem of estimating the coefficient of the variables in a system of equations.

ignoramus   *We are ignorant;* used by the grand jury to dismiss a bill of indictment meaning not a true bill or not found.

ignorance of fact   Lack of knowledge of the fact in question. In law, to be excusable, such want of knowledge must not arise from the intentional neglect of the party to investigate.

ignorance of the law   Lack of knowledge of the law of one's own country or state.

ignorantia   Ignorance.

ignorantia eorum quae quis scire tenetur non excusat   *Ignorance of that which is known to all affords no excuse.*

ignorantia facti excusat, ignorantia juris non excusat   *Ignorance of fact excuses while ignorance of law does not.*

illegal   Forbidden by law; contrary to law; unlawful.

illegal contract   Agreement to do any act forbidden by law; an agreement that has an unlawful purpose (e.g., a contract to commit a crime or tort, one that amounts to an unlawful restraint of trade, or one to distribute pornographic material). An illegal contract confers no rights on the parties and no action can be founded on it.

illegal dividend   *investing* A dividend which is declared by the Board of Directors of a corporation in violation of its own charter, or of state laws. Most states require that dividends be paid out of current earnings or retained earnings. This is to prevent them from being paid out of capital surplus, or any other fund which might tend to weaken the financial structure of the company.

illegal interest   Rate of interest higher than the law allows; usury.

ill-gotten   Acquired by improper or illegal means.

illicit   Contrary to law, morals, or public order. Frequently used as a synonym for illegal.

illicitum collegium   Illegal corporation.

illness frequency rates   *economics; management* The number of illnesses suffered by the employees of a company per million man-hours of work, calculated on an annual basis.

illness severity rate   *economics; management* The number of days of work lost because of disabling illnesses or death per thousand man-hours of work, with six thousand charged to a death, calculated on an annual basis.

illusion of value   A deceptive concept of the true worth of an asset during a time when inflation is rapidly pushing up prices.

illusory   Having a false appearance of validity or of conforming to a valid legal act. Deceiving or tending to deceive; fallacious.

imbalance of orders   *investing* A situation in which there are too many orders either to sell or to buy a stock, without other orders to balance out the market. This often happens as a result of an event in the life of a company which might tend to move its stock price either up quickly or down quickly.

imitation   A thing in similitude or likeness of another.

immaterial   Unimportant; not essential or pertinent; of no substantial consequence. An averment is said to be immaterial when it is unnecessary in regard to the matters in issue; an issue is said to be immaterial when it will not decide the action at hand.

immediate   *law, insurance* Acting without intervention of another object, cause, or agency, as an immediate cause; adjoining; nearest; next; in relation to space, in uninterrupted relation, continuous, direct, as the immediate contact of two objects; in relation to time, occurring without delay, made or done at once.

immediate annuity   Annuity in which benefits are purchased with a single premium and begin at the end of the first income period.

immediate cause   Last event in a series of events which, without further events, produced the result in question.

immediate insurance needs   Catch-all phrase indicating certain types of insurance coverage one cannot be without.

immediately   Straightaway or without any delay or lapse of time; the act to be done should be done at all convenient speed. "Immediately" and "forthwith" are synonymous and import a greater urgency than "within a reasonable time."

immediate or cancel order   *investing* A buy or sell order which requires that the broker execute the order immediately, in whole or in part, and that the remainder be cancelled. Often this will be a large buy or sell order, which may be difficult to fill completely in a short period of time.

immediate payment annuity   *investing* An annuity contract bought with only a single premium and with a specified pay-out plan, sometimes beginning immediately. Payments, usually on a monthly basis, might continue for a specified period of time or for the life of the annuitant.

immediate vesting   *pension plans* An alternative to bringing employees into a plan after one year's service. Three years' service may be required prior to participation, provided that the participant becomes immediately 100% vested at the end of three years (i.e., from the beginning of participation).

immemorial   *law* Before the time of legal memory.

imminent   *law* About to happen; near at hand; close rather than touching; impending; menacingly near.

immobile   Immovable.

immobilis   *Immovable.*

immoral contract   Contract founded upon an immoral consideration.

immovable   Incapable of being moved. The term includes land, that which is affixed to land, that which is incidental or appurtenant to land, and that which is immovable by law.

immunity   Freedom from duty or penalty; special privilege; exemption, as from tax.

immunization   *investing* A method of equalizing the maturities for assets and liabilities in order to reduce interest-rate risk.

impact day   *finance* The date of the public issue of new stock offerings by a corporation. (The term is used in England, and other countries, but rarely in the United States.)

impair   To make worse; to diminish in quality, value, excellence, or strength; to weaken or deteriorate.

impaired capital   *economics* A negative surplus account. Capital stock whose value has been reduced below the level of the initial purchase price of the stock when issued.

imparity   Lack of parity or equality; disparity.

impartial   Favoring neither; treating all alike; unbiased.

impeach   To bring charges of misconduct in office against a public official.

impeachment   Proceedings for the removal of a state or federal officer for misconduct in office or for a crime.

impeachment of waste   *law* Liability of a life tenant or tenant with a limited estate for committing waste on the demised premises.

impede   To obstruct; to hinder; to check; to delay.

imperative   Mandatory; as contrasted with "directory," which is a direction or instruction of no obligatory force.

imperfect   Not complete; lacking in

some essential; defective; not enforceable in law. An obligation is said to be imperfect when it is in the nature of a moral, charitable, or similar obligation which cannot be enforced by law.

imperfect mortgage   Legal title which a vendor holds under an unexecuted contract for the conveyance of land upon payment of the purchase money, in which case the vendor's interest in the land is nothing more than a security; the security is said to be stronger than a mortgage, because the legal title is retained as security.

imperfect title   *law; real estate* Title which requires a further exercise of granting power to pass fee in land or which does not convey full and absolute dominion, not only as against private persons, but as against the government, or one which may consequently be affirmed or disavowed by political or granting authority.

imperialism   *economics* The expanding of industries or trade into less advanced countries for the purpose of: (a) the development of outlets for the investment of excessive savings of the developed country, or (b) the development of markets for the excess production of the advanced country, or both.

implicit rent   *economics; accounting* In calculating the income of a business which owns its own lands (and buildings, probably) the amount of rent it would have to pay on the land if it were leased or rented instead of owned.

implicit wages   Income which is the result of labor input that is not received as wages or salary but in some other form, such as net proprietor's income (profits).

implied agency   Agency in fact found to be so by a court drawing reasonable deductions from disclosed facts. May spring from acts within control of the principal and permitted over course of time by acquiescence, although it cannot exist contrary to the principal's express will.

implied authority   Powers directly connected with and essential to the business specifically designated to an agent and that can be inferred and proven by circumstantial evidence such as the conduct of the principal.

implied contract   *law* A contract

which, according to the actions of the parties, appears to be in force though no written agreement has been made. (E.g., if a contractor is furnished with building materials by a dealer, and the contractor accepts, signs for, and uses the materials, it must be assumed that some kind of contract exists, even though no formal agreement has been signed.)

implied notice   Knowledge by inference.

implied powers contract   *law* A concept of the U.S. Constitution developed early in the nineteenth century which follows the principle that the means to an end are implied as correct if the end is an express power in the Constitution.

implied terms   *contract* Conditions that, although not expressly agreed upon between parties, would be inferred by law to be part of the engagement between them. Such terms are divided into two classes: those which are applied by formula to all contracts of a certain class by reason of general rules of law, unless inconsistent with the express terms (e.g., implied warranties on the sale of goods); and those which are the product of the interpretation of the express terms of the individual contract read in the light of its subject matter and the circumstances under which it was made, necessary to give the contract efficacy and produce a workable agreement.

implied trust   Trust arising from an equitable construction put upon the facts, conduct, or situation of the parties; may arise as a result of the intention of parties as inferred or presumed by law. If one buys and pays for a property and has the conveyance made to another party, that party is presumed to hold the property as trustee for the party who bought and paid for same, unless a contrary intention is shown.

implied warranty   *law* Conditions surrounding the sale, ownership, and disposition of goods which the buyer may assume to be true when not expressly denied by the seller. Warranty that is not written but exists under the law.

imply   To indicate indirectly; to suggest without explicitly stating.

import   1. To bring goods into a country from outside its geographical and political limits. 2. Good or service purchased from foreign suppliers.

import quotas *economics* A fixed amount of a specific good which may be imported during a given period of time. A restriction often used in lieu of tariffs to limit imported goods which may be in competition with domestic goods.

impose To levy or exact a tax, duty, or penalty.

impossibility *law* That which, in the constitution and course of nature or the law, no person can do or perform.

impossibilium nulla obligatio est *The law imposes no obligation to do what is impossible.*

impost Levy, tax imposed; generally used in relation to tax on goods imported or exported.

imposta complementare progressiva sul reddito complessivo A complementary tax or progressive surtax charged on an individual's total income from all sources in Italy.

imposto profissional A professional tax on earned income in Portugal.

impot des personnes physiques The Belgian income tax, which is a progressive tax on total net income from real estate and personal property including capital and income from miscellaneous sources. There is also a surcharge on high incomes.

impot federal pour la defense nationale A Swiss national defense tax charged on total income from all sources.

impot sur le revenu A principal income tax levied in both France and Luxembourg which is progressive in nature and which is levied on income from any source, including capital gains.

imprest fund *accounting* A fund created for purposes of internal control, withdrawals from which can only be made as authorized and supported by documents. Usually, the fund is brought back to its normal level by periodic payments into the fund.

improved land Land that has been partially or fully developed for use.

improved pension program Program for armed services personnel which went into effect on January 1, 1979, in which benefits are generally paid monthly and reduced by the annual accountable income of the surviving spouse and dependent children; however, there are a number of income exclusions. Certain educational expenses and unreimbursed medical expenses are not included in determining income. In addition, the pension may be denied or discontinued if the claimant's net worth is such that it is reasonable that some portion of the estate be used for the claimant's support. Additional pension for a child may be denied if the child's net worth is excessive. A child's net worth would probably be classified as excessive if the assets owned produced as much annual income as the $1,239 payment for the dependent child. Pensioners must provide income and net worth reports annually to the Veterans Administration.

improvement 1. Act of making or becoming better; a process, change, or addition by which the value or excellence of a thing is increased; that by which anything is made better. 2. Addition to raw land tending to increase value (e.g., buildings, streets, and sewers).

improvidence Want of foresight or thrift.

impuesto general sobre la renta de las personasfisicas The general income tax of Spain, which is a progressive tax charged on all income.

impugn To assail by words or arguments; to draw into question.

impulse goods *marketing* Consumer goods of the type which are normally purchased on whim, or the feeling of the purchaser at the time. Unplanned buying done on the spur of the moment. These products, such as candy, periodicals, gadgets, and cigarettes, are often displayed near store cash registers to induce spur-of-the-moment purchases.

impunity Exemption or protection from penalty or punishment.

imputed costs *accounting* Those costs incurred in the normal process of running a business, but which are not directly related to the production or marketing of products. Interest paid on loans is an example.

imputed income *finance* Wages, or other payments, received in a form other than money. Goods or services are given in lieu of money. (E.g., the employer may furnish a dwelling as part of the employee's wages.) These and many other forms of implied income never enter the national income accounts.

imputed interest Implied interest; in a mortgage with an insufficient interest rate, the law will impute the rate is higher and the principal is less.

imputed knowledge Knowledge assumed on the part of a principal for having been received by one's agents acting within the scope of their authority.

imputed negligence Legal fiction whereby negligence of one person is charged to another because of a legal relationship existing between them, such as between parent and child, husband and wife, driver and passenger, owner of a vehicle and driver, bailor and bailee, or master and servant.

inactive post *investing* A post on the trading floor of the New York Stock Exchange where inactive stocks are traded in lots of ten shares rather than in round lots of one hundred shares.

inadmissable That which, under established rules of law, cannot be received or admitted as evidence in a court of law.

inadvertence *law* Heedlessness; lack of attention; carelessness; oversight.

in aequali jure melior est conditio possidentis *Where rights are equal, the party in possession is favored.*

inalienability Impediment of the right to freely transfer property. The rule against inalienability is often confused with the rule against perpetuities but is directed against a different evil, i.e., the making of a devise, gift, transfer, or trust of property in tenure which prevents or fetters the free disposition of the property.

inalienable Incapable of being transferred to another.

in-and-out trader *investing* Someone who buys and sells stock on the same day, hoping to profit from sudden price fluctuations.

in articulo mortis *At the point of death.*

in bond Describes goods on which custom duties have not been paid and which are stored in the customs' bonded warehouse.

incapacity Legal disability; want of capacity.

incestuous share dealing *finance* Buying and selling of each other's stock by closely related companies for the purpose of seeking some tax advantage, or some other financial advantage.

inchmaree Clause(s) in an ocean marine insurance policy covering the risks other than perils at sea.

inchoate Unfinished; begun but not completed, as a contract that has not been executed by all parties involved.

inchoate right 1. *law* A right which is not yet complete. (E.g., the interest of a wife in the lands and tenements of her husband during his lifetime is said to be an inchoate right to dower, since the interest is not complete until his death.) 2. *patent law* The right of an inventor to use the invention while application for patent is pending.

incidence of a tax Amount of a tax that ultimately falls on households, irrespective of who initially pays the tax.

incident Connected, as a condition or event. A happening which is dependent upon or follows another is said to be incident to it.

incident of ownership Any degree of control over an asset. Generally, has reference to an insurance policy which would normally be outside one's probate estate. If the policyholder maintains any degree of control, such as the receipt of dividends, the policyholder is considered to still have incident of ownership.

inclosure Land surrounded by a visible obstruction, such as a fence. Also spelled enclosure.

inclusive Comprehensive; taking in the stated limits or extremes.

income The return to a factor of production as a result of productive activity, such as the return in money from one's business, labor, or capital invested.

income and expenditure statement *finance; accounting* A form similar to a profit and loss (P/L) statement issued by a for-profit business, but issued by a non-profit organization to account for both monies received and monies expended.

income approach Method appraising real estate based on the property's anticipated future income. (*See* Appendix C)

income averaging Method of computing income tax which allows the qualified taxpayer to reduce the tax liability in peak income years by spreading the taxable income evenly over five years. (*See* Appendix G)

income bond Bond that has a stated rate of interest with principal due at maturity with the interest payable only as earned by the corporation.

income effect Increase or decrease in a buyer's real income (i.e., in goods purchased) resulting from a change in the price of a commodity while the buyer's money income, tastes, and the prices of all other goods remain the same.

income elasticity of demand *economics* With all prices constant, the relative change in quantity demanded of a good consumed compared with the relative change in income, assuming all prices remain constant.

income fund *investing* A unit trust or mutual fund whose primary objective is to produce income for the shareholders, as opposed to capital growth. At times, the fund ends up producing both.

income in respect of a decedent (IRD) Items of income, or items for deduction, which would have been either receivable or payable to the decedent had that person lived. Such items must be either received or paid by the estate, and taxes paid, in the same proportion the decedent would have paid them.

income leakage *economics* Leakage from the national income as graphically illustrated in the circular flow of income chart. Leakages may be accounted for by savings (money not spent), taxes (money the individual cannot spend), or anything that is not consumption in the period being calculated. It must be noted, however, that the leakages may be offset by investment, by government purchases or transfer payments, or in other ways. If income from the flow were not put back into the flow in some manner, the flow in the subsequent year would be lowered by the amount of the leakage.

income program Income producer. (E.g., an oil and gas income program involves the purchase of existing, produc-

ing wells with investors taking no drilling risks.)

income property Real estate that generates rental income.

income splitting Shifting a portion of the high marginal income taxpayer's unearned income (i.e., passive investment income) to related persons in a lower tax bracket. This can be accomplished by creating a trust or a custodial account under the Uniform Gifts to Minors Act or by making outright gifts of income-producing assets to family members. Income splitting is often utilized to reduce the tax burden on the donor, while at the same time creating funds to meet specific needs of the donee. (*See* Appendix G)

income statement Report of a company's revenues, associated expenses, and resulting income or loss for a period of time. Also called profit and loss statement.

income stock *investing* 1. Stock of well-known company which has a long history of paying regular and substantial dividends, as compared to a young company where the primary return may be in capital growth. 2. A stock that pays a higher-than-average return; stocks that yield generous current returns in the form of dividends.

income stream Regular flow of money generated by a business or investment.

income summary *accounting* A statement (or account) used at the end of an accounting period which summarizes and clears the revenue and expense accounts.

income velocity of money *economics* The ratio of income generating expenditures in a time period to the quantity of money. Income generation expenditures include both expenditures on consumer's goods and expenditures on investment goods.

in common Owned, used, or enjoyed by several persons without division into individual parts.

incompetence Lack of ability, fitness, or some legal qualification necessary for the performance of an act or the discharge of a responsibility.

incompetent *law* Lacking ability; lacking in skill; wanting in legal capacity. A person who has not realized the age of majority is legally incompetent to execute a contract or sue on his or her own behalf in court. In law of evidence, an incompetent witness is one whose testimony is not admissible under law.

incomplete gift Gift in which the donor reserves some interest in or power over the property. If the gift is not considered complete, there will be no gift tax liability, but there may be an estate tax liability if the owner does not consume the property in his or her lifetime.

incontestability clause 1. Provision in a life insurance policy whereby an insurer cannot contest a policy after a certain date or after issuance of the policy. 2. Provision in an insurance policy which prohibits the insurer from contesting statements made by the insured after a stated period of time, such as two years.

inconvertible paper standard Monetary standard under which the nation's unit of currency may or may not be defined in terms of any metal or other precious substance; however, there is no free convertibility into these other forms. This standard has existed on a domestic basis in all countries since the worldwide abandonment of gold in the 1930s.

incorporate 1. To create a legal entity or body recognized by law; to form a corporation. 2. To take into or include as part of a whole.

incorporation by reference *law* Doctrine of interpretation of testamentary instruments whereby a testamentary document, if in existence when a will is executed and is sufficiently identified in the will, may, though neither attested nor subscribed, be probated as part of a validly executed will.

incorporators Three or more people who subscribe funds for a proposed business which will be chartered by the state as a corporation.

incorporeal chattel Class of incorporeal rights growing out of or incident to things personal, such as copyrights and patent rights.

incorporeal hereditament Anything which is inheritable and is not tangible or visible, such as rights and profits annexed to or issuing out of land.

incorporeal right Right issuing out of and annexed to or exercised with incorporeal inheritances, as for example annuities and right-of-way.

increasing cost *economics* A situation in which the average total costs per unit in a business increase as the volume of business increases. Extractive industries (mining, etc.) are specifically affected by this problem.

increasing returns *economics* When product output increases more, proportionately, than do factor inputs.

increment Increasing growth in bulk, number, or value.

incremental cost of capital *finance* The weighted cost related to different issues of securities put on the market in a given period. Usually, costs relate to different types of debt or equity instruments.

incremental pricing *finance* The use of a two-tier pricing scheme with one tier covering the full cost of production, and the second tier covering the marginal cost of further production.

incroachment Unlawful intrusion upon the right or possession of another.

incumbent 1. Imposed as an obligation of office or role. 2. Holding a benefice (an endowed church position) or any office.

incumber To make something subject to a charge or liability (e.g., by mortgaging land).

incumbrance *See* encumbrance.

incur To become liable for; to bring upon oneself.

indebitatus *Indebted.*

indebtedness The state of being in debt. Anything that is due and owing; a debt.

indefeasible *law* Something which cannot be annulled or declared void, such as an indefeasible deed to certain property.

in delicto *In default; in fault.*

indemnify 1. To compensate for loss or damage that has already occurred; to reimburse. 2. To give security against future loss or damage. 3. To protect another person against loss or damage.

indemnity 1. Contract or agreement by which one party agrees to secure another against an anticipated loss or to protect the party from the legal consequences of the act or omission of one of the parties or of some third person. 2. Compensation given for loss or damage already sustained. 3. *insurance* Legal doctrine limiting recovery under an insurance policy to the lesser of the sum which will restore the insured to his or her financial position prior to the loss or to the actual cash value of the loss.

indemnity benefit basis Reimbursement method for medical insurance coverage in which the insured is paid a stated sum of money for each day spent in the hospital.

indemnity benefit plan *insurance* Government-wide plan, administered by Aetna Life Insurance Company and underwritten by 130 carriers, offering reimbursement for expenses of hospital care, surgical and medical care and treatment, obstetrical benefits, prescribed drugs, medicines and prosthetic devices, and other medical supplies and services.

indemnity insurance Form of liability insurance obligating the insurer to reimburse or indemnify the insured only to the extent that the insured has actually paid damages.

indenture 1. *investments* Legal document that specifies the terms of a bond issue including the principal amount, maturity date, interest rate, any qualifications and duties of the trustee, and the rights and obligations of the issuers and the holders. 2. Legal document, such as a deed or contract, to which two or more persons are parties and which is executed by all parties involved. Originally, the document was in duplicate with the edges of the two copies indented for the purpose of making identification of the various parts easier. 3. *trusts* An agreement between two or more persons or legal entities which stipulates reciprocal rights and duties.

independent adjuster *insurance* Insurance adjuster who operates independently of any insurer (although the insurer is responsible for paying the adjuster's fees) and whose sole duty is to settle claims between the insurer and insured.

independent agent *insurance* Insurance agent operating under the American Agency System who will represent several companies in the property and liability insurance business and whose duty is to assist the insured by seeking out the best company and coverage for that individual.

independent contractor 1. Person who contracts to do certain work without control by the employer except as to the result or product. The test which distinguishes an independent contractor from a servant or agent is the degree of control which the employer is entitled to exercise. 2. *real estate* One who contracts or enters into agreements for building or renovating, who is unconnected with a large firm and does business in his own name.

independent executor *law* A position recognized in only a few states, where the executor of a will makes no more reports to the probate court after filing the inventory of the assets of the estate.

independent union *economics* A union which is not affiliated with some federation, or congress, of unions.

independent variable *statistics* A variable which is not dependent upon another variable for its value. (E.g., in a time series where the output of wheat per year and rainfall per year are charted, wheat is the dependent variable and rainfall is the independent variable.)

index fund *investing* A mutual fund whose portfolio matches the securities found in a broad-based stock index such as Standard and Poor's, and which portfolio therefore matches the market as a whole.

indexing System of adjusting incomes to stay in line with inflation.

indexing contracts Labor contracts which take into consideration increases in the cost of living over the period of the contract and make provision for wage increases based on those rises relative to the base year.

index-linked products *insurance* Insurance products designed with a cost-of-living index attached, so that the face amount of insurance automatically increases every three years based on changes in the Consumer Price Index during that period.

index number *statistics; economics* A mathematical device or number which is used to represent the price level, volume of trade, etc., of a given period, in comparison with that of a base period, the value for which is always 100%.

index of disparity *economics* A scale

159

for comparing the size of the leading firms of different industries with each other.

index of industrial production *economics* Using a base year equaling 100%, the positive or negative changes in any prior or subsequent year of total industrial production.

index of multiple correlation *statistics* The square root of the index of multiple determination.

index option *investing* Puts and calls on indices of stocks. Such options are traded on the New York, American, and Chicago Board Options Exchanges, among others. They may be broad-based indices covering a wide range of industries and companies, or a narrow range which may cover a single industry or one sector of the economy.

indicate To give reason to expect; to give a knowledge of; to show as something existing or taking place; to suggest.

indicated yield *investing* The coupon or dividend rate as a percentage of the current market price of the security. On a fixed rate bond, the indicated yield is the same as the current yield. (*See* current yield)

indication of interest *securities* A term used in securities underwriting meaning that the potential investor is interested, even while the securities are still in registration (or awaiting SEC approval). The broker will usually send the interested party a preliminary prospectus on the securities.

indictment Accusation by a grand jury.

indifference curve Using a graph with quantity of commodity "A" on one axis and quantity of commodity "B" on the other axis, the locus of all points indicating those combinations of the two variables which will yield equal satisfaction to a given individual.

indifference map *economics* A series of indifference curves for one individual with regard to consumption preferences as to two commodities with each curve revealing the various combinations of the two goods which are considered equal in value by the individual, but each separate curve indicating a higher level of satisfaction as the curves move farther from the origin.

indigent Destitute of property or means of comfortable subsistence; needy; poor.

indirect business tax *economics* 1. Land real property tax, excluding income tax. National income is determined after the deduction of indirect business taxes (as well as depreciation) from the gross national product. 2. Tax extracted from business, yet normally built into the selling price of the end product.

indirect cost *accounting; finance* Expenditure which is not directly attributable to any specific product or department, but which is attributable to the entire production of the plant. The accounting department will usually prorate the expenditure among the products or departments on a proportionate basis. Also known as overhead.

indirect demand *See* derived demand.

indirect expenses *accounting* Expenses that are incurred by the business for the benefit of all departments and thus become an indirect expense to each (e.g., electricity, heat, rent, etc.).

indirect labor *accounting* The amount of wages paid to employees which cannot be charged to specific finished goods because the wages do not vary proportionately with the units of the products made, but must be allocated in some logical manner to all existing jobs.

indirect tax Tax collected from businesses that are ultimately paid in full or in part by someone other than the business from which the tax is collected. All taxes, other than polls, are either direct or indirect taxes. A direct tax is imposed directly upon property according to its value or on the person who it is intended shall pay the same; an indirect tax is upon some right, privilege, corporate franchise, or persons who can shift the burden on someone else, such as an excise tax or sales tax.

indirect transfer Transfer of savings from savers to borrowers through a financial intermediary.

individual annuity Annuity purchased by an individual in which the individual pays an insurance company a specified capital sum in exchange for a promise that the insurer will make a series of periodic payments to the individual (the annuitant) for as long as the annuitant lives.

individual expectancy chart *management; psychology* A chart, often showing the results of psychological testing, which attempts to predict how an individual, or a group, will succeed in a specific occupation.

individual investor   Any person who puts money into a business, whether through buying stocks or bonds, government debt instruments, or bank vehicles that pay interest.

individualism   *economics; politics* 1. Similar to laissez-faire. 2. Any system opposed to collectivism.

individual program   *agriculture* Program set up by an individual in which a farm, or some semblance of a farm such as the ownership of cattle, is used as a tax shelter rather than a profit-making venture. Individuals involved in such programs are similar to passive partners in limited partnerships except they operate on their own. While there is considerable doubt as to what constitutes a farmer with respect to tax law, two prerequisites seem to stand out: how much the individual has to do with the workings of the project, and does whether the individual actively participates in management decisions. The 1984 Tax Act was a major attack on shelters taking advantage of prepaid expenses, one of which was cattle feeding. Since 1984, the definition of what a real farmer is has been narrowed, but is still not complete. This often requires that each case be examined according to its own merits. (*See* Appendix G)

individual retirement account (IRA)   Plan instituted by the Employee Retirement Income Security Act in 1974, and greatly expanded by the Economic Recovery Tax Act of 1981, allowing people with earned income, regardless of whether they are covered by another retirement plan, to establish a retirement account with a bank or another responsible organization as trustee or custodian. The individual may put into this account $2,000 per year or 100% of income, whichever is less. No income tax is paid on the funds until they are withdrawn. The individual may contribute an additional $250 per year for a spouse who does not work outside the house. When both spouses work, $4,000 per year may be saved in an IRA. (*See* Appendix G)

indorse   *See* endorse.

induced investment   *economics* New dollars invested in capital goods in response to increased consumer spending. This does not always ensue, however, since the increased consumption may just put back to work the idle capacity that already exists.

inducement   Form of influence brought by threats or promises. In inducing infringement of patent, must be active steps knowingly taken, in the sense of being purposeful or intentional, as distinguished from accidental or inadvertent.

industrial   Concerning manufacture or commercial production in general; of or pertaining to industry or labor.

industrial bank   *economics* A somewhat antiquated term denoting a type of bank that was organized to receive small deposits from industrial workers and make small loans. This function has now largely been taken over by full-service commercial banks.

industrial espionage   *economics* Deliberate attempts on the part of one company to acquire the secrets of another company, by devious means. This is sometimes done by electronic methods or by bribing an employee of the target company who has access to strategic information.

industrial life insurance   A type of life insurance sold in the past to industrial workers that was of generally small face values. Collections were generally made by a personal call by the agent who called weekly or monthly. This type policy made it possible for low income families to have some degree of protection. But it was expensive insurance and has now generally been replaced with other type policies, such as low-cost term insurance.

industrial park   Area designed and zoned for manufacturing and associated activities.

industrial property   Property used for industrial purposes, such as factories.

industrial revenue bonds   Bonds issued by a municipality to enable a business to build or expand facilities in accordance with the present existent laws of the federal government. Issuance through a municipality gives the bonds the status of a tax-free municipal bond. (*See* Appendix G)

Industrial Revolution   *economics* The dramatic technological advances of the nineteenth century and the economic and

161

social changes which accompanied them and led to the modern age. Among these changes were the factory system, specialization in production, and industrial capitalism.

industrials   Classification of securities usually covering manufacturers; most commonly used in reference to the standing of the Dow Jones Industrial Averages.

inefficiency in the market   *securities* A failure on the part of market investors to recognize either that a security has excellent prospects or that it may be headed for trouble. Though the market is supposed to be "efficient," in that its prices are supposed to reflect all information available, this information does not always get to the market first. Any investor who gets information before it reaches the market can often make good profits.

inelastic demand   *economics* Demand condition in which the quantity demanded does not change proportionately with the change in prices. (E.g., the price of bread increases by 10%, but there is no change in the demand for bread.)

inertia selling   *marketing* A highly unethical method of selling in which goods are shipped to possible purchasers without their consent, after which they are pressured to pay for the goods. The recipients will often pay for the goods rather than go to the trouble to return it.

in extremis   *In the last extremity*; at the point of death.

infans   *An infant.*

infant   *law* Person under the age of legal majority.

infant industry argument   Contention that it is economically justified to provide trade protection to a new industry in a country to enable it to grow to a size that would result in economies of scale competitive with foreign producers.

in fee simple   Absolute ownership of an estate in land.

in flagrante delicto   In the act.

inflation   Continuously rising general price level resulting in a loss of the purchasing power of money. (*See* demand-pull inflation, cost-push inflation)

inflationary gap   Amount by which aggregate demand exceeds aggregate supply at full employment, thereby causing inflationary pressures. Also called demand pull inflation.

inflation premium   Increased return on a security required to compensate investors for expected inflation.

inflow   Entry on a cash flow statement showing the amount of income for a specified period of time.

influence   *law* To effect, modify, or act upon by physical, mental, or moral power, especially in some gentle, subtle, and gradual way.

informal communication network   *communication* The "grapevine"; network that concerns itself with official matters when the formal channels of communication fail to deliver, are not understood, or are not accepted.

informative institutional advertising   Type of promotion concerned with increasing public knowledge of a concept, political viewpoint, industry, or company.

informative product advertising   Type of promotion that seeks to develop initial demand for a product. Used in the introduction phase of the product's life.

informed consent doctrine   General principle of law that a physician has a duty to disclose to the patient, within reason, whatever grave risks of injury might be incurred from a proposed course of treatment, so that the patient, faced with a choice of undergoing the proposed treatment, an alternative treatment, or none at all, may intelligently exercise judgment by reasonably balancing the probable risks against the probable benefits.

infraction   Violation, breach, or infringement, as of a law, obligation, or contract.

infra furorem   *During insanity.*

infrastructure   *economics* A nation's basic system of communications, transportation, and other aspects of its total physical make-up. The infrastructure requires vast amounts of capital to build and maintain, but provides millions of jobs, some continuing. Before a nation can develop, it must have a basic infrastructure sufficient to support a growing economy.

infringement   *law* 1. Trespass or encroachment upon; a violation of law, regulation, or contractual right. 2. In copyright, patent, or trademark law, the unauthorized invasion of the exclusive right of the owner to the privileges and benefits accompanying a copyright, patent, or trademark. The owner of such rights may permit, in some cases, the privilege to use the above, but may generally refuse if he or she desires.

in futuro   *At a future time.*

in gross   At large; personal. I.e., a right such as an easement is in gross when it is a personal right and not running with the land on the benefit side.

inhabitant   One who actually and permanently resides in a given place and has one's domicile there.

in haec verba   *In the same words.*

inherit   1. To take either by devise or descent from one's ancestor. 2. To take as an heir at law solely by descent rather than by devise.

inheritance   The passing of real property by descent. More broadly, may be either real property or personal property passed by will or through the intestacy of the former owner to heirs designated by law.

inheritance tax   Burden imposed by government on all gifts, legacies, and successions whether of real or personal property or both or any interest therein passing to certain persons (other than those specially excepted) by will, by intestate law, or by deed or assignment made inter vivos, intended to take effect at or after the death of the grantor. A tax levied by many states on the passing of property (not on the property itself) by descent or will. The tax is levied on the amount the beneficiary receives, and the percentage of the tax is usually quite small, and differs state by state.

initial margin requirement   *investing*   Good faith deposit made by an investor before engaging in margin transactions. (*See* margin)

initial public offering (IPO)   A corporation's first stock offering to the public. Often such an offering gives owners and first investors opportunities to make large profits, particularly if the company is doing well with respect to profits.

initiative   Power of the people to propose bills and laws and to enact or reject them at the polls, independent of legislative assembly. Right to propose laws to be enacted by the legislature reserved to the people themselves.

injunction   Order of the court ordering a party to do or refrain from doing a particular act.

in jure   *In law;* according to law.

in jure alterius   *In the right of another.*

injury   Infringement of some legal right; a wrong or damage done to another, either in one's person, rights, reputation, or property.

in kind   In commodities, produce, labor, etc., instead of in money, as payment in kind, in-kind income.

inland bill of exchange   Bill of exchange made in the United States and drawn on a person within the United States, though not in the same state as the drawer.

in loco parentis   *law In place of a parent.* This can refer to the guardian of a child, or a master/servant relationship.

inner city   Older, more urbanized area of a large city, often surrounding the central business district.

innkeeper's lien   *law; economics*   The right usually given an innkeeper to keep baggage or other possessions of a guest for charges unpaid.

innocent purchaser   Person who, by an honest contract, purchases property without knowledge or means of knowledge sufficient to be charged in law with notice of any infirmity in the title of the seller; such purchaser must have no reasonable basis to suspect that the seller did not have good title.

innovation   1. Adoption of a new or different product, or a new or different method of production, marketing, financing, etc., establishing a new relation between output and various kinds of input (capital, land, labor, etc.) in a production process. 2. The setting up of a new production function.

innovation theory of the business cycle   *economics*   Theory originated by Joseph Schumpeter (1883–1950) which attributes business cycles and economic development to innovations that were adopted to reduce costs and increase profits. Once an innovation proves successful, other businesses follow with the same or similar techniques, causing fluctuations in investment which result in business cycles. The innovation theory has also been used as a partial explanation of how profits arise in a competitive capitalistic system.

innuendo   Hinting, insinuation, or intimation.

in pari causa possessor potior haberl debet   *Where causes are equal, the persons in possession should be favored.*

in personam   *law Against the person.* A legal proceeding against a person, which, if the person should lose, he or she will be personally bound with a judgment. (Cf. in rem)

in-plant banking   *banking* A service which is provided by a bank for its employees, on the premises of the bank.

in praesenti   *At the present time.*

in principio   *At the beginning.*

in promptu   *In readiness.*

in re   *In the matter of;* concerning. Frequently abbreviated as "re."

in rem   *law* A legal proceeding against a specific property, as opposed to a person. (Cf. in personam)

inscription   1. Anything written or engraved upon a metallic object or other solid substance intended for great durability (e.g., on a tombstone, tablet, pillar, medal, ring, etc.). 2. In jurisdictions where civil law is prevalent, the entry of a mortgage, lien, or other document at large in a book of public record. 3. Anything written on a single surface.

inside limits   *insurance* Under major medical plans, maximum amount to be paid for certain types of services such as daily room and board, private nursing care, etc.

inside market   *investing* As distinguished from the retail market, trades between dealers who are trading from their own inventories and for their own profit.

insider   Person who, by reason of the percentage of the corporation's shares that the person holds or controls or by reason of position as a company officer or director, has information on the company's affairs not available to the general public. (*See* insider trading)

insider trading   *investing* A situation in which the directors or officers of a corpo-ration, or relatives and friends, use information from inside the company which is not available to outsiders to make a profit from dealing in that stock on the basis of the information. An insider is required to follow strict regulations of disclosure before trading in the stock of that corporation.

insolvency   Condition of indebtedness greater than the realizable value of one's assets.

insolvent   1. With liabilities exceeding assets, unable to pay debts as they become due. 2. One who has committed an act of insolvency in the meaning of bankruptcy statutes. A corporation is deemed to be insolvent if its assets can never be made to pay or the corporation does not possess available resources to meet its present needs, or if it closes up its business for want of funds, or if it commits any other act of bankruptcy.

in specie   *Specific;* specifically.

installment   Part of a larger debt, payable at successive periods as agreed; payment made to reduce a mortgage.

Installment Lending Directory   A book published by the American Bankers Association which lists all the banks in the country that extend installment credit to finance dealers and purchasers of durable consumer goods.

installment sale   Sale made with the agreement that the purchased goods or services will be paid for in fractional amounts over a specified period of time. Congress has made it possible to recognize the gain on the sale proportionately in each tax year in which payments are received. Device for spreading out the taxable gain and thereby deferring the income tax on the sale of property.

Instinet   *See* Institutional Network Systems.

institutional advertising   Type of advertising concerned with promoting a concept, an idea, a philosophy, or the good will of an industry.

institutional broker   *investing* One who trades securities for institutions such as banks, insurance companies, pension funds, etc. Trades are usually in large blocks, and a smaller fee per unit is charged.

Institutional Broker's Estimate System (IBES) A service provided by the New York Stock brokerage firm of Lynch Jones and Ryan. It assembles estimates of future earnings for thousands of publicly traded companies. Estimates are tabulated, and significant differences are noted from other points in time.

institutional economics An approach to economics which emphasizes the impact of institutions such as labor unions or corporations upon the economy and its development. This stands in juxtaposition to the normal approach, which includes individual decisions by investors and consumers, profit motives, utility, value, etc.

Institutional Network Systems (Instinet) A privately owned computerized trading network which allows its subscribers to deal privately with each other in trading securities without paying a brokerage fee.

instrument 1. Formal legal document, whereby a right is created or confirmed or a fact recorded; a formal writing of any kind as an agreement, deed, charter, or record drawn up and executed in technical form. 2. A tool or article used to perform work.

instrumentality 1. A means or agency; the quality or state of being instrumental; medium. In corporate law, the instrumentality rule is that when one corporation is so dominated by another that the subservient corporation becomes a mere instrument and indistinct from the controlling corporation, than its corporate veil will be disregarded and it will be considered as part of the controlling corporation. 2. *finance* A federal agency that issues bonds, notes or certificates which are guaranteed by the federal government, and are backed by the "full faith and credit" of the government. They are not, however, direct obligations of the United States government.

instrumental variable *economics* 1. A variable which is subject to control by policy makers, for example, the rediscount rate, taxes, or the quantity of money. 2. A variable which is exogenous to the economy and significant but does not enter the equation(s) being estimated, and is used in a special way to estimate such equations.

insurable Capable of being insured against loss, damage, death, etc.

insurable interest 1. Interest in a person or property that would cause one a loss if that person or property were injured. Such an interest must be sufficient to show that an insurance contract was not taken out as a mere wager policy. 2. Any interest which would be recognized by a court of law or equity. An insurable interest is not confined to a strict legal right of property.

insurable title Title that can be insured by a title insurance company.

insurance Contract of indemnity whereby for a stipulated consideration one party, called the insurer, undertakes to indemnify the other, called the insured, against damage or loss, on a specified subject by specified perils. The instrument by which the contract is entered into is called a policy.

insurance adjuster Agent of the insurer who undertakes to ascertain and report actual loss of insurance subject matter due to the peril insured against.

insurance age change In life insurance, the one-year period starting one-half year before and ending one-half year after the birthday is used to determine age for premium purposes. In annuities, however, the last birthday is used.

insurance agent Person or corporation which solicits the sale of insurance of all types, counsels prospective clients concerning their insurance needs, arranges coverage, and represents a number of different insurance companies.

insurance broker Person whose functions are similar to that of an insurance agent but who is not permanently employed by any principal, holding one's self out to employment by the public; the insurance broker's employment in each case is that of a special agent for a single object.

insurance commissioner Head of the commission whose duty is to oversee insurance sold in the state. The National Organization of State Insurance Commissioners is powerful in the insurance company decision-making process.

insurance company Company whose primary business activity is the writing of insurance or the reinsuring of risks underwritten by other insurance companies.

Insurance companies are subject to supervision by the insurance commissioner or a similar official or agency of a state, territory, or the District of Columbia.

insurance company rating service Company that makes annual reviews of insurance companies and reports on the conditions related to comparative financial standing and cost of policies among various insurance companies. *Best's Insurance Reports* concentrates on financial standing and *Consumers Union Report on Life Insurance* reports on the costs. *Best's* uses rating symbols from A+ (highest) to C (lowest). *Best's* also assigns each company a financial size category which groups the company into one of fifteen net safety ratings.

insurance coverage Total amount and type of insurance carried.

insurance poor A slang expression denoting that the person is carrying and paying for so much insurance that other needs in life are neglected.

insurance trust An inter vivos trust which is funded by an insurance policy. Used by both individuals and business firms to meet needs which will occur ultimately, but of uncertain date, but which will require a given amount of money to discharge the obligation. For example, a closed corporation might set up such a trust to have the money to buy the stock of a deceased stockholder.

Insured Income Properties A limited partnership owned by E. F. Hutton, in which shares can be purchased by subscribers, in the minimum amount of five thousand dollars. It is a real estate partnership in which all real estate is owned outright, with no mortgages. Thus the income from the shares can be guaranteed, specifically through an insurance company. (Cf. limited partnership)

insured pension plan A type of group annuity which is sold by insurance companies to firms with employee pension plans both to insure that the plan will ultimately pay the employees, and to relieve the firm of onerous book work.

insured plan Retirement plan where all contributions are invested in individual retirement income and/or retirement annuity policies. Thus, it follows that all benefits are derived from these contracts.

This approach offers a maximum of guarantees and administrative growth at a guaranteed interest rate and provides a guaranteed monthly life income and preretirement benefit.

insuring agreement Statements broadly defining coverages in an insurance policy.

insurrection Revolt of citizens or subjects against their legally constituted government.

intangible That which cannot be seen or touched, such as the good will of a business or an incorporeal right such as a bond or a bank account.

intangible asset *economics; accounting* 1. Right or nonphysical resource that is presumed to represent an advantage to the firm's position in the marketplace. Such assets include copyrights, patents, trademarks, good will, computer programs, licenses, leases, franchises, capitalized advertising costs, organization costs, exploration permits, and import and export permits. (Cf. tangible asset) 2. In law and taxation, a nonmaterial property right such as securities, notes, and other similar claims.

intangible drilling cost Cost of establishing a well (e.g., geologists costs, drilling, tests, etc.). If no oil or gas is found, there is nothing to show for the investment; however, if oil or gas is found, certain other equipment will be needed to complete the well for production. This equipment is then categorized by the Internal Revenue Service as capital equipment and must be depreciated over a period of time. (*See* Appendix G; cf. tangible drilling cost)

intangible value Benefit that cannot be seen or touched.

integration 1. *pension plans* Process of combining the benefits paid by Social Security with the benefits paid by a qualified retirement plan. The thrust of an integrated plan is to offset the discrimination against higher paid employees which occurs with Social Security benefits by adding benefits for those groups. 2. In interpreting documents, the association of disconnected writings by their internal sense, coherence, or adaptation of parts.

integration level Level at which higher-paid employees would begin losing Social Security benefits because of the covered compensation concept. This represents the level at which the employer would want to begin a first tier employer contribution for higher paid employees.

integration of industry *See* horizontal integration, vertical integration.

intensive distribution Attempt by manufacturers of convenience goods to provide saturation coverage of potential markets.

intensive growth Economic growth resulting from increased productivity and raising a country's standard of living.

intentional interference Deliberate intervention with a person or with property of another. Both are covered in the law of tort.

intent to defraud *insurance law* Action taken on the part of insured, insurer, or a third party, which action is aimed at misrepresenting facts about the case with the end that fraudulent claims will bring forth payments which are not due by the insured, or inducing the insured to accept promises which may not materialize.

inter alia *Among other things.* When used in law, the phrase refers to people who are not primarily engaged in the case at hand.

intercede To attempt to mediate or reconcile differences between two or more parties.

intercept To stop, halt, or interrupt the course, progress, or transmission of anything.

intercommodity spread *investing* Spread consisting of a long position in one commodity and a short position in another. Commodities are usually related, such as having one position in gold and the other in silver.

interdelivery spread *investing* Spread between futures contracts which may entail buying one month in a contract and selling another month in the same contract (e.g., buying a June contract and simultaneously selling a September wheat contract). The investor hopes to profit from the price differential in the contract.

interdependence *economics* Relationship between individuals and institutions that arises because of specialization of production in which each has a need for the products or services of the other.

interesse termini *law* Executory interest of a lessee in land demised to the lessee, prior to actual possession of the land. A person having a mere interesse termini has no estate and cannot bring an action of trespass, for damages, or on a covenant for quiet enjoyment.

interest 1. Objective concern in something by right or title, or a claim upon, or a share in. Legal concern in a thing; share in the ownership of property or in a commercial or financial undertaking or enterprise. 2. Factor payment for the use of capital. 3. Cost of the use of money.

interested person Heir, devisee, child, spouse, creditor, beneficiary, and any other having a property right in or claim against a trust estate or the estate of a decedent, ward, or protected person.

Interest Equalization Act (IET) *finance* A 15% tax, levied in 1963 and removed in 1974, on interest received by foreign borrowers in U.S. capital markets.

interest-only loan Loan in which interest is payable at regular intervals until loan maturity, when the full loan balance is due.

interest-only option *insurance* Policy alternative in which the proceeds are left with the insurer and only interest is paid out for a limited period, at the end of which time another option may be chosen. This might be used for the period while the surviving spouse with dependent children is collecting social security benefits.

interest rate risk Risk caused by the fluctuation of the general level of interest rates. Securities that offer purchasers a fixed periodic return are affected especially by interest rate risk. As market interest rates change, the prices of these outstanding securities fluctuate. In general, a rise in general market interest rates tends to cause a decline in market prices for existing securities, and a decline in interest rates tends to cause an increase in market values for existing securities. Thus, market prices for existing securities tend to move inversely with changes in the general level of interest rates.

interest, real rate of *See* real rate of interest.

interest reipublicae ut quilibet re sua bene utatur *It is the concern of the state that every man use his property properly.*

interfere To check; to hinder; to disturb;

to intervene; to enter into the concerns of others against their wishes. To be in opposition; to intermeddle.

interfirm comparison The practice of checking company management and production performance with other companies of like size, and other similar characteristics. Production and productivity, sales, costs, labor turnover, etc., are areas normally checked.

interim bond *investing* A temporary certificate issued in lieu of a permanent bond, which will be issued at a later date.

interim dividend *investing* A dividend declared and paid, usually quarterly, before profits are known. This is done to show consistency to shareholders. Sometimes, after year-end profits are known, an additional dividend is paid.

interim financing Loan, including a construction loan, used when a property owner is unable or unwilling to arrange permanent financing. Generally arranged for less than three years; used to gain time for financial or market conditions to improve.

interim statements *accounting* Periodic financial statements which are made up to keep management aware of the condition of the business at any point in time.

interinsurance System of insurance whereby several individuals, partnerships, and corporations underwrite each other's risks against various hazards common to all, under an agreement that each underwriter acts separately and severally and not jointly with any other, and all subscribers are insured and insurers at the same time.

interlineation *law* Writing between the lines. An interlineation in a will raises a rebuttable presumption that it was made after the will.

interlocking directorates *finance* Directorates of several businesses involved in the same, or similar, activities that have some of the same people serving on the boards of the various companies. This tends to decrease competition between the firms, and otherwise causes them to act like monopolies. Steps have been taken to eliminate this practice, and it is thus much less prevalent than it was twenty years ago.

interlocutory *law* Temporary or provi-

sional. A judgment is said to be interlocutory when it determines less than all issues as to all parties, thereby leaving something further to be determined and adjudicated by the court.

Intermarket Trading System (ITS) *finance* A video-computer display that links the posts of specialists (market makers) at the New York, American, Boston, Midwest, Philadelphia, and Pacific stock exchanges who trade in the same securities. Orders may be sent and received electronically, greatly facilitating trade.

intermediate goods *economics* Goods which exist at some stage between raw materials and the finished product.

intermediate targets *finance; monetary policy* Goals which are set by the Federal Reserve System for an intermediate period (usually less than one year) for growth in the money supply, interest rates, etc. The purpose of this monetary policy is to help achieve and maintain equilibrium in the economy.

intermediation 1. *finance* The process of transferring funds from the ultimate lender to the ultimate borrower. Thus, a bank engages in intermediation when it accepts deposits and makes loans. 2. *investing* The placement of money with a bank, broker, or some institution for the purpose of achieving a specifically required return. (Cf. disintermediation)

internal audit *accounting; finance* An audit carried out by employees of the firm, sometimes perennially, rather than by an outside agency.

internal control *accounting* Procedures and techniques developed by a business to provide control for operations, financial management, and the safeguard of company assets.

internal diseconomies Decreases in production, productivity, or profitability with the use of the same resources as before.

internal economies Increases in production, productivity, or profitability relating to the scale of operations of the firm.

internal limit *insurance* Limit which applies to certain kinds of property covered by a homeowner's policy. The effect of internal limits may be to make it necessary to schedule specific additional amounts of insurance on certain policy items. (E.g., a stamp collection is valued at three thousand dollars, but the homeowner's policy allowed only five hundred dollars.) Also called sublimit.

internal rate of return (IRR) 1. Discount rate at which project's net present value equals zero. 2. Rate at which funds in a project are compounding. (*See* rate of return)

Internal Revenue Code Law as passed by Congress that specifies how and what income is to be taxed and what may be deducted from taxable income.

Internal Revenue Service (IRS) Agency of the federal government responsible for the administration and collection of federal income taxes. The IRS prints and distributes tax forms and audits tax returns.

internal sources Cash available to a company through cash flow from operations.

international balance of payments A summary accounting statement showing all transactions (debits and credits) between one nation and all other nations of the world, with surplus and deficit balances for each of the various kinds of current and capital transactions. The balance of payments shows how the nation received and used foreign money and whether there was a surplus or deficit which had to be balanced out by "official reserve transactions."

international balance of trade The total of goods and services exports minus goods and services imports. (The largest part of the international balance of payments, but excludes capital items.)

International Bank for Reconstruction and Development (IBRD) Institution which grew out of the Bretton Woods Conference and was established by the United Nations in 1945 to provide loans for postwar reconstruction and to promote development of less developed countries. The bank's chief function is to aid the financing of basic development projects such as dams, communication and transportation facilities, and health programs, by insuring or otherwise guaranteeing private loans or, when private capital is not available, by providing loans from its own resources and credit. Affiliated agencies also exist to help finance higher-risk investment projects in underdeveloped countries. Also known as the World Bank.

international banking facility (IBF) Facility which can accept time deposits from foreign customers free of reserve requirements and interest rate limitations and can lend to foreigners if the funds are for the conduct of foreign business outside of the United States. Net borrowing from these facilities by domestic banking offices is subject to reserve requirements.

international bank rate *finance* That rate of interest at which a nation's central bank is willing to loan to similar banks in other countries.

international law System of laws, or more often the customs and usages, that regulates affairs among nations.

International Monetary Fund (IMF) Organization of 146 member nations established in 1946 to assist in operation of the world monetary system by regulating the exchange practices of countries and providing liquidity to member countries that have payment problems. The main functions of the International Monetary Fund are to lend funds to member nations to finance temporary balance-of-payment problems, to facilitate the expansion and balanced growth of international trade, and to promote international monetary cooperation among nations. The IMF also creates special drawing rights (SDRs) which provide member nations with a source of additional reserves. Member nations are required to subscribe to a fund quota, paid mainly in their own currency. The IMF grew out of the Bretton Woods Conference of 1944.

International Monetary Market (IMM) A division of the Chicago Mercantile Exchange that trades in futures in United States treasury bills, foreign currency, certificates of deposit, and Eurodollar deposits.

international mutual fund *investing* A mutual fund that invests in securities markets around the world, thus hedging against a slump in any specific market. This is a highly complex type of investing, which demands an hour-to-hour knowledge of the value of foreign currencies.

interpleader *law* Proceeding by which a person who has money or goods claimed by two or more other persons may, for personal protection, ask that the claimants be required to litigate their title among themselves instead of litigating it with the person.

interpolate To insert words in an already completed document.

interpolated terminal reserve Method by which life insurance and annuity contracts are valued. Except at the onset of most contracts, the interpolated terminal reserve is roughly equivalent to the policy's cash value. If at the time of transfer the policy is in a premium-paying stage, the gift's value is usually equal to the interpolated terminal reserve plus unearned premiums on the date of the gift.

interpolation *statistics* The method of estimating unknown values which lie between known data points.

interpositioning *securities* The placement of a second broker in a securities transaction between two principals or between a client and a market maker. This practice becomes illegal if the additional broker is used simply to generate more fees and is deemed unnecessary.

interpretatio chartarum benigne facidena est, ut res magis valeat quam pereat *Deeds are to be interpreted liberally so that they may have effect rather than fail.*

interrogatories *law* Questions presented in writing to one who is going to testify in a case so that the person will be prepared to answer.

interruption In the law relating to prescription and adverse possession, some event, act, or occurrence which breaks the continuity of the use or possession.

inter se; inter sese *Among themselves.*

interstate commerce Commerce and traffic between citizens or inhabitants of different states of the United States; refers to not only interstate movement but interstate business as well. Includes the passage of property, persons, or messages from within one state to another.

Interstate Commerce Act (1887) Nineteenth-century law enacted by U.S. Congress to curb monopolistic and discriminatory shipping practices to railroads and to prohibit arrangements among competing railroads for sharing traffic and

earnings. The Interstate Commerce Commission was created by the act.

Interstate Commerce Commission (ICC) Regulatory body established by the Interstate Commerce Act to enforce the provisions of the act; now regulates not only the railroads but also motor carriers, express companies, and interstate fuel pipelines.

Interstate Land Sales Act Federal law, administered by the Department of Housing and Urban Development (HUD), which requires certain disclosures and advertising procedures when selling land to purchasers in other states.

intervener *law* A third party brought into a legal proceeding between two other parties. This person must have the permission of the court to intervene and must do so voluntarily because of some special interest in the proceeding.

intervention *law* The act of bringing into a legal proceeding between two parties, the defendant and the plaintiff, a third party, the intervener.

inter vivos *Between the living.* (*See* donatio inter vivos, inter vivos trust)

inter vivos trust Living trust, set up during one's lifetime to benefit one's self or someone else.

intestacy State or condition of dying without having made a valid will, or without having disposed by will of part of the decedent's property.

in testamentis plenius testatoris intentionem scrutamur *In wills, we seek out more fully the intention of the testator.*

intestate distribution Apportionment a state will make of an estate when the deceased has died without leaving a will. Although state laws differ somewhat, there is usually a typical order of intestate distribution.

intestate estate Estate left by a decedent who did not leave a valid will. The court will divide the estate according to the state statutes.

intestate succession *law* The procedure used by the court to divide the property of a decedent who dies leaving no valid will. This procedure varies among the states.

in testimonium *In witness; in evidence whereof.*

in-the-money 1. Call option contract for which the striking (exercise) price of the call is below the market price of the underlying security. 2. Put option contract for which the striking (exercise) price of the put is above the market price of the underlying security. 3. Market condition when the market price of the underlying stock has risen above the strike price of the option.

in toto *In the whole;* completely.

intracommodity spread *securities* A futures position in which a trader buys and sells contracts on the same commodity, and on the same exchange, in one day. (E.g., a trader would place an intracommodity spread if the trader buys wheat contracts expiring in December, and sold contracts for wheat expiring in April.) This is another method of hedging.

intraday *securities* Occurring over the course of one day (e.g., the phenomenon of a stock hitting a new low during the day but recovering before the market closes).

in transit privileges *economics* The rights of a shipper related to detaining goods in transit for the purpose of performing further processing.

in transitu *In transit;* on the way.

intrastate Wholly within the boundaries of one of the states of the United States.

intra vires *Within the power.* A statute is said to be intra vires when its subject matter is within the competence of the legislative body enacting the law under the British North America Act.

intrinsic evidence That which is derived from a document without anything to explain it.

intrinsic fraud *law* In relation to trials, type of fraud employed during the course of a hearing which provides a forum for the truth to appear, even though the truth was distorted by the fraud. (*See* extrinsic fraud)

intrinsic value 1. Value inherent in something by its nature. 2. Amount by which a call or put stock option is in-the-money; the difference between the current market value of the underlying security and strike (exercise) price of the option. 3. Professional valuation which is valid by the facts or the underlying

assumptions in a specific examination. 4. Worth of an asset.

inure *law* To take effect in such a way as to benefit a person, especially when the benefit is not specifically intended. To come into use.

invadiare To mortgage or create a charge upon lands.

invalid Of no binding force; having no legal efficacy; without authority; null and void.

invention In patent law, creation of something which did not exist before and which possesses elements of novelty and utility in kind and measure different from anything preceding.

inventory Itemized list of goods, showing the number and usually the value; the goods and stock so itemized. Inventories may be made of raw materials, goods-in-process, or finished goods.

inventory asset Asset used in the normal conduct of business; this can be raw material waiting to be processed, material in the process of production, or finished goods waiting to be sold.

inventory cycle *economics* 1. A term relating to the business cycle where the cycle is measured in terms of fluctuations in inventories. 2. The same as inventory turnover when applied to a single business firm.

inventory turnover *accounting* The number of times the average inventory of a business is sold (turned over) during each accounting period.

inventory turnover ratio Measure of management's control of its investment in inventory, computed by dividing cost of goods sold by ending inventory.

inventory valuation adjustment Adjustment to historical-cost financial statements to correct for the possible understatement of inventory and cost of goods sold during periods of inflation.

inverse condemnation *law* Cause of action against a governmental agency to recover the value of property taken by such agency without the formal exercise of power of eminent domain.

inverse order of alienation doctrine Doctrine which holds that where land subject to lien has been conveyed in whole or

171

in part, a lienholder must satisfy the debt out of land remaining in the grantor, if possible, but if such remaining land is insufficient to satisfy the debt, the lienholder must resort to separate parcels which have been conveyed successively in inverse order of alienation

inverted funnel sequence *communication* Order of questions moving from the specific to the general.

inverted scale *securities* A serial bond offering where earlier maturities have higher yields than late maturities. (Cf. serial bonds)

inverted yield curve *securities* A graphic presentation of a situation in which short-term interest rates are higher than long-term rates. Usually short-term rates are lower. However, when investors show a lack of confidence in the future of the economy, they will invest for short terms, demanding the highest possible yield, and will be reluctant to commit money for the long-term.

invest *economics* To place capital in such a way that it will secure income or profit for the investor. To put money into a new or expanding business, or in debt or equity vehicles.

invested asset Entry in a statement of financial position which shows assets currently invested and in what kind of investment vehicles.

investiture *law; real estate* Ceremony formerly part of the grant of land whereby the grantee was given possession in the presence of witnesses.

investment 1. *economics* Purchase of plants, equipment, or inventory. 2. The purchase of an asset such as a stock or a bond. 3. Corporate security held by a firm and reported on the firm's balance sheet.

investment advisory service A service supplying investment advice for a fee. The advice may be in-office, with the advisor speaking to the client, or it may be in a newsletter to which one can subscribe. Any person supplying this service must be registered with the Securities and Exchange Commission, in compliance with the Investment Advisors Act.

investment advisory services Persons or business firms who offer investment advice for a fee. Such services must abide by state and Securities and Exchange Commission regulations.

investment appraisal *investing; management* Generally, a complete review of an investment portfolio, with respect to how well it is achieving the goals set for it. The same term, however, is used in evaluating personnel and all the other activities of a business firm.

investment bank Financial institution specializing in the original sale and subsequent trading of company securities.

investment banker *investments* Underwriter, or a firm that sells new issues of securities to the general public. These securities may be sold on a best-effort agreement; i.e., the investment banker may pledge his best effort in getting the securities sold. Sometimes these people buy the issue and sell the securities on their own. Also, in large transactions, syndicates of investment bankers may be formed between several companies to carry out the sale.

investment banking *finance* The process of underwriting and marketing new issues of securities to investors.

investment club A group of people who pool their funds for the purpose of making investments on behalf of the group. There will often be an Investment Committee within the group that will actually do the investing. However, in the periodic meetings of the group, any member can make suggestions with respect to investments made.

Investment Company Act (1940) Act of Congress requiring registration of and setting regulations for investment companies.

investment constraints Personal factors which govern or limit how every investor will approach the total matter of investing (e.g., the ability to risk loss of income or principal; the degree of liquidity and marketability necessary; the ability to weather the ups and downs in the securities markets; overall tax and estate status; and attitudes and emotional tolerance for risk).

investment contract Investment of money in common enterprise where the investor expects to reap profits from the efforts of the promoter or a third party.

investment credits Reduction in income tax liability granted by the federal government to firms that make new investments in certain asset categories. The tax credit is based on a percentage of the purchase price of the asset. (*See* Appendix G)

investment-GNP ratio Proportion of gross national product which is allocated to private investment.

investment grade Describes bonds suitable to a conservative investor. Standard & Poor's rating service looks upon all bonds between the AAA and BBB ratings as investment grade. Generally speaking, any bonds graded below BBB are junk bonds.

investment-grade securities Securities which are debt instruments that are considered to be of high enough quality to be eligible for investment by banks. These include U.S. Treasury and government agency bonds, notes, or bills, plus state and municipal bonds of the four highest ratings, and corporate bonds, also highly rated.

investment history A body of knowledge gained through the experience between a client and the brokerage house.

investment interest expense Interest paid to carry passive investments such as undeveloped land and net-leased rental property. Tax deductions for such interest are limited.

investment letter When new securities are placed privately, there must be a letter of intent in which the buyer affirms he or she is buying the issue for investment and not for resale. When this is done, the securities do not have to be registered with the Securities and Exchange Commission.

investment life cycle Time span from the acquisition of an investment to the final disposition.

investment multiplier *economics* In essence this is the reciprocal of the marginal propensity to save. The ratio of the change in national income ensuing from a change in investment to that change in investment.

investment objective What an investor hopes to accomplish through investing (e.g., to maximize current income; to average current income with moderate capital growth; to obtain long-term capital growth or aggressive capital growth; and to acquire tax-sheltered

investments). Objectives are different for every investor.

investment policies Guidelines for investment, established in light of investment objectives.

investment relations department Department, in major companies listed on an exchange, that usually handles the public relations activities relative to the company's stock and shareholders or potential buyers. The duties generally include: (a) to present a positive image of the company, with respect to its activities and its objectives; (b) to work with the legal staff on reports and projects required by the SEC, stock exchanges, and all other regulatory authorities; (c) to respond to requests for reports and other information from shareholders, professional investors, brokers, and the financial media; (d) to maintain good relationships with investment bankers, market makers, major brokerage houses, and institutional investors who are interested in the stock; (e) to take whatever measures necessary to see that the company's stock is properly valued.

investment strategy Method of action used in portfolio construction and management to implement an overall plan.

investment strategy committee A committee working out of the research department of a brokerage house that sets the overall investment strategy the brokers will use with their clients.

investment tax credit 1. Tax break given to encourage investment in equipment and the restoration of certain kinds of buildings. 2. Credit, available to the taxpayer involved in business ventures, equal to a percentage of the cost of investment in qualified tangible personal property acquired and placed in service at any time during the tax year. 3. First-year tax credit of 10% of the purchase price of art. (*See* Appendix G)

investment tax credit recapture Tax credit earned at the rate of 2% per year by holding equipment. If a three-year property is held for only two years, there is a 2% ITC recapture. (*See* Appendix G)

investment value Value of a convertible security based solely on its characteristics as a fixed-income security, ignoring the value of the conversion feature.

investment vehicle Any investment

asset chosen for a portfolio, such as a stock, bond, money market certificate, or savings account.

Investors Advisors Act (1940) Act requiring registration and reporting of firms and individuals who provide investment advice for a fee.

invisible exports *economics* Exports of nontangible services from one country to another. These may consist of insurance, freight, etc. They are called invisible because they do not pass through customs.

invisible hand theory *economics* Concept described by Adam Smith of England in his economics book *Wealth of Nations,* which appeared in 1776. He proposed the idea that, though businesses were there to make a profit, their actions of hiring people to work and using natural resources in the end increased the wealth of the nation and all the people; i.e., while the economy is guided by the self-interest of individuals, this ultimately leads to benefits to all society, as though guided by an invisible hand.

invisible imports *economics* Services, financial or personal, provided by one country to another. They may consist of insurance, freight, etc., and because they are intangible, they do not go through customs.

invisible trade *economics* Transactions with foreign countries in intangible items such as insurance, interest, dividends, travel, etc.

invitee *law* One who may come onto the property of another without fear of being accused of trespass because he or she is doing so by invitation or because the business of the other demands that he or she do so in order to transact business. An invitation does not have to be direct but can be implied, such as that given by a church, theater, or mall. Concept may be important in insurance cases, particularly when one is accused of being liable for an accident to another person on the property of the first person.

invito beneficium non datur *A gift cannot be made without the consent of the donee.*

invoice *accounting* An itemized list sent to a purchaser of goods received or sold or services rendered or received, showing both quantity and price, and often stating the terms of the sales agreement.

invoice approval form *accounting* A form used to indicate that the terms of a sales or purchase agreement have been met, and affirming the fact that all required procedures have been carried out. Also called a voucher.

involuntary payment Payment which has been obtained by fraud, oppression, or extortion or made to secure a right which the party was entitled to without such payment and which right was withheld until such payment was made. An involuntary payment may be recovered by the payer.

involuntary trust Trust in which the intention of the parties is not expressed and is therefore implied by law as in a resulting trust or is imposed by law regardless of intention as in a constructive trust.

IOU *law; finance* I owe you. Recognized as a form of admission of debt, and will be so considered by the law.

ipso facto *By the fact itself; by the act itself.* Arising from the very fact.

iron law of wages *See* subsistence theory of wages.

irrecusable *law* Describes obligations imposed upon a person or without the person's consent or action.

irredeemable bond *investing* A perpetual bond; a bond without a call feature. Only a few such issues exist, some originating in England many years ago.

irrevocable beneficiary Beneficiary designation where all policy rights are vested in the beneficiary; the policy owner may not assign the policy or borrow on it without the beneficiary's consent.

irrevocable letter of credit *economics; finance* A letter of credit which cannot be cancelled until after a stated date without the consent of the person in whose favor it is drawn. (*See* letter of credit)

irrevocable living trust Trust in which the settlor (or grantor) while still living gives up property forever without reserving any right to revoke or alter the trust. The estate thus avoids probate. It is normally supervised on a professional level with currently distributed income taxed to the beneficiary. Rights to all or part of the advantages of an irrevocable trust would be lost if the grantor (settlor) retained any interest in the property at all.

irrigation works   Man-made water conduits designed to divert the flow of water to areas where it would otherwise not flow because of the configuration of the land. Unlike some natural watercourses, all ditches and canals are capable of being owned.

iso-outlay curve   *economics; statistics* Curve plotted on a graph with a vertical "Y" axis and a horizontal "X" axis, and charting quantities of factor "A" and factor "B" which are used in the production of a good. The resulting curves from any point on "Y" to any point on "X" will denote all combinations of A and B which can be purchased for the same amount of money.

isoquant   *economics; statistics* 1. Iso-product curve. 2. Any curve representing equal quantities of anything, not just quantities produced.

issue   *law* 1. Single, certain material point, affirmed by one side and denied by the other in a legal action which is to be decided at the conclusion of the pleadings or the trial. 2. Offspring. 3. To put into circulation, as stock. 4. Securities offered by a company at one time.

issued and outstanding   Describes those stocks or bonds which have been approved for sale by the board of directors of a corporation, and which have been sold and are currently held by the public, and on which dividends or interest is paid.

ita utere tuo ut alienum non laedas   *Use your own property so as not to injure your neighbor's.*

itemized deductions   Specific amounts which may be subtracted from gross income to calculate net income. Itemized deductions fall into three categories: deductions for personal expenditures, expenses incurred by employees in connection with their employment, and expenses incurred in connection with income-producing activities not constituting a trade or business and not involving rents or royalties.

J

jactus   Throwing away of goods to lighten or save a vessel.

jason clause   Clause in bills of lading which obligates cargo owners to contribute in general average in cases of danger, damage, or disaster resulting from faults or errors in navigation or in management of a vessel, her machinery, or appurtenances, provided that the owner shall have exercised due diligence to make the vessel seaworthy in all respects and to have her properly manned, equipped, and supplied.

jeopardy   1. Danger; hazard; peril. 2. *law* The risk traditionally associated with criminal prosecution and proceedings to invoke criminal punishment for vindication of public justice.

jeopardy assessments   *economics* A power vested in the federal government to make an immediate assessment and seizure upon claim of income taxes where there appears to be a danger of either the taxpayer leaving the country or of assets disappearing.

jettison   To cast (goods) overboard.

jobber   *marketing* 1. Wholesaler. 2. Middle-man dealing in relatively small job lots who buys from a manufacturer, importer, or wholesaler and then resells to a retailer. In England, this term is used on the London Stock Exchange to denote a market-maker.

job classification   1. Process of describing the duties, responsibilities, and characteristics of jobs; point-rating them (perhaps by established formulas based on engineering time-studies of workers in such jobs); and grouping the jobs into graduated classifications with corresponding wage rates and ranges. 2. The rank assigned a job by such a process.

job cost ledger   *accounting* A special type subsidiary ledger which lists the jobs in progress by name or number and keeps a running account of the accumulated costs on each job.

job description *management* A broad, written analysis of a specific job, usually accompanied by a listing of the various facets of the job in order of their priority.

job lot A specific number of identical items manufactured to fill an order, or which constitutes the most cost effective way of producing the good, even if it is going into inventory.

job order cost system *accounting* A method of assembling costs as they relate to a specific order, or to a job that is going into inventory.

jockey *investing* Investment manager, particularly one of those who manage mutual funds. The name suggests that investors should probably pick the best "jockeys" instead of the best "horses," i.e. stocks.

Johari Window *communication* Concept (named for the originators, Joe Luft and Harry Ingham) that illustrates the quality of a person's relationships or how open a person is while communicating.

joint account *banking* An account carrying the names of two or more people, each of whom has unlimited access to the account. Generally, any type of account to which two or more people have access, either in the rights or the liabilities.

joint account agreement *banking* A form used to open a joint account at a bank or a brokerage house. All pertinent signatures are required, without regard to which signers will have checking privileges or authority to change the account.

joint and last survivor life income option *insurance* Options under which the insured may elect to have the proceeds paid during the lifetimes of two or more recipients.

joint and several Binding two or more persons both collectively and individually.

joint and several liability Situation in which, in a suit against joint and several tort feasors, a successful plaintiff may recover damages from any or all defendants separately or as a group, and in which a creditor can demand full repayment from any and all of those who have borrowed, each borrower of a common loan being liable for the full debt, not just the prorated share.

joint and survivor annuity Annuity which covers the life of the primary annuitant plus that of one or more survivors. The annuity payment is computed by taking into account that the life expectancies of two persons will be greater than that of one, making the periodic annuity payments smaller. The persons named are provided a specified amount of income over their lifetimes with the income (or reduced amount) continuing to the survivor after the death of one of the covered persons.

joint bond *investing* A bond used when a parent company wishes to guarantee a bond issue of a subsidiary.

joint correlation *statistics* Where three variables are involved, the situation in which the difference between two variables depends on what the level of the third variable is.

joint liability *law* The liability of two or more persons arising from their association with regard to a contract, tort, or other legal relationship. Whether each is liable for the whole or only part of the liability depends upon the law of the state, but at common law, each is liable for the whole. (Cf. joint and several)

jointly owned property Property that is owned by two or more persons, regardless of the nature of their relationship or how that relationship came into being.

joint ownership *law* A common type of ownership of real or personal property by two or more people. The people are either joint tenants or tenants in common.

joint-product method of cost accounting A system of allocation costs between two or more products produced simultaneously by distributing costs on some index basis, which might be selling price, space occupancy, direct labor, etc.

joint return Income tax return reporting the income of both the husband and the wife, making each fully liable for the total tax due.

joint stock company A corporate form that has characteristics both of a corporation and a partnership. There is unlimited liability, yet stock can be issued and traded.

joint tenancy *law; real estate* Type of ownership of real or personal property by two or more persons in which each owns an undivided interest in the whole and attached to which is the right of survivorship.

joint tenancy bank account   Account created when two or more persons enter into an agreement, usually through the completion of a uniform signature card, with a financial institution. Upon the death of one, the survivor has full access to the account. These proceeds pass outside the probate estate of the decedent and may be the most widely used substitute for a will.

jointure   *law* An agreement made before marriage between persons intending to become husband and wife, providing lands for the wife upon the death of the husband, for the life of the wife. When this is in operation, it eliminates dower.

joint venture   1. Type of international enterprise in which a company shares the risks, costs, and management of the foreign operation with a partner who is usually a national of the host nation. 2. Agreement between two or more parties who invest in a single business or property. (*See* tenancy in common, limited partnership) 3. Association of two or more persons to carry out a single business enterprise for profit for which purpose their property and services are combined.

joint will   Single instrument executed as the will of two or more individuals, jointly signed by them. Such wills are usually executed to make testamentary disposition of joint property.

joint work   *law* In the context of copyright legislation, a work prepared by two or more authors with the intent that their contributions be merged into inseparable or interdependent parts of a unitary whole.

journal   A book which records the original business transaction, and which normally contains numbers of items, cost, etc.

journeyman   Worker hired for a given time period, such as by the day.

judge   *law* Officer of the court, at some level, who may be either appointed or elected, but who is commissioned to carry out the judicial functions of a specific court. A judge has numerous powers, such as the power to perform weddings, etc.

judgment   *law* 1. Judicial determination; the decision of a court upon the respective claims and rights to an action litigated and submitted for its determination. 2. A sum due for collection or payment as a result of a court order.

judgmental forecasting   *economics* A method of forecasting which places the major emphasis upon human judgment, in the light of knowledge and experience, as opposed to the interpretation of statistical data alone. Sometimes called qualitative forecasting.

judgmental system of evaluating applicants   *finance* A method, referred to in the Equal Credit Opportunity Act, of determining the credit worthiness of a loan applicant other than by quantitative methods alone. It takes into consideration any action taken which in any way demonstrates the creditworthiness of the individual.

judgment creditor   An individual or entity who has proven a debt in court, has obtained a judgment for its recovery, and is entitled to use court process for collection. (Cf. judgment debtor)

judgment debt   Debt for the recovery of which a judgment has been obtained from a court. Sometimes, even if the action itself was not for the recovery of monies, if costs had been awarded to the successful party and the costs had been taxed, then those costs would be a judgment debt.

judgment debtor   *law* A debtor against whom an individual or entity has obtained a legal judgment. (Cf. judgment creditor)

judgment in personam   *law* Judgment against a person, against something, or against the defendant's interest. Judgments are generally divided into three categories: judgment in personam, judgments in rem, and judgments in quasi rem.

judgment in quasi rem   *law* Judgments in the nature of a judgment in rem against a person with respect to particular property.

judgment in rem   *law* Judgment pronounced upon the status of some particular matter, rendered in a proceeding instituted against property, or brought to enforce a right. Thus a judgment of adjudication in bankruptcy is a judgment in rem, since it determines the status of the bankrupt. (*See* jus in re)

judgment lien   *law* Lien on property, arising from the operation of law as a result of judgment rendered by a court of record; not a lien known to common law but one created by statutes.

judicial foreclosure   *law* Having a defaulted debtor's property sold where the court ratifies the price paid.

judicial settlement   *law* The settlement of any type of account which comes by the direct order of a proper court.

judiciary supervised personal trust   *law* Trust management in which the trustee must periodically report to the court. This is most common when the trust beneficiary is an infant or an incompetent.

Julliard cycle   *economics* A ten-year business cycle predicated upon a large number of time series presented as statistical evidence.

jumbo certificate of deposit   *investing* A certificate with a minimum denomination of $100,000, usually bought by institutions, such as banks, pension funds, insurance companies, etc.

jumbo group   *insurance* High individual coverage much in demand by group insurance purchasers. Large term policies cut down the market for permanent individual insurance and consequently, as argued by some insurers, are detrimental to the public in the long run. Premiums for group term are tax deductible by the employer, but are not taxed to the employee on coverage over fifty thousand dollars. (Up to fifty thousand dollars in premiums paid by employer are not recognized as income to the employee. Over fifty thousand dollars in premiums paid are taxable to the employee.)

junior   *securities* Describes a security, debt instrument, or lien whose claim on the assets of the issuer is subordinate to some other claim. (E.g., common stock is junior to a preferred stock.)

junior bond   *securities* Bond of a specific issue which are subordinated to another issue from the same firm.

junior issue   *securities* An issue of debt or equity which is subordinate to prior issues, in event of the liquidation of the company.

junior mortgage   Mortgage whose claim against a property will be satisfied only after prior mortgages have been repaid.

junior refunding   *finance* The refinancing of short-term government debt by issuing new long-term debt instruments.

junior security   A security which is subordinate to other securities with respect to claims on assets of the company.

junk bond   *investing* A low-rated bond, often from a relatively new company, which is speculative in nature. Generally any bonds graded below BBB. In the event of the company's success the bonds can return outstanding profits. (*See* investment grade)

jura   *Rights.*

jura rerum   Those rights which one may acquire over things, unconnected with one's person.

jure uxoris   *In the right of a wife.*

juridical   Relating to the administration of justice.

juridical day   Days on which legal business can be transacted (does not include Sundays, Christmas Day, New Year's Day, etc.).

jurisdiction   1. *law* Legal right by which courts and judicial officers exercise authority; the extent of legal authority and power. 2. *banking; investing* Authority of some agencies to regulate certain aspects of the banking or investments business. (E.g., margin accounts are controlled by regulations issued by the Federal Reserve Banking System rather than the Securities and Exchange Commission.) The term also has significance with respect to Eurocurrency; while a loan may be funded in one country, it may require the participation of banks in several countries and be made to a borrower in still another country. Thus, the ability to agree on jurisdiction becomes of primary importance.

jurisprudence   Science of law which treats the principles of positive and substantive law and legal relations. Its function is to ascertain the principles on which legal rules are based, to classify them in their proper order, and to show the relation in which they stand to one another.

jurisprudentia   *Jurisprudence.*

jurist   Civil lawyer; one who is versed and skilled in law.

juror One who has been selected and sworn as a member of jury in a particular case.

jury of executive opinion A situation in which several senior corporate financial executives are asked to submit individual opinions and forecasts on a given problem. Each will then read the opinions of all the others, and eventually a consensus will be reached. Sometimes called a Delphi forecast. (*See* Delphi technique)

jus *Right; justice, law.* Particularly law in the abstract, as a body of law.

jus accrescendi *Right of survivorship.*

jus accrescendi inter mercatores, pro beneficio commercii, locum non habet *In the interest of commerce, the right of survivorship has no application between merchants.* Thus, there is no right of survivorship among partners.

jus accrescendi praefertur ultimae voluntati *Right of survivorship is preferred to the last will.* Thus a joint tenant cannot by will convey interest in a joint estate, for that would be in violation of the concept of survivorship.

jus disponendi The right of alienation, of disposing. In the sale of goods, an unpaid vendor may reserve to one's self the jus disponendi; i.e., the right of preventing the ownership from passing to the purchaser even after the vendor has parted with the goods, until payment is received.

jus dividendi Right of disposing of real estate by will.

jus habendi et retinendi The right to have possession of property and to retain the profits thereof.

jus in re *A right in a thing.* Right relating to a thing, arising out of a person's relation to it, implying complete ownership with possession, and available against all the world.

jus in re aliena Right in another's property, such as an easement.

jus legitimum *A legal right.* A right enforceable in a court of law.

jus mariti *The right of a husband.* This relates particularly to the wife's movable goods.

jus merum A bare right in lands without possession or even the right of possession.

jus non scriptum *Unwritten law.*

jus pascendi The right of grazing cattle.

jus possessionis *Right of possession.*

jus publicum The law relating to public affairs, the constitution and functions of government, and administration of criminal justice; public ownership and those rights to be exercised by the state in the interest or for the benefit of the public.

jus quentium *law The law of nations.* In old Roman law, this concept was broader than today when it is generally used to denote all relations between the citizens of one state and another state. (Cf. international law)

just Legal or lawful; morally right; fair.

just compensation Fair cash market value on the date of taking property for public use; that compensation which places the owner of property in as good a position financially after the property is taken and improvement made as the owner was prior thereto.

jus tertii *law The right of the third party.* The position of the defendant denying that the plaintiff is entitled to the property and claiming that the right is in the third party.

justice of the peace *law* Officer of the court at a low level, usually a governmental area comprising a township. The civil codes of the state will be quite specific as to the powers and duties of such an officer of the court. As is true with a judge, a justice of the peace may perform weddings and do other prescribed functions for society.

justifiable Sanctioned by law; defensible; lawful.

justified price *investing* A price which a well-informed customer will be willing to pay for a security, real estate, etc.

just price Concept held by early philosophers that there was one fair price for each good or service.

K

kaffir *finance* British term for South African gold mining share. Such shares are sold over the counter in the United States in the form of American Depository Receipts.

Kaiser plan *management* An arrangement which was worked out between Kaiser Steel Company and the steelworkers union to guarantee that employees would not lose earnings or employment because of the introduction of new technology.

Kefauver–Celler Act (1950) *economics* An amendment to the Clayton Antitrust Act of 1914 for the purpose of remedying a loophole in the 1914 act. This act forbids the acquisition of the assets of another company if the effect is to lessen competition in that industry.

Kennedy Round *economics* A series of meetings held by the organization General Agreement on Tariffs and Trade (GATT) which were initiated by President John F. Kennedy while in office, which produced agreements on the sale of cereal grains and anti-dumping agreements.

Keogh Plan Formal arrangement, made possible by the Self-employed Individuals Retirement Act of 1962, whereby owners of an unincorporated business establish a program to provide tax-favored retirement benefits for themselves and any eligible employees. Prior to 1963, sole proprietors could have qualified pension and profit-sharing plans covering their employees, but the owners of these businesses could not get the tax benefits of these plans. The Keogh Act and its subsequent amendments made it possible for owner-employees of unincorporated businesses and other self-employed persons to be covered under qualified retirement plans. These plans allow them to annually set aside tax deferred 25% of net earnings or thirty thousand dollars, whichever is less. In 1984, the act was broadened to include more employees in different categories who wished to save more money under this tax-deferred plan. The Tax Reform Act of 1986 made many changes, however, and should be consulted for the full range of those changes. (*See* Appendix G)

key currency *finance* A strong currency which is used as a standard of value for other currencies. Nations belonging to a trading block may peg their currencies to the strongest currency in the group.

keyed advertisement *marketing* An advertisement that is coded so the response to it can be traced. Often each periodical carrying the ad will have a different code so that the results in each market can be traced.

key individual insurance Insurance purchased to cover the life of a key person in a company, the death of whom might cause the company to incur undue losses or difficulty in continuing business.

key industry *economics* An industry considered to be vital to the economic health of a nation. Defense industries are arguably included in this group, as is the auto industry, since so many jobs in the nation are directly or indirectly related to it.

key man insurance *See* key individual insurance.

Keynesian cross *economics* A graph with consumption plotted on the vertical "Y" axis, and income on the horizontal "X" axis. The intersection of the curve traces (a) the path of consumption as income increases, with (b) a straight line from the origin at forty-five degrees (to either axis.)

Keynesian economics The body of economic thought originating in the economic philosophy of John Maynard Keynes (1883–1946) of England. Keynes' most important publication was *The General Theory of Employment, Interest and Money*, published in 1935. Keynes, who came into real prominence during the Great Depression, opposed idea of Adam Smith that a private enterprise economy was self-regulating and would eventually return to near equilibrium from any setback it might suffer. Keynes attempted to prove this theory wrong, opting rather for government intervention where drastic disequilibrium occurred. Keynes advocated "easy money" and averred that government spending would increase employment and consumer demand and stimulate saving and investment. Before the 1930s were over, Keynesian economics had inundated the world.

keystone pricing *marketing* Nominal price in which the marked price is higher than the intended selling price to make the buyer feel he or she is getting a bargain.

kickback A payment of money, or reward in some other form, which is paid to a person to influence some business deal. This practice is often illegal and is usually against standard business practices.

kicker 1. Payment required by a mortgage in addition to the normal principal and interest. 2. *finance* A feature of debt obligation which will often promise equity participation for loan participation.

kick-out clause *finance* Wording in a trust instrument which allows the trustee to terminate the trust and distribute its assets if the cost of maintaining the trust becomes impractical.

killer bee *investing* Investment banker who helps one company thwart take-over bids by another company. Usually the strategy is to make the intended target less appealing.

kinked demand *economics* The demand curve of a firm which becomes discontinuous at the market price. This occurs in an industry with few firms, but no price leader. Here, if a firm raises a price, the others will not follow, but if the price is cut, others will follow.

kinsman 1. Person related by blood or, in some cases, by marriage. 2. One of the same racial or cultural background.

kitchen cabinet *general business* An informal group of people who become the confidants of the top officer in a business or government and advise the officer in his or her actions, though they may have no formal place in the company.

Kitchen cycle *economics* A thirty-seven-month cycle based upon the same kind of statistical evidence used in the Juilliard cycle.

kite 1. To obtain money by passing bad checks. 3. To fraudulently deposit checks drawn on various banks into accounts in other banks under the same name in order to give the false impression that there are funds in each account.

Knights of Labor National labor organization founded in Philadelphia 1869 that rejected the traditional organizing of workers by crafts, preferring instead the mass unionization of both unskilled and skilled workers. The Knights championed the cause of workers and achieved many liberal improvements and reforms, but began to decline in the late 1880s due to opposition by craft leaders who preferred organization along craft lines, internal dissension among leading members and groups, and the unproven suspicion of its involvement in Chicago's Haymarket riot and bombing of 1886. By 1917, it ceased to exist.

Kondratieff cycle Business cycle, proposed by Russian economist Nicolai Kondratieff in 1926, which was thought to occur every fifty years, bringing a prolonged recession. Kondratieff deduced that business cycles only existed in the long-term. In recent years, some economists are turning back to the study of Kondratieff's theories.

Koopsman principle *economics; statistics* A hypothetical model specifying that the relations among variables should be such as to allow for the identification of parameters.

K ratio The reciprocal of velocity of circulation. (Cf. velocity of money circulation)

krona The basic unit of currency of Sweden.

krone The basic unit of currencies in Denmark and Norway.

Krugerrand Gold coins minted in South Africa in fractional sizes of one-half, one-quarter, and one-tenth of an ounce. The principal Krugerrand is one troy ounce of pure gold. Krugerrands were banned from further import to the United States in 1985.

L

L Measure of money supply, which includes M³ plus commercial paper, savings bonds, and Treasury obligations with maturities of eighteen months or less. (*See* M³)

labor dispute Controversy concerning terms, tenure, or conditions of employment or the association or representation of persons in negotiating, fixing, maintaining, changing, or seeking to arrange terms or conditions of employment regardless of whether the disputants stand in the proximate relation of employer and employee.

laborer   Person who does work that requires strength or repeated motion rather than skill, as distinguished from artisans and professionals.

labor force   *economics*   1. The total number of workers who are willing to work under prevailing wage scales.   2. In census definition, all persons between the ages of sixteen and sixty-five years of age not institutionalized and not in the military service on an active basis, who hold themselves out as being ready, willing, and able to work.

labor-intensive   Requiring much labor relative to the amount of capital equipment.

Labor Management Relations Act   *See* Taft-Hartley Act.

Labor Management Reporting and Disclosure Act (1959)   *See* Landrum-Griffin Act.

labor relations consultant   Person who for compensation advises or represents an employer, employer organization, or labor organization concerning employee organizing, concerted activities, or collective bargaining activities.

labor stability index   *economics*   The ratio of the number of employees who have been with the company at least a year to the number of employees one year earlier.

labor time ticket   *accounting*   A record of how and for what purpose a worker used time on a job, usually for one day. Such a record is used to allocate labor costs to different jobs which an employee may work in a day.

laches   *law*   Such neglect, omission, or unreasonable delay in asserting a right or claiming a privilege as to warrant or justify the withholding of relief. Laches is a defense against various kinds of suits.

lack of marketability discount   Discount sometimes given to closely held stock due to the necessity of having a low selling price. If the executor tries to sell it on an exchange or in a sale to the public, the selling price must be lower than mar-

ket prices for comparable stock due to the additional costs of Securities and Exchange Commission registration, preparation of a prospectus, underwriter's commissions, etc. The cost for taking a stock public can range from 10% to 25% of the selling price.

laddered maturities   *investing*   The spacing of the maturities of securities in a portfolio which is reasonably equal so that over time their maturities produce a steady flow of funds into the liquidity account.

laden in bulk   Lying loose in the hold (of a ship), protected from moisture by a number of mats and quantity of dunnage, as with corn, salt, etc.

Laffer curve   *economics*   A graphic presentation of the postulate, devised by economist Arthur Laffer, that economic output will grow if marginal tax rates are cut. The Laffer curve is used in explaining supply-side economics, a theory which, among other things, avers that noninflationary growth is stimulated when national tax policies encourage productivity and investment.   (*See* supply-side economics)

laga   Law. (A Saxon word.)

lagged reserve requirements   *banking*   A reserve system that requires that banks hold reserves in the current period against deposits outstanding in an earlier period.   Somewhat antiquated.

lagging indicator   *economics*   A series of economic data that moves with the general economy, but which tends to move either up or down later than the economy as a whole.   (Cf. leading indicator.)

laissez faire   *economics; politics*   A concept of nonintervention by government developed by the eighteenth-century French physiocrats in reaction to mercantilism and incorporated into classical economic writings by Adam Smith and others. Today the phrase is interpreted to mean freedom from government intervention in all economic affairs.

laissez-faire economy   *See* laissez faire, capitalism.

laissez-faire leader   *communication*   A superior who follows a leadership style of initial guidance and directions with a general "hands-off" policy after that. Such a leader supplies information and material when asked but does not take part in or direct decisions of the group.

lame duck A broker or jobber who cannot fulfill contracts.

land Any part of the surface of the earth, including buildings, trees, and herbage. Land is divisible not only horizontally but also vertically, so that one may own the fee and yet another may be entitled to all the minerals below the surface of the land. Equally one may own one story of a building while another may own the story below or above.

land contract *law* A written agreement for the sale of land. The purpose for using a contract sale instead of a deed with a mortgage is that the seller can foreclose more easily and get one's money back much quicker through a contract.

land court *law* A court of law that has jurisdiction over issues pertaining to, and interests in, real property.

land department Department of the United States government having jurisdiction over public lands.

land-grant railroads *economics* Railroads built on land granted by Congress from 1850 to 1900, obliging the railroads in turn to handle government freight at reduced costs. The land grant act was repealed in 1946.

landlord Owner who grants to another the right to use real property; the owner of an estate in land who has leased it for an agreed period at a specific rental to another person (the tenant or lessee).

landmark Fixed object serving as a boundary mark for a tract of land.

land patent A legal document used by the Federal government to convey title to lands to individuals.

Landrum-Griffin Act *law* A 1959 federal law providing for disclosures of certain financial transactions and administrative practices of labor organizations and employers and setting standards for election of officers of labor organizations. Also known as the Labor Management Reporting and Disclosure Act of 1959.

land trust An association of land owners which is unincorporated and which has as its purpose the holding of the title to land. Usually, the title for the land is held by one or more trustees for the benefit of association members. Members' interest in the land is evidenced by land-trust certificates.

land use regulation Government ordinances, codes, and permit requirements intended to make the private use of land and natural resources conform to policy standards.

lane Narrow way, which may be either public or, more frequently, private.

Laplace criterion A principle stating that where there is uncertainty with respect to the probabilities of eventualities, particularly in states of nature, it should be assumed that each eventuality is equally probable.

lapse 1. Termination of some right or privilege; forfeiture caused by the failure to perform some act or by the failure of some contingency. 2. To pass; to become forfeit or terminated. (E.g., a power of appointment lapses when, under the normal gift tax rules, the holder loses all power to determine the beneficiaries of all or of any portion of the property in question.)

lapsed legacy *law* A legacy which falls back into the residue of the estate because the donee predeceased the donor.

lapsed option *investing* An option that has reached its expiration date without being exercised and is therefore without value.

lapse ratio *insurance* The ratio of the number of life insurance policies lapsed without value or surrendered for cash during a year to the number of policies in force at the beginning of the year.

larceny *common law* The carrying away of another's personal property without consent with the intent of depriving the owner and of converting the property to a use other than that of the owner.

large blocks *investing* A large number of shares of stock bought or sold in one trade, and defined by the New York Stock Exchange as a trade for ten thousand or more shares.

large-loss principle *insurance* Principle which causes the buyer to purchase insurance to cover the large losses and not the small but more probable losses.

last-in, first-out (LIFO) Method of inventory accounting in which the newest item in inventory is assumed to be sold first. (See first-in, first-out)

last sale   *investing* The most recent sale of a specific security. It is to be differentiated from the closing sale of the day on an exchange.

last trading day   *investing* The final day for a futures contract to be settled. Without some kind of agreement between the buyer and the seller, the commodity must be physically delivered. (*See* commodity futures, futures contract)

lata culpa dolo aequiparatur   *Gross negligence is equivalent to fraud.*

latent   Potential but not presently visible, as in latent defects.

laudare   To cite, to show one's title or authority.

laundering money   *banking; law* The action of depositing and withdrawing funds from numerous accounts, usually in numerous banks, in an attempt to hide the source of the money. Usually, the money is the result of some kind of illegal transaction, such as drug trafficking.

law   1. A rule which must be obeyed and conformed to by citizens, on peril of sanctions and legal consequences. 2. The body of all such rules. 3. The study of jurisprudence. 4. The legal profession. 5. Principle of conduct observed habitually by an individual or class.

lawful   Warranted or authorized by law; not contrary to or forbidden by law.

lawful age   Age at which, in a given jurisdiction, one attains particular rights and/or responsibilities.

lawful issue   *common law* Legitimate descendants of a person.

law merchant   Commercial and trade regulations based upon the traditions of the past.

law of demand   Principle which states that the quantity demanded of a commodity varies inversely with its price, assuming that all other things which may affect demand remain the same.

law of diminishing marginal productivity   *economics* The hypothesis that when successive units of one or more variable factors are applied to a fixed factor in production, output will follow three stages: (a) it will increase at an increasing rate, (b) it will increase at a decreasing rate, and (c) it will reach a maximum and decrease thereafter.

law of diminishing marginal utility   *economics* The hypothesis that consumption of each succeeding unit of a good will yield less satisfaction than the preceding unit. Thus, total utility will increase at a decreasing rate. Also called law of variable proportions.

law of diminishing return   Common condition in which additional inputs produce successively smaller increments of output. If some of the factors of production are fixed (buildings and machinery), output can be increased by adding more variable inputs (labor and materials). But as more variable inputs are added and output is expanded, eventually a point will be reached beyond which the returns from each additional unit of variable input will diminish.

law of large numbers   *marketing* The concept that the larger the number of samples one uses, the closer the results should be to the total population.

law of the trivial many and the critical few   *See* Pareto's law.

law of variable proportions   *See* law of diminishing marginal utility.

lawyer   *law* One who is licensed to practice law in a state by virtue of completing certain prescribed courses of study, passing a comprehensive examination, usually called the bar exam, and who is required to live up to a certain code of professional conduct.

layered trusts   Independent trusts, each of which is created for the benefit of one generation of beneficiaries, usually done to avoid the application of the generation-skipping tax.

layoff   1. Temporary suspension of employment at an employer's will. 2. *finance* A process by which investment bankers agree to purchase and resell to the public any portion of a stock issue not subscribed to by shareholders who hold the rights. To hedge against any loss during the layoff period, the bankers will usually engage in buying the rights and, at the same time, sell shares represented by those rights. (Cf. hedge, investment banker)

leading indicator   *economics* Signal of economic change that tends to move ahead of aggregate economic activity, thus reaching peaks and troughs before the economy as a whole. The U.S. Department of Commerce Bureau of Economic analysis releases a monthly index of twelve leading indicators. In 1985 they were listed as: average workweek of production workers, average weekly claims for state unemployment insurance, new orders for consumer goods and materials, vendor performance, new business formation, contracts for new plant and equipment, new building permits, inventory changes, sensitive materials prices, stock prices, money supply, and business and consumer borrowing.

lead-lag technique   A method used in forecasting based on the proposition that a stable relationship exists between one economic series (the indicator) and another series which is being forecast on the basis of the first.

leakage   *economics* The removal of funds from the income stream for repayment of debts previously contracted or for additions to savings.

lease   Contract for the use and enjoyment of property at an agreed rental for a specific period, or at the pleasure of the parties.

leaseback   *economics; investing* A method of selling assets to an investor, and then immediately leasing them back. This gives the seller a better cash flow and gives the investor a good rate of interest plus the other privileges of owning assets, such as claiming depreciation, etc.

leased department   *economics; marketing* A department in a store, which is leased and operated by specialists in the business of that department.

leasehold   Land held by lease; the estate in real property of a lessee created by a lease. Generally refers to an estate whose duration is fixed but may also be used to describe a tenancy at will; i.e., a month to month or periodic tenancy.

leasehold interest policy   *insurance* Policy protecting a tenant who has a bargain created by a long-term lease on a property with the present rental value greater than the amount agreed upon in the lease. The value of this bargain (the leasehold interest) is measured by the excess value between the market rate and the contractual rate. The lease may allow for cancellation by the landlord but with a leasehold interest policy the tenant can be protected against loss of the favored position.

leasehold mortgage   *banking* A loan made to the lessee of property secured by personal leasehold interest in the property.

lease with option to purchase   Lease that gives the lessee the right to purchase the property at an agreed-upon price under certain conditions.

left-hand side   *banking* The rate at which a bank sells specific foreign currencies.

legabilis   That which may be the subject of a bequest.

legable   That which is capable of being bequeathed.

legacy   Gift of personal property by will. (*See* legatee, bequest)

LEGAL   A computerized data base used by the New York Stock Exchange to track enforcement actions against member firms, audits of member firms, and customer complaints.

legal capacity   The capacity to participate in a legal contract.

legal description   Legally acceptable identification of real estate.

legal ethics   Body of usages and rules, written or unwritten, governing the conduct of lawyers in their dealings with one another, with their clients, and with the court. The Code of Professional Conduct as written by the American Bar Association has been adopted in many jurisdictions.

legal interest   *See* legal title.

legal investment   Investment to which savings banks, trust funds, insurance reserves, and the like are restricted by law. These usually consist of U.S. government debt instruments, certain municipal bonds, real estate first mortgages, etc. (*See* legal list)

legal liability   Liability which is recognized and enforced by the courts.

legal list   *finance* A listing of legal investments. (*See* legal investment)

legal monopoly   *economics; law* A monopoly which is created by law in the public interest, including public utilities, patents, copyrights, etc.

legal name One's name used for official purposes. The name on one's birth certificate, unless changed through marriage, adoption, or court action.

legal notice Notification of others, using the method required by law.

legal purpose *insurance* Purpose of a policy which is acceptable within the framework of law.

legal rate of interest *finance* That maximum rate of interest which may be charged on specific types of loans, which rate is established by state law.

legal remonetization *See* remonetization.

legal representative 1. Executor and administrator of a decedent's estate. 2. One who stands in the place of another, such as an assignee in bankruptcy.

legal reserves *finance* Monies that an insurance company, a bank, or a savings and loan company must retain as a security for the conduct of its business.

legal tender All coins and currencies lawful within a given country.

legal title Title or interest that is recognized by common law, as distinguished from an equitable title or interest. Also called legal interest.

legatee One to whom a legacy is given.

legatum morte testatoris tantum confirmatur, sicut donatio inter vivos traditione solo *A legacy is confirmed (takes effect) by the death of the testator, even as a gift from a living person is by delivery alone.*

legend securities Securities bearing restrictive covenants of varying natures.

legislation Act of making laws and passing enactments by legislative body.

legislature *law* Elected body of officials, usually convening in the national or state capitol, whose duty it is to pass the laws of the nation or state, within the context of the constitution governing that nation or state.

legitimi haeredes *Legitimate heirs.*

legitimus *Lawful; legitimate.*

leisure class *economics* A term first coined by Thorstein Veblen to describe a social group who, because of income from whatever source, eschews work and seeks pleasure in leisure time.

lender of last resort Institution having authority and financial resources to credit to depository institutions or other entities in unusual circumstances involving a national or regional emergency, where failure to obtain credit would have a severe adverse impact on the economy. In the United States, such authority is held by the Federal Reserve System.

lending at a premium *securities* Loaning of shares of stock by a broker to another broker to help that broker cover short positions; a fee or premium is charged for this service.

lending at a rate *investing* The action of paying a client interest on the credit balance from proceeds from a short sale. This action does not occur often.

lending securities The practice of a broker lending stocks to a client who has made a short sale and must deliver the shares. Such clients have cash and stock accounts with the broker, the cash account being sufficient to cover the cost of shares borrowed.

leonina societas Partnership in which one partner takes all the profits and doesn't share in the losses; not a true partnership.

lessee One to whom a lease is granted; a tenant holding property by lease.

lesser-developed country Country in which development lies somewhere between industrialized countries and Third World countries, which are virtually undeveloped.

lessor One who grants a lease; a landlord letting property under a lease.

lestagium Duty levied on the cargo of a ship.

let To demise or lease. In a lease, the letting of the premises occurs at the beginning of the tenancy with the subsequent payment of rent merely an incident of the letting.

letter of administration *law* Document issued by a probate court authorizing a specified person or persons to administer the estate of a person who dies intestate. The person to whom such authority is granted is called the administrator and upon such grant being made, acquires all the powers, rights, and duties of an executor. Sometimes an administrator is appointed by the court to fulfill the duties of an executor who dies before the estate is fully settled.

letter of credit 1. An arrangement with specified conditions whereby a bank agrees to substitute its credit for a customer's. 2. Letter in the nature of a negotiable instrument whereby a person requests another to advance money or give credit to a third person and promises to repay the former the amount of the advance.

letter of exchange Bill of exchange.

letter of indemnity *law* A contract by which one party agrees to reimburse another party for a loss suffered, under specific circumstances, usually for a stated period of time. In effect, an insurance contract.

letter of intent Expression of a desire to enter into a contract without actually doing so, ordinarily represented by a brief memorandum of the preliminary understanding of the parties who intend to enter into a contract.

letter security *finance* A security which a corporation is allowed to sell to a small group of private investors without having it registered with the SEC. Normally, the SEC must be assured by the buyers that the security is to be held and not resold.

letter testamentary Document issued by a probate court authorizing the executor of a will to act as such.

level debt service *finance* A provision in a municipal charter stating that payment on the municipal debt will be approximately the same every year, thus making it easier for the municipality to budget annual expendable funds.

level payment amortization *finance* A plan for amortizing a loan in which the mortgage payments are constant but the percentage of the payment going to principal and interest changes with each payment.

level payment mortgage Lien requiring the same payment each month (or other period) for full amortization.

level premium insurance A fixed premium rate on a life insurance policy which is determined by the age of the person at the time the policy is taken out and which remains the same so long as the policy is in force.

leverage 1. Use of borrowed funds to increase purchasing power and profitability of an investment; the amount of leverage capital has a definite impact on market price of common stock. If a large debt must be serviced and earnings are low, market price will often come down. 2. Control of large resources with a minimal investment. 3. Amount of money borrowed by a business party in excess of money or assets invested in the business. For leverage to be profitable, the investment's realized rate of return must be higher than the cost of the money borrowed. 4. Borrowing of money for investment. Leverage is widely used in business and has increased tremendously in recent years. (*See* positive leverage, reverse leverage)

leverage coefficient The ratio of the total increase in national income to an increase in initial expenditures. (Cf. acceleration principle)

leveraged buy-out *finance* The buy-out of one business entity by another, with the use of borrowed money when the assets of the acquired company serve as collateral for the loan or stock in the merged companies is used for the pay-off.

leveraged employee stock ownership plan (LESOP) Plan prevalent in medium and small businesses where a trust can acquire blocks of employer securities through the use of borrowing—even if the collateral used is the acquired shares. While the characteristics of LESOPs are many, one of the most important is that the maximum annual contribution is 15% of eligible payroll. However, if the funds are used to purchase securities an employer can contribute up to 25% of payroll to a LESOP for the principal component of purchased shares and an unlimited amount for interest. Thus, a LESOP represents a powerful tool for the tax-deductible acquisition of employer securities. (*See* Appendix G)

leveraged investment company *finance* An open end investment company, or mutual fund, which is empowered by its charter to borrow funds from a bank or some other lender. Or a dual-purpose investment company which issues both income and capital shares. Holders of income shares receive dividends and interest on investments, and holders of capital

187

shares receive all capital gains on investments. Essentially, each class of shareholder leverages the other.

leverage factor 1. *finance* The extent to which a corporation can effect, by the use of bonds and preferred stocks (both essentially debt instruments), proportionate changes in return to common stock greater than the changes in operating income. If corporate capital is largely represented by bonds and preferred stock, the corporation has a high leverage factor. This process is termed "trading on the equity." 2. The increase in the rate of profit which follows an increase in the volume of sales or production when fixed costs are spread over more units.

leverage fund Mutual fund that is allowed by its charter to borrow money to increase the quantity of securities purchased with the aim of increasing return.

leverage ratios *accounting* Relationships among balance sheet values that measure the degree to which owners rather than creditors finance a business.

levy To collect or obtain money by seizure; to legally impose or collect that which is due.

lex loci *law The law of the place.* With regard to contracts, the place was where the contract was made.

lex loci contractus The proper law applicable in deciding upon the rights and liabilities of the contracting parties; would also decide such matters as the essential validity of the contract.

lex succurrit ignoranti *Law assists the ignorant* (which is not to excuse ignorance of the law).

lex terrae *Law of the land.*

liability 1. Obligation to pay an amount or perform a service. The claim of a creditor against an individual or a business, whose assets are subject to payments for the claim. Liabilities are shown on financial statements by category and amount and balanced against assets to obtain net worth. In a business, especially a corporation, liability refers to bonded indebtedness as opposed to equity investment. 2. Condition of being responsible for damages resulting from an intentional tort or a negligent act or for the discharging of an obligation or the payment of some debt.

liability exclusions *insurance* Item which is not included in a homeowner's policy, which may mean the necessity of having further liability insurance. Two common exclusions are aircraft and certain types and sizes of watercrafts.

liability on an account Legal responsibility to repay debt.

liability without fault Liability imposed regardless of negligence or intentions; absolute or strict liability. Applies to dangerous instruments, extra hazardous operations, and defective products.

liable Bound; responsible; answerable; chargeable in law or in equity. This is not a legal term and has no technical meaning.

libel Defamation expressed in a permanent form—such as published writing, printing, or other graphic representation—that damages a reputation or exposes one to public ridicule. (Cf. slander)

libera batella Liberty of free fishery in certain waters.

liberata pecunia non liberat offerentem *Money tendered does not release the tenderor* (from the debt).

libertas est naturalis facultas ejus quod cuique facere libet, nisi quod de jure aut vi prohibetur *Liberty is that natural attribute which allows everyone to do what he pleases, save that which is restrained by law.*

libertas inestimabilis res est *Freedom is a priceless thing.*

license 1. Permission granted by an authorized official to perform some act or engage in some business activity. 2. Document that grants such permission. 3. Written authorization by the owner of a patent empowering another person to make or use the patented article or process for a limited period of time in a limited area.

licensee Person to whom a license has been granted.

licensing fee Amount of money, usually stated as a percentage of sales, which an investor can collect by letting other people put a plan into operation. If the property is deemed to have a short life, the licensing fee may be large; if it has a longer life, the fee will be smaller.

lien Charge against property, making it

security for the payment of a debt, judgment, mortgage, or taxes under which claim the property may be seized and sold to satisfy the debt. (*See* specific lien, general lien)

life annuity 1. Engagement to make an annual payment, sometimes by monthly installments, during the continuance of any given life. 2. An annuity not limited as to time. (*See* straight life annuity, guaranteed minimum annuity)

life annuity certain *insurance* An annuity policy that provides for payments of income for the life of the annuitant but guarantees a minimum number of payments so that if the annuitant dies within the guaranteed period, the balance of the payments are made to the estate.

life estate 1. Freehold interest (in real property) that expires upon the death of the owner or some other specified person (pur autre vie). 2. An estate held for the life of the holding party or for the life of some other person or persons.

life income annuity A program under which the holder of the annuity is promised a life income with no benefits accruing to a beneficiary.

life income with period certain option Insurance option in which payments are guaranteed for as long as the recipient lives; however, if the recipient should die before the end of a specified period, such as ten or twenty years, payments would continue to a second payee for this balance of the period.

life insurance Contract for payment whereby a specified sum of money becomes payable upon death of the insured. An absolute engagement to pay a certain sum at the end of a definite or indefinite period; not in essence a contract of indemnity but frequently characterized as such.

life insurance trust Agreement between an insured person and a trustee according to which, upon the death of the former, the trustee is to be paid the insurance policy's proceeds for investment and distribution to beneficiaries named by the insured. This is generally a living trust, which may be revocable or irrevocable, funded or unfunded, or a short-term, reversionary type trust; also embraces trusts set up by will—testamentary trusts to receive, hold, and distribute life insurance proceeds.

life interest Interest in property entitling the holder to the income from or the use of property, or a portion of the property, for his or her lifetime. This does not amount to ownership.

life table *insurance* A table showing the mortality and survivorship characteristics of a given population. The years' experience these tables are based on change over time.

life tenant 1. Person who holds an estate for life or a life interest. 2. One who is allowed to use property for life or the lifetime of another designated person. (*See* life estate)

lifetime transfers Transfers made during the lifetime of the estate owner to some person or entity, the chief aim of which is to avoid or diminish the estate tax owed upon death.

lifting a leg *investing* The closing of one side of a hedge position.

like-kind property Property legally transferred which is similar but not identical to the property received. Like-kind requirements limit tax-free exchanges to the exchange of real estate for real estate and personal property for personal property. An exchange of an apartment building for vacant farmland is considered to be like-kind.

limitation *real estate* The extreme period during which an estate or interest is to continue, as specified in the conveyance, will, etc. Thus, if there is a devise to A for life and then to B absolutely, there is a limitation of a life interest to A and the remainder to B.

limited company *finance* A form of business entity found primarily in Great Britain where registration under the Companies Act is comparable to incorporation under the state laws in the United States. It is usually abbreviated Ltd. or Plc.

limited discretion *investing* An agreement between a broker and client giving the broker the right to make certain limited trades without consulting the client, as in the case of an option nearing expiration.

limited liability 1. Restriction of one's potential losses to the amount invested. In a partnership, the general partner is responsible in an unlimited manner for the debts of the partnership, and a limited partner's liability can be no greater than the investment in the partnership. 2. Legal provision that protects individual stockholders of a corporation from being sued by creditors of the corporation to collect unpaid debts of the firm. (*See* at-risk rules)

limited line store Retail store that competes with larger stores by offering a complete selection of a few related lines of merchandise, such as clothing, hardware, or sporting goods.

limited open-end indenture *finance* An arrangement which controls the number of mortgage bonds that may be issued in the future under the same indenture and with the same priority lien on the assets of the corporation.

limited owner Person whose interest in land is less than fee simple, such as a tenant for life.

limited partner One whose liabilities are limited to the investment in the partnership and who usually has no responsibility for its management. Losses and profits are in proportion to the investment made by the partner.

limited partnership Form of business in which certain partners are liable only to the extent of their investment and usually do not participate in the management of the business. One or more general partners would be fully responsible for the debts of the business. While civil law recognizes limited partnerships, common law does not, and limited partnership in common law jurisdictions is purely a creature of statute. (*See* general partner, partnership)

limited partnership interest *real estate* Interest of the investors, with the promoters, builders, or developers being the general partners. The limited partners can invest their money with only limited liability for partnership debts, and the earnings (and tax losses) from the real estate can be passed through to these partners without being taxed to the partnership. The earnings or losses are either taxable or deductible to the individual partnerships.

limited partnership resyndication A partnership in which existing properties

are sold to new limited partners, who can get tax advantages that had been exhausted by the previous partnership. This is often found in privately financed government housing projects.

limited-pay life Insurance policy on which the premiums are paid only for a specified number of years.

limited payment *life insurance* Life insurance on which payment is made for a limited length of time (e.g., twenty years), at which time the policy is paid up.

limited policy Health insurance policy with unusual exclusions, limitations, restrictions, or reductions in coverage.

limited power of appointment Special power of appointment conferred on a person where the power can be exercised only in favor of a specified class of individuals or for specific purposes.

limited tax bond *finance* A municipal bond which is backed by the full faith of the municipality, but which is not backed by its full taxing power. Usually, only specified taxes can be used to discharge the bond obligation.

limit order Buy or sell order for a stated number of shares of a specific security placed at a specified price. The order is to be executed at the specified (limit) price or better. Typically the buy limit order is placed below current market price and states the maximum purchase price. The sell limit order is placed above the current market price and sets the minimum sale price. When the limit is not within the current quote, the order is said to be "away from the market."

linea recta semper praefertur transversali *The direct line of descendent is always preferred to the collateral.* A maxim applicable to devolution of estates of intestates.

linear programming *statistics* A system of concluding the maximum output and the minimum cost, giving specific recognition to the fact that at any given point in time methods of production, supplies of factors, or other elements are fixed and the paths of expansion are linear. The system uses constraints (limitations that must be met by the answer), and an "objective function" (that will be maximized or minimized) which are then controlled by matrix algebra.

line limit Maximum amount of insurance any one insurer will issue on any one exposure.

line of credit 1. Fixed limit of credit prearranged between lender and borrower. 2. *finance* A formal commitment by a bank or other financial institution to a borrower to lend on future request on currently agreed terms, up to a specific amount of money. These loans are normally secured, but might not be, and the continuance of the agreement is contingent upon the borrower maintaining a sound financial condition.

Lipper mutual fund industry average *finance* The average performance level of all mutual funds, as reported by Lipper Analytical Services of New York. Mutual fund performance is ranked quarterly and annually, by type of fund, such as aggressive growth fund or income fund. Obviously it is to the advantage of mutual fund managers to surpass the average of such funds, since these reports are given wide publicity.

Lipsey equation A theory set forth by R. G. Lipsey in 1960, which, like the Phillips curve, relates wage rates to unemployment, with the added dimension of taking into consideration changes in retail prices during the preceding twelve months.

liquid asset Any asset that can be quickly converted to cash without significant loss of value.

liquidate 1. To dissolve a business. 2. To pay and settle; to adjust. To collect and realize upon the assets and settle with the creditors, and, if there is a surplus, to distribute among owners.

liquidated damages Fixed sum of money specifically agreed upon between parties at the time of entering into a contract, to be paid in the event of the nonperformance of the contract by either party, as distinguished from a penalty, which is nonenforceable.

liquidating value *finance* The value of a company after it ceases to operate, sells all assets, and settles with all creditors.

liquidation 1. Process by which the affairs of a debtor are settled, leading to the closing of financial accounts by converting assets into cash for distribution to creditors, stockholders, etc. 2. Process of closing down a company, selling the assets, paying off creditors, and distributing any remaining cash to owners.

liquidator Person appointed to close a corporation's business.

liquidity *finance* 1. Ability of the marketplace to absorb the selling of an issue. 2. The ease with which assets can be converted into cash without loss of principal (e.g., an investor's ability to convert securities into cash on short notice with minimal or no loss in current market value). The desire or need for liquidity is somewhat controlled by the nature and immediacy of financial obligations, the nature of other assets, the age and liquidity needs of estate, what credit facilities may be available, and availability of adequate health insurance and other insurance coverages to meet emergencies. Of all types of investments, tax shelters are the least liquid.

liquidity needs *estate planning* Amount of cash, or near cash, one would need immediately upon the death of the estate owner to be used to pay bills owed, funeral expenses, etc.

liquidity ratio Any ratio used to estimate a company's cash position. (*See* acid test, current ratio)

liquidity preference *finance* The percentage of a person's assets, or those of a business, which will be kept in the form of cash under varying sets of circumstances.

liquidity trap *finance* The point at which the demand for money, or liquidity, is infinitely elastic with respect to the interest rate and further increases in the money supply will not result in falling interest rates. This situation can arise when the yield on earning assets is so low that the risk of holding such assets is thought to be so high that investors would prefer to hold any increases in the money supply in liquid form. This is generally a Keynesian theory.

lis pendens *law A pending suit.* In relation to real estate, this is a notice of public record of property on which questions have been raised bearing on the title of the property so that the buyer will take the risk of what the ultimate decision of the case might be.

listed agent; listed broker *real estate* One who takes the listing on a specific piece of real estate, ordinarily getting a small percentage of the sales commission.

listed option Stock option contracts, issued by the Options Clearing Corporation, traded in an organized auction market on the floor of a member exchange. The striking prices and expiration dates are set in advance, and adjustments are made in the event of a stock split or a stock dividend. Listed options trade in a liquid market, which allows the buyers and sellers to close out their positions at any time or to exercise their contracts at will.

listed security *investing* A security which has met the qualifications for listing on a stock exchange. Such requirements include the submitting of financial reports, consent to periodic supervision, etc.

listing 1. Written engagement contract between a principal and an agent, authorizing the agent to perform services for the principal involving the latter's property. 2. A record of property for sale by a broker who has been authorized to sell. 3. The property so listed. 4. Contract made between the owner of realty and a real estate broker, whereby the owner binds himself or herself to sell the land to a purchaser procured by the broker or the broker's agent on the terms set out in the contract. (Not an offer to sell which may be accepted and converted into a binding agreement of sale.)

list renting *marketing* The action of purchasing the use of a specific list of names and addresses (such as all the people subscribing to a certain periodical) for the purpose of doing direct mailing. Frequently, the owner of a list will do the mailing so that the list is not actually released to the purchaser.

lite pendente *law Pending the suit.* In law, a court may issue orders for the duration of a suit, i.e., until the matter is fully resolved.

literary property right 1. Exclusive right of an author to possess, use, and dispose of the author's literary compositions. 2. Natural right of an author or the author's assigns to the exclusive use of and profit from the author's work.

livery of seisin Formal or actual delivery of corporeal possession of the interest in land; essential at common law for a conveyance. An incorporeal hereditament could, on the other hand, be effectively conveyed at common law by an instrument under seal.

livestock Any creature kept for the production of food, wool, skins, or fur, or for its use in the farming of land.

living trust A written agreement under which a donor sets apart a certain portion of the donor's estate, income from those assets to be paid to others through a trustee. Also called an inter vivos trust.

Lloyd's, Corporation of A company that originated in London, dealing originally in marine insurance, but which has grown to be worldwide and deals in virtually all types of property and casualty insurance. Lloyd's is not an insurance company per se, but provides a clearinghouse for many companies dealing in insurance. It can still be said that Lloyd's has the most comprehensive programs of marine statistics and insurance coverage to be found in the world. Also called Lloyd's of London.

load factor *economics* The ratio of the average output to the peak output for a given period of time. Used to differentiate between classes of customers with respect to rates.

load fund Mutual fund that charges a fee (load) for the transaction. Normally, the price of a load fund is the net asset value price plus the load, which may run 8½ or 8¼% of the public offering price. Open-end mutual funds are infrequently sold on a no-load basis.

load line Line along the side of a ship used as a guide to determine the amount of load that can be safely carried. When loaded, the ship should not sink below this line.

loan Anything lent or given to another on condition that it be returned or repaid, either with or without interest.

loanable funds theory of interest *finance* An explanation of interest as the price adjusting the demand for and supply of loanable funds available at any particular time, with demand determined mainly by investment opportunities and supply by savings and credit creations.

loan officer *banking* Person who makes loans. Most often, a short tenure loan officer may only have power to make suggestions with respect to making loans. Generally, the loan officer, after some degree of experience, will be given the title assistant vice president and, ultimately, vice president, and perhaps, at some point in time, senior vice president. Normally loan officers, regardless of title, will operate in a specialized field of lending, such as consumer lending, commercial lending, agricultural loans, real estate loans, etc.

loan standby fees Fees paid on a loan which "stands by" to be paid out as needed, as on a construction project. The fees are incorporated in the ultimate mortgage loan.

loan-to-value ratio *finance* The ratio between the amount of a loan and the appraised value of the asset which serves as security for the loan, expressed as a percentage of the asset value.

loan value *insurance* The cash value of a policy at any given point in time.

loan warehousing Packaging of a number of mortgage loans for sale in the secondary mortgage market by a financial institution or mortgage banker who has originated the loans.

lobbying Addressing or soliciting members of a legislative body for the purpose of influencing a vote.

local agent *insurance* Insurance agent, usually dealing in life insurance, representing several insurers in a restricted geographical area, primarily performing sales functions. Such agents are often capable of building up a sizeable business over time.

locked in *investing* A stock market term describing an investor who owns securities which that investor has a profit on but is unwilling to sell because of capital gains taxes. (Cf. capital gain)

lockout Refusal by an employer to furnish available work to its regular employees, usually motivated by employers' desire to protect itself in bargaining with employees.

locus Place; location; area.

locus sigilii *law* *The place of the seal.*

lode Any zone or belt of mineralized rock clearly separating same from neighboring rock.

lodger Tenant of part of a premises that is in the possession of a landlord, with exclusive possession of that part.

logical In accordance with inferences reasonably drawn from preceding or surrounding events.

logical analysis *marketing* An analytical approach to a market survey, which survey may result in an advertising campaign. Normally, the analysis is nothing more than the company applying the knowledge of the market, and the product in question, which it already has.

logistic curve A modified exponential curve; a series in which progression is, by small absolute amounts in the early stages, followed by larger absolute amounts, and finally again by smaller absolute amounts until an upper limit or saturation is approached. This curve approximates the growth pattern of new companies, new products, or new industries over time.

Lombard Street A street in London named after the money changers who came to London from Lombardy (France) in the eighteenth century. The street is currently the financial and banking center of London, the British equivalent of Wall Street.

London Interbank Offered Rate (LIBOR) Rate of interest that most credit worthy international banks dealing in Eurodollars charge each other for large loans.

long Having a large holding of a particular security or commodity. (E.g., to be long five hundred shares of ABC Corporation is to own those five hundred shares.)

longa possessio parit jus possidendi, et tollit actionem vero domino *Long possession produces the right of possession and takes his action away from the true owner long-term assets.* Asset expected to last (or to be held) by the taxpayer for more than one year, such as plant and equipment.

long coupon *investing* A bond so issued that the first interest payment covers a longer length of time than subsequent payments.

longevity pay *economics* A differential in pay among employees which is based on years of service and favors those employees with the longest tenure.

long hedge position Method of protecting against a rise in the cost of honoring a future commitment. (Also called a buy hedge.) The hedger benefits from a narrowing of the basis (difference between cash price and future price) if the future is bought below the cash price, and from the widening of the basis if the future is bought above the cash price.

long leg *investing* A part of an option spread representing a commitment to buy the underlying security and consisting of a long call option and a short put option.

long position The position of owning a large portion of securities. (*See* long)

long run *economics* A sufficiently long period of time that the amount of all factor inputs can be varied.

long-term capital gain Gain on a capital asset which has been held by the taxpayer for six months or more. (*See* Appendix G)

long-term capital loss Loss on a capital asset which has been held by the taxpayer for six months or more. (*See* Appendix G)

long-term disability Contract paying monthly indemnity after an employee has been totally disabled for a stipulated period (such as 60, 90, or 180 days); frequently takes over after a short-term plan which may have been insured or self-funded by the employer. The amount is usually equal to 50–60% of base pay. Frequently, benefits are integrated with worker's compensation, Social Security, statutory benefits, veteran's disability benefits, and other employer retirement and government provided disability plans.

long-term investments *finance* Assets which are owned by a business but which will not be turned into cash during the current accounting period. Depending on context, may refer to time periods anywhere from one year to forty years or more.

long-term liability Debt obligation that will come due in more than one year. Generally speaking, long-term debts are those due in ten or more years.

Lorenz curve *economics; statistics* Diagram of statistical data showing the distribution of income among population groups, with cumulated percent of population shown on the horizontal axis and cumulated percent of income shown on the vertical axis. A curve which was completely uniform would appear as a straight line of forty-five degrees. The more hollow the curve the more unequal the distribution. The curve is most often used to show the effect of a tax on the distribution of income.

loss 1. Unintentional decline in or disappearance of value. 2. Any deprivation, decrease in value, depreciation, liability actually incurred. 3. The act of losing or the thing lost. 4. Uncollectable debt.

loss carry-forward *finance* Business losses in past years which can be deducted from profits in this year, and in subsequent years, thus effectively reducing taxable income.

loss exposure Situations under which the possibility of loss exists. The number and type of such exposures determine how a risk-management program may be put together.

loss leader Retail good priced at less than cost so as to attract customers who will possibly then buy other merchandise at the regular price.

loss leader price *marketing* A popular, fast moving item in a store which may be sold for less than its cost to attract people to the store on the assumption that they will buy other items while there.

loss reduction *insurance* Measures taken to minimize future loss, such as having fire extinguishers in buildings.

loss-unit concept The principle of aggregating diverse losses resulting from a single event.

lost grant *law* Doctrine whereby courts presume, from the long possession and exercise of a right by a claimant with the acquiescence of the owner, that there must have originally been a grant by the owner to the claimant, which was lost.

lot and block *real estate* Method of locating a parcel or land. (*See* legal description)

lottery Distribution of prizes by lot or chance; a game of hazard in which small sums are ventured for the chance of obtaining a larger value either in money or other articles; an allotment or distribution of anything by chance; the drawing of lots.

lower of cost or market *accounting* A conservative approach to the valuation of inventory, which usually means that the inventory will be priced at replacement cost, or market price, if lower than replacement cost.

low interest loan Loan made, usually by one family member to another, bearing interest at a very low rate. The Tax Recovery Act of 1984 has provided new income and gift tax rules that severely limit, but do not destroy, the benefits of such loans in intra-family gift transactions. Under this law, such loans generally are recharacterized as arm's length transactions in which the lender is deemed to have made a lesser loan to the borrower at a statutory interest rate, and the borrower is deemed to have paid such an amount back to the lender as interest. The deemed interest is taxed to the lender and may be deductible by the borrower. It may also be treated as a gift to the borrower. The statutory rate is determined by reference to federal rates with corresponding terms. (*See* Appendix G)

lucrative Yielding gain or profit; profitable; bearing or yielding a revenue, salary, or wages.

lucri causa *For the sake of gain;* for the sake of profit.

lucrum *law Profit loss.* One element of damages in the breech of a contract.

lucrum facere ex pupilli tutela tutor non debet *A guardian ought not to profit from the estate of his ward.*

Luddite 1. A person belonging to a group in nineteenth-century England that objected to the new technology being brought into the hosiery industry. 2. A person who objects to the introduction of new technology to industry.

Ludwig von Mises Institute *economics* An organization located at Auburn University, in memory of Ludwig von Mises, and dedicated to the propagation of von Mises' economic theories and those of the Austrian school in general.

lump of labor theory of wages *economics* A highly generalized view that, at one point in time, the amount of labor demanded by producers is fixed and does not change with the rate of pay demanded by the workers, but that increased productivity would shorten the number of hours of work available.

lump-sum distribution Situation in which all the proceeds of a pension or profit-sharing plan are paid to the recipient at one time during a tax year. Most qualified plans allow lump-sum distributions as one of the methods of payout. Such a provision in the plan is necessary for the employee to draw benefits in this form; otherwise, he or she will be limited to an installment annuity. To qualify for a lump-sum distribution for income tax purposes, the entire balance in an employee's account must be paid out within one taxable year of the recipient's retirement age after fifty-nine years and six months. All qualified plans of the employee that are of the same type must be combined to determine whether an employee's entire balance has been distributed. In determining what plans are of the same type, all pension plans, including defined-benefit and money-purchase plans, are treated as a single type; and all stock bonus plans are treated as a single type. If the distribution qualified as a lump sum, Internal Revenue Code Section 402(a) divides the distribution into two parts; contributions and accumulations to the plan prior to January 1, 1974, will receive long-term capital gain treatment, and the amount of distribution attributable to income and accumulations on or after January 1, 1974, will be separately taxed as ordinary income. Once this distribution has been properly allocated, the pre-1974 capital gain portion is included in an employee's income along with other capital gains and losses. The post-1973 portion is taxed as deferred compensation at ordinary income rates subject to the employee's election to use ten-year forward income averaging, which reduces the tax liability on the distribution. (*See* Appendix G)

lump-sum settlement Sum, due by installments, which is paid at one time, usually a lesser amount than was originally due.

lunar month Period consisting of twenty-eight days.

M

M¹ *finance* Symbol for the basic money supply, which is made up of demand deposits and currency in circulation in the economy.

M² *finance* Symbol for the money supply which includes all of M¹, plus time deposits in commercial banks, excluding large certificates of deposit.

M³ *finance* Symbol for the money supply which includes M², plus the beginning of the month and the end of the month deposits in savings and loans and mutual savings banks.

M⁴ *finance* Symbol for the money supply which includes M², plus negotiable certificates of deposit of $100,000 or more, with large, weekly reporting banks.

M⁵ *finance* Symbol for the money supply which includes M³, plus negotiable certificates of deposits of $100,000 or more held with large, weekly reporting, banks.

machine ancillary time *economics* Production time lost when the plant is shut down for clean-up, preventive maintenance, and other planned activities which will guarantee continuing efficient production. (Cf. machine downtime)

machine downtime *economics* That time in which a machine is not in production because of a breakdown. Downtime is usually unplanned. (Cf. machine ancillary time)

machine idletime *economics* Any time when equipment is available for production work but is not in use because of lack of materials, or lack of orders, etc.

macroeconomics The study of the nation's economy as a whole, in which aggregate data such as price levels, unemployment, industrial production, productivity, and inflation are analyzed. Sometimes called national income economics.

Magna Carta Charter granted by King John of England in 1215 A.D. at his barons' compulsion; consisted of a collection of statutes declaring the ancient liberties and customs of England, providing for the regulation of the administration of justice, defining the temporal and ecclesiastical jurisdictions, and securing the personal liberty of each subject, the subject's rights of property, and the limits of taxation.

Magyar Nemzeti Bank The national (central) bank of Hungary, established in 1924.

mail float *banking* The float, or lag, that occurs while a check is still in the mail from the payer to the payee.

mail fraud Using or causing to be used the postal service of the United States government in furtherance of a scheme to swindle.

mail order selling *marketing* Goods sold via direct mail order, catalog, or other type of advertisement which requires only the use of the postal service, with no direct contact between the buyer and the seller.

mail teller *banking* A bank employee responsible for processing all mail deposits.

maintain To keep up; to bear cost of; to keep in good order; to support or supply with means of support; to provide for and sustain; to uphold, carry on, or continue.

maintenance margin *investing* The cash or securities which a trader must keep with the trader's broker to insure the payment of margin or credit accounts.

maintenance margin requirements Minimum level of funds in a margin account that triggers a margin call. (*See* margin account)

maintenance of membership *labor law* Clause in a labor contract providing that once an employee joins a union the employee must remain a union member for the term of the current contract, usually under penalty of losing the job. Sometimes an escape period is granted an employee between contracts.

maintenance shift A period of work time specifically set aside for maintaining and repairing machines and plant so as not to interfere with the production schedule.

major One who is of legal age.

major dispute Under the Railway Labor Act, a dispute arising out of the formation or change of collective agreements covering rates of pay, rules, or working conditions, or efforts to secure collective agreements.

majority 1. Age at which the law recognizes one's ability to manage one's own affairs and enjoy civic rights. 2. The greater number; greater than half of any total.

major medical expense Expense separately covered in insurance policies in either of two ways: an integrated major medical plan, whereby expenses are reimbursed according to a priority established in the plan, or a comprehensive major medical approach, which combines all expenses into a single plan of reimbursement.

major medical insurance Insurance covering most types of medical expenses up to a high overall maximum limit of liability using a deductible and coinsurance provision.

make-bulk center Central distribution center where small shipments of products shipped over a short distance are consolidated into economical carload or truckload quantities.

maker Person who signs and binds himself or herself by a bill of exchange.

mal Prefix meaning bad, wrong, or fraudulent, as in malfeasance or malpractice.

mala fides *Bad faith;* the opposite of bona fides.

mala in se *Wrong in itself;* morally wrong.

mala praxis *Malpractice;* lack of skill in one's profession.

Malartic Hygrade (MHG) A goldproducing company that sells its stock on the American Stock Exchange and is considered by some investors to be a superior gold stock.

malfeasance An unlawful act; malfeasance in office is the wrongful or unjust official act accompanied by evil intent.

malice 1. Ill will; a preconceived design to do harm or mischief to another; evil motive; wanton or reckless disregard of rights of others. 2. Intention or desire to injure another by deliberately doing a wrongful act without any legal justification or excuse.

malicious abuse of process *law* Improper use of process where probable cause exists for its issue but where the intent is to secure ends other than those intended by law.

Malkiel method of buying stocks A method devised by Burton Malkiel, a former member of the President's Council of Economic Advisors and author of *The Inflation Beater's Investment Guide,* which includes four rules: (a) Confine stock purchases to companies that appear to be able to sustain above-average earnings growth for at least five years. (b) Never pay more for a stock than can be reasonably justified by a firm foundation of value. (c) Buy stocks whose stories of anticipated growth are ones on which investors can build castles in the air. (Malkiel considers this a psychological help.) (d) Trade as little as possible, since switching too often subsidizes one's broker and increases one's tax burden.

malo animo *With an evil mind;* with malice.

Maloney Act (1938) *securities* A legislative act, also known as the Maloney Amendment, enacted to amend the Securities and Exchange Act of 1934 by adding Section 15a. Section 15a provides for the regulation of the over-the-counter (OTC) market through national securities associations registered with the Securities and Exchange Commission.

malpractice Improper, injurious, negligent, or immoral conduct in the performance of professional or fiduciary duties; the failure of a lawyer, doctor, or other professional person to exercise, on behalf of a client or patient, the knowledge, ability, skill, and standard of care commonly applied by similar members of the profession in the area.

malpractice insurance Insurance designed to protect certain professional people against claims resulting from negligent performance of professional duty or suspicion of same.

Malthusian theory of population Theory published by Thomas Malthus in 1798 and revised in 1803, stating that population tends to increase as a geometric progression (1, 2, 4, 16, 32, etc.) while the means of subsistence increase at most as an arithmetic progression (1, 2, 3, 4, 5, etc.). Human beings are therefore destined to misery and poverty unless the population growth rate is retarded, to be accomplished either by preventive checks such as moral restraint, late marriages, and celibacy, or by positive checks such as wars, famines, and disease.

managed change technique (MCT) Methods developed by Westinghouse

197

which concerned themselves with getting full cooperation of both managers and employees in implementing effective changes within the organization.

managed costs   Those costs over which management has some discretion once a project is started, as opposed to costs that are committed and which cannot be changed once the project is underway.

managed currency   *finance* Any monetary system in which the money supply is regulated by the government or a central bank, as opposed to being on a gold standard.

management   Control, superintendence, government. Person or body of persons in charge.

management accounting   That branch of accounting which is specifically directed at supplying management personnel with detailed statistical information they need to assess a project, a department, or the whole firm.

management audit   A periodic, or sometimes perennial, assessment of the standards and techniques of the management of a firm and their effectiveness.

management by crisis   A style of management that tends to concentrate only on serious problems when they arise. Such a style shows a lack of planning, or even a lack of perception of what the goals of the company are.

management by exception   A management method centered around reports by employees to management on only exceptional problems, while they assume responsibility for usual problems. This has been effective in some instances, but is still not practiced widely.

management by objectives (MBO)   A technique of setting goals for executives and their employees so that top executives will have a quantifiable method of judging performance.

management development   Usually a company-wide plan for giving management personnel various experiences in the company, along with additional training, to make them more effective on their present jobs, and more promotable in the future.

management fees   *limited partnerships* Fees charged to care for a business.

management planning   An analysis of present and future manpower requirements and the formation of plans to meet those needs.

management ratio   The ratio of the number of management personnel in a company to employees. This is often further broken down as to top-management and middle-management per thousand employees. A means of observing the correlation, or lack of it, between management and quantifiable production results.

management succession   A method of continually assessing the ranks of management to ascertain whether future needs of the company can be met by current management talent, or whether outside talent may need to be brought in from the outside.

manager   A person who has the responsibility of controlling and coordinating the activities of other people.

managing underwriter   *securities* An investment banking firm that takes the leadership position in putting together a syndicate (a group of underwriters) for the purpose of purchasing and selling a new issue of securities.

Manchester school   *economics* An English school of nineteenth-century economists who applied the doctrines of the classical school to achieve certain economic reforms, such as the repeal of the Corn Laws.

mandamus   *law We command.* Court order directing a public official to perform an act in regard to which no discretion is permitted and which, upon the facts existing, the official is bound to perform. Corporate officers are usually held to be officials for the purpose of this type of action.

mandate   1. Specific instructions given to the representative(s) of an organization as to how to vote on issues in a meeting. (This situation could occur when one or more people act as the official representatives to a meeting of a larger group.) 2. Command; a direction of some authority. 3. Bailment of personal property, without reward, whereby a bailee undertakes to carry the property from one place to another or to have some act performed on the property.

mandatory 1. One to whom a mandate, charge, or commandment is given; the person who obtains a benefice by mandamus. 2. Required as if by mandate; obligatory; containing, in the nature of, or pertaining to, a mandate or command. (Frequently used in contradistinction to directory.)

manifest 1. List of goods that make up the cargo of a vessel. 2. That which is apparent, evident to the senses, especially to the sight.

manipulation *securities* The buying and selling of securities by an individual or group, to make it appear that the activity in the market for a specific stock is vigorous. This often influences persons to buy or sell the stock on the basis of their observations. This is an illegal activity, and persons engaging in manipulating the market in such a manner are subject to both criminal and civil penalties.

manpower analysis *management* The first stage in the process of manpower planning in a firm, inasmuch as it allows management to see their entire work force, properly categorized, and lets them see their needs, if any, and how they may possibly be met.

mansuetae natura *Of a tame nature.* Tamed or domesticated animals in which a person may acquire special property.

manufacture To make or fashion by hand or machinery; to create by artifice. Production of articles for use from raw or prepared materials by giving to these materials new form, qualities, and properties or combinations, whether by hand or machinery.

Maple Leaf A gold coin minted in Canada which, like the South Africa Krugerrand, has one full troy ounce of gold. It is regularly traded.

margin Borrower's equity representing the amount that must be deposited in cash or in other securities along with the purchased securities or commodities to furnish collateral for a loan. In the stock market, an equity position amounting to a percentage of the purchase price must be established. In the commodities market it is a deposit, and the amounts of the deposits are set by the exchange and differ among commodities. (*See* initial margin requirement)

margin account *investing* Account with a broker in which the investor pays for securities partly with cash and partly with credit supplied by the broker. To open a margin account, the investor signs an agreement with the broker that gives use of the securities and some control of the account to the broker. The margin requirement for such an account is set by the Federal Reserve Board, but individual brokers may require more than this minimum if they wish. Investors who use the margin accounts are usually aggressive, considered speculators, and normally hold the stock for a short period of time. Sometimes margin accounts are used to purchase stock for long-term holding, if it is felt the stock is currently underpriced.

marginal analysis *economics* A type of analysis of economic data in terms of the addition to the value of one variable (e.g., to output, revenue, or costs) resulting from the addition of one unit to another variable (e.g. to input, prices, or output).

marginal contribution per unit 1. The contribution that one unit of sales adds toward the payment of fixed expenses. 2. The difference between the selling price and the variable cost per unit of production.

marginal contribution rate The marginal contribution of a product expressed as a percentage of the sales price.

marginal cost *economics* The increase or decrease in total costs of a firm which comes as a result of producing one more or one less of a specific unit of output.

marginal costing A method of accounting for variable costs in relation to various levels of output.

marginal efficiency of capital *economics* The annual percentage earned on the last additional unit of capital utilized by a firm.

marginal farmers *economics* Farmers who cultivate or graze land which produces just enough to cover costs of production at given prices. When prices fall, marginal land is idled, or it is farmed at a loss.

marginal income tax rate 1. Income tax rate payable on the last increment of income which is taxable; the tax rate paid on an additional last dollar of taxable income. 2. The top income tax bracket for each income.

marginalist school Significant development in neoclassical economic theory that led to the market theory of supply and demand, the acceptance of the equilibria concept, and possible expansion of economic theory through the use of differential calculus.

marginal output curve *economics* At any given volume of production, the increase in production which is the direct result of the last factor unit added. To arrive at this, all other factors of production must remain constant, while one changes.

marginal pricing A method of fixing the selling price in relation to marginal costs. At best, this can only be used in the short-term, since, in the long-term, total revenues will have to exceed total costs in order for the company to be profitable.

marginal productivity theory of interest *economics* A theory of interest that proposes that interest rates tend to be equal to the value of production of the last unit of capital added. It is assumed that leverage might continue to be used up to the point where the value of the increase in production is equal to the rate of interest charged on the capital.

marginal productivity theory of wages *economics* A wage theory which holds that the wages of all workers under competitive conditions will equal the marginal addition to production attributed to the marginal laborer.

marginal propensity to consume *economics* The ratio between the increase in consumption occasioned by an increase in income.

marginal property Property that is barely profitable to use.

marginal rate of substitution *economics* A refinement of the concept of diminishing marginal utility. (Cf. law of diminishing marginal utility)

marginal rate of tax *economics* Ratio of the change in total personal income to the change in total taxable income.

marginal revenue product *economics* At any given point on a schedule which relates revenue and input, this is the addition to total revenue occasioned by the last unit of input.

marginal utility *economics* 1. That production, added to total production, occasioned by the last unit of a production resource added. 2. Change in total utility resulting from a unit change in the quantity consumed; measures the gain (or loss) in satisfaction from an additional unit of a good.

marginal utility school *economics* A nineteenth-century school of economists led by W. S. Jevons of England, Leon Walras of France, and Carl von Menger of Austria, who related prices and product preferences through marginal utility; i.e., the added amount of satisfaction obtained from the addition of one more unit of a good.

margin call *investing* A demand made by a broker to an investor for additional collateral in the investor's margin account.

margin department *securities* A section within a brokerage firm that keeps check on the compliance of customers with the margin requirements. (Cf. margin requirement)

margin of cultivation, extensive *See* extensive margin of cultivation.

margin of profit *economics* The relationship of gross profits to net sales.

margin requirement *investing* The minimum deposit an investor must make with a broker to purchase securities on credit. The minimum percentage is determined by the Federal Reserve System, but brokers may require more than the minimum set if they wish.

margin stock Any stock listed on a national securities exchange; any over-the-counter security approved by the Securities and Exchange Commission trading in the national market system.

marine insurance Insurance against the losses incident to maritime adventure.

marital deduction Tax-free amount one transfers by will to one's spouse. A provision in the Economic Recovery Tax Act of 1981 allows all assets of the marriage partner to go to the surviving spouse free of estate taxes. Previously, a portion of the estate was taxed. The change eliminated double taxation of the surviving spouse's estate. Analysis of whether a transfer qualifies for the estate tax marital deduction requires consideration of whether the decedent is a United States citizen, the beneficiary is a surviving spouse, the property was included in the decedent's gross estate, the property did pass from the decedent to the surviving spouse, and the transfer violated the terminable interest rule. Another factor to be considered is the amount of marital deduction.

marital trust Trust applicable to the disposition of large estates, usually related to and used in conjunction with a nonmarital trust. To keep a certain amount of income out of the spouse's estate, the donor will set up a nonmarital trust for the spouse for her lifetime with the remaining proceeds of the trust going to the children after her death. (The trust will usually be in about the same amount as the exemption equivalent of the unified credit.) When the second spouse dies, the trust will pay the estate tax, and the children will receive the remainder. The remainder of the donor's estate, after the nonmarital trust has been set up, will go into a marital trust. The marital trust will usually be given to the spouse under a general power of appointment. All income from the trust must go to the spouse at least annually during her lifetime, and the assets left upon her death will be included in her estate.

Maritime Administration A branch of the U.S. Department of Commerce that issues notes, bonds, or other obligations secured by mortgages on ships and directly guaranteed by the federal government.

maritime contract Contract pertaining to navigation, business, or commerce of the sea.

maritime law System of law which particularly relates to commerce and navigation, to harbors, ships, and seamen, to business transacted at sea or relating to navigation, to the transportation of persons and property by sea, and to marine affairs generally.

maritime lien The legal appropriation of a vessel as security for a debt or claim. This creates a remedy for claim against the vessel herself and vests in the creditor a special property in the vessel subsisting from the moment the debt arises and following the vessel into the hands of an innocent purchaser.

mark 1. Token, evidence, or proof. 2. Measure of weight of gold or silver consisting of twenty-four carats. 3. A character, usually in the form of a cross, made as a substitute for a signature by a person who cannot write in executing a legal document. 4. British measure of weight consisting of two-thirds of the pound weight. 5. A monetary unit in both East and West Germany.

market 1. Public place of commercial activity where goods are bought and sold. 2. Public time and appointed place of buying and selling. 3. In the stock market, the range of bid and asked prices reported by brokers making the market in over-the-counter securities. 4. Customers who possess purchasing power and both willingness and authority to buy. The population within which one can find prospective buyers for one's product, at any stage of its manufacture or distribution.

marketability A measure of the ease with which a security can be converted into cash with minimal or no loss in current market value.

marketable title Land title free from reasonable doubt in law and in fact, which can readily be sold or mortgaged to a prudent purchaser or mortgagee; one that is free from material defects or grave doubts, and reasonably free from litigation. Such title as a court of equity, when asked to decree specific performance of the contract of sale, will compel the purchaser to accept as sufficient. (*See* cloud on title)

market area *marketing* Geographic region from which one can expect the primary demand for a specific product or service provided at a fixed location.

market basket plan *See* cafeteria plan.

market economy 1. An economy where goods and services are produced for sale, rather than for consumption by the producer. 2. An economy where the decisions about what will be produced, how it will be produced, and who will get what is produced is decided in the marketplace, rather than by central planning.

market equilibrium *See* monetary equilibrium.

market if touched (MIT) order *securities* An order to buy or sell a security or commodity as soon as a specified price is reached, at which point the MIT becomes a market order.

marketing The economic activities related to the movement of goods and services from the producer to the consumer, including buying, selling, advertising, standardizing and grading, transporting, warehousing, financing, and providing marketing information.

marketing audit Thorough objective evaluation of an organization's marketing philosophy, goals, policies, tactics, practices, and results.

marketing concept Consumer-oriented managerial philosophy based on the premise that planning begins with an analysis of the consumer and that company objectives involve satisfying consumer wants and achieving long-run profits.

marketing cooperative An association of producers, often of farm products, who cooperate to market their products jointly (e.g., Sunkist oranges). Often, the cooperative will have a trademark, an advertising program, and whatever is necessary to keep the products of the members moving well.

marketing director *banking* Person who surveys current markets periodically, seeks new markets and new methods of marketing, and who may, in small banks, serve as public affairs officer. This position is vital in a period of rapid economic and social change. The marketing director must be adept in all areas of human relations.

marketing research Systematic gathering, recording, and analyzing of data relating to the marketing of goods and services. A composite of all the techniques used in evaluating a market, with a high degree of study of consumer motivation to buy. It gives marketing some semblance of being scientific while it remains, to some degree, an art.

marketing strategy An overall plan for maximizing the impact on the market for a good or a service, both in the short-term and in the long-term.

market line Line representing the relationship between expected return and B-risk or systematic risk. (Cf. expected return, systematic risk)

market maker 1. Broker/dealer who makes a market to buy and sell a stock for the broker's own account. 2. Dealer or specialist who buys and sells certain securi-

ties to and/or from investors from their own accounts. Through this inventory of shares, the market maker attempts to stabilize volatile price fluctuations by buying and selling from the broker's own account to narrow the spread between bid and asked prices and to make the market more liquid. (*See* dealer, specialist)

market norms *investing* Somewhat fictional estimates of what the normal price of a specific stock should be.

market order Buy or sell order for a stated number of shares of a particular security placed at the market. The order is to be executed at the best possible price at the time it reaches the post or desk at which the stock is traded. (*See* market)

market out clause *securities* An escape clause sometimes written into firm commitment underwriting agreements which would allow the underwriter to be released by an agreement if the general condition of the market should suddenly turn bad. This method of opting out is seldom used, since the ability of the underwriter to do the job under all conditions is something the issuers have come to expect.

market penetration *marketing* The proportionate share of a specific market held by one firm.

market potential The size of the entire universe in which prospective buyers of your product exist. (Cf. universe)

market price 1. Actual price that prevails in a market at any particular moment. 2. The price at which a seller is ready and willing to sell and a buyer is ready and willing to buy in the ordinary course of trade.

market rate Rate a well-informed buyer is willing to pay, and a well informed seller is willing to take.

market rate for bond interest The rate which bond purchasers are willing to take, and bond issuers are willing to pay. This is a prime determinant of the effective interest rate of bonds, since the demand and supply in a bond market ultimately decide the going rate.

market risk 1. Loss or gain of capital resulting from changes in the prices of investments and properties. Market risk is caused by investor reaction to tangible as well as intangible events—factors independent of a particular security or property, such as political, economic, and social events, or changes in investors' preferences. 2. Risk related to the fluctuations of the market itself. No person is able to accurately forecast this; therefore, virtually every security traded on the market is subject to some risk. The market is known as an efficient market because it supposedly has all the information which might influence the price of the stock before sellers or buyers do. No system devised to date, and no survey, has been able to chart the market accurately, and thus beat the market risk. 3. Systematic risk. Risk associated with the tendency of a stock's price to fluctuate with the market.

market share objective   Goal set for the control of a portion of the market for the firm's product.

market tone   The general health, vigor and outlook of the market. This "general health and vigor" is supposed to be good when dealers and market makers are trading on small spreads.

market value   1. Price at which an item can be sold. (*See* book value) 2. Price which a property might be expected to bring if offered for sale in a fair market where both seller and buyer have full knowledge of the situation, and where neither is under duress to buy or sell. The price is fixed by agreement between a willing buyer and a vendor who is willing but not compelled to sell.

market value per share   The price at which a share of stock can be sold, assuming both buyer and seller are well informed.

market value–weighted index   A securities index in which the components are weighted according to the market value of their outstanding shares.

mark-on   Markup based on cost.

mark to market   *securities* To put a value on a portfolio of securities by multiplying the number of specific securities by the market value, and adding them to the total.

markup   Amount added to cost to determine selling price.

married out   *securities* Describes an option to sell a given number of shares at a specified price by a specified time, bought at the same time as shares of the underlying company so as to provide a

hedge for the price paid for the shares.

marshal   To arrange; to rank assets, funds, claims, or interests in such an order of consequence as secures justice to all concerned.

Marshall, Alfred (1837–1924)   Neoclassical economist. Marshall's methods were primarily analytical, emphasizing the pricing process and partial equilibrium analysis. Marshall defined economics as the story of people in everyday business life.

Marshallian cross   *economics* Where a price is charted on the vertical axis and quantity on the horizontal axis, the point at which the curves intersect. Also called the equilibrium point.

Marshallian school   *economics* The neoclassical school of economic thought espoused by Alfred Marshall. Generally the school is analytical rather than historical and puts primary emphasis on the pricing process and partial equilibrium analysis.

Marshall Plan   *See* European Recovery Program.

martial law   Military law; temporary jurisdiction or rule by military forces in an area where civil law and order do not exist or have broken down.

Maslow's hierarchy of human needs   *management* A theory advanced by Abraham Maslow classifying human needs into five basic levels, each of which must be at least partially satisfied before proceeding to the next; thus people are most apt to be motivated in the area of their greatest need at the time. These five needs are: (a) basic physiological needs; (b) safety and security needs; (c) belongingness needs; (d) self-esteem and status needs; and (e) self-actualization needs.

Massachusetts Rule   *investing* Method of investing securities in a trust fund. The rule was established by the Supreme Court of Massachusetts in 1830. (*See* prudent-man rule)

mass production   *economics* The manufacture of a product on a massive scale made possible by standard specifications in product design and in method of production.

master contract   *group insurance* Contract between insurer and employer covering all terms of a group insurance contract. The individual employee is not issued a contract but receives a certificate explaining the coverage.

matched and lost   *securities* A report of the results of flipping a coin by two securities brokers competing for the privilege of executing equal trades.

matched book   *securities* A term used for the accounts of securities dealers when their borrowing costs are equal to the interest earned on loans to customers and other brokers.

matched sale-purchase agreements Sale by the Federal Reserve of a security, outright, for immediate delivery to a dealer or foreign central bank, with an agreement to buy back on a specific date (usually within seven days) at the same price. Matched sale-purchase agreements are the reverse of repurchase agreements and allow the Federal Reserve to withdraw funds on a temporary basis.

matching principle   A concept in accounting that requires the costs of a specific period to be matched with the revenues for the same period in order to know what net income for that period was.

material   Substantive; going to the merits; dealing with matter as distinguished from form.

material evidence   *law* Evidence material to a question which must necessarily enter into consideration of a controversy and which by itself or in connection with other evidence is determinative of the case.

material fact   1. *insurance* A fact the knowledge or ignorance of which would naturally influence the judgment of the underwriter in estimating the degree and character of a risk, in fixing the rate of the premium, or in making the contract at all. In insurance law, the suppression of a material fact by an insured at the time of entering into the contract will void it.   2. *law* A fact germane to a particular situation; one that participants in a legal proceeding may reasonably be expected to consider.

materiality   1. The state or quality of having substance. 2. Matter. 3. Importance.

material man   *law* One who supplies materials, either manufactured or fabricated, for use in a building.

materials handling   *economics* The application of analytical methods and equipment design technology to the problems of storing, packaging, and movement of products or materials in any form. It is desirable to incorporate efficiency and safety in the methodology.

Mates Fund   One of the go-go funds in 1968 which achieved a number one standing among mutual funds, but which sold in 1974 for about a fifteenth of its 1968 value.

mathematical economics   The use of mathematical analysis in the study of economics, particularly the use of equations, symbols, etc., most specifically in the handling of relationships between a number of variable factors.

matrix trading   *securities* A method of bond trading where traders seek to take advantage of temporary aberrations in yield spread differentials between bonds of the same class but with different ratings or between bonds of different classes.

mature economy   Any economy of any nation which has ceased to grow, and thus has become stagnant, nor because of a temporary recession, but because of lack of economic energy and the desire to do better. Most western European nations are now considered mature, as is the United States. The Far Eastern nations are generally still young, economically, and are outdoing Western nations.

maturity   1. Date on which a bond is scheduled to mature or be redeemed; due date of a loan. 2. Legal age.

maximum benefit period   Greatest period of time during which disability benefits will be paid to a disabled person. It may be expressed in weeks or months or as extending to a specific age. Sometimes disability benefits are payable for as long as the insured remains disabled as defined in the plan.

May Day   *securities* May 1, 1975; the date when fixed minimum brokerage commissions ended in the United States. This ushered in the discount brokerage era in the nation.

McFadden Act (1927)   *banking* Act of Congress giving the power to control the branching of banks to the states, whether the banks are state or federally chartered.

mean   Middle between two extremes, whether applied to persons, things, or time; an average.

mean deviation   *See* average deviation.

mean return   In security analysis, expected value, or mean, of all the likely returns of investments comprising a portfolio.

means   That through which, or by the help of which, an end is attained; intermediate agency or measure; necessary condition or co-agent; instrument.

means-end analysis   A technique of questioning decision making to ascertain if there is a vital connection between the desired end and the actions proposed to achieve the results.

means of support   All those resources from which the necessities and comforts of living are or may be supplied, such as lands, goods, salaries, wages, or other sources of income.

measure of damages   Test which determines the amount of damages to be given in any action, suit, or cause.

measures of central tendency   Data in an array which most nearly are descriptive of the average of the data. (*See* average, mean, median, mode)

measures of variability   Methods of determining how far individual values in a distribution vary from the mean or the measure of central tendency. (Cf. measures of central tendency)

mechanic's lien   *economics; law*   A lien which a workman, or supplier of materials, can levy against the property worked on or supplied in the event the buyer does not pay. Such a lien attaches to the land as well as the buildings constructed thereon.

mechanistic organization   *management*   Bureaucratic organization. A highly structured organization where virtually every job and function is specifically defined, and where communications are allowed to flow along prescribed routes.

median   Special type of average that divides a distribution of numbers into two equal parts, one-half of all cases being equal to or greater than the median value and one-half being equal to or less than it.

mediation   A process by which a third party attempts to bring two parties in disagreement into agreement.

mediator   One who tries to bring about an agreement between two adversary parties by reconciling differences.

Medicaid   A federal-state program in which participating states furnish assistance to individuals whose economic resources are insufficient to meet the cost of medical services. (*See* Medicare)

medical/hospital service plan   Nonprofit medical and hospital plan organized under special state statutes, a hybrid of mutual and proprietary forms. The best known is Blue Cross, organized by members of the American Hospital Association. Such plans differ from regular insurance plans in that service, not insurance, is sold.

Medical Information Bureau (MIB)   Cooperative organization of life insurers, with centralized information on the physical condition of previous applicants for life insurance in a member company. Insurer's action on the application is not recorded.

Medicare   A two-part federal health insurance program for those sixty-five or older and disabled persons. Part A consists of basic hospital insurance benefits, largely financed by social security taxes. Part B (Supplemental Medical Insurance) covers certain other medical expenses. Part B, which is voluntary (but must be specifically declined if not desired), is financed partly by quarterly payments by the insured and partly by the federal government. (*See* Medicaid)

medium-term debt   A term not specifically defined, but normally refers to debt which matures from one to five years.

megalopolis   Extensive contiguous urban-suburban strip of population, the largest of which extends from Boston to Washington, D.C.

member bank   Depository institution that is a member of the Federal Reserve, as all national federally chartered banks must be. Member banks own stock in Federal Reserve banks and elect some of the directors.

member firm   *securities*   A brokerage firm that has at least one membership on a major stock exchange; although that membership may be held in the name of an individual in the firm, the firm has all the rights and privileges of membership.

member of household Person living under the same roof and in a close intimate and informal relationship with others.

member short sale ratio *securities* A ratio of the total shares sold short for the accounts of members of the New York Stock Exchange in a week, divided by short sales from the same week. A high ratio is considered bearish, and a low ratio, bullish.

mental anguish *law* Mental suffering resulting from emotions such as grief and despair; it must be real, with cause, and more than the normal grief occasioned by the loss of a loved one. The statutes of each jurisdiction differ in the degree to which mental anguish is a compensable element in actions for damages based on personal injury or death.

mental capacity *law* Degree of intelligence and memory as necessary to understand the nature and effect of an act.

mental competency *law* In relation to testamentary instruments, as common testator, sufficient intelligence and memory to comprehend, without prompting, the condition of property and relations to those who might be beneficiaries, to form some rational judgment in regard to them.

mental incompetence Unsoundness of mind; lunacy; idiocy; imbecility. Inability to transact the ordinary affairs of life, to understand their nature and effect, and to exercise will in relation to them. A person who has been adjudged to be mentally incompetent has no legal capacity and can act only through a guardian or committee.

mercantile Having to do with trade or commerce or the business of buying and selling merchandise; commercial; based on business principles.

mercantile agency *finance* Establishment in the business of collecting information relating to credit, character, responsibility, general reputation, and other matters affecting persons, firms, and corporations engaged in business, the purpose of which is to enable subscribers to conduct business safely with unfamiliar customers.

mercantilism *economics* A doctrine, prevalent in Europe during the sixteenth and seventeenth centuries, holding that exports should be maximized and imports minimized to generate an inflow of gold, and exports of machinery and technology prohibited to prevent competition from foreign producers. The fallacy of the theory is that the nation that imports everything and exports nothing will soon be unable to pay for imports, and trade will effectively halt. Later trade theories centered more on having a balance of trade, that is, to having imports and exports about equal.

merchandise Goods, commodities, and wares that are ordinarily the objects of trade and commerce, whether sold wholesale or retail.

merchandise inventory account An account that shows the cost of merchandise on hand which is available for sale.

merchant One engaged in the business of buying commodities and selling them for the sake of profit. One whose business is to buy and sell merchandise; a trader.

merchantability Implied warranty held to be extended by the seller relating that the thing sold is reasonably fit for the general purpose for which it is manufactured and sold, that it will conform to ordinary standards, and that it will be of the same average grade, quality, and value as similar goods sold under similar circumstances.

merchant bank A European type of bank that engages in investment banking, counseling, negotiating mergers and acquisitions, and other services including securities portfolio management, insurance, accepting foreign bills of exchange, etc.

merger 1. Combining of two or more commercial interests or corporations into one, by which procedure all properties are transferred to the surviving corporation. The surviving corporation retains its name and corporate identity with the added capital, franchises, and powers of the merged corporation, and is liable for the debts and contracts of the absorbed corporation, which disappears. 2. Absorption of any entity, such as an estate, right, or liability, into another of greater importance or dignity.

merit goods Goods and services which have a social value over and above their utility for the individual consumer.

merits   *law*   Real or substantial elements of a controversy; the real or substantial grounds of action or defense.

Merrick multiple piece rate plan   *economics*   Historically, an incentive wage plan deriving from the Taylor differential piece rate plan and providing for progressively increasing piece rates for varying ranges of output.

mesne profits   *economics*   1. Profits which are taken by virtue of the wrongful possession of land. Usually such profits can be recovered in the same suit in which the land is recovered. 2. Intermediate profits; i.e., profits accrued between two given periods.

metayer system   *economics*   European system similar to sharecropping in the United States.

metes and bounds   Measurements and boundaries; boundary lines of land, with their terminal points and angles. (E.g., a widow entitled to dower of land who had her share ascertained and set apart to be held by her in severalty was then said to hold the land by metes and bounds.)

metric system   Standard of weights and measures based on the number ten and its multiples; used throughout most of the world.

mezzanine financing   *banking*   Preferential treatment by a bank's senior officer of a loan which has already been rejected by junior officers. So called because the offices of the senior officers are often on the mezzanine level of the building.

mezzanine level   *economics*   The stage of a firm's development just before it goes public. Capital invested at that point is lower risk capital than the start-up investment.

middleman   1. One who buys at one price from a manufacturer or a wholesaler for resale at a higher price. 2. Person who acts as an agent in bringing two parties together to negotiate their own contract.

Midwest Securities Trust Company (MSTC)   A regional depository founded in 1973 which serves the securities exchanges in Chicago.

mile   Measure of distance containing eight furlongs, 1,760 yards, 5,280 feet, or 1.6093 kilometers.

mileage   1. Allowance for traveling expenses at a specified rate per mile. 2. Number of miles traveled by an automobile per gallon of fuel used. 3. Distance in miles.

mill   1. Machine for reducing grain, fruit, or other substances to fine particles or for performing other such operations by means of wheels and a circular motion, as a grist mill, a coffee mill, a cider mill, etc; to operate such a machine. 2. House or building that contains the machinery for grinding. 3. One tenth of one cent, a monetary measure used frequently in the field of taxation.

mine   1. To excavate in the earth for the purpose of extracting ores, coal, or other mineral substances. 2. Such an excavation.

mineral estate   Estate in fee simple in and to minerals. The conveyance or reservation of estate gives title to minerals in place.

minerals   Any inert part of the earth formed or deposited through natural agencies alone and which is capable of being extracted from beneath the surface for the purpose of profit.

mini-manipulation   *securities*   An action of trading in a security underlying an option contract so as to manipulate the stock's price and increase the value per share.

minimum   Least quantity assignable, admissible, or possible in a given case; opposite of maximum.

minimum deposit   Plan under which individuals purchase cash value insurance under the agreement that, if they pay four out of the first seven premiums, they will never have to pay another premium. In addition, it is assumed that the annual after-tax expense on the policy loans used to finance all the other premiums will be modest in comparison to the annual premium amount.

minimum legal capital   Normally, the par value of the stock issued. In many states this is considered the minimum investment.

mining claim   Claim, on public lands of the United States, which is a possessory interest in land that is mineral in character and as respects which discovery within the limits of the claim has been made.

minor Person who is below the age, usually eighteen years, when civil and personal rights may be legally exercised.

minor dispute Under the Railway Labor Act, dispute which contemplates existence of a collective agreement already concluded and which relates either to the interpretation or to the application of the agreement's provision. Under the statute the jurisdiction of the adjustment board may be invoked, thereby bringing the dispute to arbitration.

minority 1. The state of being under legal age. 2. The smaller part or number.

minority interest The percentage of a subsidiary's common stock and retained earnings accounts not owned by the parent company.

minority interest discount Discount sometimes given for estate tax purposes on stock held by a minority stockholder in a closely held corporation, premised upon the minority stockholder's inability to influence corporate policy, compel dividend distributions, or force corporate liquidation, merger, consolidation, or sale.

minor minorem custodire non debet, alios enim praesumitur male regere qui seipsum regere nescit *A minor must not be guardian to another minor, for he who knows not how to govern himself is presumed to be unfit to govern others.*

mint 1. Place where money is coined. 2. To produce coinage.

minutes Record of the proceedings of a meeting, as of directors or shareholders of a corporation.

misappropriation *law* Conversion of property for improper or illegal use.

misconduct Transgression of some established rule of action; a dereliction of duty; unlawful behavior. In the area of employer-employee relationship, an intentional or deliberate wrongful act, wanton negligence, or neglectful failure in performance of an employee's duties.

misfeasance 1. Trespass; the improper performance of a lawful act. 2. Act of misconduct which causes injury to another. (*See* nonfeasance)

misnomer A name wrongly applied.

misrepresentation 1. Untrue statement, whether unintentional or deliberate. 2. Any representation by words or conduct that misleads the party to whom it is made.

missing the market *investing* Failing to execute a transaction on terms favorable to a customer, and thus being accused of broker negligence.

mistake 1. Unintentional error made in preparing a contract; may be corrected by mutual consent of all parties without voiding the contract. 2. Valid justification under limited conditions for an intentional tort.

mitigation of damages *law* A reduction in damages or a lessening of punishment as a result of facts or circumstances of an extenuating nature.

mixed economy Economic system in which the basic questions of what, how, and for whom to produce are resolved by a mixture of market forces with government direction and/or custom and tradition.

mixed estate *law* Compound of realty and personal property, particularly used in relation to devolution and testamentary instruments.

mixed property Property which has both the characteristics of real property and personal property, which may include keys to the property, certain fixtures, etc.

mobilia non habent situm *Movable things have no locale.*

mobilia sequuntur personam *Movable things follow the laws of the person,* i.e., the owner. The devolution of movable property is usually governed by the laws of the owner's domicile.

mobilization system A system of cash management which is designed to transfer funds collected in the field to the concentration bank.

mode The most frequently encountered value in an array.

model *economics* The consideration of quantifiable factors which may be either variables or constants and the construction of relations among them that may be expressed in the form of an equation.

model unit Representative home, apartment, or office space used as part of a sales campaign to demonstrate the design, structure, and appearance of units in a development.

Modified Accelerated Cost Recovery System (MACRS) System using the declining method and longer lives to determine depreciation expense under the 1986 Tax Reform Act.

modular housing Dwelling units constructed from components prefabricated in a factory and erected on the site.

moisture barrier Layer of foil, plastic, or paper used in construction of exterior walls, ceilings, and foundations to prevent moisture penetration into wooden members or insulation.

monetarism Economic theory that emphasizes the importance of changes in the money supply and their impact on the aggregate economy. Closely linked to economist Milton Friedman, monetarism employs the equation of exchange (PQ = MV) as an analytical device. (*See* Chicago school of economics)

monetarist Economist or other person who believes that economic equilibrium can be achieved and maintained by manipulating the money supply.

monetary asset *finance* Asset having a value defined in units of currency. Cash and accounts receivable are monetary assets; inventories and plant and equipment are physical assets.

monetary base *banking* Assets which can be used by a bank to meet required reserve deposits. On a national basis, the composite of all accepted reserves held by all banks, which consists of reserves held by the various Federal Reserve banks, and coin and currency.

monetary equilibrium *economics* The immediate price in the market at which exchange of goods currently takes place and the goods are cleared from the market. Also known as market equilibrium.

monetary liabilities Fixed amounts of money that are owed by the company to the suppliers, bondholders, etc.

monetary policy 1. Policies implemented by the Federal Reserve Board to increase or decrease the supply of money and credit. 2. Policy that advocates the manipulation of the money supply to achieve and maintain economic equilibrium.

monetary theory of business cycles *economics* Theory which attributes business cycles to monetary factors, such as

changes in the quantity of money and credit or in interest rates, holding that upswings occur when credit and borrowing conditions become favorable enough for businessmen to borrow and that downswings occur when the banking system begins to restrict its expansion of money and credit.

money 1. Any currency, tokens, bank notes, or other circulating medium in use as the representative of value. 2. Coined metal, usually gold or silver, upon which the government stamp has been impressed to indicate its value.

money bill Bill imposing a direct tax on people; one for raising revenue, levying a tax on all or some of the people, property, or business for a public purpose.

money broker *finance* A financial institution that deals primarily in the money market in short-term securities and loans and in the gold and foreign exchange markets.

money center *finance* A city large enough to support an active money market and financial community, such as New York, San Francisco, etc.

money center bank A bank located in one of the major financial centers of the world, such as New York, London, Paris, or Tokyo, and which deals voluminously in foreign exchange, and in large foreign loans to both businesses and governments.

money changers Persons in the business of exchanging kinds or denominations of currency.

money demand *law* Claim for a liquidated or fixed sum of money enforceable by action.

money expansion multiplier *banking* The ability of banks to expand their deposit base by fractionally more than the reserves held due to a fractional reserve system. (E.g., if the required reserve ratio is 20%, banks can expand their deposit base by making loans up to five times the reserve requirement.)

money market *finance* A loose network of institutions or individuals who buy and sell financial securities and debt instruments, usually short-term. The typical security is for ninety days or less.

money market certificate (MMC) A type of certificate of deposit offered by

209

banks and savings and loan associations. A fixed interest rate is determined each week by rates offered on United States treasury bills. MMCs carry a six-month term and require a ten thousand dollar deposit.

money market fund Mutual fund that invests in short-term (usually thirty days to one year) United States government securities, bank money instruments, and commercial debt instruments. The minimum balance is usually five hundred dollars or larger with withdrawals allowed with no notice and no penalty. Interest rates change daily or weekly, reflecting earnings of the fund.

money market instrument *finance* Short-term debt instrument, types of which include negotiable certificates of deposit, Eurodollar certificates, commercial paper, banker's acceptances, and Treasury bills.

money-market mutual fund Fund that invests in large bank CDs, commercial paper, and government securities and that sells shares to investors. Yields in the late 1970s and the early 1980s were about 12 to 13%. Yields vary with time and the general fluctuation of the interest rates. Most such funds allow limited checking in large amounts, usually of five hundred dollars or more. Such funds may well be popular for the next decade because of their safety, regardless of yield.

money market trusts Six-month certificates offered by brokerage firms. These funds are not continuously managed, but buy a package of high-yielding instruments and then liquidate the fund at the end of six months. They offer individual investors with as little as one thousand dollars to buy in. The investment vehicles in these trusts are usually more speculative than other types of funds, thus they often yield slightly higher returns.

money multiplier *finance* The ratio between the monetary base and the nation's money supply, normally using the M^1 measure.

money order Form of credit instrument calling for payment to the named payee; encompasses non-negotiable as well as negotiable instruments.

money purchase formula *pensions* Defined contribution plan in which a stat-

ed amount of money is paid purchasing a certain amount of retirement income.

money purchase plan *pensions* A plan in which employer contribution is fixed as a percent of the eligible payroll, adding an additional element to profit-sharing plans. Money purchase plans are subject to the Employee Retirement Income Security Act's minimum funding standard. An employer who adopts a money-purchase plan has a fixed, measurable, and ongoing contribution commitment, notwithstanding fluctuations in business. This inflexibility can limit options for cash flow management and be troublesome in time of recession or rapid growth when cash may be in short supply.

money wages *economics* Wages expressed in terms of a monetary unit without regard to changes in the purchasing power of money. Also called nominal wages.

monitoring *financial planning* Process involving periodic review with a client so that a financial planner is aware of changes in goals and constraints, requiring continuous review of economic conditions and expectations.

monometalism *economics* A monetary system in which only one metal is used to coin standard money (i.e., only one metal can be coined or melted down in unlimited amounts).

monopoly Power to exclude competition and to control prices; situation in which a product or service is controlled by one interest and no substitutes are available in the market. This power may be vested by privilege (as by a government grant) or by peculiar advantage (as a corner on the market). (*See* Sherman Antitrust Act, Clayton Antitrust Act)

monopsony *economics* A market in which there is only one buyer for a commodity.

Monte Carlo simulation Computer-based extension of sensitivity analysis that calculates the probability distribution of a forecast outcome.

monument 1. Fixed object and point established by surveyors to determine land locations. 2. Any visible mark or indication left on natural or other objects indicating the line of a survey.

Moody's Investment Grade Ratings assigned to certain municipal short-term securities by Moody's Investors Service. Classifications such as MIG-l, 2, 3, and 4 indicate best, high, favorable, and adequate quality.

Moody's Investors' Services, Inc. A large investment advisory organization which publishes financial manuals that analyse thousands of securities firms that sell securities to the public. The service also rates the investment quality of debt instruments.

moonlighting Working at a second job after regular work hours.

moot 1. Open to discussion; not yet settled; undecided; debatable. A moot point is one that has not been settled by judicial decisions. 2. Hypothetical. 3. To bring up for discussion.

moral duress Imposition, oppression, undue influence; undue advantage of business or financial stress, extreme necessity, or weakness of another whereby one's free agency is overcome.

moral hazard *insurance* The risk an insurer takes that either the insured or the beneficiary will cause a loss in order to collect on the policy.

moral law Law of conscience; rules and principles of ethics.

moral obligation 1. Duty assumed in obedience to the rules of right conduct. 2. Obligation which cannot be enforced by action, but which is binding on a party who incurs it in conscience and according to natural justice. 3. Duty which would be enforceable at law but for some positive rule which exempts the party in that instance from legal liability.

moral suasion *economics* Oral or written appeals by the Federal Reserve Board to member banks, urging them to expand or restrict credit but without requiring them to comply.

moral turpitude Conduct contrary to justice, honesty, modesty, or good morals.

moratorium 1. Time period during which a certain activity is not allowed. 2. Authorized postponement or suspension of all or of certain legal remedies, usually against debtors.

mortality tables Account kept for a great number of consecutive years of the ages at which men and women die, taking the average of all such ages. By this means, the probable number of years any man or woman of a given age and of ordinary health will live may be arrived at with reasonable certainty.

mortgage 1. Lien upon land or other property as security for the performance of some obligation, usually the repayment of a loan, to become void upon such performance. 2. Written instrument that creates a lien upon real estate as security for the payment of a specified debt.

mortgage banker One who originates, sells, and services mortgage loans. The mortgage may be kept and serviced by the mortgage banker, but such mortgages are usually bundled and sold to other investors. Most loans are insured or guaranteed by a government agency or private mortgage insurer.

Mortgage Bankers' Association (MBA) Organization that provides educational programs and other services for mortgage bankers. It also offers the Certified Mortgage Banker (CMB) designation and publishes the magazine *Mortgage Banker.*

mortgage bond 1. Bond backed by specific property of the issuing corporation. 2. Tax-exempt security sold by municipal and state authorities for the purpose of providing low-interest rate mortgage loans to qualified individuals. For most programs, mortgage borrowers must be first-time home buyers with moderate income.

mortgage broker *real estate* A person or entity that arranges for a mortgage loan for a fee but does not own or service the mortgage.

mortgage certificate *See* guaranteed mortgage certificate.

mortgage, closed-end *See* closed-end mortgage.

mortgage discount Amount of principal deducted at the beginning of the loan. (*See* discount point)

mortgagee Person who takes a mortgage as security for a loan; the holder of a mortgage.

Mortgage Guarantee Insurance Co. (MGIC) Private company that insures loan repayment to lenders in the event of default and/or foreclosure.

mortgage lien Encumbrance on property used to secure a loan.

mortgage loan commitment Lender's written statement agreeing to grant a specific loan amount at a given rate for a certain term secured by a specific property, if the real property transaction is closed before the expiration date.

mortgage out To obtain financing in excess of the cost to construct a project. In the early 1970s, developers could mortgage out by obtaining a permanent loan commitment based on a high percentage of the completed project's value. This enabled the developer to borrow more than the cost of developing the project. Since then, opportunities to mortgage out have been virtually eliminated by lower loan-to-value ratios, higher capitalization rates, and higher construction costs.

mortgage portfolio *finance* The total number of mortgages held by the original lender, or the mortgage loans serviced by a mortgage banker.

mortgage trust Real estate investment trust that specializes in loans secured by mortgages on real estate.

mortgagor Owner of property mortgaged as security for a loan.

mortis causa *By reason of (or in contemplation of) death.* (*See* donatio mortis causa)

mortis est *He is dead.*

mortmain *Dead hand.* Sale or gift of lands or tenements to any corporation, sole or aggregate, ecclesiastical or temporal, so that the land becomes nontransferable (i.e., said to be in a dead hand).

mortmain statute Statute prohibiting excessive charitable bequests when the decedent is survived by a spouse, children, or other heirs. Typically, the mortmain statute provides that if the charitable bequest exceeds a certain percentage of the net estate (25% is common), then a spouse, child, grandchild, parent, or other recognized heir has a personal right to make an election and set aside that portion of the net estate going to charity in excess of the statutory percentage limit. (E.g., if a decedent's will left 35% of the net estate to a charity, a designated heir could elect to set aside that portion of the charitable bequest in excess of the statutory limit—in this case, 10% of the estate.)

most-favored-nation clause *economics* A clause in trade agreements between two countries specifying that if subsequently either party grants a favor, such as a tariff reduction, to another country, it will immediately grant the same to the other country which is party to the agreement.

motion 1. Application for a rule or order, made viva voce or in writing to a court or judge, in an action or special proceedings. 2. Proposal for action by a deliberative assembly.

motivation research *marketing* A study used in many facets of the economy in an attempt to discover why people act the way they do in a myriad of circumstances. While much useful knowledge has been gained in this manner, we are still compelled to say that we really don't know why people respond the way they do in different circumstances in the market.

motive An inner state that directs people toward satisfaction of a felt need; cause or reason for a person's behavior.

motor vehicle Any vehicle driven or drawn by mechanical power manufactured primarily for use on public streets, roads, and highways, excluding any vehicle operated exclusively on a rail or rails.

movable That which can be changed in place, such as goods, furniture, and personal chattels.

moving average *securities* Average in which the most recent observation is added and the most distant is deleted before computing. These are continually updated for a specified period of time. The average is calculated daily, and as a new current price is added, the oldest price is deleted from the average. This method smooths out short-term movements and therefore represents truer current values.

multicurrency clause *finance* A clause which allows a borrower in the Eurobond market to make payments in a different currency or to borrow in a different currency on rollover at maturity.

multifamily housing Type of residential structure with more than one dwelling unit in the same building.

multinational corporation (MNC) A business firm that has production facilities in more than one country and makes management decisions on the basis of the world economy, not just on the domestic economy.

multiple capital structure company *finance* A business firm having more than one class of securities outstanding.

multiple hurdle rates *investing* Use of different hurdle rates for new investments to reflect differing levels of risk. (*See* required rate of return)

multiple listing Arrangement among a group of real estate brokers devised to give side exposure to properties listed for sale. Participants agree in advance to provide information about some or all of their listings to the others and also agree that commissions on sales of such listings will be split between listing and selling brokers.

multiple-location forms *insurance* Policies developed for a business wanting full coverage for many outlets, such as a chain store. Formerly, they would be forced to buy an amount of insurance for each store unit equal to the maximum value of goods expected in any one store. This approach would require a larger amount of total insurance than the average amount of exposure justifies. With the multi-location forms came the development of reporting forms. (*See* reporting forms)

multiple plan limits *employee benefit plans* Rules developed over time to limit the large deductions and unreasonable accumulations which would occur with no constraint on plans. These rules place limits on benefits by imposing the requirement that the percentage utilization of maximum benefits under combined plans can't exceed 1.0, under a complicated formula. (*See* 1.0 rule)

municipal Pertaining to a local government unit, such as that of a city, town, or village.

municipal bond Bond issued by a government authority such as a state, county, city, or subdivision other than the federal government. Carries a lower rate of interest than other bonds, which is generally free from federal taxes and sometimes from state and local taxes. Municipal bonds fall into four main categories: general obligation, revenue, industrial revenue, and public housing authority. Most municipal bonds mature serially; i.e., a

certain number of bonds will mature each year from one year to as many as fifty.

municipal corporation Public corporation formed by charter from a sovereign government for purposes of local civil government.

Municipal Securities Rulemaking Board (MSRB) An independent, self-regulated organization which sets the rules for investment bankers, brokers, and dealers active in the municipal bond market. Though "unofficial" in nature, the MSRB does cooperate with the Securities and Exchange Commission.

muniments of title *law* 1. Documents, such as deeds or contracts, used to indicate ownership. 2. Instruments of writing and written evidence which the owner of lands, possessions, or inheritances has, by which the title to the estate can be defended.

mutatis mutandis *statistics Changing those things that must be changed.* An economic analysis which proceeds by assuming constant all things except the variables being studied; a change in a variable may necessarily involve a change in other conditions which are not within the particular consequences being studied.

mutilate To render imperfect, as by cutting, tearing, burning, or erasing part of a document or negotiable instrument.

mutilated security A securities certificate which has been so badly damaged that there is nothing legible on it to assure the name of the owner or the denomination of the security, or to provide other meaningful information to identify the owner or make the security transferable. It is incumbent on the owner to work out the matter with the official transfer agent.

mutual account Account that arises where there are mutual dealings between parties and an account is permitted to run with a view to an ultimate adjustment of balance between parties. An account where each party has extended credit to another and in which there have been reciprocal demands.

mutual agency A business partnership where every member is an agent of the partnership and can bind it to any contract within the scope of the business.

mutual fund 1. Fund that sells its own shares on a continued basis and offers the privilege of redemption of the shares at prices reflecting asset values. 2. *See* closed-end investment fund. 3. *See* open-end company.

mutual insurance company Insurance company which issues no stock and, theoretically, is owned by the policyholders. Initially, mutual companies pooled the premiums and paid claims out of them. If claims were low, the companies would usually return dividends to the policyholders. If the cost of claims was high, assessments would be made of the holders. Most mutual companies now are nonassessable and operate much like stock companies. (*See* cooperative)

mutual insurer Incorporated cooperative insurer with no stockholders.

mutuality 1. Reciprocity; state or quality of being mutual. 2. Requirement in a contract that each party to it is bound to action under the contract. To be valid, all contracts require mutuality of assent, meaning that both parties to the transaction must know what the other is to do.

mutually exclusive alternatives Two projects which accomplish the same objective, so that only one will be undertaken.

mutual mistake *contracts* Mistake common to both parties to a contract, each laboring under the same misconception.

mutual savings bank Type of state-chartered bank, found mainly in the northeastern United States, owned by the depositors and operated for their benefit. Most of these banks accept deposits primarily from individuals and hold a large portion of their assets in home mortgage loans. Savings banks generally have broader asset and liability powers than savings and loan associations but narrower powers than commercial banks. Savings banks are authorized to offer checking-type accounts.

mutual will Will made pursuant to an agreement between two or more individuals, often spouses, to dispose of their property in a special way; accomplished either by a joint will or by separate wills contain similar or identical provisions in favor of each other or some other beneficiary.

N

naïve forecast A projection made on the basis of past trends.

naked *law* Bare, involving no active duties, such as a naked or passive trust; powers that are personal to a person, such as a trustee, which cannot be exercised by the court or a successor.

naked debenture A simple certificate of indebtedness issued against an unsecured loan.

naked option *See* uncovered option.

naked position An unhedged position in the commodities market.

namium vetitum *law* Unlawful or unjust taking of the cattle of another and driving them to an unlawful place on the pretext that they have done damage.

narrowing the spread *securities* Closing the spread between a bid and asked price on a security as a result of bidding and offering by the market makers and specialists in that specific security.

narrow market *securities* A securities or commodities market marked by light trading and greater fluctuations in prices relative to the trading volume than would be the case if the trading were heavier.

NASD Form FR-1 A form required of foreign dealers in securities subscribing to new securities issues in the process of distribution, wherein they agree to abide by National Association of Securities Dealers rules concerning a hot issue. (*See* hot issue)

National Association of Home Builders (NAHB) Organization providing educational and political information and research services; publishes *Builder*, a monthly magazine.

National Association of Insurance Commissioners Voluntary organization, comprised of all heads of state insurance commissions, formed to achieve some uniformity in state insurance laws. An organization of increasing importance with a number of task forces made up of individuals from government and private industry.

National Association of Investment Clubs A national group that assists investment clubs in getting started.

National Association of Manufacturers (NAM) Organization formed in 1895 that serves all fields of industry.

National Association of Realtors (NAR) Organization devoted to encouraging professionalism in real estate activities, with over 600,000 members, fifty state associations, and several affiliates. Members are required to abide by the organization's code of ethics.

National Association of Securities Dealers (NASD) Self-regulatory organization with jurisdiction over certain broker-dealers. NASD requires member brokers to register and conducts examinations for compliance with net capital requirements and worth regulations. It also conducts market surveillance of over-the-counter (OTC) securities market. (*See* National Association of Security Dealers Automated Quotations)

National Association of Security Dealers Automated Quotations (NASDAQ) Securities quotation system, a subsidiary of the NASD, for reporting trades on over five thousand domestic over-the-counter securities most active over-the-counter issues through. NASDAQ issues four or five identifying symbols for the various securities. Three levels of subscription service are available: level one for member firm offices; level two intended for institutional and certain retail traders; level three, to provide market makers a system to enter their firm bid and asked prices. (*See* market maker, National Association of Securities Dealers)

national bank 1. A central bank of a country. 2. In the United States, a bank which by law must be a member of the Federal Reserve System and the Federal Deposit Insurance Corporation.

National Credit Union Administration (NCUA) Federal agency that supervises, charters, and insures federal credit unions applying and qualifying for insurance. NCUA also operates a credit facility for member credit unions.

National Credit Union Association (NCUA) The agency which regulates federally chartered and federally insured Credit Unions.

national debt crisis *economics* A situation in a country where unchecked spending has created a huge national debt. This debt and the cost of annual debt service make planning for the future difficult and almost assure continuing high interest rates and the danger of spiraling inflation.

National Flood Insurance Act A law which established an insurance program for homeowners whose houses are located in flood-prone areas, and which is administered by the Federal Insurance Administration. (This was done to make insurance available to people who could not buy insurance through other carriers.)

National Fraternal Congress Table of Mortality A mortality table prepared in 1898 for the use of fraternal organizations engaged in insurance writing.

national income *economics* Total payments made to factors of production—namely to land, labor, capital, and entrepreneurship—in a specified period of time, usually a year. (*See* factor of production)

national income economics *See* macroeconomics.

National Industrial Recovery Act (NIRA) An act passed by Congress in 1933 giving President Franklin Roosevelt great power to regulate trade, industry, labor, and prices through appointed agencies. The act was declared unconstitutional by the Supreme Court in 1935 on two counts: (a) Congress cannot relegate legislative powers. (b) Congress cannot regulate interstate commerce.

National Institutional Delivery System (NIDS) A central securities joint industry service which simplifies the process of comparing and settling broker-to-institution trades.

nationalization *economics* The process by which the government of a nation assumes ownership and control of specific industries within the country.

nationalized industries Industries which have been transformed from private to public ownership.

National Labor Relations Act (1935)
Basic labor relations law of the United States. Provisions of the act guarantee the right of workers to organize and bargain collectively through representatives of their choosing, forbid employers to engage in unfair labor practices such as discrimination or interference, and authorize the National Labor Relations Board to enforce the act and supervise free elections among a company's employees. Also called the Wagner Act.

National Labor Relations Board
Government agency established under the National Labor Relations Act of 1935 to enforce that act, investigate violations, and supervise free elections among a company's employees to determine which union, if any, is to represent them in collective bargaining.

National Market Advisory Board
A board appointed by the Securities and Exchange Commission as a result of the 1975 Securities Act. The purpose of the board is to advise the SEC on an automated national exchange market system (NEMS).

National Quotation Bureau (NQB)
An organization that provides a daily service to subscribers listing bid and offer quotes from market makers in stocks and bonds traded over-the-counter.

National Securities Clearing Corporation (NSCC)
A clearinghouse formed in 1977 by subsidiaries of the New York Stock Exchange, the American Stock Exchange, and the National Clearing Corporation. The purpose is to facilitate the settling of accounts between brokerages, exchanges, etc.

National Student Marketing (NSM)
A conglomerate of companies serving the needs of young people. Born in the 1960s as the brainchild of Cortess W. Randell, it was enormously popular for some time, with many seasoned investment managers buying into the firm. Various subsidiaries deal with such things as magazine subscriptions, guidebooks for summer jobs, books, records, etc.

natural child Child in fact; the child of one's body who may or may not be legitimate.

natural heir Heir of the body, as distinguished from those entitled to succeed to the grantee's estate in testacy.

naturalization Act of admitting an alien to citizenship; the final judicial act whereby the applicant is accepted and admitted to the taking of the oath of allegiance.

natural law 1. System of rules and principles for the guidance of human conduct which, independently of enacted laws or of the system peculiar to any one people, are generally held to be true. 2. Well-established and universally recognized physical, mechanical, and mathematical principles; regular behavior of nature and natural phenomena of which the courts will take judicial notice.

natural monopoly Legal monopoly established by a state or federal government usually for one of two reasons: (a) there are increasing economies of scale over a wide range of output, so that one firm can supply the market more efficiently than several or (b) unrestricted competition among firms in the industry is deemed socially undesirable. Natural monopolies are generally public utilities.

natural person Human being, as distinguished from artificial persons or corporations recognized by the law.

natural resource Any form of naturally created wealth such as timber, gas, oil, minerals, lakes, land, etc.

natural-resource stocks Stocks representing firms that own natural resources, such as land, minerals, timber, etc., or that do research in natural resources. It is believed by some stock market experts that natural resource stocks are often overlooked and underpriced.

natural rights Rights which pertain originally and essentially to each person, which are inherent in human nature, as contrasted to civil rights which are given, defined, and circumscribed by laws enacted by civilized communities as necessary to the maintenance of organized government.

nautical Pertaining to ships, to the art of navigation, or to the business of carriage by sea.

nautica pecunia Monies advanced to the owner of a ship, repayable upon completion of the voyage, and by nature of the inherent risks of the sea, carrying what would otherwise be an extraordinary rate of interest.

navigable Describes watercourses, rivers, or lakes susceptible of being used in their ordinary condition as routes for commerce, and over which trade and travel may be conducted in customary modes.

nearby contract A futures contract that is nearing maturity.

nearest month *securities* In stock options or commodity futures, the expiration dates, expressed in months, nearest to the present date.

near money Assets with a specified monetary value which can be readily redeemable as cash (e.g., savings accounts, certificates of deposit, and shares in money market mutual funds).

necessaries Purchases made by minors and married women whereby the estate of the minor, the parent, or the husband is bound to pay for them.

nec vi, nec clam, nec precario *Not by violence, stealth, or permission.* In order that a person may acquire title to land by adverse possession, one's possession must be characterized by these attributes.

ne exeat *law He does not leave.* A writ enjoining a person from leaving the jurisdiction of the court.

negative amortization Increase in the outstanding balance of a loan resulting from the failure of periodic debt service payments to cover required interest charged on the loan. The repayment schedule calls for periodic payments insufficient to fully amortize the loan. Earned but unpaid interest is added to the principal, increasing the debt. Eventually payments must be rescheduled to fully pay off the debt.

negative carry *securities* A situation where the cost of borrowed money to purchase securities is higher than the return on the securities.

negative cash flow 1. A condition in business where the cash flowing out is more than the cash flowing in. Obviously, this condition cannot be tolerated over a long period of time. 2. *real estate* Situation in which a property owner must make an outlay of funds to operate a property.

negative factor or value With regard to the Equal Credit Opportunity Act, this is some bit of information, either qualitative or quantitative, which casts a less favorable light on a prospective debtor than the information the creditor already has.

negative gap A mismatch in the maturity dates of securities wherein the maturity dates of interest-sensitive liabilities exceed the maturity dates of interest-sensitive assets.

negative income tax A proposed system of income taxes whereby the Internal Revenue Service would be used to collect taxes from those above a given income level and distribute income to those below a certain level, providing a guaranteed minimum income for eligible families with no other income and a supplement for families with incomes below a predetermined level. Proponents argue that such a system would simplify social welfare and eliminate much of the welfare hierarchy. Opponents argue that giving cash to people who might not be very responsible would not guarantee that either they or their families would be taken care of with respect to life's necessities.

negatively sloped yield curve Graphic expression of the relationship between yield and maturity that indicates instances when investors do not require a premium for the length of time to maturity.

negative pickup *tax shelters* Shelter deal in which the investor in a motion picture does not put up money until the production is finished and then filed "in the can." The studio takes a finished product and sells an interest in it as a means of spreading risk.

negative pledge clause One of the covenants in an indenture which promises that the corporation will not pledge any of its assets unless the notes or debentures outstanding under this particular indenture are equally covered by such a pledge. (Cf. indenture)

negative yield curve *securities* A situation in which yields on short-term securities are higher than yields on long-term securities, the reverse of normal securities activities. Usually, long-term investors require a greater yield to induce them to tie up their money for a long period. However, when interest rates are high, investors may accept the short-term yield, avoiding the long-term securities because of uncertainties in the securities market and the underlying economy.

neglect *law* 1. To fail to do something; to leave out; to omit through carelessness. 2. Fault; imprudence. A disregard of duty owing to indifference or willfulness.

neglected stocks Stocks of dull, neglected, or even bankrupt companies which may hold out the possibility of yielding great returns in the future. This is an area constantly explored by contrarian investors. (*See* pariah stocks)

negligence 1. Act of an unreasonable and imprudent person, often resulting from carelessness or thoughtlessness, but also due to forgetfulness, bad temper, ignorance, bad judgment, or stupidity. Never involves intent. 2. The omitting to do something which a reasonable person would do or the doing of something which a reasonable person would not do under the existing circumstances. The failure to exercise the standard of care that would be expected of a normally reasonable and prudent person in a particular set of circumstances.

negotiable bond Bond on which coupons can be detached, making it immediately convertible to cash. (*See* coupon bond)

negotiable certificate of deposit CD in which the rate and the term are individually negotiated between bank and lender.

negotiable instrument 1. Check, note, bill of exchange, or any other written security transferable by endorsement and delivery, or by delivery only, which gives the person to whom it is transferred legal ownership, enabling the person to demand the full amount called for on the face of the instrument. A document which represents freely assignable rights in a debt instrument, i.e., instruments which can be cashed freely by the bearer. 2. Promise to pay money, transferable from one person to another.

negotiable order of withdrawal (NOW) account Interest-earning account on which checks may be drawn. Withdrawals from NOW accounts may be subject to a notice requirement of fourteen-days or more, although this is rarely imposed. NOW accounts may be offered by commercial banks, mutual savings banks, and savings and loan associations and may be owned only by individuals and certain nonprofit organizations and governmental units. Such accounts were introduced in the late 1970s and were nationwide in the 1980s. Account owners were thus induced to keep money in checking accounts, in spite of inflation. (Cf. disintermediation)

negotiate To discuss, arrange, or conduct a business transaction, sale, or contract.

negotiated underwriting *securities* When underwriting new securities the investment banker (or syndicate) may negotiate the price of the securities privately rather than to seek competitive bids on the issue.

neighborhood life cycle Generalized pattern describing the physical and social changes that residential areas experience over time.

nemo dat qui non habet *He who hath not cannot give.*

nemo plus commodi haeredi suo relinquit quam ipse habuit *No man can confer a greater benefit to his heir than he himself had.*

nemo potest esse dominus et haeres *No man can be both owner and heir.*

neoclassical economics Approach to economics which flourished in Europe and the United States between 1870 and World War I. Among its leaders were William Stanley Jevons in England, Carl von Menger in Austria, Leon Walras in France, Vilfredo Pareto in Switzerland, Alfred Marshall in England, and John Bates Clark and Irving Fisher in the United States. The neoclassicists were primarily concerned with refining the principles of price and allocation theory, marginalism, the theory of capital, and related aspects of economics. They made early and extensive use of mathematics, especially differential and integral calculus, in the development of their analyses and models. Much of the structure of modern economic science was built on their pioneering work.

nepotism Bestowal of patronage by public officers in appointing others to position by reason of blood or marital relationship to the appointing authority.

net 1. Portion of original gross income or assets that remains after deduction of expenses or losses. 2. Clear of anything extraneous.

net asset value (NAV) 1. Market value (usually of a mutual fund) at a given time plus cash the fund holds divided by the total number of shares the fund has outstanding. 2. Asset value of a share of an investment company; total assets minus total liabilities divided by the number of shares outstanding.

net asset value per share Book value per share.

net book amount; net book value The value of a fixed asset after allowing for the amount written off for depreciation.

net capital gain Capital gain realized after computing capital gains and capital losses for both long-term and short-term, and adjusting for the purpose of taxation. (*See* Appendix G)

net capital loss Capital loss experienced after computing capital gains and capital losses for both long-term and short-term and adjusting for the purpose of taxation. If the loss is long-term, it can be deducted from ordinary income at the rate of two to one. If it is short-term in nature, it can be deducted from ordinary income on a one to one basis. (*See* Appendix G)

net capital requirement; net capital rule *securities* A requirement of the Securities and Exchange Commission that member firms and nonmember broker-dealers, trading in securities, do not exceed a maximum ratio of indebtedness to liquid capital of fifteen to one.

net domestic product *economics* A figure arrived at by deducting the depreciation of capital assets from the gross domestic product. (Cf. gross national product)

net estate Assets going to one's heirs after payment of the costs of dying (i.e., debts, claims, administration fees, and taxes); that part of the total estate that actually becomes available to the heirs.

net exports of goods and services *economics* Total exports in a year minus total imports.

net gift Gift conditioned upon the donee's payment of the gift taxes. The value of a net gift is the fair market value of the property minus the gift tax the donee must pay. This type of gift is made when a donor does not have enough liquid assets to pay an anticipated gift tax. This technique, due to a ruling and a Supreme Court decision in 1982, now has two disadvantages: under the revenue ruling, the donor's unified credit must first be exhausted before there is any gift tax payable by the donee; and under the Supreme Court decision resolving a conflict in the circuit court of appeal, when a donor makes a gift and the donee pays the federal gift tax due, the donor has taxable income to the extent that the gift tax paid exceeds the donor's adjustable base in the gift property.

net income Profit remaining after all deductions for operations, taxes, interest, and reserves; often called earnings or earnings-per-share.

net inflow Balance of inflow over outflow in a cash flow statement.

net investment An important figure which subtracts the previous year's depreciation of capital assets from the amount of investment in capital assets being made during the current year. This gives a truer picture of what the real annual investment figure is.

net investment income per share The income received by an investment company during an accounting period, derived from interest and dividends paid on their securities portfolio, less management fees and administrative expenses, divided by the number of outstanding shares to determine net investment income per share. This income is then paid out as dividends to shareholders in the investment company according to the equity position each one holds.

net leasable area Floor space in a building or project that may be rented to tenants; the area upon which rental payments are based. This generally excludes common areas and areas devoted to space equipment, such as for heating and air conditioning.

net lease Lease whereby, in addition to the rent stipulated, the tenant pays such expenses as taxes, insurance, and maintenance. The landlord's rent receipt is thereby net of those expenses.

net lease transactions High tax write-off real estate investments. In the 1980–83 period, these transactions came to dominate the real estate investment area. Usually such deals are so large that two or more brokerage houses will combine to offer them. A transaction will involve the selling of a building by a major credit worthy tenant. The new landlord (the passive investor) rents the building back to the occupying firm which agrees to maintain the building and pay all expenses. The risk of ownership, maintenance, and spiraling costs are on the tenant. Virtually all economic benefits (as distinct from tax benefits) are also enjoyed by the tenant. The tenant sells the building without giving up ownership.

net listing   Listing in which the broker's commission is the excess of the sale price over an agreed-upon (net) price to the seller; illegal in some states.

net monetary creditor   Economic agent having monetary assets in excess of liabilities.

net monetary debtor   Economic agent having monetary assets less than liabilities.

net national debt   The total national debt minus that part held by the government in various trust funds.

net national product (NNP)   *economics* Gross national product minus depreciation of capital goods in a year or minus capital consumption allowances.

net operating income (NOI)   Income from property or business after operating expenses have been deducted, but before deducting income taxes and financing expenses (interest and principal payments).

net present value (NPV)   *investing* The expected future payments from an investment, discounted by the marginal cost of capital to the firm, less the cost of the investment. This represents the increase in wealth accruing to an investor and is a method of determining whether expected performance of a proposed investment promises to be adequate. (*See* internal rate of return)

net profit margin   1. Ratio of earnings, after interest and taxes, to sales.   2. Earnings after all operations costs and debt service have been taken into account. The figure is sometimes used before federal taxes have been paid but most often is quoted as an after-tax profit.

net regression coefficient   *statistics* In multiple correlation, the coefficient of each independent variable in the regression equation is the net regression coefficient.

net rentable area   *real estate* That part of an office building, or an apartment building which is available for rental to tenants, which naturally excludes foyers, staircases, elevator shafts, areas used for maintenance equipment, hallways and any other public area.

net reproduction rate   The ratio of the number of females who will become mothers to the number of females who produced them. When the rate is one, the population is stationary, if less than one, the population is declining, and if more than one, the population is increasing.

net sales   Total sales revenue less certain offsetting items such as returns and allowances and sales discounts.

net trades   Trade on which no commission is charged.

net transaction   A securities transaction in which neither the buyer nor the seller pay commissions. (E.g., on a new issue the offering price is all that is paid; there is no commission added.)

net worth   1. Equity; shareholders' equity.   2. Excess of assets over liabilities.

net yield   Return on an investment after subtracting all expenses.

neutral equilibrium   *economics* A condition which, once achieved, will continue indefinitely unless one of the variables (economic or noneconomic) changes, at which time the system will come to rest at a new equilibrium.

ne varietur   *It must not be altered.*   A notary public after authenticating a document may write these words on the document.

New Deal   The economic, social, and political program and philosophy of Franklin D. Roosevelt, carried out after his election in 1932 through legislation, administrative actions, and court decisions.

New Economics   Body of economic thought which originated with the British economist John Maynard Keynes (1883–1946) in the 1930s. It has since been extended and modified, and its basic analytical tools and methods are now used by many economists. In contrast to classical economics, which emphasized the automatic tendency of the economy to achieve full employment equilibrium under a government policy of laissez faire, the New Economics demonstrates that an economy may be in equilibrium at any level of employment. It therefore concludes that appropriate government fiscal and monetary policies are needed in order to maintain full employment and steady economic growth with a minimum of inflation.

new investment technology (NIT) An idea, held by many stock market analysts, that security markets are very efficient, and that it is generally futile to try to use any method to outsmart the market. While the core theme is not new, it does now stand in a position diametrically opposed to the views that various methods, with some use of new technology such as the computer, can indeed outdo the market.

new issue market Bond or stock issue offered for sale for the first time in a market, created by an agreement between a business entity and an investment banker or underwriter.

new money That amount of an issue of money which remains after reducing the original amount by the amount necessary to redeem maturing or refunded issues.

new money preferred Preferred stock issued after October 1, 1942, when the tax exclusion for corporate investors having preferred stock dividends was raised from 65% to 85%. This is the same percentage as common stock. Some financial institutions, or quasi-financial institutions, are allowed to hold only so much common stock in their portfolios. The new law allowed them to own preferred stock and still get the maximum tax exemption. (In 1987, the corporate tax exclusion on dividends was lowered to 80%.)

new town Large mixed-use development designed to provide residences, general shopping, services, and employment. The basic concept of a new town is to construct a community in a previously undeveloped area under a central plan to avoid unplanned development. Used somewhat in the United States in a few urban areas of the East and Southwest.

New York Stock Exchange (NYSE) The largest securities exchange in the United States; often called the Exchange or Big Board.

New York Stock Exchange Composite Index A weighted average of prices of all common stocks listed on the New York Stock Exchange, the sum of which indicates trends and conditions in the market. There are four sub-group indexes: NYSE Industrials, NYSE Transportations, NYSE Utilities, and NYSE Financial.

New York Stock Exchange Composite Transactions A total listing of the activities of the New York, Philadelphia, Boston, Cincinnati, Midwestern, and Pacific stock exchanges for a given period of time.

next devisee *estate planning* Person who will receive the remainder of the estate devised by will after the first devisee.

next of kin 1. Person or persons most nearly related to a decedent by blood. 2. Those entitled to share in the decedent's estate according to the applicable laws of distribution; may include a relationship existing by reason of marriage.

Nielson ratings A rating system, primarily for radio and television, which attempts to determine who is listening to the radio or viewing the television at any given point in time, and what program they are hearing or viewing.

nifty fifty *investing* The fifty stocks most favored by institutional investors. While membership in the nifty fifty is constantly changing, securities from this group generally pay competitive and consistent dividends or interest, and thus are a safe haven for institutions.

night 1. *law* Period between sunset and sunrise. Various statutes have defined it as having a specific starting and stopping time. 2. *common law* The condition of not having enough daylight to discern a person's face.

nine-bond rule A rule on the New York Stock Exchange requiring that an order of nine bonds or less (ten is considered a round lot, as is one hundred shares of stock) be taken to the floor where an attempt is made to get the best possible price for the customer. Such customers are normally small investors, and the NYSE tries to protect them with this rule.

no-action letter *securities* A letter requested by sellers of certain types of investments of the Securities and Exchange Commission that the commission will not take action against the sellers in the event their securities appear unique. This is often done with limited partnerships which may be exploring somewhat untested territory.

no-brainer A term describing the market when its course seems to be set and in which any analysis would appear unnecessary.

no-fault insurance plans Plans relieving the wrongdoer from the consequences of an act by paying defense costs and assessed damages. No-fault plans now exist in a number of different forms.

no-load funds Mutual funds which do not charge a sales commission (load) when the shares are purchased or redeemed. Thus, both transactions would occur at the fund's net asset value per share.

nolo contendere *I do not contest it.* Constitutes an implied confession of guilt but leaves the defendant free to deny guilt in other arenas.

nominal amount 1. Yield received on an investment without reference to the rate of inflation. For example, if the coupon rate of a bond is 10% and one hundred dollars is received annually as interest on a thousand dollar bond, it is yielding the nominal rate. 2. Any quantity not adjusted for changes in the purchasing power of the currency due to inflation. (*See* real amount)

nominal capital The total paper value of the shares in a company at any given time. (It should be kept in mind that nominal value and market value are rarely the same.)

nominal damages *law* Damages awarded when the court has negated real damage but is affirming that there is an infraction of a legal right. It is a trivial amount awarded to vindicate an invasion of one's legal rights where, although no physical or financial injury has been inflicted, the underlying cause of action has been proved to the satisfaction of a jury.

nominal group technique *communication* Form of brainstorming with the idea of generating lists of ideas as a method of decision making. Ideas are generated and listed by each participant secretly and then orally offered to the group coordinator. These, along with others in the group, are put on a board or flipchart and discussed openly.

nominal rate of interest The currently quoted rate of interest.

nominal wages *See* money wages.

nominal yield Annual amount of interest or dividends paid compared with a security's par or face value.

nonaccredited investors *limited partnerships* Investors who cannot meet a test as accredited. Accredited investors must meet one of three financial tests: having a net worth of an excess of $1,000,000; having an income in excess of $200,000 for the present year; or investing $150,000 or more in the program in question.

nonaccrual asset *banking* An asset, usually a debt, which may not be collected. Banks set up reserves for this.

nonadmitted insurer *insurance* Describes companies which are not licensed to operate within a state; including by mail-order solicitation. Unauthorized insurers are subject to the laws of the state, and therefore subject to fines and court actions for infractions. Also called unauthorized insurer.

nonage Minority.

nonborrowed reserves *banking* Total reserves of member banks of the Federal Reserve Banking System, minus bank borrowings.

noncancelable Provision under which the insured is guaranteed that the policy will be renewed up to an age specified in the policy. Premium rates are also guaranteed unless the insurer raises rates for an entire class of insured.

noncash charge Expense recorded by an accountant not matched by a cash outflow during the account period.

noncash fringe benefits Benefits taxed on their fair market value under provisions added to the Internal Revenue Code by the Tax Reform Act of 1984 (Deficit Reduction Act of 1984). Congress also established categories of noncash benefits that will not be considered taxable income to an employee. The categories of noncash benefits to be excluded from an employee's taxable income are: (a) no-additional-cost services; i.e., services of a type normally provided to the public by an employer; (b) qualified employee discounts; (c) working condition fringe benefits; e.g., business but not personal use of a company car, parking, etc.; and (d) de minimus fringe benefits; i.e., benefits so small that accounting would be impractical or unreasonable. (*See* Appendix G)

noncharitable beneficiaries Persons named in the charitable trust who are income beneficiaries of the trust but are not part of the charitable organization (i.e., spouse, child, etc.). The only way one can get an income, estate, or gift tax deduction for a contribution to a charitable remainder trust that has one or more noncharitable income beneficiaries is if the trust qualifies as either an annuity trust or a unitrust under the Internal Revenue Code.

noncompetitive bid *investing* A process used by small investors who use Federal Reserve banks to purchase government securities, thus avoiding the large auctions, which appeal only to very large investors.

non compos mentis *Not sound of mind*; insane. General phrase used to refer to all varieties of mental incapacity. There are said to be four different classes of persons who are non compos mentis: (a) an idiot, one who has suffered mental incapacity from birth; (b) one who has lost one's reason by an act of God; (c) an insane person or a lunatic who is given to lucid intervals; and (d) one who deprives him- or herself of reason, such as a drunkard.

nonconforming use Pre-existing use of land permitted to continue after enactment of a zoning ordinance which prohibits this use.

noncontributary plan Group insurance plan in which the employer pays the entire insurance premium for the employee. One rationale is that employees show greater appreciation for the benefits financed entirely by the employer. Another is that a noncontributary plan is easier to administer—there are no payroll deductions and 100% of the employees are covered. Employer contributions are normally deductible for federal income tax purposes, and not taxable to the employee for federal income tax purposes on coverage up to fifty thousand dollars.

noncontributory pension plan One in which all monetary additions to the pension trust are made by the employer, while none are made by the employee.

noncupative will *law* An oral testament made by a person who feels he or she may die; i.e., a deathbed declaration of how the estate is to be distributed. The oral testament must be made before a sufficient number of witnesses, who may reduce the oral declaration to writing at a later time. In some states, this is not considered a legal will, and in others it will be accepted under the proper circumstances.

nondeductible expenses Expenses related to the settling up of the business syndicate, such as registration fees or brokerage fees, which are never deductible for tax purposes at any time.

nondisturbance clause Agreement in mortgage contracts on income-producing property that provides for the continuation of leases in the event of loan foreclosure.

nondiversifiable Unable to be diversified. For a portfolio to be truly diversifiable, it may need to contain real estate, precious metals, collectibles, etc.

nondiversifiable risk B-risk; systematic risk.

non est factum *It is not his deed.* Plea whereby a defendant either alleges that he or she did not execute the deed in question, or that the defendant was laboring under a mistake as to its nature when the deed was executed.

nonexempt employee An employee qualified under the Fair Labor Standards Act to receive compensation for overtime work.

nonfeasance *law* The failure to perform a legal or official duty. (*See* malfeasance, misfeasance)

nonforfeiture Cash values that are not forfeited if the policy is discontinued, with the policyowner choosing among various options for receiving cash value of the policy.

nonforfeiture options *insurance* Provisions in a policy designed to protect the policyholder who has accumulated cash value in the policy, but who opts to discontinue paying premiums. The three options usually are cash surrender value, reduced paid life insurance, and extended term insurance.

nonfunctional roles *communication* Roles often in evidence in group meetings which impede rather than encourage the progress of the group (e.g., the blocker, the aggressor, the storyteller, the recognition seeker, the mute, the special-interest pleader, the dominator, the confessor, and the playperson).

nonmarital trust *See* bypass trust.

nonmember depository institution Depository institution that is not a member of the Federal Reserve System. Nonmember depository institutions that offer transaction accounts or nonpersonal time deposits are subject to reserve requirements set by the Federal Reserve; they also have access to the Federal Reserve discount window and Federal Reserve services on the same terms as member banks.

nonmonetary asset *accounting* A company asset which has value, but is neither money nor near money (e.g., land, a plant, and most fixed assets). While these assets have value they are not easily converted into cash.

nonmonetary liabilities *accounting* Obligations of the company which change in value, sometimes as general price levels change. A primary example is a stockholder's equity, which must be shown on the company books as a liability, though that liability changes in amount from day to day.

nonnegotiable A term denoting a document lacking in some requisite to make it freely transferable. The document can be transferred by assignment. Often erroneously understood to mean nontransferable.

nonnotification plan *banking* A method used by dealers to sell sales contracts of consumers to banks without notifying the customer. The customer continues to make payments to the dealer.

nonowner occupied residential real estate Residential rental property.

nonpar life policy Policy which does not make provision for the participation of the policy in the company earnings.

nonprofit corporation A corporation organized for religious, educational, or charitable purposes. Usually is a nonstock company, and does not pay income taxes, but may be required to pay taxes on income earned from property or other income-yielding operations.

nonpublic information Information about a company which might influence the price of its stock, but which is not yet available to the public. Insiders are prohibited by law from trading on such information until it has been made public.

nonpurpose loan A loan for which securities are pledged as collateral, but the money obtained by the loan will not be used to purchase other securities.

nonqualified deferred compensation plan Agreement whereby an employer promises to pay an employee in the future for services rendered today. The plan is usually set up to provide for salary continuation over a period of years following retirement or other termination of employment. Such plans are called nonqualified because they do not meet the requirements for a tax-favored qualified retirement plan. These payments are usually limited to highly paid executives.

nonqualifying annuity An annuity purchased with after-tax dollars because it is not qualified by the IRS for use in an approved pension plan.

nonrecourse agreement *banking* A retailer dealer financing pact where the dealer accepts no responsibility for collections once the paper is sold to the bank. While the dealer must be liable for the authenticity of the sale, in all regards, the dealer will not be liable for nonpayment of contracts.

nonrecourse notes Loan for which the borrower bears no liability for beyond the amount invested. Lenders may take the property pledged as collateral to satisfy a debt, but have no recourse to other assets of the borrower.

non refert an quis assensum suum praefert verbis, aut rebus ipsis et factis *It is immaterial whether a man give consent by words or by acts and deeds.*

nonresident One who does not reside in a particular place. The residence or non-residence of an individual or a corporation is important in determining the jurisdiction of a court in matters where a judgment in personam is sought against such individual or corporation.

non sequitur *It does not follow.*

non sui juris *Not of his own right* (e.g., a minor or an insane person).

nonsuit *law* Judgment brought against a plaintiff who has failed to prove his or her case or has defaulted.

nontaxable income Income benefit which is excluded for purposes of income tax; e.g., interest income on municipal bonds.

nontenure Species of plea in a real action whereby a defendant pleaded that he or she was never a tenant of the lands in question or was not a tenant on the day the writ was issued.

nonuser Reason a right is extinguished where a person ceases to exercise such right, as an easement, profits a prendre, or other similar right, within the prescribed number of years so that the right is not perfected.

non valet donatio nisi subsequatur traditio *A gift is not valid unless accompanied by possession.* This refers only to gifts inter vivos and not to testamentary gifts.

nonverbal communication All intentional and unintentional messages that are neither written nor spoken. May include facial expressions, posture, body movements, or any manner other than verbalizing. Sometimes referred to as body language.

no-par stock *finance* Shares of stock issued by a corporation which have no par value shown on the face of the share. Such stock is sold for whatever the market will bring at time of issue.

normal distribution *statistics* The curve expressing the relationship between the frequency (measured on the "Y" axis) and the deviation, positive or negative, from the mean (measured on the "X" axis). In a normal distribution, 99% will lie within a range of three standard deviations either side of the arithmetic mean, 95% within two standard deviations, and 68% within one standard deviation.

normal rate of return Rate of earnings on invested capital that is normal for a given degree of risk.

normative economics Approach to economics which deals with what ought to be as compared to what is. It involves statements which are value judgments, making empirical verification sometimes impossible. (*See* positive economics)

nostro account *banking Our account;* denotes an account held by a bank with a foreign bank.

nota bene *law Mark well,* observe, take note.

notarius A scribe; a notary.

notarize To attest in the capacity of a notary public to the genuineness of a signature.

notary public A minor public official who is commissioned by law to attest and certify documents under an official seal in order to give them credit and authenticity, to take acknowledgments of deeds and other conveyances and certify them, and to perform certain official acts, chiefly in commercial matters, such as administering oaths, protesting of notes and bills, the noting of foreign drafts, and protesting marine cases of loss or damage. Many common documents must be witnessed and stamped by a notary public before they can be considered legally valid. A commission of a notary public is for a specified period of time.

note 1. Signed promise by one party to pay a certain sum of money at a specified place and time. 2. Written instrument that acknowledges a debt and promises to pay. 3. Brief memorandum or writing.

notes payable *accounting* Debt instruments indicating that the company owes a specific amount of money to specific creditors at specific times. Normally, the face amount of the debt, the rate of interest, and the date due will appear on the face of the promissory note, etc.

notes receivable *accounting* A promissory note owned by the company as a creditor, which is due from a specific debtor, in a given face amount, at a given interest rate, on a specific date.

not held (NH) Instructions on a market order declaring that the broker will not be held responsible for the way the order is carried out. The broker is required to use due diligence in making the best possible trade for the client, but will not be held responsible if the trade is not as good as the client expected.

notice Information about or knowledge of the existence of some fact or condition. This can be any fact which would put an ordinary prudent person on inquiry. Notice may be actual or constructive. (*See* actual notice, constructive notice)

notice of default Letter sent to a defaulting party as a reminder of the default; may state a grace period and the penalties for failing to cure the default.

notice of dishonor Notice given by or on behalf of the holder, any party who has received notice, or any other party who can be compelled to pay the instrument to the maker, the endorser, and any other person who may be liable on the instrument of the fact of dishonor. Such a notice may be given in any reasonable manner, may be oral or written, and may be in any terms which identify the instrument and state that it has been dishonored.

notice of loss Requirement under most insurance policies that the policyholder give immediate written notice to the insurer. In some cases, specific time limits are given.

notice to creditors A notice, usually posted in a prominent public place and printed in a newspaper, whereby the executor or the administrator of an estate requests creditors to submit their claims for payment. Normally the same notice is a signal for debtors to pay the estate what they owe.

notice to quit Notice of termination of a tenancy given by a lessor to a lessee. A notice given privately by one party to another terminating or attempting to terminate a landlord-tenant relationship; not the equivalent of a court process.

notification plan Plan in which a business sells accounts receivable to a bank, and so notifies the debtors, who then make their payments directly to the bank rather than to the business firm.

notorious possession Generally acknowledged possession of real estate; one of the requirements to gain ownership of real estate through adverse possession. (*See* adverse possession)

not otherwise indexed by name (NOIBN) *transportation* A freight classification that applies if no specific class exists.

not rated (NR) An indication used by some securities rating services that a specific security, or company, has not been rated, denoting neither positive nor negative opinions.

novation 1. An agreement to replace one party to a contract with another party who assumes all the obligations of the contract. 2. The replacement of an older debt, or obligation, with a new one.

nuda pactio obligationem non parit *A nude agreement* (i.e., an agreement without consideration) *does not give rise to an obligation.*

nudum pactum *law A naked promise.* A promise which is unsupported by consideration; a voluntary promise, not legally binding. In short, a promise but not a contract.

nuisance 1. Land use whose associated activities are incompatible with surrounding land uses. 2. An actionable wrong, distinct from trespass and negligence. Consists in the wrongful act or omission on the part of the defendant which indirectly impairs the use and enjoyment by the plaintiff of personal property or affects the plaintiff's health, comfort, or convenience. 3. Any thing or practice that by its existence or use causes annoyance, harm, inconvenience, or damage. A nuisance is often a valid basis for a civil suit.

nuisance tax A tax, often small, placed on items of ordinary use which involves annoying complexities in the way the tax is collected.

null Of no legal force or effect; invalid.

null and void Not legally enforceable, as with a contract provision that is not in conformance with the law.

nulla pactione effici potest ut dolus praestetur *No contract can provide that a fraud shall be committed.*

null hypothesis An assumption that the difference between two measures is zero.

nullity *law* Nonexistence; invalidity.

numeraire A commodity chosen as a medium of exchange or a standard of value in the place of money.

numismatic market The worldwide arena in which gold and silver coins are traded. This market deals primarily in rare coins, since less-than-rare coins have little margin for going up or down in price.

numismatic value Properties of coins which satisfy the desires of collectors and investors as well. Coins may be valued for their beauty, their immediate and future value, or for themselves.

nuncupate *law* To declare publicly and solemnly.

nuncupative will Unwritten will which declares orally or verbally in front of witnesses by the testator in a last illness, in the manner specified by statute, sometimes later put in writing. Many states do not honor a noncupative will and regard the maker as having died intestate; others will honor it only in specific situations.

O

oath 1. Pledge or promise by which a person swears that a statement made or about to be made is true. 2. A solemn affirmation by which an individual certifies that the individual is bound in conscience to do something in good faith.

objective indicators *banking* A collection of statistical data series designed to forecast changes in the exchange rate.

objectives *financial planning* Goals, especially specific measurable targets, that a client hopes to achieve through use of the client's assets.

obligate To bind in a legal or moral sense.

obligation 1. A debt. 2. Legal relationship subsisting between two persons by which one is bound to the other for a certain performance. Signifies not only the duty of the debtor but also the right of the creditor. 3. *law* The act of obliging or binding; that which obligates; the binding power of a vow, promise, oath, or contract.

obligation bond *securities* A situation in which the face value of a bond is greater than the underlying property which guarantees the bond. The difference between the two compensates the bondholder for costs exceeding the mortgage value of the property.

obligor Person who is liable under an indenture security; if such security is a certificate of interest or participation, person who is liable upon the security or securities in which such certificate evidences an interest or participation. This does not include the trustee on an indenture under which certificates of interest or participation, equipment trust certificates, or like securities are outstanding.

obliterate To blot out; to cancel; to cross out.

obscure Not clear, full, or distinct; clouded; imperfect.

obsolescence 1. Condition or process by which anything gradually ceases to be useful or profitable because of changed conditions. May also arise as a result of laws regulating or forbidding a particular use of property. 2. Loss in value due to reduced desirability and usefulness of a structure because the design and construction have become outmoded. 3. *economics* A decrease in value of a capital asset, or a good, because of a change in technology, in demand, or in some other factor.

obstruct To hinder or prevent from progress; to check; to stop; to retard the progress of or make accomplishment difficult and slow.

obstructing justice *law* Interfering with the orderly administration of law.

occupancy 1. Actual possession of real property without implication of ownership, as in the case of a tenant's occupancy of a rented apartment. Though a house is considered occupied when some person is dwelling therein, the dweller need not be there continuously, for temporary absence may not necessarily change the occupied character of the premises. For a dwelling house to be in a state of occupation, it must have the presence of human beings as the customary place of residence, not absolutely and uninterruptedly continuous, but as a place of usual return and normal occupation. (Cf. vacant, unoccupied) 2. The act of taking possession of something unowned so as to become its owner.

227

occupancy level Percentage of currently rented units in a building, city, neighborhood, or complex.

occupation A vocation; the particular business, profession, trade, or calling in which a person is regularly or usually engaged.

occupational profile *management* An analysis of a breakdown of all the occupations within a company, expressed in ratios and proportions.

occupational psychologist One who engages in the study of ergonomics.

odd lot An amount of stock that is less than the round (one hundred shares) or full lot unit of trading. Typically nine to ninety-nine shares of stock is considered an odd lot.

odd-lot dealers Brokerage houses that specialize in buying or selling less than a round lot (one hundred shares).

odd-lot doctrine *insurance* Principle stating that if a worker is physically capable of performing some work but, due to lack of skills and intelligence and/or advanced age, finds it impossible to obtain suitable work, the court may find permanent and total disability.

odd-lot short-sale ratio A ratio obtained by dividing odd-lot short-sales by total odd-lot sales during a certain period.

odd-lot short selling *investments* Short sales of shares of stock in amounts less than one hundred shares by individuals. Since odd-lot sellers are usually not expert, they tend to sell short at the bottom of the cycle and buy at the top, negating any opportunity to make a profit, and almost assuring loss.

odd-lot theory *investments* Technical approach to the stock market that purports to predict security prices on the basis of odd-lot sales and purchases. The theory states that investors who purchase odd-lot quantities of securities are usually late in the timing of their investments, that the sophisticated investor should move in the opposite direction of the odd-lot investor. However, data has shown that at almost every major market bottom, odd-lot investors have been buyers rather than sellers, and, at almost every major market top, there is a lower buy-to-sell ratio.

odd-lot transactions Stock market transactions which are made for less than a round lot (one hundred shares).

odd pricing Pricing that uses prices with odd endings, such as $16.95, $17.99, or $18.98, under the assumption that these prices appear lower and therefore more appealing. Originally, odd pricing was initiated to force sales clerks to make change, thus serving as a cash control device within the firm.

oeconomicus The executor of a will.

of counsel *law* Phrase describing an attorney who is not the principal attorney but is retained or employed as an expert or specialist to assist the principal attorney in the preparation or management of a case or matter where the attorney's special knowledge applies.

offer 1. Expression of willingness to purchase a property at a specified price. 2. Proposal to make a contract containing within itself all the terms of the contract. Acceptance of such a proposal creates the contract. (*See* contract)

offer for sale *securities* A situation in which an investment bank buys all the new issue of stock of a corporation, and assumes the responsibility for selling the stock.

offering circular *securities* A somewhat informal document which alerts prospective investors of a municipal bond issue. Municipal governments are not required to prepare and issue a prospectus as are corporations.

offering memorandum *tax shelters* A book required by the Securities and Exchange Commission on all offerings made to the public, containing information about the workings of the shelter, fees, management, legal liability, profits, problems, and everything crucial to making an educated investment.

offer wanted (OW) A notice given by a potential buyer of a security that the buyer is looking for a potential seller of that security.

off-floor order An order to buy or sell a security that originates off the floor of an exchange. Such orders are sent from customers to brokers, as opposed to brokers trading with each other on the floor. Rules of the exchange require that off-floor orders be executed before floor orders.

Office of Management and Budget (OMB) A department within the executive branch of the federal government which is responsible for preparing and presenting the President's budget to Congress. Other duties are: (a) working with the Treasury Department and the Council of Economic Advisors to develop a fiscal program, and (b) reviewing the policies and performances of the various departments in the executive branch.

offset Legal claim that balances, diminishes, or cancels another claim.

offset method of integration *pension; profit sharing* Plan which theoretically provide benefits for all plan participants under a traditional nonintegrated unit or flat-benefit formula. There is no annual computation of spread or excess benefit rates. Whenever a participant reaches retirement age, however, benefits are reduced by a portion of the employee's Social Security payments. The maximum reduction, or offset, is 83.33% of the primary Social Security amount.

offshore *finance* Describes a financial institution outside the country. (E.g., a mutual fund with headquarters in another country is an offshore fund.)

off-site costs Expenditures related to construction that are incurred away from the place of construction.

off-the-book payments Payments for labor, goods, or services, often in cash, that are not accounted for in the company books. Usually illegal, since the purpose often is to evade taxation.

oil and gas lease Agreement that gives the right to explore for and extract from the ground oil, gas, or other minerals.

oil and gas lottery A program run by the Department of Land Management of the Interior Department in which drawings are held for the privilege of exploring for oil or gas on certain parcels of government owned land. Any company, large or small, can enter the lottery with an equal chance to win.

oil and gas shelter Tax shelter vehicle attractive to high-income bracket investors. There are two primary aspects to this type of shelter: (a) if the project fails, there is a large first-year write-off, and (b) if it should prove successful, it can offer large returns on investment.

oligarchy Form of government in which supreme power is restricted to a few.

oligopoly 1. Shared monopoly in which there is no explicit agreement among the firms. 2. *economics* A situation in which the number of sellers of goods or services is limited, giving the sellers the tacit opportunity to control prices without collusion.

oligopsony A market situation in which the number of buyers is limited.

ombudsman Government official appointed to receive, investigate, and report upon grievances of private citizens against the government.

omission *law* Nonperformance of a duty required of a person when there is an awareness on the person's part that performance is required or needful; failure to do what the law requires.

omitted dividend A situation in which a corporation has planned a dividend, and perhaps even announced it, only to have it rescinded by the board of directors, usually because of some late-emerging financial problem.

omne testamentum morte consummatum est *Every will is completed by death.* Every will takes effect from or becomes operative upon the death of the testator.

omnia quae sunt uxoris sunt ipsius viri *All things which belong to the wife belong to the husband.*

omnibus clause *insurance* In an auto policy, the clause providing that the insurance protection also extends to those persons (other than the owner/insured) who are using the auto with the consent of the insured and within the conditions of the policy.

on account Partial satisfaction of an account as contrasted to payment in full.

on-approval sale Sales transaction of goods in which a seller takes a business risk in delivering goods on the understanding that they are to remain the property of the seller until accepted by the purchaser on satisfaction of the appearance, quality, or performance of the goods.

on arrival Within reasonable time. This phrase is used to require the collecting bank to present drafts and bills of exchange payment upon receiving goods to which the draft relates.

on-balance volume *securities* A method of technical analysis that attempts to pinpoint whether a stock or bond or commodity is being bought and held by many buyers or is being widely sold.

on call Obligation that is to be met or is payable when demanded.

one bank holding company A corporation that controls one commercial bank, or that owns 25% or more of the stock of one commercial bank.

one-decision stock Stock of such blue ribbon caliber that it can be bought at any price level and held with a maximum of safety, thus requiring only one decision. Such stocks prove to be security blankets for many institutional investors. (Cf. institutional investor)

one-hundred-percent location Point in space where a retail establishment achieves maximum sales volume compared to other locations in the local market area.

100% reserve money *banking* An archaic plan, never used, to require commercial banks to hold reserves equal to their deposits. (Cf. fractional reserves)

one-name paper A negotiable instrument which has not as yet been endorsed, and which changes to a two-name instrument when it is endorsed.

1.0 rule *pension plans* Complex rule comparing the utilization percentage of the multiple plans. If a plan is set up to provide benefits of 50% of the average salary (over a working lifetime), then 50% of the available benefits would have been used. Thus, depending upon the percentage which is to be utilized, multiple plans may not exceed 100% of allowable benefits under the law.

one-tier method of integration Method by which an employer may fund an employee's pension plan above the taxable wage base to assure that the higher-paid employees are not discriminated against because of limitations on covered compensation under Federal Insurance Contributions Act deductions.

open account credit Credit arrangement used by many retailers. Customers may purchase goods at any time, up to a certain limit, with payment made for all purchases within thirty days with no interest charge applied or in stated monthly payments, based on the current account balance plus interest.

open contract Contract where the parties, the subject matter of a contract, and the consideration for the contract are ascertained, leaving other terms to be implied by law.

open corporation A corporation whose stock is widely held, such as General Motors, AT&T, etc.

open dating Practice in the marketing of perishable or semiperishable food in which the last date the item can be sold is shown on the package.

open-end company A management company, incorporated under the Investment Company Act of 1940, offering for sale or having outstanding any redeemable security of which it is the issuer; one that continuously offers its securities for sale. An open-end company redeems its own shares, thereby allowing an investor to sell back the shares to the company. Commonly called a mutual fund. (Cf. closed-end company)

open-end credit Line of credit that may be used repeatedly up to a certain limit. Also called charge account or revolving credit.

open-end credit plan Consumer credit plan prescribing the terms of credit transactions which may be made and under the terms of which a finance charge may be computed on the outstanding unpaid balance. The creditor may permit the customer to make purchases or obtain loans directly from the creditor or indirectly by use of a credit card, check, or other device, as the plan may provide. The customer has the privilege of paying the balance in full or in installments. Negotiated advances under an open end real estate mortgage or a letter of credit are not included.

open-ended question *communication* Broad general questions that allow the respondent maximum freedom in deciding how much and what kind of information to give.

open-end fund A mutual fund that issues and sells new shares to each new investor and redeems shares from investors when they wish to sell. Assets held by the fund increase and decrease as investors move into, or out of, the market.

open-end investment fund Investment fund in which the number of outstanding shares, or capitalization, is not fixed. Instead, the number of shares continually changes as investors purchase new shares or redeem old ones. When shares are purchased in an open-end fund, they are purchased from the fund itself. When shares are redeemed the fund must stand ready to buy them back. The price of purchases or sales of open-end fund shares is based on the most recently computed net asset value (NAV) of the fund. Net asset value per share is the total value of all securities and other assets held by the fund divided by the number of outstanding shares and is calculated twice daily.

open-end lease Lease which may involve an additional payment based on the value of property when returned.

open-end mortgage Mortgage under which the mortgagor (borrower) may secure additional funds from the mortgagee (lender), usually stipulating a ceiling amount that can be borrowed.

open-end mortgage bonds Bonds issued under an indenture which allows additional bonds to be issued under the same indenture at some future date.

open house *real estate* Method of showing a home for sale whereby the home is left open for inspection by interested parties.

open housing Condition under which housing units may be purchased or leased without regard to racial, ethnic, color, or religious characteristics of the buyers or tenants.

open indent The purchase order of an importer indicating that the order may be filled with goods from any manufacturer so long as the specifications are met.

open insurance policy Policy of insurance whereby the maximum limit of the insurer's liability is set forth in the policy, obliging the insurer to pay the actual value of the loss up to the maximum limit. Ordinarily, policies of fire insurance fall under this category. Also called unvalued policy.

open interest The total number of open contracts (i.e., unliquidated purchases and sales) on a commodities futures market. When this figure is published it ostensibly assists investors to better evaluate the market.

open listing *real estate* Listing given to any number of brokers without liability to compensate any except the one who first secures a buyer who is ready, willing, and able to meet the terms of the listing or secures the seller's acceptance of another offer. The sale of the property automatically terminates all open listings.

open market operations *banking* The buying and selling of government debt instruments by a branch of the central bank of a country, to brokers who deal in such instruments. In the United States this is done by the Open Market Committee of the Federal Reserve System for the purpose of influencing the money supply.

open market operations The Federal Reserve activity of buying and selling government securities on the open market as a means of expanding or contracting the credit supply.

open market rates *securities* The interest rates on various types of securities sold on the open market that are directly influenced by supply and demand.

open mine Mine which is in operation for the extraction of minerals by any method employed by miners for that purpose. A mine is open as soon as mineral right operations are begun upon it to extract the minerals from the soil, either by open cut or ground sluicing.

open mortgage Mortgage that has matured or is overdue and is therefore open to foreclosure at any time.

open order Any order that has not yet been executed to buy or sell securities, either for the day or until cancelled.

open outcry *commodities* A method of trading on a commodity exchange in which traders cry out their buy or sell orders, other traders cry out a response, and on this basis, a trade is made and duly recorded.

open policy *insurance* A policy covering a risk for a specified time or a stated value, but allowing interchange of the goods insured. Used in the transportation industry, among others.

open-rate method *securities* A technique used by dealers to sell commercial paper in which, essentially, the issuer receives a partial payment when the paper is delivered to the dealer and the remainder when the notes are sold.

open repo A repurchase agreement in which the repurchase date is not specified and the agreement can be terminated by either party at any time. The agreement continues from day to day, and the interest rate is adjusted according to the market.

open shop An establishment employing both union and nonunion labor.

open space Land within a developed area left undeveloped, serving as an amenity to surrounding occupants.

operating expenses Amounts paid to maintain property, such as property taxes, utilities, and hazard insurance. This excludes financing expenses and depreciation.

operating lease A lease which can be cancelled by the lessee and in which the lessor maintains the asset.

operating leverage Fixed operating costs which tend to increase the variation in profits. (*See* financial leverage)

operating profit Amount found by deducting operating expenses (overhead) from gross profit.

operating profit margin Percentage earned on sales before deducting interest expenses and taxes.

operating ratio Total operating expenses divided by operating revenues. Ratio of the cost of goods sold plus selling and administrative and general expenses to net sales.

operational targets *finance* The current, primary concern of Federal Reserve monetary policy. Usually the focus is on bank reserves or the Federal fund rate. The current concern must coincide with intermediate and long-range objectives.

operations research (OR) The use of statistical methods of analysis to attempt to solve operational problems in a company. The goal is to provide management with a logical basis for making decisions.

opinion of title Certificate, generally from an attorney, as to the validity of the title to property being sold.

opportunity cost *economics* 1. The cost of an alternative use of resources; difference between revenues returned when resources are used for one purpose and those that would have been returned had the same resources been used for another purpose. Also called alternative cost. 2. Income foregone by an investor when one action is chosen as opposed to another. Expected income on next best alternative. 3. Real economic cost of a good or service produced measured by the value of the sacrificed alternative.

option 1. Right to purchase or lease a property upon specified terms within a specified period. 2. Privilege, for which one usually pays, of either buying or selling something at a specified price within a specified time. This has become a significant way of trading common stocks in recent years. Option buying and selling is usually done by market speculators in blocks of one hundred shares. (*See* call option, put option, striking price)

optionally renewable *insurance* Situation in which the insured has no rights concerning renewal or premium levels. The insurer may deny renewal, increase premiums for all or any of the classes of insureds, and add restrictive policy conditions.

options clearing corporation (OCC) A corporation operating on behalf of an exchange that handles options transactions. Each exchange will own its own clearing corporation. The organizations handle all options transactions from beginning to end.

oral Uttered through the mouth; consisting of spoken as opposed to written words, as oral testimony.

oral contract Spoken agreement, not expressed in writing.

or better (OB) Code marked on order ticket of a customer indicating to the broker that the transaction should be carried out at a better price than that listed on the limit order, when that is possible, but not at a poorer price.

orderly market *securities* A market that maintains a degree of stability because the specialist involved buys or sells the security according to the need, even in the face of heavy buying or selling. (Cf. specialist, market-maker)

order of distribution *law* A directive by a court (usually probate) which has jurisdiction over an estate to begin the process of distributing the assets to those entitled to receive them.

order paper A negotiable instrument requiring an endorsement by the payee or indorsee. Order paper can be converted to bearer paper by a blank endorsement.

ordinal utility theory *economics* The hypothesis that economic analysis must proceed from a ranking of pleasurable alternatives since there is no unit for the measurement of pleasure.

ordinance 1. Law or statute; an enactment of the lawmaking body of a municipal corporation. 2. A subordinate legislation promulgated with the authority of a properly established body of the government, such as a city or town.

ordinary annuity 1. Series of equal payments, each payment occurring at the end of an equally spaced period. 2. An annuity which stipulates that the payments be made at the end of the period (e.g., a mortgage note payment).

ordinary asset Any asset which is not specifically a capital asset. An example of an ordinary asset is an inventory item.

ordinary gain Gain on the sale of an ordinary asset.

ordinary income Income which is defined by the Internal Revenue Code to include salaries, fees, commissions, interest, dividends, and many other items. This is taxed at regular tax rates as contrasted with long-term capital gains which receive more favorable tax treatment. (*See* Appendix G)

ordinary insurance Policy on which the insured is to pay premiums until death. Also called straight life insurance.

ordinary loss 1. Loss on the sale of an ordinary asset. 2. *income tax* Loss deductible against ordinary income.

organization chart *management* A graphic presentation of the formal structure of a company which reveals where specific people are to function. The chart forms the backdrop for communications within the company.

organization costs The costs related to organizing a corporation, which include legal fees, charter costs, etc. The sum of these costs is considered an intangible

asset to a corporation and is kept on the books as such.

organized exchange Formal market for buying or selling securities or commodities.

original cost theory of rate making *economics* In public utility and railroad rate making, original cost is the cost of the property at the time it was first devoted to public service, less accrued depreciation. The rate of return is allowed on this basis.

original issue discount *securities* The amount an original issue of bonds is discounted per bond to make the initial sales.

original maturity *securities* The interval between the issue date and the maturity date of a bond. (Cf. current maturity)

originating house Investment banker that makes an agreement with a firm to sell a new issue and forms the syndicate to sell the securities.

orphan's deduction; orphan's exclusion A deduction from the gross estate of a decedent for amounts passing to a child of the decedent, when the child is under twenty-one years of age, there is no spouse of the decedent, and there is no known living parent of the child.

ouster Dispossession. Generally, a wrongful dispossession in respect to which the aggrieved party becomes entitled to maintain an action.

outflow All cash flowing out for any purpose, shown on a cash flow statement.

out-of-pocket costs Costs related to a present or future decision which will require an outlay of money, such as the purchase of a piece of new office equipment. (Cf. sunk cost)

out of the money *securities* 1. Describes a call option contract for which the striking (exercise) price of the call is above the market price of the underlying security. 2. Describes a put option contract for which the striking (exercise) price of the put is below the market price of the underlying security.

outright ownership Highest form of ownership; property held in the owner's name, with the right to deal with it as the owner wishes during his or her lifetime.

outright sale Sale of commercial paper through a dealer in which the issuer sells directly to the dealer and receives immedi-

233

ate payment for the paper, less the dealer's fees.

outside financing Process used by a corporation to raise expansion funds through issues of securities rather than through the use of retained earnings.

outstanding Remaining undischarged, unpaid, or uncollected. Existing as an adverse claim.

outstanding balance Amount owed on a debt.

out the window *securities* Describes rapid sale of a new issue of securities. Sometimes called a blowout.

overage Amounts to be paid, based on gross sales, over the base rent, in leases for retail stores.

over age fifty-five home sale exemption *income tax* Exemption given an individual over age fifty-five allowing for the sale of the principal residence at a gain and excluding up to $125,000 of the gain from taxation.

overall market capacity *marketing* The total amount of a good or a service which could possibly be absorbed by the market under current circumstances.

overall market price coverage *securities* The extent to which the market value of a particular class of securities is met in the event of liquidation.

overall rate of return (OAR) The percentage relationship of net operating income divided by the purchase price of property.

overapplied overhead A credit balance in the manufacturing overhead account of overhead cost applied to work in process that is greater than the amount of overhead cost actually incurred during a period.

overcapacity The existence of so many firms in a specific industry, with so much productive capacity, that it is impossible to run each plant at capacity because the demand is not great enough for the supply, and a profit cannot be made. Also called excess capacity.

overcapitalized A situation in which a corporation has too much invested capital in relation to its expected earnings or its income producing assets.

overdetermined system *economics* A system of equations, even though consis-

tent and independent, such that the number of the equation is greater than the number of variables and different solutions are obtained, depending on which variable is eliminated first.

overdraft Any adverse balance in a customer's general account, whether the balance was created by charging up checks of the customer or debiting past due bills and notes to that account.

overdraft banking A service offered to customers by some commercial banks where accounts that are overdrawn are backed by a line of credit to the customer. This service relieves the customer of the embarrassment of having checks returned, inasmuch as the line of credit picks up when the funds in the account become insufficient.

overdraft checking Line of credit permitting a person to write checks for more than the account balance, with interest charged on the amount borrowed.

overdraft system A custom widespread in Europe in which checks are cleared through accounts which frequently have negative balances. This is an arrangement made between the bank and the customer, and interest is paid on the overdrafts.

overdue 1. Past maturation in relation to the time for its performance. 2. More than due; delayed or unpaid. 3. In circulation for an unreasonable length of time.

overhang A block of securities or commodities large enough to depress prices if released on the market all at one time.

overhead 1. Any cost not specifically associated with production (e.g., administrative cost). 2. *See* indirect cost.

overheating *economics* The condition of an economy that is expanding so rapidly that inflation can result.

overimprovement Land use considered too intense for the land.

overinvestment theory *economics* Theory of business cycles which holds that economic fluctuations are caused by too much investment in the economy as businessmen try to anticipate rising demands during an upswing, and from sharp cutbacks in investment during a downswing when businessmen realize they expanded too much in the previous prosperity.

overissue Shares of capital stock issued

in excess of the number of shares authorized.

overlapping debt *accounting* In municipal government accounting, total debt of the subdivisions and special districts sharing the same geographic area.

overlay An amount included in tax levies on general property to cover abatements and uncollected taxes. (Cf. abatement)

overnight repo A repurchase agreement used by securities dealers and financial institutions to finance their treasury bills, notes, or bonds. These repos are sold one evening and repurchased the next morning. (Cf. repurchase agreement)

overrule To supersede; to annul; to make void; to reject by subsequent action or decision.

oversubscription *securities* An issue of securities that attracts more buyers than the amount of the issue can accommodate.

overt 1. Open to view; observable; manifest. 2. *law* Done openly and publicly, without attempt at concealment and with evident intent.

over the counter (OTC) Process for handling trades in securities not listed on a registered stock exchange. Such trades are handled through negotiations among dealers who make a market in a particular security rather than by the auction system of a stock exchange. Most new issues and smaller issues are handled through the over-the-counter market.

over-the-counter margin bond Debt security not traded on the national securities exchange which meets certain Regulation T requirements as to size of the original offering, available information, and status of interest payments.

over-the-counter market Informal market for trading in securities which are not listed on organized exchanges.

over-the-counter stocks Stocks not traded on a national securities exchange.

overtime Hours worked in excess of number of hours fixed as the regular work period. Work done after hours or on Sundays and holidays.

overwriting A speculative venture by an options writer who believes a security to be overpriced or underpriced and sells call or put options in quantity on the security, assuming they never will be exercised.

owe To be indebted; to be bound to do; to omit something.

owned real estate *banking* Real property which the bank has acquired by virtue of the foreclosure on a mortgage, or in settlement for some other obligation owed the bank.

owner 1. Person with legal or rightful title to property or who is beneficially entitled to such right. 2. Person beneficially entitled to any corporeal thing such as land, chattels, goods, animals, etc. 3. Person with dominion or control over a thing, although the title to the same may be with another, such as a conditional sales purchaser; may include a person whose right to a thing is short of entire beneficial ownership, such as a lessee, for a term of years. 4. *real estate* One who owns property as opposed to one who leases or rents property. An owner can mortgage, lease, or sell the property, whereas renters have no jurisdiction over the property they use except for the present interest allowed by the rental or lease agreement.

owner-occupied residential *real estate* Residential property occupied by the person who owns the property.

owner's equity Owner's vested interest in property.

ownership Right of a person to possess, enjoy, and dispose of property to the exclusion of all other persons; legal claim or title.

ownership form Method of owning real estate, which affects income tax, estate tax, continuity, liability, survivorship, transferability, disposition at death, and disposition at bankruptcy.

own occupation definition *See* definition of disability.

P

pace Measure of length containing two and one-half feet, the ordinary length of a step. The geometrical pace is five feet long.

pacers Workers in a plant who have established a reputation for working fast and are used by management to set the production pace at the plant. Usage primarily British.

Pacific Securities Depository Trust Company (PSDTC) The securities depository used by the Pacific Stock Exchange and its members.

pacing The time taken to complete each specific task on an assembly line.

package car *transportation* A car designed for less-than-carload lots, destined for distant points, and supposedly moving on fast trains.

package deal A business agreement which may cover several issues in order to prevent argument on small specific issues. All concerned feel it is better to get a complete package deal without argument than to hash over small specifics and perhaps get no agreement.

package mortgage A mortgage which may include real property and durable personal property such as appliances, etc.

package pay Particularly with reference to executive pay, the components of non-salary compensation which may be larger in total than the salary. May include pensions, stock options, etc.

packaging 1. Process in the film and television industry of developing and assembling talent and scripts for a particular program or programs. 2. Process in the publishing industry of preparing a finished, edited, and designed book to be sold to a publisher for marketing. 3. *marketing* Box, container, or wrapping in which a product is sold. A sophisticated marketing tool, as well as a necessary step in getting products from producers to consumers. Facets of good packaging are aesthetic value, protection of the product, storability, etc.

pac-man strategy A technique used by a corporation which is a takeover target in an attempt to thwart that attempt. The strategy is to have the corporation begin to purchase shares of the acquirer's stock, accompanied by the threat to take over the acquirer. The name is taken from the popular electronic game.

pact An agreement; covenant; compact; bargain.

pacta conventa quae neque contra leges neque dolo malo inita sunt omni modo observando sunt *Contracts which are not in contravention of the laws or entered into with a fraudulent intent should in all respects be observed.*

pacta dant legem contractui *Agreements of the parties constitute the law of the contract.*

Page rule *insurance* Rule stating that, where there is a blanket policy and a specific policy covering one potential loss, if a loss occurs the two policies will contribute proportionately according to their face amounts.

paid-in capital That portion of shareholders' worth which has been paid in directly, as opposed to earned profits retained in the business.

paid-in surplus Capital accumulated by a corporation in excess of that credited to capital stock. May come from par stock selling above par, or from non-par stock which was sold at prices above the estimated share price, from forfeited payments made upon subscribed stock, or from contributions from stockholders or people outside the corporation.

paid-in surplus account Account where minimum paid-in fund for mutual insurers is assigned. This fund is assigned entirely to paid-in surplus.

paid-up additions *life insurance* Units of a single premium policy bought by application of the dividends to the policy under the insured's option as to the disposition of dividends.

paid-up capital Capital derived from the sale of shares of a corporation's stock that have been completely paid for.

paid-up insurance A life policy for which the insured has paid all premiums, but which has not yet matured. Sometimes a policyholder may cancel a policy and use the cash value to pay for a paid-up term policy.

painting the tape *securities* An illegal practice sometimes used by market manip-

236

ulators who trade certain stocks among themselves to make it appear that there is activity in the security. Consecutive or repeated trading in a security causes its frequent appearance on the ticker tape. Usually this activity is supported by a special investor interest in the security.

paired shares Common stocks of two companies under the same management that are sold as a unit, usually appearing on one stock certificate, printed on front and back.

pallet Platform, usually made of wood, on which products are transported.

panic *stock market* A situation in which stockholders will sell stock irrationally to avoid some real or imagined threat to the value of the stock. The same thing can happen when a run on a bank is precipitated by rumors that the bank may be in trouble.

panoramic office planning (POP) Open office plan which was popular for several years. Recent trends in some industries is to go back to enclosed office space.

pantry check A method used in market research in which door-to-door callers or telephone interviewers ask consumers if they currently have a specific product in the pantry.

paper Credit given, evidenced by a written obligation that is backed by property.

paper gain *securities* Unrealized gain on securities in a portfolio which is currently selling for price more than that paid for them. The gain will simply be on paper, and not realized, until the securities are sold.

paper gold *See* special drawing right.

paper loss *securities* Unrealized loss on securities in a portfolio which is currently selling for price less than that paid for them. The loss will simply be on paper, and not realized, until the securities are sold.

paper standard Monetary system using any paper currency that has no commodity backing and is therefore not exchangeable for any commodity. Paper money is backed by the full faith and credit of the country issuing it.

parallelism A tendency for stocks to move upward or downward together, mak-

ing diversification in the portfolio necessary. A portfolio lacking in absolute parallelism would contain stocks that do not move in the same direction at the same time as others.

parameter 1. Boundaries within which one is expected to operate. Parameters qualify or quantify the constraints and are derived from specific facts unique to the client's situation. The parameters for a portfolio manager would be the boundaries set up by the goals, constraints, etc., of the client. 2. *econometrics* A constant or the coefficient of a variable in a model or system of equations.

paramount title Title superior to another in that the latter is derived from the former.

parcella terrae *Parcel of land.*

parent corporation One corporation which owns more than 50% of the voting stock of another corporation and thus controls the activities and the resources of that corporation.

parent-sub controlled group Relationship existing for a group of organizations with a common parent, with each of these under control of one or more of the other, and with the common parent having direct control over at least one member of the group.

Pareto's law Hypothesis that the pattern of income distribution is constant, both historically and geographically, regardless of taxation or welfare policies; also called the law of the trivial many and the critical few, or the 80/20 law.

pariah stocks Stocks of dull, neglected, or even bankrupt companies which may hold out the possibility of yielding great returns in the future. This is an area constantly explored by contrarian investors. Basically, pariah stocks are outcast stocks.

parity 1. *foreign exchange* Equality between the market values or the declared values of two nations' currencies. 2. *agriculture* In farm subsidy programs, comparison of cost/sale prices during a past period with current cost/price needs.

parking The placing of assets in a safe investment while looking about for an investment yielding a greater return. For example, one might leave ten thousand dollars in a bank savings account while awaiting a more lucrative investment possibility.

par life policy   Life insurance policy which makes provisions for the policy to participate in the earnings of the company.

parol evidence   1. Oral evidence. 2. The testimony of a witness by word of mouth. (*See* parol evidence rule)

parol evidence rule   *law*   Rule that prohibits the change or modification of a written agreement by an oral agreement made by the parties or their agents prior the writing, in the absence of a plea of mistake, ambiguity, or fraud in the writing.

pars rationabilis   Personal goods and chattels which by law devolve to a person's surviving spouse and children.

partial call   *securities*   The redemption of a portion of a callable bond issue prior to the maturity date; an action which does not completely eliminate the debt. Still outstanding as debt instruments are the bonds of the same issue not called.

partial interest gift   Gift of a portion of a property which qualifies for a gift deduction if it is the donor's entire interest in the property.

partial oligopoly   *economics*   A situation in which a few sellers dominate the market for a product on the selling side but do not act in such a way as to maximize profits of the group due to the uncertainty of the actions of the whole group on the part of one who might wish to make some changes on one's own.

partial release   Provision in a mortgage that allows some of the property pledged to be freed from serving as collateral.

partial taking   Acquisition by condemnation of only part of a property or some property rights.

participating policy   Insurance policy which returns to the insured a portion of the gross premium in the form of policy dividends based on the insurer's actual mortality experience.

participating preferred stock   A unique type of preferred stock that allows holders to receive dividends in addition to the normal fixed amount during years in which the common stock dividend exceeds that of preferred stock.

participation   *banking*   A loan funded by more than one lender, but serviced by only one. Banks, especially small banks, often ask for assistance in funding a loan which is too large for them to fund alone.

participation certificate (PC)   *See* guaranteed mortgage certificate.

participation mortgage   Mortgage that allows the lender to share in part of the income or resale proceeds.

particular average   *marine insurance*   Average used to distinguish damage sustained by specified interest as distinct from general average charges. Any loss resulting from accident other than normal perils of the sea (such as water leakage) is not apportioned among the shippers but borne by the particular owner of the damaged goods.

particulars   Details of a claim. In the phrase "bill of particulars," refers to a written statement of the details in the claim of a plaintiff or the counterclaim of a defendant.

partition   1. Division between the property of several persons which belongs to them as co-owners; may be compulsory as per judicial process or voluntary. Severance of the unity of possession or title or both, between co-owners, enabling them to hold severally their respective shares. 2. *real estate*   A method of dividing property among two or more persons who are entitled to fractional interests in the property. (E.g., five people own undivided interests in a piece of real property. If one dies, or wants the money back, the entire property may be sold, and the proceeds divided among the five on a pro rata basis.)

partner   Person who has joined with another or others to form a partnership.

partnership   Voluntary contract between two or more competent persons to place their money, effects, labor, and skill or some one or all of them in lawful commerce or business, and to divide the profit and bear the loss in certain proportions, according to the interest of each in the partnership. A partnership does not survive the death of any partner. (A legal form of business enterprise, as opposed to a proprietorship, yet not having the status of being a legal entity, such as a corporation.)

partnership capital account   That percentage of the partnership owned by a partner, represented by the amount of capital the partner has invested in the partnership.

partnership capital freeze Technique used by partners who choose to give away (usually to a child or other family member) their share of the partnership, creating frozen partnership interest. This should have a relatively clear-cut value (not more than the value of its fixed liquidation preference) for estate tax purposes.

party *law* Person who takes part in a legal transaction or who is named as such in a legal proceeding. At common law, an action must be brought in the name of the party who has the legal right.

party wall Division wall between two connected and mutually supporting buildings of different owners, or intended to be between a building actually constructed and a contemplated one, which stands half on the land of each and which is maintained at mutual cost.

par value 1. Arbitrary value set on the trade of a security. Bondholders receive par value for their bonds on maturity. 2. Face value or nominal value. The dollar value assigned per share when issued, as stated in the corporate charter and printed on the face of the certificate. Par value is the minimum price at which a share may be issued and be fully paid; usually the value assigned is arbitrary, and may bear no relationship to the market value. Today most shares have a par value of one dollar to five dollars. The proceeds received from the sale of shares higher than par result in paid-in surplus.

pass To transfer or be transferred.

passenger mile cost Total cost of passenger travel divided by the total number of miles traveled.

passing the dividend Failing to declare a customary dividend. Directors of corporations are reluctant to take this step because it usually reveals that the company is losing money, or is marginal, and such action may damage the stock price for a considerable time in the future.

passive 1. Inactive; permissive; subjected to a burden or charge. 2. Describes income or loss from economic activities in which a taxpayer does not materially participate, such as a limited partnership. This type of income (or loss) is differenti-

ated from investment income or from earned income from a trade or business.

passive equity management strategy Investment situation in which neither the design of the portfolio nor its ongoing operation is based on any attempt to assess whether or not the underlying fundamentals of its holdings are reflected fairly in prices. Index funds designed to track the performance of a defined market of stocks (e.g., Standard and Poor's 500 Index) constitute the only widely accepted current form of passive equity management.

passive income Income from investments for which no active work is now being done, but which is the result of retention and investment of past funds earned.

passive investor *real estate* One who invests in property for income, but who does not wish to play any role in the management of the property.

passive negligence A failure to take that degree of care in relation to the plaintiff as the law requires or to do something that should have been done and which failure amounts to a breach of the duty of care.

passive solar heating System of features incorporated into a building's design which uses and maximizes the effects of the sun's natural heating capability.

passive trust Trust that imposes no affirmative duties upon the trustee but merely conveys the bare legal title with all beneficial use passing to the beneficiary of the trust.

passive trustee Trustee in whom property is vested simply for the benefit of another person. In a passive trust, the beneficiary has the entire management of the estate. (*See* trustee)

pass off To sell goods and carry on business in such a manner, under such name, mark, description, or otherwise as to mislead the public into believing that a person's goods or business are those of another person.

passport Document identifying one as a citizen of the issuing country recognizing the right of the bearer to the protection and guidance of the country's diplomatic and consular offices. Required in application for a visa permitting travel in another country.

pass-through account Reserve account that a bank which is not a member of the Federal Reserve System is required by the Fed to hold at a member bank holding an equivalent amount on deposit at the Federal Reserve Bank.

pass-through certificate Certificate showing interest in a pool of mortgages sold by mortgage bankers to investors. Money collected as monthly mortgage payments is distributed to those who own certificates. (*See* Ginnie Mae pass-through)

past-service benefit The credit toward a pension, given by an employer to an employee, for all or part of the employee's past service prior to the time when a pension plan was adopted.

past-service credit *pension plans; profit sharing* Credit, based on the assumption that the employee was earning the present salary in each of the previous years, which makes available to the employee the unused portion of exclusion allowances for previous years.

past-service liability Unfunded "pot" of money based on the hypothesis that it is possible to pretend that an employee always had a money-purchase plan in place. Given that hypothesis, one may reasonably ask what would cumulatively have been contributed to the plan in the past.

patent 1. Government grant to an inventor, securing for a limited time (normally seventeen years) the exclusive right to make, use, sell, and license the invention. Confers a statutory monopoly protecting the patentee against unlicensed use of the patented device or process. 2. Conveyance of title to government land.

patrimony 1. Hereditary estate that has descended in a direct line from the father. (May also be applied to that which has descended from the mother or other ancestor.) 2. Totality of assets and liabilities given to monetary evaluation consisting of assets which are subject to execution for the benefit of creditors.

patron 1. Regular customer. 2. Protector or benefactor.

pauper One who has no means and is completely dependent upon charity.

pawn *law* Pledge; a bailment of personal property as a security for some debt or engagement, the property being re-deemable on specified terms and subject to sale in the event of default.

pawnbroker Person who is in the trade or business of lending money at a legally specified rate of interest on an article or articles of personal property left with the person as security.

pay Fixed and defined amount given as compensation for services.

payable Describes sum of money a person is under an obligation to pay.

payable on death (p.o.d.) account Account in which an individual deposits funds with a financial institution for the benefit of another, payable on the death of the depositor. The primary weakness of such an account is that it may be considered testamentary in nature.

payables *See* accounts payable.

payables period Measure of a company's use of trade credit financing calculated by dividing accounts payable by purchases per day.

pay-as-you-go plan *See* current disbursement plan.

payback An estimated time when a business will reach its break-even point and begin to make a profit.

payback period Time an investor must wait to recoup an initial investment. Estimates of this time are used by management to evaluate the profitability of alternative investment proposals.

payee Person in whose favor a bill of exchange, promissory note, or check is made payable.

paying agent An intermediary, usually a bank, that receives funds from an issuer of bonds or stock and in turn pays out principal and interest, or dividends. A fee is charged for the service. Sometimes called a disbursing agent.

payment Transfer of money from one party to another with the assent of both parties. A transfer made without such assent does not constitute payment.

payment by result A system of wage payment in which the employee is paid according to the employee's production; similar to piecework.

payment mechanism System designed for the movement of funds, payments, and money between financial institutions throughout the nation. The Federal

Reserve plays a major role in the nation's payments mechanism; services are made available to both member banks and non-member depository institutions on the basis of uniform pricing schedules.

payment supra protest A payment after protest. An endorser liable on a dishonored negotiable instrument which has been protested receives a right to reimbursement from the drawer for paying the instrument.

payoff matrix A table with situations that may develop classified by rows against available alternative strategies classified by columns for the purpose of analysis in view of the probability attaching to each of the situations.

payor bank Bank by which an item is payable as drawn or accepted.

payout Amount received on an instrument equal to that invested.

payout ratio The percentage of a firm's annual earnings per share which are paid out in dividends to stockholders. (E.g., if a corporation earns $3.00 per share and pays a dividend of $.50 per share, it has a payout ratio of 16.6%.)

pay-related stock ownership plan (PAYSOP) Tax credit employee stock ownership plan used infrequently in small and medium-sized businesses. Instead of PAYSOP's contributions being deducted from corporate income, they are deducted from corporate taxes. (For contributions to an employee stock ownership plan made in 1983 through 1987, a corporation may elect to claim a credit based on the lesser of the total value of employer securities transferred to the plan each year or 0.5% of the annual compensation of all employees covered by the plan.) (*See* Appendix G)

payroll register *accounting* A multicolumn disbursements journal used in recording the payroll, the multicolumn being necessary for registering hours of work, rate of pay, deductions, etc.

peak load In public utilities, the maximum demand for services during a given unit of time.

peculiar Particular; special.

pecuniary Relating to money or monetary affairs.

pecuniary bequest A gift of property, often made in connection with a marital deduction trust, which is expressed in terms of dollars instead of a fractional amount of the estate.

pecuniary emulation *See* conspicuous consumption.

peg An exchange rate on the currency of a country which is acceptable to the central bank of that country.

pegging The act of stabilizing the price of a security, commodity, or currency by intervening in the market. (E.g., the price of gold was once pegged at thirty-five dollars an ounce in the world, with the United States being the prime mover behind the action. Later, in 1971, governments pegged the price of gold in order to stabilize their currencies. They would buy gold when the price dropped, and sell when the price rose, thus, through the laws of supply and demand, keep the price within the pegged rate.)

penalty 1. Punishment set by statute for the commission of some offense. 2. Sum of money stipulated to be forfeited and paid in case of the nonperformance of the conditions or obligations of a contract. 3. Sum of money fixed by statute to be forfeited as a punishment.

penetration pricing New product pricing policy that uses an entry price lower than what is intended as the long-term price. The premise is that the initially lower price will help secure market acceptance.

penny stock A low-priced and usually highly speculative stock, often from a new company, which can be purchased for less than a dollar per share.

pension Deferred portion of the compensation earned for services rendered; i.e., a sum of money paid a retired or disabled employee by the company, or by some organization empowered by the company, which is symbolic of services rendered, and which is intended to assist the retiree in matters of personal income after retirement.

Pension Benefit Guaranty Corporation (PBGC) A federal corporation, authorized by the Employee Retirement Income Security Act of 1974 (ERISA), to guarantee basic pension benefits in covered plans by administering terminated plans and placing liens on corporate assets for certain pension liabilities that were not funded. In order to be covered, a plan must promise clearly defined benefits to more than twenty-five employees. Should a company go out of business, up to 30% of its net worth can be taken by the government and applied toward the pension plan. This program provides a major additional element of safety. (*See* Appendix G)

pensioner   A person supported by an allowance at the will of another; a dependent; one who receives periodic payments from a government, a company, or an employer of labor in consideration of one's past service. (*See* pension)

penthouse   Luxury housing unit located on the top floor of a high-rise building.

per capita   *law*   By the heads or polls according to the number of individuals; share and share alike. To take per capita of an estate means to take equally with other children and in one's right.

per capita debt   The total bonded debt of a municipality divided by its population.

per cent   Per hundred.

percentage   Rate per hundred; proportion in the hundred parts. A portion or proportion of what is under consideration.

percentage depletion   Method of computing the depletion allowance in which a fixed percentage of the gross income earned is excluded from taxability.

percentage lease   Lease of property in which the rental is based on a percentage of the sales volume made upon the leased premises. It usually stipulates a minimum rental and is regularly used for retailers who are tenants.

percolation test   Procedure to measure the drainage characteristics of the soil on a lot; required in the proper design of septic tank drainfield.

per diem   *By the day.*   May refer to charges made for a day on a loan, expenses allowed per day for business trips, or payment for a service per day.

perdurable   Estate that lasts long or forever.

peremptory   Imperative; not admitting of question, delay, or reconsideration; final; arbitrary; not subject to debate.

perfect   To file a security in the office of the Secretary of State, where such filing is required, or to take possession of a security.

perfect competition   *economics*   1. Pure competition. 2. A market situation in which there is perfect knowledge of the market by both buyers and sellers and a relatively unlimited supply of the ingredients of production at current prices. (Cf. pure competition)

perfect elasticity   *economics*   Demand or supply elasticity when the quantity demanded or offered at a given price is not limited. Also called finite elasticity.

Perfect Investment, The   A 1983 book by Lowell Miller that deals with the buying of stocks of troubled companies.

perfectly inelastic demand   *economics*   A situation in which a small change in price will result in virtually no change in demand.

perfectly inelastic supply   *economics*   A situation in which a small change in price will result in virtually no change in supply.

performance   Fulfillment or accomplishment of that which is required by a contracting party under a condition.

performance bond   Bond posted by a party who is to perform certain work. If the work is not performed, the insurer promises to complete the work or pay damages up to the amount of the bond.

performance, defined   See defined performance.

performance fund   A mutual fund designed to invest in firms expecting large capital growth. These are often growing firms that do not pay dividends, or, if dividends are paid, they are quite small. The firm will generally be plowing its profits back into capital investments designed to guarantee the growth and development of the firm over time.

peril   Cause of a loss. (Causes of loss are often loosely called risks. Correctly, risk is the uncertainty about the occurrence of the event that creates the loss, while the peril is the loss-producing agent.)

peril point   *economics*   A point beyond which the lowering of tariffs could substantially injure certain domestic industries. This is usually monitored closely, and in recent years the tendency has been in the direction of free trade.

per industriam   Qualified property in wild animals that have been tamed or contained by the art and industry of humanity.

periodic payment　1. Plan offered by many mutual funds for the purchase of additional shares of the fund at regular intervals.　2. Payment which must be made at specified times to discharge the obligations of an annuity.

period of digestion　A time period after the release of a new issue of securities during which the trading price is being established in the market.

perjury　Willful giving of false testimony by a witness under oath in a court proceeding about some matter material to the issue or point of inquiry.

perk　Perquisite. Benefit from a job which is above and beyond normal wages. While they may be termed fringe benefits, they are usually of an informal, unstructured type.

permanent　Stable; enduring. Generally used in distinction to temporary, but does not always mean perpetual.

permanent alimony　Alimony provision for the support and maintenance of a former spouse during his or her lifetime or until remarriage.

permanent benefit　*insurance* Benefit that provides an economic value extended beyond one policy year; for example, a paid-up cash surrender value. The regulations specify three things which may be provided in connection with a group-term life insurance policy but which will not be considered permanent benefits: a right to convert (or continue) life insurance after group life insurance coverage terminates; any other feature that provides the employee with no economic benefit other than current insurance protection; a feature under which term life insurance is provided at a level premium for a period of five years or less.

permanent disability　Degree of incapacity or disability as a result of which the worker's earning power is wholly destroyed. However, this does not exclude the employee from being able to perform light work or deny that there is still some remaining usefulness in the injured member of the worker's body.

permanent income hypothesis　The theory that people gear their expenditures not just to the income of the current peri od but to average actual and anticipated income over several periods.

permanent mortgage　Mortgage for a long period of time, usually more than ten years.

permit　License; an instrument of license or warrant issued by a person in authority empowering the grantee to do some act that is not forbidden by law but is not allowable without such authority.

per my et per tout　*law By the half and by the whole.* Describes the mode in which property is held in joint tenancy. For possession and survivorship, each joint tenant holds the whole, but for purposes of conveyance, each owns half.

perpetual annuity　Annuities which continue forever.

perpetual bond　Bond which has no maturity date. These bonds pay only period interest, never principal. England is one country which has issued such bonds. Simplistically, the present value of a perpetual bond is equal to the income received from it divided by the interest you might be receiving at the time from a similar investment.

perpetual debt　Bond that never matures or is so long-lived it is considered perpetual. The issuer never has to retire the principal; it has only to meet the interest payments and other terms of the indenture. Although rare, there are some in existence. (E.g., the British government issued perpetual bonds called consols to refinance the debt that was issued to support the Napoleonic Wars. These bonds will never mature, but they do pay interest, and there is an active secondary market for them.)

perpetual inventory　An inventory system that results in having an accurate account of inventory at any point in time. Normally, a card or sheet is used for each product, and the incoming and outgoing items are logged as they are moved. If accurately kept, the precise inventory will be available for scrutiny at any given moment.

perpetual policy　Policy provided by a mutual insurer which requires a very large initial payment and provides coverage with no termination date, assuming the dividend income will be adequate to cover all expenses incurred.

perpetual succession Continuous succession; the capacity to continue in business as long as the corporation exists. (A corporation does not die because of the death of the founder or of specific stockholders.)

perpetuities, rule against *See* rule against perpetuities.

perpetuity 1. Endless duration. 2. Annuity paid for life. 3. *law* An agreement keeping property in a family permanently or for a very long time.

perpetuity annuity An annuity, the income stream from which is unending.

person *law* Entity having legal responsibility. (*See* natural person, artificial person)

personal auto policy (PAP) Coverage designed to be the standard form for insuring eligible vehicles. The provisions of the PAP include: (a) single limit of liability per accident for bodily injury and/or property damage; (b) liability coverage provided for property damage to nonowned private passenger autos, trailers, and small trucks in the custody of the insured; (c) nonowned vehicles covered under liability coverage on an excess basis; (d) medical expenses incurred within three years from the date of accident covered under medical payments; (e) medical payments coverage made primary with respect to automobile accidents; (f) physical damage coverage provided under a single insuring agreement, though collision coverage is optional; (g) first-aid coverage not included as a supplementary payment; (h) no personal-effects coverage under the physical damage section; (i) no coverage for persons using a vehicle without reasonable belief that they are entitled to do so; (j) vehicles acquired during term of policy to be reported within thirty days for coverage. Because many insurers use nonstandard forms, and the PAP has not been approved by all states, this form has not been universally adopted. The Insurance Services Office will discontinue the FAP when all states accept the PAP. Because of this, many insurers continue to use the Family Auto Plan and the Standard Auto Plan to cover private passenger automobiles and certain kinds of light trucks.

personal banker A bank employee, usually of middle management or above, who is assigned specific customers, for whom the employee oversees all banking transactions and may serve the same general purpose as a financial planner. Found particularly in larger banks in metropolitan areas. Also called private banker.

personal consumption expenditure *economics* Personal disposable income less personal saving and interest paid by an individual. That part of disposable personal income which is spent in a given year.

personal contract Contract in auto insurance made for individuals or married couples to cover private passenger autos and certain types of nonbusiness trucks owned or rented under a long-term lease.

personal exemption *income tax* The amount allowed to be deducted for an individual in order to determine taxable income. (*See* Appendix G)

personal holding company A corporation in which more than 50% of its outstanding stock is owned directly or indirectly by not more than five individuals at any time during the last half of a taxable year, and in which 60% test; at least 60% or more of the corporation's adjusted ordinary gross income is personal holding company income (such as dividends, interest, rents, or amounts received in return for a certain type of personal services). Both tests must be met in the same taxable year. Status as a personal holding company attained in one year does not automatically continue into the next.

personal income *economics* National income minus undistributed corporate profits, contributions for social insurance, and corporate income taxes, plus transfer payments.

personal income distribution Pattern of income distribution according to the relative size of people's income.

personal liability forms Coverage provided for liability losses from bodily injury and property damage to others.

personal needs approach *insurance* Approach to the purchase of insurance based on a consideration of the type and amount which most nearly meets the needs of the insured.

personal property Any property which is not specifically designated by law as real property. Property that is movable, such as goods, chattels, securities, shares, dividends, premiums, bonuses in any bank, company, or corporation, any interest therein, and any chose in possession or in action. It is subject to ownership, is portable, and can be either tangible or intangible. (*See* chattel)

personal residence Dwelling in which the owner usually resides. While neither depreciation nor upkeep can be claimed since it is not a business, it does have two strong points as a personal investment. One can deduct interest on the mortgage from federal income tax and can be the sole recipient of any increase in the value of the property. (*See* Appendix G)

personal saving *economics* Disposable personal income less personal consumption expenditures and interest paid.

personalty Personal property as distinguished from realty or real property. (*See* chattel)

per stirpes *By the roots; by representation.* A legal method of distributing an estate to include the descendants of a deceased legatee, whose share is apportioned among linear descendants.

persuasive institutional advertising Type of promotion used to advance the interests of a particular institution within a competitive environment.

petition *bankruptcy law* Application to the bankruptcy court by a debtor or a creditor for a decision against debtor.

petitory *law* Action brought by one who claims to own property who is out of possession against another having possession to determine legal ownership of the property.

petty cash fund A fund of cash that is kept supplied in a given amount to pay for small purchases without writing a check. The petty cash would be accounted for by notations, receipts, etc.

phantom income 1. Any tax which experiences burnout but then continues to generate taxable income without any positive cash flow. 2. *real estate* Income which occurs because total dividends paid and loan disbursements exceed the amount paid in premiums. The phantom income will be treated as capital gains if straight line depreciation was taken, and ordinary income if accelerated depreciation was taken.

phantom stock plan A type of employee bonus plan in which a certain amount of company stock, often stated in terms of units, is set aside each year, on the books of the company only, though the employee does not get immediate possession of the stock. IRS rulings, to date, have allowed a plan to be tax deferred since the employee does not get constructive possession of the stock.

Phillips curve *economics* A graphic presentation of the inverse relation between the rate of the money wage increase (plotted on one axis) and the unemployment rate (plotted on the other axis). The curve in the United States seems to indicate that with 5–6% unemployment the price level will remain stable, but when unemployment is reduced to 3%, there will be an increase in the price level. This relationship was first set out by Phillips, in 1958, for England. In more recent years, though numbers may be altered, there still seems to be a relationship between the level of employment and the level of prices.

physical asset Asset a collectible may have which makes it physically attractive and displayable.

physical damage coverage *See* comprehensive insurance.

physical distribution concept Total cost approach to physical distribution, integrating the fixed cost, variable cost, and nonvariable cost involved in the physical distribution of goods.

physical distribution management (PDM) The study, control, and coordination of methods used in the distribution of materials and finished products (i.e., the science of materials handling).

physiocrat school *economics* A school of economic thought which holds that only land is value-creating in its product, which was called the product net. The school also holds that economics should always analyse transactions in terms of flows of income to get at the fundamental changes in relationships. This was done by a chart called "tableau économique" attributed to many French economists of the seventeenth and eighteenth centuries.

pickup The value gained in an exchange of bonds. Bonds with identical coupon rates and face values will have different values on the market. Thus it is possible at times to trade bonds whose values seem the same but market-wise are not.

picture   Wall Street slang used to ask about bid and asked prices, and quantity information, from a specialist or from a dealer on a specific security.

piggyback   Intermodal coordination of truck trailers on railroad freight cars allowing the shipper to obtain the benefits of both transportation modes.

piggybacking   1. Adding products to one's line which are related to primary products in order to optimize business efforts. 2. In direct mail selling, the adding of a secondary product to the primary product to maximize the selling effort at very little more cost.

piggyback loan   Combination of the construction loan with the permanent loan commitment.

pignorative contract   *European law*   A pledge of property as security. Counterpart of the American term mortgage.

Pigou effect   *economics*   The hypothesis that a fall in the price level will increase consumption due to the lower prices, in sufficient amount to prevent a drop in employment.

pilferage   Petty stealing; stealing property of minor value.

pilot production   The first unit produced under shop conditions, in order to test production methods.

pink sheets   A daily publication listing over-the-counter stocks, market makers (dealers), and prices. (*See* Yellow Sheet)

pip   *securities*   The smallest possible change in a quoted price for a specific currency. (E.g., if one currency is quoted in terms of a second currency at .9766, an increase to .9767 would be a pip.)

piracy   Infringement of copyright.

piscary   The right to fish in the waters of another nation.

pit   *See* ring.

Pittsburgh-plus pricing   Well-known basing point system used in the steel industry for many years in which steel price quotations contained freight charges from Pittsburgh regardless of where the steel was produced.

placer claim   Claim wherein valuable mineral is not found in the veins, lodes, or ledges within the rock, but in a loose condition in the softer materials that cover the surface of the earth.

place utility   Utility created by marketers who have products available where the consumers want to buy, i.e., at the right place at the right time.

plaintiff   *law*   Person or legal entity lodging a complaint with the court against another person or entity who is accused of wrong doing with respect to the plaintiff. The accused is called the defendant. It is incumbent upon the plaintiff to prove his case, and the defendant to protest it.

planned economy   An economy in which the productive resources are controlled by government to the extent that it can plan the use of them. In highly socialistic economies, the resources are owned by the government, and the use of them thus planned by government.

planned obsolescence   Practice of producing goods or services that are deliberately designed for limited use, thereby requiring replacement or repair.

planned unit development   Tract of land relieved from conventional zoning to permit clustering of residential uses, compatible commercial and industrial uses, and structures of varying heights.

planning   Systematic development of a community or an area with particular reference to the location, type, and extent of streets, squares, and parks and to related mapping and charting. The term refers to broad systematic municipal development to insure well-balanced land use in the community and is designed for the social and economic betterment of the community. (A planning board or commission is usually appointed to oversee such matters.)

plant   Fixtures, tools, machinery, and apparatus which are necessary to carry on a trade or business.

plat   Plan or map of a specific land area.

plat book   Public record containing maps of land, showing the division of the land into streets, blocks, and lots, and indicating the measurements of the individual parcels.

plebiscite Vote by all eligible voters in a state or nation on a matter of great importance to the public interest, such as a proposed change in its constitution.

pledge 1. Delivery of personal property as a security for some debt or engagement, the property being redeemable on specified terms and subject to sale in the event of default. 2. Security consisting of personal property for some debt or other obligation.

pledgee One who receives a pledge.

pledgery *law* Guarantee; an undertaking or answering for another.

pledgor One who offers or gives a pledge.

plena aetas *Full age.* Age of majority.

plenary Full in all respects; absolute; complete; unqualified, as certain confessions.

plimsoll mark Load line or mark along a ship's side to show the depth to which the proper cargo causes her to sink.

pliopoly *economics* A condition in which the probability grows that new companies will come into the industry as the profitability of the existing ones grow.

plottage *real estate* Increase of value which may accrue to two or more vacant and unimproved contiguous parcels of land held in one ownership because of their potentially greater use adaptability as a single unit.

plug *finance* The unknown quantity in a pro forma forecast.

pluralistic theory A theory in the field of industrial relations which denotes that though there are divergent interests in industry, as between labor and management, there is also a broad framework of common interests.

plurality State of being numerous; a large number or quantity; it may mean two but also includes any number in excess of two.

plus tick *See* uptick.

poaching Offense of unlawfully taking or destroying game on someone else's land.

pocket card *real estate* Card identifying its holder as a licensee of the state licensing agency which must be carried by salespersons and bankers in most states at all times.

point 1. Fee paid to induce lenders to make mortgage loans. Each point equals 1% of the loan principal. Points have the effect of reducing the amount of money advance by the lender. Also called discount point. 2. *stocks* In reference to a share of stock, the equivalent of one dollar. 3. *See* basis point.

point and figure chart A graphic technique used by technical analysts to follow the up or down movement in the price movements of a security. Time is disregarded, plus signs are used to represent an upward move, and minus signs are used for downward movements.

Point Four Program Program, which is part of the Foreign Economic Assistance Act of 1950, that seeks to raise living standards in the underdeveloped countries by making available United States technical and financial assistance, largely in the areas of agriculture, public health, and education. Much of this work is now carried out by agencies of the United Nations and by the United States Agency for International Development.

police power Power of government to make and enforce all laws and regulations necessary for the good and welfare of the state and its citizens.

policy cost per thousand Benchmarks established in a table for persons at least thirty years of age, up to eighty-four years old, derived from certain United States population death rates. Guidelines are then created to allow one to decide whether the rates are low or high. (*See* Appendix C)

policy limits Limits in insurance policies which are usually set out in the declarations. There may be a face amount limit in the policy, and it may also include internal limits applying to particular types of property, losses, locations, perils, or hazards.

policy loan provision Life insurance provision allowing the policyholder to take a loan (technically an advance because it does not have to be repaid) on the sole security of the policy up to an amount that with interest, as specified in the contract, will not exceed the cash value of the policy at the next anniversary date.

247

policy of insurance 1. Contract of insurance whereby for a specific monetary consideration, one party (the insurer) undertakes to indemnify the other (the insured) against damage or loss on a certain subject by certain perils. 2. Actual instrument embodying the contract.

policy replacement Practice of replacing one life insurance policy with another; historically frowned upon by insurance companies and discouraged by many state insurance commissioners. In a changing and highly competitive market, replacing a policy is not only possible, but advisable under proper circumstances.

politiae legibus non leges politiis adaptandae *Politics are to be adapted to the laws and not laws to politics.*

political economy Currently a synonym for economics, but originally denoting the growing partnership between pure economics and politics.

political union The unification of two or more countries or territories under a common government. When the Treaty of Rome was signed in 1957, establishing the European Economic Community, it was the purpose of many engaged in the meeting to eventually see political unification of Western Europe.

politics Science of government; the art or practice of administering public affairs.

poll Describes deeded land cut smooth or in a straight line without indentation or defacement.

poll tax Tax on a person as distinguished from a tax on property. This was a method once used to prevent minorities from voting, since they could not pay the tax.

pollute To make foul or unclean; to wrongfully contaminate the atmosphere, water, soil, or any matter or substance to the material injury of the right of an individual or to animal or vegetable life. (*See* Environmental Protection Agency)

polyopsony *economics* A market situation in which the number of buyers is so small that the actions of one can impact on the marketplace, but where the market is just large enough that individual buyers cannot predict what their actions might have on other buyers.

polypoly *economics* A market situation in which the number of sellers is so small that the actions of any one can impact on the market, but where the number of sellers is just large enough to preclude one seller from determining how that seller's actions will impact on the conduct of other sellers.

pooled income fund Trust formed to pay income to noncharitable beneficiaries. While the charitable remainder trusts may be viewed as going private (making an individual, private contribution), pooled income funds allow contributors to benefit both charity and contributors by pooling the funds of several contributors.

population 1. *statistics* All of the people, items, or whatever from which a sample is drawn to determine the characteristics of the whole. 2. *economics* Total number of the inhabitants of a country.

port Place where a vessel can remain in a position of shelter from the elements with the purpose of loading or discharge of cargo, for servicing, and for loading provisions.

portfolio Holdings of a diverse group of assets by an individual or a company.

portfolio beta score The relative volatility of a securities portfolio, taken as a whole, as measured by the beta coefficients of the securities making it up. (Cf. beta coefficient)

portfolio construction Creation and maintenance, through a logical sequence of steps, of optimal combinations of investment vehicles to achieve stated goals. The operation, by a stockbroker or some other person or institution, of handling the investments of a person or a trust. Also called portfolio management.

portfolio investment Purchase of a range or variety of stock shares and/or other securities in order to broaden the spread of the risk.

portfolio management *See* portfolio construction.

portfolio revision Steps taken to alter investment vehicles in order to put them in line with objectives or constraints which have changed since the portfolio was set up.

portfolio risk The total risk associated with owning a portfolio; the sum of systematic and unsystematic risk.

portfolio theory A sophisticated investment decision taking a complex approach that permits an investor to classify, estimate, and control both the kind and the amount of the expected risk and return.

portion 1. Allotted part; a share; a parcel. 2. Share falling to a child from a parent's estate or the estate of anyone bearing a similar relation.

positive carry A situation in which the interest cost of money borrowed to buy securities is less than the yield on the securities.

positive cash flow A situation where more money is flowing into a project or business than is being spent.

positive economics The discipline of economics as it concentrates on the analysis of what is with no particular reference to what ought to be.

positive gap *securities* A mismatch in a securities portfolio wherein interest-sensitive assets exceed interest-sensitive liabilities.

positive leverage Use of borrowed funds that increases the return on an investment.

positively sloped yield curve Graphic demonstration indicating instances where the investor apparently requires a premium for the length of time to maturity.

possession 1. The having, holding, or detaining of property in one's power or command; the detention or enjoyment of property by a person or by another in that person's name; the condition under which one may exercise power over a thing at one's pleasure to the exclusion of all others. 2. Something that a person owns, controls, or occupies; property. In every case, possession must be considered with reference to the peculiar circumstances, the character and value of the property, and the suitable and natural mode of its use.

possession utility That aspect of utility that arises from the fact of possession of the one desiring to use the good or service.

possessory title *law* Title acquired by one who is not the owner but who is in actual, open, adverse, exclusive, and uninterrupted possession of the land, which possession is not consistent with the exis-

tence of title in another and is under a claim of right or title for the period of time prescribed by the Statute of Limitations.

possibility of reverter *law* Interest remaining in a grantor who has conveyed a determinable fee.

post A horseshoe-shaped enclosure on the main floor of a stock exchange around which trading in specific stocks takes place.

postdate To date an instrument later than its actual date. Postdating normally does not affect the negotiability of the instrument.

posting The process of transferring data from the journal to the general ledger. The journal is set up to accommodate initial entries, and the ledger to accommodate final entries.

postmortem expense Expense which will accrue to a family after the death of a family member (e.g., last illness expenses, household support if the earner dies, and extra expenses for running a household). This risk of loss can be insured against with integrated insurance programs.

postselection Act by underwriters of reviewing renewal applications using techniques similar to those employed in considering whether to renew or decline the coverage for new applicants. They also review claims to determine whether to cancel a policy before it expires.

posttest *marketing* A survey taken after a sales or advertising promotion to ascertain its effectiveness.

pot *securities* That portion of a securities issue which is returned to the managing underwriter by participating investment bankers to facilitate sales to an institutional investor.

potentia *Possibility; power.*

potestas *Power;* authority; domination.

pot is clean A term describing the fact that all the securities sent to the managing underwriter for sale to Institutional Investors have been sold.

pound sterling The basic unit of currency in the United Kingdom.

pourover trust Trust into which assets are poured from another source. The pourover may be from the settlor's will or

249

from a source completely outside the testamentary estate. It is most useful as a receptacle for benefits from a qualified employee benefit plan, Keogh plans, individual retirement accounts, or insurance proceeds. It may receive assets from other trusts or estates.

power of alienation The power, legally recognized, to assign, transfer, or otherwise dispose of property.

power of appointment 1. Lifetime or testamentary right given by one person to another person authorizing the holder of the power to dispose of property over which he or she does not have a fee simple title. 2. An authority enabling one person to dispose of the interest in property which is vested in another.

power of attorney *law* 1. Instrument authorizing a person to act as the agent of the person granting it, conferring the authority to perform certain specified acts or kinds of acts on behalf of the principal (i.e., to act as attorney in fact). 2. The authority to act as an attorney-in-fact. (*See* general power of attorney, special power of attorney)

power of sale A clause sometimes inserted in mortgages or deeds of trust granting the lender (or trustee) the right to sell the property upon certain default. The property is to be sold at auction but court authority is unnecessary.

power to revoke or change Right retained by a grantor to alter, amend, or terminate the trust. If such power exists it must be relinquished more than three years prior to death to keep the corpus of the trust out of the grantor's estate.

practitioner A person engaged in the exercise or employment of any art or profession, but most often a profession, such as physician or a certified public accountant.

praedial servitude Easement; a servitude affecting land.

praedium Lands and tenements; tract of land.

praedium dominans *Dominant tenement* in an easement.

praedium serviens *Servient tenement* in an easement.

preamble Preliminary part or clause at the beginning of a statute or legal document giving the reasons for the statute or legal document or reciting the facts leading to such instrument. (*See* United States Constitution)

precatory language Language in a will found by the court to express wishful thinking. May also connote something stronger than a wish, but less than a command or direction.

precatory trust Trust created when property is given absolutely to any person who is to dispose of that property in favor of another. The trust will hold if the words so used might be looked upon as an explicit order, if the subject of the recommendation or wish is certain, and if the identity of the objects or persons intended to have the benefit of the recommendation or wish is also certain.

precautionary motive Desire on the part of households and businesses to hold part of their assets in liquid form so that they can be prepared for adverse contingencies. This motive is influenced primarily by income levels rather than by changes in the interest rate and is one of the chief sources of demand for loanable funds in the modern theory of interest.

precedent Adjudged case or judicial decision that furnishes a rule or model for deciding a subsequent case that presents the same or a similar legal problem.

preceding year basis A situation in which income tax, or any other tax or expense of business, is calculated (forecast) on the basis of the figures from the preceding year.

precept A mandate or command; an order or direction given by a person in authority to another requiring the latter to do some act within the scope of his or her powers.

precious metals Grouping of metals considered valuable, including gold, silver, platinum, and its related metals (rhodium, iridium, osmium, palladium, and ruthenium).

precompute *installment lending* 1. To subtract interest from the principal sum at the time of the loan. 2. To add interest to the principal sum and amortize the loan by payments of equal amounts over a period of time.

predecessor One who has preceded another.

predetermined overhead application rate   A rate used to charge overhead costs to jobs in production; the rate is established in advance for each period by use of estimates of manufacturing overhead cost and production activity for the period.

preemption   1. Privilege accorded by United States law to an actual settler upon public lands to purchase the tract settled upon at a fixed price in preference to all other applicants. 2. Privilege given to existing shareholders to purchase or subscribe for newly issued stock before such stock is sold or subscribed to by those who are not current stockholders.

preemptive right   *investing* The right of a shareholder, granted by the corporation, to purchase any additional shares of common stock necessary to maintain a proportionate interest in the corporation.

preference share   Share of a company which by the articles of incorporation confer on the holder a preference over other classes of shareholders in regard to payment of dividends, repayment of capital, or both. (*See* preferred stock)

preference stock   Security ranking after a preferred stock issuance of a company.

preferential creditor   One who owns debt instruments of a company which give that person preference over unsecured creditors. Usually, the preference will be in the form of a debenture on the assets of the debtor.

preferred dividend coverage   The degree to which a corporation's income is sufficient to cover dividends on preferred stock. Can be calculated by dividing net income after taxes and interest by preferred dividends payable.

preferred risk   Insurance applicant possessing lower-than-average loss expectancy.

preferred stock   *securities* Equity security that ranks above common stock in the payment of dividends and claims on the assets of a corporation. Preferred stock combines features of common stock and corporate bonds. Such stock usually has a par value and no voting rights. The claim that preferred stockholders have against the assets of the corporation follows the claim of bondholders but precedes that of common stockholders. Dividend rates on preferred stock are usually fixed, and, if the stock is cumulative, dividends in arrears must be paid before dividends on common stocks. Preferred stock usually does not have maturity dates, but it may be subject to call. It may also have a sinking fund which will retire a given number of the stocks each year.

preferred stock, participating   *See* participating preferred stock.

preliminary prospectus   The first document released by the underwriter to prospective investors on a new issue of securities. Because portions of the front cover of this prospectus are printed in red ink, it is sometimes called a red herring.

premature distribution   Distribution made from a regular or spousal individual retirement account or individual retirement annuity to the individual for whom the plan is maintained before the amount of the distribution which is includable in gross income in the tax year. Generally carries a penalty for early withdrawal. (*See* Appendix G)

premeditation   *law* Plan, deliberation, or decision made in advance; a plot, plan, or thought conceived beforehand.

premises   1. All the statements of the deed preceding the habendum including the date of the instrument, the names of the parties, the preliminary statements, the consideration, and the grant, release, or other operative portions. 2. The ground immediately surrounding a house which may include the house itself, a building, a room, or a place. (*See* habendum)

premium   1. The amount above list price or face value. This can be the amount a bond sells for above its face value, the amount a preferred stock sells for above its par value, or the amount by which a new security issue exceeds its offering price shortly after issuance. 2. The price at which option contracts are bought and sold; the money that the writer (seller) of the stock option received from the holder (buyer). 3. Consideration; a reward for an act done; a bounty or bonus. 4. Bonus item given free with the purchase of another product. 5. Annual or periodic payment made by an insured to the insurer in consideration of the insurer's issuing the policy of insurance or renewing the same.

premium over bond sale The upward difference between a convertible bond's market value and the price at which a straight bond would sell for in the same market.

premium over conversion value The amount by which the market price of a convertible bond or preferred stock exceeds the price at which it is convertible.

premium raid A surprise attempt to acquire a position in a firm's stock by offering stockholders a premium over market price for the stock.

prenuptial agreement *See* antenuptial settlement.

prepaid expense Expense which can be paid in advance and deducted in the year it is paid. Item which is an asset when it is purchased but becomes an expense as it is used. (E.g., cattle feed could be purchased in December, taken as a deduction off that year's income tax, and then used the next year.) (*See* Appendix G)

prepaid fee Expense incurred which relates to assets having a useful life of more than one year; often these are expenses related to a construction project. Financing fees and loan standby fees are so categorized.

prepaid interest Interest paid in advance of the time it is earned.

prepaid legal insurance Plan providing group members with coverage for legal fees up to a specified amount. Five types of legal work are usually covered: civil, criminal, clerical, counseling, and preventive law. Although this type of insurance was first introduced about 1900, it has begun to gain popularity only recently.

prepayment clause Clause in a mortgage that gives a mortgagor (borrower) the privilege of paying the mortgage indebtedness before it becomes due. Sometimes there is a penalty for prepayment, with a waiver of the interest that is not yet due.

prepayment penalty Fee paid by a borrower for the privilege of retiring a loan early.

preponderance *civil law* Greater weight, credit, and value of the aggregate evidence on either side.

prepurchase activity *marketing* The period of time in which a consumer becomes aware of a good or a service which the consumer believes will satisfy a need. During this time, the consumer is sensitive to sales or other promotions which will better enable the consumer to acquire the good or service.

prerogative *law* Exceptional powers, advantages, and privileges which the law gives the government; that special preeminence which the government has over and above all other persons in rights and dignity.

presale The sale of proposed properties, such as condominiums, before construction begins.

prescription 1. Method of acquiring an interest in land or a right with respect to land by using and enjoying it for a period set by statute. 2. Acquiring rights through adverse possession.

preselection Procedure followed in selecting new applicants for insurance.

present 1. To tender or offer. (E.g., a bill of exchange is said to be presented for acceptance when it is tendered or exhibited to the drawee with an express or implied demand for acceptance or payment.) 2. A gift; gratuity. 3. Now existing; at hand; relating to the present time.

presentation Step in the sales process when the salesperson gives the sales message to the prospective customer. The presentation covers the product's major features and how they relate to the customer's needs.

present interest Situation in which the holder has an immediate right to use or enjoy the property.

presentment *law* A requirement in the law of negotiable instruments that, in order to bind endorsers on their liability, the instruments must be presented to the maker or other party primarily liable for payment as specified on the document. A failure to do this promptly discharges the liability of the endorsers for the default of the drawer or acceptor.

present sum Specific amount of money existing in the present which may be used as a base to determine future value.

present value Present worth of a sum to be received in the future when discounted for a given number of periods and at a given interest rate. (*See* discounted cash flow)

present value equation Method used to find the present value of a future sum. (*See* Appendix C)

present value of an annuity Value of the annuity in the future discounted by the number of periods between that future time and the present. The present value of an annuity will depend upon whether it is an ordinary annuity or an annuity due. In the first year of an ordinary annuity, the value is less than unity, due to the fact that the compounding does not begin until the end of the first period when the first payment is made. After that, the value will increase, compounded by whatever rate of interest you are working with. In an annuity due, the value is the present sum, because no interest has yet been paid. Thus, it will equal 100% of the first annuity payment. Subsequently, the values will always be greater than 100% because they represent multiple payments at a specified rate of interest.

present value of an annuity factor For any period n, the sum of the present factors for periods 1 through n.

present value of a serial payment Value of a serial payment, such as an annuity payment, which will begin at some future time, but is presently discounted by the number of periods until the first payment. In the first year of an ordinary annuity, the serial payment will be less than unity, and subsequent payments will be more than unity. In an annuity due, the value will be unity first year (i.e.,the present sum is equal to the present sum) and greater than unity in subsequent payments.

present value of interest factor Today's value of an interest payment which will not be paid until some future time. This value is always less than unity because the interest rate must be discounted by the number of periods separating the future period from the present. The present value of interest factor is the reciprocal of the future value, with the same interest rate, and the same number of time periods. (*See* reciprocal, future value)

present value table Table using the present value factor to show present values at different time periods and at different rates of interest.

president *banking* Top officer in a bank who is usually also the chief executive officer and who answers only to the board of directors. Three chief functions for which this person is accountable are: (a) providing leadership and general direction to the bank, in order that profitability may be reasonably assured, both in the short- and long-term; (b) employee development, and maintaining the morale of the employees; and (c) maintaining a posture for the bank as being a good citizen of the community. While many of the functions under these three broad categories may be carried out by subordinate personnel, the responsibility rests upon the president to see that they are done.

presidential election cycle theory A hypothesis of investment advisors that major market moves can be anticipated after the election of a new president. It assumes that the market will be bearish for the first two years of the president's term because of the hard decisions the president may have to make relative to new taxes, the budget deficit, etc. Then, during the last two years, the view is that the market will be bullish due to efforts of the president to get the economy moving prior to another election.

prestige advertising A methodology of promoting the image of either a company or a product, which makes it appear that the company or the product, or both, are superior in nature, and thus should appeal to superior people.

prestige pricing Premium pricing, or charging a high price for a good or a service, which is assumed to make potential buyers believe they are getting a superior product. This ploy most often succeeds in times of affluence, when many people practice conspicuous consumption. (Cf. conspicuous consumption)

presumed negligence Doctrine which, in the absence of the proof of negligence, assumes the allegedly responsible party could have intervened at some point in the sequence of events to prevent the occurrence if the injured party lacked such ability.

presumption *law* Conclusion, either of fact or of law. (*See* presumption of fact, presumption of law)

presumption of advancement *estate law* Rebuttable presumption, except where excluded by law, that a parent who during the parent's lifetime makes a substantial gift to a child intends that such gift shall be an advancement (i.e., that such gift shall represent the whole or the portion of the parent's estate which the child will be entitled to inherit upon the parent's death intestate).

presumption of continuance of life *law* Inference that a person alive and in good health at a certain time was alive a short time after.

presumption of death *common law* Legal conclusion that a person is dead if it is proved that for a period of seven years no information concerning this person has been received by those who would naturally hear from the person if alive and that such inquiries and searches naturally suggested by the circumstances have been made.

presumption of fact *law* Conclusion which a court is at liberty, but not compelled, to draw from the facts proven before it.

presumption of innocence *law* Fundamental doctrine of law stating that no person shall, in the absence of substantial proof, be supposed to have done any act which amounts to a violation of the criminal law, which would subject the person to any type of punishment, or would involve any penalty or forfeiture. (I.e., a person is innocent until proven guilty.) This is so, even where the act charged is only one of omission, and whether the guilt of the party comes in question directly or in a secondary manner.

presumption of law *law* Inference drawn from a particular fact or evidence, unless or until the truth of such inference is disproved.

presumption of survivorship *common law* Doctrine that when two or more persons, especially two relatives, perish in the same calamity, no presumption of survivorship is recognized; in the total absence of all evidence regarding the particular circumstances of the calamity, the matter will be treated as if both persons had perished at the same moment, and because of this, neither of the parties will be held to have transmitted any rights to the other.

presumptive heir One who, if the ancestor had died immediately, would have been the ancestor's heir, but whose right of inheritance might be defeated by the uncertain event of some nearer heir being born.

pretensed right or title *law* A claim where one is in possession of land and another, who is out of possession, claims and sues for same. At common law, the sale of any pretensed right or title was void unless the vendor was actually receiving the profits or had been in possession of the land or of the reversion or remainder.

pretermit *law* To omit; to leave out; to pass by.

pretermitted heir Child or a descendant who would normally have received a share in the parent's estate had the parent died intestate, but in respect of whom the parent's will makes no provision. The rights of such an heir are governed by statutes.

prevent To hinder, frustrate, prohibit, preclude, obstruct, or intercept.

price 1. Consideration given in exchange or sale of anything. 2. Rate of exchange estimated by dollars or any other medium.

price-consumption curve *economics* Indifference curve plotting quantities of commodity "A" on one axis, and quantities of commodity "B" on the other axis; reveals all the combinations of the two commodities which will yield equal satisfaction to the individual.

price/earnings (P/E) ratio 1. The relationship between the current market price of a stock and its annual earnings per share found by dividing the market price of the stock by the annual per share earnings of the corporation. (E.g., a stock selling at thirty dollars per share and earning three dollars per share has a P/E ratio of ten.) This ratio is a conventional and highly regarded measure of stock value because it gives an indication of stock prices measured against the earning power of the company. A high P/E ratio often exists in a growth company.

2. Amount investors are willing to pay for one dollar of a firm's current earnings calculated by dividing the price per share by earnings per share over the most recent twelve months.

price elasticity of demand and supply *economics* The measurement of a small relative price change as being accompanied by a proportionately smaller, equal, or larger change in quantity demanded. The result would be an elasticity less than unity, equal to unity, or greater than unity respectively. Sometimes used synonymously with sensitivity to price change.

price fixing *economics* 1. An action by a central government, usually during a time of war or other crisis, to fix the prices of some goods to inhibit demand. 2. Sometimes industries, or companies, will conspire to fix prices and avoid competition. This is an illegal act for which both the companies and top management people can be held liable.

price leadership *marketing* A situation in which one company, which is a leader in that industry, can set prices and expect that other companies in the industry will follow. Price leadership does not connote price fixing or collusion.

price limit Price range within which a consumer's perception product quality varies directly with the price. A price below the lower limit is regarded as too cheap, while one above the higher limit is too expensive.

price plateau A price level, or strata, which is acceptable to consumers with regard to specific products with specific quality levels. If prices do not remain within this acceptable range, consumers may seek a substitute for the product.

price rigidity *economics* The tendency of the prices of certain goods not to respond to changes in the cost of producing the goods or in conditions determining the demand for such goods. When this rigidity of price is intentional it is known as an administered price.

price sensitive Describes a good or service which is especially vulnerable to price changes, particularly if there is an increase in price. A price increase will usually result in a percentage drop in demand greater than the percentage change in price,

denoting that the product or service is subject to demand elasticity.

price-volume system A system, actually composed of a number of different systems, which attempts to predict a stock's performance by how the price is acting now, and in what volume shares are currently being traded.

pricey 1. Unrealistically low, in reference to a bid price. 2. Unrealistically high, in reference to an offer price.

pricing objectives Goals a company seeks to reach through implementation of its pricing strategy. Pricing objectives can be related to volume, social and ethical considerations, status quo, and prestige.

prima facie *At first sight;* on the first appearance; on the face of it.

primary boycott Refusal to purchase or handle the products of a firm which is undergoing a labor conflict. (Cf. boycott, secondary boycott)

primary capital Equity plus long-term debt; viewed as the most important measure of the sufficiency of capital. Term used by the Federal Reserve, the FDIC, and the comptroller of the currency.

primary data Data collected for the first time during a marketing research study.

primary evidence *law* That kind of evidence which, under every possible circumstance, affords the greatest certainty of the fact in question. A deed of land is a conspicuous instance of a document which, if possible, must be produced as being the primary and best evidence of its existence and its contents. It is at the same time the direct and most convincing proof of its own being and the most satisfactory evidence of its contents.

primary market *securities* Situation in which a new issue of securities is sold to investment banks, investors, etc.

primary mortgage market An unorganized market in which new mortgages are bought and sold. (Cf. secondary mortgage market)

prime rate Lowest commercial interest rate charged by banks on short-term loans to their most creditworthy customers.

prime tenant *real estate* Chief occupant in a shopping center. Tenant who may occupy the most space, have a reputation that draws other tenants, or attracts traffic which may affect the surrounding tenants. Also known as an anchor tenant.

primogeniture 1. The state of being the firstborn child among several children of the same parents. 2. The right of the eldest son to inherit the property or title of a parent to the exclusion of all other children.

primogenitus A first born; eldest son.

principal 1. Trade in which the broker acts as if in his or her own behalf rather than as an agent. 2. Property or capital, as distinguished from interest or income. 3. *insurance* Applicant for insurance, or the insured, to whom the agent is ostensibly responsible.

principal beneficiary The grantee who receives the principal of an estate.

principal broker *real estate* Broker who owns or manages the real estate company. Although there may be other brokers in the firm, as well as salespersons, all answer to the principal broker.

principal meridian A prime meridian used in the government rectangular survey method of land description to locate range lines.

principal residence Place one lives most of the time.

principle of materiality A rule in accounting which states that the strict adherence to any accounting principle is not required if the cost to adhere is proportionately great or the lack of adherence will not materially affect the business's financial position. If the cost of holding to an accounting rule in specific matters is greater than the benefit it would produce, there is no need to follow such rule, if the financial position of the company is not materially changed.

prior That which precedes; the former; earlier.

priority 1. Precedence; going before. 2. Legal precedence; having preferred status. Generally, upon foreclosure, lenders are repaid according to priority.

prior redemption privilege A special privilege sometimes extended to callable bond holders allowing them to redeem their holdings before the call date or the maturity date.

private annuity Annuity issued by someone not in the annuity business that can be acquired in exchange for a transfer of property. The party making a promise to pay the annuity (the obligor) is usually a member of the annuitant's family, typically a junior member, but can be someone outside the family.

private banker *See* personal banker.

private company Company, often a research organization, created for private activities as distinguished from purely public purposes, its character being determined by the terms of its charter and the general law under which it is organized.

private enterprise *See* capitalism.

private mortgage *insurance* Default insurance on conventional loans provided by private insurance companies.

private non-operating foundation Foundation which does not distribute money or operate in the public sector. Frequently it is an educational or scientific charity which receives funds and carries on its own programs of research. In the Master Tax Guide it is defined negatively; private foundation includes all Code Sec. 501(c)(3) organizations other than those in four distinct categories: maximum (50%) charitable deduction donees; broadly (publicly) supported organizations receiving more than one-third of their annual support from members and the public and less than one-third from investment income and unrelated business income; supporting organizations; and public safety organizations.

private nuisance *law; real estate* Unlawful interference with a person's use or enjoyment of land, or of some right over, or in connection with, same.

private placement Nonpublic sale of securities to a financial institution. For a deal to qualify as a private placement, there are several requirements to meet. A private offering may be made only to a limited number of sophisticated investors who meet certain financial suitability standards. A private placement does not go through a brokerage house, nor is it registered with the Securities and Exchange Commission. However, all SEC regulations which apply to public placements also apply to private placements.

privilege 1. Freedom for a person to act in a given manner. An individual will not be held liable for an intentional tort if the conduct is privileged. 2. An exceptional or extraordinary advantage or right; an exemption from some duty, burden, liability, or attendance to which certain persons are entitled.

privilegium est beneficium personale, et extinguitur cum persona *A privilege is a personal benefit and dies with the person.*

privity *law* 1. A mutual or successive relationship to the same property rights. An heir is in privity with his or her ancestor. 2. Participation in interest or knowledge; the sharing of some knowledge or concern. (*See* privity of blood, privity of contract, privity of estate, privity in representation, privity in tenure)

privity of blood Privity which exists between an heir and his or her ancestor and between coparceners.

privity of contract 1. Principle which historically prevented direct action by a consumer against a manufacturer of a defective product; allowed only a party to the contract to bring action for its breach. This has changed over time to the point where consumers, in most states, can sue the manufacturer of a defective product for breach of implied warranty. 2. Privity which exists between the immediate parties to a contract.

privity of estate Privity which exists between a lessor and lessee, between a tenant for life and remainderman, between joint tenants, etc.

privity in representation Privity which exists between a testator and the executor.

privity in tenure Privity which exists between a lord and a tenant.

pro *For;* in respect of; on account of; in behalf of.

probable error *statistics* The range (plus and minus from the mean of the measure) within which there is one chance in two that the particular statistical measure (such as the arithmetic mean) of a sample will fall when drawn from such a universe. The probable error is 0.6745 times the standard deviation of the particular distribution involved if it is normal.

probability theory A statistical technique for establishing the likelihood of certain events taking place. This is a valuable tool in the field of insurance.

probate *law* 1. Court procedure by which a will is proved and legally established, generally including all matters and proceedings pertaining to administration of estates. 2. Related to proof. The judicial process whereby a will is adjudged valid and ordered to be recorded.

probate estate Property that is handled and distributed by a personal representative (executor if there is a will, or administrator if there is not) upon a person's death. The property that can be disposed of by will, including property owned outright in one's own name; interest in property held as a tenant in common with others; and life insurance (or other death proceeds) payable to one's estate at death.

procedure *law* Method by which the successive steps in litigation are taken. That which regulates the formal steps in an action or other judicial proceeding. The law of procedure is also called adjective law, as opposed to substantive law.

proceeds 1. Sum, amount, or value of land, investment, or goods sold and converted into money. 2. Whatever is derived from or obtained as a result of the sale of property.

process costing system A costing system used in those manufacturing situations where a single, homogeneous product (such as cement or flour) is produced for long periods of time.

process of creative destruction Expression coined by the economist Joseph Schumpeter (1883–1950) to describe the growth of a capitalistic economy as a process of replacing the old with the new (i.e., replacing old methods of production, old sources of supply, and old skills and resources with new ones).

proctor Manager of another person's affairs. A procurator, proxy, or attorney.

procuracy Writing or instrument which authorizes a procurator to act.

procurare To manage another person's affairs; to superintend.

procuration Agency; proxy; the administration of business of another.

procurator Agent or attorney; servant; one who has a charge committed to him or her by any person.

prodigal *civil law* Person who, for reasons of extravagant habits, is adjudged to be incapable of managing personal affairs and for whom a guardian (often temporary) is therefore appointed.

prodition   Treason; an act contrary to the interests of one's own country, usually on behalf of another country, such as an enemy in time of war.

proditor   Traitor. (*See* prodition)

produce   1. To create something of exchange value; to bring about the accrual of, as income. 2. Foodstuff produced or grown from or on the soil or found in the soil.

producer   *insurance* Agent or salesperson for an insurance company who produces business for the company.

product   Something produced by physical labor, by intellectual effort, naturally, or as a result of natural process as by generation or growth.

product differentiation   *marketing* The process of attempting to make similar products dissimilar, with one appearing to have a value above the other. This may be done through advertising, through giving better after-the-sale service, or by the personality of the seller.

product homogeneity   A situation in which products are actually similar and without specific distinction, one over the other, or are perceived by the public as being the same.

production   *law* Right of each party to call upon the other to produce for inspection all such documents as may be in the possession of or under the control of such other party that have any meaningful relationship to the matters in dispute in the litigation.

production coefficient   As related to a given factor of production, the quantity of that factor necessary to produce one unit of that product.

production credit association (PCA)   Local farm credit cooperative associations which are chartered by the Farm Credit Administration to make secured, non-real estate loans to members.

production possibilities curve   Curve which depicts all possible combinations of total output for an economy, assuming that there is a choice between producing either one or both of two kinds of goods, full and efficient employment of all resources, a fixed supply of resources, and a given state of technological knowledge.

production revenue contour   An indifference curve with selling costs on one axis and output prices on the other axis, tracing all combinations of selling costs and output prices which will yield the seller a given production revenue.

production unit method of depreciation   Method of determining depreciation per unit, calculated as the difference between the initial cost of the capital asset and the salvage value, divided by the number of product units produced by the asset.

productivity   1. Amount of physical output for each unit of productive input. 2. *economics* Measure of the value of goods and services which are produced with one man-hour's work.

product life cycle   Path of a product through four stages—introduction, growth, maturity, and decline—before its death.

product mix   The range of products produced by a company. Companies seek to find a product mix which maximizes profitability.

produit net   The net product of extracting industries such as mining.

profession   1. Vocation or occupation requiring certain degrees of training and/or education which holds itself forth to be able to properly conduct certain types of activities. 2. Vocation, calling, occupation, or employment involving labor, skill education, special knowledge, and compensation or profit in which the labor and skill involved is predominantly mental or intellectual rather than physical or manual (e.g., physicians and attorneys).

professional corporation   Incorporated organization composed of professional people. Although there are many considerations relative to setting up a professional corporation, if one is set up, the professional becomes a stockholder employee of the corporation and is able to participate in employee benefit plans along with regular employees. The following benefits normally apply to the stockholder/employee: qualified retirement plans, group term life insurance, medical expense insurance disability income insurance, and five thousand dollar death benefit.

professional liability forms Policies for professional people providing liability protection against malpractice suits. The suit must result either from faulty services or failure to meet the standard of service expected under the circumstances. Liability policies are written on either a claims-made basis or an occurrence basis.

profit Return on investment that accrues to the entrepreneur (risk bearer) after all other factors of production have been paid.

profit and loss statement *See* income statement.

profit a prendre *law* Right to enter on the land of another person to take some profit of the soil, such as minerals, oil, stones, trees, turf, fish or game, for the use of the owner of the right.

profit center 1. Organizational unit within a company that produces revenue and for which a profit can be calculated. 2. Any part of the organization to which revenue and controllable costs can be assigned, such as a department. This can be a department of a company, or a subsidiary, where accounting is done as though the entity existed alone. Thus the entity can produce a profit and loss statement. Some firms prefer to have many profit centers, while others prefer centralized accounting and budgetary control.

profit margin Proportion of each sales dollar that filters down to income; income divided by net sales.

profit maximization Traditional pricing objective in classic economic theory; the assumption that all firms need to maximize their gains or minimize their losses.

profits 1. Earnings; merit; present value of cash inflows divided by present value of cash outflows. 2. A payment made to the entrepreneur (risk bearer) in a business for that person's contribution to the total productive process. 3. That money which remains from revenue received by a business after all business expenses have been paid.

profits and commission form Insurance that protects against loss if the goods being sold are destroyed and cannot be replaced in time to fill orders.

profit squeeze A situation which occurs during a period of inflation because income is overstated due to the inclusion of inventory profits, and depreciation charges are understated because they are based on original cost rather than on replacement costs. This results in higher taxes for the firm, and less retained earnings for the ultimate replacement of buildings and equipment. Thus a profit that appeared healthy on paper actually puts the firm in a profit squeeze.

profit taking An action by short-term securities or commodities traders to take advantage of an uptrend in the market by selling and taking the profits. The action tends to turn the market downward in the short-term.

pro forma *As a matter of form.* 1. Used in relation to certain decisions rendered to facilitate further proceedings. 2. Describes an invoice submitted to the purchaser before goods are delivered.

pro forma statement A statement of financial position which makes assumptions about future events in order to show the position of the company as a result of those events.

progeny Descendants; offspring.

program evaluation and review technique (PERT) Commonly used planning and scheduling technique, which came into prominence in World War II, applied in a variety of industries to minimize project completion time.

programming *insurance* Putting together an integrated plan for the coverage of losses applicable to the insured. In family needs coverage, five issues must be considered: determination of the amount of post-loss resources needed to satisfy each purpose, determination of the amount of resources available, determination of the amount of additional resources required, coordination of the post-loss resources into a plan, and arrangement of safeguards to protect the plan.

program trading *securities* Trading of securities, particularly stocks, by use of a computer. Computers are programmed to buy and sell automatically at predetermined prices and do so almost instantaneously. This practice can induce volatility in the market by trading large blocks of stock quickly.

259

progress payments *construction* Loan payments issued to the builder as a building is completed.

Pro Hac Vice (P.H.V.) *law For this purpose.*

pro indiviso *Undivided.* The interest of coparceners and tenants in common is said to be held pro indiviso.

projection *economics* Estimation of future performances made by economists, corporate planners, credit and security analysts, etc. Although the future is unknown, estimates must be made for purposes of long term planning. Usually the estimates are not "seat of the pants" guesses but have foundations in past performances.

proletariat People who, as described by Karl Marx, own no capital goods and depend entirely upon wages for a living. (Cf. bourgeois)

proletarius *civil law* Person of poor means, one who had no property to be taxed.

promise An expression of an intention to do or refrain from doing some act, made by one person to another. Where such a proposed intent is made by deed, it is called a covenant.

promisee One to whom a promise has been made by another.

promisor One who makes a promise to another person or persons.

promissory estoppel Doctrine stating that a promise which the promisor should reasonably expect to bring about action or forbearance of a definite or substantial nature on the part of the promisee, and which does induce such action or forbearance, is binding if injustice can be avoided only by enforcement of the promise. (*See* estoppel)

promissory note Unconditional written promise to pay by one person to another, or to the person's order or to the bearer, a certain sum of money at a specified time or on demand. Distinct from a bill of exchange in that the maker of a promissory note is primarily liable on the note while the liability of the drawer of the bill of exchange is not primary but secondary, particularly after acceptance.

promoter *corporate law* Person who sets in motion the machinery by which a company is created and brings together investors to contribute capital of the corporation. (*See* entrepreneur)

promotion Function of informing, persuading, and influencing the consumer's purchase decision.

promotional elasticity *economics* A measure of the relative change in the consumption of a good as relative expenditures for advertising and/or selling are increased while price and other factors remain the same.

proof-of-loss statement Verification of loss required by insurers. Under some policies, policyholders are required to furnish a signed and sworn statement within sixty days after the insurer requests it. Proof-of-loss statements usually include the following items: time and cause of loss, the interest of the policyholder and all others in the property and all encumbrances on the property, other insurance that may cover the loss, specifications of any property damage and detailed estimates for repair of the damage, any receipts there may be for extra expenses incurred and records supporting fair rental value losses, and receipts for medical expenses. Proof-of-loss statements vary as to the time limit for submitting the statement and the information required.

propensity to consume, average *See* average propensity to consume.

propensity to invest, average *See* average propensity to invest.

propensity to save, average *See* average propensity to save.

property 1. That which is owned. 2. Dominion or indefinite right of user; control and disposition which one may lawfully exercise over particular things or objects (i.e., things one owns, whether personal or real).

property interests Interests owned by legal right in property, real or personal.

property qualifying for exchange treatment *tax law* Property that qualifies under the stipulation that real property must be exchanged for real property and personal property for personal property. (E.g., while a drill press might be exchanged for a pickup truck, the same truck would not qualify as like-kind property if exchanged for a tract of land.) Qualifying property does not include inventory or other property held primarily for sale. In addition, negotiable and non-negotiable securities, stocks, bonds, notes, or other forms of indebtedness or indicia of ownership do not qualify. This latter rule prevents investors from diversifying their holdings without recognizing taxable income when a particular security is involved.

property residual technique Method for estimating the value of property in appraisal, based on estimated future income and the reversionary value of the building and land.

property tax Government levy based on the market value of privately owned property. Sometimes referred to as ad valorem tax or real estate tax.

propinqui et consanguinei Nearest of kin to a deceased person.

proportional representation In corporations, a method of voting for members of the board of directors of a firm which gives small shareholders greater influence than does the normal "one share, one vote" process. Normally, the number of shares owned is multiplied by the number of seats to be filled in the election, and all the cumulative votes can be cast for one new director.

proposal Offer by one person to another, often either to buy or to sell something.

Proposition 13 revolts Citizens' revolts which occur because they feel taxes are too high. The name derives from a revolt in California under the leadership of Howard Jarvis that succeeded in getting taxes lowered through a legislative measure called Proposition 13.

propound To produce as authentic. To offer, to propose. (E.g., an executor is said to propound a will or other testamentary instrument when he institutes an action for obtaining probate.)

propria persona *law His own person.* The force of this in law is that a person may conduct his own suit and need not be represented by an attorney.

proprietary 1. Belonging or pertaining to ownership; relating to a certain owner or proprietor. (*See* proprietary rights) 2. A person having the exclusive title or legal right to something; an owner.

proprietary rights Those rights which an owner of property has by virtue of ownership of the property.

proprietas *Ownership, property*. (*See* proprietas nuda, proprietas plena)

proprietas nuda A mere ownership without usufruct or possession.

proprietas plena Full property combining within itself the ownership and possession of the thing.

proprietorship certificate A writing filed with a bank as evidence of the private, individual ownership of a business.

pro rata *In proportion;* proportionately; according to a given proportion, rate, or percentage.

pro rate To divide, distribute, or assess proportionately.

pro se *For himself;* in person.

Prospector Fund A no-load mutual fund that invests only in North American mines.

prospectus 1. Printed descriptive statement about a business or investment that is for sale, to invite the interest of prospective investors. 2. Any offer or confirmation, made in writing or through the medium of television or radio, of the sale of any security of a corporation. Essentially, a document required to be published by a corporation offering its securities to the public containing the nature and objects of the issue of shares or other securities and complying with the requirements of law in that behalf. 3. A statement of the current condition of a company or some other organization, normally used in an attempt to raise additional capital.

prosperity Upper phase of a business cycle in which the economy is operating at or near full employment and a high degree of business and consumer optimism is reflected by a vigorous rate of capital investment and consumption.

protection of property *insurance* Action taken after a loss occurs which according to declarations in the policy can determine liability. When reasonable steps are taken to protect the covered property, the insurer pays for all reasonable expenses plus indemnity for losses incurred up to the limits of the policy.

protective covenant Covenant including a clause binding the signatories to protest some common interest, as a park area shared by adjacent landowners.

protectorate State or region which has transferred the management of its own important international affairs to a stronger state. (The stronger state proposes to watch over and protect the interests of the weaker state.)

pro tempore *For the time being;* temporarily.

protest *law* 1. Solemn declaration of dissent. 2. To object to, especially in a formal statement.

protocol 1. Original record or register. In international law, the first or original draft of an instrument or transaction. 2. The form of ceremony used by heads of state or by diplomats.

provide 1. To afford or yield; to prepare, make ready, or procure beforehand. 2. To set down as a condition; to stipulate. 3. To supply means of subsistence.

provision 1. Clause in a legal document. 2. Stipulation or qualification.

proviso Clause in a legal document or a statute, the effect of which is to revoke or leave out some earlier stipulation.

proviso for re-entry Provision contained in leases empowering the lessor to re-enter the demised premises for breach of the covenants contained in the lease, especially for non-payment of rents.

proximate Immediate; nearest; direct; next in order.

proximate cause Direct, immediate cause to which the injury or loss can be attributed and without which the injury or loss would not have occurred.

proximity Nearness in time, place, causation, influence, etc.

proxy 1. Person who stands in the place of another to complete a business deal or to vote in that person's place and stead. (Widely used practice in corporation stockholder's meetings.) 2. The document giving to another the authority to represent. An authorization given by a stockholder to enable someone to act as the stockholder's representative.

prudent Wise in adapting means to ends; careful in action or in determining any line of conduct; wise in a pragmatic way; judicious; careful; sensible.

prudent-man rule A standard adopted by some states to guide those people who have responsibility for investing the money of others. Such people, including executors of wills, trustees of trusts, etc., are required to act as a prudent man or woman would act to secure for the client the highest possible return with the least possible risk. (*See* Massachusetts Rule)

psychic income Personal gratification or satisfaction which a good or a service gives the owner or receiver.

psychic reward Psychological satisfaction that a worker derives from the job.

psychographics Psychological profiles of different consumer types developed from quantitative research; sometimes referred to as AIO (attitudes, interests, and opinions) statements.

psychological pricing Pricing procedure based on the belief that certain prices or price ranges are more appealing than others to buyers.

psychological theory of business cycles *economics* Theory which holds that business cycles arise from people's responses to political, social, and economics events. These responses become cumulative waves of optimism and pessimism, setting off cycles of economic activity.

psychophysics Study of the relationship between the actual physical stimulus and the corresponding sensation produced in the individual. (*See* Weber's law)

public All the inhabitants of a particular place. The whole body politic; the total number of the citizens of a state, district, or municipality.

public adjuster *insurance* Insurance adjuster who ostensibly represents the insured rather than the insurer.

public charity Organizations including churches, temples, nonprofit colleges, universities and other schools, hospitals and medical research organizations, government units, private operating foundations, private distributing foundations, along with private foundations maintaining a common fund. They also include a broad range of organizations not meeting specific criteria for public charities that have over a four-year period received a substantial amount of public support, normally one third of total support, excluding amounts received from their exempt function or activities.

public domain 1. Status of a work or design after its copyright or patent has expired; the ideas involved are considered to be public and may be used by anyone. 2. Land owned by the government.

public housing Government-owned housing units made available to low-income individuals and families at no cost or for nominal rental rates.

public issue Newly issued securities sold directly to the public. (*See* private placement)

public lands Such government or state lands as are open to public sale or other disposition under general laws and which are not held back or reserved for any governmental or public purpose.

public monopoly A product or service for which the government may choose to be the only producer, ostensibly for the benefit of society.

public offering Solicitation of the general public for the sale of investment units.

public policy Course of action covering all principles under which the freedom of contract or private dealings is restricted by law for the good of the community. The principle which declares that no one can lawfully do that which has a tendency to be harmful to public welfare.

public record Land transaction records kept at the county courthouse.

public sale Auction sale of property with notice to the general public.

public utility Business or service which is engaged in regularly supplying the public with some commodity or service of public consequence, such as electricity, gas, water, transportation, telephone, or telegraph service. (*See* legal monopoly)

public works Government-sponsored construction, defense, or development projects which usually entail public investment expenditures that would not ordinarily be undertaken by the private sector of the economy.

Public Works Administration (PWA) A program started by the National Industrial Recovery Act which administered billions of dollars appropriated during the 1930s for public works.

publisher One who is in the business of producing and selling books, pamphlets, magazines, newspapers, etc. One who publishes or causes to be published any matter, usually printed.

puer Child between the age of seven and fourteen.

pueritia Childhood; the age from seven to fourteen years.

puffing 1. Exaggerated claim of excellence made by a seller of goods or services (i.e., making something sound or appear superior or better than it really is). 2. Overstating the qualities of a property.

puisne Later born; junior; inferior; lower in rank. The title by which the justices of the courts are distinguished from the chief justice thereof.

puisne mortgage Mortgage subsequent to the mortgage of a legal estate.

pump priming Attempting to increase incomes during a depression by having government pump money into the economy through spending. It is assumed that the money so expended will have a multiplier effect and generate more new income than the amount of money injected into the economy.

punitive damages 1. Such damages as are allowed in excess of the actual malice or deliberate violence or oppression. 2. Damages awarded to a plaintiff over and above those to which he is entitled because the defendant has violated one of the plaintiff's legal rights. Such damages are awarded because of the special character of the wrong done to the plaintiff (violent, malicious, fraudulent, or similar wrong) or to punish and thereby make an example of the defendant to deter others from acting in the same way.

pur autre vie *For the life of another.* An estate one person grants to another only for the duration of the life of a third person.

purchase 1. The acquisition of property by payment of a price of any kind. 2. To acquire property other than by inheritance or descent or by the mere operation of law. 3. To acquire anything for sale to buy. 4. That which is paid for or bought.

purchase account An account in which purchases made for resale are recorded.

purchase acquisition An accounting method whereby an acquiring company adds the assets of the acquired company to its own, at fair market value, thus treating the acquisition as an investment.

purchase money mortgage Mortgage given, concurrently with a sale of land, by the buyer to the seller on the same land to secure all or part of the purchase price.

purchase order A form used by the purchasing department of a firm to place an order with a supplier. Normally no purchase will be honored without a purchase order, and the invoice for the purchase will show the purchase order number.

purchaser One who buys property. One who acquires property in any manner other than by descent.

purchase requisition A request prepared by some department in the firm and forwarded to the purchasing department to acquire an item(s) for that department.

purchases return and allowance account An account in which a firm records merchandise returned to a supplier for credit or discount allowed by the supplier on merchandise because of its reduced quality.

purchasing power parity theory A hypothesis designed to explain the rate of exchange between currencies which have no commodity backing. A rate of exchange will be established which equates the domestic buying power of each currency.

purchasing power risk 1. Uncertainty that future inflation will erode the purchasing power of assets and income. 2. Uncertainty over the future purchasing power of the income and principal from an investment. This purchasing power depends upon the general price level changes in an economy.

pure assessment mutual insurer Cooperative insurer with few employees levying a small initial premium, subject to additional payment from policyowners to cover losses incurred. This type of insurer is usually localized, perhaps offering coverage to farms in the area.

pure competition Condition prevailing in an industry in which there are a large number of firms producing a standardized product; no single firm can noticeably affect the market price by changing its

output. An industry in which firms can easily enter or leave.

pure economics A theoretical study of economics, including data and principles, under a given set of assumptions.

pure life income option *insurance* Option which allows the policyholder to have the proceeds paid out over the lifetime of the recipient. There are no guarantees as to the return of the insurance proceeds.

pure play A slang expression used in the stock market denoting a firm that is devoted almost entirely to one line of business.

pure risk Risk which can only result in a loss; there is no possibility of a gain.

purpose credit Credit used for the purpose of buying, carrying, or trading in securities.

purpose statement A form filed by a borrower that denotes the purpose of a loan backed by securities. This is done to satisfy Federal Reserve Bank Regulation U.

put Contractual agreement that gives the holder the right to sell, and the writer the obligation to buy, one hundred shares of the underlying security per contract at a stated price within a specific period of time.

putative Supposed; reported; reputed.

put option Option to sell an asset at a specified exercise price on or before a specified maturity date. (*See* call option)

pyramid debt Borrowing funds, one loan at a time in somewhat rapid succession, the last of which may be used to pay off the first. This practice rapidly erodes one's financial position, and is frowned upon by banks.

pyramiding In general, a form of business expansion that makes extensive use of leverage to build a complex corporate structure.

pyramid selling *marketing* A system of selling in which a person, sometimes called an agent, buys products from a company and is then given the right not alone to sell the product but to enlist other people in the plan for a prescribed payment. This method of selling has been open to much abuse and also much criticism. In some countries, the practice is illegal.

Q

qua In the character or capacity of; in virtue of being.

quadrans Fourth part of a whole; a quarter.

quadrant Angular measure of ninety degrees.

quadrantata terrae A quarter of an acre of land.

quadripartite Divided into four parts; an agreement entered into between four parties.

quae in testamento ita sunt scripta ut intelligi non possint, perinde sunt ac si scripta non essent *Words in a will so written that they are ambiguous and have the same effect as if they had not been written at all.*

quaere *A question;* a query; a moot question. A proposition so stated as to be considered open to question.

qualification Quality which makes a person eligible for an office or profession; that which makes any person fit to do a certain act.

qualified acceptance 1. In a bill of exchange, a variation of the terms of the acceptor. The holder can then treat the bill as dishonored. 2. In contracts, a qualified acceptance is really not an acceptance but a counter offer.

qualified disclaimer A disclaimer of a bequest of property from a decedent which may be exempt from estate taxes; established by meeting the requirements of Internal Revenue Code Section 2518.

qualified endorsement An endorsement made on a negotiable instrument that contains wording, such as the phrase such words as "without recourse," designed to limit the endorser's liability (e.g., the signature on the back of a check, or other negotiable instrument, transferring the amount to someone other than the one to whom it is made payable).

qualified estate Estate limited to a person and the person's heirs, with a qualification annexed providing that such estate must determine whenever that qualification is at an end. It is an estate which may continue forever but is liable to be determined without the aid of a conveyance by some act or event circumscribing its continuance or extent.

qualified fixed asset Asset which qualifies for investment tax credits. In general, qualified investments are of three types: tangible, nonreal property for which an ACRS deduction is authorized; tangible real property other than buildings and building components—if the property is used in manufacturing, producing, extracting, or furnishing a good or utility service or if the property constitutes a research or storage facility; and an elevator or escalator. (*See* Appendix G)

qualified heir Person meeting one of five requirements for an estate being considered for special use valuation, according to the Internal Revenue code. May include ancestors, lineal descendants, spouses, cousins, daughters-in-law, sons-in-law, and other members of the immediate family. (*See* special use valuation)

qualified opinion An opinion, used often by an accounting firm or auditing firm, that disclaims any liability for items in the statement which go beyond that usual oversight of the firm. (E.g., an accounting firm may declare that the methods used to arrive at the conclusions in the statement are correct without affirming the correctness of the statement itself.) Methods can be correct, while false numbers may be used to arrive at the bottom line.

qualified pension plan 1. Plan that meets the requirements for certain tax advantages. Some of these advantages are that the employee is not considered to be receiving taxable receipts until funds are finally distributed, death benefits are payable in installments or as gross estate for federal estate tax purposes, and lump-sum distribution to an employee on account of the employee's severance of employment may be taxed on a favorable income tax basis. 2. Plan which meets the necessary Internal Revenue Service requirements for making the contributions by the employer tax deductible.

qualified pension, profit sharing, and stock bonus plans Plans that meet the requirements of Section 401 of the Internal Revenue Code so that employer's contributions are income tax deductible.

qualified report *accounting* A report by a certified public accountant (CPA) in which a part of the report may be verified as being true, but in which there is a disclaimer stating that some parts of the report have not been verified.

qualified stock option A privilege granted to an employee, or several employees, of a corporation which entitles them to purchase at a stated price a limited number of shares of the capital stock of the company, under conditions set out in the Internal Revenue Code. (Often this is used by a corporation to persuade people, particularly in the higher echelons, to come to work for the company.)

qualified stock option plan A plan devised for issuing stock options to key employees of an industry in which the plan qualifies under Internal Revenue Code 422.

qualified terminable interest property (q-tip) Property in which the donor's (or decedent's) spouse is given an absolute income interest for life. (*See* qualified terminable interest property trust)

qualified terminable interest property (q-tip) election Option of an executor of an estate, of a decedent dying after December 31, 1981, to elect to deduct the value of qualified terminable interest property passing to the surviving spouse. The interest of the surviving spouse is not a qualified terminable interest unless the executor irrevocably elects it on the estate tax return. An executor may make a partial election under temporary regulations issued by the Internal Revenue Service. According to those regulations, the partial election must be in the form of a fraction or percentage of the property.

qualified terminable interest property (q-tip) trust Trust which allows assets to be transferred between spouses. The grantor of a q-tip trust directs income from the assets to the spouse for life, but has the power to distribute the assets upon the death of the spouse. Such trusts qualify the grantor for the unlimited marital deduction if the spouse should die first. A q-tip trust is often used to provide for the welfare of a spouse while keeping the assets away from another (such as a future marriage partner) if the grantor dies first.

qualifying annuity Annuity which has been approved by the Internal Revenue Service for inclusion as an investment in Keogh plans, IRAs, and other IRS-approved pension or profit sharing plans.

qualifying distribution Relating to a private foundation, any amount paid out to accomplish a legitimate philanthropic purpose in line with the stated purpose of the foundation, plus the administrative expense related to the gift-making. Also, any asset purchased to expedite the gifting process.

qualifying for the marital deduction Exclusion allowed by a spouse when receiving outright bequests, jointly-owned property, life insurance proceeds when the spouse is the beneficiary, miscellaneous other death benefits, and qualified terminable interest property.

qualifying property *See* qualified terminal interest property.

qualifying utility Utility in which shareholders were able to defer taxes by reinvesting up to $750 in dividends ($1,500 for couples filing joint returns) in the company's stock. This was made obsolete by the 1986 Tax Reform Act. The practice became legal through the enactment of the Economic Recovery Act of 1981, as a means of helping utilities raise capital needs with little involved expense. Electric utilities were generally qualified.

qualitative analysis Evaluation of factors that cannot be precisely measured. (Cf. quantitative analysis)

qualitative forecasting *See* judgmental forecasting.

quality 1. Descriptive of organic composition or substance. 2. The character, nature, and degree of excellence of an article.

quality of a bond Relates to the degree of risk an investor entails in buying the security.

quality rating, bond *See* bond rating.

quantitative analysis A method of analyzing a firm that considers most of the measurable factors, such as the value of assets; historical and projected sales patterns plus profitability. Also, economic activities that impact directly upon the industry are considered, as is the past history of securities performance. Usually a complete analysis will consider both qualitative and quantitative factors.

quantity discount Price reduction granted for large purchases. Such a discount can be either cumulative (based on purchases over a stated period of time) or noncumulative (a one-time reduction in list price).

quantity equation *See* equation of exchange.

quantity theory of money Classical theory which holds that the level of prices in the economy is directly proportional to the quantity of money in circulation, such that a given percentage change in the money supply will cause an equal percentage change in the price level. The theory assumes that the income velocity of circulation of money remains fairly stable, and that it always tends toward full employment. (*See* equation of exchange)

quantum meruit *As much as he deserved.* Where there is no contract price stated for goods or services, and where no gift was intended, the person furnishing the goods or services can recover on a quantum meruit basis, that is, the fair value of the goods or services which are accepted

quarterly Once in a quarter, every quarter of a year.

quarterly report Financial report sent every quarter to a firm's stockholders.

quarter of coverage *social security* Three-month period ending March 31, June 30, September 30, or December 31, during which an employee earned a specified amount in covered employment. For years prior to 1978, an employee receives one quarter of coverage for each quarter in which earnings were fifty dollars or more in covered employment. In addition, each quarter of the year is counted as a quarter of coverage if the employee's total wages (or wages and self-employment income) for any calendar year equal or exceed the maximum Social Security earnings base for that year. This is true even if the employee received no wages in some quarters. For 1985, an employee receives one quarter of coverage up to a maximum of four for each $410 of earnings. (For additional information, Social Security Annual Updates are published by many sources, including the Superintendent of Documents, and are available through Social Security offices.)

quarter-section One-fourth of a section of land laid out according to the government survey, dividing a lot into four equal parts with each containing 160 acres.

quasi As if; sharing the qualities of; appearing as if; simulating in appearance. Often used in combination with other terms to suggest a lack of reality.

quasi contract *law* Contract imposed by law upon parties independent of their intention, in situations in which there is no contract between the parties, either express or implied in fact. An action for money had and received and an action based on quantum meruit are examples of actions founded on quasi contracts.

quasi corporation Body which exercises certain functions of a corporation but which is not deemed to be created a corporation by any act, general or special, of the legislative authority.

quasi-judicial *law* Describes function that is akin to those of a judge. This is frequently applied to the functions of administrative tribunals when such tribunals have to determine any substantive rights of private individuals.

quasi personalty *personal property* Things which are movable in point of law though fixed to things real either actually or fictitiously.

quasi-public corporation A corporation, the stock of which is owned by private persons and corporations, but which is run by public appointees, such as the Federal Reserve System.

quasi realty Things that are fixed in contemplation of law to realty but movable in themselves, such as title deeds, court rolls, etc.

quia *Because;* whereas; inasmuch as.

quick ratio Acid test. Cash, marketable securities, and accounts receivable divided by current liabilities.

quicquid plantatur solo, solo cedit *Whatever is affixed to the soil, belongs to the soil.*

quid pro quo *Something for something.* Mutual consideration, one thing given for another.

quiet enjoyment 1. The right of an owner or any other person legally entitled to possession to the use of property without interference. 2. Covenant contained in a lease or a grant whereby the person leasing or granting assures the lessee or grantee that the latter can peaceably and quietly enter upon, have, hold, occupy, possess, and enjoy the lands and premises conveyed and its appurtenances without any let, suit, trouble, denial, eviction, interruption, claim, or demand whatsoever of, from, or by a grantor or lessor or that person's heirs, successors, or any person claiming or to claim by, from, under, or in trust for him or her, them, or any of them.

quiet period The period during which an issuer of new securities is in registration and subject to an SEC embargo on promotional publicity. It usually dates from the preunderwriting decision to forty to ninety days after the effective date.

quiet title action *See* action to quiet title.

quit claim 1. Deed that conveys or releases the interest or title of the grantor in and to the property described in the deed as opposed to conveying the property itself. It purports to convey only such title or interest as the grantor has. 2. Deed that conveys only the grantor's rights or interest in real estate, without stating the nature of the rights and with no warranties of ownership.

quittance An acquittance, a release.

quo animo *With what intention.*

quod constat clare non debet verificari *That which is early apparent need not be proved.*

quod hoc *As to this;* with respect to this; as to such matters as were specified.

quod solo inaedificatur solo cedit *That which is built on the soil is an accessory of the soil.*

quorum Minimum number of persons required to be present in order for any assembly, such as a committee, board of directors, shareholders, or other body of persons, to legally transact business.

quota *foreign trade* The amount of a specific product a country is allowed to buy from another country. The monetary limit assigned to each member country of the International Monetary Fund for it use of the fund's reserves. This limit also prescribes the voting power and the subscription to the fund of that member country. (*See* International Monetary Fund)

quota buying A plan similar to buying to minimum inventory, which requires less supervision. In it, the best order size is determined and this is divided into annual sales to get the number of times per year for reordering.

quo warranto *By what authority.* A species of prerogative writ. A suit to test the authority of a person in office or of a corporation's franchise or charter.

R

racket Easy or lucrative means of livelihood, generally denoting something illegal or fraudulent.

rack jobber Wholesaler who markets specialized lines of merchandise to retail stores and provides the service of merchandising and arrangement, pricing, maintenance, and stocking of display racks.

rack-rent Rent of the full value of the tenement. Rent raised to the utmost

radar alert The action of close monitoring of sales activities in a firm's stock for the purpose of determining when some

unusual buying activity might presage a take-over attempt.

radius clause A clause sometimes found in an employment contract in which the employee agrees not to go to work for a competing company after termination with the present company, usually circumscribed by a set number of miles.

raffle Lottery in which several persons pay, in shares, a value of the item as a stake and then determine by chance which one of them shall become the sole possessor of it.

raider An individual or a corporation who buys enough of a company's stock to have a controlling interest and thus possesses the ability to change company management, etc. Because of the wide dispersion of a firm's stock, 5% is often enough ownership to be a controlling interest.

raiding *politics* Practice whereby voters in sympathy with one party vote in another primary in order to distort primary results.

raise 1. Passageway from a lower to a higher level. 2. To erect, build, or construct. 3. To borrow, collect, get together, levy, cause, or procure. 4. To be produced, breed, or propagate.

ranch Farm used for grazing and rearing livestock.

random sample *statistics* A number of units from a population which are chosen in such a manner as to give every unit in the population an equal chance to be chosen. (Cf. population, universe)

random walk 1. *securities* A theory about the movements in a stock market that affirms the futility of trying to judge the future by the past. This theory asserts that the market acts randomly, and therefore cannot be predicted. Technical analysts dispute this and affirm that they can make sound judgments on the basis of systematic analyses. 2. *math* A sequence of numbers produced by random process such as flipping a coin.

range 1. That which may be traversed or ranged over. 2. Large stretch of land usually unenclosed, having no fixed boundary, on which cattle run at large during the entire year.

range lines Lines parallel to a principal meridian, marking off the land into six-mile strips. These strips are called ranges and are numbered east or west of a principal meridian in the government rectangular survey.

range-of-earnings chart Graph relating earnings per share (EPS) to earnings before interest and taxes (EBIT) under alternative financing options.

ratable According to a measure which fixes proportions. (*See* rate)

ratable distribution A method of distributing the assets of an estate according to a percentage. For example, if an estate cannot fund all the legacies fully, then a proportionate share amount will be subtracted from each legacy. Thus, each legatee will receive the same percentage of the estate as if it had been fully funded.

ratable estate Property which in its quality and nature is capable of being appraised or assessed for taxation.

ratchet effect *income analysis* Establishing successive plateaus as income increases with the expectation that it will not slide back. As applied specifically to the consumption function, the concept that a change in the absolute level of income is associated with a change in the marginal propensity to consume. Derived from the analogy of an automobile jack.

rate Tax or a sum of money assessed in respect of the enjoyment or occupation of real property in proportion to its value. A form of municipal taxation levied on property owners within the limits of that municipality.

rate base Public utility companies' total investment, less depreciation, in property that is used and useful to the public in providing utility service during a given period.

ratemaking association Organization of insurers established to maintain cooperative ratemaking, openly if allowed or secretly where such organizations are illegal. A ratemaking organization may be an independent body offering advisory rates to insurers at a contract price or an organization owned by, financed by, and managed by the member insurers.

ratemaking laws Model fire and casualty insurance rating bills developed by the committees of the National Association of Investment Clubs. Filed rates, in states, can be used after a specified time unless specifically disapproved by the commissioner. However, the commissioner retains the power to disapprove rates at any time even though they had been tacitly approved by failure to act during the initial period. Model rating laws are not in force in every state.

rate of return 1. Yield obtainable on an asset. 2. Percentage by which the rate base is multiplied to provide a figure that allows a public utility to collect revenues sufficient to pay operating expenses and attract investment.

rate of return on average investment The rate of return on an asset (usually a fixed asset) which is arrived at by dividing the after-tax profit from the sale of the asset's production by the average investment in the asset.

rate of return on stockholder's equity A measure of the profit the firm earns for its common stockholders. Arrived at by dividing net income by the average stockholder's equity.

rate sensitivity The risk exposure of assets or liabilities to changes in interest rates.

ratification Act of sanctioning or affirming.

rating 1. *insurance* A term for measuring the risk to determine premium rates. 2. *television* A method of measuring how many people are viewing a program at a given time. 3. *finance* Determining credit worthiness of customers and potential customers by using trade references, credit agencies, etc.

rating bureau *insurance* An agency which collects experience on risks in an area from which it establishes rates. The agency may be formed by a group of insurers or be under close control by the states.

rating insurance Relative state of insurable quality.

ratings Rating schedule on stocks and bonds as issued by several influential publishers.

rating scale 1. A range of specific values against which a specific quality is compared. Bonds are rated from AAA to D, according to the financial strength of the company against which they are debt instruments. 2. Scale on which employees are rated against some established norm, such as how many items are to be produced each hour. 3. Scale on which applicants for employment are compared with other applicants based on their tests and general demeanor.

ratio analysis Analysis of financial statements using ratios. (*See* Appendix C, Appendix D)

ration Any method used to restrict the purchases or usage of a good when the quantity demanded exceeds the quantity supplied at a given price. (An economic device widely used in time of war or upheaval.)

rationing of exchange Government control of foreign exchange through the forced surrender of exchange by exporters for domestic currency, at the government rate. The foreign exchange is then allocated to importers according to a government schedule.

ratio writer An options writer who sells more call contracts than the writer has in underlying shares.

raw land Acreage with no added improvements such as landscaping, drainage, streets, utilities, and structures.

re *See* in re.

reachback The ability of a limited partnership, or other tax shelter, to reach back at the end of the year and offer deductions for the entire year, though the investment might have been for only part of the year.

reaction curve or function *economics* In the theory of duopoly, the reaction curve is the locus of all the points of maximum profit for each firm for each corresponding quantity of a good that its rival may produce.

real 1. Of, pertaining to or consisting of land and tenements; contrasted with things personal. 2. Actual, having an objective independent existence.

real action *real estate* Action brought for the specific recovery of lands, tenements, and hereditaments.

real amount Any quantity which has been adjusted for changes due to inflation in the purchasing power of the currency. (*See* nominal amount)

real certitude Certainty (assurance) due to an estate such as a right-of-way for railroad lines, as distinguished from a personal certitude or one which is due to persons.

real chattel Interest which is annexed to or concerns real estate.

real covenant Covenant that is annexed to the estate as incidental to its ownership and enjoyment, having as its main object some benefit, binding on subsequent grantees.

real effective exchange rate An exchange rate between foreign currencies which takes inflation into consideration and is also weighted according to the volume of trade done with the nations.

real estate 1. Land and tenements, and corporeal as well as certain incorporeal hereditaments, including, by statutes and judicial decisions, oil and gas leases. 2. *law* Land and everything more or less attached to it with ownership extending below to the center of the earth and above to the heavens.

real estate agent Person engaged in the sale or trade of real estate. Within the profession the term may denote a legal relationship the person has with the principal.

real estate broker Special agent engaged to negotiate bargains or contracts for the sale or lease of real estate between other persons for which a commission is paid, usually by the vendor.

Real Estate Commission State agency that enforces real estate license laws.

real estate investment trust (REIT) Real estate mutual fund which offers its shares to investors and invests the funds received in real estate holdings, allowed by income tax laws to avoid the corporate income tax. It must meet certain other requirements, including minimum number of shareholders, widely dispersed ownership, and asset and income tests. A REIT can give the real estate investor many of the investment advantages of corporate ownership, including centralized management, limited liability, continuity of interests, and transferability of ownership. The main advantage of the REIT over a public real estate corporation is the REIT's unique tax advantage. If it distributes 90% of its income to shareholders, it is not taxed on that income, but shareholders must include the income in their personal tax returns. However, a REIT cannot pass along an operating loss, as can a limited partnership syndicate.

Real Estate Settlement Procedures Act (RESPA) A federal law that requires lenders to provide as full information as possible, relating to closing costs, etc., to home mortgage borrowers.

real income Purchasing power of money income or the quantity of goods and service that can be bought with money income.

realize To make real; to have in hand, as a return on investment.

realized *tax law* Received, paid, debited or incurred, in accordance with method of accounting authorized for use by taxpayer.

realized gain In tax-free exchange, a gain that has occurred financially, but is not necessarily taxed.

realized income Earning of income related to a transaction as distinguished from a paper gain.

realized return Return actually taken from the sale of a security, either profit or loss. (*See* unrealized return)

real national income The national income measured in terms of unchanging purchasing power. Normally, national income in current dollars is divided by a price index.

real property Land, tenements and hereditaments, and any interest or estate therein or right or easement affecting the same, including all buildings or other things erected upon or affixed to the land. Also includes permanent fixtures such as heavy machinery firmly fixed and not easily movable; oil and gas leasehold interest, except where such is excluded by statute.

real rate of interest The nominal rate of interest (the currently quoted rate) minus the current rate of inflation. (E.g., if the nominal rate is 10% and the rate of inflation is 3%, the real rate is 7%.)

real right The right of property, jus in re. the person having such right may sue for a subject itself.

realtor *real estate* Licensed broker who belongs to the National Association of Realtors and is allowed to use the association logo on stationery, in advertising, and on business cards.

realtor associate *real estate* Licensed salesperson who belongs to the National Association of Realtors.

real wages The total amount of goods and services which one can buy with one's wages at any point in time.

reappraisal lease Lease in which the rental level is periodically reviewed by independent appraisers. Often, the lessor and lessee will each select an appraiser; if a value is not agreed on, a third appraiser will be chosen.

reasonable That which is fair, just, and proper in the given circumstances of a case; fit and appropriate to the end in view; according to reason, not immoderate or excessive.

reasonable and prudent Using common sense, proceeding cautiously in decision making.

reasonable care *law* Test to determine if the defendant breached the duty of care owed the plaintiff as may be reasonably expected of a person of ordinary prudence under like or similar circumstances.

reasonable cause *law* Under the National Labor Relations Act, in the context of grounds for issuance of temporary injunction, circumstances which would lead a reasonable person to believe that the facts alleged give rise to a violation of the act.

reasonable doubt *law* Degree of doubt that would make a reasonable and prudent person hesitate to accept the truth of a charge. Proof beyond a reasonable doubt must satisfy the judgment and conscience of the jury as to the guilt of the accused.

reasonable grounds Situation in which an officer of the law may make an arrest without a warrant, or make forcible entry into a building for the purpose of arresting the inhabitants or scrutinizing the contents thereof. In such a context, the term has been held to be substantially the equivalent of probable cause, as used in Fourth Amendment to the U.S. Constitution. (State statutes differ as to extenuating circumstances, and a court must often decide the validity of the reasonable grounds claim.)

reasonable notice Such notice or information of a fact as may fairly and properly be expected or required in particular circumstances. The length of time and contents are necessarily governed by the context.

reasonable time Such time as would be necessary under the circumstances to do conveniently what is required to be done. Meaning will vary with the context.

reassessment Process of revising or updating the value estimate of property for ad valorem tax purposes.

rebate 1. Discount, deduction, or refund, as from some stipulated payment, charge, or rate. 2. Refund by the seller of a portion of the purchase price. 3. Allowance by way of discount; a deduction from a gross amount.

rebating *insurance* Act on the part of an insurance agent of refunding to the purchaser of the policy a part of the first policy premium; this is in violation of anti-rebating laws which are designed to maintain fair competition among agents and often to protect career agents from part-time agents.

recapitalization 1. Alteration in a firm's sources of finance, such as the substitution of long-term debt for equity. 2. Change in the financial structure of a corporation made by adding more capital through the sale of additional debt or equity securities.

recapture 1. In the Internal Revenue Service code, realized depreciation, i.e., the amount of a gain on the sale of a depreciable property that represents depreciation charges previously taken for tax purposes. (E.g., if the selling price of an asset is one thousand dollars and the book value is four hundred dollars, the gain on the sale would be six hundred dollars. If the book value reflected accumulated depreciation charges of two hundred dollars, that portion of the gain would be realized depreciation, and would be taxed as ordinary income.) 2. The action of taking back the dollars one may have received in a tax-sheltered arrangement. In short, the individual may ultimately be required to pay back through taxes or in some other manner the deductions already received. 3. *tax law* Process by which income that has been deferred for taxation purposes from a taxation year is deemed to fall into taxable income at a subsequent year by process of law.

recapture clause Clause in a contract permitting the party who grants an interest or right to take it back under certain conditions.

recapture rate Rate of recovery in appraisal of an investment in a wasting asset which is added to the discount rate to derive a capitalization rate in appraisal terminology. May be based on the straight line, sinking fund, or annuity method.

receipt Written acknowledgment that a certain sum of money or goods stated thereon has been received.

receivables *See* accounts receivable.

receivable turnover Speed with which a firm collects its accounts receivable.

receiver Person appointed by a court of competent jurisdiction to collect and receive, pending the action in which the person is so appointed, the rents, issues, and profits of land or the produce of personal estate or other things in question, which it does not seem reasonable to the court that either party to the action should collect or receive or where a party is incompetent to do so, as in the case of an infant. He or she can be appointed only for the purpose of getting in and holding or securing funds or other property which the court after the trial or in the course of the action will have the means of distributing among or making over to the entitled persons. Once appointed, a person becomes an officer of the court and is not a representative of the plaintiff or the defendant. This person is not to be interfered with or dispossessed of the property he or she is directed to receive by anyone, although the order appointing this person may be erroneous.

receiver's certificate 1. Certificate issued under authority of a court enabling the receiver to raise money on the credit of the fund under control of the court. Entitles the holder of such certificate to receive from such fund the amount specified in the certificate if the fund is sufficient to pay all holders and, if not, a prorated share thereof. 2. A debt instrument used by a receiver who uses the proceeds to finance continued operations or otherwise to protect assets which are in receivership.

receiving report *accounting* A report that is designed for the receiving department to record items received. This report is normally sent to the purchasing department to compare with purchase orders on file.

recent possession Principle of evidence that property recently stolen found in a defendant's possession gives rise to the presumption that the defendant is guilty of theft.

recession 1. Period of rising unemployment and declining national output. 2. Moderate downturn in business activity evidenced by increased unemployment and reduced consumption. (Depression is a severe form of recession.) 3. Significant decline in general economic activity extending over a period of time.

reciprocal *securities* One of the quantities which, multiplied together, equal

unity. Used in determining the present value of interest factor.

reciprocal buying *marketing* The act of buying items from vendors who are also customers.

reciprocal deal Agreement between two parties facing each other as both buyer and seller in which one party offers to buy the other party's goods but only if the second party buys other goods from the first party. This serves as an effective way to improve sales and to deny competitors equal access to the market.

reciprocal demand One country's demand for a second country's product measured in terms of the first country's product. John Stuart Mill (England, 1806–1873) developed this theory, which essentially states that it is not the cost of production which establishes the value of products for international trade, but rather the costs of one product which is destined to be exchanged for another product. (Cf. comparative advantage)

reciprocal exchange *insurance* An unincorporated association writing insurance for its own members.

reciprocal insurance exchange Unincorporated cooperative insurers operated by attorneys-in-fact empowered to act on behalf of the subscribers who exchange insurance with each other to reduce the risk.

reciprocal law Law which provides that one state will extend to other states the same privileges it extends to its own citizens, often with respect to insurance or tax laws.

reciprocal trade agreement An executive agreement between countries providing for the exchange of goods at mutually lowered tariffs or other advantageous terms.

reciprocal wills Wills in which each testator names the other as beneficiary, either in a joint will or in separate wills.

reciprocity 1. Mutual agreement to accept as valid (e.g., a state's acceptance of the real estate license one has earned in another state). 2. Mutuality. In international law or conflict of laws, the relationship existing between states when each gives citizens of the other certain favors or privileges that its own citizens enjoy at hands of the other state. 3. Practice of giving favorable consideration to suppliers who are also purchasers of the firm's products.

recision Declaring of a contract as void from the beginning because of fraud or misrepresentation in the inducement to contract.

recital Narrative or introductory statement in a formal legal document introduced for the purpose of explaining or leading up to the operative part of the instrument. Such statements can be used as evidence against the parties to the instrument.

reclaim To claim or demand back. To rescue from a wild or uncultivated state; make fit for cultivation or use. (Often used in relation to strip mining.)

reclaimed animal Animal made tame by one's knowledge, industry, or education whereby a qualified property may be acquired in it.

recognizance Bond of record testifying the recognizor to owe a certain sum of money to another; such an obligation undertaken before some court of record or magistrate duly authorized. The object of a recognizance is to secure the performance of some act by the cognizor.

recognized income *income taxes* All income from whatever source derived, unless specifically excluded.

recommend To command to favorable notice of another; to present one's advice or choice with the idea that another has the final decision.

record date *securities* Date a company closes its stockholders' list for purposes of dividends or proxies.

recording Act of entering in a book of public records instruments affecting the title to real property. Recording in this manner gives notice to the world of facts recorded. (*See* constructive notice)

recourse Ability of a lender to claim money in addition to the property pledged as collateral from a borrower in default.

recovery 1. *economics* Upward phase of a business cycle in which the economy's income, output, and employment are rising, and a growing degree of business and consumer optimism is reflected by an expanding rate of capital investment and consumption. 2. *law* Restoration of a right or property taken from a person. Recovery is effected by formal judgment in a competent court, at the aggrieved or injured person's instance and suit.

recycling The processing of used materials for reuse, providing a new source of raw materials and alleviating a major factor in environmental pollution.

reddendum *Rendering; yielding.* The phrase is a term of conveyance where it is used by a grantor to denote that the grantor is reserving unto himself or herself something of what has been granted, such as the rents from the lands demised.

redeem To regain possession of something by paying a price; to repurchase as from a pawnbroker.

redemption value The per share amount a corporation is willing to pay to redeem preferred stock from stockholders. Normally this is par value plus a premium.

redeployment *management* The re-allocation and retraining of workers as changes in technology and changes in business environment demand mobility between skills.

red futures contract month A month which is just a year and a month away, for which futures contracts are traded. The red month is used to distinguish the contract from the corresponding month in the current year.

red herring *See* preliminary prospectus.

rediscount The resale of a promissory note or bill of exchange by the owner of such a document. Member banks of the Federal Reserve system often sell commercial paper to the Fed. The seller pays the buyer a fee in advance for accepting the paper, which is essentially sold at a discount.

rediscount rate Rate of interest charged to member banks when they borrow from the Federal Reserve system. Also called discount rate.

reditus assisus Set or standing rent.

redlining Illegal practice of refusing to originate mortgage loans in certain neighborhoods on the basis of race or ethnic composition.

reduced form equation *econometrics* The equation resulting from a reduction of the size of a model, namely, by reducing the number of equations in the model or system. These reductions are made by eliminating equations of equilibrium (identities) and equations which fix the value of the exogenous variables.

reduced paid-up insurance option Option permitting the policyholder to elect to take the cash value as paid-up insurance of the same type as the policy but for a reduced face value.

reductio ad absurdum Process of reasoning which if carried forward leads to absurd consequences.

re-entry, proviso for *See* proviso for re-entry.

referee Person appointed by a court to exercise judicial powers, to take testimony, to hear parties, and to report the findings to the appointing court.

Reference Book, The A directory published by the firm of Dun and Bradstreet containing the names and credit ratings of three million commercial and industrial enterprises located in the United States and Canada.

referendum Submission of an important legislative measure to a direct vote of the people. It is a right reserved by the people of a state or political subdivision to have submitted for their approval or rejection any laws passed by the legislature, with certain stated exceptions.

refinance 1. Substitution of an old loan(s) with a new loan(s). 2. To take out a new mortgage for an amount greater than the current unpaid balance. The proceeds from the new mortgage then go to pay off the old mortgage and the owner can keep the surplus. This represents one way to put off the phantom income problem. Although those principal payments that create the phantom income are the owner's money, it is not available unless the property is sold or the mortgage is refinanced.

reflation The process of managing a currency for the purpose of restoring a previously acceptable price level.

reformation *insurance* Method of changing policy terms to meet the original intentions of the insurer and the insured.

reformation of contract Remedy in equity by means of which the written instrument is made or construed so as to express or conform to the real intention of the parties when some error or mistake has been committed. This is usually worked out between parties without court intervention.

refund 1. Repayment; that which is repaid; restitution. 2. To repay, return money in restitution or repayment; to fund again.

refund annuity Annuity in which the insurance company agrees to pay an income for the life of the annuitant in return for which the purchaser of the annuity pays a single premium; if the purchaser dies before the entire principal plus interest has been paid in the form of income, then the unused part of the principal is refunded to a designated beneficiary.

refunding bond One that replaces or pays off outstanding bonds which the holder surrenders in exchange for the new security.

refunding securities Replacement or repayment of outstanding bonds by the issue of new bonds. It is thus a method of prolonging a debt by paying off old obligations with new obligations.

refund life income option *insurance* Option that provides a life income with the additional guarantee that in the event of the recipient's death before receiving the full amount of the original life insurance proceeds, the difference (original proceeds minus amount paid to date) will be paid to a second payee.

regional agent *insurance* Normally, a district agent whose status is somewhere between a local agent and a general agent.

regional check processing center (RCPC) Federal Reserve check processing operation that clears checks drawn on depository institutions located within a specified area. RCPCs expedite collection and settlement of checks within the area on an overnight basis.

register 1. Book kept by a public authority containing a record of facts or transactions as they occur. 2. To record formally and exactly; to enroll.

registered bond 1. A simple certificate of indebtedness in favor of a particular individual, payable at a date named, with interest at days named; said to be registered because the name of the payee is entered on the books of a corporation debtor as the registered owner. 2. A type of bond which is recorded by the issuing company in the names of the purchasers for the purpose of identification and preventing loss or theft.

registered competitive trader *investing* A member of a stock or commodities exchange who trades for his or her own account, or for an account controlled by that member. Because no commissions are involved in their trades, they are able to make a profit in securities with only small movements up or down in the market. This type of trading is hedged about with many regulations which keep the traders from taking advantage of their unique position in the market. Sometimes called floor trader or competitive trader.

registered representative *investments* Broker; a person registered with the Securities and Exchange Commission to buy and sell securities for a client. Commissions are higher than those of the discount broker, because advice is given to the client, and time is taken to build for the client a proper portfolio.

registered stock Stock issue, either new or as a secondary offering, which is registered with the Securities and Exchange Commission.

registered voter One who has been lawfully registered as a qualified voter and has the present right to vote. Normally, requires that one be officially enrolled at the appropriate office in the county (parish) court building.

register of deeds An office, one of which is normally found in every county or parish, where documents affecting the title to land are recorded. Some offices are also designated to record chattel mortgages and other documents affecting security rights in personal property.

register of wills A position existing as an arm of the court in some states, the main duty of which is to receive wills offered for probate and to grant letters testamentary and letters of administration.

registrar 1. Public official whose duty it is to maintain a register, such as a registrar of births, deaths, and marriages; registrar of deed, etc. 2. Trustee of records in a school. 3. Trust company or bank assigned the duty of keeping track of the owners of bonds and the issuing of stock.

registration Process of filing information with the Securities and Exchange Commission concerning a proposed sale of securities to the general public.

registry The listing of a ship under the law of the nation whose flag the ship flies, without regard to the nation of ownership. This is usually done to avoid more stringent laws in the country of ownership.

regress Re-entry; used in the phrase "free entry, egress, and regress."

regression analysis *statistics* A technique used to measure the degree of correlation between the dependent and independent variables, therefore attempting to predict, within reason, the dependent variable.

regressive tax Tax levy that takes a higher proportion of a low income than a high income.

regular Usual, customary, or general; steady or uniform in course, practice, or occurrence and not subjected to unexplained or irrational variations; conforming to prescribed rule, standard or established pattern, law, or principle; recurring without fail; methodical or orderly.

regular route *transportation law* Operation between fixed points according to a predetermined plan involving habitual use of certain fixed routes, specified highways, or highways that are on a fixed schedule.

regulate To fix, establish, or control; to adjust by rule, method, or established mold; to direct by rule or restrictions; to subject to governing principles or law.

regulated commodity Commodity which is under the jurisdiction of the Commodities Futures Trading Commission, which includes all commodities traded in organized contract markets.

regulation Subordinate legislation enacted under statutory authority by a governmental body; a rule or order having force of law issued by executive authority of government.

Regulation A 1. A Securities and Exchange Commission provision for a simplified registration procedure for small issues of securities. 2. A Federal Reserve Board statement of the means and conditions under which Federal Reserve banks make loans to members and to other banks at the discount window.

Regulation B The Federal Reserve regulation that prohibits creditors from discriminatory actions against credit applicants. It sets guidelines for the collecting of credit data on applicants and evaluating that data. When credit is denied, the applicant must be notified in written form.

Regulation D Regulation of the Securities and Exchange Commission that sets forth conditions necessary for a private offering exemption.

Regulation F The Federal Reserve regulation that establishes some control over state chartered banks, requiring that, if they have five hundred or more stockholders and at least $1 million in assets and if their securities are traded on a national exchange, they must register and file financial statements with the Federal Reserve Board of Governors.

Regulation G The Federal Reserve regulation that governs credit secured by margin securities extended or arranged by parties other than banks, brokers, and dealers. Regulations T, U, and X also deal with different facets of the same subject.

Regulation I The Federal Reserve regulation that requires banks joining the system to buy stock in the Federal Reserve System up to 6% of their capital and surplus; 3% is to be paid on joining, and 3% is "on hold" should the Fed ever need it. Ownership of Fed stock would obviously vary according to the changes in the bank's capitalization. Should the 3% on hold ever be needed, it is subject to call by the Board of Governors of the Federal Reserve System.

Regulation L The Federal Reserve regulation that seeks to promote competition among depository institutions by restricting the interlocking relationships that any management official may have with depository organizations.

Regulation 9 A regulation issued by the Comptroller of the Currency which sets standards for national banks in their use of fiduciary powers and collective investment funds. (The full title is "Regulation 9: Fiduciary Powers of National Banks and Collective Investment Funds.")

Regulation O The Federal Reserve regulation that prohibits a bank from making loans to its own executive officers, and further prohibits the making of such loans to executive officers of correspondent banks, on preferential terms.

Regulation Q Federal law that specifies the maximum interest rates that banks and savings and loan associations can pay on various types of deposits.

Regulation T A Federal Reserve regulation that deals with the extension of credit to customers by securities brokers, dealers, and members of the national securities exchanges. It sets up initial margin requirements and specifically defines registered (eligible), unregistered (ineligible), and exempt securities. Many securities dealers follow more strict rules than those laid down by the Fed.

Regulation U The Federal Reserve regulation that governs the extension of credit by banks for purchasing and carrying margin securities.

Regulation W A special Federal Reserve regulation which the Fed has used to control credit during extraordinary economic times, such as a war or the aftermath of a war. It can require minimum down payments, set length of maturities, etc. It was used during and after World War II, and during the Korean War. The authorizing legislation was repealed in 1952, but Regulation W could be reinstated in time of need.

Regulation Z Federal regulation requiring creditors to provide full disclosure of the terms of a loan. Compliance is compulsory for anyone who arranges credit for more than five sales of residential real estate in a year. The interest rate must be stated as an annual percentage rate.

rehabilitate 1. To restore a structure to a condition of good repair; often refers to historical structures. 2. To restore to a former status, capacity, right, rank, or privilege; to reinstate.

rehabilitation Restoration to a former state, capacity, privilege; making a person capable of becoming a useful member of society again. Restoration of an individual to one's greatest potential, whether physically, mentally, socially, or vocationally.

rehabilitation tax credit Tax credits provided in the 1981 Tax Act for the rehabilitation of a building. Congress created three levels of credit based on the age of the building: 15% credit for structures at least thirty years old; 20% for structures at least forty years old; 25% credit for certified historic structures. (*See* Appendix G)

rehypothecation In the stock market, the repledging of a security by a broker to whom the security has been pledged. Realistically, this is not a repledge, since possession is not surrendered, but rather the right to order sale on default is given.

reimburse To pay back that which has been expended; to refund; to place in treasury or private coffer that which has been taken, lost, or expended.

reimbursement form *medical insurance* Method used by an issuer of medical care policies to reimburse the policy holder for medical expenses incurred. According to the policy provisions, the reimbursement may be 100% of expenses or something less. If the charges are more than the policy limits, the insured bears the excess amount.

reinstatement Return to a former status, authority, or station. Restoration to a former state or position.

reinstatement provision *insurance* Provision designed to help a policyholder who has failed to pay a premium within the time allowed, including the grace period, giving the insured the right to reinstate the policy within a specified period, usually three years of any default in premium payment, subject to the furnishing of evidence of insurability.

reinsurance 1. Contract of indemnity to the person or corporation who is in the position of an original insurer, binding the reinsurer to pay to the reinsured the whole loss sustained in respect to the subject of the insurance to the extent to which he or she is reinsured. 2. Insurance procured by an insurer from another person or company against a risk that the insurer has previously assumed.

reinsurance A method of insuring insurance in which a number of different companies share the risks of large scale risks, which might be overly burdensome to one company.

reinvestment rate The rate of interest at which the funds from a maturing investment can be reinvested, or the rate of interest at which interest payments from an investment may be reinvested.

related Standing in some relation; connected; of common ancestry.

relation Person connected by blood or marriage; relative; kinsman.

relative Next-of-kin; a relation. Those connected to the person by blood or by marriage; those descended from a common ancestor, as well as in-laws.

relative income hypothesis The saving ratio of an individual depends not on the level of income but on the relative position of the individual on the income scale. Duesenberry's particular form of this theory expresses the saving ratio as a function of the ratio of current income to the highest level of income previously attained.

relative priority A principal of reorganization under which each group of creditors and stockholders, based on seniority, survives the reorganization, but the losses of each group are inversely proportional to its seniority.

relative strength system A technique used by some investors which entails the holding of stocks that are doing well and the disposing of stocks that are doing poorly. (Cf. buy-and-hold strategy)

relative volatility The comparing of returns and risks for various stocks, usually over the long term.

release 1. To surrender or relinquish some claim, privilege, or right to the person against whom such claim may have been exercised or enforced. 2. Conveyance of one person's right in property to another person who is actually in possession of the property.

relevant Pertinent; applying to the matter in question. In the law of evidence, a fact is said to be relevant if it either directly or indirectly proves or disproves a fact in issue.

reliance Belief or dependence upon certain statements of facts which tends to motivate actions.

reliction The addition to a piece of land by the receding of the waters of a river or sea.

relinquish To abandon, give up, surrender, or renounce, as of some right, interest, or title.

relocation clause Lease stipulation that allows the landlord to move the tenant within the building.

remainder 1. Estate that takes effect after the termination of a prior estate, such as a life estate. 2. That part or residue of an estate which is left after all the other provisions of a will have been satisfied. (Remainders may be vested or contingent.)

remainder beneficiary After the interest of the original donee of a trust has been satisfied, the second beneficiary named in the trust has the right to the principal of the trust.

remainder interest Right to the property itself after a life interest has ended.

remainderman Person who is to receive possession of property after the death of a life tenant.

remedy *law* Legal method for enforcing a right or for redressing, compensating, or preventing a wrong, including money damages, restitution, injunction, and performance.

remittance Monies sent by one person to another in coin, currency, by bill of exchange, check, or otherwise.

remonetization 1. Removal, by an act of legislation, of a type of currency from a country's legal tender list Also called legal remonetization. 2. Returning precious metal, which has been melted down from its coined state, to money use when the price of the precious metal falls below the mint price. Also called factual remonetization.

remoteness Lacking in close connection between a wrong and a damage, as cause and effect so that a party injured is denied any compensation from the wrongdoer.

remuneration Payment of an equivalent for services, loss, or expense. Salary, wages, commission, reward.

remunerative donation Gift, the object of which is to recompense the donee for services rendered to the donor.

rendu price The price of an imported good including all charges for tariffs and freight.

renegotiable rate Type of variable rate involving a renewable short-term balloon note. The interest rate on the loan is generally fixed during the term of the note,

but when the balloon comes due, the lender may refinance it at a higher rate. In order for the loan to be fully amortized, periodic refinancing may be necessary.

renegotiate To legally revise the terms of a contract.

renegotiated rate mortgage (RRM) A type of mortgage which must periodically be renegotiated. While the renewal of the mortgage is guaranteed, the rate of interest may be reset with each periodic renegotiation.

renew 1. To restore, or revive. 2. *insurance* To continue a policy. 3. To execute a new lease, rather than to continue with an existing lease.

renewal option Right, but not obligation, of a tenant to continue a lease at a specified term and rent.

rent 1. Charge for the use of space. 2. Money paid for the possession, use, and enjoyment of another person's property for a period of time and according to the terms of a lease. 3. Something issuing out of land as a compensation for possession during the term. A fixed sum, or property amounting to the fixed sum, to be paid at stated times for the use of property. 4. Payment for the use of property. (*See* economic rent)

rental insurance 1. Insurance available to protect a tenant whose lease requires rent payment even during a period when the property is untenable. 2. Insurance that protects the landlord from the loss of rental income if a lease does not require rent payments for untenable property.

rental-value insurance Rental insurance that protects the owner from loss of use of owner-occupied property.

rente French interest-bearing bond without a maturity date.

rentier 1. A person whose income is mostly derived from previously invested wealth. 2. Person who derives most of his or her income from the rent of land. Somewhat antiquated term.

reopening The act on the part of the Treasury Department of selling more of an already-issued security instead of issuing a new security.

reorganization Act or process of organizing again. In relation to a corporation, some process by which the corporation

279

has organized anew and yet retained some of the features of the old corporation.

reparation Restitution by making complete amends for a wrong or injury done.

replacement cost Cost of replacing lost, destroyed, or damaged property.

replacement cost accounting A type of accounting used by some firms to adjust values placed on assets or liabilities to those which most nearly reflect the value at the time the statement is made up.

replacement cost insurance Insurance providing for loss settlement on the basis of the cost of replacing damaged property without deduction for depreciation. Usually, to collect under replacement cost insurance, the insured must rebuild or replace the damaged property.

replacement cost provision *insurance* Additional conditions in homeowners' policies which permit the insured, if the proper amount of insurance is carried, to recover any loss to the dwelling and private structures on the basis of the full cost to repair or replace the damaged or destroyed property without any deduction for depreciation.

replacement reserve Amount set aside from net operating income to pay for the eventual wearing out of short-lived assets.

replevin 1. Legal action to regain possession of specific personal property alleged to have been unlawfully taken or detained. 2. Redelivery of goods; common law remedy available to a plaintiff who is seeking the recovery of the actual goods wrongfully detained or taken away from the plaintiff.

replication *law* The reply by a plaintiff in a law suit to the defendant's answer to the original charge.

report 1. Formal statement or recital of facts and findings by a judicial officer. 2. An account brought back; a story related; a tale carried. 3. Publication of a periodic nature containing a full account of judicial decisions with a statement of the facts, the decision of the court, and the reasons for such a decision arranged by a court reporter.

reporting forms *insurance* A system in which the insured submits a periodic report stating the values that have been at risk so that the premium collected can vary with the amounts at risk during a given period (usually monthly). The system was developed along with that of multiple-location forms.

repossession Act of resuming possession of property. Where goods or chattels such as automobiles are purchased on conditional sales contract, occurs when the purchaser commits default in payment of installments.

represent To stand in place of another, act that person's part, or speak with authority on behalf of another. To appear in the character of; to impersonate.

representation 1. Statement of fact, incidental or collateral to a contract, made in writing or orally and on the basis of which the contract is acceptable and entered into by proper parties. 2. *insurance* Statements by the applicant to the insurer in the process of obtaining a policy, accepted as being true to the best of knowledge and belief of the applicant but not part of the contract.

representative One person representing another, succeeding to the rights of another, or standing in the place of another.

representative firm *economics* A hypothetical device designed by Alfred Marshall (England, 1842–1924) for use in economic analysis. His definition is, "a firm that has its fair share of those external and internal economies which appertain to the aggregate scale of production in the industry to which it belongs." This would not be an average firm in the statistical sense.

representative money Money, usually in the form of paper money, which is convertible into full-bodied money. (E.g., a silver certificate, not now in circulation, could be exchanged for silver bullion.) (Cf. full-bodied money)

repressed inflation A situation in which there is limited control of prices and wages accompanied by an increase in money demand for goods relative to the supply of goods after the economy is at full employment.

repriceable *banking; investment* Describes an asset or liability on a date when its rate of interest accrual may be changed.

reprisal 1. *international law* Such actions as embargo, seizure, etc., as a means employed by one nation against another to redress a grievance. 2. *common law* The taking of one thing in satisfaction for another.

reprobata pecunia liberat solventum *The refusal of money rendered releases him who tenders it.* However, tender does not release the person tendering from the debt as such, although the person may plead tender in any action brought against him or her in order to avoid the consequences of not having paid.

republic Commonwealth; a form of government that has no monarch, where the administration of the government is carried on by elected representatives.

republication In relation to wills, the re-execution by a testator of a will or codicil.

repudiate To renounce or disavow, as a right, privilege, or duty.

repudiation Denial of an obligation or liability.

repurchase agreement In relation to conditional sales contracts, an endorsement on a contract allowing the conditional vendor to sell the contract to a finance company with the understanding that in the event of default by conditional purchaser, the conditional vendor will repurchase notes of finance company for an amount stated in the face of the note, less any installments paid, unearned insurance premiums, and unearned finance charges.

reputation Name, honor, credit. That which the public says, or feels it knows, about a person.

request To ask for earnestly; to desire for; to solicit, entreat, petition. Under certain conditions, it may impose a legal obligation to comply; in a will the term may amount to a disposition or may impose a duty.

require To demand; to ask as if by right of and by authority; call for as suitable or appropriate in a particular case; to need for some end or purpose; to demand as necessary or essential; to stand in urgent need of.

required rate of return Expected return necessary to induce the investor to purchase an asset.

requisition 1. Authoritative demand in written form, especially for military purposes. 2. In condemnation statutes, equivalent to condemnation or expropriation.

res *Thing; object;* subject matter or object against which proceedings were taken. It includes corporeal as well as incorporeal things, movables and immovables, real and personal, things in possession and choses in action.

rescind 1. To abrogate, annul, avoid, or cancel; to vacate or set aside; terminate. 2. To withdraw an offer or contract. Regulation Z allows a three-day period in which to rescind certain credit transactions. (*See* Regulation Z)

rescission 1. Act of abrogating, cancelling, vacating, or annulling; the undoing of a thing. 2. The cancellation of a contract without penalty.

rescript A duplicate of a document.

res derelicta Property that has been abandoned by its owner.

reservation Clause in a deed, usually a lease, whereby the grantor or lessor reserves a new right or thing out of that which is granted or leased.

reserve Fund set aside by depository institutions to meet reserve requirements. For member banks, reserve requirements are satisfied with holdings of vault cash and/or balances at the Federal Reserve Banks. Depository institutions that are not members of the Federal Reserve System may hold their reserves in the same manner, or they may pass the reserve balances through a correspondent institution to the Federal Reserve Banks.

reserve deficiency *banking* The amount by which the reserves of a bank, held by the Fed, fall short of reserve funds required.

reserve fund 1. Monies made, saved, or set apart, usually as a result of the operation of a commercial venture, from year to year and not paid out in dividends or otherwise to those entitled to share in the profits; the current surplus of assets over liabilities, and part of the profits, set aside to meet unforeseen contingencies, to cover losses and to pay dividends. 2. *real estate* Account maintained in order to provide funds for anticipated expenditures required to maintain a building. A reserve may be required by a lender in the form of an escrow to pay upcoming taxes and insurance costs.

reserve requirement 1. Percentage that banks must hold in reserve against their deposit liabilities. 2. Amount of money that member banks of the Federal Reserve System must hold in cash or on deposit with the Federal Reserve System. Nonmember banks hold reserves with other banks.

res fungibiles Things that can be measured, numbered, weighed, and thus can be replaced by equal quantities and qualities.

residence Place where one actually lives or has a home; the person's dwelling place or place of habitation; an abode.

residential energy credit Credit given for the installation of renewable energy source equipment in a taxpayer's principal residence, equal to 40% the first ten thousand dollars of qualifying expenditures for a maximum four thousand dollars. These credits were available through 1985, with maximum limits applied on a cumulative basis. Credits were subtracted from the tax liability on a one-for-one basis. (*See* Appendix G)

resident manager *real estate* One who lives on the premises of a multi-unit residential housing complex and manages the property.

residual Value or income remaining after deducting an amount necessary to meet fixed obligations.

residual accounts Short-term capital transfers and monetary gold transactions that compensate for the imbalance in a country's basic balance in its international payments.

residual disability benefit Benefit designed to make up income lost when insured is unable to work at full-income capacity. Reimbursement to a partially disabled insured to bring final income up to pre-disability levels. Monthly benefit payment payable is adjusted by the ratio of earnings after resuming work to predisability earnings.

residual fee Fee taken at the end of a deal; the cut taken by the promoter when the tax shelter property is sold and the tax shelter is terminated.

residual income security The type of security which has the last claim on company income, but which usually is the immediate beneficiary of company growth.

residual profit Income less the annual cost of capital employed by the profit center; an alternative to return on investment as a measure of profit center performance.

residual theory of wages A generalized theory that labor is the residual claimant to the product of industry after all capital costs have been paid.

residuary Pertaining to or constituting the residue or remainder; the part of an estate left after distribution of specific legacies.

residuary bequest Testamentary disposition of all personal property in an estate not otherwise disposed of.

residuary clause 1. Clause in a will disposing of that which remains after satisfaction of charges, debts, and particular bequests and which disposes of property not expressly disposed of by other provisions of the will. 2. *trusts* Transfer of the residue of an estate to one named beneficiary or of fractional shares to two or more named beneficiaries. The bequest may be outright or in a trust. The trust or trusts may be those created by the will, or a living trust created during the testator's lifetime may receive the bequest.

residuary devise Disposition of that which is left after payment of debts, expenses of administration, and specific and general bequests; that which is not otherwise disposed of by the will.

residuary legacy General legacy containing the assets of the estate after all other legacies have been satisfied and charges, debts, and costs have been paid.

residue That which remains after payment of all liabilities of the testator. In administering a decedent's estate, the executor or administrator has to first pay all debts of the deceased, funeral expenses, and costs of probate and then what is left as surplus of the estate is known as the residue.

res immobiles *Immovable things,* such as land and buildings.

res ipsa loquitor *The thing speaks for itself.* Doctrine nearly synonymous with presumed negligence. Under this doctrine a legally sufficient case of negligence can be established and referred to the jury if (a) the plaintiff's injury was caused by the defective object, (b) the injury could not have occurred without the defendant's negligence, and (c) the object causing the injury was controlled by the defendant.

resistance level A price ceiling at which technical analysts note persistent selling of a security or commodity. (E.g., if Acme SAC sells normally between thirty and forty dollars a share, the higher price is called the resistance level.) When the market breaks through the resistance level, it is usually assumed that the price will continue to go higher for a time. (Cf. support level)

resolution Solemn judgment or decision of a court; a formal statement of the opinion or intention of an official body or corporation.

resource 1. Money or any property which can be converted into money or supplies; available means or capability of any kind; means of raising money or supplies. 2. *financial planning* Existing assets and discretionary income which the client may wish to incorporate into a well-constructed portfolio.

respite Temporary delay or postponement, as the execution of a sentence or demand for payment.

respondeat superior *law* A principal is liable for the acts of an agent.

respondent *law* Person or entity against whom a legal proceeding has been lodged with the court.

respondent bank A bank that regularly buys the specified services of another bank, called the correspondent bank, such as trade clearing or indirect depository participation.

respondentia Form of security given on the cargo of a ship, distinct from a bottomry bond, which is a security on the ship itself.

responsibility State of being answerable for an obligation; includes judgments, ability, capacity, and experience in the particular subject. Also frequently used as synonymous for liability.

res publicae *Things that belong to the public at large.*

restitution 1. Restoration of the parties to a rescinded contract to the positions they occupied before making the contract. 2. Restoration of property to the person

entitled to it after reversal of a judgment under which the property was taken. 3. Restoration of anything to its rightful owner. Act of compensating or making good any loss or damage to property.

restrain To prohibit an action; to restrict or limit. To check, curb, stay.

restraint of trade 1. Agreement or understanding between companies designed to stifle competition, fix prices, or otherwise obstruct the natural course of commercial and business activity. 2. *common law* Contract with a stranger to the contractor's business which wholly or partially restricts the freedom of the contractor in carrying on that business.

restraint on alienation Limiting condition on the right to transfer property. If the condition is against public policy or is unreasonable, courts will void the condition.

res transit cum suo onere *The thing passes with its burden.* Thus, a mortgage or an easement passes with the land.

restrict To restrain within bounds; to limit, confine.

restricted allotment Patent issued to a native American conveying to that person land in fee and imposing restriction upon its disposal for twenty-five years or some other stated period.

restriction 1. Limitation placed upon the use of property, contained in the deed or other written instrument in the chain of title or in local ordinances pertaining to land use. 2. *financial planning* Restraint followed by investment companies and individual investors which dictates the types of securities invested in.

restrictive covenant Mutual agreement, often between owners in a housing development and the developer, whereby certain activities are prohibited within the development.

restrictive endorsement Endorsement of negotiable paper which limits the negotiability of the paper (e.g., the words "for deposit only" on the back of a check).

resulting trust Trust implied by law arising from the nature or circumstances of consideration involved in a transaction. This trust may be categorized in two classes: (a) one in which a person buys and pays for a property and has the conveyance made to another party, obligating the latter to hold the legal title for the benefit of the former in equity; or (b) one in which a person makes or causes to be made a disposition of property under circumstances which raise an inference that one does not intend that person taking or holding property to have beneficial interest therein unless inference is formally contradicted.

resyndication, limited partnership *See* limited partnership resyndication.

retail To sell in small quantities directly to the consumer, as opposed to selling in bulk or wholesale. May include providing services as well. (*See* Fair Labor Standards Act)

retail banking Banking services that are offered to the general public, including consumers, businesses, and other commercial enterprises.

retail cooperative Contractual agreement between a group of retailers in which, in order to compete with chain operations, each retailer purchases stock in a retail-owned wholesaling operation and agrees to purchase a minimum percentage of supplies from the operation.

retail house A brokerage firm that caters to individual (retail) investors as opposed to institutional investors. Such firms can run the gamut from large houses with many research people, who may major in phone-in business, to a small house which caters to a small and select clientele.

retail investor An individual investor who buys stocks or commodities on the investor's own behalf, and not for any type of organization.

retail method of inventory *accounting* A method of approximating the inventory by records kept at retail prices. The cost value of the inventory is determined by applying to the inventory at retail a percentage which is the cost complement of the average rate of gross profit.

retain 1. To hold or keep that which one already has, not to lose, part with, or dismiss it. 2. To detain. 3. To engage an attorney or other professional advisor.

retainage In a construction contract, money earned by but not paid to the contractor until the completion of construction or at some other agreed-upon date.

retained earnings 1. Earnings that are reinvested back into a business for expansion and working capital after having paid all expenses, taxes, interest, and dividends to shareholders. Also called surplus or earned surplus. 2. Net profits allowed to accumulate in a business after dividends are paid. The corporate form of business allows it to retain earnings at a lower marginal tax rate than is available to individuals.

retained life interest Condition existing when the grantor retains an interest in the possession or enjoyment of, the right to the income from the property, or the right, either alone or with anyone else, to dictate who's going to enjoy or possess the property or its income.

retainer 1. Act of employing an attorney or counsel. 2. Fee which a client pays an attorney for acting as the client's advocate. (May refer to many types of professionals.) 3. *estates* Common law right of an executor or administrator who is also a creditor of the deceased to retain as much of the estate as is sufficient to pay the debt, in preference to all other creditors of equal degree. 4. Duty of an executor or administrator to hold back from a legatee's share any amount of debt owed to the deceased by the legatee.

retaining lien Right of an attorney to retain possession of clients' documents, money, or other property which comes into the attorney's hands professionally, until a general balance due to the attorney for professional services is paid.

retaliatory duty *economics* A duty imposed by an importing country to punish another country which already has such a duty. (Circumstances must dictate whether this is wise, either in the short-term, long-term, or both.)

retention of risk *insurance* Conscious act of keeping or assuming risk rather than transferring it.

retire 1. To withdraw from active service in an office or a profession. 2. To take or pay up, as to retire a bond. 3. To pay off the principal on a loan, thereby fulfilling the obligation under the loan contract. (*See* amortization)

retired lives reserve Irrevocable trust funded by deductible employer contributions which are accumulated to fund post-retirement death benefits or to continue group life insurance for retired employees. Trust investment earnings are exempt from federal income tax and are not treated as taxable income to employees as long as the trust money is not paid to them. Unlike other irrevocable trusts, retired lives reserve tax shield is preserved as long as trust income is restricted to providing death benefits.

retirement plan trust A trust established to hold funds which are periodically paid out to retired employees of a business, as a pension. The trust may be composed of funds paid by the employer, the employee, or both.

retraction 1. Taking back of a previous position or stand. A withdrawal. 2. In probate practice, a withdrawal or a renunciation.

retroactive Describes that which takes effect as of a prior date.

retrocession That which encompasses the past. As applied to statute, when the effect is to take away, limit, or impair rights which have vested; or which creates a new obligation or liability in respect to transactions already concluded.

return 1. To bring back or restore. 2. Product, yield, income, realization, receipts (e.g., return on investments). 3. Income plus capital gains earned on an investment in an asset.

return on assets (ROA) 1. Income divided by total assets; measure of the productivity of assets. 2. The sum of income, interest expense, and preferred dividends divided by total assets. 3. The ratio of earnings to total assets.

return on assets managed (ROAM) A measure of performance of a company or management team expressed as net operating income divided by average operating assets.

return on equity (ROE) 1. Income divided by equity, measure of the productivity or efficiency with which shareholders' equity is employed. 2. Ratio of earnings to stockholder's equity. 3. Net income after debt service, expressed as a percentage of the owner's equity.

return on income *security* Security which has last claim on company income, usually the primary beneficiary of company growth.

return on investment (ROI) Income divided by book value of an investment or a profit center; measures of productivity on an investment or a profit center. (*See* return on assets)

returns to scale *economics* Comparing the returns of an enterprise (if all factors of production are proportionately increased or decreased) to the scale of operations.

revaluation *economics* Official upward adjustment in the value of a nation's currency in relation to other currencies or to gold.

revendication *law* Right of a credit seller of goods to take the goods if the bill for the goods is not paid on time.

revenue 1. Return, profit, or yield of land or other funds; income. 2. Cash received in a period, distinguished from income which includes noncash items as well as items for which cash was received in an earlier period and items earned in this period but not yet paid for. 3. *See* sales.

revenue anticipation note (RAN) Short-term municipal government note which is sold in anticipation of revenues and is paid from the proceeds of those revenues. The source of the revenues is usually specific, rather than general.

revenue bill Any bill whose principal object is to raise funds, not taking into consideration bills for other purposes which may incidentally create or affect revenue.

revenue bond 1. Special obligation bond, generally issued by a municipality, intended to be retired from operating proceeds of the public project which the bond is issued to finance. 2. Bond issued to finance any of several different kinds of projects, usually state or municipal, such as a water bond. The principal and interest of such bonds are payable solely from revenues produced by the project. (Perhaps the largest and best-known kind of agency using revenue bonds is the toll road or turnpike authority.)

Revenue Ruling 60-31 Ruling making it clear that a mere promise to pay in the future, if it is unfunded and unsecured, is not of sufficient economic benefit to be taxable even if it is nonforfeitable at the time it is made.

reverse To annul, set aside, or revoke, as a judgment or decree.

reverse annuity mortgage Type of mortgage, designed for elderly homeowners with substantial equity, by which a lender periodically (monthly, for example) pays an amount to the borrower. The loan balance increases with interest and periodic payments, causing negative amortization.

reverse a swap The action of restoring a bond portfolio to its original state following the swapping of one bond for another, to gain the advantage of either a yield spread or a tax loss.

reverse leverage Situation in which financial benefits from ownership accrue at a lower rate than the mortgage interest rate.

reverse reciprocity Practice of giving favorable consideration to purchasers who supply the firm with needed supplies and raw materials.

reverse stock split Division of the number of shares authorized to a lesser number. Shareholders continue to maintain their proportionate ratio of ownership, but it is represented by fewer shares. (E.g., in a five for one reverse split, a shareholder previously owning one thousand shares would then own two hundred shares.)

reversion *real estate* 1. Return of an estate to the grantor or the grantor's heirs after expiration of the term of the grant. Thus a lease for a term of years creates a particular estate, but, on the termination of the lease, the land reverts back to the lessor in whom the residue always vested. 2. Estate so returned to its original owner.

reversionary interest Interest a person has in property upon termination of the preceding estate. Under Code 2037, any possibility that the property will return to the descendant or the descendant's estate, or be subject to the descendant's power of disposition. The meaning of reversion is broader than its meaning under property law. For tax purposes, a reversion includes any reserved right or power to reacquire control over the property, whether arising by express terms or implied by state law. An implied reversionary interest arises when a trust fails to dispose of all interests in the corpus and,

under applicable state law, the grantor is deemed to have retained the right to any interests which fail to vest.

revert To return to; go back to a former owner; turn back. Pass or go.

revival 1. To renew a writ after its expiration. 2. To renew by debtor's acknowledgment of a debt or by debtor's making part payment, a debt that is barred by the statute of limitations.

revocable beneficiary *insurance* Named beneficiary of an insurance policy which may have this right revoked by the insured, who is the owner of the policy.

revocable living trust Trust made during the lifetime of the grantor, which can be revoked at the settlor's discretion. The trust may be funded or unfunded, avoids probate, usually has supervised control and investment, is taxable to the settlor, and is includable in the settlor's estate.

revocable trust 1. Trust in which the settlor reserves the right to revoke. Such provisions may have tax implications, depending upon the time following its creation within which the settlor may revoke. In a typical revocable trust arrangement, the grantor transfers assets to a trustee but retains the right to revoke the trust at any time. 2. A trust which can be changed or revoked during the lifetime of the donor.

revocation The recall, cancellation, destruction, or making void of some power, authority, thing or deed.

revolving credit *See* open-end credit.

rezoning Legislative change in existing zoning rules and regulations within a comparatively large area in a governmental unit, which before rezoning had been uniformly zoned in its entirety.

Ricardian theory of rent *economics* David Ricardo's (England, 1772–1823) explanation of differences in land rent as reflecting the differing levels of productivity of land over no-rent or marginal land.

Ricardo effect *economics* The proposition that a rise in real wages will encourage capitalists to substitute machinery for labor.

rich 1. Describes a security whose price seems too high in light of its historic price. 2. Describes an interest rate which seems exorbitant in relation to the borrower's risk. 3. Wealthy.

rider 1. Addition or amendment, as to an insurance policy, contract, or legislative bill. 2. *insurance* A written attachment to a life or health policy that changes the original policy to meet special conditions.

right *stock* A privilege granted by a corporation to current stockholders to buy shares of a new issue at some price below the subscription price for the new issue. This is done to allow the current stockholders to retain their current equity position in the company. Stockholder loyalty is enhanced by this action.

right-hand side The rate at which a bank will buy foreign exchange; i.e., foreign currencies.

right of common Right exercised in the land of another with the additional right to participate in the profits of the soil, or take a part thereof of some of the produce of the land.

right of election The right of a surviving spouse, under the decedent's estate law, to take his or her intestate share in preference to the amount given in the decedent's will.

right of entry Interest which remains in the grantor or the grantor's successor or the successors of estate, where an estate on condition subsequent has been created and is exercisable on failure of the condition. It is a right of power to terminate the estate of the grantee and retake the same if there is a breach of the condition. Also called the right of re-entry.

right of first publication Author's proprietary interest in the author's literary or art creation before it has been made generally available to the public.

right of first refusal Opportunity of a party to match the terms of a proposed contract before the contract is executed.

right of presentment The right, usually related to oil and gas shelters, which gives an investor the right to sell back to a general partner the interests in the project at specified times. (*See* Appendix G)

right of retainer Right of executor to retain a legacy against a debt owing by the legatee to the deceased.

right of survivorship Right of a surviving joint tenant to acquire the interest of a deceased joint owner; distinguishing feature of both joint tenancy and tenancy by the entirety.

right of way 1. A right to pass from one point to another across another person's land in a course defined either expressly in the grant or by implication, according to the use to which it is to be put. The right exists even though the one using it has no other right in the land. 2. The ground over which a right of way exists, such as the strip of land over which a railway lays its track.

rights of absolute priority Specification in bankruptcy law stating that each class of claimants with a prior claim on assets in liquidation will be paid off in full before any junior claimants receive any proceeds.

right-to-work laws Provisions in some state statutes or constitutions outlawing the closed shop clause in labor contracts. This right extended to the states by the Taft-Hartley Labor Act of 1947.

ring The location on the floor of an exchange where trades are executed. It is circular in form and is often called a pit.

riparia Water running between two banks.

riparian Belonging to, relating to, or connected with the banks of a river or other watercourse.

riparian owner; riparian proprietor One who owns land on the banks of a river, stream, or a small pond. Also called riparian proprietor.

riparian rights 1. Rights pertaining to the use of water on, under, or adjacent to one's land. May be qualified to avoid nuisance and pollution. Riparian rights are recognized in most eastern states but rarely in western states, which recognize usufructuary rights. 2. The rights relating to the use of water of a person whose property borders on a watercourse.

rising yield curve A graphic presentation which indicates that rates on long-term maturities are higher than rates on shorter maturities.

risk 1. Hazard, danger, or exposure to loss, injury, disadvantage, or destruction; comprises all elements of danger. 2. Uncertainty concerning loss or the exposure to adversity or danger. 3. The possibility of loss; the uncertainty of future returns.

risk-adjusted discount rate A discount rate that includes a premium for risk. Also called cost of capital, hurdle rate. (Cf. discount rate)

risk analysis Process of locating loss exposures, measuring the amount of losses that can result from these exposures, estimating the probability that losses will occur, and evaluating the exposures to determine actions necessary to meet family or business risk management objectives.

risk and return Generally, the unfixed ratio between risk and rate of return. A rule of thumb is that the greater the return required, the greater the risk one must take to get it.

risk assumption Risk one is willing to assume rather than mitigate through insurance or some other vehicle.

risk aversion The unwillingness on the part of an investor to bear risk without compensation in some form.

risk avoidance Analysis made as to how best to escape the probability of a loss. For example, a company may incorporate to avoid risks existing in proprietorships and partnerships. This could also qualify as a transfer of risk.

risk capital Capital invested with the hope of some return in an enterprise over whose risk the investor has no control.

risk diversification *investing* The action of an investor to invest in various types of securities to reduce the total risk exposure.

risk economist An insurance specialist who attempts to diagnose the risks to which a project or business may be subject and then prescribe appropriate action.

risk-free interest rate Interest rate prevailing on a default-free bond in the absence of inflation.

risk management Use of all the alternative methods of dealing with risk, consisting of knowledge of the existence of various forms of risk and their magnitude and the management of the various methods of dealing with those risks.

risk management program Process requiring setting and achieving goals of maintaining a sufficient cash flow to enable families or businesses to meet objectives with minimum of interruption following a loss.

risk premium Increased return on a security required to compensate investors for the risk borne.

risk reduction 1. Steps taken to specifically reduce the possibility of loss because of risk (e.g., installing smoke alarms in the home). 2. *insurance* Loss prevention; consists of all activities intended to prevent the occurrence of a loss.

risk retention 1. Conscious act of keeping or assuming risk. 2. The decision, made by persons or businesses exposed to risk, to retain that risk in hope of saving money or in the hope that the loss may never come to them.

risk-return tradeoff 1. Conscious decision in investing to trade the possibility of greater returns for some greater degree of safety, or vice versa. 2. Ratio between the degree of risk involved in buying a specific security and the return expected. It is usually necessary to accept a greater degree of risk for the possibility of receiving a greater return.

risk tolerance level Subjective constraint based upon the client's emotional temperament and attitudes with respect to any type of risk but referring most often to making investments.

risk transfer Act of transferring all or part of the risk of loss to another.

road Highway; a strip of land appropriated and used for travel between different places.

roadway Strip of land over which a road is constructed; a road; that part of the road open to public travel.

rod Linear unit of measurement equal to 16½ feet, otherwise called a perch (5.029 meters).

roll call vote Parliamentary procedure. A vote taken in a formal meeting by calling out the names of all eligible voters and recording the vote with the name.

rolling stock *limited partnerships* Movable property belonging to railroad corporations; such property (such as cars, locomotives, and their attachments and usual accompaniments) in ordinary use is taken from one part of the line to another.

rollover Movement of funds from one investment to another. For example, an Individual Retirement Account may be rolled over when a person retires, into an annuity or other form of pension payout system.

rollover IRA   *profit sharing* Lump-sum distribution received from a qualified plan which is not taxable to the employee if the employee transfers the distribution to a different qualified retirement plan, including an Individual Retirement Account separately established for the purpose of receiving the distribution. This separate Individual Retirement Account may not be co-mingled with any other existing Individual Retirement Account funds. The distribution qualifying for rollover treatment may be either the employee's total balance under the plan, or as a result of the 1984 Tax Act, a partial balance if it exceeds 50%. The lump-sum distribution requirement of five or more years in plan participation by an employee does not apply for rollover purposes. This provides important tax deferral opportunities for employees of short duration receiving distribution from a qualified plan. An employee has sixty days from receipt of the lump-sum distribution to rollover the amount to another qualified corporate plan or individual IRA. If a rollover is not accomplished within sixty days, the employee has only certain options to minimize the tax impact of the distribution. The employee may rollover all or part of the distribution; however, the part not rolled over is fully includable in income without the benefit of capital gain treatment or ten-year forward income averaging. Amounts distributed from an IRA, even after a tax-free rollover, are taxed at ordinary income rates. Therefore, a rollover of the distribution to another qualified corporate plan may be more beneficial to the employee since the employee still will have the option of ten-year forward income averaging. The spouse (but no other beneficiary) of a deceased employee who receives a lump-sum distribution after the employee's death also may elect to establish a rollover IRA under the rules described above. Rollover treatment is limited to one time only; transfers are not subject to such limitation, so they should be utilized when merely a change of investment assets is desired or trustee-to-trustee transfer is otherwise available. (*See* Appendix G)

rollover loan   Type of mortgage loan, commonly used in Canada, in which the amortization of principal is based on a long term but the interest rate is established for a much shorter term. The loan may be extended, or rolled over, at the end of the shorter term at the current market interest rate.

rooming house   House or building where there are one or more bedrooms which the owner lets out for lodging.

roughneck   Laborer who under the supervision and direction of a superior known as a driller engages in rigging up or installing and operating drilling rigs in the search and exploration for oil and gas.

round lot   Standard unit of trading. A round lot is usually one hundred shares in the case of stocks and a thousand dollars face value in bond. A few inactive shares have a standard unit of ten, twenty-five, or fifty shares.

route   Trodden or usual way. A designated course over a way or right-of-way. A course, line of travel, or transit.

row house   Single-family dwelling units attached to one another by common walls, generally with a common façade.

royalty   Percentage paid to a property owner for extraction of some valuable resource from the land, or to an author for publication rights.

rule   Formula to which conduct must be conformed; a minor law; canon or regulation, especially a regulation which a person imposes on one's self.

rule against perpetuities   Rule providing that a trust created for a named beneficiary or class of beneficiaries can exist only for a given length of time not exceeding the lives of any of the beneficiaries alive at the time the trust was created plus twenty-one years and nine months. If a trust is created to be of perpetual duration, it will violate this rule if any of the beneficiaries comes into existence more than twenty-one years and nine months after the creation of the trust. Such a trust would be invalid and unenforcable. One of the few exceptions to this rule occurs when the trust is established for the benefit of a charitable beneficiary. Conceivably, the trust could last as long as the charitable beneficiary exists.

rule against suspension of the power of alienation Rule in some states, as an alternate or supplement to the rule against perpetuities, limiting the period during which the power to deal with land can be suspended in order to avoid the social problems involved with the non-salability of land. This rule can be simply avoided by giving the grantee the power to sell the land and imposing the control on the proceeds of the sale.

Rule 405 A concept codified by the New York Stock Exchange that urges those firms doing business with individual investors to know their customers so well that they will be able to recognize what might be a good or bad investment for them.

rule of 45 Rule under which a participant becomes partially vested at the earlier of either the time when the sum of the participant's age and years of service equals forty-five or the completion of ten years of service.

rule of reason Interpretation of the courts (first announced in the Standard Oil case of 1911) that the mere size of a corporation is no offense and that it requires unreasonable behavior in the form of actual exertion of monopoly power, as shown by unfair practices, for a firm to be held in violation of the antitrust laws. This interpretation, also known as the "good-trust-versus-bad-trust" criterion, was largely reversed in the Aluminum Company of America case in 1945, as well as in subsequent cases.

rule of 78s A method for determining the amount of interest to be deducted from a prepaid loan contract by allocating $^{12}\!/_{78}$ of a year's interest in the first month, $^{11}\!/_{78}$ in the second, $^{10}\!/_{78}$ in the third, etc.

rule of 72 Approximate guideline for determining how long it will take an investment to double in value or for determining the interest rate required for an investment to double in value, in which the number seventy-two is divided by the interest rate. (E.g., if a client invests one thousand dollars at 8% compounded annually and wants to double the investment to two thousand dollars, seventy-two is divided by eight to arrive at the answer of nine years to double the original sum.) If the years are known but not the percent, seventy-two is divided by the number of years, and the total is the rate of interest necessary to double the investment.

runaway inflation *See* hyperinflation.

running account Mutual account between creditor and debtor which shows all transactions between parties; the continuous record of the entry of the charges as well as payments on account.

running with the land Covenant that is either leased or conveyed when either the liability to perform it or the right to take advantage of it passes to the assignee of that land.

run with the land 1. Expression indicating a right or restriction that affects all current and future owners of a property. 2. Phrase used to describe a covenant or undertaking that goes with the land and passes to each successive owner of the land, thus making the purchaser subject to whatever contractual obligation the former owner had.

rural 1. Of or pertaining to the country as distinguished from a city or town. 2. Of or pertaining to farms.

Rural Electrification Administration (REA) Agency created in the Department of Agriculture in 1935, with its chief duty being that of making loans to finance the cost of putting electricity and telephones into rural areas.

S

sabotage Malicious damaging of property or deliberate slowdown of work, either to interfere with or to halt industrial production.

sacrifice tax theory The view that taxes should be so levied as to cause equal sacrifice for all taxpayers.

safe harbor 1. Moves that can be made

in accounting or finance to avoid specific legal or tax consequences, as when a capital-short company will allow another company to buy capital equipment and then lease the equipment, thus avoiding the need for investment. This practice was severely curtailed by the Tax Equity and Fiscal Responsibility Act of 1982. 2. Certain provisions of law that excuse liability if promises or projections have been made in good faith, as when a broker projects earnings on a given security in error but in good faith. 3. A form of defense for a company targeted to be acquired, where the target company is so regulated that it repels the prospective acquirer. Sometimes referred to as shark repellent.

safekeeping *banking* A service offered by some banks which entails storing in the vault, for the customers, valuables which are too large to be put in a safety deposit box.

safe place of work Place of work that, though not absolutely free from danger, is reasonably safe. Under common law, a master is under a duty to provide a fit and proper place to work and a fit and proper system and suitable materials with which to work. If the master chooses to delegate this duty, the master is still liable to a workman who is injured by a breach of that duty.

safety factor *finance* The ratio of interest on funded debt to net income before taxes but after such interest has been deducted.

safety fund system A system of bank insurance used in New York in the nineteenth century. The fund was held by the state treasurer and was funded by 3% of each bank's capital stock. The fund guaranteed the bank notes issued by bank members of the same system.

salary Remuneration (wages) made periodically to a person under a contract for service to be distinguished from a fee which is payable on a contract for services, such as that of a lawyer or a surgeon. A salary is payable to an employee under a contract for service, under which contract the employee obeys all lawful orders of the employer and submits to the employer's supervision and direction.

salary compression *management* A situation in which very high salaries at the top echelons of management reduce the opportunity for salary increases at lower echelons.

salary continuation plan Fringe benefit provided by the employer in addition to all other forms of compensation under which the employer promises to pay a deferred benefit with no reduction in the employee's present compensation, raise, or bonus.

salary progression curve A graphic presentation of current employees and their salaries, as they relate to age, experience, education, and other variables.

salary reduction Mechanism allowing an individual employee to elect to reduce salary by some percentage on a prospective basis with taxes deferred on these contributions.

salary reduction plan Virtually synonymous with the 401(k) plan which allows certain employees to contribute pre-tax funds to a qualified tax-deferred retirement plan. In the Tax Reform Act of 1986, the amount of pre-tax money to be saved was severely limited, and employees of the state, municipalities, and not-for-profit organizations were prohibited from setting up the 401(k). The 403(b), which they are allowed to use, limits the annual contribution to $9,300. Subsequent tax laws may again change the limits or the plans proper.

salary review *management* A re-examination of the salaries of employees with regard to their past performance, inflation, and perhaps other variables. Most companies have salary reviews annually.

salary sacrifice A situation in which an employee relinquishes a portion of his or her current salary, which is usually matched by the employer, for the purpose of buying an endowment insurance policy that will increase retirement pay.

salary structure A method of setting the ranges of salaries in a business, where there are progressions in grade and also progression within grades.

sale 1. Contract under which property is transferred from one person (the seller or vendor) to another (the buyer or purchaser) in return for the latter's payment or promise of payment of a fixed price of money or property. 2. The transmutation or transfer of the property in a personal chattel from one person to another for a consideration paid or agreed to be paid.

saleable   Fit for sale in the usual course of trade at usual selling prices.

sale at arms length   Sale between parties with opposing economic interests.

sale-lease back   Arrangement in which a business decides to sell to a group of investors equipment which has been previously purchased and used with the intention and understanding that the business would continue to lease the equipment from the investors, generally on a long-term basis. This type of transaction is usually intended to secure either income or estate tax advantages or both. This may be used when: (a) lessor is rich in assets and poor in cash, (b) a person is in a high income tax bracket and wishes to divert highly taxed income to a family member, (c) a person who has property which is appreciating rapidly in value would like to escape estate taxes on that future growth, or (d) a person would like to find an alternative to financing business property through a mortgage.

sale of goods   Transaction between the owner and the buyer of goods in which the property shall for some price or consideration be transferred to the other at such time and in such manner as is agreed. To be distinguished from an exchange or barter.

sale on condition   Executory contract where title does not vest in the buyer at the time of the transaction of sale but only on the happening of a future condition and buyer does not hold title to the property but is in a position similar to a bailee or lessee.

sale or return   *marketing* A clause in a sales contract or a general posted agreement stating that, though the ownership of the merchandise sold passes directly to the buyer, the merchandise can be returned if the goods prove to be unsatisfactory to the buyer. Some retail establishments find this a major selling point. Usually, the notice is posted conspicuously in the place of business.

sales   Inflow of resources to a business for a period from the sale of goods or provision of services. Also called revenue. (*See* net sales)

sales analysis   In-depth evaluation of a firm's sales. This involves breaking aggregate data down into component parts.

sales chain   *marketing* The path along which a product will pass in going from the producer to the consumer.

sales charge   *finance* An initial charge made by some investment companies to cover commissions and other costs related to setting up the account.

sales contour   *See* sales line.

sales finance company   A company that buys the installment paper from retailers who sell durable goods to consumers. In recent years, that finance company has usually been a subsidiary of the company producing the durable goods, since the financing tends to be more profitable than the production and marketing of goods.

sales forecast   Estimate of a company's sales for a specified future period under a proposed marketing plan and an assumed set of economic and other influences. The forecast may be for an individual product or for an entire line of products.

sales line   An indifference curve with selling costs on one axis and output prices on the other axis that traces all combinations of selling costs and output prices which will enable a seller to dispose of a given quantity of output. Also called sales contour.

sales manual   *marketing* A book, put out by a company, that outlines the sales policies of the company and suggested techniques to be used by salespersons.

sales maximization   Pricing philosophy analyzed by economist William J. Baumol under which firms set what they consider the lowest acceptable profit level and then seek to maximize sales in the belief that increased sales are more important than immediate high profits to the long-run competitive picture.

salesperson   *real estate* One who is licensed to buy, sell, or list real estate, while connected with and under the supervision of a licensed broker.

sales-purchase curve   Curve with price on the "Y" axis, quantity purchased on the positive side of the "X" axis, and quantity sold on the negative side of the "X" axis tracing the quantities that an individual is able to buy or sell at various prices.

sales quota   Level of expected sales to which actual sales are compared; a standard of comparison used in sales analysis.

sales tax   A tax levied on the retail price of a good or a service and collected by the retailer. Generally these are either state or local taxes.

salus populi suprema lex   *The welfare of the people is the supreme law.*

salvage   Property transferred to an insurer to reduce loss. Property remaining after some casualty or loss, often the loss of a building, from the damage done by wind, hail, fire, etc., which may have some value to the insurer.

salvage loss   Difference between the amount of salvage after deducting the charges and the original value of the property.

salvage value   1. Estimated value that an asset will have at the end of its useful life. 2. Value which property used in the production of income has after it is no longer useful to the taxpayer. 3. *marine law* Amount of reward or compensation given to those who have successfully rescued the cargo, the ship, or both from threatened, impending, or actual loss or injury.

same-day substitution   Offsetting changes in a margin account in the same day, resulting in neither a margin call nor a credit to the special miscellaneous account.

sample   1. Relatively small quantity of anything from which the quantity of the mass, group, or species which it represents may be judged for quality; a specimen. 2. Small quantity of some commodity presented or sold to customers as a specimen of goods offered for sale.

sample reliability   *statistics* The reliability of the arithmetic mean of a sample can be judged by dividing the estimated standard deviation of the items in the universe by the square root of the number of cases in the sample.

sampling error   *statistics* The difference between the sample drawn from a portion of the population and the whole population. While the sample is meant to be representative, and usually is, it will rarely coincide with the whole population, and is therefore subject to degrees of error.

sampling frame   *statistics* Information gained from sampling a population used to define and assemble a sample for the purpose of the survey.

Samuelson-Stolper effect   *economics* The proposition that under free trade (i.e., no tariffs on imports) goods may serve as a partial substitute for immigration of labor into a labor-scarce economy, and hence that real wages may fall under free trade. (The relative and absolute share of the labor might go down although real national product would go up under free trade in such a situation.)

Samuelson substitution theorem   *economics* In input-output analysis, the proposition that even where variation of input proportion is possible, it will never be advantageous to vary input proportions when there are constant returns to scale, only one scarce input, and no joint products.

sanction   1. To concur, confirm, consent to, assent, ratify. 2. A penalty or punishment provided as a means of enforcing obedience to a law.

sandwich course   A course of study, normally at the undergraduate level, in which part of the time is spent in classroom work and the other part in gaining practical experience in the plant, business, or enterprise. This British term corresponds closely to cooperative education in the United States.

sandwich lease   When land is leased to a lessee, who in turn releases the land to a releasee, the first lease is called a sandwich lease.

satisfaction of judgment   *law* A document which states that payment has been received and signed by a judgment creditor and filed in the same court or courts where the judgment is docketed.

Saturday-night special   A colloquialism denoting the sudden attempt to take over a company by a public tender offer. The term was first used in the 1960s when a plethora of such deals were put together and posed during a week-end. In 1968, the Williams Act placed tough restrictions on tender offers and required disclosure of direct or indirect ownership of 5% or more of any class of equity.

save   1. To economize. 2. To reserve or except, as in conveyance of land which conveys part of the holding of the grantor, saving or reserving to the grantor the rest of the holding. 3. *economics* To buy debt instruments to make a profit.

savings *economics* That portion of income which is not currently spent. Economists use the term "savings" with regard to consumers, and "investment" with regard to business.

savings account One of the most popular forms of fixed-income investments. A highly safe and liquid investment outlet offering almost complete flexibility to the depositor. These conveniences must be weighed against other factors, the principal one being rate of return. Savings accounts traditionally return lower yields than many other forms of fixed-income investments.

savings and loan association Financial institution which accepts deposits primarily from individuals and channels the funds chiefly into residential mortgage loans. Most savings and loan associations are technically owned by the depositors who receive shares in the association for their deposits. Sometimes called building and loan association, cooperative bank, or homestead association.

savings bank insurance Type of insurance, not lawful in all states, in which a bank writes small face policies on depositors with insurance funds and bank funds kept separate. Because of the desire to keep costs low, salespeople are not used, but banks do advertise this service. (Some state laws do not demand that the insured be depositors, making it possible to buy from several different banks.)

savings bond Bond issued by the United States Treasury that is not traded on the open market and is redeemable only by the government.

savings club A special kind of account offered by a bank which allows the customer to make periodic deposits, usually small, to meet a specific future need. Christmas clubs and vacation clubs are among these special programs.

Say's law of markets Theory of the French economist J. B. Say which holds that, when goods or services are produced, enough income is generated to purchase what is produced, thereby eliminating the problem of overproduction.

scab *labor law* 1. Laborer who replaces a worker on strike. 2. Laborer who works for lower wages than or under conditions contrary to those prescribed by a trade union.

scalar principle *communications* The concept that employees should communicate with their superiors only through their immediate superiors, thus strictly following the formal chain of command.

scale 1. *labor* A wage rate for a specific type of employee. 2. *economics* The amount of production, as in economy or diseconomy of scale. 3. *serial bonds* Important data for each of the scheduled maturities in a new serial bond issue, which includes the number of bonds, the dates they mature, the coupon rate, and the offering price.

scale line *economic* Indifference curve, with quantities of one factor of production on one axis and quantities of another factor on the other axis, tracing all combinations of the two factors which can be purchased with the same amount of money.

scalp To trade for small gains in securities markets. The process usually is one of buying and selling securities in a short period of time, often one day.

scalper 1. A speculator who enters into a quasi-legal or illegal transaction in order to turn a quick and often unreasonable profit. 2. *securities* An investment advisor who takes a position in a security prior to recommending it, and sells out after the price has risen because of those recommendations. 3. A market maker who, in violation of the Rules of Fair Practice of the National Association of Securities Dealers, adds an excessive markup or takes an excessive markdown on a transaction. 4. A commodity trader who trades for small gains, usually gaining a position and quitting a position in one day's trading.

Scanlon plan A cash incentive plan, devised by Joseph Scanlon in the 1930s and 1940s while he was at the Massachusetts Institute of Technology, for employees who share in reductions in labor costs experienced by a company.

scarce currency *international finance* A situation in a country in which the demand for a certain currency threatens to exhaust the supply at the usual rate of exchange.

scarcity Limitation of resources for production relative to the unlimited wants for goods and services.

scatter diagram *statistics* A graphic presentation which shows the relationship between two or more variables. Also shows how data vary in a frequency distribution. (Cf. frequency distribution)

scenic easement Encumbrance on title to a property requiring its preservation in a more-or-less natural or undeveloped state. Often related to a historic site or a natural phenomenon. (*See* easement)

schedule A Income tax form for reporting itemized deductions used with Form 1040.

schedule C—Form 1040 Income tax form for reporting profit or loss on business or profession.

schedule for amounts of insurance Formula for determining the amount of life insurance a company may wish to buy for employees, with the plan usually being contributory. The normal three matters for such consideration are: (a) current earnings (of the employee), (b) length of service with the firm, (c) position in firm. (Some plans give a flat amount of insurance to each employee regardless of any considerations, which plans are usually non-contributory.)

schedule W deduction A method for managing the tax liability of married couples who both work and file a joint return allowing a deduction of the lesser of 10% of thirty thousand or 10% of the earned income of the lower-earning spouse. (*See* Appendix G)

scope of authority In the law of agency, authority, both actual and/or implied, conferred upon the agent by the principal.

scope of employment Activities that fairly and reasonably may be said to be incident to employment or logically and naturally connected with same; acts of some general nature as that authorized or incidental to the conduct authorized.

scorched-earth policy A technique of a company which has become the target of another to make itself less attractive to the prospective suitor. This may include selling off profitable and attractive parts of the firm, etc.

S corporation *See* subchapter S corporation.

scrambled merchandising *marketing* An offering for sale by a retail outlet which is outside the scope of its usual merchandising. (E.g., a small shoe outlet has the opportunity to buy rainwear at deeply discounted prices, does so, and markets them until they are gone. The act might not ever be repeated.)

screening 1. *personnel* Making a preliminary assessment of job applicants and making a decision as to those who may be suitable. 2. *management* Assessing ideas, suggestions, and requests in order to eliminate those considered unworkable.

scrip Certificate of acknowledgment issued by a company or other body corporate evidencing the person named therein or the holder to a specified number of shares, bonds, or debentures upon payment of all the installments or the unpaid amount owing on such shares, bonds, or debentures.

scripophily The practice of a few people of collecting bond and stock certificates for their scarcity value, rather than for their value in trade. Early issues of old but still operating companies are much in demand.

scrivener Agent who, until the middle of the eighteenth century, traded in money, both receiving money from clients and investing money for clients. The scriveners' services were similar to that of present-day bankers. They were free to use the money without having to account for any profit until it was actually invested.

seal Originally, wax or a wafer with an impression. To constitute a valid seal in modern times, neither wax, wafer, nor other adhesive substance is required. All that is needed is the impression, and this may be visible by means of an indentation on the face of the instrument.

search and seizure Examination of a person's premises or of his or her person in an effort to find stolen or illicit property or contraband, or to discover evidence of guilt that may be used in prosecuting a crime with which the person is charged.

search warrant Written judicial order directing an officer to search a house or

295

other specified place for certain specified goods or documents alleged to be unlawfully concealed there.

seasonal index *economics* A seasonal pattern of business which can be observed by comparing business done by the month, for several years until a pattern has been established.

seasonal variation *economics* Those changes in economic activity which are occasioned by adverse weather accompanying certain seasons, vacations, etc. (E.g., many plants now practice closing down for two weeks each summer while all employees take vacations at the same time. Quite naturally, the economic activity of that plant for that quarter would be considerably diminished.)

seasoned securities Securities which have been bought and sold on the market long enough to be considered safe investments and which tend to be held by the type of investors seeking permanent investments (e.g., blue chip stocks representing firms like IBM, AT&T, etc., since they pay good dividends and some capital growth).

seat A traditional figure of speech for a membership on a stock exchange. The price of a seat is high, and admissions fees vary but are considered quite high.

Seat-of-the-Pants Management, Inc. An investment game, produced by a firm in 1979, the essence of which was to have one group of investors throw darts at a board containing the name of the stocks, and compare results with another group using a set of so-called advisor darts.

seaworthiness *marine law* Readiness of a ship and all its appurtenances, hull, decks, machinery, tools, stowage, and cargo containers, for the purpose for which they are to be used.

sec Sometimes used as an abbreviation for security. When the word appears after the signature of a party on the face of the instrument, it is to be construed as indicative of a relationship of principal and surety between that party and others who signed the same instrument.

secondary boycott Refusal to deal with a firm that does business with another firm which is under boycott. Usually in a labor dispute. (*See* boycott)

secondary evidence rule *law* The rule of admitting copies (or other secondary evidence) when sufficient explanation is offered as to why the original or other primary evidence is not available.

secondary market Market for buying and selling previously issued securities (e.g., the New York Stock Exchange).

secondary mortgage market An unorganized market in which existing mortgages are bought and sold. (Cf. primary mortgage market)

second disposition Transaction occurring when a parent sells property to a child, with the child reselling the property for a higher figure. Under certain circumstances a part of the gain is attributed to the donor, though usually at a rate lower than the donor would have had had the donor retained the property, usually resulting in a tax saving for the donor.

second-injury law Legislation which says in essence that if a worker suffers an injury which aggravates an injury previously incurred under another employer, both companies may be required to pay compensation to the worker.

second mortgage Subordinated lien, created by a mortgage loan, over the amount of a first mortgage. Second mortgages are used at purchase to reduce the amount of a cash down payment or in refinancing to raise cash for any purpose.

section Square mile in the government rectangular survey with thirty-six sections in a six-mile square township.

sectional tariff *transportation* A tariff made in sections, with each section containing different rates between the same points for alternative application.

section B housing Privately owned rental dwelling units participating in the low-income rental assistance program created by 1974 amendments to Section 8 of the 1937 Housing Act. Under the program, landlords receive rent subsidies on behalf of qualified low-income tenants, allowing the tenants to pay a limited proportion of their incomes toward the rent.

section 37 Section of the Internal Revenue Code stating that civil service annuities are includable in gross income but may qualify for the tax credit for the elderly and the permanently and totally disabled if: (a) the retiree is age sixty-five or over; (b) the retiree is under age sixty-five, retired on disability and considered permanently and totally disabled; or (c) the retiree is under age sixty-five and receiving taxable pensions under the civil service retirement system.

section 167 Section of the Internal Revenue Code that deals with depreciation.

section 179 Section of the Internal Revenue Code that allows the cost of certain qualifying property to be treated as an expense rather than as a capital expenditure; this election must be taken in the first tax year the property is placed in service.

section 303 A section of Internal Revenue Code relevant when the value of the stock in the decedent's estate for federal estate tax purposes is more than 35% of the value of the adjusted gross estate. The redeeming shareholder will receive capital gains treatment only to the extent that the shareholder's interest is reduced directly (or through a binding obligation to contribute) by payment of death taxes or funeral or administrative expenses. The redemption must take place after the decedent's death and within the three year period allowed for the assessment of the estate tax, running from the time the estate tax return is filed (normally within nine months of death) plus ninety days, or, if an appeal from an IRS determination of estate tax is taken to Tax Court, within sixty days of its final decision, whichever period is longer.

section 306 Serviceman's pension law prior to 1979.

section 403(B) Section of Internal Revenue Code allowing an employee to exclude from gross income the premiums paid on a contract that will provide the employee with an annuity for retirement or amounts paid to a custodian for purchase of stock in regulated investment companies.

section 501(C)(3) Section of Internal Revenue Code allowing exemption of non-profit organizations that are organized and operated exclusively for religious, charitable, scientific, literary, educational, or safety testing purposes, or for the prevention of cruelty to children or animals.

section 1031 Section of Internal Revenue Code that deals with tax-free exchanges of certain property.

section 1034 Section of Internal Revenue Code dealing with sales of personal residences.

section 1221 Section of Internal Revenue Code that defines a capital asset.

section 1231 Section of Internal Revenue Code that deals with assets used in trade or business.

section 1231 property Property used in trade or business including real property and cost recovery personal property, but not property held for sale to customers. Real property includes all interests such as easements, leaseholds, or water rights that are recognized as real property under applicable state laws. Cost recovery property includes most assets used to carry on one's trade or business for which one expects to get back most or all of one's investment through cost recovery deductions.

section 1245 Section of Internal Revenue Code dealing with gains from personal property on which depreciation has been claimed.

section 1250 Section of Internal Revenue Code dealing with gains from real estate on which accelerated depreciation had been claimed.

section 2503(C) trust Trust with particular provisions allowing a donor the annual gift exclusion for gifts made to such a trust. The trust must provide that income be paid for the benefit of the minor beneficiary at the trustee's discretion and, upon reaching the age of twenty-one, the proceeds of the trust must be paid over to the beneficiary.

secular stagnation theory *economics* Theory concerned not with the business cycle, per se, but with the view that the economy has reached maturity; i.e., the frontier is gone, the population is static or declining, important discoveries are lacking, etc. This posture of an economy is usually accompanied by prolonged recessions and only spasmodic periods of prosperity, lasting but a short time.

secular trend 1.*statistics* A time series line which is a simplification portraying data with disregard for minor variation on one side of the trend line or the other, and steering a middle course through the scatter points representing the values in a series. 2. *economics* The average course that would be followed by economic activities over a period of several business cycles. The trend can be calculated by fitting a line by the least squares method to the deseasonalized data.

secundum *According to.*

secundum aequum et bonum *According to what is just and right.*

secundum forman chartae *According to the form of the charter (or deed).*

secundum legem communem *According to the common law.*

secundum norman legis *According to the rule of law.*

secured creditor 1. Creditor whose obligation is backed by the pledge of some asset. In liquidation the secured creditor receives the cash from the sale of the pledged asset to the extent of the loan. 2. Creditor who holds a mortgage or lien upon property of the debtor as security for payment of the debt.

Securities Act (1933) Act of Congress that provides for registration of a security for public offering and for full and fair disclosure of material information on all initial security distributions. The Securities and Exchange Commission enforces provisions of the act.

Securities and Exchange Commission (SEC) Federal agency created in 1934 to carry out the provisions of the Securities Exchange Act; among its duties are the enforcement of the federal securities laws and the regulation of securities markets. Generally, the agency seeks to protect the investing public by preventing misrepresentation, fraud, manipulation, and other abuses in the securities markets.

Securities Exchange Act (1934) Act of Congress that regulates activities dealing with trading of outstanding shares. The act regulates securities exchanges, the over-the-counter market, and those persons and firms involved in selling securities. The Securities and Exchange Commission enforces the provisions of the act. Under this act publicly held companies are required to keep current information on file with the SEC. This is achieved by having the firm file a 10K report annually with the SEC.

Securities Industry Association (SIA) A trade association that represents broker-dealers. It serves as a political action committee, does public education in securities, and maintains statistical data on members.

Securities Investor Protection Act (1970) Federal act creating an agency to insure brokerage firms. The SIPC is managed by a seven member board of directors. Five members are appointed by the president of the United States with confirmation by the Senate, with two members representing the general public and three representing the securities industry. The insurance provided by SIPC protects a customer's cash (up to $100,000) and cash and securities combined for a total of $500,000. If a brokerage firm fails, the customers are reimbursed up to the maximum amount. If a customer's claims exceed the $500,000 limit, that customer becomes a general creditor for the remaining funds.

Securities Investor Protection Corporation (SIPC) Government sponsored membership insurance corporation designed to protect clients of SIPC member firms from certain losses should a member firm fail. All brokers and dealers registered with the Securities Exchange Commission and all members of national stock exchanges are required to be members of SIPC. SIPC does not protect an investor from any loss due to fluctuations in market value.

securities law Any of those laws which govern the issuance and sale of securities that came into being with and are administered by the Securities and Exchange Commission. (*See* blue-sky law)

securities market line *See* market line.

security 1. Something deposited or pledged as a guarantee of payment, performance, or appearance; a guarantor. 2. Instrument that signifies an ownership position in a corporation (a stock), a creditor relationship with a corporation or government body (a bond), or rights of ownership such as those represented by an option, subscription right, and subscription warrant.

security agreement Agreement creating or providing for a security interest.

security analysis Steps taken and methods used to attempt to determine the future of a stock or bond. Such analysis is usually done to assist buyers in making a decision with respect to buying or selling a stock or bond.

security analysts Persons who derive investment strategy by the use of techniques which, in their opinion, give them an advantage over other investors.

security deposit Pledge of property or additional personal obligation by the debtor to make the enforcement or promise more certain.

security interest 1. Interest in real estate in which the real estate serves as collateral. 2. Interest of a creditor in personal property or fixtures which secures payment or performance of an obligation.

Security Investors Protection Corporation (SIPC) A non-profit corporation established by Congress, under the Securities Investors Protection Act of 1970, that secures the customer accounts of member brokerage firms against the failure of those firms. All brokers and dealers registered with the Securities and Exchange Commission and with national stock exchanges are required to be members of SIPC. Each customer's account is secured up to $100,000 on cash or cash equivalents, and up to $500,000 on overall losses.

security markets Exchange on which stocks and/or bonds are traded.

security of principal Assurance to investors that they will get their money back along with dividends or interest. In times of inflation, however, one can get the principal sum back and lose purchasing power.

security of tenure The strength of a tenant's rights to hold onto property the tenant is occupying, or an employee's right to continue to hold the job. Such rights may be statutory, traditional, or by contractual agreement.

seed money Funds provided by a venture capitalist for the start-up of a new company. The funds may come as a loan, as an investment in preferred stock, or in bonds.

seigniorage A situation in which the market value of new coinage is greater than the cost of the metal content, which yields a profit to the country minting the coin.

seisin 1. Possession of land or a freehold tenure. 2. Possession of realty by one who claims to own a fee simple estate, a life estate, or other saleable interest.

seisin, livery of *See* livery of seisin.

seizure Act of forcibly taking real or personal property into legal possession.

selection consultant *management* A person who specializes in searching out middle management personnel, and top executives for companies. Such a person is usually well schooled in all types of selection processes, including psychological testing, plus old-fashioned "seat of the pants" intuition. Usually, the consultant, or head-hunter, is compensated by the company, and such compensation is often a percentage of the first year's salary of the person selected.

selective distribution Selection of a small number of retailers to handle a firm's product or product line.

selective taxes Sales taxes confined to a particular commodity or a limited number of commodities as distinguished from general sales taxes which apply to goods or commodities in general. Thus, sales tax imposed on cigarettes and tobacco products and gasoline and other petroleum products are selective taxes.

self-amortizing mortgage Mortgage that will retire itself through regular principal and interest payments. (*See* balloon mortgage)

self-concept theory Theory that the way people picture themselves influences the manner in which they act as consumers.

self-defense Criminal law defense or the right to such defense of oneself or one's family from personal assault or of one's property from destructive violence by another party or parties. Permitted by the law within reason and without punishment. The force employed by the person pleading self-defense must not be out of proportion to the apparent urgency of the occasion.

self-directed IRA An Individual Retirement Account the assets of which can be managed by the account holder. This is normally done through a financial institution to which the holder pays a small annual fee, plus transaction fees.

self-incrimination Giving testimony that would involve oneself in criminal prosecution or the danger thereof. The Fifth Amendment to the Constitution guarantees that one is not bound to give self-incriminating testimony, and this right is further protected by the Fourteenth Amendment.

self-insurance Insurance plan where the assured does not transfer the risk to a professional risk bearer but assumes all risks personally. When such a plan is adopted, a regular deposit is put into a self-insurance fund. Self-insurers provide efficient loss-inspection and loss-prevention activities that for some coverages is as important as indemnity. The self-insured obviously must have the financial strength to fund the plan and absorb the losses. (Some firms, in states where it is allowed, choose to self-insure in workmen's compensation insurance.) One disadvantage of self-insurance is the lack of an impersonal claims service, particularly in workmen's compensation and group health insurance.

self-liquidating loan A loan that will be liquidated by the revenue generated by the activity for which the loan was made.

self-regulation Act of cooperative organizations of insurers and agents who work to exert some control over the business through codes of ethics and various cooperative agreements. For example, standards for policy forms, advertising, and education have been adopted to protect the public. The fear of more regulation has instilled a conscience into some individual insurers, forcing them to act in the public interest. Self-regulation was the first type of regulation in the United States.

self-regulatory organizations (SRO) Nongovernment organizations that have statutory responsibility to regulate their own members such as the New York Stock Exchange, the American Stock Exchange, and the National Association of Securities Dealers.

sell To give up or hand over something to another person for money or something that is reckoned as money. In extended form, may also mean to agree to sell. To pass title from the seller to the buyer for a price.

seller's market Economic conditions that favor sellers, reflecting rising prices and market activity.

seller's points Lump sum paid by the seller to the buyer's creditor to reduce the cost of the loan to the buyer. This payment is either required by the creditor or volunteered by the seller, usually in a loan to buy real estate. Generally, one point equals one percent of the loan amount.

selling against the box *securities* A practice used primarily by large stockholders of selling short and delivering borrowed certificates rather than the shares the stockholder may have in possession. A method of shielding shares held.

selling agent; selling broker *real estate* Licensed broker who actually makes the sale, as opposed to the one who lists it.

selling climax A sudden precipitous drop in the price of a security brought on by panic selling by a number of stockholders. Since the drop in prices is counterbalanced by an increase in volume selling, some analysts see this movement as presaging a short-term rally. This is based on the fact that there are few shareholders left after the plunge, and when people begin to buy in at the lower prices, a new rally, though short, may ensue.

selling fee A fee received by the seller for marketing commercial paper. Fees usually represent a very small percentage, or fraction thereof, of the price of the paper, since the sums are usually large, and the holding times by the buyer are short. (Cf. commercial paper)

selling group A group of dealers appointed by a syndicate manager to act as agents for other underwriters in selling a new or secondary issue to the buying public. The selling group normally operates under a set of rules arranged by the group itself. (Cf. underwriter, syndicate)

selling on the good news *securities* The somewhat strange practice of selling a stock shortly after good news about the company represented by the stock is made public. It is assumed by this group that the stock will hit a new high within a specified time after the good news is out, because of buyers rushing into the market. They thus believe that the stock will soon be at its new high and sell at that point believing the stock will soon decrease in price.

selling short   Selling securities that the investor either does not have, and therefore must borrow to settle the account, or does possess but does not wish to deliver.

selling syndicate   A group of securities dealers who buy new security issues from underwriters and sell them to the public. The underwriters usually also participate in selling, though normally in larger blocks of securities. This market is called a primary market.

selling up   Technique of convincing the customer to buy a higher priced item than he or she originally intended to buy.

sell short   To sell securities that the investor does not own at a certain price in anticipation of buying back those same securities at a lower price.

sell the book   An order to a broker by the holder of a large number of shares of a specific stock to sell off as big a block as can be absorbed by the market at the current bid price.

semantic differential   Scaling device that uses a number of bipolar adjectives—such as hot and cold—to rank consumer attitudes.

semiaverages method of fitting a straight line   *statistics*   The division of data into two equal groups (the upper half and the lower half) with the arithmetic mean to be established for each group. Then a straight line through the two means will give an approximation of a linear regression line.

semilogarithmic chart   A graph in which one axis is scaled in logarithms and the other axis is scaled arithmetically with natural numbers.

semimanufacturers   A manufacturer who processes raw materials to a point at which they can be further processed.

semi-strong-form efficient market   Market in which prices instantaneously reflect all publicly available information.

semi-variable cost   A cost which is not constant, but which does not vary directly with an increase or decrease in production as do other costs. (E.g., while electric power used will vary according to production, a 10% increase in production will usually not result in a 10% increase in the use of power.)

semper paratus   *Always ready.*   The phrase is applicable to situations in which a tender is made in order to demonstrate the readiness of the party tendering to perform one's obligations under a contract.

senility   Mental and physical infirmity due to old age, often characterized by total incompetence to enter into a binding contract or execute a will.

senior creditor   Any creditor who has a claim on income or assets prior to that of any general creditor.

senior equity   Usually, preferred stock which holds a superior position to junior (common) stock, in the event of the liquidation of the firm.

Senior Real Estate Analyst (SREA)   This is the highest designation of a member of the Society of Real Estate Appraisers. The major designations of the society are Senior Residential Appraiser (SRA), Senior Real Property Appraiser (SRPA), and Senior Real Estate Analyst.

senior residential appraiser (SRA)   *real estate*   Designation given by the Society of Real Estate Appraisers to one who is skilled in the appraisal of residential housing. Specific courses of study usually accompany such a designation.

senior secured debt   *banking*   A loan with strong collateral, payment for which takes priority over ensuing debts. Usually finances real estate or equipment.

senior vice president   *banking*   Title given to a person of long tenure who is thoroughly acquainted with the institution, the industry, and the community. Some banks, however, give this title to vice presidents who are heads of departments, such as trust, marketing, etc. In any case, the title denotes a person who has given long service to the institution, or who, by virtue of heading a department, requires this particular title of distinction.

senior vice president for administration   See executive vice president.

sensitivity analysis   The analysis of how much impact some change in an input variable will have on a proposed plan or project.

sensitivity to price change   See price elasticity of demand and supply.

sensitivity training   *management*   A group training method designed to develop

301

social skills and to see one's self through the eyes of others.

separated manager One in a managerial position who tends to shun the company of employees and who tends to judge all work done by the company manual. A non-personal method of managing.

separate estate Property belonging to one spouse over which the other spouse has no right in equity. At common law, a married woman was not allowed to own any property independently of her husband.

separate property Property acquired by either spouse prior to marriage or by gift or devise after marriage, as distinct from community property.

separate trading of registered interest and principal of securities (STRIPS) U.S. Treasury securities, the records for which are kept on computer, that are sold by dealers. The unique thing about these securities is that the interest and principal are sold separately, with separate identification numbers.

separation rate *management* The ratio of the number of employees terminating work during the month to the average work force in the same month. Normally, separations are broken down into three categories—resignation, discharge, and layoff—and a separate rate for each category is computed in a parallel manner.

sequence analysis *economics* A study of the causal connection of the economic events of one period with the economic events of the succeeding period or periods.

sequential analysis *statistics* A method of sampling in which a terminal decision depends not on the size of the sample, as in conventional sampling, but on the values of successive observations. As each item is tested, a decision is made on the basis of values observed up to that point as to whether to continue sampling or terminate.

sequestration *law* A writ installing representatives of a court to compel performance of a court order, usually with regard to property being seized upon some judgment of the court.

serial bonds 1. Issue of bonds in which specified bonds mature each year. 2. Single bond issue offered at one time that has a portion maturing on successive dates until it is fully retired.

serial correlation *statistics* A situation in which two different time series are correlated when the values of one series are lagged by a fixed time interval with the values of the other series.

series EE bond Nontransferable United States Government savings bonds that are issued at a discount. Sold in denominations of fifty dollars (twenty-five dollars cost) or more and maturing in seven to ten years. Series EE bonds which have matured may be exchanged for Series HH bonds if the owner wishes to hold bonds, or cashed in for the face amount of the bond.

series HH bonds Nontransferable United States Government current income bonds that are sold at face value and pay interest semi-annually. Sold in denominations of five hundred dollars or more and maturing in ten years.

servant One who performs duties about the person or home of a master or personal employer. The master not only prescribes to the servant the results of the servant's work but directs or may direct the means; i.e., retains the power of controlling.

service 1. Intangible task that satisfies consumer and industrial user needs when efficiently developed and distributed to chosen market segments. Services are included in the marketing definition of product. 2. *international trade* Item which is intangible, but which is still sold internationally, such as transportation, information, insurance, etc.

service benefit basis Basis on which benefits are provided over a prescribed number of days (such as sixty days) by certain insurers, such as Blue Cross/Blue Shield. Normally, the insured is entitled to get the prescribed service benefits paid for, regardless of the rate the hospital might charge someone else. This type of service benefits is usually provided when the insurer has an agreement with the hospital in question.

service benefit plan Government-wide plan, written by Blue Cross/Blue Shield, offering hospital, surgical, and medical services and maternity and supplemental benefits. This plan is available to all eligible civil service personnel, and payments for benefits are made directly to the doctor or hospital.

service charge Component of some finance charges, such as the fee for triggering an overdraft checking account into use.

service connected death benefits System of compensation for dependents of personnel whose death is service-connected, established by the Servicemen's and Veteran's Survivor Act of 1956, effective January 1, 1957. The amount of benefits no longer differs according to whether death occurs during wartime or peacetime and, in most cases, are higher than before. There are three kinds of death benefits: burial allowance, lump sum death gratuity, and dependency and indemnity compensation.

service connected disability benefit Any of three kinds of benefits for a military disability, including compensation (paid by the Veterans Administration), severance pay, and retirement pay.

service forms *health insurance* Plan in which payments are made directly to the hospital and doctors for services rendered and not to the patient. This payment arrangement is found in some Blue Cross (hospital) and Blue Shield (physicians and surgeons) plans as well as some independent plans, health maintenance organizations' plans (HMOs), and in some insurer plans.

service partner Member of a partnership whose contribution is mainly in the form of services or knowledge rendered. In such a case, the partners must agree on the percentage of ownership of the service partner.

service reduction *retirement plans* Internal Revenue Service requirement that benefits be reduced by one-tenth for each year of service less than ten years. Therefore, an employee hired at age fifty-nine by an employer whose benefit plan specified a normal retirement age of sixty-five will be entitled to only six-tenths of the normal retirement benefit. As a practical matter, this restriction seldom applies, since many defined-benefit plans set requirement age as the latter of sixty-five or completion of ten years of plan participation.

servitus actus *Privilege of walking*, riding, or driving over another's ground.

servitus aquae dusendae *Privilege of leading water* to one's land through another's land.

servitus itineris *Privilege of walking* or riding on another's ground.

servitus ne luminibus officatur *Easement of light.* A right not to have light to one's land obstructed by the neighbor.

servitus viae *Right of way.*

set *statistics* A grouping of data, all of which pertains to a common base, such as data on teenagers, senior citizens, etc.

setback Distance from the curb or the established line within which no buildings may be erected.

set-off Discharge or reduction of one demand by an opposite one, or the right one party has against another to use the claim in full or partial satisfaction of what that party owes to the other.

settle 1. To adjust an account, not necessarily to pay it. 2. To limit real property or the income thereof to several persons in succession, thereby ensuring that no one person can deprive the others of their right of future enjoyment. 3. To make a document correct in form and substance. 4. To effect an extra-judicial arrangement between the parties to an action in relation to the subject matter, thereby terminating the action.

settlement date Date upon which the payment for the security purchased becomes due.

settlement option Life insurance policies option providing that, when the proceeds become payable, the insured or beneficiary may elect to have such proceeds paid in some form other than a lump sum. Some of these include a fixed amount option, a fixed period option, an interest, and a life income option.

setup time The time involved in changing a machine, method, or technique from the production of one type of item to another.

seven-point plan *personnel* A method of testing the potential for employment of an individual based on the following seven points: (a) general intelligence, (b) special attitudes, (c) attainments, (d) health,

(e) interests, (f) disposition, (g) circumstances.

70%–80% test   *pension plans* Test for qualification for a tax-exempt pension plan required after the employees in the excluded class are subtracted. Seventy percent of all employees must be eligible for the plan, and of that 70%, 80% must be participating in the plan. (*See* excluded class)

76 Series   *See* Homeowners' Series.

sever   *law* To divide, set apart, disjoin; to deliver a plea distinct from that of other co-defendants.

several   Describes an obligation that is not joint and can be enforced independently.

severally but not jointly   Phrase used in a form of agreement that establishes responsibility for selling a portion of the securities in an underwriting. While members agree to buy a certain portion of the issues severally, they do not agree to any joint liability for shares not sold by other members of the syndicate.

severalty   Ownership of real property by an individual as an individual.

severance   1. Act of severing; partition; division. 2. The destruction of the unities essential for the formation and continuance of joint tenancy.

severance damages   1. Element of value arising out of a condemnation to which a tract was included. 2. Award made in condemnation proceedings to an owner to compensate the owner for a decrease in value of the remainder of the property due to the partial taking; equals and is the difference between the value of the remaining property before and after the taking.

severance pay   1. Payment to an employee of a sum of money in addition to back wages on termination for reasons not attributable to the employee. The payment may be a contract, or, in small companies, a non-contract understanding; it may be gratuitous or required by statute or some regulatory agency. 2. Pay military personnel are entitled to when separated from service for physical disability. Some may not be eligible for disability retirement pay because the rated disability is less than 30% or length-of-service credits are insufficient. Disability severance pay is

a lump sum equal to twice the monthly base and longevity pay multiplied by years of service, but not exceeding the amount of two years' basic pay. Disability severance pay is payable by the member's service branch and is deducted from any Veterans Administration compensation payable to the former member for the same disability.

severance tax   A special tax levied against forests or mines for the amount harvested or mined in a given year.

sex discrimination   Disparate employment practice giving unlawful consideration to members of one sex; prohibited by Title VII of the Civil Rights Act of 1964.

shadow calendar   A backlog of securities issues which have been registered by the Securities and Exchange Commission, but for which no offerings date has been set because they have not been cleared for sale.

shake-out   A process of streamlining the employment needs of a company to make certain jobs, and therefore employees, redundant. This has been a hallmark of industry in the 1980s and will continue throughout the 1990s.

shall   *law* Verb form that, when used in statutes, makes the provision imperative.

share   1. A person's portion of anything owned in common by several persons. 2. Definite fractional part of the capital of a corporation conferring upon the holder certain rights to a proportionate part of the assets of the corporation, whether by way of dividend or on distribution of assets in dissolution. While the capital of the corporation is its property, the share is the property of the shareholder.

share averaging   System for accumulation of shares in which the investor periodically buys the same number of shares of stock without regard to price.

share certificate   Instrument under the seal of the company certifying that the person named is entitled to a certain number of shares as specified.

shared equity mortgage   Home loan in which the lender is granted a share of the equity, thereby allowing the lender to participate in the proceeds from resale.

share draft   A check-like certificate issued by some credit unions to members, who then use the drafts like checks to draw against their savings share account.

shared values theory   *industrial psychology* A view held by the structural-functionalist school that a society can maintain stability and equilibrium since all members of society have certain basic shared values. This view is often argued against by those who say that the differences between the strata of society are sufficient to disturb the equilibrium at any given point in time.

share elasticity   *economics* The ratio of the change in the percentage of the market that a specific producer has to the change in the percentage of the price differential between the producer's price and the price schedules of competitors.

shareholder   One who owns one or more shares of capital stock of a corporation. Includes one who has subscribed for a share or shares and who is entered on the books of the corporation as a stockholder, although the stock certificate has not yet been issued to that person.

shareholders' equity   The net worth of a company, less preferred stock.

share warrant   Warrant or certification under the seal of the issuing company evidencing that the bearer of the warrant is entitled to a certain number or amount of fully paid-up shares of stock of that company.

shark watcher   A firm that specializes in the early detection of takeover activity. These firms have a primary business of soliciting proxies, but also watch the markets for trading patterns in a client's stock and for identifying parties trading in the stock.

shark repellent   *See* safe harbor.

shelf registration   Experimental Securities and Exchange commission program under which companies can file a general-purpose prospectus describing their possible financing plans for up to the next two years.

shell   Special envelope designed to hold bond coupons which are being presented for payment. Each envelope must contain coupons from only one specific bond issue. Pertinent information such as the name and address of the bond holder and the paying agent is printed on the envelope. A filled shell (i.e., one completed and holding the coupons) must be handled just as cash is handled.

shell corporation   A firm that is incorporated, but appears to have few assets and few operations. Sometimes these corporations are set up to solicit cash for starting operations, in which case the business could be considered highly risky. They are also sometimes set up to attempt to evade taxes or in a manner totally fraudulent.

sheriff sale   Sale, often by auction, conducted by an authorized officer to carry out a decree, execution, or foreclosure issued by a court.

Sherman Antitrust Act (1890)   Major antitrust law of the United States intended to secure equality of opportunity and to protect the public against the evils commonly incident to monopolies. Prohibits contracts, combinations, and conspiracies in restraint of trade, as well as monopolization or attempts to monopolize in interstate trade or foreign commerce. Violations are punishable by fines and/or imprisonment. Other relevant statutes are the Robinson-Patman Act and the Clayton Act.

shifting risk   Moving risks by hedging, subcontracting, or holding harmless agreements or surety bonding agreements. In this type of action, a part of the risk is legally placed upon others with their knowledge through some contractual arrangement or agreement.

shifting the tax burden   Plans basically intended to shift income from persons in higher tax brackets to those in lower brackets. This is normally done within the family so that the economic benefits remain at home. (This is normally done by having family members in higher tax brackets transfer assets, by gift or otherwise, to those in lower brackets—parents or children—in order to reduce the income taxes of the donors.) (The 1986 Tax Reform Act has limited this somewhat.)

shilling   A unit of English money. There are twenty shillings in an English pound sterling. The abbreviation is "s."

shipper   One who transports goods for a fee.

shipping and forwarding agent   *See* freight forwarder.

shock and error model   *econometrics* A system of equations containing random disturbances of specific variables and errors in the specific equations.

shop 1. Building appropriated to the selling of wares at retail; a store. 2. Building in which making or repairing of an article is carried on or in which an industry is pursued, such as a machine shop or barber shop.

shoplift To willfully and unlawfully take possession of merchandise offered for sale in a mercantile establishment with the intention of not paying the purchase price.

shopping center Collection of retail stores with a common parking area and generally one or more large department, discount, or food stores. Sometimes enclosed as a mall where covered access to all establishments is available. Most shopping centers have an anchor tenant which is expected to draw the traffic, used as a selling point to get other stores to come into the center. Many shopping centers are owned by real estate investment trusts.

shop right value Form of implied license to freely use the subject of a patent, such right founded on application of equitable principles where an employee has used an employer's time, money, tools, and materials to produce a useful result and where it is only fair and equitable that the employer should be entitled to use produce of the employer's own property and to duplicate it in the employer's business.

short bond 1. A bond with a maturity date usually no more than two years. 2. A bond which is repayable within one year, and is thus listed as a current liability.

short hedge position Position that limits or eliminates the risk of declining value in a security or commodity without entailing ownership. (E.g., buying a futures contract on raw materials at a specific price protects a manufacturer who is committed to selling a product at a certain price at a specified time but who cannot buy the raw materials at the time of the commitment. Thus, if the price of the material goes up the manufacturer makes a profit on the contract; if the price goes down the manufacturer makes a profit on the product.)

short run Period of time so short that the amount of some factor inputs cannot be varied.

short sale 1. Sale of shares which the seller does not own for future delivery at a time when such delivery must be made under the rules of the Stock Exchange. Normally the broker will guarantee the shares to cover the short sale. 2. Sale of securities that the investor does not own at a certain price in anticipation of buying back those same securities at a lower price. The profit or loss is the difference between purchase and sale prices. The brokerage house will loan the seller the securities that must be delivered to the buyer. A short sale may only be made in a margin account.

short swing profits *corporate law* Profits made by an insider on the purchase and sale or sale and purchase of securities of the corporation within a period of less than six months. This practice is considered questionable.

short term 1. *accounting* Describes assets which can be expected to be converted into cash within a year, or liabilities coming due in one year or less. 2. *investment* Describes an investment with a maturity of one year or less or, in the case of bonds, two years or less. 3. *taxes* Formerly described assets held for six months or less, distinguishing short term gains or losses from long term gains or losses, with regard to income taxes. This distinction was removed by the 1986 Tax Reform Act.

short-term capital gain Gain on assets which have been held for less than six months at the time of their disposition. The gain is treated as ordinary income. (*See* Appendix G)

short-term capital loss Loss on a capital asset which has been held for less than six months at the time of its disposition. This loss is a deduction against ordinary income.

short-term disability benefits Coverage providing weekly indemnity to employees in amounts seldom exceeding two-thirds of normal earnings. The most common plans provide protection for twelve, twenty-six, or fifty-two weeks. These benefits are usually offered in two ways: (a) on a scheduled basis of $X weekly, or (b) on a percentage of earnings basis, such as 66⅔% of salary.

short-term investment instrument Type of vehicle which allows for short-term investing of from twenty-four hours to possibly six months. These will differ between individual investors and corporations, or institutions. They include such instruments as commercial paper, bank certificates, money-market trusts, tax-exempt money-market funds, treasuries, etc. They make earnings possible on cash which can be invested for only a short time.

short-term speculators Those traders in the market who usually use six weeks as a turning point. In short, they are in and out of the market quickly, hoping that they are accurately reading the trends.

short-term trust *See* Clifford trust.

short ton Unit of weight equal to two thousand pounds. This is opposed to a long ton, 2,240 pounds, a weight normally confined to water transportation.

sight draft A draft payable on presentment.

sigma The eighteenth letter in the Greek alphabet. The capital sigma (Σ) denotes a sum. The small sigma (σ) denotes the standard deviation.

significance ratio *statistics* A percentage of difference between variables obtained in a random sampling which is considered to be sufficient to reject the null hypothesis. (Cf. null hypothesis)

silent partner A partner who does not actively participate in the business. Unless the silent partner is a limited partner, he or she will have the same liability as the active partner. Also called sleeping partner.

silver Precious metal historically known and used almost as much as gold but with less monetary value. Enormous quantities of silver are used in industry, especially in film manufacturing and in electrical and electronic products. Silver is classified by the United States government as a strategic material because of its use in the defense industry.

silver-indexed bonds Bonds issued by the Sunshine Mining Company, in the form of a convertible security. In essence, these bonds are coupled with eleven-year call options on silver bullion. At maturity the bonds can be exchanged for fifty ounces of silver, at the option of the owner.

Silver Purchase Act (1934) An act authorizing and directing the Secretary of the Treasury to purchase silver at home and abroad until the proportion of silver in the combined stocks of gold and silver in the United States is one-fourth the total monetary value of such stocks or until the price of silver reached $1.295 an ounce.

simple annuity Straight annuity paying only until death (i.e., straight life annuity), as distinguished from a refund annuity.

simple contract Any contract which is not of record or contract under seal or specialty. Includes such instruments as promissory notes, bills of exchange, and bills of lading.

simple debenture *See* naked debenture.

simple interest Interest computed on the principal only, without compounding arrears of interest.

simple license Authority, without reward or consideration, to do a particular act or series of acts on another's land without passing any interest in the land, which need not be in writing. (*See* Appendix G)

simple negligence Negligence which is neither gross nor wanton; failure to undertake a course of conduct which a reasonable and prudent person would take, knowing one's acts might result in injury to persons or property.

simple random sample Sample chosen in such a way that every member of a representative group has an equal chance of being included.

simple trust *tax law* A trust that distributes all of its income on a current basis, and does not provide for a charitable distribution.

simplex commendatio non obligat *Mere recommendation does not bind.* The maxim has reference to exaggerated commendations of a vendor of goods, which in the absence of material misrepresentation or fraud does not render the vendor liable.

simplified employee pension (SEP) Plan that utilizes employee-owned Individual Retirement Accounts which are allowed to accept employer contributions. Federal reporting requirements are considered less burdensome in SEPs than in other plans.

simulation *See* Monte Carlo simulation.

simultaneous death The deaths of two or more persons in a common disaster or under circumstances in which it cannot be ascertained who was the first to die or who survived the other. Under statutes relating to simultaneous deaths, generally in such instances the property of each is to be disposed of as if that person had survived.

sine *Without.*

sinecure Office or position for which compensation is received but which involves few or no duties.

sine die *Without day.* Describes an adjournment in which the court has not fixed a day for the hearing of the cause.

sine qua non *Without which not.* An indispensable thing or condition without which the event would have never occurred; invoked in determining liability.

single life annuity Annuity written on the life of a single annuitant who alone can receive the annuity payments. Normally, annuity payments will be paid only until the death of the annuitant.

single life pension A situation in which the pension annuity is written on one life only (such as the life of the employee), and for which payments stop when that one person dies.

single premium contract According to the Internal Revenue Code (Section 264), a contract in which substantially all of the premiums are paid within four years or in which a substantial number of future premiums are prepaid. Under the Code, interest expense incurred to pay for such a contract is denied on contracts purchased after March 1, 1954.

single-premium deferred annuity (SPDA) A tax deferred investment somewhat similar to an IRA, without many of the IRA restrictions. A lump sum payment may be made to an insurance company and can be invested in either a fixed-return instrument or a variable-return portfolio. Proceeds are taxed only when distributions are made. There is a 10% tax penalty on distributions made before 59.5 years of age.

single publication rule Rule stating that where an issue of a newspaper or an edition of a book contains a libelous statement, the plaintiff has a single cause of action and the number of copies distributed is considered relevant for damages but not as a new cause of action. However, jurisdictions follow the common law rule that each communication of written or printed matter is a distinct and separate publication of a libel contained therein.

single-state municipal bond fund A mutual fund which invests only in state or municipal bonds issued in one state. Dividends paid on the bonds are not taxable by either state or federal governments, when the bond-holders are residents of that state.

single tax Proposal advanced by the American economist Henry George (1839–1897) that the only tax a society should impose is a tax on land, because all rent on land is unearned surplus which increases as a result of natural progress and economic growth. Three major shortcomings leveled against this thesis are that the single tax would: (a) not yield enough revenues to meet government's spending needs; (b) be unjust, because surpluses may accrue to other resource owners besides landlords if the owners can gain some monopolistic control over the sale of their resources in the market place; and (c) be difficult to administer because it does not distinguish between land and capital—that is, between the proportion that results from improvements made on the land.

sinking fund 1. Fund of cash set aside for the payment of a future obligation. 2. Series of periodic payments to retire a bond issue. 3. Cash or cash equivalent regularly set aside in a separate fund (usually held by an independent trustee) that is to be used to redeem debt securities or to retire preferred stock. 4. Aggregate of sums of money from particular taxes or uses of revenue, set apart and invested, usually at fixed intervals, for the extinguishment of the debt of a government or corporation by the accumulation of interest; it is utilized towards the payment of the interest due on the debt and for the gradual payment of the principal. 5. Account that, when compounded, will equal a specified sum after a specified time period. (*See* compound interest) 6. Savings account with which the manager of a business hopes to offset the need for insurance. This rarely works well and increases the risk burden of the business.

sinking fund provision Provision designed to retire a substantial portion of many bonds before maturity. Bonds in a designated amount are selected by lot for retirement at fixed intervals; in that way the issuer repays the debt gradually. Sinking fund provisions have become less popular because investors prefer to preserve liberal terms for a long time.

sin tax Excise tax levied on commodities that public policy deems undesirable in order to limit their consumption, such as taxes on cigarettes and alcohol.

sit-down strike A method used by unions where workers occupy a plant but refuse to work. Unions do this to stop the production flow leaving the plant. The plan became popular during the 1930s in the U.S. Also called sit-in.

situs *Location; situation.* In relation to personal property, its *situs* is said to be the domicile of its owner.

six-year graded vesting Method providing a graded schedule with vesting not less rapid than 20% after two years of service, with 20% additional vesting for each subsequent year (full vesting after six years); designed for top-heavy plans.

size-effect theory The theory that industrial relations problems increase as the size of the plant increases.

skewness *statistics* The degree to which a frequency curve lacks symmetry. The most common measure of skewness is the difference between the arithmetic mean and the mode and, for relative measure, dividing this result by the standard deviation. In mathematics, skewness is the fourth moment around the arithmetic mean.

skimming A sales method in which the product is originally sold at a high price, and then the price is periodically reduced until it appears that the market is saturated.

skip-payment privilege 1. A clause in some mortgage contracts and installment loan agreements that allows the borrower to miss a payment if payments are ahead of schedule. 2. An option sometimes offered a bank credit card holder to defer the December payment.

skip-tracing agency Business which provides creditors with mailing materials and other services to assist them in the collection of accounts by helping them locate delinquent debtors and by uncovering financial and other information about such debtors. It is not directly concerned with the business of attempting to collect the debt from the debtor.

slander Defamation by spoken word. (Cf. libel)

slander of property False and malicious statement which tends to disparage the quality, condition, or value of the property of another, and which causes special injury or damage. Such statements are actionable.

slander of title False and malicious statements, oral or written, made in disparagement of a person's title to real or personal property, causing injury.

slander per quod Words which are not defamatory on their face without the aid of extrinsic evidence but which by inference or imputations amount to defamation.

slander per se Statements which are defamatory on their face without aid of extrinsic evidence.

sleeping partner *See* silent partner.

sliding parity *foreign exchange* A concept that offers a compromise between a fixed parity and a floating exchange rate. Normally, it tends to spread the revaluation or devaluation of a currency over a period of months, thus avoiding the shock of a sudden drop in, or rise of, the value of a currency.

sliding-scale tariff A tariff so designed that the duty varies with the price of the good, whether the duty is ad valorem or specific.

slip chart A graphic method of recording progress, particularly on a research and development project.

slope *statistics* The slope of a curve at a point is the change of the dependent variable (Y axis) divided by the change of the independent variable (X axis). The slope of a straight line is the same at all points.

slowdown A labor union substitute for a strike, wherein the workers do not leave their jobs but reduce the amount of production, usually to emphasize some grievance.

Slutsky theorem *economics* The proposition that the fall in the price of a good will lead to the substitution of some quantity of that good for the near substitutes of that good.

Slutsky-Yule effect *economics* Cyclical behavior in a series (even though the resulting oscillation is nonexistent) resulting from the very fact of summing or averaging successive values of a random series.

Small Business Act Federal statute whose object is to protect the interests of small business concerns in order to preserve free competitive enterprise.

Small Business Administration (SBA) Independent agency of the federal government whose duties are to make guaranteed loans to small businesses and to assist them with certain management and financial problems. The agency is relatively small with about five thousand employees.

small saver certificate Certificate of deposit with a minimum maturity of two half-year Treasury securities, in accordance with regulations. There is no minimum denomination required on these certificates.

Smith-Connaly Act (1943) A federal law enacted as a war measure justifying government seizure of plants affected by a labor dispute and forbidding strikes unless thirty days' notice is given. Government seizure and wage and price controls were a part of an integrated program.

smuggling 1. *common law* The bringing on shore or carrying from shore goods, wares, and merchandise for which duty has not been paid or goods on which importation or exportation has been prohibited. 2. The act of surreptitiously and by concealment or fraud avoiding customs and introducing goods into a country.

snowballing A rush of selling downward.

social accounting A situation in which the economic evaluation of a project also attempts to consider the social costs. (Cf. social costs)

social audit The study of the impact upon society of a company or an industry, which may include a review of what society expects of the company or industry, as well as all other facets which may have an impact directly upon society, either positive or negative.

social class Relatively permanent division of a society into which individuals or families are categorized on the basis of prestige and community status.

social costs The costs to society, often difficult to quantify, of a given company or industry, and the negative impact it has on the health and happiness of society.

social responsibility Obligation of a person to promote those things which are in the best interest of society.

social security General term applied to the whole area of federal and state legislations providing for assistance to people on account of their disability, old age, survivor's insurance benefits, unemployment compensation administration, dependent children, maternal and child welfare, and services to crippled children; aid to the states for services to the aged, blind or disabled, for planning comprehensive action to combat mental retardation, health insurance for the aged, and medical assistance programs.

socioeconomic differences and market segmentation Dividing the total population into segments according to the economic position they occupy in society for the purpose of deciding the products or services each stratum of society is apt to buy.

socioeconomic status Social strata into which a household falls, relative to annual income, and the standard of living such an income will buy.

socius *A partner.*

soft currency A situation in which a currency may be losing its purchasing power, or its value as related to other currencies, because of a deficit balance of payments problem. Soft currencies are subject to devaluation.

soft goods Nondurable consumer goods, normally.

soft loan 1. A long-term loan, particularly to a developing country, made at a low, if any, interest rate. 2. A loan made in international trade which can be repaid in the currency of the borrower. Since the borrower's currency may have questionable value, the loan may sometimes be looked upon as foreign aid, since the loan will not be repaid.

soft money   In a development or an investment, money contributed that is tax-deductible.

soil bank   Land held out of agricultural production in an effort to stabilize commodity prices and promote soil conservation. Subsidies to farmers participating in the soil bank program are provided by the United States Department of Agriculture.

Soil Bank Act   Federal statute enacted to promote soil conservation by paying farmers to divert a portion of their crop land from production.

solar day   That period of time which begins at sunrise and ends at sunset.

solar year   Period of time consisting of 365 days, except in leap years, which consist of 366 days.

sole ownership   Situation in which only one person has interest in a property as owner.

sole proprietor   Individual engaged in a business without associates or a corporate charter.

sole proprietorship   Individual and exclusive ownership of a business. All income passes through to the owner as ordinary income for tax purposes (with business expenses being deductible). A sole proprietorship is not a business entity as is a partnership or corporation, but is indistinguishable from the individual who owns it.

solicit   To entreat, implore, urge; to make petitions to; to try to obtain; to tempt.

solicitor   *insurance* Individual appointed by an agent and authorized to solicit and receive applications as a representative of the agent with no authority to obligate the insurer in any way.

solvency   1. Financial status in which assets exceed liabilities. 2. The ability to pay all debts or just claims, generally determined by the standard of whether one owns more than one owes, even if what one owns cannot be subject to legal process.

sophisticated investor   *tax shelters* Investor who has knowledge of tax laws and other matters which would give the investor the ability to invest personally without professional help. The financial status of the individual is also vital.

sound mind   1. Condition in which mental faculties are developed to a normal extent and not impaired by a severe mental illness. 2. In the law of wills, a degree of mind and memory that allows for a clear understanding and a recollection or realization of the property to be devised or bequeathed, of the persons who are to receive the bequests, and of the manner in which the property is to be distributed among them.

source of working capital   Origin of a firm's funds, consisting of the firm's income and the funds generated by the sale of long-term assets. Long-term borrowing and the sale of new securities are also vital sources.

sources and uses statement   Document showing where a company got and where it spent its cash over a specific period of time. It is constructed by segregating all changes in balance sheet accounts into those that provided cash and those that consumed cash.

sources of investment risk   Risks in constructing and managing an investment portfolio, particularly marketability and liquidity. If all risk factors are studied closely, one can see that they all fit under one or both of the two primary risks.

sovereign   *law* An ultimate power with respect to the ability to rule or govern. A governmental body, in total, as set forth by a constitution, can be referred to as sovereign.

span of control   A concept borrowed from the military which asserts that an executive or supervisor cannot function efficiently if that person has more than a certain number of subordinates.

span of managerial responsibility This is a concept set out by Peter Drucker which attempts to assess subordinates' need for assistance and teaching.

spec house   *real estate* Single-family dwelling constructed in anticipation of finding a buyer.

special administrator   Administrator with limited authority to care for and preserve the estate until an executor or general administrator is ascertained or appointed as its proper legal representative. Such an administrator does not have the power to administer the estate other than to take such steps necessary for its preservation.

311

special agent 1. One whose authority is for a single act not involving continuity of service. Company employee who maintains contact with agents, introduces new products and procedures, and acts as an intermediary in resolving problems. 2. *law* Person appointed to act for specific duties with his power of appointment extending no further. 3. *insurance* Agent with a role similar to that of a field representative. This person travels around a specified district, supervising agents, and otherwise promoting the interests of the company.

special allocation Agreement between partners resulting from differences in contributions to and receipts from a partnership as one may bring a money-partner into the partnership and allocate that partner 80% of the losses and 50% of the income.

special assessment Assessment made against a property to pay for a public improvement meant to enhance the value of all property within that area.

special assessment bond A type of municipal bond issued for the purpose of performing some public work which is repaid from fees charged those who benefit directly from the public work. (E.g., a bond issue to build a sewer system would be paid by the individual residences and businesses which were tied to the system.)

special auto policy *insurance* Auto policy, soon to be extinct, that has the following provisions: (a) Single limit of liability per occurrence for bodily injury and/or property damage. (b) No liability coverage for property in the care, custody, or control of insured. (c) Named insured and relatives covered under physical damage coverage while using nonowned private passenger autos only if legally liable. (d) Medical expenses incurred within one year from date of accident covered under medical payments coverage. (e) Medical payments coverage on excess over accident, disability, or hospitalization insurance available to an insured. (f) First-aid coverage is included as a supplementary payment. (g) Collision and comprehensive coverages are written as separate insuring agreements. (h) Personal effects covered from loss by fire, lightning, flood, earthquake, theft of auto, and collision. (i) Persons (other than relatives) must have permission to use the vehicle of named insured before coverage applies. (j) Vehicles acquired during the term of the policy must be reported within thirty days for coverage.

special counsel Attorney employed by the attorney general of the United States or of a state to assist in a particular case where required by the public interest.

special damages Damages which are the natural but not the necessary result of the injury.

special deposit Deposit made and intended for special purpose by both the depositor and the bank, in the nature of a bailment.

special drawing right (SDR) Supplementary reserve established in 1969 in the form of account entries on the books of the International Monetary Fund. They are allocated among participating countries in accordance with their quotas, and can be drawn upon by governments to help finance balance-of-payments deficits. They are meant to promote an orderly growth of reserves that will help the long-run expanding needs of world trade. Also called paper gold.

special indorsement Indorsement which specifies the person to whom or to whose order the instrument is to be payable.

special interest Interest in property other than full ownership.

specialist *stock exchange* Member of the exchange who makes a market in one or more securities and presides over a trading post. The function of specialists is to maintain a fair and orderly market in those securities. They are expected to risk their own capital by buying or selling those securities with their own funds, or facilitating exchange among other buyers or sellers. Each stock exchange sets specific regulations regarding specialists' activities.

special miscellaneous account (SMA) A memorandum account held by a broker of the funds in excess of the margin requirement. The account is generally maintained so that the broker can gauge how close the customer might be to a margin call. Withdrawals require the permission of the broker.

special power of appointment A specification of what a donee can do in disposing of property. Property can be appointed only to certain persons; the donee, the donee's estate, and the donee's creditors do not qualify as those who can receive such property.

special power of attorney Power of attorney by which the attorney-in-fact has authority to act only in specific matters.

special purpose or use Principle that, in eminent domain proceedings, while the compensation payable to the owner for property that has been appropriated is generally the fair market value of the property, property adjacent to the condemned must be evaluated with respect to the value added to or taken away by the condemnation.

special reduction election Principle that on capital gain property contributed to a charitable organization, the donor may deduct up to the 50% ceiling if the donor elects to reduce the contribution by 40% of the amount of the appreciation on the property, notwithstanding the general 30% limitation.

special risk policy *insurance* Policy covering hazards excluded in usual health policies, such as war, accidents to those engaged in dangerous scientific experiments, and travel to the moon. Many persons with incomes dependent on some special talent or personal characteristics buy high-benefit limit special-task forms to cover their exposure. Lloyd's of London provides underwriting facilities for many of these exposures.

Special Supervisory Examination The examination of a bank when such bank has shown evidence of problems which require more than one review per year.

special trust Trust requiring the trustee to exert himself or herself to accomplish the purpose of the trust, such as a devise to a trustee upon a trust to sell and convert said trust into money.

specialty Contract under seal.

special use valuation Method of valuation eligible for real estate in a closely held business or for farming purposes. If elected by the decedent's executor, this may result in significant estate tax savings because the real estate is valued at its actu-al use rather than its highest value. A maximum reduction of $750,000 from the value of the decedent's gross estate is allowed in 1983 and later years for real estate that qualifies for special use valuation. The requirements are: (a) On the date of the decedent's death, the property must be involved in a "qualified use," either for farming purposes or in a closely held corporation. (b) The value of the qualified property minus debts and unpaid mortgages must equal at least 50% of the decedent's gross estate. (c) At least 25% of the gross estate must be qualified real estate. (d) The property must pass to a "qualified heir," defined by the Internal Revenue Code to include ancestors, lineal descendants, spouses, cousins, daughters-in-law, sons-in-law, and other members of the immediate family. (e) The property must have been owned by the decedent or a family member and used as a farm or a closely held business for five years prior to the date of the decedent's death. The decedent or family member must have been a material participant in the operation of the farm or business for five of the past eight years. The time during which the property was owned by another family member may be traced to the time the decedent held the property to satisfy the time requirement.

special use valuation election *estate planning* Principle specifying that, if certain conditions are met, the executor may elect to value real property included in the decedent's estate which is devoted to farming or closely held business use on the basis of the property's value as a farm or its value in the closely held business, rather than its fair market value determined on the basis of its highest and best use. (Stipulations are to be found in the Internal Revenue Code Section 2032A.)

special value In connection with compensation to the owner of property expropriated, value applied to present use of the land and its added worth to the owner for the actual and particular use and use for which it is specially fit.

special verdict *law* A verdict that makes separate findings on a number of the issues of a case as well as a final finding for one party or the other. A special verdict must be consistent in all of its parts, or it can be set aside by the court.

special warranty deed Deed in which the grantor declares that he or she will defend the grantee only against acts of the grantor and persons claiming under the grantor. The grantor does not warrant against title defects arising from conditions that existed before the grantor owned the property. Essentially, this is a quitclaim deed.

specification 1. Particular or detailed statement of the various elements or a description of the constituent parts of a patent or building. 2. Written description of item or job that a government unit or industrial firm wishes to acquire for use in competitive bidding.

specific bequest Gift by will of a particular item of personal property

specific devise Gift by will of a particular item of real property.

specific goods Goods identified and agreed upon at the time a contract of sale is made.

specific lien Lien against certain property only.

specific performance 1. Legal action in which the court requires a party to a contract to perform the terms of the contract when that party has refused to fulfill his or her obligations. Used in real estate, since each parcel of land is unique. 2. The actual carrying out, or a proceeding to compel the actual carrying out, of an agreement (e.g., the purchase and sale of real performance rather than for damages).

specified perils coverage *insurance* Policy covering the insured against only the perils specifically named in the policy.

speculation 1. Type of investment that offers a potentially large return but is also very risky. 2. Reasonable probability that an investment will produce a loss.

speculation, ten commandments of See ten commandments of speculation.

speculative motive Desire on the part of households and businesses to hold part of their assets in liquid form so that they can undertake financial investments at higher returns when the interest rate rises. This motive is influenced directly by the interest rate and is one of the chief sources of demand for loanable funds in the modern theory of interest.

speculative risk Chance which is inherent in business speculation, whether an on-going business or a special project. (Cf. pure risk)

speculative stock Stock with a variable, rather than a fixed, income. Stocks marked by high price/earnings ratios. Hot new stocks are considered speculative, as are penny stocks, especially in mining shares and stocks from glamour companies.

speculator 1. One who invests with the anticipation that an event or series of events will occur to increase the value of the investment. 2. Individual who is willing to accept substantial risks for the possibility of a large return. 3. Investor who is generally knowledgeable in market activities and is able to weigh risks involved rather than just gamble. The speculator's investment process includes the use of leverage, margin buying, and short selling. 4. Person who purchases goods or financial assets in anticipation that prices will rise and that he or she can sell at a profit; speculators can also speculate on a fall in prices. 5. *investments* Individual in the market who is willing to take long chances on securities in the hope of reaping large returns. Speculators normally are not interested in holding a security for the long-term, but jump in and out of the market, making mostly short-term gains or losses. 6. *real estate* One who invests money with the hope of a quick and large profit. During periods of high inflation, people buy residential housing and hold it for a time for the price increase. While this "profit" is often phantom in nature, the appearance is of a large profit in a short time.

spendthrift trust 1. Trust created to provide a fund for the maintenance of an incapable or improvident person. The trustee of such a fund is given the power to distribute only the income to the beneficiary; thus, the principal is kept free from the reach of creditors. 2. Trust established to provide a fund for the maintenance of the beneficiary and at the same time to secure it against the beneficiary's improvidence or incapacity.

spin off The severing, by a corporation, of part of its operation which will then form a new corporation. This may be done for several reasons, including establishment of a new profit center. If the part of the corporation severed is then sold, it is usually to enhance the cash position of the parent firm.

split commissions A commission divided between the broker who carried out the transaction and the person, such as a financial advisor, who brought the broker the order. Split commissions are also common in real estate transactions.

split-dollar plan Arrangement between an employer and employee whereby the cost of an insurance policy on the employee is divided between employee and employer, and whereby the proceeds from the policy upon the death of the employee may also be split. Under the basic plan, the employer pays that part of the annual premium which equals the current year's increase in the cash surrender value of the policy and the employee pays the balance. If the employee dies while the split dollar plan is in effect, the employer receives from the proceeds an amount equal to the cash value of the policy or at least the premium payments, and the employee's beneficiary receives the balance of the proceeds.

split-funded Describes a plan in which both trust companies and insurance companies are used as funding agencies. (Usually a part of the plan is made up of a whole-life insurance policy on the individual, combined with a separate equity investment.)

split gift Method of giving in which donor's spouse consents to treatment as the donor of one-half of any taxable gift made to a third person. This allows a married couple to use two annual per-donee exclusions and two unified credits with a single gift. A donor can gift-split only if both the donor and spouse are United States citizens or resident aliens at the time the gift is made. The couple must be married at the time the gift is made.

split life insurance Permanent insurance acquired under an arrangement by which the company and the executive split the premium cost and the company and the executive's beneficiaries split the proceeds on an agreed basis, usually with the company being reimbursed for its payments. Either the company or the executive may own the policy.

sponsor One who makes a promise or gives a security for another; a surety. Also one who advertises a product or service in the media.

spontaneous sources of cash Liabilities such as accounts payable and accrued wages that arise automatically without negotiation in the course of doing business.

spot market A situation in which goods or securities are dealt in at prices for immediate delivery. (Cf. futures)

spot zoning Method of rezoning a parcel of land where all surrounding parcels are zoned for a different use, particularly where the rezoning creates a use which is incompatible with surrounding land uses.

spousal IRA *tax law* Type of contribution to an individual retirement plan on behalf of an individual's employed spouse. Individual is allowed to deduct amounts contributed in cash up to the lesser of $2,250 or 100% of the includable compensation, reduced by the sum of (a) contributions made for the taxable year by the spouse, or on the spouse's behalf, to the individual retirement account (other than employer contributions to a simplified employee pension) and (b) the total amount of the deductible employee contributions for the tax year. In no event may the deduction for contributions on behalf of a nonemployed spouse exceed $2,000 for the tax year. In order to take full advantage of the deduction, at least $250 must be contributed on behalf of the nonemployed spouse.

spousal remainder trust Trust under which the child gets an income interest for a short term (e.g., five years) and the remainder passes to the spouse. The child's interest may be sheltered from gift tax by the annual exclusion, depending upon the amount transferred and the term of the income interest, and the remainder trust will qualify for the marital deduction.

spouse's allowance A sum of money granted to the spouse of a decedent by the court of jurisdiction to defray expenses of the living spouse while the estate is being settled.

spread 1. Difference between the bid price and the asked price for a security. 2. Option position that involves the simultaneous purchase and sale of options within the same class on the same underlying security. They may have the same or different striking price with the same or different expiration month. 3. *investment banking* Difference between the issue price on a new security and the net to the company.

sprinkling trust One in which the income and/or principal is divided among several members of a designated class (such as grandchildren) in amounts and proportions decided upon by the trustee.

spud-in To penetrate the surface of the soil of an oil field with the drill in place.

squatter One who takes possession of another's land without obtaining legal authority.

squatter's rights Legal allowance to use the property of another in absence of an attempt by the owner to force eviction; this right may eventually be converted to title to the property over time by adverse possession if recognized by state law.

staff adjuster *insurance* One who is employed by the company full time to adjust claims between the company and the insured.

stag A speculator who buys new issues of stock, in whole or in part, to sell immediately at a profit, rather than to hold for an extended period of time.

stagflation Situation of simultaneous economic stagnation, high unemployment, and inflation.

stagnation *economics* A situation in which per capita real income is static or declining.

stagnation thesis The proposition that American per capita income of the decade of the 1930s would not rise in the future because of (a) a declining rate of population growth, (b) the disappearance of the geographic frontier, (c) the growth of the absolute volume of savings, and (d) the tendency of new techniques of production to be capital-saving rather than capital-using.

stake Deposit made to answer an event, as on a wager. Deposit with a third person on condition that it is to be delivered to the one who shall become entitled to it by the happening of a specified contingent event.

stamp Paper sold by the government for attachment to letters and packages for postage purposes.

stamp-duties Impost raised from stamps upon parchment and paper and forming a branch of the perpetual revenue of the state.

stamp tax Excise on the act of issuance of corporate stock; to be imposed only when the original certificate of stock is issued.

standard That which is of authority; that which is accepted as correct or normal. Conforming to established practice or usage.

Standard & Poor's 500 Stock Index Value-weighted index of five hundred stocks. The index is set at ten for the base year, 1943. Thus, if the index is currently one hundred, the value of these stocks has risen ten times over their value in 1943.

standard deviation *statistics* A measure of the degree to which an individual value in a probability distribution tends to deviate from the mean of the distribution.

standard deviation of return A measure of variability. The square root of the mean squared deviation from the expected return.

standard fire policy (SFP) *insurance* Policy first prescribed in Massachusetts in 1873 which became known as the New England standard form. In 1887, New York required the use of the first New York standard fire policy, which was then modified in 1918. Currently, the 1943 New York standard fire policy is used verbatim in thirty-five states and with minor variations in the rest of the states.

standard industrial classification (SIC) Series of industrial classifications (called S/C codes) developed by the federal government for use in collecting detailed statistics for each industry.

standard of living The necessities, comforts, and luxuries which a special social or economic group regards as essential for its well-being.

standard orders Procedures set up by a firm to control the conduct of meetings. May refer to the number which constitutes a quorum, the rules for debate, etc.

standard risk Potential average loss experience.

startup costs The expenditures associated with the starting of a business, as opposed to the normal costs which will occur once the business is operating as planned.

state Complete body of free persons united together for the common benefit; a unit of government.

state insurance commissioner *See* insurance commissioner.

statement of changes in financial position Financial statement showing sources and uses of working capital for a period of time.

statement of condition *banking* A daily condensation of all the general ledger sheets of a bank, used primarily to reveal the reserve position of the bank, which reserves are required by law.

statement of financial position Financial statement, used frequently in the field of insurance, which reveals assets, liabilities, and net worth at any given point in time.

statement of retained earnings Financial statement that highlights whether a firm distributed or retained its earnings. (*See* retained earnings)

states' rights Those rights and powers not delegated to the federal government by the United States Constitution nor prohibited by it to the respective states.

static equilibrium *economics* Equilibrium such that population and its composition, stocks of capital and its composition, consumption and its composition, prices, the quantity of money, and other economic variables are constant.

statics *economics* The analysis of economic situations without regard to changes over time.

statistical illusions Charts or statistical tables that tend to create an atmosphere around a stock, or the entire market, which is more imaginary than factual. Such materials can make the individual stock or the market look better or worse than it really is.

statistical quality control A highly complex mathematical method for determining costs of producing a product as related to the elimination of faulty products. In brief, it might be more cost-efficient for the company to produce products with a possible 5% fault average than to attempt to eliminate all faults.

statistical sampling A mathematical procedure in which a small group of items is used to represent the entire population, or all of the items being considered, in order to get a view of the characteristics of the population without dealing with each item individually. Since it is usually impossible to consider each item in the population individually, sampling must often suffice. If the sample is taken randomly, it may give a reasonably true picture of the population. (Cf. random sample)

statistics 1. Science of collecting and arranging facts illustrative of any condition, resource, class, or section of the people or the population as a whole. 2. Numerical values derived from a sample.

status 1. Legal standing or position of a person as determined by membership in some class of persons legally enjoying certain rights or subject to certain limitations or conditions in respect, e.g., of liberty or servitude, marriage or celibacy, infancy or majority. 2. Relative position in the group of any individual member.

status symbol A prestigious product which may be purchased more for the image it has and what it implies about the buyer than for its utility. Applies also to the type of office a specific executive has and the perks that go with the position.

statute Written law proclaimed and enforced by legislative authority.

statute of frauds 1. State law providing that certain contracts must be in writing in order to be enforceable. Applied to deeds, mortgages, and other real estate contracts with the exception of leases for periods shorter than one year. 2. Statute requiring that certain classes of contract and engagements and certain memoranda of sales be in writing and signed by the party to be charged or by the party's agent.

statute of limitations 1. Specified statutory period after which a claimant is barred from enforcing his or her claim by suit or a state from prosecuting. 2. Statute that imposes time limits upon the right to sue in certain cases, such as the requirement that the victim in an automobile accident sue to collect damages within a specified time after the accident.

statutory exemption Specified article of personal property of a decedent, along with a specified amount of cash, which is set aside for the use of the decedent's family and is not available to settle the claims of creditors.

staying power The financial ability of an investor to stay with a security that has gone down in price in the belief that it will go back up again. This includes the ability to meet margin calls, etc.

steal To take or appropriate property of another without right or leave and with intent to make use of it personally or to dispose of it for profit.

stealth Any secret, sly, or clandestine act.

steering *real estate* Illegal practice of limiting the housing shown to a certain ethnic group.

stepped-up basis Income tax term used to describe a change in the adjusted tax basis of property allowed for certain transactions. The old basis is increased to market value upon inheritance, as opposed to a carryover basis in the event of a tax-free exchange.

sterling Silver of a high standard of fineness; genuine, standard rate.

sticker An employee who does not want to be promoted.

stimulus 1. *communication* Something, either internal or external, which causes activity. 2. A factor in the work environment that provokes a response.

sting tax Tax on passive investment income earned by an S corporation. To be subject to the sting tax, the S corporation must have C corporation accumulated earnings and profits from prior periods, and more than 25% of the S corporation's gross receipts must be from passive investment income. If the corporation meets both requirements, then the tax applied is the lesser of the net passive income or the entire taxable income of the corporation at the highest corporate marginal tax rate.

stipend Salary; settled pay.

stipulation Agreement, admission, or concession made in a judicial proceeding by the parties or their attorneys, incidental to the proceedings.

stochastic *statistics* A term describing a variation that is random as opposed to determined or biased.

stochastic model *statistics* A model using random variables.

stochastic process Random changes which follow certain events in a highly predictable pattern. (E.g., when interest rates rise or fall, short term rates tend to change more than long term rates.)

stock 1. Capital or principal fund raised by a corporation through the contribution of subscribers or the sale of shares. 2. Proportional part of capital credited to an individual stockholder and represented by the number of shares the stockholder owns. 3. Total merchandise or goods that a merchant or other commercial establishment has on hand.

stock bonus plan Benefit plan similar to a profit sharing plan but with distributions in stock; employer contributions are not necessarily dependent upon profits.

stockbroker One who buys and sells stocks as an agent for others.

stock dividend Dividend paid in the form of additional shares of stock instead of cash. It is usually expressed as a percentage of shares.

stock exchange Association of stockbrokers and dealers who have for convenience grouped together for the transaction of their business of buying and selling stocks that are publicly traded. As any other voluntary association, a stock exchange is governed by the rules set by itself. A stock exchange itself does not buy or sell but only furnishes a place for its members to meet and to deal certain hours of the day.

stock exchange seat The privilege, for which one pays a specified amount of money, of trading on the exchange floor. Usually, the owner of the seat is a part of a larger company, and his or her seat entitles the company to operate on the exchange as a member. Seats often sell for several hundred thousand of dollars.

stockholder Owner of shares in a corporation which has a capital stock. Stock may be preferred or common, but is common stock in the vast majority of cases.

stockholder of record Owner of stock on the date as declared by the corporation. The stockholder of record will be the recipient of dividends paid.

stockholder's equity Stockholder's investment in a firm; the sum of stock, paid-in capital, and retained earnings.

stock index futures A security that combines features of traditional commodity futures trading with securities trading using composite stock indexes. Investors can speculate on general market performance or can buy an index future contract to hedge a long or a short position against a decline in value.

stock insurance company Legal form of business entity engaged in the insurance business which issues stock to purchasers. The stockholders become equity owners, and their stock constitutes an investment, the dividends from which are usually taxable.

stock market timing An attempt to time the movements of the market to enhance one's position as an investor. As a rule, it is virtually impossible to time the markets, since stocks tend to move upward and downward together. There are exceptions, but the chance of finding those exceptions is more luck than expertise.

stock option Contractual privilege sometimes provided to company officers giving the holder the right to purchase a specified number of shares at a specified price and for a stated period of time.

stock ownership plan Defined contribution plan which meets the following requirements: (a) It must be a qualified stock bonus plan or a qualified stock bonus plan and a qualified money-purchase plan. (b) It must be designed to invest primarily in qualifying employer securities. (c) The plan must give participants the right to demand benefits in the form of employer securities, and if employer securities are not readily tradable on an established market, the participant must have the right to require the employer (not the plan) to repurchase employer securities under a fair valuation formula. (d) The plan must pass through certain voting rights to participants. (e) The plan must meet requirements set forth in Treasury regulations.

stock purchase plan Organized program for employees to buy shares of company stock. The plan could take the form of compensation if the employer matches the employee stock purchase.

stock redemption agreement Means by which a corporation under Section 303 of the Internal Revenue Code may make a distribution of a portion of the stock of a decedent that will not be taxed as a dividend. A Section 303 partial redemption can provide cash and/or other property from the corporation without resulting in dividend treatment and provides cash for the decedent shareholder's executor to use to pay death taxes and other expenses. A redemption under Section 303 will qualify for favorable tax treatment only to the extent that the interest of a shareholder whose stock is redeemed is reduced either directly or indirectly through a binding obligation to contribute toward the payment of the decedent's administrative expenses and death taxes.

stock repurchase Buying and retiring of stock by the issuing corporation.

stock split Recapitalization that affects the number of shares outstanding, their par value, the earnings per share, and the price of the stock. Corporate action of dividing shares authorized into a larger number with a lower market value. Shareholders continue to maintain their percentage of ownership but it is represented by a greater number of shares. For example, in a two-for-one split a shareholder with five hundred shares valued at thirty dollars would then have one thousand shares valued at fifteen dollars per share.

stock turnover Unit measure of number of times an average inventory is sold annually.

stop clause In a lease, stipulation of an amount of operating expense above which the tenant must bear. Often the base amount is the amount of expense for the first full year of operation under the lease.

stop limit order Stop order and limit order combined. As soon as the market price equals the stop price, the order becomes a limit order to either buy or sell.

stop loss *See* breakpoint.

stop loss order Stop order or stop limit order placed at a price below current market price. The order is placed to protect a profit or minimize a loss.

stop order Order issued by competent authority to prevent the doing of an act, such as the trading in the shares of a particular corporation in the stock exchange or the continuance of building operations without obtaining a building permit or complying with a work order.

stoppage in transity   Act by which the unpaid vendor of goods stops goods in transit before delivery to the purchaser where the purchaser has become insolvent. The right to stop goods is lost if the goods have been delivered to the purchaser.

stowage   1. Money paid for a room where goods are deposited.   2. The mode of landing of a ship.

straddle   To possess a put and a call option on the same asset at the same strike price. The purpose of a straddle is to profit from a large swing in the price of the stock, either up or down.

straight life annuity   Life annuity under which the annuitant is paid only until death.

straight life insurance   *See* ordinary insurance.

straight-line depreciation   *accounting* Equal annual reduction in book value of property.

straight-line recapture rate   Part of a capitalization rate that accounts for the annual erosion of a wasting asset by assuming an equal amount of loss in value each year of the useful life of the asset.

strap   An option contract that combines one put option and two call options of the same series, which can be bought at a lower total premium than if the three options were bought individually.

stratification   *marketing* A technique which divides the universe (population) into categories with similar characteristics in order to more accurately decide whether the samples taken are representative of their strata.

stratified sample   *statistics* Using the characteristics of the universe to guide the selection of a sample. (a) Division of the universe into groups (strata), each containing the known characteristic. (b) Selection of the percentage of items from the sample from each group which the group bears in the universe. Or, if different sample sizes are taken from each stratum, then weighing the results in the proportion that the group bears to the universe.

straw man   One who purchases property that is, in turn, conveyed to another for the purpose of concealing the identity of the eventual purchaser.

street certificate   Stock or share certificate endorsed in blank. Transferable by delivery as a negotiable instrument.

street name   Name, of brokerage firm or some other nominee, in which stock is registered rather than the shareholder's name.

strict liability   Liability imposed when public policy demands a person be held liable for injury to others even though the injury may be neither intentionally nor negligently inflicted; liability without fault.

strike   *labor law* Quitting of work by a body of workers in order to force their employer to comply with a demand for higher wages, better working conditions, or other benefits.

striking price   Price per share at which the holder of a stock option contract may purchase the underlying security on a call option or sell the underlying security on a put option; the exercise price.

strip   Bearer bond from which the coupons have been removed in order to sell them separately from the bonds.

strip mining   Method of extraction of mineral from the surface of the earth involving stripping off the earth, known as overburden, which lies over the mineral.

stripping   *securities* The act of removing interest coupons from bonds, with the intent of selling the coupons apart from the bonds.

strong-form efficient market   A market in which the prices instantaneously reflect all information both public and private. (*See* semi-strong-form efficient market)

structural equation   *econometrics* An equation stating the relationship between variables in an economic system.

structural-functionalist school   *industrial psychology* A school of thought which says that stability and equilibrium are the norm in society and industry due to the shared values of all members of society.

structural inflation   *See* bottleneck inflation.

structural unemployment A situation in which unemployment is the result of long-term or permanent changes in the demand for certain products.

Student Loan Marketing Association (SLMA) A publicly traded stock corporation that guarantees student loans traded in the secondary market. It was established by a decree from the federal government in 1972 to increase the availability of loan funds for students in colleges and universities.

subchapter M An Internal Revenue Service regulation dealing with the so-called conduit theory. This theory deals with qualifying investment companies and real estate investment trusts to avoid double taxation by passing through to shareholders profits which will then be taxed to them as individuals.

subchapter S corporation Corporation meeting certain qualification requirements that is taxed much like a partnership, with the profits passing through to the stockholders, who pay taxes on them as individual, ordinary income. The Sub-Chapter S Revision Act of 1982 made the necessary changes for this corporation to work like a partnership. Each item of income, deduction, and credit retains its character as it is passed through to shareholders. An S corporation can have no more than thirty-five shareholders, who must be citizens or residents of the United States. Only one kind of stock can be sold, but at times there may be a difference of voting rights even with only one class of stock. (A subchapter S corporation may not receive more than 20% of its income from passive sources.)

subcontracting Situation in which the primary contractor enters into an agreement for specified work to be done with a secondary contractor. A method of shifting risk.

subcontractor Person who enters into a contract with a principal contractor to do work specified in the latter's contract.

subculture A social subgroup with distinguishing modes of behavior, existing within the prevailing culture.

subdivide To divide land into lots for sale or improvement.

subdivision Any land which is divided or proposed to be divided into fifty or more lots, contiguous or not, for the purpose of sale or lease as part of a common promotional plan. Where subdivided land is offered for sale or lease by a single developer or a group of developers acting in concert and such land is contiguous or is known, designated, or advertised as a common unit or by a common name, such land shall be presumed, without regard to the number of lots covered by each individual offering, as being offered for sale or lease as part of a common promotional plan.

subject 1. One who is under the governing power of another; a person owing allegiance to a monarch. 2. Liable, subordinate, subservient, answerable for. 3. Topic or thing under consideration.

sublease 1. Lease from a lessee to another lessee. The new lessee is a sublessee or subtenant. 2. Lease granted by a lessee to another person of all or part of the leased premises for a term no longer than that for which the lessee holds it.

subliminal advertising The presentation of images which change so rapidly on the television or theater screen that only the subconscious is aware of them. This practice to illegal in some countries.

subliminal perception Communication at a subconscious level of awareness.

submarginal land Land so poor that it will not pay the cost of cultivation.

subordinate Inferior in order, nature, rank, dignity, or importance.

subordinated creditor Creditor holding a debenture having a lower chance of payment than other liabilities of the firm.

subordinated debt *banking* A loan which will not be repaid until previous debts are settled.

subordination Move to a lower priority, as a lien would if it changes from a first mortgage to a second mortgage.

subordination clause Clause of document that permits a mortgage recorded at a later date to take priority over an existing mortgage.

subpoena A summons issued in an action or other judicial proceeding requiring the person to whom it is directed to be present at a specified place and time for a specified purpose under a penalty for nonattendance.

subpoena duces tecum   *law* A court order directing the witness to present certain named papers or objects.

subrogation   1. Legal fiction denoting those changes by which another person is put into the place of a creditor so that the rights and securities of the creditor pass to the person, who, by being subrogated to the creditor, enters into his or her rights. 2. The placing of a person who, acting as a surety, has paid the debt of another in the same legal position as the original creditor, thus giving that person the same right to collect on the debt. 3. The right of an insurer to substitute for the victim in recovering the amount of the loss paid from a third party responsible for the loss.

subscribe   1. To attest; to agree in writing to furnish money or its equivalent. 2. To write or inscribe something, such as a name; especially, to write one's signature at the end of a written or printed instrument.

subscription   1. Written contract by which one party agrees to furnish a sum of money for a particular purpose, such as a contribution of money to a charitable institution or for the regular receipt of a publication. 2. Act of writing one's name under a written instrument; the act of witnessing a document.

subsidiary   Corporation controlled by another corporation that owns the greater part of its shares and thus has control. For legal purposes, a subsidiary corporation is a distinct legal entity from the parent corporation.

subsidy   Grant of funds or property from a government to a private person or corporation to assist in the establishment or support of an enterprise deemed advantageous to the public.

subsistence theory of wages   *economics* A theory attributed to David Ricardo, but probably formulated by Torrens, in the early nineteenth century which held that wages per worker tend to equal what the worker needs to subsist—to maintain the worker and to rear children. If wages per worker rose above the subsistence level, people would tend to have more children and the population would increase, thereby lowering per capita real

incomes; conversely, if wages per worker fell below the subsistence level, people would tend to have fewer children and the population would decline, thereby increasing per capita real incomes. Wages per worker would thus tend to remain at the subsistence level over the long run. Also known as the brazen or iron law of wages.

substance   1. Matter. 2. Essence of a thing as opposed to its form; gist.

substandard policy   Insurance policy written for physically impaired people who have had a serious illness which is now arrested, such as cancer or heart trouble. Generally, higher premiums are charged or a waiver of coverage is required for the arrested disease. These policies may cover both income and expense losses.

substandard risk   Higher than average loss expectancy.

substantial risk of forfeiture   Likelihood that property can be lost for some reason. Thus the promise of deferred compensation to an employee is not considered to give a present interest to the employee if the employee is terminated or dies, and never receives the compensation.

substantive motion   A motion passed in amended form, after the amendment(s) has been moved and carried.

substituted basis   Adjusted basis (value) of property transferred. Since basis in most cases is the cost or purchase price of property, the adjusted basis equals the basis plus or minus any improvements or depreciation taken on the property. When the adjusted basis is different from the original basis in the property, the last basis is known as the substituted basis.

subsurface rights   Mineral rights.

succession   1. Acquiring of property from the estate of a decedent by will, inheritance, or operation of the law. 2. Act or right of legally or officially coming into a predecessor's office, dignity, possessions, or functions.

succession duty   Tax on the privilege of acquiring property by inheritance. A tax upon the taking of property by a beneficiary or one to whom it is distributed.

sue   To institute a civil action.

sufferance, tenancy at   *See* tenancy at sufferance.

suffrage   Political right or privilege, conferred by the Constitution and statutes, to participate, by means of voting in elections, in the establishment or management of government.

sui juris *law Of his own right.* Describes one who is legally competent to act.

suit Any legal proceeding, including an action in law as well as in equity.

summary An abridgment. Legal proceedings without all of the formalities of a trial.

summary of the offering *investments* Review of the pertinent parts of the offering memorandum, with emphasis on those parts of vital interest to lawyers, accountants, or other professionals in a position of advising potential investors on shelter investment.

summer fallow Cultivation method whereby in each year a certain acreage of farmland is set aside, on which no crop at all is attempted to be grown. This portion is plowed before the weeds come to seed and cultivated throughout the whole season as required to keep the weeds down and to conserve the moisture for the crop of the ensuing season or seasons.

summing up 1. Recapitulation of evidence by counsel of both parties at the end of the trial, aimed at assisting the trier of facts to find in favor of their client. 2. The recapitulation of all or part of the evidence by the judge to the jury subsequent to the closing statements by counsel.

summons Notification issued from the office of a Court of Justice, calling upon the person to whom it is directed to appear before a judge or officer of the court for a certain purpose. The failure to obey the summons is usually visited with penalties.

sum-of-years-digits depreciation *tax accounting* Method of allocating the cost of an asset over its useful life by computing a fraction each year, which is applied against the depreciable amount.

sumptuary law A law designed to prevent the consumption of goods considered to be harmful to the health or welfare of society.

sunk cost 1. Previous outlay that cannot be changed by any current or future action. 2. Cost related to a past decision. (Cf. out-of-pocket costs)

sunrise industry Industry among those which are expected to be mainstays of the economy in the future, such as electronics and other computer-related industries, service industries, etc. This does not mean that the older "sunset" industries, such as steel and autos, will disappear, but that they will no longer lead the economy as they have done for many years in the past.

sunspot theory Theory of business cycles, proposed in England during the late nineteenth century, which held that sunspot cycles exhibited an extremely high correlation with agricultural cycles for a number of years; therefore, sunspots must affect the weather, the weather influences agricultural crops, and the crops affect business conditions. This theory received worldwide popularity when it was first introduced, but then fell into disrepute because the high correlation between sunspots and agricultural cycles did not endure; it was the result of accidental rather than causal factors.

superintendence Care and supervision for the purpose of direction of workmen, carrying the authority to direct and control.

superintendent One employed to direct the course and oversee details; to manage, overlook with the power of direction, regulate with authority the work and the conduct of workmen.

superior court Court of general jurisdiction. In some jurisdictions, it is an appellate court, while in others, a court intermediate between the final appellate court and the court of original jurisdiction.

supersede 1. To sit above, be superior to, precede, or have priority over. 2. To obliterate, set aside, annul, repeal.

superstore A large store, smaller than a hypermarket, which may have a combination of a discount grocery and a discount general merchandise store. Usually marked by a large parking lot and a large number of checkout lanes.

super top-heavy plan Plan in which 90% of the benefits accrue for key employees. These are common in small professional corporations.

supervisor Under the National Labor Relations Act, an individual having authority to use independent judgment in interest of management to hire, transfer, suspend, lay off, recall, promote, discharge, assign, reward, or discipline other employees, or having the responsibility to direct them, to adjust their grievances, or to effectively recommend such action.

supervisor of bank properties *banking* Job encompassing the tasks of looking after all bank properties, supervising maintenance and custodial activities, and generally supervising in-bank renovation. Normally does not include the supervision of the main building, with regard to leasing space to tenants, nor does it usually relate to any decision making with regard to building renovation or furniture or equipment changes or purchases. After these decisions are made, however, it is usually the task of the person holding this position to supervise the activities related to making the changes. (Cf. director of building and equipment)

supplement 1. To add on. 2. That which is added.

supplemental accident expense Coverage designed to fill the gap left by the deductible on group comprehensive medical expense plans; it provides first dollar coverage for expenses incurred as the result of an accident. This coverage may be purchased as a part of the travel accident or voluntary accident plan; however, this is becoming less popular.

supplementary medical insurance plan *Medicare* Medical coverage, called Part B, on items of expense and services not covered by the Basic Hospital Insurance Plan, Part A. Available to all who are on Medicare; one must apply for Part B and pay a monthly fee.

supplementary proceedings Legal procedure designed to discover the extent of a debtor's property and to apply it to the execution or carrying out of a judgment that has been entered against the debtor by a court.

supply-side economics 1. Economic theory which emphasizes that the creation of supply will create demand. It is derived mainly from Say's Law, which states that supply creates its own demand. 2. An approach to macroeconomic problems that focuses on the importance of increasing the supply of goods and service in order to increase governmental revenues.

supply-side economics A theory which, among other things, avers that non-inflationary growth is stimulated when national tax policies encourage productivity and investment.

support 1. Sustenance, source, or means of living. 2. To furnish sustenance, source, or means of livelihood.

support activities Indirect labor used in producing a product, as opposed to the direct labor.

support level Bottom of the price range at which technical analysts note persistent selling of a security or commodity. (E.g., if Acme SAC sells normally between thirty and forty dollars a share, the lower price is called the support level.) (Cf. resistance level)

Supreme Court In the federal judiciary and in some states, a court of the last resort. In others, such as New York, it is not the court of last resort but a court of general jurisdiction.

surcharge 1. Extra charge, currently prohibited by law, on those who purchase with a credit card instead of cash. 2. To show that an item is missing from and should be included in a supposedly complete accounting presented to a court for approval, as by the executor of an estate. 3. To overcharge or to charge again as in an accounting between parties. 4. To put more cattle upon a common than the pasture or herbage will sustain or than the commoner has the right to do.

surety Person who agrees to be responsible for the obligation, default, wrongdoing, or other performance of another.

surety bond Bond that guarantees the principal will accomplish certain tasks.

surgical expense Coverage provided on a usual, customary, and reasonable expense basis for surgical services; however, benefits provided may be on the basis of a limited schedule of surgical procedures with a dollar limit placed on the expense which will be reimbursed for each procedure.

surname Family name; in Western culture, the last name of a person.

surplus 1. The remainder of a thing; the residue. 2. Any type of excess, e.g., the amount by which the quantity supplied of a commodity exceeds the quantity demanded at a given price, as when the given price is above the free-market equilibrium price. 3. That which remains of a fund after provisions for all liabilities. 4. Excess of assets over the outstanding liabilities. 5. *trust* Amount of trust fund in excess of the capital or corpus of the trust. 6. *See* retained earnings.

surplus broker/agent Insurance procurement specialist who obtains unusual or marginally profitable coverages from insurers not licensed to operate in the state of location. Also called excess-line broker/agent.

surrender To yield or restore an estate to the person entitled to the immediate reversion or remainder.

surrender cost method Method resembling the traditional cost concept but using interest assumptions to avoid some of the major deficiencies of the traditional cost method. Differs from the traditional method in three respects: (a) the premiums are accumulated at interest, (b) dividends are also accumulated at interest, and (c) instead of dividing the total by twenty (for a twenty-year comparison), the new sum is divided by the amount to which one per annum payable in advance will accumulate in twenty years at the assumed interest rate.

surrogate Judge or judicial officer who has jurisdiction over the probate or proving of wills, administration of estates, and guardianship.

surrogate court Court having jurisdiction in matters relating to grant and revocation of probates, letters of administration, the administration of estates, and the custody and care of infants and mentally incompetent persons.

surtax A tax which is sometimes applied to the incomes of individuals or businesses who have achieved a certain level of income (E.g., a 10% surtax on an individual who had an adjusted gross income of forty thousand dollars). Usually such a surtax is used to bolster normal income taxes which are not, in the opinion of Congress, growing rapidly enough.

survival and wrongful death Concept under the common law of negligence providing only the injured person with a right of action against the wrongdoer; this right terminated with the death of the injured person or the wrongdoer. Today, all states have statutes providing a remedy for wrongful death.

survivor annuity Survivor benefits for eligible widows, widowers, and dependent children of eligible military personnel. Benefits are essentially the same as those provided civil service employees.

survivor benefit plan Plan, effective September 21, 1972, replacing Retired Servicemen's Family Protection plan.

survivor income benefit insurance Benefit offered by many insurers providing a monthly income for surviving spouses and children of covered employees instead of a lump-sum death benefit. The chief features which distinguish this benefit from group insurance are that the employee has no choice of beneficiary; benefits are paid only if there is a survivor. Benefits for children cease at age eighteen or prior death or marriage, and the spouse's benefit is paid to age sixty-two or sixty-five or until prior death or remarriage. Benefits may be provided for the surviving family as a unit. The monthly benefit may be a specific percentage of the employee's basic monthly earnings at death, generally ranging between 10% and 40%, subject to either a maximum basic monthly earnings to which the percentage is applied. The benefit may be a specified monthly sum according to predetermined salary brackets, a flat amount for all employees regardless of monthly pay, or based on a percentage of group term life insurance coverage.

survivorship 1. State or condition of being the one person out of two or more who remains alive after the death of the other or others. 2. The right of a surviving party having a joint interest with others in an estate to take the whole estate. 3. The right of a joint tenant or tenants to maintain ownership rights following the death of another joint tenant. Survivorship prevents heirs of the deceased from making claims against the property.

survivorship benefit That part of a life insurance premium payment made by the deceased policyholder allocated to the account of surviving policyholders.

suspended trading A temporary halt in the trading of a security because of some news release which might send the stock in an upward surge or a downward plunge. Normally such halts in trading are not of long duration, but may last for a few hours, or usually no more than a day.

suspense account A temporary arrangement used to account for monies spent before they are allocated permanently to the proper account.

sustainable growth rate Rate of increase in sales a company can attain without changing its profit margin, assets-to-sales ratio, debt-to-equity ratio, or dividend payout ratio; the rate of growth a company can finance without excessive borrowing or a new stock issue.

swamp Tract or region of spongy ground so saturated with water as to be unfit for tillage, commonly abounding with certain species of trees and coarse grasses; wet bog, morass, marsh.

swap arrangements Short-term reciprocal lines of credit between the Federal Reserve and fourteen foreign central banks as well as the Bank for International Settlements. Through a swap transaction, the Federal Reserve can, in effect, borrow foreign currency in order to purchase dollars in the foreign exchange market. In doing so the demand for dollars is increased and the dollar's foreign exchange value is increased. Similarly, the Federal Reserve can temporarily provide dollars to foreign central banks through swap arrangements.

sweat equity Value added to a property due to improvements as a result of work performed personally by the owner.

Swedish budget *economics* A governmental budget which is balanced over a period of years rather than in each particular year. (Archaic.)

sweetheart contract An agreement accepted by both labor and management which tends to favor management rather than labor.

Swift Message writing system that connects worldwide participating banks primarily for the purpose of communicating the payment process, which might also employ a system such as Clearinghouse Interbank Payments Systems to fully implement the transaction.

swindle To cheat or defraud to obtain any property.

symbol 1. *communication* Vehicle by which a concept is transmitted by one person to another. 2. Letters as assigned to a corporation's stock to facilitate trading of shares of the corporation.

symbolic delivery Constructive delivery of anything cumbersome or inaccessible by delivering something conventionally accepted as a symbol or representative of the actual thing to be delivered (e.g., a key to an automobile).

symmetallism A monetary standard in a nation whereby the government will redeem specie with proportionate shares of both gold and silver. Different from bimetallism, which allows for the redemption of specie with either gold or silver.

syndicalism A movement in a number of countries in the 1920s and 1930s which advocated the ownership of industry by workers, which would ultimately evolve into the running of the government by workers, also.

syndicate 1. An association of business organizations to control a project, or to buy a new stock or bond issue. 2. A small group of delegates separated from the rest for the purpose of carrying out a special project. 3. *investments* Selling group, usually made up of investment banking firms, which is assembled to sell a new issue of securities. 4. Association of individuals united to negotiate some business or prosecute some enterprise. An association of persons jointly taking part in some venture or undertaking, ordinarily of a commercial or financial character.

syndicated research A situation in which several companies may pool funds to carry out specific research on a certain project.

syndication Method of selling property whereby a sponsor (or syndicator) sells interest to investors. May take the form of a partnership, limited partnership, tenancy in common, corporation, or subchapter S corporation.

syndication fees *limited partnerships* Nondeductible fees related to syndicating the partnership or putting the partnership together.

synergism Simultaneous action of two agencies which together produce a total effect greater than the sum of their individual effects.

synergy The simultaneous pursuit of two or more courses of action toward the same goal.

systematic borrowing Borrowing the funds to pay premiums for more than three years.

systematic risk Risk associated with fluctuations in the market; market risks.

Systematic risk is present in varying degrees in nearly all securities because comparable securities generally move together in a systematic manner.

systematic sample *statistics* Arranging a population in some objective order and then taking every "nth" item.

T

table 1. Collection of related numbers, values, signs, or items of any kind arranged for ease of reference or comparison, often in parallel columns. 2. A synoptical statement. 3. *parliamentary law* To postpone consideration of a bill or resolution.

tableau économique A flow chart presentation of income, used by many members of the (French) Physiocratic school of economic thought. Groups receiving income are divided into three categories: (a) The productive class, i.e., agriculture and mining. (b) The property owning class. (c) The sterile class, i.e., merchants and servants. The income distribution from the first class to the other two classes is shown as well as the return of this income to the first class through purchases of its output, the net product.

tacit *communication* Communicated in silence; implied or indicated but not actually expressed.

tack 1. To add on to a time period. 2. To unite securities given at different times in order to acquire priority over any intermediate liens. (E.g., a third mortgagee buys the first lien and unites it with his or her own, thereby gaining priority over the second mortgage.) 3. *law* To add a more current claim to an earlier one to lengthen the period claimed under adverse possession.

Taft-Hartley Act A federal law enacted in 1947 in an attempt to establish equity in labor/management relations. Generally, Taft-Hartley prohibited organized labor from: (a) refusing to bargain in good faith, (b) coercing employees to join a union, (c) imposing excessive or discriminatory dues and initiation fees, (d) coerc-

ing employers to hire union workers to perform unneeded or nonexistent jobs (i.e., featherbedding), and (e) striking to influence a bargaining unit's choice between two competing unions (i.e., jurisdictional disputes). One of the most protective provisions of the act for both workers and management was Section 14(b), the so-called right-to-work law, which gave states the right to prohibit closed shops. Also called the Labor Management Relations Act.

tail 1. Limitation; abridgment; reduction. An estate in tail was a mode of keeping property in the direct lineal descendants of an ancestor. Inheritance gifted to a person and the heirs of his or her body, general or special, male or female, so that if the donee dies without leaving descendants answering to the condition annexed to the estate on its creation, it reverted to the remainder man or the reversioner. 2. *insurance* The interval between receiving premium income by the companies and payment of claims. 3. The spread in price between the lowest competitive bid accepted by the U.S. Treasury for new issues of bills, bonds, or notes and the average bid by all those offering to buy such securities. 4. *underwriting* The decimal places following the rounded dollar amount bid by an underwriter for new-issue securities in a competitive situation (e.g., $59.6625, with .6625 being the tail).

tailgating *securities* A practice, considered unethical, by which a broker will duplicate for himself or herself a buy or sell order received from a client, on the assumption that the client may have information which the broker does not have.

take a bath To suffer a large loss, usually on a speculative investment.

327

take a loss To sell a security for less than its purchase price, as opposed to holding a depreciated security.

take a position To buy a block of a specific stock, either as a principal, a dealer, or a broker.

takedown method A method wherein an underwriter sells as much of the new issue as possible and receives a fee for doing so. Nearly synonymous with best-effort sale.

take-home pay The total residual amount of wages an employee receives after all deductions, including taxes.

takeout financing Means of providing permanent financing following construction of a planned project. The takeout commitment is generally predicated upon specific conditions, such as a certain percentage of unit sales or leases, for the permanent loan to take out the construction loan. Most construction lenders require takeout financing.

takeover bid 1. Attempt by a minority group of stockholders not in control of a corporation to acquire control. 2. Attempt on the part of one company to acquire another by offering cash or other assets to the desired company, which assets normally relate to the market price of the stock at the time. Sometimes the bid is made to the shareholders who may put pressure on the company either to sell or refuse to sell.

take profits To sell a stock for more than was paid for it, as opposed to holding a security in which one has a paper profit.

tale quale *In such shape as it is.* Term used in commodity trading.

tally Ancient form of keeping accounts between a debtor and a creditor.

tally trade System of selling goods on credit for payment by weekly or monthly installments.

tandem plan Program of the Government National Mortgage Association (GNMA) working together with the Federal National Mortgage Association (FNMA) to provide low interest rate home loans.

tangible Corporeal; capable of being touched; real; substantial.

tangible asset Asset having physical existence (e.g., buildings, machinery, cash, etc.). Not all accountants look upon the distinction between tangible and intangible assets in the same way. (Cf. intangible asset)

tangible drilling cost With reference to the oil and gas business, cost relating to items that are used over a period of time (e.g., machinery, casings, well fittings, etc.). (Cf. intangible drilling cost)

tangible fixed asset Asset having physical form on which immediate liquidity is unlikely; fixed assets.

tangible personal property Movable wealth, such as household furniture, farm machinery, automobiles, farm animals, jewelry, etc.

tape *stock market* Originally a printout of market data on paper tape; now refers to an electronic display of trading activity.

tape reader Person who sits in the board room and watches stock activity on the electronic display of the trading activity of stocks.

tare weight 1. The weight of a container and material for packing. 2. The weight of a vehicle exclusive of contents.

target benefit plan Plan of the pension industry which shares characteristics of both defined-benefit and defined-contribution plans. (These cannot be defined, but must be examined to determine any advantages over defined-benefit or defined-contributions plans.)

target pricing *marketing* A policy of pricing products so as to earn a targeted rate of return on the capital invested in the production and sale of goods.

tariff A list or schedule of merchandise with the rates of duty to be paid to the government upon their importation into another country.

tariff war The use of tariffs to enhance the competitive position of a country, particularly in response to similar actions by another country.

task analysis The assessing of a task or project for the purpose of determining the skills needed, or the training which will be necessary to prepare someone to do the job.

tax 1. Charge levied upon persons or things by a government. 2. An impost, a tribute imposed upon the subject. 3. An enforced contribution to provide for the support of the government.

tax abatement The reduction of a tax because it was levied improperly, or because of a legislative directive to do so.

taxable distribution Any distribution in a tax year of money or other assets either from an estate or from some type of fund (e.g., an Individual Retirement Account) which will be taxable in the year of its distribution.

taxable estate Gross estate minus deductions allowed.

taxable gift Amount by which the value of the property transferred exceeds the value of the consideration. A transfer for full and adequate consideration in money or money's worth is not a taxable gift.

taxable income A person's gross income minus a standard deduction or itemized deductions and exemptions for the taxpayer and the taxpayer's dependents.

taxable municipal bonds Bonds issued by a municipality, the funds from which will be used not for public purposes, but for private purposes. A new water treatment plant is for public use, and therefore the bonds issued to pay for such are federally income tax exempt, and if bought by a citizen of the same state are usually also state income tax exempt. The 1986 Tax Reform Act, however, does not allow tax exempt status for municipal bonds issued for industrial parks, sports complexes, etc.

tax anticipation bill A special class of Treasury bill, sold primarily to large corporations. These bills are sold in anticipation of a particular tax date, at which time the bills will be redeemed.

tax anticipation note (TAN) Usually short-term note sold by a municipal government in anticipation of specific tax revenues to be received on or about a certain date.

tax assessment The valuation placed upon property as a base for levying a tax on it is known as assessed valuation. Applying a tax rate to this valuation determines the tax load.

taxation The raising of monies by the government for public purposes by the imposition of a levy.

tax avoidance A legal method of avoiding tax. (Cf. tax evasion)

tax base The value of a unit of an asset to which the tax rate is applied to arrive at the tax owed. In property taxes, the base is property valuation. In income taxes, it is net taxable income.

tax bracket *income tax* Various income categories designed by Congress and enforced by the IRS, dictating the bracket an individual or business falls within. The Tax Reform Act of 1986 dictated three brackets for individuals—15%, 28%, and 33%. For businesses (corporations), brackets were reduced from five to three—15%, 25%, and 34%.

tax consequences *financial planning* Considerations primary to the building of an investment portfolio. The degree of importance of tax considerations will differ among portfolios. It is therefore necessary to know a client's financial and tax posture, and to assemble vehicles in the portfolio representing asset categories and investment vehicles which fit the goals of the investor with regard to tax problems.

tax credit Dollar-for-dollar offset against the tax liability determined by use of a formula—often a percentage of the base amount. Tax credits are allowed for investments in qualified real or personal property used in a trade or business, research and development expenditures in business, political contributions, child and dependent care expenses, and expenditures for residential energy conservation or the installation of renewable energy source equipment. (*See* Appendix G)

tax deduction A type of expense that can be used to remove income from taxation.

tax deed Type of instrument given to a grantee by a government that had claimed the property for unpaid taxes.

tax deferral Postponement of federal income taxes accomplished in various ways, including interest accrued on Series EE savings bonds which may be deferred to redemption of HH bonds; Keogh and IRA accounts; and dividend reinvestment and stock purchase in qualified companies.

tax effect Technically, the tax effect is the change in output as a result of the tax change. The resultant price change is called incidence.

tax elimination Tax-saving techniques aimed at producing income tax reduction through deductions, exemptions, and credits that reduce taxable income (or the tax itself), and techniques that result in non-taxable income. Economic benefits which are not taxable are perhaps the most desirable because they avoid tax altogether. An example of tax-elimination in perhaps the most pure form is the interest on municipal bonds.

tax evasion An illegal method of avoiding a tax, as distinguished from a legal method of avoiding a tax.

tax exemption 1. Total tax freedom as is granted to education, charitable, religious, and similar non-profit organizations. 2. Partial exemption or freedom from tax such as personal exemptions on income taxes, etc.

tax-exempt property Real property not subject to ad valorem property taxes.

tax-exempt securities Securities issued by state and local governments, interest on which is currently exempt from federal income tax, and usually state income tax if the securities are intrastate. Capital gains on such securities, if any, are not tax-exempt.

tax-free exchange An exchange of goods between persons in which there is no perceptible gain for either, and thus no present recognition for tax purposes.

tax-free exchange fund Fund created to allow investors to exchange stock they owned for fund shares without incurring capital gains liability at that time. Adverse tax rulings have chilled the market for these funds. (*See* Appendix G)

tax-free incorporation A corporation in which one or more persons transfer cash or property to the corporation solely in exchange for that corporation's stock or securities. In addition, the transferors must be in control of the corporation immediately after the transfer, meaning that they own at least 80% of all other stock of the corporation. Mechanism used to shift potential ordinary income items from the individual taxpayer to the corporate taxpayer.

tax haven A country which offers low tax rates and other advantages to foreign countries, or businesses and individuals from foreign countries.

tax impact The immediate obligation of a tax; the immediate effect of the tax.

tax incidence 1. The final resting place of a tax after all shifting has occurred. 2. The price change resulting from the tax change. (The output change is the tax effect.)

tax, inheritance *See* inheritance tax.

tax levy 1. *law* The formal order for tax payment upon the assessed base. 2. *property taxes* The determination of the total revenue which will be realized by the property tax.

tax liability Amount of income tax due for the year.

tax lien Debt attached against property for failure to pay taxes.

tax limit A limit, constitutional or statutory, which is placed on the kind or maximum amount of tax which can be imposed.

tax loophole An exemption from a tax which is obviously discriminatory, and perhaps was unintended.

tax-loss carryback A provision in the tax laws which allows a business to write off losses in a given year against a previous year. This recognizes genuine business losses and allows them to be written off in more profitable years. (Cf. tax-loss carryforward)

tax-loss carryforward A provision in the tax laws which allows a business to write off losses in a given year against a subsequent year. This recognizes genuine business losses and allows them to be written off in more profitable years. (Cf. tax-loss carryback)

tax map Document showing the location, dimensions, and other information pertaining to a parcel of land subject to property taxes.

tax offset A form of tax cancellation or exemption. A tax is levied, but it is remitted in whole or in part, usually on the basis of another tax paid.

taxpayer 1. Person chargeable with a tax; one who owns property in a town or municipality subject to taxation; one from whom government demands a pecuniary contribution towards its support. 3. One who pays any tax or taxes.

tax postponement Tax-saving techniques basically involving the delaying of taxes until the future rather than the reduction or elimination of taxes now. Tax postponement can be advantageous to taxpayers in that they may be in a lower tax bracket in the future, especially after retirement.

tax preference item 1. In Internal Revenue Service code, item which must be considered by a person calculating alternative minimum tax liability; deduction that is taxed severely. There are various items of tax preference, one of which is excess depreciation. 2. Certain type of income or deductions that is added to adjusted gross income to calculate the alternative minimum tax.

tax pyramiding A situation in which the tax imposed on a good or service is used as part of the base for the markup on that good or service; thus a tax is being paid on the tax.

tax rate Specific percentage or, in the case of the progressive tax, series of percentages which the law stipulates as the appropriate multiplier in the determination of a gross tax liability.

tax-rate schedule Schedule prepared for different categories of taxpayers, showing the percentages and amounts payable for specific levels of taxable income.

Tax Reform Act (1986) The last of three important pieces of tax legislation (1976, '84, '86). (*See* Appendix G)

tax roll A listing of taxpayers with a statement opposite each name indicating the total assessment and the amount of the tax due on this assessment.

tax sale Sale of delinquent taxpayer's property to collect payment of a tax due.

tax, severance *See* severance tax.

tax shelter 1. Investment opportunity approved by the Internal Revenue Service with provisions for tax-free or tax-favored income. Usually the purpose is to attract investors to higher risk investments (e.g., oil drilling, agriculture, or real estate development). 2. An asset or investment that defers, reduces, or avoids taxation. 3. Investment of a given amount of one's income in a specifically designed fund, such as an Individual Retirement Account. A person who does this postpones the

income tax on the amount invested until the investment income plus dividends and/or interest are received. 4. An investment that produces after-tax income that is greater than before-tax income. The investment may produce before-tax cash flow while generating losses to shield from taxation income from sources outside the investment.

tax sheltered annuity (TSA) Arrangement permitted under federal law whereby an employee of a qualified organization can enter into an agreement with his or her employer to have part of the employee's earnings set aside each year for retirement. No federal income tax is payable on the amount set aside each year to purchase retirement benefits provided (a) the amounts are used to buy an annuity contract, a retirement income insurance policy, or regulated investment company shares (e.g. mutual funds); and (b) the contribution amounts do not exceed the employee's exclusion allowance. Thus, a TSA plan enables employees of qualified organizations to save for retirement with before-tax dollars. Such plans are considered by many to be one of the most advantageous and flexible tax-deferral devices available, provided the employee is eligible.

tax shield In the capital budgeting of a company, expenditures that are deductible for income tax purposes (e.g., start-up costs for a new plant), and are recognized as reducing (shielding against) income taxes that would otherwise be due. Depreciation of capital assets is treated in the same manner.

tax shifting The action of passing a tax from the one who first paid it to the person who purchases the good or service. (E.g., tax on gasoline is paid by the consumer at the pump because it is included in the price of the product.)

tax swap A method of selling a security and reinvesting the money in another security to try to gain a tax advantage.

tax table Schedules prepared by the Internal Revenue Service which place incomes into specific categories and then show the amount of tax payable for different categories of taxpayers.

tax umbrella Business losses of past years carried forward to shield profits and ease tax burdens in the current year or subsequent years.

tax waiver A written permit, issued by a state tax department, for certain property to be taken off tax rolls for the purpose of assembling the assets of the estate and distributing them.

Taylor differential piece rate plan *historic* A rate of pay for employees based on production, named after Frederick W. Taylor (1856-1915), the first proponent of scientific management. Included in the plan are efficient machinery, plant layout, time-motion studies, etc.

T-bill *See* treasury bill.

T curve *statistics* The adaptation of the Gaussian curve or normal distribution to small samples.

teamster 1. Driver of a truck or other commercial vehicle who is a member of the Teamsters' Union. 2. Anyone who drives a commercial vehicle.

technical analysis 1. Analysis of past volume and/or price behavior to identify assets and the best time to purchase them. 2. Examination and interpretation of market prices and indexes related to the actual supply of and demand for securities. Charts and various indicators are used in an attempt to forecast future price movements. Technical analysis is usually concerned with near-to-intermediate-term movements. (*See* fundamental analysis)

technocracy Economic concept originated in the 1930s in which the efficiencies of labor-saving devices are not passed on to consumers, resulting in insufficient purchasing power.

technological forecasting Assessing in advance what technological changes are apt to come in an industry, and their implications for employees, firms, products, etc.

technological unemployment Lack of employment possibilities caused by a change or cumulative changes in technology.

telemarketing 1. Marketing technique in which orders are both placed and received by computers. 2. *See* telephone advertising. 3. A method of marketing in which a prospective customer is first sent a card stating that the customer has won a prize and asking the customer to call some telephone number, often a toll-free "800"

number. When the call is made, the sales pitch" is made. Most telemarketing is legal, but much of it tends to take advantage of prospective customers, and thus may not be ethical. 4. Direct marketing through television, with many types of products and services being pitched to viewers, who can call and give a credit card number, or make some other form of payment, to receive the product. Includes auctions carried on by television. (*See* teleshopping)

telephone advertising Telephone solicitation of prospective customers for some good or service. (E.g., magazines use this method, as do many charities, etc.)

telephone survey A technique for soliciting from people, by telephone, information relating to their buying habits, etc. This is a most disconcerting practice, widely used, but with questionable results due to the disturbing influence of the unwanted telephone call.

teleprocessing The use of computers and terminals in various places, for data input and output.

teleshopping Type of shopping made possible by cable television whereby consumers can order by phone merchandise displayed on television sets. (*See* telemarketing)

telex A telegraph service which gives instant printed communications between subscribers.

teller 1. One who keeps a tally; one who numbers. 2. *banking* In a bank, one who receives and pays out money. May be an all-purpose teller or one who specializes in a particular area. In small banks, all-purpose tellers are the general rule. In larger banks, there may be exchange tellers, coupon tellers, note tellers, savings account tellers, etc. These people have constant and direct contact with customers, and thus must have good social skills. The teller will almost always be responsible for a cash fund, and will usually answer to the head or chief teller, who reports to the cashier.

temporary administrator A person or institution appointed by a court to oversee the assets of an estate while there is litigation over a will, or where some named executor or administrator is being challenged. This may also occur when probate has to be delayed because of the difficulty of locating the heirs.

temporary bond Bond, usually devoid of coupons, which is issued to purchasers before the regular issue has been printed.

temporary exports Goods taken into a country tariff-free inasmuch as the goods are not to be sold, but to be used in trade fairs, etc.

temporary injunction *law* A court order restraining conduct until a hearing can be held on whether or not the injunction should be permanent. The one seeking the injunction must usually furnish a bond to cover any damage that might result if it appears at the hearing that he or she is not entitled to the injunction.

temporary investment Investment made by a firm in short-term securities to avoid having sums of cash which are not earning interest. The term may often be as short as twenty-four hours.

Temporary National Economic Committee (TNEC) A committee created by Congress in 1938 to study monopolies and the concentration of economic power. Publications from the work of this committee constitute important references for scholarly study.

temporary staff contracting service A firm that supplies temporary employees to other companies. Usually the temporary employees are hired by the contracting service who then sells their services for so much per hour, etc.

tenancy 1. Possession of lands or buildings by any kind of right or title. 2. The period during which a tenant holds or possesses land or a building. 3. The relationship between a tenant and the tenant's landlord.

tenancy at sufferance Tenancy established when a person who had been a lawful tenant wrongfully remains in possession of property after expiration of a lease.

tenancy at will License to use or occupy lands and buildings at the will of the owner. The duration of term is uncertain as the tenant may decide to leave the property at any time or must leave at the landlord's will. Agreement may be oral or written.

tenancy by the entirety Estate held by husband and wife as a fictitious unity with right of survivorship. This stems from the common law concept that a man and wife have a single legal existence and the estate is held by them by virtue of title acquired jointly after marriage. Upon death of either, the survivor takes sole ownership of the whole to exclusion of deceased heirs. This form of ownership is not applicable to all states, but where applicable, two things might apply: (a) survivorship rights can only be terminated by the consent of both parties and (b) the husband may have full control over the property during their joint lives and be entitled to all of the income from it.

tenancy for years A type of tenancy which is uncertain as to duration, and which may be cancelled by proper notice of either party.

tenancy from period to period A type of tenancy which continues from one period to another, automatically, until a legal termination notice is given.

tenancy from year to year Contract between a lessor and lessee by which the lessor grants possession and enjoyment of land or hereditaments of the temporary nature for a certain period of years for a consideration, usually a rent in money payable at the end of stated periods of a year or more during the term.

tenancy in common Form of ownership whereby each tenant holds an undivided interest in property. Unlike a joint tenancy or a tenancy by the entirety, the interest of a tenant in common does not terminate upon his or her death (there is no right of survivorship). (E.g., if Bill and Pete, brothers, own property as tenants in common and Bill dies, his portion of the property will go to his heirs.)

tenant 1. Person who has temporary occupation and use of another person's real property, usually under terms fixed by an instrument called a lease. 2. One who holds, uses, or enjoys the property of another with that person's consent or by permission or letting; a lessee.

tenantable repair Repair necessary to render a house fit for present habitation.

tenant at sufferance *common law* Tenant who originally comes into possession under a lawful title but holds possession after his or her right has terminated;

333

the lessor is entitled to evict the tenant at sufferance at any time.

tenant at will One who holds possession of the premises by permission of the owner or landlord but without a fixed term.

tenant by courtesy *common law* Freehold interest of a husband in his wife's real estate on her death after the birth of issue capable of inheriting. This gives the husband the right to hold the land and tenements for the rest of his life. The common law requisites of this estate are marriage, seisin of wife, birth of live child capable of inheriting from the mother, and death of wife during lifetime of the husband.

tenant for life One to whom land or tenements are granted or devised, or who derives title to land by operation of law for the term of his or her own life or the life of another.

tenants in common Tenants who have, together, an undivided possession of land, but who hold it by several and distinct titles.

ten commandments of speculation Rules, the original source of which is unknown, propounded by Charles Stahl, and Richard E. Band. They are: (a) Speculate with money you can afford to lose. (b) Always keep more than the broker's required margin on deposit in your account. (c) Limit your losses. (d) Never speculate if your personal life is in disarray. (e) Don't play every horse. (f) Undertrade. (g) Fear the market. (h) Don't worship charts. (i) When you make a profit, withdraw half of it. (j) Resist the impulses of the crowd.

tender 1. Formal offer, of money or property, in satisfaction of some claim or demand. 2. An offer of the amount of a debt by the debtor to the creditor. To constitute a valid tender, the amount of money must be actually produced and seen, except where the party to whom tender is made has, by his or her conduct, relieved the debtor from the necessity for producing it.

tender offer 1. An offer to buy controlling interest in a corporation through the purchase of shares of stock in the market at a stated price by a specified date. Oftentimes this type of tender offer is hos-

tile in that it is not in line with the wishes of the present management. 2. An offer by a corporation to buy back its outstanding stock at a specified price by a specified date. This tender offer may be for all outstanding stock, but it is usually only for a percentage of the outstanding stock.

tenement 1. That which is the subject of tenure. Includes both corporeal and incorporeal hereditaments such as rents and profits issuing out of land or office or dignities concerning land. 2. A possession that is permanent and fixed; structure attached to land.

tenendum clause *real estate law* A clause in a deed no longer having meaning but originally describing the tenure by which the land was held.

1040 form The basic tax return that may be used by any individual taxpayer. Consists of a two-page form with various supporting schedules.

10-K report Annual report that all corporations with listed securities must file with the Securities and Exchange Commission.

Tennessee Valley Authority (TVA) A government corporation, created in 1933, operating water control properties in the watershed of the Tennessee River for national defense, navigation, and the development of hydroelectric power for agriculture and industry in the Tennessee Valley.

tenor True intent and meaning of a document, its purport and effect.

10-Q report Required quarterly report filed with the Securities and Exchange Commission by publicly held firms. Both the 10-K (annual) and 10-Q (quarterly) reports are more detailed than the annual report sent to the stockholders.

tentative tax Tax computed against which the descendant's available estate tax credits are applied to arrive at the estate tax that is due.

tentative tax base *estate planning* Taxable estate, prior to the deduction of available tax credits.

tenure 1. Fact, manner, or term of holding or occupying some particular office. 2. Permanent status granted to an employee after a specified trial period of employment. 3. The nature of an occupant's ownership rights; an indication of whether one is an owner or a tenant.

tenure in land Mode in which a person holds an estate in lands.

ten-year cliff vesting Plan under which a participant's accrued benefits must be 100% vested upon completion of ten years of service.

ten-year forward income averaging *profit sharing* Special method of tax computation allowed on distribution if the employee has been a participant in the plan for at least five years prior to the distribution. The election to take the ten-year averaging must be made by the employee by the attachment of Form 4972 to the employee's income tax return. The result of this election is to tax the lump-sum distribution, less the minimum distribution allowance, as if it has been received evenly over a ten-year period by a single individual with income of only the zero-bracket amount. The tax as computed is then added to the tax liability on the employee's other income. There is a minimum distribution allowance of a lump-sum payment which is received tax free. This allowance presently is the lesser of ten thousand dollars or one-half of the total taxable amount of the distribution. To arrive at the minimum distribution allowance, this amount is then reduced by 20% of the total taxable amount in excess of twenty thousand dollars. The minimum distribution allowance makes rollover treatment of small distribution amounts much more advantageous to the employee than ten-year forward income averaging. (*See* Appendix G)

term 1. Interval allowed a debtor to meet obligation. 2. One of the prescribed periods of the year during which a court may hold a session. 3. The specific extent of time (as a year or a definite number of years) for which an estate is granted; also, an estate or interest held for such a time. 4. A fixed period, a prescribed duration. 5. Length of time designated for total repayment of a loan.

term, amortization *See* amortization term.

term bonds Bonds issued at one time and which fall due at one time.

term certificate *See* certificate of deposit.

term health *insurance* Policy with no provision for cancellation. A travel-accident policy purchased at the airport provides an example of a term policy.

terminable interest An interest which will lapse after a given period of time or one which is contingent upon an event happening or an event not happening.

terminal value The worth of a sum of money or cash flow at a specified time in the future allowing for the appreciation at compound interest; i.e., the future value of a present sum, or of a periodic flow of funds.

term life *insurance* Form of life insurance issued for a period of time specified in the contract or to subject's age sixty-five or seventy. If death should occur during that time period, the face amount of the policy is paid. Term policies generally have no cash or loan values and are looked upon as pure protection insurance.

term of court *law* The specified number of days, or periods, the court meets (sets) each year. This is important because of the rule restricting the judge as to changing the judgment after the term in which it was entered, except for statutory reasons.

term of years Estate limited in advance to endure for a definite and ascertained period of time. Also called term for years.

terms Conditions and arrangements specified in a contract.

terms of trade The relationship between the price level of exports and the price level of imports. The terms of trade are said to be positive if the prices of exports increase relative to the price of imports.

territorial waters That part of the sea adjacent to the coast of a given country which is by international law declared to be within that country's jurisdiction, thereby giving its courts legal authority over offenses committed on those waters. (Generally, a three-mile limit.)

testacy Leaving of a will at one's death.

testament Written instrument by means of which a person disposes of his or her estate, such disposition to take effect after the person's death. In modern usage, "testament" is synonymous with "will" and with "last will and testament"; strictly speaking, however, the terms are different in that a testament bequeaths personal property only.

testamentary 1. Of or pertaining to a will or testament, as a document. 2. Provided or appointed by a will, as a guardian. 3. Founded on, derived from, or created by a will, as a testamentary trust.

testamentary capacity Ability of the testator to understand the nature of the act and its effects and the extent of the property that is being disposed of. The testator should be able to comprehend and appreciate the claims to which the testator should give effect and have such memory as to be able to carry in mind and appreciate the extent and nature of the estate and the people who normally should be the objects of largess. The testator should be of reasonably sound mind, memory, and understanding.

testamentary disposition Gift made by will to take effect upon the death of the person making the disposition. This is temporarily revocable in character, and the person making the disposition has substantially entire control until death.

testamentary document Document executed in compliance with the formalities of a will, to take effect after the death of the maker, and revocable during the maker's lifetime.

testamentary guardian One appointed as guardian over a child by a parent's will.

testamentary trust Trust included in the body of a will, intended to protect the estate left by the deceased by having the proceeds managed by someone other than the beneficiary. While the testamentary trust does not result in any immediate estate or income tax saving when the will is executed, it may in the future by protecting the estate as it is passed from one generation to another.

testate 1. Having made a valid will. 2. One who dies leaving a will.

testation Witness, evidence.

testator Person who makes or has made a will or testament; person who dies leaving a will or testament.

testatrix Sometimes used to designate female testator.

test in depth To audit an entire firm or a specific project, going into great depths to trace every transaction related to the firm or project.

test marketing The introduction of a product into a particular city or area considered typical of the total market, and the observation and tabulation of the results of the promotional campaign in that area. The results determine whether the product will be introduced on a larger scale.

T-group training Group training in human relations which directs the group's attention to interpersonal events and relations.

theft Unlawful taking of or exercising unlawful control over movable property of another with intent to deprive the owner of its continued use; larceny; stealing.

theft by false pretenses Crime consisting of the making of a false pretense or representation by the defendant with the intent to defraud the owner of property and actual reliance by the owner on the false pretense.

theory of concentration Theory of Karl Marx that larger capitalistic structures will usually take over smaller and weaker capitalistic structures in order to concentrate power in their hands.

Theory X and Theory Y *management* Concepts propounded by Douglas McGregor, management specialist and author, in which he divides management philosophies into two groups: Theory X, which is authoritarian in nature, and Theory Y, which takes a broader view of a person's capacity to work and to innovate. As a basic authoritarian system, Theory X sees people as lazy, naturally lacking in ambition, and needing a strong hand to get them to carry out their assignments. Theory Y takes a better view of human nature and declares that people are ambitious and innovative and will do good things if the proper atmosphere is provided for them.

Theory Z *management* A hypothesis, propounded by William Ouchi, combining certain aspects of both Theory X and Theory Y. Included in the theory are trust (in management by employees), participation in management, etc.; yet Ouchi retains some aspects both of paternalism and authoritarianism.

thesaurus inenetus est vetus dispositio pecujniae, etc., cujus non extat modo memoria, adeo ut jam dominum non habeat *Treasury is long hidden money, etc., of which non-recollection exists, so that it now has no owner.*

thing in action Thing which is not in the possession or actual enjoyment of a person, but which a person has a right to or a right to demand by an action at law.

thin market A market in which there are few bids to buy and few offers to sell. May apply to the entire market, a specific type of securities, or a specific stock.

third market When securities which are sold on a stock exchange are sold off that exchange they are said to be sold in the third market.

third-party beneficiary One for whose benefit a promise is made in a contract but who is not a party to the contract.

third-party beneficiary contract Contract in which the promisor has a legal interest in performance in favor of a third party and in which performance of terms of the contract between the two parties must necessarily result in direct benefit to the third party as intended by the parties.

third-party transaction 1. Transaction which involves three people: a buyer, a seller, and a lender. 2. Transaction which may affect a third party, but in which the third party is not a direct participant. (E.g., an apartment building owner may sell the apartment building to another person, which will affect the tenant, but the tenant is not a party to the transaction.)

third world Underdeveloped, non-aligned nations in Asia, Africa, and Latin America.

thirty-day wash rule Internal Revenue Service rule which forbids taking losses (for tax purposes) to offset gains if equivalent stock is purchased within thirty days before or after the date of sale.

thoroughfare Highway, footpath, or navigable river used by the public; a passage through; an unobstructed way open to the public; a public road or street open at both ends, especially where there is much traffic.

three-party paper A consumer sales contract owned by a dealer (usually in hard goods) and then sold to the bank or finance company.

thrift institution Organization formed and chartered to accept consumer deposits (e.g., mutual savings banks, savings and loan associations, and credit unions). Except for credit unions, the deposits in thrift institutions have historically been used to make loans on residential property.

Thrift Institutions Advisory Council (TIAC) Council, established following the passage of the Monetary Control Act of 1980, whose purpose is to provide information and views on the special needs and problems of thrifts. The group is comprised of representatives of savings and loan associations and credit unions.

thrift savings plan Employee savings plan, growing in popularity, which technically must be formulated as a pension, profit sharing, or stock-bonus plan. The employer may or may not contribute to the plan. While the employees' contributions are made with after-tax dollars, they do get the benefit of tax-deferred interest, compounded, until such time as the funds are distributed.

throat That part of an investment vehicle on which is printed the name of the registered holder and the par value of the security.

throwback rule Principle by which taxing is distributed by a trust of previously accumulated income in substantially the same way as the distributions would have been taxed if made when the income was earned by the trust.

thruster A manager or a complete organization which is dynamic, acts aggressively, and exploits opportunities.

tick *stock market* A movement upward or downward in a security's trades. Analysts often watch the ticks to get a feel for the stock's trend.

tight money A situation in which the money supply is limited, and interest rates go up. This often arises as a part of monetary policy, such as combating inflation.

timber property Property that provides some cash flow in the selling of timber and may also allow for capital appreciation. Since, like farm land, timber land is looked upon as a business, there are tax benefits not available for raw land.

time deposit *banking* A deposit which demands a set rate of interest and which requires (theoretically) a thirty-day notice for withdrawal. The thirty-day limit is meant to be the dividing line between a demand deposit and a time deposit, but in recent years this requirement has generally not been followed.

time horizon Investment holding period attained.

time indifference curve *statistics* Using an indifference map with consumption expenditure in year one on the "X" axis, and consumption expenditure in year two on the "Y" axis, a time indifference curve traces all the combinations of consumption expenditures in the two years that give equal satisfaction, or utility. The slope of the indifference curve is the rate of time substitution.

time is of the essence Phrase that, when inserted in a contract, requires that all references to specific dates and times of day noted in the contract be adhered to exactly. In its absence, delays might be acceptable.

time marine policy Marine insurance policy which limits the duration of the risk by fixing dates or time for its beginning and end and covering any voyage or voyages undertaken within that time period.

time preference theory of interest An explanation of interest that reveals what additional price people are willing to pay for the immediate satisfaction of an economic want or need. Also, an explanation of what people will demand in the way of payment for foregoing consumption at this time in order to save.

time reversal test *statistic* A method of testing the mathematical validity of an index number. The base period data are changed in identification to the later period and the later period's data are treated as the base period's. Then if the index number computed for the former base period is multiplied by the index number originally computed and the result is unity, the test is met.

times burden covered Coverage ratio measure of financial leverage, defined as earnings before interest and taxes divided by interest expense plus principal payments, grossed up to their before-tax equivalents.

time series *statistics* A gathering of data with time as the independent variable and some other factor as the dependent variable, as contrasted to a frequency distribution in which data is presented without regard for the time factor.

time series bar charts A graphic illustration of individual differences in values over time using a bar method of charting. This has the significance of illustrating the differences in magnitude of values.

time series data *statistics* The observations of the values of economic variables over a series of successive time intervals.

time series forecasting A sophisticated method of forecasting the future which takes into consideration past experience, but also seasonal and cyclical movements in the products or industries.

time-sharing Form of property ownership under which a property is held by a number of people, each with the right of possession for a specified time interval. Time-sharing is most commonly applied to resort and vacation properties.

times interest earned 1. Ratio of earnings before interest and taxes divided by interest expense; a coverage ratio that measures the safety of debt. 2. Ratio of pre-tax income plus interest charges to the interest charges on long-term obligations.

Times 1000 An annual publication giving financial and other pertinent information on one thousand leading British companies.

times preferred dividend earned *securities* An often-used measure of the earnings protection of preferred stock. The figure is computed by dividing the net earnings per year (after taxes, interest, and any prior dividends) by the preferred dividend requirements of that issue for that year.

time utility That aspect of utility which puts the good or service at the disposal of the consumer at the proper time. (*See* utility)

tip Sum of money given to a worker in appreciation of service.

title 1. Name by which anything is known. 2. An identifying mark of honor or dignity. 3. A right, particularly the right of ownership of property. 4. Evidence that the owner of land is in lawful possession thereof; evidence of ownership.

title, absolute *See* absolute title.

title company *real estate* Company that specializes in examining titles and issuing insurance on them.

title search Examination of the records of the registry of deeds, or some other office which maintains records of title documents, to see whether the title to the property is good; i.e., whether or not there are any defects in the title.

to have and to hold Phrase used in conveyancing of realty followed by a description of the estate intended to be conveyed.

token money Any object (usually a coin) whose value as money is greater than the market value of the materials of which it is composed (e.g., pennies, nickels, etc.). Tokens, especially during time of war, may have virtually no intrinsic value.

tolerance The limit in variance of size or quality permitted in the specifications for producing a product.

toll Sum of money paid for some privilege, as for the use of a road or bridge.

tombstone advertising 1. An ad announcing a new issue of securities and naming the underwriters. 2. A "business card" ad, usually put in a newspaper by a professional who wants to give only a name, business, phone, and address.

tom next *banking* An abbreviation of "tomorrow next," used by banks to indicate the delivery date on Eurodollar deposits and foreign exchange transactions on the next business day.

ton mile *transportation* Unit of measurement indicating the movement of one ton of freight a distance of one mile.

top-down method *economics* Method used to forecast industry sales and to develop a forecast of company and product sales.

top-heavy plan *pensions* Plan in which 60% or more of specifically enumerated benefits (account balance, in the case of a defined-contribution plan; present value of accrued benefits, in the case of a defined-benefit plan) inure to the benefit of key employees.

Torrens title system Title registration system in some states by which the court of

jurisdiction issues a certificate of title, along with a duplicate copy, to the owner of the land. The condition of the title can easily be discovered without resorting to a title search.

tort 1. Any private or civil wrong by act or omission, not including breach of contract. 2. A wrongful act, other than a breach of contract, committed by one person against another creating a possible legal liability. A wrongful act that is neither a crime nor a breach of contract, but that renders the perpetrator liable to the victim for damages.

tortfeasor *law* A person who has committed a tort. (Cf. tort)

total cost approach to distribution A sophisticated management technique used to identify and aggregate the more obscure distribution-related costs as well as the more obvious ones. This is used to plan cost-cutting procedures, particularly in large and complex business enterprises.

total gift Situation in which an insurance policy is the subject of a gift; the total value is the policy's replacement value (i.e., the cost of similar or comparable policies issued by the same company). The total gift of the insurance policy would have to be calculated at the time it was given.

total income for tax purposes All recognized income from whatever source derived, unless specifically excluded.

total investment risk Sum of systematic and unsystematic risk (i.e., portfolio risk). (*See* systematic risk)

totalitarian Describes a government in which state controls or ownership have been extended to virtually every facet of life.

total output curve Graphed curve that, by holding some factors of production fixed (such as plant size) and permitting one or more factors of production to vary in physical units (such as labor and materials), traces the quantities of output in physical units that result as the number of units of the variable factor is varied. With units of output on the "Y" axis and units of the variable factor on the "X" axis the total output will rise at a faster rate, reach a maximum, and then descend because of, first, the less efficient use and, finally, inefficiency of the fixed factor.

total remuneration concept A method of combining gross compensation with the expenditures made on fringe benefits to reveal to employees the complete compensation package they receive for their services.

total revenue curve Graphed curve on which, with total revenue on the "Y" axis and quantity of units on the "X" axis, the total revenue starts at the origin and traces the total receipts from different quantities of the good sold. If the price received per unit sold is constant, the total revenue curve will be a straight line starting at the origin and rising at an angle. If the price received for successively larger quantities is lower, the curve will taper away from the "Y" axis.

total tax due Amount determined after subtracting credits from the tax liability and then adding other types of taxes to the balance. These taxes include such things as the Social Security self-employment tax, the alternative minimum tax, and recapture of the investment tax credit.

total utility Amount of satisfaction a consumer derives from all of the units of a particular good or service consumed in a given time period.

totten trust Trust created when an individual deposits money in a bank or savings account for another person's benefit, and the individual names himself or herself as trustee of the account.

town Thickly settled area, regardless of its legal boundaries or the form of municipal government.

town house Dwelling unit, generally having two or more floors and attached to other similar units via party walls. Town houses are often used in planned unit developments and condominium developments, which provide for clustered or attached housing and common open space.

township 1. Six-mile square tract delineated by government rectangle survey. 2. A civil and political division of a county, created by state legislature, and sometimes vested with certain powers of local government.

tract 1. Parcel of land, generally held for subdividing; a subdivision. 2. Abstract space as opposed to specific space or relative space; as applied to land, means contiguity of parcel of property.

tract book A book containing the plats of the land parcels in certain areas.

trade Commerce; the business of selling, with a view to profit, goods which the trader has either manufactured or purchased.

trade acceptance Evidence of agreement to trade, given as draft or bill of exchange drawn by seller on the purchaser of goods sold and accepted by such purchaser.

trade association An association of dealers or manufacturers engaged in a particular trade formed for the interchange of information, establishment of product and ethical standards, and other activities of mutual concern to the members. Many of these organizations also serve as political action committees.

trade date A day on which a commodity or security futures trade actually takes place. Total settlement usually follows the trade date by five business days.

trade deficit Amount by which merchandise imports exceed merchandise exports.

trade discount A deduction from a list price or a catalog price which determines the ultimate selling price of goods. The discount may be for early payment of an invoice, a volume discount, etc.

trade dollar A special silver coin minted by the United States from 1873 to 1885 with more silver content than the standard silver dollar and intended for use in trading with the Orient.

Trade Expansion Act (1962) Act broadening the powers of the President to negotiate further tariff reductions on broad categories of goods; to lower or eliminate tariffs on those goods which account for at least 80% of total world exports; to lower tariffs by as much as 50% on the basis of reciprocal trade agreements, provided that such agreements include most-favored-nation clauses so that the benefits of reduced tariffs are extended to other countries; and to grant vocational, technical, and financial assistance to American employees and businessmen whose industries are adversely affected by tariff reduction.

trade fixture Article placed in rented

building by the tenant to help carry out trade or business. The tenant can remove the fixtures before the expiration of the lease, but if the tenant fails to do so shortly after the lease expires, the fixtures become the landlord's property. The time element would probably have to be settled by the court if lease was unclear on the matter.

trade-in Type of price allowance that preserves the list price of the new item while cutting the amount the customer has to pay by allowing credit on a used object, usually of the kind being purchased.

trademark Distinctive name, mark, or other symbol, which is affixed by a manufacturer to goods to identify them and to distinguish them from those made by other manufacturers. Includes not only the pictorial design but also the brand name. Such trademarks can be registered under U.S. law, and also in some states. In the United States the first person to use a trademark in a given area (geographic or product-wise) normally has the exclusive right to it regardless of who registers it. Canadian and Latin-American laws extend the right to the first registrant.

trade name 1. Word, name, symbol, device, or any combination thereof in any form or arrangement used by a person to identify that person's business, vocation, or occupation and distinguish same from the business, vocation, or occupation of others. 2. The name used in trade to identify a particular business, its products, or the place where the business is located. A trade name differs from a trademark in that it is not affixed to merchandise or because it is incapable of exclusive appropriation by anyone as a trademark.

trade payable Account payable.

trader *investments* Individual who buys and sells securities and commodities for himself, generally not as a representative for a client.

trade secret Any formula, patent, device, plan, process, tool, mechanism, or compound known only to its owner and those of its employees to whom it is necessary to confide the information, and which gives the owner an opportunity to obtain an advantage over competitors who do not know or use same. Contractual agreements between employers and employees often contain provisions of trade secrets, especially when innovative discoveries are made by the employee.

trade union 1. Labor organization; a combination of workers usually of the same trade or allied trade for the purpose of securing by united action the most favorable wages and conditions of labor. 2. An organization of people from the same trade or several allied trades, the purpose of which is the protection and promotion of the members' common interests, especially the increase of wages, better working conditions, shorter hours of labor, mutual insurance, and fringe benefits. (*See* union)

trade usage Custom or usage of the trade in question, which usage or custom is widely known, certain, and reasonable.

trading down The action of selling securities from a portfolio and buying securities of a lower value. The reason usually is based on the belief of the buyer that the lower priced securities have a greater opportunity to increase in value than the ones sold.

trading limits *commodities* 1. Prices above or below which trading is not permitted during any one day. 2. The maximum quantity of commodities futures which may be purchased or sold by one person or on any one trading day. Both are fixed by the Commodity Exchange Commission.

trading on equity Using borrowed funds to increase business activity where funds in use yield more in profits than the borrowed money costs in interest.

trading stamp 1. Coupon or a memorandum in writing given by a merchant which expresses in money value a small percentage of the price of goods bought and paid for by the customer. The holder is entitled, generally after accumulating a number of such memoranda or coupons, to redeem the same for other goods of the merchant or goods of some other person or trading company that has undertaken to redeem the coupons. (The popularity of trading stamps rises and falls with the cycles of the economy.) 2. Sales promotion premiums offered by some retailers with a purchase. These stamps can be exchanged for items of value at stamp redemption centers.

341

trading up   A method of merchandising which concentrates on high-priced merchandise combined with a wide variety of customer services.

traditio   *Delivery.* Method of transferring movable goods; i.e., by delivery of the same for a lawful consideration.

traditional cost method   *insurance* Established method of comparing life insurance costs per thousand dollars of insurance, taking the sum of all the premiums for a specified period (usually ten or twenty years) less (a) the cash value at the end of the period, (b) the sum of the policy dividends for the period, and (c) the current applicable dividend.

traditional economy   Economic system in which the basic questions of what, how, and for whom to produce are resolved primarily by custom and tradition.

traffic   Trade; commerce; exchange of goods or merchandise for an equivalent. The movement or passing of goods from one person to another, from one place to another.

trainability test   Test designed to assess the ability of a person for learning new skills.

tramp steamer   A cargo vessel that does not operate on a regular route but whose ports of call are dictated by what cargo it picks up from one port to the next.

transaction   Sequential group of events so connected as to be referred to as a single event, as the sale of a house.

transaction account   Checking account or similar account from which transfers can be made to third parties (e.g., demand deposit accounts, negotiable order of withdrawal accounts, automatic transfer service accounts, and credit union share draft accounts).

transcript   Official copy of proceedings in court.

transfer   Act by which a right, title, or interest in real or personal property is conveyed from one person to another.

transferability   The ability of ownership or title to be transferred. This can be restricted by provisions in the contract making them nonassignable.

transfer agent   1. Bank or trust department that acts similar to, and in conjunction with, a registrar. (*See* registrar) 2.

investments One who keeps the records of a firm and of stockholders and who transfers the certificates as they are bought and sold.

transferee   One to whom a transfer is made.

transfer for value rule   Rule stating that where prior to death a policy or an interest in a policy has been sold or otherwise transferred for valuable consideration, the death proceeds will be exempt only to the extent of (a) the consideration paid by the transferee and (b) the net premiums paid by the transferee after the transfer. The balance of death proceeds are taxed at ordinary income rates (income averaging may be available). (*See* Appendix G)

transfer in contemplation of death   Transfer made to prevent the avoidance of death taxes when it appears that death is imminent. The rule of transfer in contemplation of death levies a tax on such a transfer as though it were made at death. Often, any transfer made during the two years prior to death is looked upon as in contemplation of death.

transfer journal   A book kept by a corporation or an agent for a corporation to show stock certificates issued, transferred, or cancelled.

transfer of risk   *risk management* Any measure by which the risk of one party actually is transferred to another. Insurance remains the most used vehicle for the transfer of risk.

transferor   One who makes a transfer.

transfer payment   *economics* Payment made to an individual by government and business for which no productive work is currently being performed (e.g., welfare, Social Security, and unemployment compensation are government transfer payments). Expenditure for which no goods or services are exchanged.

transfer price   Charge for sending goods from one company profit center to another, for which an accounting must be made if year-end figures for each profit center are to be exact.

transfer tax   Tax paid upon the passing of title to property or a valuable interest. A tax upon a transfer made out of or from a decedent's estate by inheritance, bequest, or devise.

transformation curve 1. Graphed curve, with military goods on the "Y" axis and civilian goods on the "X" axis, tracing all the combinations of both types of goods which the economy can produce. 2. Graph, with product "x" on the "X" axis and product "y" on the "Y" axis, on which a series of nonparallel straight lines from a point on one axis to a point on the other axis will each trace the output of a common component of the two products, which use a common component, that the plant can produce.

transformation functions Those functions that define the attainable positions to which a firm can move in terms of the structure of its assets, liabilities, and other variables. There are two transformation functions, namely, the product function and the market function.

transient Passing, temporary, not lasting.

transitivity *statistics* A situation in which if a = b and b = c, a will also equal c. For this condition to exist, both of the prior statements must be in the same dimension; e.g., length measured linearly, etc.

transit number *banking* The identification number of a bank which is printed on its checks under the national numerical system. The number has three parts, the first denoting the location of the bank, the second the bank's name, and the third (below the line) the Federal Reserve District. These numbers facilitate the routing of out-of-town checks.

transitory action Action founded on a transaction that took place not necessarily within the jurisdiction of the court or that has no locality in the consideration of the law.

transmission 1. Transfer, not by the voluntary act of parties but by implication of law. 2. Act of sending or transferring from one person or place to another.

transmit To transfer; to communicate as by wire or cable.

transplacement An error caused by moving all digits to the right or to the left of the proper columns without changing the order of the digits.

transport To move from one place to another.

transportation Business of moving goods or people from one place to another.

transportation ratio Regarding railroads, the ratio of transportation expenses to operating revenues. Transportation expense includes the cost of moving trains, but not depreciation, repairs, or maintenance.

transportation terms Terms which designate the party (buyer or seller) who is responsible for transportation charges. May be stated as "f.o.b. shipping point" or "f.o.b. destination."

trap *law* Concealed danger or hidden evil involving a deliberate intent to surprise the victim.

traveler's check Check-size document issued by various large banks and other companies designed for the use of travelers who do not wish to carry cash and from whom a personal check would not be acceptable in a foreign place. They come in several denominations and can be purchased, often from a bank, for a relatively small fee. They must be signed once by the purchaser in the presence of the seller and again when cashed. The full value is guaranteed by the issuing institution.

traveler's letter of credit A letter of credit which is addressed to a corresponding bank. The traveler can then present the letter to any one of the banks, along with a signature card from the issuing bank for identification, and draw credit.

treasurer's drafts Checks which are written on a corporation rather than a bank, but which are payable through a bank.

treasury 1. Place where money or other valuables are deposited. 2. Department of the government in charge of receipt and disbursement of all public monies.

treasury bill Short-term debt instrument with maturity of one year or less issued weekly by the United States government on a discount basis with full face value due at maturity. T-bills are issued in denominations of ten thousand dollars with income exempt from state and local income taxes. Maturities range from 91 to 182 to 359 days. They are the main instruments used by the Federal Reserve to control the money supply through the operations of the Open Market Committee, and they comprise the bulk of government's short-term debt.

treasury bond Long-term debt instrument issued by the United States Treasury with maturity of ten years or longer. These bonds are issued at par with semi-annual interest payments being exempt from state and local taxes. Bonds and notes are quoted in points and thirty-seconds. (E.g., a quote of 93.8 would equal 93%₃₂, or $932.50.) These bonds, which constitute the largest segment of the government's public debt, may be purchased in denominations of a thousand dollars and up. Many of the bonds are callable at par five years before maturity on interest payment dates.

Treasury Investors Growth Receipt (TIGER) A form of zero-coupon security first created by Merrill Lynch, Pierce, Fenner, and Smith. These securities are U.S. government backed bonds which have been stripped of their coupons. Both coupons and bonds are sold at deep discounts. Holders of the securities receive face value for the securities at maturity, devoid of interest. Since zero-coupon bonds must pay imputed interest annually, TIGERs also must do this, according to the IRS. To avoid paying tax on this interest, some holders put the securities in IRA plans, Keoghs, or other tax deferred accounts.

treasury note Intermediate-term debt instrument issued by the United States government with maturities of over one year and up to ten years. These notes are issued at par in denominations of five thousand dollars and ten thousand dollars, with interest payments semiannually being exempt from state and local taxes. The notes, issued in bearer or registered form, constitute the bulk of the intermediate-term debt of the government.

treasury securities Interest-bearing obligations of the United States government issued by the Treasury as a means of borrowing money to meet government expenditures not covered by tax revenues. Marketable Treasury securities fall into three categories: bills, notes, and bonds. The Federal Reserve System holds more than $125 billion of these obligations, acquired through open market operations. Marketable Treasury obligations are currently issued in book-entry form only; i.e., the purchaser receives a statement, rather than an engraved certificate.

treasury stock Shares of a corporation's own stock which have been reacquired by the corporation either by direct purchase or gift, and that have not been cancelled.

Treasury tax and loan (TT&L) accounts Accounts in which tax deposits may be made through any depository institution which is authorized to do so. The deposits will remain there until withdrawn, on a predetermined schedule, by the treasury department.

Treaty of Paris (1951) Treaty that established the European Coal and Steel Community. It was signed in April 1951 and became operative in August 1952. Founding members were France, West Germany, Italy, the Netherlands, Belgium, and Luxembourg. Predated the Treaty of Rome of 1957, which created the European Economic Community, or Common Market.

Treaty of Rome (1957) Treaty signed in Rome in 1957 which formed the backdrop for the Common Market (European Economic Community).

treaty reinsurance Agreement between a direct insurer (the company that writes the insurance) and a reinsurer (a company that shares in the risk of a direct company agreeing to accept a certain portion of the amount of insurance written) in which there is a sharing of the risk of a certain insurance policy.

trend, arithmetic straight line See arithmetic straight line trend.

trespass 1. Any voluntary transgression of law or rule of duty; any offense done to another's person or property. 2. Any unlawful act accompanied by force, either actual or implied, such as unauthorized entry on another person's land either intentionally or unintentionally. 3. Unlawful entry or possession of property.

triadic product test A type of product assessment in which two samples of the same product are given to a person, along with one of a different kind, to determine whether the difference is discovered by the one doing the sampling.

trial The examination of a cause, civil or criminal, before a judge who has jurisdiction, according to the laws of the land, to determine which of two opposing sides is entitled to succeed and thereby justify its cause.

trial balance *accounting* A listing of all the accounts and their balances which is used to test the equality of debits and credits.

tribal land Lands within the boundaries of an Indian reservation held in trust by the federal government of the United States for the Indian tribe as a community. Such lands grant to the various tribes all mineral rights and all other rights held by fee simple deed.

tributary A stream which empties into or feeds another stream. A consideration in buying land, due to the danger of flooding.

tripartite 1. Consisting of or divided into three parts and having three corresponding copies. 2. An agreement to which there are three different parties.

triple tax exempt A feature of some municipal bonds which exempts them from federal, state, and local taxes, if the bonds are held by residents of the states and municipalities involved. These bonds are particularly popular in states which have high income tax rates, and where larger municipalities may have the same.

triple witching hour The last trading hour on the third Friday in March, June, September, and December, when options and futures on stock indexes expire concurrently.

trivial Minor, insignificant, of little worth or importance.

trover and conversion *law* A type of action at common law the purpose for which is to recover damages for personal property wrongfully appropriated.

true bill *law* The verdict of a grand jury that there is sufficient evidence to warrant a trial.

true copy Copy that is exact in all essential particulars so that no one can be misled as to the effect of the instrument. A true copy and a duplicate are not synonymous, since a duplicate means an exact double of the original; a true copy may vary from the original.

true value rule Rule relating to corporate stock stating that where the corporation becomes insolvent, the holder of corporate stock, in order to be absolved from further liability, must have paid in full in money or money's worth the true value of the property irrespective of any

questions of fraud, mistake, error in judgment, or cheerful optimism.

truncation A shortening of operating procedures in order to reduce paperwork and reduce expenses.

trust 1. Right of property held by one person (trustee) for the benefit of another (beneficiary). 2. The confidence placed in a trustee that the trustee will faithfully apply the property to the benefit of the beneficiary. 3. The property so held; also, the relationship between the holder of the property and the property so held. 4. Confidence reposed by one person in another in relation to any right in property held by the latter for the benefit of the former or for the benefit of a third person known as the cestui que trust. A fiduciary relationship with respect to property, subjecting the person by whom it is held to equitable duties to deal with it for the benefit of another. 5. Fiduciary arrangement set up by someone called the grantor, creator, or settlor of trust, whereby a person, corporation, or other organization, called the trustee, has legal right (title) to property placed in the trust by the grantor.

trust account *real estate* Separate bank account segregated from a broker's own funds in which the broker is required by state law to deposit all monies collected for clients. In some states called an escrow account.

trust deed Means of conveyance of real estate to a third party to be held for the benefit of another. Commonly used in some states in place of mortgages that conditionally convey title to the lender.

trustee 1. Person in whom an estate, interest, or power is vested under an agreement to manage it for the benefit of another; one who is appointed or required to carry out a trust. 2. Person who holds property upon trust. (*See* passive trustee)

trustee in bankruptcy Person in whom the property of the bankrupt is vested in trust for creditors. The powers and duties of a trustee in bankruptcy are provided for in the Federal Bankruptcy Law.

trust for sale Fiduciary agreement whereby the trustee is directed by the creator of the agreement to sell real estate and convert the same into personal chattels.

trust fund Fund held by a trustee for the specific purposes set forth in the document; a fund which is to be devoted to a particular purpose and not to be diverted from that purpose for any reason.

trust fund doctrine Rule of equity by which all assets of an insolvent corporation pass to a receiver to be equitably distributed to innocent creditors; these assets are a trust fund for the benefit of creditors.

Trust Indenture Act (1939) A federal law which requires all corporate bonds and other debt instruments to be issued under an indenture agreement approved by the Securities and Exchange Commission and naming a qualified trustee for the issue, free of any connection with or obligation to the issuing company.

trust officer *banking* Head of the trust department, usually a senior vice president in larger banks. Under him will be other trust officers. Several trust officers, however, will be either assistant vice presidents or vice presidents. In large banks, there will be specialized departments within the trust department. It is not uncommon for the head of the trust department to be a member of the board of directors. Regardless of how the department is set up, its function is to hold property in trust for clients, either individuals or corporations. It is common for several of the people in the trust department to be attorneys.

trustor Person who creates a trust either by will or by another trust instrument; often called a grantor.

trust receipt Method of securing a debt or financing commercial transactions by means of which title passes directly from the manufacturer or seller to the banker or lender who as owner delivers goods to the dealer, in whose behalf the banker or lender is acting and to whom the title will pass when the primary right of the banker or lender has been satisfied.

truth Veracity; sincerity in character, action, and speech; genuineness in expression.

turbary Common law right of ancient origin to dig turf upon another person's ground.

turnkey project Development in which a developer completes an entire project on behalf of a buyer, with the keys turned over to the buyer at completion.

turnover of accounts receivable An accounting for the rapidity of the collection of accounts receivable. Credit sales divided by the average receivables balance. (*See* Appendix D)

turnover tax A sales tax levied on every transaction, whether at wholesale or retail.

turnpike Highway, maintenance costs for which are collected from the tolls levied upon those who use it.

turpitude Depravity of principles or actions. Moral turpitude consists of any behavior done contrary to justice, honesty, modesty, or good morals.

tutela actio Action by a ward against a guardian to compel an accounting.

tutela testamentaria Guardianship created by a will.

12b-1 mutual fund A type of mutual fund which may assess shareholders for some of its promotional expenses. Such funds must be registered as such.

twenty-five percent rule A rule held by municipal bond analysts that bonded indebtedness over 25% of a municipality's annual budget is excessive.

twenty-percent cushion rule A guideline used by municipal indebtedness analysts which states that the project financed by the bond issue funds should produce 20% more revenue than it takes to finance the bond issue and keep up the facility.

twisting *insurance* Misrepresentation by an agent persuading a policyholder to drop one policy and take another; includes failure to disclose facts. In the insurance industry, this was once frowned upon, but has become less so as policies have changed, and as the policyholder's need for such changes has increased.

two-earner married couple deduction Special deduction from gross income that may be taken by a two-earner married couple who file a joint return, provided neither claims foreign-earned income exclusions. The deduction is an amount equal to 10% of the lesser of thirty thousand dollars or the earned income of the lower earning spouse's income. (*See* Appendix G)

2503(b) trust Trust that makes the annual exclusion available only for gifts of present interests and so mandates current income distributions to satisfy that requirement. This and 2503(c) are widely used as vehicles for gifts to minors. (*See* Appendix G)

2503(c) trust Trust that deals with the availability of the annual gift tax exclusion for the benefit of minors. The section itself says nothing about trusts; merely describes a specific form of transfer for the minor's benefit that will qualify as a gift of present interest to make the annual exclusion available. (*See* Appendix G)

two-sided market A market in stocks in which both the bid and asked sides are firm. Specialists and others who make markets must maintain their stocks in this way. Thus, both buyers and sellers are assured that they will be able to complete their transactions.

two-tiered method of integration *pension plans* Combination of plans designed to generate one properly integrated plan. The first tier of the plan makes up for compensation not covered by Social Security. The second tier provides uniform contributions above and beyond the first tier.

tying agreement Agreement requiring a dealer who wishes to become the exclusive dealer for specific products of a manufacturer to carry other of the manufacturer's products in inventory. The legality of a tying agreement is based on whether it restricts competitors from major markets.

U

uberrima fides *The most good faith.* Contracts of life insurance and marine insurance are said to be contracts of the most good faith in that any material misrepresentation made by the insured to the insurer at the time of entering into the contract will entitle the insurer to avoid liability.

ubiquity Omnipresence; present in several places.

ullage 1. Quantity of the loss of fluid from a cask as a result of leakage or evaporation. 2. The distance from the oil level in a tank to the top of the tank.

ultimate The last in train of progression or sequence, tending toward all that preceded; arrived at as the last result. Final.

ultimate beneficiary A trust beneficiary who is meant to receive the principal of the trust property in a final distribution.

ultimate facts *law* Final facts essential to the maintenance of the cause of action or determination as a successful defense.

ultimate purchaser Final consumer to whom a product is sold for use or consumption.

ultimate targets The final objectives of the Federal Reserve System in its use of monetary policy: real output, employment, price stability, and growth.

ultra vires *Beyond powers.* In relation to corporations, an action is said to be ultra vires when it is beyond the purpose or power of a corporation, when such actions, though not illegal, are outside the scope of general express or implied authority, as defined by its charter or bylaws or the statute under which it is incorporated.

umpire *insurance* One having the authority to render the final decision where two or more arbitrators are unable to agree.

unaccrued Describes income received before it is due (e.g., a rental payment made before it is due). To the payor, this is a prepaid expense.

unamortized bond discount The difference between the par value (face value) of a bond and the proceeds received from the sale of the bond issue, less whatever amount has been amortized, i.e., written off to expense as recorded in the periodic profit and loss statement.

unamortized premiums on investments The unexpensed portion of the amount by which the sale price of a security exceeded its par, or face value, if the issue is a bond or preferred stock, or the market value if it is a common stock.

unassociated variance *statistics* The sum of the squares of that part of the deviation of a variable from its arithmetic mean represented by the distance from a line of least squares to the actual values of the variable divided by the number of items.

unassociated variation *statistics* The unassociated variance times the number of items.

unauthorized insurer *See* nonadmitted insurer.

unauthorized investment An investment made in favor of a trust that the trust instrument does not authorize.

unavoidable accident *law; insurance* Accident that results without any negligence on the part of either plaintiff or defendant; one that occurs when all persons concerned are exercising ordinary care and which could not have been prevented by any means suggested by common prudence.

unbalanced bid Bid based on a nominal price for some work and an enhanced price for other work; where such a method results in a material enhancement of the gross price, it is open to criticism and review.

unbundled premium *insurance* Component of universal life in which the insurance contract is broken down into three components: interest, administrative costs, and pure death protection. Thus the policyholder knows exactly where premium dollars are going. The effect of the interest rate on the policy's cash value also can be determined. (Report is made annually to policyholders.)

uncalled capital The capital of a company which has been authorized but which is not yet subscribed.

uncollected premium *insurance* For the purpose of income taxation of life insurance companies, premium which falls due on or before the thirty-first day of December in a given year but which has not been paid by year's end, due to the life insurer's policy of allowing a grace period for payment, and which the insurance company has no contractual or other right to collect prior to the year end.

unconditional and sole ownership *insurance* Phrase used in fire insurance policies meaning that the ownership of the property insured is in those on whom the loss insured would certainly fall, not as a matter of mere contract obligation, but as a result of real, bona fide rights in insured property.

unconfirmed letter of credit A letter of credit for which credit has been established but on which the advising bank does not guarantee payment.

uncontrollable costs Expenditures which cannot be controlled by one firm because it is a subsidiary of another company and therefore must submit to plans laid down by the parent company. This often incurs costs which the subsidiary company would like to avoid but cannot. Also, there are times when governmental decisions result in additional costs to a firm which it had not planned to make.

uncovered option Short stock option position for which the writer (seller) does not hold a hedged position in the underlying security. Also called naked option.

underapplied overhead A situation in which there is a debit balance in the overhead cost account, indicating that actual overhead incurred was greater than overhead applied.

underbanked A situation in which the underwriter of a new issue of security is having difficulty getting participation from other underwriters.

undercapitalized A business lacking in capital for the scope of the business it is trying to carry on.

underconsumption Condition in which consumers do not purchase all production in an economy in a given period of time. This may be a result of saving too much income, inequity of distribution of income or overproduction.

underconsumption theory Theory of business cycles which holds that recessions result from consumer expenditures lagging behind output because too large a proportion of society's income is not spent on consumption. According to the theory, society distributes income too inequitably to enable people to purchase all the goods produced. (*See* underconsumption)

underdetermined system *econometrics* A system of equations (even though consistent and independent) such that the number of variables is greater than the number of equations and hence in the final equation (after elimination of all the other variables possible), more than one variable is left. There can be, therefore, an infinite number of solutions.

underemployed Describes workers unable to obtain full-time employment or who are working at jobs for which they are overqualified. A condition most prevalent during a recession; it exists sometimes due to monumental changes in an economy.

underground economy *See* black market.

underinsurance Insurance held for less than the value of the property or the amount of the risk.

underlying bonds A bond issue, when a company has more than one issue outstanding, which has the first priority as to income.

underpricing *securities* A policy which is common in the public offering of a new security. As an incentive to the prospective buyer, the underwriter (or issuer) of new securities, either as to an issue already publicly held or an issue of a company being offered to the public for the first time, deliberately seeks to offer the issue at a discount of up to 10% below the underwriter's estimate of the probable price at the time of issuance.

under protest A condition in which the payor of a note holds the right to contest at a later date.

undertaker's receipt A document which allows a bank to pay the funeral bill of a decedent directly from that person's account.

undervalued Depressed in price, and that for which a higher current market value and price/earnings ratio would be justified.

underwrite 1. To assume a risk by way of insurance; to insure life or property. 2. To agree to purchase the unsold shares of a certain number of securities to be offered for sale to the public. 3. To guarantee the sale of an new issue of securities. 4. To classify and rate each loss exposure to maintain a semblance of equity toward policyholders. The success of a cooperative plan like insurance requires an equitable distribution of cost among participants.

underwriter 1. An insurer, especially one who joins with other insurers in entering into a policy of insurance. Particularly used in relation to marine insurance policies which generally are subscribed to by more than one insurer. 2. *real estate* In mortgage lending, one who approves or denies the loan. Normally, there are one or more specialists in a financial institution to deal with such matters.

underwriting associations Associations formed to provide underwriting facilities for a particular industry or for a special class of property.

underwriting syndicate Group of investment banks that bands together for a brief time to guarantee a specified price to a company for newly issued securities.

undifferentiated marketing Practice of firms that produce only one product and market it to all customers with a single marketing mix.

undigested securities Newly issued securities which remain unsold because of insufficient public demand.

undistributed corporate profits *economics* Corporate profits which are not paid out in dividends and which are usually kept in a retained earnings account.

undistributed net income (UNI) That amount by which the amount of distributable income for a year exceeds any distributions which are required to be made.

undistributed profit Profits retained by a business and not paid out as dividends to stockholders.

undistributed profits tax A tax designed by the Internal Revenue Service to discourage the holding by a firm of profits in excess of that needed to continue the business as a growing concern.

undivided interest Ownership right to the use and possession of property that is shared among co-owners, with no one co-owner having exclusive rights to any portion of the property.

undivided profits A part of the capital structure of a bank; profits earned which have not been paid out in dividends or transferred to the bank's surplus account.

undue influence *law* Such influence by one party on another that the latter, acting under the influence, may be said not to be exercising free and independent will.

unearned charges Describes obligations incurred but not covered by earnings

349

(e.g., bond interest incurred when the firm is losing money).

unearned discount *accounting* Interest in the form of a discount, already collected but not yet earned.

unearned income 1. In accounting, income received in advance of the accounting period to which it is allocable. 2. In some forms of income taxation, a preferential treatment is given to earned income defined as income from services performed, and all other income is considered unearned for this purpose.

unearned increment Increase in the value of real estate unrelated to effort on the part of the owner; often due to an increase in population which pushes property price up.

unearned premium *insurance* That part of a premium which is allocable to the part of the policy period which has not yet expired.

unemployment *economics* That percentage of the labor force not employed at any given time.

unemployment compensation Payments made to workers while they are unemployed. Certain criteria must be met: (a) The worker cannot be unemployed voluntarily. (b) The worker must have been employed in a firm covered by insurance. (c) The worker must be willing and able to accept work offered. (d) A waiting period must have elapsed before payments can begin. Unemployment compensation laws differ from one state to another.

unemployment insurance Premiums collected by state and federal governments from business firms out of which unemployment compensation is paid.

unencumbered property Real estate with free and clear title.

unenforcable *law* Describes that which cannot be enforced in a court. A contract is said to be unenforcable when it cannot form the basis of an action, although in other respects it may be a valid contract; e.g., an agreement for the sale of land which is required to be in writing by the statutes of fraud; where it is not in writing, it is unenforcable.

unequivocal Not ambiguous, clear.

unfair competition Attempt to divert customers from another seller by representing that what one sells is the same as, or actually comes from, the same producer.

unfair labor practice A practice that restrains or coerces employees in the exercise of their rights guaranteed by the National Labor Relations Act. Section 7 of that act declares it the policy of the United States to protect the exercise by workers of full freedom of association, self organization, and designation of representatives of their own choosing for the purpose of regulating the terms and conditions of their employment and other material and/or protection. The interference with these rights whether by an employer or by a union can constitute an unfair labor practice. (A most common accusation in labor disputes.)

unfair method of competition Phrase used in Federal Trade Commission Act that has broader meaning than the common law term "unfair competition." Its scope cannot be precisely defined and what constitutes unfair methods must be determined in particular competitive conditions of what is found to be a specific and substantial public interest.

unfit Unsuitable, incompetent, or not adapted for a particular use or service.

unfunded agreement *employee benefits* Plan under which there has been no constructive receipt of compensation or economic benefits. A properly planned deferred compensation agreement postpones until a future date payment for current rendered services, with the effect of postponing taxation of the deferred compensation until it is received. Under a typical deferred compensation agreement, an employer promises to pay an employee fixed or variable amounts for life or for a guaranteed number of years.

unfunded insurance trust A personal trust which will ultimately be funded by the proceeds of an insurance policy, upon the death of the donor. The donor, not the trustee, is responsible for the premium payments of the policy.

unified credit Federal estate tax credit that may be applied against the gift tax, the estate tax, and, under specified conditions, the generation-skipping transfer tax. The amount of the unified credit was substantially raised by the Economic Tax

Recovery Act, and under that law it will increase in steps from 1982 to 1987, and thereafter, when it will reach a maximum of $192,800. (Please note that the unified credit is actually worth $600,000 in estate tax exemption dollars, thereby leaving estates tax free which do not exceed that amount.) The unified estate and gift tax credit is subtracted from the taxable estate to arrive at the actual federal estate otherwise payable.

unified gift and estate tax system A system established by the Tax Reform Act of 1976 by which estate taxes and gift taxes are combined in an amount called the unified credit, which credit has an exemption equivalent deductible from the tentative gross estate to arrive at the true taxable estate. (*See* unified credit)

unified tax system System under the Tax Reform Act of 1976 which replaced the separate gift and estate tax rate schedules with a single unified rate schedule applicable to gifts made after 1976 and to estates of descendants dying after 1976.

Uniform Commercial Code (UCC)
Group of laws aimed at standardizing the state laws that are applicable to commercial transactions.

Uniform Consumer Credit Code
Laws passed at the state level which attempt to standardize laws in all the states with regard to consumer credit.

uniform contract   *commodity trading* Contract meeting requirement that for a particular commodity the contracts must be identical. Besides specifying delivery month, contracts must specify grade and type of commodity (e.g., a particular type of wheat) and the units of the commodity (e.g., five thousand bushels).

Uniform Gifts to Minors Act (UGMA)
Law adopted by most United States jurisdictions that sets up rules for the distribution and administration of assets in the name of a child. The act provides for a custodian of the assets, often the parents, but sometimes an independent trustee. Securities are frequently transferred to a UGMA account from a parent's account, which is taxed at high rates compared with the low bracket of a child. When the child reaches the age of majority, the assets in the account can be disposed of as the child pleases, unless specific prohibitions

have been agreed upon. Many states have amended their acts to expand the type of property to include real property, personal property, and intangibles, and a few states permit transfers to custodians from other sources, such as trusts and estates, as well as lifetime gifts. (*See* Appendix G)

uniform laws   *insurance* Laws approved by the National Conference of Commissioners on Uniform State Laws and adopted by one or more jurisdictions in the United States and its possessions. Their aim is to make laws consistent from state to state.

unilateral   Binding or obligatory on one party only, as certain contracts; one-sided, having relation to only one of two or more persons or things. (Cf. bilateral contract)

unilateral contract   Contractual agreement in which it is agreed to exchange an act for a promise. (Cf. bilateral contract)

unilateral mistake   Error on the part of only one party to a contract, made under a mistaken belief as to one of the essential terms of the contract (e.g., the price, quantity, or quality of the subject matter or the other party).

unimodal   *statistics* A frequency distribution with a single mode.

unimproved land   Land not cleared and with no improvements (e.g., curbs or gutters).

unincorporated association   *tax law* An organization, without a charter, formed by a group of people for the purpose of meeting common needs, such as one might find in a real estate residential development. (Cf. corporation)

uninsured motorists insurance Insurance required in several states on all auto policies covering the policyholder and family members if hit by a hit-and-run driver, an uninsured motorist, a motorist who has insurance below the limits required by financial responsibility laws, or a driver insured by a financially irresponsible insurer.

union   An association, as of persons, parties, states, or nations, combined for some mutual interest or purpose. (*See* trade union)

union certification   A decision by the National Labor Relations Board (or a similar state agency) that a specific union has

351

qualified under the law as a representative of employees in a given firm.

union label   An imprint inside or on a product which states that it was produced by a particular trade union.

union shop   A firm in which all workers, excluding supervisory and management personnel, must belong to the union in order to be employed. Also called closed shop.

unique-product production   One of the three major methods of production propounded by Peter Drucker, identified by the various independent stages of production which go into the final product. The other two methods of production are mass production and process production.

unit allocated system   *employee benefits* Profit-sharing system under which deposits are allocated according to something other than pure compensation ratios such as years of service. (E.g., the plan may credit participants with a nonmonetary unit for each hundred dollars of compensation and a unit for each year of service with the employer.) Plan contributions (e.g., 15% of payroll) are allocated according to the ratio that each participant's units bear to the units of all participants. Unit allocations introduce the most rudimentary form of recognizing long-standing service.

unit bank   A bank with only one place of business.

unit-benefit formula   *employee benefits* Plans that reward long-standing service in the most direct and visible way by providing retirement income based on a multiple of compensation and years of service or participation.

United Kingdom Central Bank   The Bank of England.

United States Constitution   Document containing the principles by which the United States is governed. The Constitution was written in Philadelphia in 1787 during a summer meeting of the Constitutional Convention, and became the supreme law of the land in 1791 after ratification by the states that year. The first ten amendments, called the Bill of Rights, were added in 1791 and ratified in December 1791.

U.S. treasury bill   (*See* treasury bill)

U.S. treasury bond   (*See* treasury bond)

U.S. treasury note   (*See* treasury note)

unitizing   Combination of as many packages as possible into one load, preferably on a pallet. Unitizing promotes faster product movement, requires less labor in materials handling, and reduces damage and pilfering.

unit of trading   *securities* The normal number of shares of stock, dollar amount of bonds, or units of commodities comprising the minimum unit of trading on an exchange. For stocks, this is usually a round lot (one hundred shares), though on less active stocks units of ten shares are sometimes traded. In bonds, the dollar amount is one thousand dollars or five thousand dollars, face value. Commodity futures units of trade vary according to the commodity.

unit pricing   Pricing of items in terms of some recognized unit of measure (e.g., a pound or quart) or a standard numerical count (e.g., a dozen).

unit purchase plan   *insurance* Group plan combining employer-financed decreasing term insurance and employee-financed paid-up units of whole life insurance.

unit trust   An organization that buys a wide variety of securities and then sells shares in the company called units. The units denote some degree of ownership in the organization. Sometimes small investors like this arrangement since each unit of ownership is diversified because of the diversified investment of the organization. Usually such an organization will buy back units from investors upon request.

unit-value basis   One method of determining a beneficiary's share in a pension plan in which certain credit is given for past service; i.e., service to the company before the pension plan was established.

unity   One.

unity of interest   Situation in which all joint tenants have the same interest in the property jointly held; one of the four essential requirements of joint tenancy. (*See* joint tenancy)

unity of possession   Situation in which all joint tenants are equally in possession of the entire property and not merely in respect of a share; an essential requirement of joint tenancy.

unity of seisin *law* Situation occurring when a person who possesses land subject to an easement, right of entry, or similar right also becomes the possessor of the essential service, thereby extinguishing the easement, right of entry, or other such rights.

unity of title Incident of joint tenancy requiring that all the joint tenants have right of title under the same instrument (unlike tenants in common who may take property by different titles). (*See* tenancy in common)

univariate analysis *statistics* The analysis of values of one variable; e.g., determination of the standard deviation.

universal agent Agent appointed to do all the acts which the principal can do. It is a rare kind of agency since in effect the universal agent becomes the master of all the rights and property of the principal. It is to be distinguished from a general agency where there is a delegation by the principal of power to do all acts connected with a particular trade, business, or employment.

universal legacy Term used in civil law denoting a disposition of all one's property to one or more persons.

universal life Policy combining pure life protection (term) with a cash value fund that accumulates interest tax-free. By 1990 universal life is expected to account for 90% of new business for all non-term sales.

universal life insurance Policy officially classified as flexible premium adjustable life. The premium the policyholder may pay is completely flexible. The cash value is related to the premiums actually paid. The plan of insurance does not specify the progression of cash values. The cash value depends on the premiums actually paid minus the loading charge, the insurance charge, policy loans and unpaid interest thereon, plus new interest.

universal partnership Unusual procedure known to civil law whereby all partners put up all their properties in common towards the partnership.

universe *statistics* The entire body of possible data. Used to distinguish between all the data and a sample taken from all the data.

universitas A corporation aggregate.

unjust enrichment A benefit gained by a person by imposing an improper and unjust loss on another.

unlawful Contrary to law; that which is illegal; that which violates some legal right. No action can be founded upon any transaction that is unlawful.

unlawful assembly *common law* Meeting of three or more persons with a common plan in mind which, if carried out, will result in a riot or some act detrimental to the whole of society or to specific persons.

unlawful detainer *real estate* Illegal retention of possession of real property by a person whose right to such possession has terminated and who refuses to quit the property.

unlimited marital deduction Deduction allowed a surviving spouse of a decedent who dies after December 31, 1981. The estate deducts the full value of all qualifying property passing to the surviving spouse, including community property, without limitation as to amount.

unlimited personal liability Characteristic of sole proprietorships and partnerships giving unlimited liability for the debts of the business. (Contrarily, limited partnerships exist in which one general partner has unlimited liability and limited partners have limited liability.)

unlimited tax general-obligation (G.O.) bond A general-obligation bond of a municipality which has no ceiling on the amount of general revenue it may obtain through taxes to discharge the interest and principal obligations of the issue.

unliquidated Unascertained as to amount; undetermined or not settled or liquidated.

unliquidated damages Damages or compensation which must be ascertained by the court after trial as distinguished from special damages.

unlisted security Security which is not listed on a major exchange, but which is sold in the over-the-counter market.

unmarketable title Title that if accepted by the purchaser would lay him or her open to a fair possibility of aggravating litigation with a possibility of serious loss.

unnatural Contrary to the laws of nature; inconsistent with attitudes, feelings, or actions considered natural or normal. Thus a provision in a will giving a stranger a substantial part of the estate while the members of the immediate family of the testator are omitted is said to be unnatural.

unoccupied *insurance* In a policy of fire insurance, the state of being without animate occupancy. (Cf. vacant, occupancy)

unproductive labor *economics* 1. The expenditure of human energy on the production of something that has no economic value. 2. In a comparative sense, labor wasted through efficiency. 3. Colloquially, work that does not involve a material product.

unrealized income Income earned but for which there is no confirming transaction; a paper gain.

unrealized return Expected return not yet actually taken from the sale of a security, either profit or loss. Until the profits or losses are actually taken, they are considered unrealized profits or losses. (Cf. realized return)

unrecorded deed *real estate* Instrument transferring title from one party (grantor) to another party (grantee) without providing public notice of change in ownership. Recording is essential to protect one's interest in real estate.

unrelated business taxable income Income considered ancillary or extraneous to the operation of a tax-exempt institution or to the creation of secure retirement benefits for employees.

unsatisfied-judgment funds Funds available to accident victims who cannot collect judgments from drivers with insufficient resources, usually because they have no collectible insurance plan.

unsatisfied need *consumer economics* A concept which assumes that the buyer will not make a purchase until he or she perceives a need for the product.

unseasoned securities Securities which have not been on the market long enough to establish a reputation.

unsecured With no security, collateral, or pledge held by the creditor.

unsecured note Loan granted on the basis of a borrower's creditworthiness and signature; a loan not secured by collateral.

unsocial hours Unusual working schedules which may cause the employee to be working during times normally used for social purposes. A British term.

unstable equilibrium *economics* Principle stating that a condition, when once achieved, will continue indefinitely unless one of the variables (economic or noneconomic) is altered, and then the system will not return to the original equilibrium and will not come to rest unless there is further alteration of a variable.

unstated interest Interest included in payments received in excess of the taxpayer's basis on property sold on a deferred basis. The interest is treated as ordinary income; the other portion of the payment will constitute gain on the sale, which qualifies for long-term capital gains treatment. (*See* Appendix G)

unsystematic risk Risk associated with individual events that affect a particular security.

unvalued policy *See* open insurance policy.

upset price Price at which property is offered at an auction or foreclosure sale, such price being the lowest at which the property may be sold. Also known as the reserve price.

upside potential The amount of the upward price movement an analyst or an investor anticipates on a specific stock. This anticipation may be the result of technical analysis, fundamental analysis, or speculation.

upstairs market A securities transaction which takes place within the broker-dealer's firm without using an exchange.

uptick A stock transaction made at a price higher than the previous transaction for that stock. Also called a plus tick.

upward communication *communication* Communication which flows from subordinates to superiors.

urban life Period of time over which a building is expected to provide a competitive return.

urban property Real estate located in an urban area, generally characterized by relatively high-density development and extensive availability of city water and sewer services.

urban renewal Process of redeveloping deteriorated sections of a city, often through demolition and new construction. Although urban renewal may be privately funded, it is most often associated with government renewal programs.

usage 1. Customary or habitual practice that is lawful, reasonable, and either known to the involved parties or so well established that it is presumed that the parties have acted in accordance with it; evidence of an existing standard of practice. 2. Practice of customs that have endured for a long time; must be well known, certain, and, above all things, reasonable and not contrary to the intention of any legislative enactment.

use 1. To put into practice; employ habitually. To occupy and enjoy the fruits of, as in using lands and tenements. 2. Right of one person (the beneficiary) to the enjoyment of the rents and profits of lands and buildings, the legal title to and the possession of which are vested in another in trust for the beneficiary.

use and occupation *real estate* Action maintained by a landlord in the absence of a lease or other agreement against a person who is in occupation of the landlord's land for liability to pay for damages. An agreement to pay for such use is implied by law.

use asset Asset which one uses in everyday life (e.g., a house, car, personal property, etc.); shown on a statement of financial position with other assets.

useful life Length of the useful period of a depreciable asset as estimated with reasonable accuracy based upon the evidence of past experience with other properties. Useful life provides the basis for allowable depreciation deductions on properties acquired prior to 1981.

use of funds Transactions of a business firm which cause an outflow of funds (for purposes other than current asset acquisitions or the payment of current liabilities) and decreasing working capital.

use tax Tax levied on the use, storage, or consumption of tangible personal property within the boundaries of taxing jurisdiction irrespective of whether the property is purchased within those boundaries.

usufruct The right to the fruits of things belonging to others without destroying or wasting the property over which such right extends, and without changing what is substantive in the property.

usufructuary rights Interest that provides for the use of property that belongs to another.

usura est commodum certum quod propter usum rei mutuatae recipitur *Usury is a certain benefit received for the use a thing lent.*

usura manifesta *Manifest interest.* Interest that is fully disclosed.

usurpation Unlawful use of authority or property of another.

usury Interest beyond that allowed by law charged to a person who borrows money. In most states, usury limits vary according to the type of lender and type of loan. Federal laws have passed to preempt certain usury limits under certain conditions. Originally the term meant interest charged on any loan.

usus fructus Usufruct.

utility *consumer economics* The ability of an economic good or service to satisfy human wants or needs.

utility easement Use of another's property for the purpose of laying gas, electric, water, and sewer lines.

utility, place *See* place utility.

utility, possession *See* possession utility.

utility, time *See* time utility.

utmost good faith *insurance* Greatest degree of good faith needed in insurance contracts. This faith must be present in the negotiations before the insurance contract is issued and must be observed until the objectives of the policy have been attained.

utopian Ideal; illusory in nature and impractical in government and business.

utopian socialism Philosophy advanced by a group of English and French writers in the early nineteenth century which advocated the creation of model communities, largely self-contained, in which the instruments of production were collectively owned and government was primarily on a voluntary and wholly democratic basis. The leading propagators were Robert Owen (1771– 1858) in England and Charles Fourier (1772–1837) in France. (*See* utopian)

utter *law* To pass or attempt to pass counterfeit money and/or forged documents as genuine (i.e., to pretend something is good or true when it is not).

V

vacancy ratio The percentage of housing units that are fit for use but unoccupied.

vacant As occurring in a fire insurance policy, the absence of inanimate objects. (Cf. unoccupied)

vacate 1. To set aside; to annul; to declare void; to rescind or cancel, as a judgment. 2. To make vacant; to move out; to surrender possession of by removal.

vacation club account Funds deposited periodically in a bank in an interest-paying savings account for special events, such as vacations. (Cf. Christmas club)

vacua possessio *Vacant possession.* In the absence of a stipulation to the contrary in the contract, a vendor of land has to give vacant possession of the lands to the purchaser upon closing the transaction of sale.

vadium 1. Pledge, pawn, or security. 2. Security by the pledge of property.

vagrant Idle wanderer; a vagabond; a person with no fixed place of residence (i.e., bum or hobo).

vagueness doctrine *law* Doctrine stating that a law which does not precisely and clearly indicate what is forbidden violates the due process clause of the Constitution.

valid 1. Authorized by law; legally sufficient or efficacious; executed with proper formality; sustainable and effective in law. 2. Legally binding; sound, as to form and substance; that which will be upheld by the courts.

validate To make valid; to confirm.

validation *management* An assessment of a specific training program, judging its validity internally, by its success in teaching what it set out to teach, or externally, by whether or not the training was needed at all under existing circumstances.

validation proceedings Proceedings required in some states wherein the courts pass on proposed bond issues.

valid date *banking* Date indicating the time after which a bank card is not valid or the date on which the card will be valid. Usually only the month and year indicated.

validity 1. Being sound and well grounded in law; the quality of being valid. 2. *statistics* The degree to which a test measures the objective which it is intended to measure.

valorization scheme Either direct government or cartel intervention in the world markets to attempt to maintain the price of a product. This has been done many times in the past, particularly by nations whose exports consist of one major product (e.g., Brazil's coffee and mid-eastern oil).

valuable 1. Of financial or market value. 2. Capable of being evaluated.

valuable consideration 1. Type of promised payment upon which a promisee can enforce a claim against an unwilling promisor. Includes money, extension of time, and other equivalents for the grant. 2. Some right, interest, profit, or benefit accruing to the one party or some forbearance, detriment, loss, or responsibility given, suffered, or undertaken by the other party to a contract. (*See* consideration)

valuation Estimated worth or price.

value *See* value in use, value in exchange.

value added *economics* The difference between the purchase price of raw materials or finished parts and the sale price of the product. On a national basis, when depreciation and indirect business taxes are deducted from the value added, the national income is the result.

value added tax (VAT) A method of taxation used widely in western Europe in which each stage of the production is taxed according to the value added, and all such tax in the production process is added to the price of the finished product.

value analysis A technique used to assess the design, production and marketing of a specific product to determine if the most efficient methods are being used.

value date 1. The date on which a sum of money is transferred to a beneficiary from some fund allocated to him or her. 2. The date funds will be available to a receiving bank.

valued forms *insurance* Health policy providing a flat amount per day for a maximum number of days while the insured is in the hospital. These specific benefits are paid regardless of the incurred expenses. (E.g., an American Association of Retired Persons hospitalization policy which would pay fifty dollars per day while hospitalized, for a specified number of days.) The payment is usually to the insured, rather than to the hospital.

valued policy Policy of insurance in which the sum payable in the event of a loss is fixed and is expressed in the policy itself.

value in exchange The power of purchasing other goods or services which the possession of the object conveys.

value in use Utility of an object in direct or indirect relation to the needs or desires of human beings.

Value Line *investments* Private company which issues a periodic advisory service paper ranking hundreds of stocks for timeliness and safety. The company uses a computerized model for judging the value of the stocks. Each stock is assigned a risk rating. (*See* Value Line index)

Value Line index Index of over seventeen hundred stocks computed by Value Line. These include not only stocks listed on the New York Stock Exchange but also securities traded on AMEX and over-the-counter stocks. (*See* Value Line)

value of marginal product *See* marginal revenue product.

value of money The purchasing power of a specific monetary unit; i.e., the amount of goods and services it will buy at any given point in time.

value of service principle Setting of railroad or utility rates by establishing the rate at what is thought to be the upper limit of what the great bulk of buyers is willing to pay (i.e., what the traffic will bear).

value received Something taken in exchange for valuable consideration.

value satisfaction *marketing* A consumer's satisfaction with or reasons for buying a specific product.

vandal Ruthless plunderer; one who willfully destroys or disfigures anything, particularly things of value. The destruction is usually wanton and without cause.

vandalism Unauthorized, willful, or ruthless damaging, defacing, or disfiguring of property belonging to another, wantonly done.

vandalism or malicious mischief endorsement *insurance* Endorsement which provides coverage against direct loss caused by the willful and malicious damage to or destruction of the covered property. Specifically excluded is damage to glass (other than glass building blocks) constituting part of a building or an outdoor sign. Coverage is suspended if the property had been vacant or unoccupied beyond a period of thirty consecutive days immediately preceding the loss.

variability, measures of *See* measures of variability.

variable A measure whose value changes.

variable annuity Annuity upon which the benefits may vary according to the insurer's earnings on the supporting investment portfolio.

variable cost Expense that varies with sales over the observation period. (*See* fixed cost)

variable dollar investment Investment which promises no specific rate of return, if any (e.g., common stocks and real estate).

variable factor programming (VFP) A method involving the use of the study of the performance of clerical workers to determine productivity.

variable interest rate Amount of compensation to a lender that is allowed to vary over the maturity of a loan. The amount of variation is generally governed by an appropriate index.

variable life *insurance* Insurance policy basically designed to combine the traditional protection and savings functions of life insurance with the growth potential of equities, in particular, common stocks.

variable markup pricing *See* cost-plus pricing.

variable proportions, law of *See* law of diminishing marginal utility.

variable rate agreement Agreement which calls for an interest rate that may fluctuate over the life of the loan. The rate is often tied to an index that reflects changes in market rates of interest. A fluctuation in the rate causes changes in either the payments or the length of the loan term. Limits are often placed on the degree to which the interest rate or the payments can vary. (Cf. fixed rate agreement)

variable rate mortgage (VRM) *See* adjustable rate mortgage.

variance 1. *accounting* The difference between the standard cost and the actual cost in the areas of direct material, direct labor, and direct overhead. A positive variation (when the actual cost is below the standard cost) would yield higher profits unless offset by negative variations in other areas of the business. 2. *finance* The difference between corresponding items on a comparative balance sheet and a profit and loss statement. 3. *finance* The difference between budgeted figures and actual experience in any financial category. 4. *statistics* The measure of the dispersion of a distribution. Essentially, the sum of the squares of the deviation from the mean. 5. *law* Discrepancy between allegations in the pleading and evidence adduced at the trial in support of the same. 6. Use of property which is otherwise expressly prohibited by zoning law. 7. Permission granted by a zoning authority to a property owner to allow for a specified violation of the zoning requirements.

variance analysis *statistics* The separation of total variance (the sum of the squares of deviations of observed data from their arithmetic mean divided by the number of items) into components associated with the several sources of such variance on the basis of classification of the observations.

variation *statistics* The variance times the number of items. (Cf. variance)

variety Number of product lines carried by a retailer.

vastum *A waste;* i.e., a tract of land open to all the tenants for pasturage.

Veblenian school School of institutional economics, established by Thorstein Veblen (1857–1929), emphasizing the sociological overtones of economics. Veblen coined the term "conspicuous consumption" to describe the economic activity of the leisure class of his day.

velocity Rate at which money balances turn over in a period for expenditures on goods and services (often measured as the ratio of GNP to the money stock). A larger velocity means that a given quantity of money is associated with a greater dollar volume of transactions.

velocity of money circulation Average rate at which money changes hands.

vendee Person to whom something is sold.

vendor 1. One who sells anything. 2. One who sells land as opposed to goods. (Cf. seller)

vendor rating Method of ranking suppliers' performance, reliability in meeting delivery dates, and standards of quality.

vendor's lien Implied lien the law allows a vendor for the purchase price of property for which the vendee has not paid. At common law, the vendor of land has a lien over the land which is the subject matter of the sale, for any part of the purchase money that remains unpaid on the closing of the transaction of sale. Such a lien has priority over the claim of an execution creditor of the purchaser.

venture capital Money raised for high risk investments, capital which people choose to risk, usually on a new and risky venture.

venture capitalist Individual or firm providing financing for new business ventures for a share in the returns if the business succeeds.

venture capital limited partnership An investment vehicle, usually organized by a brokerage firm or some entrepreneurial company, to raise capital for start-up ventures or companies in the early stages of product development and production. Often the capital is exchanged for stock in the company to whom it is supplied.

venture team A planning and execution group formed for developing new-product areas by combining the management resources of technological innovations, capital, management, and marketing expertise. Venture teams, composed of specialists from different areas of the organization, are physically separated from the permanent organization and linked directly with top management.

venue *law* Geographic area in whose court a case must be tried. Concept derived from the common-law rule that the case must be tried where the events occurred.

verification *law* 1. Confirmation of the correctness, truth, or authenticity of a pleading by means of an affidavit. 2. Examination of anything for the purpose of ascertaining the truth. 3. Sworn statements before a duly qualified officer that the contents of an instrument are correct. 4. Testing of alternative hypotheses or conclusions by means of actual observation or experimentation, i.e., by reference to the facts.

vertical combination A combination of companies that unites under one ownership a number of plants which are engaged in various stages of the production and marketing of a product.

vertical integration Combining under one management the various stages of a production process, often beginning with the raw resources used in the industry. (Cf. horizontal integration)

vertical marketing system (VMS) Professionally managed and centrally programmed network set up to achieve operating economies and maximum impact in the marketing channels.

vertical merger Joining of two firms in which the output of one firm is an input of the other firm. (*See* vertical integration)

vessel deadweight tonnage *economics* 1. Deadweight. 2. Tons of water a ship displaces when empty, and when loaded to the load line.

vest To have ownership of, as property, upon a person; to invest a person with the full title to property.

vested Entitled to a right, estate, interest, etc., either in interest or in possession. The present right to the future possession of property is said to be vested in interest, while the present right to the immediate possession of property is said to be vested in possession.

vested interest Fixed and present right to the present or future enjoyment of property.

vested remainder *law* An interest in property to commence in enjoyment at some time in the future but with the person who is to enjoy it determined at present and no condition attached to the interest.

vested right Immediate fixed right to present or future enjoyment, held by a tenure that is subject to no condition or contingency.

vestibule training The training of an employee by an employer in a company school prior to actual experience in the shop or plant.

vesting order Order passed by a court of competent jurisdiction vesting title to lands in a person, instead of giving a conveyance.

vesture The corn, grass, underwood, sweepage, and the like of land but not including house, timber, trees, mines, and other real things which fall part of an inheritance.

Veterans Administration (VA) Agency of the federal government that provides services for eligible veterans. Generally, a veteran who has served (beyond basic training) more than 120 days active duty in the armed forces is eligible for a home loan with no down payment, plus other benefits.

Veterans Administration (VA) loan Home loan guaranteed by the United States Veterans Administration under the Servicemen's Readjustment Act of 1944 and later. The VA guarantees restitution of a certain percentage to the lender in the event of default.

veto Right of forbidding or denying without assigning any reason.

vexatious action *law* 1. Action that is not bona fide but is intended to harass the other person(s) or is brought without reasonable grounds. 2. New action brought for a cause which might have been included in an earlier action; considered an abuse of the process of the court.

V formation A technical chart pattern that forms the shape of a V. The pattern indicates that the security being charted has bottomed out and that it is now in a bullish or rising trend.

via By way of.

via publica A public way or road.

via servitus A right of way or easement over another's land.

vicarious liability Liability of one person for the wrongs of another (e.g., the liability of the employer for a tort committed by an employee in the course and within the scope of his or her employment).

vice Defect; a fault.

vice president *banking* Normally, the head of a department with tenure being either long or short with the institution. The title is not simply a title of distinction, but one that carries with it certain authority, usually within one department.

vicinity Quality or state of being near or not remote; neighborhood.

vi et armis *With force and arms.* Phrase used in common law action for damages for trespass to the person or property of the plaintiff, alleging that the defendant caused the damage with direct force or violence.

vintner One who sells wine.

violate To breach a duty opposed by law or otherwise. To breach an obligation or a contract.

visa Authentication of a passport by a foreign authority signifying the permission granted by such authority to the passport holder to enter and travel in and through a foreign country.

visceral drives Instinctive or innate drives of a human being, including hunger, thirst, the need for air, temperature regulation, sexual satisfaction, etc.

visible supply The total amount of municipal bond sales scheduled for the next thirty days.

vital statistics Those figures, usually collected and kept by some agency of government, which denote births, deaths, divorce, etc., usually for the entire nation, but often broken down to regions and states.

vocational training Training specifically designed to enable one to do a particular kind of work.

voice-recognition system A complex system which allows a computer to react to verbal instructions.

void Null, ineffectual; having no legal force or efficacy. A transaction is void when it does not confer rights, nor can it be the basis of any action.

voidable Capable of being made void, although not necessarily void in itself. A transaction or agreement is said to be voidable when one of the parties to it is entitled to rescind it, and until such rescission it continues to have full legal validity.

void contract *law* An effort by parties to enter into an agreement which is contrary to law or to public policy as interpreted by the courts. Since no contract ever really exists, the court merely calls the agreement a void contract.

volatility *investments* Measure of the rise and fall, and frequency of such, in stocks, bonds, and commodities. (*See* B-risk)

Volcker, Paul Chairman of the Federal Reserve Board of Governors, appointed in 1979 and replaced in 1987 by Alan Greenspan. First a proponent of a tight money supply to combat inflation, he allowed the money supply to increase to over $700 billion in 1986.

volume The number of shares traded in a stock market, in a group of stocks, or in an individual issue.

volume checking An auditing method in which every aspect of a company's transactions are examined as opposed to only the accounting methods, or a partial audit of departments of the firm.

voluntary 1. Without compulsion; in the absence of fear, prejudice, or hope of advantage; inadequacy of consideration. 2. Done knowingly, willfully.

voluntary accumulation plan *investing* A method by which an investor can make periodic deposits in some mutual funds, after the initial deposit has been made. There is usually a minimum deposit involved, and the additional deposits can be made monthly, quarterly, etc.

voluntary assumption of risk A situation in which an employee says in advance of undertaking a task that the employer will not be responsible in the event of an accident. Legally, this would be highly questionable as a means of absolving the employer from responsibility.

voluntary bankruptcy *law* Proceedings begun by the debtor who wishes to wind up his or her affairs.

voluntary conveyance *law* A transfer of property without consideration.

voluntary employees' beneficiary association (VEBA) A tax-exempt entity, formed by a tax-exempt, 501 (c) (9) organization, that puts together funds for members of the formed association. These association funds may be used, according to association rules, for members, dependents, or designated beneficiaries, and may include life, illness, accident, or other benefits.

voluntary trust A trust account established voluntarily by a donor which is not conditioned on his or her death.

voluntas donaris in charta doni sui manifeste express observetur *The will of the donor as expressed in his deed gift is to be observed.*

voluntas facit quod in testamento scriptum valeat *The intention of the testator gives effect to the words of the will.*

voluntas testatoris est ambulatoria usque ad extremum vita exitum *The will of a testator is ambulatory until the last moment of life;* i.e., a will may bechanged at any time by the testator during his or her life.

volunteer Person who gives services without express or implied promise of remuneration.

vostro account *banking Your account with us.* An account belonging to the bank which is held in deposit by a bank in a foreign country.

voting security Corporate stock entitling the owner to vote at shareholders' meetings.

voting trust A trust created by agreement of a number of shareholders to deposit stock in the hands of a trustee or trustees. Under such an agreement, the shareholders retain ownership of the stock but delegate their power of voting it to the trustee or trustees.

voucher 1. Receipt for payment of money. An acquittance or release which serves as evidence of the discharge of a debt. 2. Certification of the correctness of accounts. 3. *See* invoice approval form.

voucher to warranty Formerly, when a person holding land was sued for the recovery of that land, the right to require the person who warranted the land to either defend the title or give the person land of equal value.

vulture fund A type of limited partnership that invests in depressed property, usually real estate, expecting to make large profits when prices begin to rise.

W

wages Compensation payable by an employer to employees in consideration of their services. Under equal pay provisions of Fair Labor Standards Act, wages which must be paid at equal rates to both sexes if work performed is equal include all payments made to or on behalf of employee as remuneration for employment.

Wage-Hour Law *See* Fair Labor Standards Act.

wages-fund theory Classical theory of wages, articulated by John Stuart Mill in 1848, that held that producers set aside a portion of their capital funds for the purpose of hiring workers needed for production. The amount of the fund depends on the stock of capital relative to the number of workers. In the long run, however, the accumulation of capital is itself limited or determined by the tendency toward a minimum subsistence rate of profits; hence the only effective way to raise real wages is to reduce the number of workers or size of the population. This theory was a reformulation of the subsistence theory of wages.

Wagner Act *See* National Labor Relations Act.

waiting period *See* elimination period.

waive To intentionally give up or not insist on some right, claim, or privilege that one is otherwise entitled to enforce.

waiver 1. Voluntary relinquishment or abandonment of a right, privilege, claim, or advantage, as in a waiver of immunity. 2. The instrument that evidences such relinquishment.

waiver of premium 1. Provision that after a period of total disability of a stated duration, usually ninety days, premiums will be waived. In some policies the insurer agrees to refund premiums paid during the waiting period. Waiver of premium is usually automatically included in non-cancelable and guaranteed renewable policies. 2. Rider added to an insurance policy for an extra premium which provides that in the event the insured becomes totally disabled before a certain age, typically sixty or sixty-five, premiums on the life insurance policy will be waived (i.e., not required to be paid by the insured) during the continuance of disability after six months. In addition, premiums are normally waived retroactively for this six months.

wanton Reckless, heedless, or malicious disregard of the rights or safety of others or of consequences.

ward 1. Territorial division of most American cities, made for convenience of management and government. 2. A person, usually a minor, who is in the charge or under the protection of a guardian.

wardship Guardianship.

warehouse Building used for the purpose of receiving and keeping goods for storage, particularly wares and merchandise.

warehouse receipt Receipt for goods issued by a warehouseman evidencing that goods are in the warehouseman's custody.

warehousing, loan *See* loan warehousing.

wares Tangible, moveable, personal property having intrinsic value.

warrant 1. Certificate issued by a corporation that represents an option to buy a stated number of shares of stock at a specified price on or before a specified date.

(A few are perpetual.) Warrants have a value of their own and may be traded on the open market. 2. *law* A judicial writ or order authorizing arrest, search, seizure, or any other designated act in aid of the administration of justice. It is the authority under which the person to whom it is directed acts. 3. *real estate law* A covenant in a deed whereby the grantor binds himself or herself and his or her heirs to secure to the grantee the estate conveyed to him or her and pledges, in the event of eviction of the grantee by paramount title, to recompense the grantee with other land of equivalent value. 4. An assurance or undertaking, either express or implied, by the seller of property, that the property is or shall be as it is represented or promised to be. 5. *insurance* Pledge or stipulation on the part of the insured that the facts in relation to the person or thing insured or to the risk are as stated; the validity of the insurance contract depends upon the literal truth of such a pledge.

warranty 1. Promise contained in a contract. 2. Undertaking to indemnify or make good the party assured against some possible default or defect in the contemplation of the parties. 3. Stipulation in an insurance policy that some statement about the subject matter is true. 4. Guarantee to the buyer that the manufacturer will replace the product or refund its purchase price if it proves to be defective during a specified period of time.

wash a dog *banking* To finance a company that is in such poor condition that it would ordinarily have already been shut down.

waste 1. Act or omission causing injury to property by a person in rightful possession (e.g., damage or destruction done or permitted to lands or houses by the tenant or to corporate assets by the corporation's management). 2. The destruction, misuse, alteration, or neglect of premises by one lawfully in possession thereof, to the prejudice of the estate or interest therein of another.

wasting assets Property that is perishable; assets of a wasting character such as leaseholds.

watercourse 1. Stream containing a definite bed, banks, and channel which flows into some other river, stream, lake, or the sea. 2. Channel by means of which a particular watershed is drained, although it may be dry in certain seasons and despite the fact that it may not empty into any other river, stream, lake, or body of water.

watered stock   Stock representing ownership in a company whose assets are overvalued, resulting in the company's assets being worth less than the issued stock.

water's edge   Boundaries to a body of water. In a deed, land granted fixing its boundaries to water's edge will generally act to convey title to and fix the boundaries of land by the center of the thread of the body of water or watercourse if grantor's title extends thereto.

way   Defined passage, path; a right of passage over land. It may be either a public way or a private one.

Wealth of Nations   Shortened title of the first economics book of which there is record, published by Adam Smith in 1776. Smith's general view of government was that it should promote international commerce, care for the defense of the nation, and keep up the post roads. (*See* invisible hand theory)

wear and tear   Deterioration or depreciation in value of anything by the ordinary use of it. The phrase occurs in leases, usually exempting the tenant from any liability for ordinary wear and tear.

Weber's law   *communication*   Proposition that the higher the initial intensity of a stimulus, the greater the amount of change in intensity necessary for a difference to be noticed.

weighted-average cost of capital   Cost of capital when each increment borrowed is measured as to amount and interest paid.

weighted-average expected return   Expected return an investor makes on different investment sums. The expected return on stock for which ten dollars a share was paid and ten shares purchased would be twice as great as that expected on five shares for which ten dollars per share was paid.

Welsh mortgage   Form of mortgage in which the mortgagee is given possession of the lands mortgaged, redeemable at any time by the mortgagor, with no corresponding right in the mortgagee to compel redemption or foreclosure. The mortgagee, while in possession, receives

the rents and profits of the land in satisfaction of interest. The mortgagee is not entitled to anything over and above the rents and profits on account of the mortgagee's interest.

wet-field   Field where the natural gas comes to the surface and holds crude naptha in suspension.

wetlands   Land, such as a marsh or swamp, normally saturated with water.

wharfage   Money paid for landing goods upon or loading them from a wharf.

wheel of retailing   Hypothesis by M. P. McNair that attempts to explain patterns of change in retailing. According to the hypothesis, new types of retailers gain a competitive foothold by offering lower prices to their customers through the reduction or elimination of services. Once they become vulnerable to a new low-price retailer who enters with minimum services, the wheel turns.

whiplash injury   Injury sustained by a person by having his or her head thrown violently forward and back or from side to side, usually as the result of an auto accident when the car is hit from behind by a second car.

whole life insurance   Policy which furnishes protection for the whole of life regardless of how premiums are paid, whether for all of life, a stated number of years such as ten, twenty, or thirty years, or by one lump sum at the inception of the policy. Death benefits and maturity date are fixed; there are fixed level premiums and a fixed progression of cash values. (Most whole life policies are endowment policies, paid up at either age ninety-five or one hundred.) (*See* cash value insurance; cf. straight life insurance)

wholesale   Purchase or sale in bulk or in large quantities, usually for the purpose of reselling in retail.

wholesale health insurance; wholesale life insurance   *See* franchise life insurance.

widow's election   *See* election.

width   Complementary products carried by the retailer within a merchandise line.

will   Legal declaration of a person's intentions as to the disposal of that person's estate after the person's death. This instrument states what people want done with their property and their instructions as to other matters when they die. The will does not take effect until the person's death and may be changed or revoked at any time up until that death. Its validity insofar as its execution is concerned depends entirely upon its compliance at the time of its execution. (*See* codicil)

will contest Attempt to shift property interests from one beneficiary to another. Will contests are the result of supervised court litigation and quite often are hostile in nature, as opposed to family settlement agreements.

will substitute Method used by an individual who wants to transfer his or her estate without being governed by a particular state's laws of intestacy. Also called poor man's will.

winding up Cessation of a corporation's business, the collecting in and realization of all its assets, the payment of all its liabilities, and the distribution of the surplus among the shareholders.

windstorm *insurance* Storm characterized by high winds with little or no precipitation.

without prejudice *law* Describes a judicial determination that in no way harms or cancels the legal rights or privileges of the parties concerned except as expressly stated. If a case is dismissed without prejudice, the plaintiff can bring suit again on the same cause of action. The person or the party on whose behalf the offer is made is not waiving any rights. Overtures of pacification and any other offers or propositions between litigating parties expressly or implicitly made without prejudice are inadmissable in evidence on grounds of public policy.

without recourse Mode of endorsement of a negotiable instrument by which the endorser merely passes it on but accepts no liability to subsequent holders for its payment. The holder is not to look to the debtor personally in the event of nonpayment; the creditor has recourse only to the property. A form of exculpation. (*See* exculpate)

without reserve Phrase used in auctions meaning that the vendor or anyone on the vendor's behalf shall not bid; the property shall be sold to the highest bid-

der, whether the sum bid is equivalent to the real value or not.

with-without principle Principle defining those cash flows which are relevant to an investment decision. It states that if there are two worlds, one with the investment and one without it, all cash flows that differ in these two worlds are relevant and all cash flows that are the same are irrelevant.

witness 1. One whose statements and declarations under oath are received as evidence for some purpose, whether such statements or declarations are made on oral examination, by deposition, or by affidavit. 2. One who subscribes in attestation of a document.

words of limitation *law* Words in a conveyance or a will that specify or have the effect of marking the duration of an estate.

words of purchase *law* Words in a conveyance or a will designating the person who is to take the estate.

work Any form of physical or mental exertion, or both combined, for attainment of some object other than recreation or amusement.

worker's compensation Program of compensation designed for workers who are injured or become ill while working. In some states, the compensation law is not compulsory, but where it is not, the company is denied the use of the common-law defenses. A company may choose to be self-insured (if allowable), or the insurance may be purchased from a carrier. Some states also finance their own programs, and carriers are not allowed to solicit business in that state. Benefit amounts are not always the same, but, for disability, a percentage of the wages is common, subject to a maximum. Loss of a limb, an eye, etc., is also covered. Survivorship benefits, including burial expenses, exist for fatal injuries and provide a partial replacement for the deceased worker's weekly wages.

working capital Excess of current assets over current liabilities. Working capital can be used to pay cash dividends, to purchase property, equipment, or a plant, or to pay a debt. Also called net working capital.

working capital cycle Periodic transformation of cash through current assets and current liabilities and back to cash. (*See* cash flow principle)

work-product *law* Class of materials that are given protection from discovery in civil practice and which have been prepared by an attorney in the anticipation of litigation.

world anxiety coefficient Indication of level of political tension. One of the factors Dr. Horace W. Brock postulated would affect the future price of gold.

worthless Destitute of value; of no value or use.

wraparound Financing device that permits an existing loan to be refinanced and new money to be advanced at an interest rate between the rate charged on the old loan and the current market interest rate. The creditor combines or wraps the remainder of the old loan with the new loan at the intermediate rate.

wraparound mortgage Second mortgage that increases a borrower's indebtedness while leaving the original mortgage contract in force. This is done by a loan arrangement in which an existing loan is retained and an additional loan, larger than the existing loan, is made. The new lender accepts the obligation to make payments on the old loan. The existing loan generally carries an interest rate below the rate charged on the new loan. Sellers are the most common wraparound lenders.

writ 1. Command or precept from a sovereign. 2. Document issued out of a court, commanding the person to whom it is addressed to do or forbear from doing some act.

write-down To diminish in amount on the records generally to reflect a market value loss.

writer 1. A person who sells put and call options contracts and collects premium income. 2. An insurance underwriter.

writing naked A strategy used by an options seller in which the trader does not own the underlying security. This kind of strategy can lead to huge profits or huge losses, depending upon the movement of the market.

writ of summons Judicial writ, issued out of a superior court, commencing a legal proceeding and addressed to the defendants commanding them to appear and answer the case of the plaintiff.

X

X-O chart Chart used in technical analysis to summarize price movements.

X; XD 1. A symbol used in bond tables to indicate bonds trading without interest. 2. *See* XD.

XD A symbol used in newspapers to indicate that stocks are trading ex-dividend, i.e., without dividend.

XR A symbol used in newspapers denoting that the stock is trading ex-rights, i.e., without rights.

XW A symbol used in newspapers to denote that a stock is trading ex-warrants, i.e., without warrants attached.

Y

yard 1. Measure of length consisting of three feet or thirty-six inches or 0.9144 meters. 2. Enclosed space of ground such as a courtyard or a front yard.

year Period of 365 days (or, in a leap year, 366 days). The calendar year commences on the first day of January ending with the thirty-first day of December.

year to year, tenancy from *See* tenancy from year to year.

Yellow Sheet A daily publication, similar to pink sheets, which lists bonds.

yen bond Any bond denominated in Japanese yen.

yield 1. To give way; to give up the contest; to submit; to surrender; to succumb; to cease opposition. 2. A measurement of the rate of earnings from an investment. (*See* current yield, yield to maturity)

yield advantage The extra amount of return an investor will earn by purchasing a convertible security instead of the common stock of the same issuing corporation.

yield curve Graphic expression of the relationship between yield and maturity. This curve is plotted on a graph with the vertical axis showing the percentage of yield and the horizontal axis showing the years to maturity. Normally depicts fixed-income securities of the same quality for a wide range of maturities.

yield to call Yield earned on a bond from the time it is acquired until the time it is called and retired by the firm. Measures the return on a bond investment an investor would receive stated as an average yearly return from purchase date to call date. Similar to yield to maturity.

yield to maturity Internal rate of return on a bond when held to maturity. A measure of the average compounded yearly return on a bond based on purchase price, maturity value, time to maturity, and coupon yield. This calculation takes into consideration all interest to be received from purchase date to maturity, plus or minus any discount or premium paid for the bond and redemption value at maturity.

yo-yo stock A stock that rises and falls quickly and uncertainly, as a yo-yo might go up and down.

Z

zero-based budgeting Method of arriving at the expenditures for a year in which every line item must be justified, without regard to past experience in that area.

zero-bracket amount Deduction generally available to individual taxpayers in arriving at taxable income. The amount of the deduction is $2,300 for single persons and those who qualify for head-of-household status; $3,400 for married persons filing jointly; and $1,700 for married persons filing separate returns. The zero bracket amount is built into the tax table and the tax rate schedules. It is subtracted from total itemized deductions to arrive at the amount of excess itemized deductions. The excess itemized deduction amount appears on Form 1040. (*See* Appendix G)

zero coupon bond Corporate and government bond issued at a deep discount from maturity value paying no interest during the life of the bond; redeemable at full face value. Tax consequences vary according to the type of security, but typi-

cally the holder must declare the unpaid interest as ordinary income for tax purposes, annually.

zero lot line Form of cluster housing development in which individual dwelling units are placed on separately plotted lots but are attached to one another.

zero net outlay *insurance* Unusual form of minimum deposit financing under which the policyholder borrows the after-tax cost of the policy loan interest expense in addition to borrowing the premium. A tax-reduction method sometimes practiced by those in higher income tax brackets and frowned upon by the Internal Revenue Service.

zero population growth Point at which the number of live births equals the current death rate.

zone Area set off by local ordinance for specific use, subject to certain restrictions or conditions.

zone pricing Modification of uniform delivered price system in which the market is divided into different regions and a price is set within each region.

zoning 1. Partition of a municipality into zones by ordinance. 2. Prescription of the purposes to which land and buildings in designated areas may be put and regulation of the structure and design of buildings.

zoning map Map of local jurisdiction indicating current zoning designations.

zoning ordinance Act of city, county, or other authorities specifying the type of use to which property may be put in specific areas.

Appendix A

Abbreviations

ab. abridgment

AAII American Association of Individual Investors

ABA American Bankers Association; American Bar Association

A/C air conditioning

ACE AMEX Commodities Exchange

ACH automated clearinghouse

ACRS accelerated cost recovery system

ADR asset depreciation range

A.E. account executive

AFDC Aid to Families with Dependent Children

AFL-CIO American Federation of Labor and Congress of Industrial Organizations

AICPA American Institute of Certified Public Accountants

AID Agency for International Development

AIM American Institute for Management

AIME average index monthly earnings

AIO attitudes, interests, and opinions

AIREA American Institute of Real Estate Appraisers

ALTA American Land Title Association

AMA American Management Association

AMBAC American Municipal Bond Assurance Corporation

Amex American Stock Exchange

AMI alternative mortgage instrument

AML adjustable mortgage loan

APA American Planning Association

APB Accounting Principles Board

app. appreciation

APR annual percentage rate

arb arbitrageur

AREUEA American Real Estate and Urban Economics Association

ARM adjustable rate mortgage

ARPS adjustable rate preferred stock

ASA American Society of Appraisers

ASAP as soon as possible

ASE American Stock Exchange

ASO administrative services only; associated service organization

ASREC American Society of Real Estate Counselors

ATM automated teller machine

ATS automatic transfer service

BAN bond anticipation note
BD bank draft; bills discontinued
B/D broker-dealer
BE bill of exchange
B/F brought forward
BIC Bank Investment Contract
BIS Bank for International Settlement
B/L bill of lading
BLS Bureau of Labor Statistics
BO buyer's option
BOMA Building Owners and Managers Association
BOP balance of payments
BOT balance of trade; board of trade
BPW Business and Professional Women's Foundation
BS balance sheet; Bureau of Standards

CAB Civil Aeronautics Board
CAC Consumer Advisory Council
CACM Central American Common Market
CAD cash against documents
CAI Community Associations Institute
C. & F. cost and freight
CATS Certificate of Accrual on Treasury Securities
CATV community antenna television
CBA cost benefit analysis
CBD central business district
CBOE Chicago Board Options Exchange
CBT Chicago Board of Trade
CC chamber of commerce
CCH commerce clearinghouse
CCIM Certified Commercial-Investment Member
CD certificate of deposit
CEA Council of Economic Advisors
CEO chief executive officer
CFC consolidated freight classification
C.F.I. cost, freight, and insurance
CFO chief financial officer
C.F.P. Certified Financial Planner
CFTC Commodities Futures Trading Commission
CH clearinghouse
CHIPS Clearinghouse Interbank Payments Systems
c.i.f. cost, insurance, and freight
cld. called

CLU Certified Life Underwriter; Chartered Life Underwriter
CMB Certified Mortgage Banker
CME Chicago Mercantile Exchange
CMV current market value
C/O certificate of origin
Co. company
COB close of business
COBOL Common Business Oriented Language
c.o.d. cash on delivery
CODA cash or deferred arrangement
COLA cost-of-living adjustment
COMEX Commodity Exchange (New York)
COMSAT Communication Satellite Corporation
CPA Certified Public Accountant
CPI consumer price index
CPM Certified Property Manager
CR current rate
CRA Community Reinvestment Act
CRB certified real estate brokerage manager; certified residential broker
CRE counselor of real estate; coefficient of relative effectiveness
CRS certified residential specialist
CSE Cincinnati Stock Exchange
CSVLI cash surrender value of life insurance
CUNA Credit Union National Association
CUSIP Committee on Uniform Securities Identification Procedures
C.W.O. cash with order

DA deposit account
D & B Dun and Bradstreet
DB&C dwelling, building, and contents
DCFM discounted cash flow method
DCR debt coverage ratio
DDB double declining balance
depr. depreciation
DIDC Depository Institutions Deregulatory Committee
DJIA Dow-Jones Industrial Average
DJTA Dow-Jones Transportation Average
DJUA Dow-Jones Utility Average
DNR do not reduce
DPI disposable personal income

EBIT earnings before interest and taxes
ECM European Common Market

ECOA Equal Credit Opportunity Act
EDD estimated delivery date
EEC European Economic Community
EEOC Equal Employment Opportunity Commission
EFT electronic fund transfer
EFTA European Free Trade Association
EIPSL entry age normal with frozen initial past service liability
EIS environmental impact statement
EPA Environmental Protection Agency
EPR earnings price ratio
EPS earnings per share
ERISA Employee Retirement Income Security Act
ERP European Recovery Program
ERTA Economic Recovery Tax Act
ESOP employee stock ownership plan
ETA estimated time of arrival
ETD estimated time of departure
Eximbank Export-Import Bank

FA free alongside
FAA Federal Aviation Administration; free of all average
FAP family auto plan
FAR floor-area ratio
F.A.S. free alongside
FASB Financial Accounting Standards Board
FAX facsimile
FCA Farm Credit Administration; Fellow of the Institute of Chartered Accountants
FCC Federal Communications Commission
FCM Futures Commission Merchant
FCUA Federal Credit Union Administration
FDA Food and Drug Administration
FDIC Federal Deposit Insurance Corporation
Fed Federal Reserve Board; Federal Reserve System
FFB Federal Financing Bank
FFCS Federal Farm Credit System
F.G.A. foreign general average; free of general average
FGIC Financial Guarantee Insurance Corporation
FHA Farmers Home Administration; Federal Housing Administration
FHLB Federal Home Loan Bank
FHLBB Federal Home Loan Bank Board
FHLMC Federal Home Loan Mortgage Corporation
FICA Federal Insurance Contributions Act

FICB Federal Intermediate Credit Bank
FIFO first-in, first-out
FITW federal income tax withholding
FLB Federal Land Bank
FMC Federal Maritime Commission
FMCS Federal Mediation and Conciliation Service
FmHA Farmers Home Administration
FMRR financial management rate of return
FMV fair market value
FNMA Federal National Mortgage Association
f.o.b. free on board
F.O.I.A. Freedom of Information Act
FOMC Federal Open Market Committee
F.P.A. free of particular average
FPM flexible payment mortgage
FRA Federal Reserve Act
FRB Federal Reserve Board; Federal Reserve Bank
FRD Federal Reserve district
FRIET Finite Real Estate Investment Trust
FRS Federal Reserve System
FS final settlement
FSLIC Federal Savings and Loan Insurance Corporation
FTC Federal Trade Commission
FVO for valuation only
FX foreign exchange
FY fiscal year
FYI for your information

GAAP generally accepted accounting principles
GAAS generally accepted auditing standards
GAI guaranteed annual income
GAO General Accounting Office
GATT General Agreement of Tariffs and Trade
GEM growing equity mortgage
GIM gross income multiplier
GM general manager
GNMA Government National Mortgage Association
GNP gross national product
G.O. general obligation
GPM Graduated Payment Mortgage
G.R.I. Graduate Realtors Institute
GRM gross rent multiplier

HFR hold for release
HMO health maintenance organization
HOW homeowners warranty
HQ headquarters
HR House resolution
HUD Department of Housing and Urban Development
HVAC heating, ventilation, and air conditioning

IAAO International Association of Assessing Officers
IBES Institutional Broker's Estimate System
IBF international banking facility
IBRD International Bank for Reconstruction and Development
ICC Interstate Commerce Commission
ICMA Institute of Cost and Management Accounts
IDB industrial development bond
IET Interest Equalization Act
IFC International Finance Corporation
IMF International Monetary Fund
IMM International Monetary Market
INSTINET Institutional Networks Corporation
IOU I owe you
IPO initial public offering
IRA individual retirement account
IRB industrial revenue bond
IRC Internal Revenue Code
IRD income in respect of a decedent
IREM Institute of Real Estate Management
IRR internal rate of return
IRS Internal Revenue Service
IRWA International Right-of-Way Association
ITC investment tax credit
ITS Intermarket Trading System
IWW Industrial Workers of the World

KCBT Kansas City Board of Trade
KWH kilowatt-hour
KYC know your customer

L listed
LBO leveraged buyout
L/C letter of credit
LDC less developed country
LESOP leveraged employee stock ownership plan

LIBOR London Interbank Offered Rate
LIFO last-in, first-out
LMRA Labor-Management Relations Act
LP limited partnership
ltd. limited
L/V loan-to-value ratio

MACRS Modified Accelerated Cost Recovery System
MAI Member Appraisal Institute
MBA Mortgage Bankers Association of America
M.B.A. Master of Business Administration
MBIA Municipal Bond Insurance Association
MBO management by objective
MCA Monetary Control Act
MCT managed change technique
MFN most favored nation
MGIC Mortgage Guarantee Insurance Co.
MHG Malartic Hygrade
MHR Member of the U.S. House of Representatives
MIB Medical Information Bureau
MIG-1 Moody's Investment Grade
MIMC Member of the Institute of Management Consultants
MIS management information system
MIT municipal investment trust; market if touched
MLS multiple listing service
MMC money market certificate
MMDA money market deposit account
MNC multinational corporation
M.O. money order
MSB mutual savings bank
MSE Midwest Stock Exchange
MSRB Municipal Securities Rulemaking Board
MSTC Midwest Securities Trust Company
MTU metric units

NAA National Apartment Association
NACORE National Association of Corporate Real Estate Executives
NAHB National Association of Home Builders
NAIC National Association of Investment Clubs
NAM National Association of Manufacturers
NAPA National Association of Purchasing Agents
NAR National Association of Realtors
NAREB National Association of Real Estate Brokers

NARELLO National Association of Real Estate Licensing Law Officials
NASA National Aeronautics and Space Administration
NASD National Association of Securities Dealers
NASDAQ National Association of Securities Dealers Automated
  Quotations
NATO North Atlantic Treaty Organization
NAV net asset value
N.B. nota bene
NBS National Bureau of Standards
NC no charge
NCUA National Credit Union Association
NEMS national exchange market system
NH not held
NIDS National Institutional Delivery System
NIRA National Industrial Recovery Act.
NIT negative income tax; New Investment Technology
NL no load
NLRA National Labor Relations Act
NLRB National Labor Relations Board
NMAB National Market Advisory Board
NNP Net National Product
NOI net operating income
NOIBN not otherwise indexed by name
NOW National Organization for Women; negotiable order of withdrawal
NPV net present value; no par value
NQB National Quotation Bureau
NR not rated
NSBA National Small Business Association
NSCC National Securities Clearing Corporation
NSF not sufficient funds
NSM National Student Marketing
NSTS National Securities Trading System
NYCSCE New York Coffee, Sugar, and Cocoa Exchange
NYCTN,CA New York Cotton Exchange, Citrus Associates
NYFE New York Futures Exchange
NYM New York Mercantile Exchange
NYSE New York Stock Exchange

OAPEC Organization of Arab Petroleum Exporting Countries
OAR overall rate of return
OASI Old Age and Survivors Insurance
OB or better
OCC options clearing corporation

OECD Organization for Economic Cooperation and Development
OILSR Office of Interstate Land Sales Registration
OMB Office of Management and Budget
OPEC Organization of Petroleum Exporting Countries
OPM options pricing model
OR operations research
OTC over the counter
OW offer wanted

PA purchasing agent
P/A power of attorney
PAM pledged account mortgage
P & C put and call
P & I principal and interest
P & L profit and loss
PAP personal auto policy
PAYSOP pay-related stock ownership plan
PBGC Pension Benefit Guaranty Corporation
PC participation certificate
PCA production credit association
PDM physical distribution management
PE price earnings ratio (in stock listings of newspapers)
P/E price/earnings
PERT program evaluation and review technique
pfd. preferred
PHA Public Housing Agency
P.H.V. pro hace vice
PITI principal, interest, taxes, and insurance
Plc. public limited company
PMI private mortgage insurance
POD payable on death
POE port of entry
POP panoramic office planning
PR public relations
PSDTC Pacific Securities Depository Trust Company
PSE Pacific Stock Exchange; Philadelphia Stock Exchange
PUC public utilities commission
PUD planned unit development
PUHCA Public Utility Holding Company Act
PVR profit/volume ratio
PWA Public Works Administration

QC quality control

QTIP   qualified terminable interest property trust

RAM   reverse annuity mortgage
RAN   revenue anticipation note
R & D   research and development
RCMM   registered competitive market maker
RCPC   regional check processing center
REA   Rural Electrification Administration
REIT   real estate investment trust
REO   real estate owned
RESPA   Real Estate Settlement Procedures Act
RESSI   Real Estate Securities and Syndication Institute
RM   residential member
RNMI   Realtors National Marketing Institute
ROA   return on assets
ROAM   return on assets managed
ROE   return on equity
ROI   return on investment
RRM   renegotiated rate mortgage
RTW   right to work
RW   right-of-way

SAA   special arbitrage account
SAB   special assessment bond
SAM   shared appreciation mortgage
S & L   savings and loan association
S & P   Standard & Poor's
SAP   standard auto plan
SB   senate bill
SBA   Small Business Administration
SBIC   small business investment corporation
SBLI   savings bank life insurance
SCORE   special claim on residual equity
S.D.-B.L.   sight draft, bill of lading attached
SDR   special drawing rights
SE   shareholders' equity
sec   security
SEC   Securities and Exchange Commission
SEP   simplified employee pension
SF   sinking fund
SFP   standard fire policy
SIA   Securities Industry Association
SIAC   Securities Industry Automation Corporation

SIC standard industrial classification
SIPC Securities Investor Protection Corporation
SIR Society of Industrial Realtors
SLMA Student Loan Marketing Association
SLO stop-limit order; stop-loss order
SMA Society of Management Accountants; special miscellaneous
account
SMSA standard metropolitan statistical area
snafu situation normal, all fouled up
SOP standard operating procedure
SPDA single-premium deferred annuity
SRA senior residential appraiser
SREA Senior Real Estate Analyst; Society of Real Estate Appraisers
SRO self-regulatory organization
SRP salary reduction plan
SRPA Senior Real Property Appraiser
SRT spousal remainder trust
SS Social Security
STRIPS separate trading of registered interest and principal of securities
SYD sum-of-the-years-digits

T- Treasury (as in T-bill, T-bond, T-note)
TA trade acceptance
TAB tax anticipation bill
TAN tax anticipation note
TC Tax Court of the United States
TD time deposit
TDR transferable development rights
TEFRA Tax Equity and Fiscal Responsibility Act
TIAC Thrift Institutions Advisory Council
TIGER Treasury Investors Growth Receipt
TIL truth-in-lending law
TM trademark
TNEC Temporary National Economic Committee
TSA tax sheltered annuity
TT testamentary trust
TT&L Treasury tax and loan
TVA Tennessee Valley Authority

UAW United Automobile, Aerospace and Agricultural Implements
Workers of America
UCC Uniform Commercial Code

UGMA Uniform Gifts to Minors Act
UIT unit investment trust
UL Underwriters Laboratories
ULI Urban Land Institute
UMW United Mine Workers
UN United Nations
UNI undistributed net income
UPC Uniform Practice Code; Universal Product Code
USBS United States Bureau of Standards
USCC United States Chamber of Commerce
USIT unit share investment trust
U/w underwriter

VA Veterans Administration
VAT value-added tax
VEBA voluntary employees' beneficiary association
VFP variable factor programming
VIP very important person
VL value line
VMS vertical marketing system
VRM variable rate mortgage

W/B waybill
WCA Workmen's Compensation Act
WCR Women's Council of Realtors
WR warehouse receipt
WSJ Wall Street Journal
W/tax withholding tax
WW with warrants

x-d ex-dividend
xw ex-warrants

yld. yield
YTC yield to call
YTM yield to maturity

z. zero
ZBA zero bracket amount
ZBB zero-based budgeting

Appendix B

Simple Analysis of Various Investment Vehicles

INVESTMENT VEHICLE	LIQUIDITY	MARKET-ABILITY	SOURCES OF RISK	TAXATION
Insured savings accounts	High	N/A[1] power/ Interest rate	Purchasing income	Ordinary
Money market accounts	High	N/A[1] power/	Purchasing income Interest rate	Ordinary
EE and HH bonds	High	N/A[1]	Purchasing power/ Interest rate	Ordinary income/
Treasury bills	High	High	Purchasing power/ Interest rate	Ordinary income/ Capital gains and losses[2]
Commercial paper	High	High	Purchasing power/ Interest rate	Ordinary income/ Capital gains and losses[2]
Certificates of deposit	High	N/A[3]	Purchasing power/ interest rate	Ordinary income/ capital gains and losses[2]
Treasury notes bonds	Moderate[4]	High	Purchasing power/ interest rate	Ordinary income/ Capital gains and losses

INVESTMENT VEHICLE	LIQUIDITY	MARKET-ABILITY	SOURCES OF RISK	TAXATION
High-grade common stock	Moderate	High	Market/ Business	Ordinary income/ Capital gains and losses
High-grade corporate bonds	Moderate[4]	High	Purchasing power/ interest rate	Ordinary income/ Capital gains and losses
High-grade municipal bonds	Moderate[4]	High	Purchasing power/ interest rate	Tax-free income[5]/ Capital gains or losses
High-grade preferred stock	Moderate	High	Purchasing power/ interest rate	Ordinary income/ Capital gains or losses
Speculative common stock	Low	High	Business/ Market	Ordinary income/ Capital gains or losses
Speculative corporate bonds	Low[4]	Moderate/ High	Business/ Financial	Ordinary income/ Capital gains or losses
Puts and calls	Low	High	Market/ Business	Capital gains and losses

INVESTMENT VEHICLE	LIQUIDITY	MARKET-ABILITY	SOURCES OF RISK	TAXATION
Real estate investment properties	Low	Low	Market/ Business	Ordinary income/ Capital gains and losses
Real estate investment trusts	Moderate	High	Market/ Business	Ordinary income/ Capital gains and losses
Physical assets	Low	Low	Market/ Business	Capital gains or losses
Futures contracts	Low	High	Market/ Business	Ordinary income/ Capital gains or losses
Gold	Low	Moderate/ High	Market/ Business	Capital gains or losses
Cash value life insurance	High	N/A[1]	Depends on type chosen	Tax-deferred /Ordinary income[6]
Annuities:				
Fixed	High	N/A[1]	Interest rate/ Purchasing power	Tax-deferred /Ordinary income[6]
Variable	Moderate/ Low	N/A[1]	Depends on investment chosen	Tax-deferred /Ordinary income[6]

INVESTMENT VEHICLE	LIQUIDITY	MARKET-ABILITY	SOURCES OF RISK	TAXATION
Mortgage-backed securities	Moderate	Moderate/ High	Interest rate/ Purchasing power	Ordinary income/ Capital gains or losses
Limited partnerships	Low	N/A[7]	Market/ Business	Depends on particular partnership

1. A secondary market does not exist. However, they may be redeemed by issuer.
2. If sold prior to maturity.
3. Some brokerage firms issue CDs and maintain a secondary market in certificates of deposit, providing a high/moderate degree of marketability.
4. The longer to maturity, the less the degree of liquidity.
5. The income is free from federal income tax. Some municipal bonds also are free from state income taxes.
6. Earnings and capital gains are tax-deferred until withdrawn, at which time they are taxed as ordinary income.
7. A small number of firms provide a secondary market for some limited partnerships. Also, some partnerships permit a limited number of units to be sold back to the general partner.

Note: Mutual funds have been purposely excluded from this table because of the many types available. However, the underlying securities in a fund should be used to determine the degree of liquidity and sources of investment risk for the fund.

Appendix C

Ratios, Equations, and Formulae Used in Financial and Quasi-Financial Business Institutions

annuities While there are equations to figure the value at some point in time of an annuity, it is easier for the inquirer to consult an annuity table, since the computations can get quite complex and elongated.

beta coefficient formula

$$\frac{\% \text{ Change in Price of Security}}{\% \text{ Change in Market Index}}$$

compound value of a dollar

(year one) $Po + iPo + P1$ (year two) $P1 + iP1 + P2$

explanation (First year) initial principal + (interest rate times initial principal) = principal after one year. Proceed from there with equation for year 2, 3, etc.

current price of a bond

$$PB = (1000) \ (PVF) + (\text{Interest}) \ (PVAF)$$

PB . . . price of bond
(1000) . . . face value of bond
(PVF) . . . present value factor
(PVAF) . . . present value annuity factor

current yield

$$\frac{\text{Annual Income}}{\text{Current Price}}$$

deposit expansion multiplied

$$\frac{1}{\text{Legal Reserve Ratio}}$$

divided yield

$$\frac{\text{Dividend}}{\text{Current Price of Stock}}$$

earnings per share on preferred stock

$$\frac{\text{Earnings after Taxes}}{\text{Number of Preferred Shares Outstanding}}$$

equivalent tax benefit

$$\text{Before Tax Benefit} = \frac{\text{Tax Credit}}{\text{Marginal Income Tax Bracket}}$$

equivalent yields on municipal and corporate bonds

$$i_c (1 - t) = i_m$$

i_c . . . interest paid on corporate debt

t . . . tax bracket

i_m . . . interest paid on municipal debt

expected rate of return on common stock Expected rate of return = expected dividend yield + expected growth in earnings, or

$$= \frac{D}{P} + g$$

expected return on an investment Expected return = expected income + expected capital appreciation.

holding period return

$$\frac{\text{Income} + \text{Sale Price} - \text{Purchase Price} - \text{Interest Charges}}{\text{Initial Investment} + \text{Interest Charges}}$$

income approach to real estate appraisal

$$\text{Market Value} = \frac{\text{Expected Annual Income}}{\text{Capitalization Rate}}$$

margin requirement

$$MR = VS \times M + CC$$

interpretation of equation Margin requirement is equal to the value of the securities, times the margin requirement plus the commission.

policy cost per thousand

$$\frac{(P + CVP)\ (1 + i) - (CSV + D)}{F - (CSV)\ (.001)}$$

P . . . annual premium

CVP . . . previous cash surrender value

i . . . interest rate

CSV . . . current cash surrender value

D . . . dividend

F . . . Face value

preferred stock The ratio of dividends to earnings of preferred stock is expressed in this manner.

$$\frac{\text{Earnings after Taxes}}{\text{Dividends on Preferred Stock}}$$

present value factor

$$pvf = \frac{1}{(1 + r)n}$$

present value of a dollar   (Requires "discounting," which is the reverse of compounding.)

$$Po = \frac{Pn}{(1 + i)n}$$

explanation   Present value equals the future value divided by the discount factor expressed $(1 + i)n$.

present value of a perpetual bond

$$PV = \frac{I}{i}$$

rate of return on common stock

$$P_o (1 + g)n = P_n$$

P_o . . . cost of security

g . . . rate of return per period

n . . . number of periods (years)

P_n . . . price at which security is sold

rate of return on investment on common stocks   (holding period)

$$\frac{\text{Sale Price} - \text{Purchase Price} + \text{Income}}{\text{Purchase Price}}$$

realized return on investment

$$\text{Realized Return} = \frac{\text{Income Earned}}{\text{Amount Invested}} + \frac{\text{Gain or Loss Expected}}{\text{Amount Invested}}$$

yield to call   Same as yield to maturity, except use callable years for "N."

yield to maturity

$$i = \frac{\text{Interest} + \dfrac{1000 - \text{Price of Bond}}{N}}{\dfrac{1000 + \text{Price of Bond}}{2}}$$

yield to maturity on a zero coupon bond

$$Po (1 + g)n = Pn$$

Po . . . Current period price of bond.

$(1+g)n$ . . . One plus the current rate of interest, times the "n," number of periods to maturity.

Pn . . . Value of bond at maturity.   (Original cost plus gain.)

If you have a financial calculator, please enter the following information: PV (present value), FV (future value), and N (time) Solve for "i."

If you use an HP-12C, be sure to change the sign before trying to solve for either "n" or "i."

conclusion The inclusion of all the ratios, equations, and formulae the user might wish to use on occasions would require another book. These more common ones have been included to assist the user in saving time on the calculation of common problems.

Appendix D

Important Ratios Used to Evaluate a Business

acid test

$$\frac{Cash + Marketable + Receivables}{Current\ Liabilities}$$

average collection period

$$\frac{Receivables}{Sales\ per\ Day}$$

average propensity to consume ratio of consumption to income

$$Average\ Propensity\ to\ Consume = \frac{Consumption}{Income}$$

average propensity to save ratio of savings to income

$$Average\ Propensity\ to\ Save = \frac{Savings}{Income}$$

average revenue

$$\frac{Total\ Revenue}{Quantity} = \frac{(Price)\ (Quantity)}{Quantity} = Price$$

average tax rate

$$Average\ Personal\ Income\ Tax\ Rate = \frac{Total\ Personal\ Income\ Tax}{Total\ Taxable\ Income}$$

cost depletion

$$Depletion\ Allowance = \frac{Basis}{Total\ Estimated\ Units} \times Units\ Sold$$

current ratio

$$\frac{Current\ Assets}{Current\ Liabilities}$$

debt to equity

$$\frac{Debt}{Total\ Assets}$$

earnings per common share

$$\frac{\text{Earnings Minus Preferred Dividends}}{\text{Number of Common Shares Outstanding}}$$

fixed asset turnover

$$\frac{\text{Annual Sales}}{\text{Fixed Assets}}$$

inventory turnover

$$\frac{\text{Cost of Goods Sold}}{\text{Inventory}}$$

or

$$\frac{\text{Sales}}{\text{Inventory}}$$

marginal utility

$$\text{Marginal Utility} = \frac{\text{Change in Total Utility}}{\text{Change in Quantity Consumed}}$$

net profit margin

$$\frac{\text{Earnings after Taxes}}{\text{Sales}}$$

operating profit margin

$$\frac{\text{Earnings before Interest \& Taxes}}{\text{Annual Interest Expense}}$$

payout ratio

$$\frac{\text{Dividends}}{\text{Earnings}}$$

P/E ratio

$$\frac{\text{Price of Stock}}{\text{Earnings per Share}}$$

receivables turnover

$$\frac{\text{Annual Credit Sales}}{\text{Accounts Receivable}}$$

or

$$\frac{\text{Annual Sales}}{\text{Accounts Receivable}}$$

return on assets

$$\frac{\text{Earnings after Taxes}}{\text{Total Assets}}$$

return on equity

$$\frac{\text{Earnings after Taxes}}{\text{Equity}}$$

times-interest earned

$$\frac{\text{Earnings before Interest \& Taxes}}{\text{Annual Interest Expense}}$$

conclusion The analyzing of a business is not easy, and these ratios may make it appear that it is. Firms change over time, as do accounting methods and all changes may slant a specific ratio. However, if one is a seasoned investor, or wishes to be, then some kind of analysis should be made of a company before investing in it.

Over time, however, academicians have learned that no type of analysis is foolproof. As with the old-time airplane pilots, flying by the seat of your pants probably plays some role in most investing.

Appendix E

Investment Vehicle Pyramid

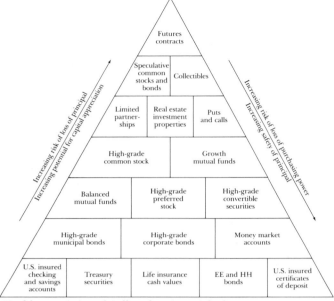

Used by permission of College for Financial Planning
Denver, Colorado. Copyright December 1985

Appendix F

Sources of Financial Information

American Stock Exchange
86 Trinity Place
New York, NY 10006

Chamber of Commerce
 of the United States
1615 H Street, N.W.
Washington, DC 20062

Chicago Board of Trade
141 West Jackson Blvd.
Chicago, IL 60606

Chicago Board Options Exchange
LaSalle at Jackson
Chicago, IL 60604

Chicago Mercantile Exchange
444 West Jackson Blvd.
Chicago, IL 60606

Dow Jones and Company, Inc.
P.O. Box 400
Princeton, NJ 08540

Dun and Bradstreet, Inc.
99 Church Street
New York, NY 10007

Federal Reserve Bank of Atlanta
104 Marietta Street
Atlanta, GA 30303

Federal Reserve Bank of Chicago
Box 834
Chicago, IL 60690

Federal Reserve Bank of Cleveland
East 6th and Superior Avenue
Cleveland, OH 44101

Federal Reserve Bank of Dallas
Station K
Dallas, TX 75222

Federal Reserve Bank of Kansas City
Federal Reserve Station
Kansas City, MO 64198

Federal Reserve Bank of Minneapolis
250 Marquette Avenue
Minneapolis, MN 55480

Federal Reserve Bank of New York
33 Liberty Street
New York, NY 10045

Federal Reserve Bank of Philadelphia
P.O. Box 66
Philadelphia, PA 19105

Federal Reserve Bank of Richmond
P.O. Box 27622
Richmond, VA 23261

Federal Reserve Bank of San Francisco
P.O. Box 7702
San Francisco, CA 94120

Federal Reserve Bank of St. Louis
P.O. Box 442
St. Louis, MO 63166

Federal Reserve System
Board of Governors
Washington, DC 20551

International Monetary Market
444 West Jackson Blvd.
Chicago, IL 60606

Investment Company Institute
1775 K Street, N. W.
Washington, DC 20006

Moody's Investor Service, Inc.
99 Church Street
New York, NY 10007

New York Stock Exchange
11 Wall Street
New York, NY 10005

No-Load Mutual Fund Association
11 Penn Plaza, Suite 2204
New York, NY 10001

Securities Investor Protection Corporation
900 17th Street, NW, Suite 800
Washington, DC 20006

Small Business Administration
1441 L Street, NW
Washington, D.C. 20416

Standard and Poor's Corporation
345 Hudson Street
New York, NY 10014

Superintendent of Documents
U.S. Government Printing Office
Washington, DC 20402

United Business Service Company
210 Newbury Street
Boston, MA 02116

U.S. Securities and Exchange Commission
500 North Capital Street
Washington, DC 20549

Value Line Services
Arnold Bernhard and Company
5 East 4th Street
New York, NY 10017

Veteran's Administration
810 Vermont Ave.
Washington, D.C. 20420

Weisenberger's Investment Companies
Warren, Gorham, and Lamont, Inc.
1633 Broadway
New York, NY 10019

Appendix G

The 1986 Tax Reform Act

On September 27, 1986, the Senate passed the 1986 Tax Reform Act. It was initially hailed as the tax reform long needed, but experiences since that time have not as yet confirmed this.

The income tax in the United States was made possible by the Sixteenth Amendment to the Constitution, and installed as a taxing vehicle in 1913. Until World War II, the income tax was little known to the average citizen. This was to change rapidly as the financial burden of the war pushed the federal government to its use as a primary taxing vehicle, which position it still holds, producing almost 50% of the revenues of the federal government, when both corporate and individual taxes are considered.

Until 1986, there had not been a major assault on the structure of the income tax. Tax rates had varied over time, and various other minor changes were periodically made to accommodate socioeconomic needs. On occasions, individual rates were changed, but the system, per se, had never had a major overhaul.

Three goals were set for the 1986 Tax Reform Act from the outset. One was that the act had to be "revenue neutral"; i.e., there would be neither a loss nor a gain in total revenues, but that the tax burden would be distributed differently. The second goal was one of "fairness"; i.e., there would be a marked degree of equity among both individual and corporate income tax payers. The third goal was "simplicity." The first two goals were not, it now appears, too far off. "Simplicity" turned out to be a different matter. Some parts of the Reform Act made certain provisions retroactive, and others were to be phased in through the year 1991.

Inasmuch as the original documents prepared for the 1986 Tax Reform Act comprised some twenty thousand pages, nothing can be done here beyond highlighting those changes which seem to be getting the most attention.

For individual taxpayers, some of the following provisions are most often discussed:

positive . . . The reduction of the number of individual tax brackets from fifteen to two, beginning in 1988.

positive . . . The repeal of the "zero bracket amount," which is being replaced with the "standard deduction."

positive . . . The retention of home mortgage interest deductions, on both first and second homes.

negative . . . The repeal of many current itemized deductions.

negative . . . Major changes in gifts of appreciated property to charitable institutions.

negative . . . Repeal of old long-term capital gains provisions. (Beginning in 1988 there will be a flat tax of 28% on long-term capital gains.)

negative . . . Family "income shifting" to be much more difficult.

      negative . . . Major changes in provisions for Individual Retirement
            Accounts and 401(k) plans.
      negative . . . A considerable "thinning out" of tax shelters.

Corporate rates are also lowered, with the lowest bracket (1988) being 15% and the highest, 34%. The top bracket is down from 46% under the old provisions.

It is generally conceded that small corporations got a break in this tax reform but that it is too early to know the ultimate effects on larger corporations.

A major "minus" for corporations was the repeal of the Investment Tax Credit. Essentially, this plan allowed corporations to take a tax credit (dollar-for-dollar decrease in tax liability) for certain types of business investments. This had originally been enacted to encourage the purchase of new technology, and to encourage research and development.

Allowable methods of depreciating different kinds of properties have changed dramatically. This is considered to be a "minus" for business.

Some of the more exotic business deductions of the past such as special boxes at sports arenas, etc., have been severely curtailed.

As stated in the first edition of this volume, it was generally believed that beginning in 1989 (1988 being a general election year), the 1986 Tax Reform Act would be attacked by special interest groups vehemently. That year did not produce another tax reform act, but some changes, worthy of the attention of both individuals and businesses, were made.

It is likely that 1990 will bring other changes, the most important of which could be a reversion to the former capital gains rates.

Changes we know of now:

      negative . . . Consumer interest deductible fell to 20% on 1989 returns
            and will fall to 10% in 1990.
      positive . . . Extended until Sept. 30, 1990, the ability of an employee to
            accept, tax-free, financial assistance (up to $5,250) for further
            education.
      positive . . . Extended till Sept. 30, 1990, the tax exemptions on premiums
            paid for life insurance for employees' spouses and
            dependents.
      positive . . . Extended, for self-employed people, until Sept. 30, 1990, the
            ability to continue a deduction for providing their own
            medical benefits.
            (25% of the cost of health insurance from taxable income.)
      positive . . . For high income persons, Congress extended through 1990
            a tax credit on low-income housing investments. The credit
            generally lets investors cut taxes over a ten-year period by up
            to 90% of their money invested in the project.
      positive (generally) . . . For people who use a private car for business

purposes, a deduction of twenty-six cents per mile for all miles travelled beginning in 1990.

positive . . . Investors in mutual funds will not be taxed on income they do receive. The 1986 law required that people count as income the management fees that mutual funds siphon off from earnings before making any payouts.

positive . . . Code Section 89. More onerous parts of this section, relating to non-discrimination in fringe benefits repealed.

While about 80% of the definitions and descriptions given in a publication such as *Dictionary for Business & Finance* will remain for decades, those related to tax laws will change, often dramatically so. The serious user will always keep a file of tax changes, and refer to a reputable tax manual.

Appendix H

Boundaries of Federal Reserve Districts and Their Branch Territories

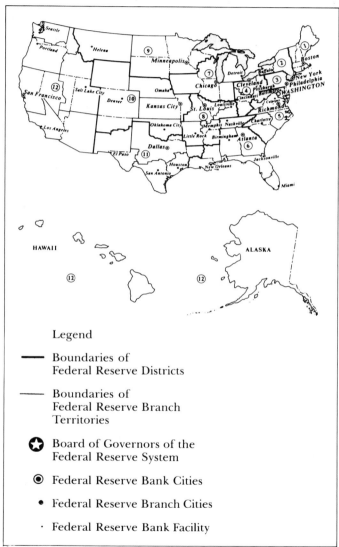

Legend

—— Boundaries of
Federal Reserve Districts

—— Boundaries of
Federal Reserve Branch
Territories

⭐ Board of Governors of the
Federal Reserve System

◉ Federal Reserve Bank Cities

• Federal Reserve Branch Cities

· Federal Reserve Bank Facility

Used by permission of the Federal Reserve Board of Governors